PRODUCT LIABILITY

PRODUCT LIABILITY

C. J. MILLER, B.A., LL.M.

of Lincoln's Inn, Barrister
Lecturer in Law in the University of Leeds

THE LATE
P. A. LOVELL, LL.B., B.C.L.
Lecturer in Law
in the University of Leeds, 1964–1975

LONDON
BUTTERWORTHS
1977

England London	Butterworth & Co., (Publishers) Ltd. 88 Kingsway, WC2B 6AB
Australia Sydney	Butterworths Pty., Ltd., 586 Pacific Highway, Chatswood, NSW 2067 Also at Melbourne, Brisbane, Adelaide and Perth
Canada Toronto	Butterworth & Co. (Canada) Ltd., 2265 Midland Avenue, Scarborough M1P 4S1
New Zealand Wellington	Butterworths of New Zealand Ltd. 26/28 Waring Taylor Street, 1.
South Africa Durban	Butterworth & Co. (South Africa) (Pty.) Ltd. 152/154 Gale Street
USA Boston	Butterworth & Co. (Publishers) Inc. 19 Cummings Park, Woburn, Mass., 01801

ISBN 0 406 29627 8

Preface

Product liability is concerned with the civil liability of manufacturers, retailers and others for damage or loss caused by products which are defective or which fail to meet the standards legitimately to be expected of them. It is only recently that the expression has become familiar to British and Commonwealth lawyers though it has long been familiar to their American counterparts. The position is, however, changing rapidly. Indeed it seems safe to predict that the subject will become increasingly important over the next few years. Thus product liability is currently being considered by both a Royal Commission sitting under the chairmanship of Lord Pearson and the Law Commission whilst there are also potentially important developments within the European Economic Communities and the Council of Europe. As a result of these deliberations English law now seems likely to follow the American pattern of imposing strict liability where a defective product causes death or personal injury and perhaps also in cases of property damage. Such a change is likely to stimulate litigation in a somewhat wider range of cases than in the past. The archetypal snail in the bottle has less potential for harm than the dangerously designed car or the drug which is marketed without adequate warnings as to possible side-effects.

For convenience in exposition we have divided the book into two main parts according to whether the liability is contractual or tortious. The former section discusses matters such as liability for misrepresentations and breach of express and implied warranties, and the common law and statutory controls over exemption clauses. The latter discusses the liability of manufacturers and others for damage or loss caused by products which are defective, whether in terms of construction or design. In discussing these matters we have sought to provide reasonably comprehensive coverage of Commonwealth, no less than English, cases and some indication of the position adopted in American case law. In this we have benefited from the writings of the authors of the standard texts on the law

v

of contract, sale of goods and tort and from discussions with our colleagues both at Leeds and elsewhere. Our access to American materials has been greatly facilitated by the benefactions of Ralph Yablon whose generosity over the years has provided the Leeds university law library with a substantial holding of American reports.

As some of our readers will be aware, the writing of this book has had a chequered and indeed tragic history. The work was begun in the autumn of 1972 and Patrick Lovell joined me as a co-author in the following year. We then worked together until Lovell's tragic death in September 1975 and I completed the work thereafter. It accordingly follows that responsibility for errors and omissions in the final text is mine alone, though it is my belief that the text expresses our joint view on matters of opinion and policy. I hope that the book will be regarded as a fitting tribute to his memory.

I am indebted to Mrs. Peggy Clapham, LL.B. for her many hours of painstaking work in typing and proof reading and to Butterworths for their unfailing courtesy, patience and assistance. As always my wife, Michèle, and my children have borne my prolonged absences with good humour and understanding and I am grateful to them.

C. J. MILLER

November 1976

Contents

vii

Table of Statutes

References in this Table of "*Statutes*" are to Halsbury's Statutes of England (Third Edition) showing the volume and page at which the annotated text of the Act will be found.

List of Cases

1 Introduction and Modern Historical Outline

There is ample room for debate over what ground ought to be covered in a book on product liability. The considerations which have guided us have been partly pragmatic or dictated by the exigencies of space and partly a reflection of our own interests. In the result we have concentrated on the civil liability of manufacturers and others where damage or loss is caused by products which fail to meet the standards claimed expressly or impliedly for them or which are defective or otherwise dangerous.

This has led us to exclude discussion of statutory provisions such as the Trade Descriptions Acts 1968 and 1972 and the Health and Safety at Work Etc. Act 1974, s.6, which impose criminal liability on suppliers of goods without providing civil remedies for breach of the duties created.[1] We have also omitted discussion of liabilities arising before the product has been marketed or "put into circulation", as where damage is caused by a product during its own production process.[2] Similarly we have not discussed the liability of vendors or lessors of real property although some consideration

---

[1] See the Trade Descriptions Act 1968, s. 35; Health and Safety at Work etc. Act 1974, s. 47 (1) (a). Contrast the Consumer Protection Act 1961, s. 3 (1), below, pp. 268–270.

[2] The phrase "put into circulation" is used in the Strasbourg Convention on Products Liability (art. 2 (d), 5 (1)) and in the EEC draft directive on liability for defective products (art. 5). The Law Commission Working Paper No. 64, Scottish Law Commission Memorandum No. 20, "Liability for Defective Products" (1975) is similarly limited in scope: see para. 64. For convenience this joint document circulated by the two Law Commissions will hereafter be referred to as Law Commission Working Paper No. 64. The phrase "put into circulation" is somewhat wider in scope than the term "marketed". The latter might be thought to exclude injuries caused in transport or before the first retail sale or hiring as in *Barnett* v. *H. and J. Packer & Co., Ltd.*, [1940] 3 All E.R. 575. For the Strasbourg Convention, the EEC draft directive and the Law Commission Working Paper No. 64, see below, pp. 3–4.

1

has been given to the position of building contractors and builder-vendors.[3] Suppliers of products such as bricks, cement or tiles which are incorporated subsequently into immovables have been regarded as falling within the scope of the subject[4] although their position has not been specially emphasised. The same is true of the producers of natural commodities such as fruit or vegetables and of livestock.[5]

A high proportion of the text deals with case law and developments in the United States of America where product liability has recently attracted an unprecedented amount of litigation and academic attention. The effect has been a transformation in the basis and scope of liability. As yet there has been no comparable development in English law or in major Commonwealth jurisdictions. Even if such a development were not forthcoming, American experience would still be relevant on a variety of matters, many of which have barely been explored in other common law jurisdictions. This would be true, for example, of actions alleging that injury has occurred because of deficiencies in a product's design or in accompanying warnings or directions for use.[6] In fact it is virtually certain that English law will see significant changes within the next few years although, in contrast to the position in the United States, they are likely to occur through legislation rather than case law. The form which any such changes will take is at present unclear. If they operate within the broad format of the present adversary system English law is likely to follow the American pattern of imposing strict liability for personal injury[7] and to have to deal with the same problems as have been faced by American courts. Consequently American cases are likely to have an increased relevance.

Product liability is currently occupying the attention of a number of bodies concerned with law reform. Thus a Royal Commission has been established under the chairmanship of Lord Pearson with the following terms of reference:[8]

> "To consider to what extent, in what circumstances and by what means compensation should be payable in respect of death or personal injury (including ante-natal injury) suffered by any person—(*a*) in the course of employment; (*b*) through the use of a motor-vehicle or other means of transport; (*c*) through the manufacture, supply or use of goods or services; (*d*) on premises belonging to

---

[3] See below, pp. 313–315. As is noted in the Law Commission Working Paper No. 64, para. 65 (citing as examples "lifts, cranes, oil-rigs and swing bridges"), the distinction between "movables" and "immovables" is by no means clear cut.
[4] As in the Strasbourg Convention, art. 2(*a*) and the EEC draft directive, art. 1. See also the Law Commission Working Paper No. 64, para. 65.
[5] As in the Strasbourg Convention art. 2(*b*) and the EEC draft directive, art. 1. See also the Law Commission Working Paper No. 64, para. 66.
[6] See below, chapters 11 and 12.
[7] See *Restatement of Torts*, 2d, ss. 402A, 402B, below, pp. 17–18 and pp. 58–59.
[8] See Hansard, H.C. Debs., Vol. 848, col. 1119, 19 December 1972.

or occupied by another; or (*e*) otherwise through the act or omission of another where compensation under the present law is recoverable only on proof of fault or under the rules of strict liability, all this having regard to the cost and other implications of the arrangements for the recovery of compensation, whether by way of compulsory insurance or otherwise."

In addition the Law Commission and the Scottish Law Commission have been charged to consider:[9]

"whether the existing law governing compensation for personal injury, damage to property or any other loss caused by defective products is adequate, and to recommend what improvements, if any, in the law are needed to ensure that additional remedies are provided and against whom such remedies should be available."

The terms of reference of these bodies overlap but are by no means identical. The Pearson Commission is concerned only with compensation for "death or personal injury (including ante-natal injury)" in the situations specified. Subject to these limitations, however, it is clearly open to it to recommend that the present adversary system be replaced by a scheme of compensating from a central source funded by the state or private insurance.[10] The Law Commission's terms of reference encompass "damage to property or any other loss" (including purely economic losses), but they assume the continuation of the present framework of inter-party litigation.[11]

Separate developments are also occuring on the European front where a committee of the Council of Europe has produced the Strasbourg draft Convention on Products Liability[12] and the Commission of the European Economic Communities has published a series of draft directives and a memorandum on the same subject.[13] The Strasbourg Convention, now adopted by the Committee of Ministers of the Council of Europe, will

---

[9] Under the Law Commissions Act 1965, s. 3 (1) (*e*).

[10] A model might perhaps be found in the New Zealand Accident Compensation Act 1972, as amended. The Act resulted from the *Report of the Royal Commission of Inquiry into Compensation for Personal Injury in New Zealand* (the Woodhouse report) (1967).

[11] At least they have been so interpreted. See Law Commission Working Paper No. 64, para. 3.

[12] The Draft European Convention on Products Liability in Regard to Personal Injury and Death and the Draft Explanatory Report (March 1975) are set out as Appendix B to the Law Commission Working Paper No. 64.

[13] The First Preliminary Draft Directive and the accompanying Memorandum on the Approximation of the Laws of Member States relating to Product Liability (August 1974) are set out as Appendix C to the Law Commission Working Paper No. 64. A second preliminary draft was published in July 1975 and final amended proposals were presented by the Commission to the Council of Ministers on 9 September 1976: see the Bulletin of the European Communities, Supplement 11/76. The present draft directive is set out as Appendix A, below. The draft directive still has to be approved by the Council of Ministers under art. 100 of the Treaty of Rome.

be open for signature by member states including the United Kingdom. Signatories would undertake to make their national laws conform to the provisions of the Convention the effect of which is to make producers strictly liable for death or personal injuries caused by a defect in their products.[14] The broad effect of the European Economic Communities draft directive in its present form would be to make producers strictly liable to any person who suffers damage as a result of a defect in their products. This goes somewhat further than the Strasbourg Convention since by art. 6 of the draft directive "damage" means not only death or personal injuries but also damage to property other than property acquired or used for the purpose of a trade, business or profession. Damages in respect of diminished value, damage to or destruction of the defective article itself would, however, be excluded.[15] Any one of these sources of possible change might lead to a substantial rewriting of English product liability law.

At a more modest level, changes are also likely to occur through the provisions of the Fair Trading Act 1973.[16] This Act creates the office of Director General of Fair Trading and requires the Director to keep under review commercial activities which relate to the supply of goods or services and which may affect adversely the economic interests of consumers in the United Kingdom.[17] Provision is also made for the Director General to refer a consumer trade practice to the Consumer Protection Advisory Committee[18] when it may have such an effect.[19] Following a report by the committee agreeing with the Director General's proposals for remedying the situation[20] the practice may be controlled or prohibited through an order of the Secretary of State approved by a resolution of both Houses of Parliament.[1] A number of references have already been made to the committee.[2] These include a reference of the practice of purporting to exclude the rights guaranteed to purchasers in consumer sales by the Sale of Goods Act 1893, s.55, as amended,[3] and a

---

[14] The Convention was adopted by the Committee of Ministers in the session 20–29 September 1976. It will be open for signature on 27 January 1977. The final version of the Convention is set out as Appendix B, below.

[15] See further below, pp. 358–359.

[16] See *Benjamin's Sale of Goods* (1974), para. 1029.

[17] Section 2.

[18] Established by s. 3 of the Act.

[19] Sections 14, 17, 19. A "consumer trade practice" is defined in s. 13 of the Act.

[20] Or agreeing subject to modifications specified in the report: s. 22(1)(b).

[1] Sections 18, 22. The affirmative resolution procedure is required by s. 22(4). Penalties for contravention of such an order are contained in s. 23 and defences in ss. 24, 25.

[2] The work of the Office of Fair Trading has been summarised in its first report, H.C. 370/1975: see Lawson, (1976), 126 N.L.J. 45.

[3] By the Supply of Goods (Implied Terms) Act 1973, s. 4. See *A Report on Practices Relating to the Purported Exclusion of Inalienable Rights of Consumers and Failure to Explain their*

reference of the practice of seeking to sell goods without revealing that they are being sold in the course of a business.[4]

Contract and tort in English product liability law

Discussion of product liability in English law may be divided into two main parts according to whether the liability is based on contract or on tort. The division is not clear cut, especially in the area of liability for misrepresentations, but it is convenient for the purposes of exposition and has been adopted in this book.

Liability under a contract for the sale of goods is associated primarily with compensating a purchaser in respect of unfulfilled expectations whilst liability in tort is associated with compensating third parties who have suffered physical injury or property damage. It is still the case that purely economic losses are not readily compensated by the law of tort although there has been a movement in the direction of compensation in recent years.[5] Whether this trend is desirable is open to debate. On the other hand contractual remedies are certainly not the exclusive preserve of purchasers who are suing in respect of a failure to confer a promised benefit. They are also available to purchasers seeking compensation for physical damage which has resulted from their use of the goods. The decision of the Court of Appeal in *Randall* v. *Newson*[6] is illustrative. Here the purchaser of a phaeton carriage was claiming damages in respect of injuries suffered by his horses when a defective pole broke. The court held that he was entitled to recover provided that the injuries were found to be a natural consequence of the defect. This was clearly an important decision since, as will frequently be the case, the loss associated with the injuries (£130–£140) was greatly in excess of the value of a replacement pole (£3).[7]

Existence, December 1974. The resulting Consumer Transactions (Restrictions on Statements) Order 1976 has now been approved by the House of Commons (H.C. Debs. Vol. 916, cols. 1161–1171, 30 July 1976) and the House of Lords (H.C. Debs. Vol. 375, cols. 97–118, 11 October 1976). See also below, p. 145.

[4] As by using the classified advertisement columns of local newspapers. See the Director-General's supporting dossier 17/3 (March 1975), and the report of the CPAC, *Disguised Business Sales* (May 1976).

[5] See, e.g., *Hedley Byrne & Co., Ltd.* v. *Heller & Partners, Ltd.*, [1964] A.C. 465; [1963] 2 All E.R. 575, H.L.; *Rivtow Marine, Ltd.* v. *Washington Iron Works* (1973), 40 D.L.R. (3d) 530 (Sup. Ct. of Canada), and in general, below, chapter 16, pp. 328–344.

[6] (1877), 2 Q.B.D. 102. See also below, p. 145. See also *Brown* v. *Edgington* (1841), 2 Man. & G. 279; *Smith* v. *Green* (1875), 1 C.P.D. 92; *Mullett* v. *Mason* (1866), L.R. 1 C.P. 559; *Randall* v. *Raper* (1858), E. B. & E. 84.

[7] An extreme example is provided by the case of *Harbutt's Plasticine, Ltd.* v. *Wayne Tank and Pump Co., Ltd.*, [1970] 1 Q.B. 447, [1970] 1 All E.R. 225, C.A., below, p. 135.

Whether physical damage to person or property is involved or not, the principal advantage of a claim in contract is that liability is strict. When the goods supplied under a contract of sale fail to correspond with the contract description, or where they fail to meet the standards of merchantable quality or reasonable fitness for purpose where such standards are applicable,[8] it will not excuse the vendor to show that he has exercised all reasonable care. Nothing less than an analysis by an expert could have revealed the arsenic in the beer in *Wren* v. *Holt*,[9] but this did not prevent liability being incurred by the defendant publican who had the misfortune to supply it. The law is admittedly open to criticism in adopting this position. An entitlement to recover the purchase price when the goods are not as promised does not necessarily carry an implication that there is a right to claim compensation for physical injury which results from their use.[10]

In English law the advantages of strict contractual liability are substantially offset by the requirements of privity which confine the benefits and liabilities of contracts to the immediate contracting parties.[11] Accordingly a purchaser may not claim under the contract of sale against anyone other than his immediate vendor (vertical privity). He could not, for example, sue a wholesaler or manufacturer in contract. Similarly a contractual remedy is denied to all but the purchaser (horizontal privity). It is not available to a third party, no matter how close his connection with the purchaser and with the product. Even in the United States where the requirements of privity have long been modified, it has been found that a contractual liability carries further limitations. For example, exemption clauses are, in principle, effective to safeguard the vendor although their effectiveness has been curtailed by both the courts and statute.[12] There may also be difficulties where the supply is not by way of a sale.[13]

The result of such considerations is that there has been a need for a liability which is based in tort and which is free from the constraints of the

---

[8] Sale of Goods Act 1893, ss. 13(1), 14(2), 14(3) as amended by the Supply of Goods (Implied Terms) Act 1973, ss. 2 and 3. See also the Consumer Credit Act 1974, s. 192(3)(a) and Sch. 4, para. 35. These implied conditions are discussed below, pp. 69–78 (correspondence with description), pp. 78–97 (merchantable quality) and pp. 98–107 (fitness for purpose).
[9] [1903] 1 K.B. 610. See further below, pp. 107–110.
[10] See Waddams, "Strict Liability, Warranties and the Sale of Goods" (1969), 19 Univ. Toronto Law Jo. 157, 159–160.
[11] Privity of contract is discussed further below, chapter 2.
[12] Exemption clauses are discussed below, chapters 7 and 8. The principal examples of statutory control are the Sale of Goods Act 1893, s. 55, as amended by the Supply of Goods (Implied Terms) Act 1973, s. 4, and, in America, the unconscionability clause of UCC art. 2–302 and UCC art. 2–316.
[13] See, e.g., *Perlmutter* v. *Beth David Hospital*, 123 N.E. 2d 792 (N.Y. 1954) (blood transfusion held to be a contract for services which did not attract strict contractual liability) and in general below, pp. 115–122.

law of contract. It was not until the decision of the House of Lords in *Donoghue* v. *Stevenson*[14] in 1932 that this need could be said to have been met in English law at least in cases of carelessly inflicted damage. The equivalent American case of *Macpherson* v. *Buick Motor Co.*[15] had been decided in the New York Court of Appeals some sixteen years earlier. The decision in *Donoghue* v. *Stevenson* will be discussed later. In this introductory chapter it is convenient to summarise the position in both the English and the American law of tort before 1932 and 1916 respectively, and then to note the main strands of later American developments.

Winterbottom v. Wright and exceptions to the early rule of non-liability

The decision in *Winterbottom* v. *Wright*[16] is generally cited to illustrate the early rule of non-liability in the English law of tort. The plaintiff was a coachman employed by persons who had contracted with the Postmaster-General to run a mail-coach between Hartford and Holyhead. The defendant had entered into a separate contract with the Postmaster-General to supply a coach for the same purpose, promising that "the said mail-coach should, during the said contract, be kept in a fit, proper, safe and secure state and condition". When the plaintiff was driving the coach he suffered injuries after it had broken down, throwing him from his seat. In his declaration he averred that this was because the defendant had "so improperly and negligently conducted himself, and so utterly disregarded his aforesaid contract, and so wholly neglected and failed to perform his duty in this behalf". The Court of Exchequer held that the declaration did not disclose a cause of action.

The form of the plaintiff's declaration makes it possible to argue that the decision of the court meant no more than that the plaintiff could not sue on the contract of supply and repair to which he was not a party. The privity of contract rule would clearly have prevented this. But this is an extremely narrow interpretation of the decision. The claim was conceived as an action on the case and it seems to have been understood that the plaintiff was pointing to the contract solely to indicate the nature of the defendant's connection with the coach and hence the origin of the duty of care for which he was contending. Indeed it was central to Lord

---

[14] [1932] A.C. 562, H.L.

[15] 217 N.Y. 382, 111 N.E. 1050 (1916).

[16] (1842), 10 M. & W. 109. For a general discussion of both *Winterbottom* v. *Wright* and *Langridge* v. *Levy* (1837), 2 M. & W. 519, affd. (1838), 4 M. & W. 337, below, p. 301, see Winfield, "Duty in Tortious Negligence" (1934), 34 Col. L.R. 41, 51 *et seq.*

Abinger's objection to recovery that it would be unjust to the defendant if, after accounts had been settled between the contracting parties, "we should subject them to be ripped open by this action of tort being brought against him".[17]

The assumption behind *Winterbottom* v. *Wright* was, it seems, that the defendant's contract with the Postmaster-General delimited his potential liability in the matter of supplying and repairing the coach. It did not permit of an independent and concurrent duty being owed to third parties. This, in any event, was how the case came to be interpreted in the years before *Donoghue* v. *Stevenson*.[18]

Whatever the precise basis for the decision it appears to have been prompted by a feeling that it was necessary to avoid a multiplicity of claims. Thus Lord Abinger observed in a much cited passage that:[19]

"There is no privity of contract between these parties; and if the plaintiff can sue, every passenger, or even any person passing along the road, who was injured by the upsetting of the coach, might bring a similar action. Unless we confine the operation of such contracts as this to the parties who entered into them, the most absurd and outrageous consequences, to which I can see no limit, would ensue."

Similarly, Alderson, B. noted that:[20]

"If we are to hold that the plaintiff could sue in such a case, there is no point at which such actions would stop. The only safe rule is to confine the right to recover to those who enter into the contract: if we go one step beyond that, there is no reason why we should not go fifty."

The argument is familiar and it may be that it was grounded on an outdated view of industry at the time it was advanced.[1] In any event it is clear that the pattern of liability produced by a combination of the rules for contract and tort was not easily justifiable. The vendor of a coach might have been strictly liable to the purchaser when damage resulted from an undetectable defect,[2] but he would not be liable to an injured driver or passengers even though he had clearly been careless.

A number of qualifications to this rule of non-liability were developed over the years.[3] Thus it was clear that a supplier was at least under a duty

---

[17] (1842) 10 M. & W. 109, 115.
[18] [1932] A.C. 562, H.L. See, e.g., *Blakemore* v. *Bristol and Exeter Rail. Co.* (1858), 8 E. & B. 1035; *Alton* v. *Midland Rail. Co.* (1865), 19 C.B. N.S. 213; *Collis* v. *Selden* (1868), L.R. 3 C.P. 495; *Earl* v. *Lubbock* [1905] 1 K.B. 253; *Blacker* v. *Lake & Elliot, Ltd.* (1912), 106 L.T. 533.
[19] (1842), 10 M. & W. 109, 114.
[20] *Ibid.*, at p. 115.
[1] See P. S. James, "The Liability of Manufacturers for Faulty Goods", [1960] J.B.L. 287, 288.
[2] *Cf. Randall* v. *Newson* (1877), 2 Q.B.D. 102, C.A., above, p. 5.
[3] For a general discussion of the development and scope of these exceptions, see Levi, *An Introduction to Legal Reasoning* (1948), at pp. 8–27. See also Bohlen, "Liability of

to refrain from deceit,[4] to disclose known dangers,[5] and not to permit a dangerous article to fall into the hands of a person who was unable to handle it with safety.[6] These basic duties which are common to all who supply or control the use of products are discussed in a later chapter.[7]

Appliances on premises

A further qualification was established by the Court of Appeal in *Heaven* v. *Pender*.[8] The defendant was the owner of a dry dock used for the painting and repair of vessels. He supplied and erected the staging necessary for such work but did so on the basis that control of the staging passed to the shipowner whose vessel was in the dock. The plaintiff was employed by a master painter who had contracted with a shipowner to paint his vessel in the defendant's dock and he was injured when a defective rope supporting the cradle on which he was working broke, throwing him to the ground. The cradle had been erected by the defendant earlier the same day.

In the resultant proceedings the Court of Appeal unanimously rejected the defendant's contention that the plaintiff was in essentially the same position as the coachman in *Winterbottom* v. *Wright*.[9] Cotton and Bowen, LL.J. relied on decisions holding that an occupier might be liable to an invitee when the source of danger remained within his own control.[10] In the light of such decisions it was a small step to subject the occupier to a similar duty of care when he handed over appliances to a third party for the immediate use of invitees on the premises.[11] Brett, M.R. concurred in the result but his reasoning was based on altogether broader grounds. In his judgment a duty of care arose because a man of ordinary sense would have recognised that if he did not use care and skill he would cause injury or damage to the person or property of another.[12]

Manufacturers to Persons Other than their Immediate Vendees" (1929), 45 L.Q.R. 343; Feezer, "Tort Liability of Manufacturers and Vendors" 10 Minn. L.R.1 (1925); Feezer, "Tort Liability of Manufacturers" 19 Minn. L.R. 752 (1935).

[4] *Langridge* v. *Levy* (1837), 2 M. & W. 519, affd. (1838) 4 M. & W. 337 is the leading case.

[5] *Clarke* v. *Army & Navy Cooperative Society*, [1903] 1 K.B. 155, C.A.

[6] *Dixon* v. *Bell* (1816), 5 M. & S. 198.

[7] See below, chapter 15, pp. 300–304.

[8] (1883), 11 Q.B.D. 503.

[9] (1842), 10 M. & W. 109, above, p. 7.

[10] Notably *Indermaur* v. *Dames* (1867), L.R. 1 C.P. 274, and *Smith* v. *London and St. Katherine Docks Co.* (1868), L.R. 3 C.P. 326.

[11] See also *Elliott* v. *Hall* (1885), 15 Q.B.D. 315, where liability was imposed when injury was suffered off the premises by an employee unloading coal from a defective truck sent out by the defendant colliery owner.

[12] *Cf.* (1883), 11 Q.B.D. 503, 509–510.

This approach and its application to a case of product liability was later to influence Lord Atkin in his speech in *McAlister (or Donoghue)* v. *Stevenson*.[13] But it was rejected by Cotton and Bowen, LL.J. as being inconsistent with existing authorities.[14] With the benefit of hindsight one can say that Brett, M.R. was some fifty years ahead of his time.

Inherently dangerous chattels

Another exception to the general rule of non-liability covered chattels which were described as "inherently" or "imminently" dangerous or as "dangerous in themselves". Judicial recognition of this mode of classifying chattels is to be found in *Longmeid* v. *Holliday*.[15] The plaintiff, Eliza Longmeid, had been burned by naphtha following the explosion of a certain "Holliday" lamp which, there was evidence to suggest, had been constructed negligently. The defendant retailer had sold the lamp to her husband, having bought in the parts and caused it to be constructed by third parties. Delivering his judgment in the Court of Exchequer Parke, B. agreed that liability might be incurred:[16]

> "when any one delivers to another without notice an instrument *in its nature dangerous* . . . as a loaded gun[17] which he himself loaded, and that other person to whom it is delivered is injured thereby . . ."

On the facts of the case, however, the lamp was not regarded as a thing which was dangerous in itself, and since the jury had negatived any question of fraud the plaintiff's claim failed.

The same distinction was taken in *Dominion Natural Gas Co., Ltd.* v. *Collins & Perkins*.[18] Here the defendants had installed apparatus to control the pressure of natural gas which they were supplying to a railway company. Normal practice would have required a pipe to have been placed on the emission nozzle of a safety valve to take escaping gas through to the open air; but the defendants allowed the valve to discharge into the enclosed chamber of a blacksmith's shop. After a resultant explosion in which one man was killed and another injured the Privy Council upheld a decision in favour of the plaintiffs on the ground that:[19]

---

[13] [1932] A.C., 562, 580–582, H.L.
[14] *Cf.* (1883), 11 Q.B.D. 503, 516 *per* Cotton, L.J. with whom Bowen, L.J. concurred.
[15] (1851), 6 Ex. 761.
[16] *Ibid.*, at p. 767. Emphasis supplied.
[17] Citing *Dixon* v. *Bell* (1816), 5 M. & S. 198.
[18] [1909] A.C. 640, P.C.
[19] *Ibid.*, at p. 646.

"in the case of articles dangerous in themselves, such as loaded firearms, poisons, explosives, and other things *ejusdem generis*, there is a peculiar duty to take precautions imposed upon those who send forth or install such articles when it is necessarily the case that other parties will come within their proximity."

Although a number of different products were classified as "dangerous in themselves",[20] the exception was applied sparingly. Thus it was held, for example, that a van which shed its wheel was not a thing dangerous in itself.[1] Neither was a brazing lamp containing inflammable mineral oil under pressure,[2] nor a domestic steam boiler without a safety valve.[3] By its very nature the exception could not cover a product whose sole danger lay in faulty workmanship on an individual item. It might, however, have been extended to cover products which, although not inevitably dangerous as a class, were nonetheless "inherently" dangerous in the sense that their danger stemmed from a general deficiency in design. This step does not, however, appear to have been taken.[4]

American developments before Macpherson v. Buick Motor Co.[5]

Early American developments followed broadly the same path as English law with the same exceptions to a general rule of non-liability,[6] although the exceptions were interpreted more liberally. Thus it was clear for

---

[20] See, e.g., *Burfitt* v. *Kille*, [1939] 2 K.B. 743; [1939] 2 All E.R. 372 (loaded gun); *Jefferson* v. *Derbyshire Farmers, Ltd.*, [1921] 2 K.B. 281, 289 (petrol); *Parry* v. *Smith* (1879), 4 C.P.D. 325 (leaking gas meter); *Anglo-Celtic Shipping Co., Ltd.* v. *Elliott and Jeffrey* (1926), 42 T.L.R. 297 (cleansing fluid which gave off explosive gases).

[1] *Earl* v. *Lubbock*, [1905] 1 K.B. 253.

[2] *Blacker* v. *Lake and Elliott, Ltd.* (1912), 106 L.T. 533.

[3] *Ball* v. *London County Council*, [1949] 2 K.B. 159; [1949] 1 All E.R. 1056, C.A. The case was criticised by Goodhart, "Dangerous Things and the Sedan Chair" (1949), 65 L.Q.R. 518 and would be decided differently today in the light of *A. C. Billings & Sons, v. Riden*, [1958] A.C. 240; [1957] 3 All E.R. 1. Excluded also, it seems are bows and arrows: *Ricketts* v. *Erith Borough Council*, [1943] 2 All E.R. 629; air rifles: *Donaldson* v. *McNiven*, [1952] 1 All E.R. 1213, 1215; and catapults: *Smith* v. *Leurs* (1945), 70 C.L.R. 256 (High Ct. of Australia), although in this latter case counsel did not argue the contrary.

[4] *Cf. Blacker* v. *Lake and Elliott, Ltd.* (1912), 106 L.T. 533 where the brazing lamp which exploded appears to have been designed dangerously. For negligence in design, see below, chapter 11. For the current status of this system of classification, see below, pp. 253–255.

[5] 217 N.Y. 382, 111 N.E. 1050 (1916) below, p. 13.

[6] See, e.g., *Goodlander Mill Co.* v. *Standard Oil Co.*, 63 F. 400 (7th Cir., 1894); *Bragdon* v. *Perkins Campbell Co.*, 87 F. 109 (3rd. Cir., 1898); *McCaffrey* v. *Mossberg and Glanville Manufacturing Co.*, 50 Atl. 651, 55 L.R.A. 822 (R.I., 1901); *Lebourdais* v. *Vitrified Wheel Co.*, 80 N.E. 482 (Mass., 1907); *Tompkins* v. *Quaker Oats Co.*, 131 N.E. 456 (Mass., 1921).

example that liability might be incurred for fraud or deceit,[7] failure to disclose known dangers,[8] supplying dangerous articles to persons who could not handle them with safety,[9] and where defective appliances injured persons on premises.[10]

The most important exception approximated to the English category of products which were dangerous in themselves. *Thomas* v. *Winchester*[11] was an early example. Here the defendant manufacturer of drugs had supplied a particular container labelled extract of dandelion when it in fact contained extract of belladonna, a deadly poison. The compound was subsequently resold by a retail druggist to the plaintiff who, having used it as the extract of dandelion for which she had a prescription, became seriously ill. Recovery was permitted in a New York court on the ground that the defendant's negligence had put human life in imminent danger.

Liability was extended beyond things which would have been classified in English law as "dangerous in themselves" to a somewhat wider category of cases. The principle was summarised by Judge Sanborn in *Huset* v. *J.I. Case Threshing Co.* in the following terms:[12]

"[An] act of negligence of a manufacturer or vendor which is imminently dangerous to the life or health of mankind, and which is committed in the preparation or sale of an article intended to preserve, destroy, or affect human life, is actionable by third parties who suffer from their negligence."

Poisons and firearms were obviously included within this description;[13] but so also were drugs, and food and drink.[14] Excluded, however, were a

---

[7] See 2 Frumer and Friedman, *Products Liability*, s. 17.01 and below p. 300. For an unusual early case, see *State to use of Hartlove* v. *Fox & Son*, 79 Md. 514 (1894). D, knowing his horse to have glanders, informed the purchaser that is was "suffering from nothing worse than a bad cold". A third party who had looked after the horse contracted glanders and died. His claim failed through incorrect pleading.

[8] See, e.g., *Lewis* v. *Terry*, 43 P. 398 (Cal., 1896). See also *Gerkin* v. *Brown and Sehler Co.*, 143 N.W. 48 (Mich., 1913); *Karsteadt* v. *Gross Co.*, 190 N.W. 844 (Wis., 1922) and, in general, Eldredge, *Modern Tort Problems* (1941), at pp. 249–253.

[9] See, e.g., *Bernard* v. *Smith*, 90 A. 657 (R.I., 1914) and, in general, below, pp. 303–304.

[10] See e.g., *Coughtry* v. *Globe Woolen Co.*, 56 N.Y. 124, 12 Am. Rep. 387 (1874); *Devlin* v. *Smith*, 89 N.Y. 470, 42 Am. Rep. 311 (1882). See also *Hayes* v. *Philadelphia and Reading Coal and Iron Co.*, 23 N.E. 225, (Mass., 1890); *Bright* v. *Barnett and Record Co.*, 26 L.R.A. 524 (Wisc., 1894).

[11] 6 N.Y. 397, 57 Am. Dec. 455 (1852).

[12] 120 F. 865, 870 (8th Cir., 1903).

[13] *Thomas* v. *Winchester* above; *Norton* v. *Sewall*, 106 Mass. 143, 8 Am. Rep. 298 (Mass., 1870) (laudanum sold as rhubarb); *Peters* v. *Jackson*, 57 L.R.A. 428 (W. Va., 1902) (saltpetre for epsom salts); *Herman* v. *Markham Air Rifle Co.*, 258 F. 475 (D.C. Mich., 1918) (loaded air rifle).

[14] *Blood Balm Co.* v. *Cooper*, 5 L.R.A. 612 (Ga., 1889) (iodide of potash); *Tonsman* v. *Greenglass*, 142 N.E. 756 (Mass., 1924) (iron in bread); *Bishop* v. *Webber*, 139 Mass. 411 (Mass., 1885) (devilled crab); *Roberts* v. *Anheuser Busch Brewing Assn.*, 98 N.E. 95 (Mass., 1912).

defective balance wheel on a circular saw,[15] a steam boiler,[16] a hot water bottle,[17] and, until *Macpherson* v. *Buick Motor Co.*,[18] a defective car.[19] The latter, unlike the former, were neither potable nor edible; nor were they regarded as inherently dangerous when constructed carefully.[20]

The major breakthrough associated with *Macpherson* v. *Buick Motor Co.*[1] came in 1916, although it had been foreshadowed in earlier cases. The plaintiff had purchased a car manufactured by the defendant corporation from an intermediate dealer and he was injured when a wheel collapsed as he was driving at some eight miles per hour. The wheel had been bought in from a reputable manufacturer and there was evidence that its defective condition could have been discovered by a reasonable inspection. There was no suggestion of fraud or knowledge on the part of the defendants. Nor could the vehicle readily be described as "dangerous in itself" in the sense of being dangerous when constructed carefully. Indeed the trial court judge had told the jury that an "automobile is not an inherently dangerous vehicle". Yet a majority of the Court of Appeals of New York affirmed a judgment holding the defendants liable.

This conclusion was justified by Justice Cardozo through reference to a series of cases[2] in which the principle of *Thomas* v. *Winchester*[3] had been pushed to its furthest limits. The inference was that that principle was "not limited to poisons, explosives, and things of like nature, to things which in their normal operation are implements of destruction". He added:[4]

> "If the nature of a thing is such that it is reasonably certain to place life and limb in peril when negligently made, it is then a thing of danger. Its nature gives warning of the consequences to be expected. If to the element of danger there is added knowledge that the thing will be used by persons other than the purchaser, and used without new tests, then, irrespective of contract, the manufacturer of this thing of danger is under a duty to make it carefully. That is as far as we are required to go for the decision of this case."

---

[15] *Loop* v. *Litchfield*, 42 N.Y. 351, 1 Am. Rep. 513 (1870).

[16] *Losee* v. *Clute*, 51 N.Y. 494, 10 Am. Rep. 638 (1873).

[17] *Smith* v. *Davidson Rubber Co.*, 35 N.E. 2d 486 (Mass., 1940).

[18] 217 N.Y. 382, 111 N.E. 1050 (N.Y.C.A., 1916), below.

[19] *Cadillac Motor Co.* v. *Johnson*, 221 F. 801 (2nd Cir., 1915). The case was reheard in the immediate aftermath of *Macpherson* v. *Buick Motor Co.* and the plaintiff obtained a reversal: 261 F. 878 (2nd Cir., 1919).

[20] Borderline cases were presented by soap, chewing tobacco, and the container for a beverage: see Prosser, *Law of Torts*, 4th edn., 1971, p. 642, notes 16–18.

[1] 217 N.Y. 382, 111 N.E. 1050 (1916).

[2] Notably, *Statler* v. *George Ray Manufacturing Co.*, 88 N.E. 1063 (N.Y.C.A., 1909) (coffee urn); *Torgensen* v. *Schultz*, 84 N.E. 956 (N.Y.C.A., 1908) (bottles of aerated water). Reliance was also placed on *Devlin* v. *Smith*, 89 N.Y. 470, 42 Am. Rep. 311 (1882).

[3] 6 N.Y. 397, 57 Am. Dec. 455 (1852), above, p. 12.

[4] 111 N.E. 1050, 1053 (1916).

On the facts of the case he concluded that an automobile "was as much a thing of danger as a defective engine for a railroad".[5] The fact that *Macpherson* v. *Buick Motor Co*, was associated with *Thomas* v. *Winchester* and its principle of imminent danger led some courts to qualify their general acceptance of the decision by construing it narrowly. Thus it was held, for example, that a bed with inadequate supports which collapsed beneath a pregnant woman was not "an article that is reasonably certain to place life and limb in peril".[6] Similarly, liability was denied in a series of cases involving shoes with protruding nails,[7] a truck with a defective door handle,[8] and a Maxwell House coffee tin with a dangerous opening key.[9]

This restrictive approach was however untypical and shortlived. In other cases recovery was permitted when injury stemmed from ordinary household items such as stools, chairs, ladders, sewing machines and dresses,[10] and when damage to property alone was in issue.[11] The decision of the Supreme Court of Massachusetts in *Carter* v. *Yardley & Co. Ltd.*[12] in 1946 was notable for its change of emphasis. Permitting recovery in negligence by a person who had suffered a second degree burn after applying the defendant's perfume to her skin, the court said:[13]

"The doctrine of the *MacPherson* case is now generally accepted. Its acceptance has brought all dangerous things into the same class as the 'inherently dangerous' things to which the principle already stated has always been applied. The *MacPherson* case caused the exception to swallow the asserted general rule of nonliability, leaving nothing upon which that rule could operate. Wherever that case is accepted, the rule in truth is abolished, and ceases to be part of the law."

---

[5] 111 N.E. 1050, 1053 (1916).
[6] *Field* v. *Empire Case Goods Co.*, 166 N.Y.S. 509 (1917).
[7] *Kerwin* v. *Chippewa Shoe Manufacturing Co.*, 157 N.W. 1101 (Wis., 1916). See also Fleming James, "Products Liability" (1955), Texas L.R. 44, 61–63.
[8] *Cohen* v. *Broakway Motor Truck Corporation*, 268 N.Y.S. 545 (1934).
[9] *Boyd* v. *American Can. Co.*, 291 N.Y.S. 205 (1936).
[10] *Blickman Inc.* v. *Chilton*, 114 S.W. 2d 646 (Tex. Civ. App., 1938); *Okker* v. *Chrome Furniture Manufacturing Co.*, 97 A. 2d 699 (N.J., 1953) (stools); *Sheward* v. *Virtue*, 126 P. 2d 345 (Cal., 1942) (chair); *Kalash* v. *Los Angeles Ladder Co.*, 34 P. 2d 481 (Cal., 1934) (ladder); *White Sewing Machine Co.* v. *Feisel*, 162 N.E. 633 (Ohio App., 1927) (sewing machine); *Noone* v. *Fred Perlberg Inc.*, 49 N.Y.S. 2d 460, affd. 60 N.E. 2d 839 (N.Y., 1945) (inflammable dress). See also *United States Radiator Corporation* v. *Henderson*, 68 F. 2d 87 (10th Cir., 1933) (domestic boiler).
[11] *Kolberg* v. *Sherwin Williams Co.*, 269 P. 975 (Cal., 1928) (spray for fruit trees); *Du Pont de Nemours & Co.* v. *Baridon*, 73 F. 2d 26 (8th Cir., 1934) (disinfectant for bulbs). In other cases recovery had been denied, as in *Windram Manufacturing Co.* v. *Boston Blacking Co.*, 131 N.E. 454 (Mass., 1921).
[12] 64 N.E. 2d 693 (Mass., 1946).
[13] *Ibid.*, at p. 700.

American developments after Macpherson v. Buick Motor Co.

English law has not made any significant advance beyond the position reached in the United States of America at the time of *Macpherson* v. *Buick Motor Co.*[14] In the United States itself, however, the law has been transformed by a series of developments all of which have led to the gradual substitution of strict liability for liability dependent on proof of negligence.[15] Since frequent reference will be made to these developments it is convenient to summarise them at this stage.

The process of imposing liability without fault began in cases involving adulterated food and drink.[16] Thereafter a separate strand of cases associated with the decision in *Baxter* v. *Ford Motor Co.*[17] began to impose liability on manufacturers in respect of claims made when advertising their products. Liability was imposed for breach of express warranties and it was justified on the basis that manufacturers ought not to be free to represent that their products possess qualities which they do not possess and at the same time be able to point to the absence of privity as a reason for denying liability to those who consume or use the products. English law could accommodate a similar liability without undue difficulty[18] and it is strange that it has not done so.

Any clear distinction between express and implied warranties is difficult to maintain especially where the former are to be found in promotional literature and other advertising. This was perhaps a reason underlying the gradual development of an implied warranty theory of liability. Beginning with the early food and drink cases the process was extended so that

---

[14] 217 N.Y. 382, 111 N.E. 1050 (1916).

[15] For a selection of articles in American periodicals, see Prosser, "The Assault upon the Citadel (Strict Liability to the Consumer)", 69 Yale L. Jo. 1099, (1960); Prosser, "The Fall of the Citadel (Strict Liability to the Consumer)", 50 Minn. L. Rev. 791 (1966); Kessler, "Products Liability", 76 Yale L. Jo. 887 (1967); Traynor, "The Ways and Meanings of Defective Products and Strict Liability", 32 Tenn. L. Rev. 363 (1965); Wade "Strict Tort Liability of Manufacturers", 19 Sw. L. Jo. 5 (1965). For contributions in English periodicals, see Legh-Jones, "Products Liability: Consumer Protection in America", [1969] C.L.J. 54; Pasley "The Protection of the Purchaser and Consumer under the Law of the USA" (1969), 32 M.L.R. 241; Waddams, "The Strict Liability of Suppliers of Goods" (1974), 37 M.L.R. 154. See also Jolowicz, "The Protection of the Consumer and Purchaser of Goods under English Law" (1969) 32 M.L.R. 1.

[16] See, e.g., *Mazetti* v. *Armour & Co.*, 75 Wash. 622, 135 Pac. 633 (1913); Prosser, 69 Yale L. Jo. 1099, 1103–1110, *Law of Torts*, 4th edn., 1971, pp. 653–656.

[17] 12 P. 2d 409, 88 A.L.R. 521 (1932); 15 P. 2d 1118 (1932) (rehearing); 35 P. 2d 1090 (1934) (second appeal), below, pp. 58–62.

[18] The obvious basis for such liability is the offer of a unilateral contract to whoever buys (or perhaps uses) the goods: see *Carlill* v. *Carbolic Smoke Ball Co.*, [1893] 1 Q.B. 256; *Wells (Merstham), Ltd.* v. *Buckland Sand and Silica, Ltd.*, [1965] 2 Q.B. 170; [1964] 1 All E.R. 41, and below, pp. 64–65.

manufacturers, generally, were taken to warrant that their products were of merchantable quality and reasonably fit for their purpose.[19] *Henningsen* v. *Bloomfield Motors Inc.*[20] is the leading case. Here the plaintiffs had acquired a new Plymouth sedan car manufactured by the Chrysler Corporation and sold through an authorised dealer. The car had been purchased by a husband as a gift for his wife and the wife was injured when faulty steering caused it to go out of control as she was driving it. There was no evidence of negligence to go to the jury but the Supreme Court of New Jersey upheld verdicts for both plaintiffs against the manufacturer and the dealer and in respect of the breach of an implied warranty of merchantability. Dealing with the position as between the plaintiff purchaser and the manufacturer the court said, "an implied warranty that it is reasonably suitable for use as such accompanies [the car] into the hands of the ultimate purchaser. Absence of agency between the manufacturer and the dealer who makes the ultimate sale is immaterial."[1] The breadth of the principle is well illustrated by the fact that the wife was similarly entitled to recover against both manufacturer and dealer although she was not herself a purchaser. Dealing with her position the court added:[2]

> "[It] is our opinion that an implied warranty of merchantability chargeable to either an automobile manufacturer or a dealer extends to the purchaser of the car, members of his family, and to other persons occupying or using it with his consent. . . . Those persons must be considered within the distributive chain."

Had these facts occurred in an English case the requirement of privity of contract would have led to a markedly different result. The husband alone would have had the benefit of strict contractual liability and only then in a claim against the dealer, whilst the wife would have failed through inability to establish negligence.[3]

Although breach of implied warranty is still regularly pleaded in personal injury cases the adaptation of sales warranties to non-sales relationships was not always free from difficulty. Whether the claim is under the *Henningsen* doctrine or under the third party beneficiary provisions of Article 2–318 of the Uniform Commercial Code[4] there is a danger that it may fail through restrictions imported from either the law of sales or the general law of contract.[5] Indeed Prosser has said that as a device for the justification of strict liability to the consumer the warranty "carries far too much luggage in

---

[19] See 2 Frumer and Friedman, *Products Liability*, s. 16.04 [2]; 2 Harper and James, *Law of Torts*, (1956 with 1968 supplement), ss. 28.15–28.25.
[20] 161 A. 2d 69 (1960).
[1] *Ibid.*, at p. 84.
[2] *Ibid.*, at p. 100.
[3] Privity of contract is discussed below, chapter 2.
[4] See below, p. 28.
[5] Apart from the privity problem some of the more important obstacles include the

the way of undesirable complications, and it is more trouble than it is worth."[6] Strict liability in tort is undoubtedly a more appropriate way of achieving the same goal and the emphasis has now changed to this theory of liability. *Greenman* v. *Yuba Power Products Inc.*[7] is the leading case. The plaintiff was suing in respect of injuries received from a combination power tool which had been manufactured by the defendants and purchased by the plaintiff's wife from a retailer. A piece of wood had flown out of the tool as he was using it and severely injured his forehead. His claim for the breach of an express warranty contained in the manufacturer's brochure[8] succeeded despite a contention that he had not given notice of breach in accordance with the requirements of sales legislation. But, in any event, the Supreme Court of California believed that "the remedies of injured consumers ought not to be made to depend upon the intricacies of the law of sale".[9] In the words of Justice Traynor:[10]

> "A manufacturer is strictly liable in tort when an article he places on the market, knowing that it is to be used without inspection for defects, proves to have a defect that causes injury to a human being."

Although there is no definitive version of the rule for strict liability in tort the American Law Institute, *Restatement of Torts,* 2d, s. 402A, is usually cited although not invariably followed. It provides that:

> "(1) One who sells any product in a defective condition unreasonably dangerous[11] to the user or consumer or to his property is subject to liability for physical harm thereby caused to the ultimate user or consumer, or to his property, if
>   (a) the seller is engaged in the business of selling such a product, and
>   (b) it is expected to and does reach the user or consumer without substantial change in the condition in which it is sold.
> (2) The rule stated in Subsection (1) applies although
>   (a) the seller has exercised all possible care in the preparation and sale of his product, and
>   (b) the user or consumer has not bought the product from or entered into any contractual relation with the seller."

---

following: (i) the necessity for a "sale" (see *Lasky* v. *Economy Grocery Stores,* 65 N.E. 2d 305 (Mass., 1946)); (ii) the procedural rules of U.C.C. art. 2–607(3) requiring adequate notice of breach; (iii) exemption clauses.
[6] *Law of Torts,* 4th edn., 1971, p. 656.
[7] 27 Cal. Rptr. 697 (1963).
[8] For manufacturers' express warranties, see below, pp. 58–62.
[9] Citing *Ketterer* v. *Armour & Co.,* 200 F. 322, 323 (1912).
[10] 27 Cal. Rptr. 697, 700 (1962).
[11] For discussion of the words "defective condition unreasonably dangerous to the user etc.", see below, pp. 186–189.

Section 402A is followed by a caveat stating that:

"The Institute expresses no opinion as to whether the rules stated in this section may not apply:
(1) to harm to persons other than users or consumers;
(2) to the seller of a product expected to be processed or otherwise substantially changed before it reaches the user or consumer; or
(3) to the seller of a component part of a product to be assembled."

Similar principles have been developed to cover persons such as retailers and lessors of defective products[12] whilst liability has been extended, predictably, to benefit bystanders and others who neither "use" nor "consume".[13] More difficulty has been experienced with manufacturers of component parts and of products which require processing.[14] This is to be expected since there is little in common between the manufacturer of, say, a defective car tyre and the manufacturer of a nut and bolt which might be used for a multiplicity of purposes. There has also been difficulty in finding a uniform approach to economic loss[15] and to the problems of contributory negligence and abnormal use.[16]

---

[12] See, e.g., *Vandermark v. Ford Motor Co.*, 37 Cal. Rptr. 896 (Sup. Ct. California, 1964) (retailer) (below, p. 307); *Cintrone v. Hertz Truck Leasing and Rental Service*, 212 A. 2d 769 (N.J., 1965) (lessor) (below, p. 308); *Canifax v. Hercules Powder Co.*, 46 Cal. Rptr. 552 (1965) (wholesaler) (below, p. 311); *Stuart v. Crestview Mutual Water Co.*, 110 Cal. Rptr. 543 (1973) (land developer); *Realmuto v. Straub Motors Inc.*, 322 A. 2d 440 (N.J., 1974) (used car dealer); 2 *Frumer and Friedman*, s. 16A [4] [b].

[13] See, e.g., *Elmore v. American Motors Corporation*, 75 Cal. Rptr. 652 (1969); *Sills v. Massey Ferguson Inc.*, 296 F. Supp. 776 (1969); 2 *Frumer and Friedman*, s. 16.04 [2] [c], 16A [4] [c]. See also below, pp. 29–30, notes 14–15 and cases there cited.

[14] See *Restatement of Torts*, 2d s. 402A, comments p and q. *Goldberg v. Kollsman Instrument Corporation*, 240 N.Y.S. 2d 592, 191 N.E. 2d 81 (1963) (altimeter) is a leading case denying recovery under a strict liability theory on the facts. *Cf.*, however, *Suvada v. White Motor Co.*, 201 N.E. 2d 313 (Ill., 1965) (brake system); *Haley v. Merit Chevrolet Inc.*, 214 N.E. 2d 347 (Ill., 1966) (car tyre), and below, pp. 227–228.

[15] See below, chapter 16, at pp. 338–342 especially.

[16] See below, pp. 295–296.

Part I
Liability in Contract
and for Misrepresentations

2 Privity of Contract

Introduction

The first part of this book covers the liability of a vendor of goods for misrepresentations and for breaches of the express and implied terms of a contract of sale. Reference is also made to certain analogous transactions such as contracts for the hire-purchase or hire of goods and contracts for work and materials.

Although a vendor's liability will normally be contractual, it will be seen later that a more widespread liability may also be incurred in tort. Thus liability may be imposed for deceit,[1] for failing to disclose known dangers,[2] supplying a dangerous article into incompetent hands,[3] omitting to inspect or to warn that an inspection has not been undertaken,[4] and for representing that a product is safe for its intended use when it is not.[5] In all such cases fraud or negligence must be established and this may be especially difficult where goods are marketed in sealed containers.[6] Sometimes a would-be purchaser will have to sue in tort if he is to sue at all. This would be true for example of a customer who is injured by a bottle which explodes as he is taking it off a supermarket shelf and hence before the conclusion of the

---

[1] *Langridge* v. *Levy* (1837), 2 M. & W. 519; affd. (1838), 4 M. & W. 337.

[2] *Clarke* v. *Army and Navy Cooperative Society*, [1903] 1 K.B. 155, C.A.

[3] *Burfitt* v. *Kille*, [1939] 2 K.B. 743; [1939] 2 All E.R. 372. See also *Dixon* v. *Bell* (1816), 5 M. & W. 198.

[4] *Andrews* v. *Hopkinson*, [1957] 1 Q.B. 229; [1956] 3 All E.R. 422.

[5] *Watson* v. *Buckley, Osborne, Garret & Co., Ltd., and Wyrovoys Products, Ltd.*, [1940] 1 All E.R. 174. See, in general, below, pp. 304–307.

[6] See, e.g., *Gordon* v. *M'Hardy* 1903, 6 F. (Ct. of Sess.) 210; *Kratz* v. *American Stores Co.*, 59 A. 2d 138 (Pa., 1948) and, in general, below, pp. 305–307. The other side of the coin is, of course, that the manufacturer is unlikely to be exempted on the ground that there was an opportunity for intermediate inspection (see below, pp. 284–290), whilst the defect will be readily traceable to the manufacturer (see below, pp. 279–281).

contract of sale.[7] In other cases a purchaser will have a claim in both contract and tort arising out of the same facts. This has caused some difficulty, especially where the action in tort is founded on a negligent misrepresentation under the *Hedley Byrne* doctrine.[8] But generally the possibility of concurrent liability must be conceded. Where this overlap exists, a plaintiff will concentrate on the theory of liability most favourable to him. An exemption clause may, for example, be apt to cover a defendant's strict contractual liability but not liability in negligence.[9] The rules for remoteness of damage differ as between contract and tort[10] and so may the application of limitation periods[11] and of defences.[12] Again, the quantum of damages may differ, since an award of damages for breach of contract is intended to make good the contractual promise whereas damages in tort are intended to compensate for losses actually suffered.[13] These points are developed later. Initially, however, it is convenient to discuss the implications of the privity requirement to which reference was made in the introductory chapter.

Privity of contract

It has been seen that the general pattern of English product liability law is to impose strict liability for breach of express and implied warranties as between parties to a contract of sale, but to require proof of fault or negligence in the absence of a contract between the parties. There is nothing necessarily indefensible about treating a purchaser who has furnished

---

[7] *Pharmaceutical Society of Great Britain* v. *Boots*, [1953] 1 Q.B. 401; [1953] 1 All E.R. 482. For examples see *Hart* v. *Dominion Stores* (1968), 67 D.L.R. (2d) 675; *Lasky* v. *Economy Grocery Stores*, 65 N.E. 2d 305 (Mass., 1946). Similar problems might arise with "free samples" and "trial runs". See Waddams, "Strict Liability, Warranties and the Sale of Goods" (1969), 19 Univ. Toronto L.J. 157, 163–166, 183–198, and below, pp. 115–116 and pp. 308–309.

[8] *Hedley Byrne & Co.* v. *Heller & Partners*, [1964] A.C. 465; [1963] 2 All E.R. 575, H.L., below, pp. 43–45, and pp. 337–338.

[9] As in *White* v. *John Warrick & Co., Ltd.*, [1953] 2 All E.R. 1021; [1953] 1 W.L.R. 1285 where the contract was one of hire. The point is less important now that liability for breach of the conditions implied by the Sale of Goods Act 1893, ss. 13–15, as amended, cannot be excluded in consumer sales: see below, pp. 142–150.

[10] In contract the position is judged as at the date when the contract was made, whereas in tort it is judged at the date of the tortious act. And in tort there is a greater willingness to hold that damage is foreseeable: see *The Heron II*, [1969] 1 A.C. 350; [1967] 3 All E.R. 686, H.L.

[11] See below, pp. 296–299.

[12] Notably the defence of contributory negligence: see below, p. 97, note 4.

[13] See Ogus, *The Law of Damages* (1973), pp. 286–288; Cheshire & Fifoot, *Law of Contract* (9th edn., 1976), pp. 274, 588–604, and cases there cited, *Fillmore's Valley Nurseries, Ltd.* v. *North American Cyanamid, Ltd.* (1958), 14 D.L.R. (2d) 297 provides a good example of the different approach to quantifying damages in contract and tort respectively: see below, pp. 53–56.

consideration more favourably *vis-à-vis* the vendor than a third party who has not. Nor is there necessarily anything indefensible about treating a third party on the same basis as the purchaser, whether the third party be a sub-purchaser of the product, a donee, employee, passenger in a car, bystander, or indeed anyone else. Yet nowadays the full implications of the privity requirement are difficult to defend. This is especially so in a "consumer sale" where the basic terms of the contract are imposed by law rather than as a matter of genuine agreement between the parties,[14] and where the product is frequently purchased for the use of a family as a whole. The privity rules are that much less defensible since the contractual régime does not concern itself solely with the protection of economic or expectation interests. It covers personal injury and property damage as well.[15]

The implications of the privity requirement may be conveniently illustrated by reference to the case of *Daniels and Daniels* v. *R. White & Sons, Ltd. and Tarbard*,[16] an example which is also taken in the Law Commission Working Paper,[17] Mr Daniels, a street trader, had purchased from Mrs Tarbard, the licensee of a public house, a bottle of lemonade which had been manufactured and bottled by R. White & Sons Ltd. The bottle contained a quantity of carbolic acid and Mr and Mrs Daniels had both become ill on drinking it. On such facts Mr Daniels could sue Mrs Tarbard in contract and he recovered in respect of his illness without proof of negligence.[18] Neither Mr nor Mrs Daniels could sue the manufacturers R. White & Sons Ltd. in contract, although Whites might have broken their own contract by supplying contaminated lemonade to their immediate purchaser. Mr Daniels was not a party to this contract and Mrs Daniels was not a party to any contract. Both Mr and Mrs Daniels could, however, sue Whites in tort in respect of their illness, but proof of negligence was required and the claim failed on the facts.[19] It is unlikely that Mr Daniels could have recovered the value of the lemonade, as such, from Whites (even on proof of negligence) and substantially certain that Mrs Daniels could not have done so had she been a disappointed donee.

---

[14] Since the coming into force of the Supply of Goods (Implied Terms) Act 1973 the implied conditions imposed by ss. 13–15 of the Sale of Goods Act 1893 cannot be excluded in the case of consumer sales: see below, pp. 142–150. For the definition of a "consumer sale", see below, pp. 147–150.

[15] See *Randall* v. *Newson* (1877), 2 Q.B.D. 102; *Wren* v. *Holt*, [1903] 1 K.B. 610.

[16] [1938] 4 All E.R. 258.

[17] See Working Paper No. 64, "Liability for Defective Products" (1975), paras. 8, 120.

[18] Recovery was based on the breach of the implied condition of merchantable quality imposed by s. 14(2) of the 1893 Act. The plaintiff failed to establish a breach of an implied condition of reasonable fitness for purpose since reliance on the seller's skill or judgment could not be shown: see further below, pp. 102–105.

[19] The case has been criticised and the unwillingness of Lewis, J. to infer negligence is out of step with the general trend of cases: see below, p. 258.

The loss would have been purely financial and the law of tort does not readily compensate such losses.[20] Mrs Daniels could not sue Mrs Tarbard, the licensee, in contract in respect of her illness since she was not a party to the contract between Mrs Tarbard and Mr Daniels. She might have sued her in tort (as might her husband), but on the facts of the case it was unlikely that she would have succeeded in proving negligence. In the result she did not obtain compensation from anyone.

The consequence of Mr Daniels suing Mrs Tarbard was not necessarily that she would have been burdened with the cost of compensating him. In the normal course of events she would have sued her own supplier for breach of warranty, and so through third and, if necessary, fourth party proceedings the loss would be passed down the line to the manufacturers themselves.[1] Admittedly, this might not always be possible. The chain might be broken by an effective exemption clause,[2] insolvency, or by an intermediary going out of business. The loss would then lie at the point immediately before the break. Furthermore, Mr Daniels's position of apparent strength might have proved illusory for a number of reasons. In the first place, Mrs Tarbard might have become insolvent,[3] or have been otherwise unable to meet a claim. Secondly, she might have escaped liability by showing that Mr Daniels had inspected the goods before purchase (there being in consequence no liability for such defects as that examination ought to have revealed), or, alternatively, that his attention had been drawn to particular defects.[4] This was admittedly unlikely on the facts. Thirdly, Mr. Daniels, being a person who had purchased the goods before the coming into force of the Supply of Goods (Implied Terms) Act 1973, might have been defeated by a term in the contract exempting the vendor from liability.[5] Finally, had Mr Daniels been a litigant in the

---

[20] See below, pp. 328–344. Conceivably, recovery might have been granted to at least Mr Daniels on the theory that physical harm was threatened, although it did not, on the assumed facts, materialise: see below, p. 336, note 13 and cases there cited.

[1] *Kasler and Cohen* v. *Slavouski*, [1928] 1 K.B. 78; *Dodd and Dodd* v. *Wilson and McWilliam*, [1946] 2 All E.R. 691. The retailer may commence entirely separate proceedings against his own supplier or institute third party proceedings in the original action. U.C.C., art. 2–607(5) provides for a "vouching-in" procedure whereby the buyer may give his seller written notice of the litigation and the seller may become bound by any determination of fact common to the two litigants.

[2] The Supply of Goods (Implied Terms) Act 1973 still permits reliance on such clauses in non-consumer sales to the extent that this is fair or reasonable: see below, pp. 150–158.

[3] As occurred in *International Harvester Co. of Australia Pty., Ltd.* v. *Carrigan's Hazeldene Pastoral Co.* (1958), 100 C.L.R. 644 (High Ct. Australia) discussed below, p. 63. See also Stoljar (1959), 32 A.L.J. 307.

[4] See, respectively, s. 14(2)(*b*) and s. 14(2)(*a*) of the 1893 Act, as amended.

[5] Since this was a consumer sale exemption clauses would no longer be effective. But the courts may still have to deal with cases such as *Cehave N.V.* v. *Bremer Handelsgesellschaft m.b.H.*, [1976] Q.B. 44, [1975] 3 All E.R. 739, below, p. 42 in which the relevant contract pre-dated the coming into force of the Act.

United States, he might have been defeated in his contract claim by the requirement of the Uniform Commercial Code that notice of breach must be given to the seller within a reasonable time after the buyer has actual or constructive knowledge of it.[6]

In these circumstances a number of possibilities have been discussed and a number of developments have occurred. These have been aimed first and foremost at an extension of the rights of buyers against manufacturers, and thereafter at an extension of the rights of third parties against both retailers and manufacturers. The process is generally known as dispensing with the requirements of "vertical" and "horizontal" privity. The meaning of these terms is not self-evident, but they are explained by the Law Commission as follows:[7]

> "If the manufactured product is thought of as descending a chain of distribution from the producer to the middleman and on to the retailer who sells to the public, 'vertical privity' is the privity which each of these persons has with his predecessor and successor, and 'horizontal privity' is the ensuing privity of contract between the retailer and the first domestic consumer who buys from him, and then between that consumer and any sub-consumer, if such there be."

Dispensing with vertical privity requirements[8]

In the belief that it is wrong that the manufacturer of a product should be held liable only on proof of negligence whilst a retail seller is held strictly liable,[9] it might be suggested that an ultimate purchaser should be able to sue the manufacturer on the latter's contract of sale. All that would then need to be established would be a breach of the manufacturer's contract with his own commercial buyer (whether a retailer or an intermediate wholesaler), the requirements of "vertical" privity having been waived.

---

[6] See U.C.C., art. 2–607 (3) (a). Official Comment No. 4 states that the provision is "designed to defeat commercial bad faith, not to deprive a good faith consumer of his remedy". But Prosser has described the earlier provision in the Uniform Sales Act, s. 49 as a "booby-trap for the unwary": see "The Assault upon the Citadel: Strict Liability to the Consumer", 69 Yale L.J. 1099, 1130 (1960).

[7] See Working Paper No. 64, "Liability for Defective Products", para. 120.

[8] On the relaxation of vertical and horizontal privity generally, see Law Commission Working Paper No. 64, paras. 119–135; Working Paper No. 18, paras. 32–41; Legh Jones, "Products Liability: Consumer Protection in America" (1969), C.L.J. 54, 56–57; Waddams, *Products Liability* (1974), pp. 208–213, Waddams, "Strict Liability of Suppliers of Goods" (1974), 37 M.L.R. 154, 157–159; Pasley, "The Protection of the Purchaser and the Consumer under the Law of the USA" (1969), 32 M.L.R. 241, 246–249; Pelster, "The Contractual Aspect of Consumer Protection: Recent Developments in the Law of Sales Warranties", 64 Mich. L.R. 1430 (1966): Note, 42 Wash. L.R. 253 (1966).

[9] The arguments in favour of imposing strict liability on the manufacturer are noted below, p. 357.

In *Daniels and Daniels* v. *R. White & Sons, Ltd. and Tarbard*,[10] Mr Daniels might then have sued Whites directly, and in contract. Similar reasoning might be applied, *mutatis mutandis,* to enable an ultimate purchaser to sue an intermediate distributor. As applied to manufacturers the immediate practical consequences would include (i) the imposition of a measure of strict liability; (ii) the "leapfrogging" of intermediate parties, so avoiding circuity of action; and (iii) the possible facilitation of recovery for economic losses.

A proposal along these lines is at first sight attractive. But a moment's reflection reveals a number of drawbacks or limitations. These stem largely from the fact that such an approach does not impose a direct and separate duty on the manufacturer. It merely extends to the consumer buyer the benefit of such obligations as the manufacturer may have assumed towards his own buyer. In this the approach differs from the strict tort theory of *Greenman* v. *Yuba Power Products Inc.*,[11] and probably also from the theory associated with *Henningsen* v. *Bloomfield Motors Inc.*,[12] whereby manufacturers are subjected to duties similar to the implied warranties of sales legislation.[13] The consequences of this approach include the following. Firstly, whilst the retail seller cannot now exclude his liability under a consumer sale, the manufacturer may (albeit subject to certain safeguards) and might have done so. Hence had Whites excluded their contractual liability Mr Daniels could not have sued on that contract.[14] Secondly, the manufacturer's own buyer may have assumed certain risks or have undertaken to prepare the goods for further distribution, the result being that there is no breach of contract by the manufacturer at all. Thirdly, the time lag between the two contracts of sale may be so substantial that the limitation period governing the first contract has already run its course by the time the second contract is entered into; or, if not, will have done so very shortly thereafter.[15] Further, as the Law Commission notes, the buyer may experience difficulty in obtaining precise knowledge of the manufacturer's contract,[16] and a relaxation of vertical privity which is confined to consumer sales may involve "separating contracts for the supply of goods from other contracts, such as contracts for the supply of services".[17] This

---

[10] [1938] 4 All E.R. 258, above, p. 23.

[11] 27 Cal. Rptr. 697 (Cal. Sup. Ct., 1963), above, p. 17.

[12] 161 A. 2d 69 (N.J., 1960), above, p. 16.

[13] The approach has been favoured recently by the Ontario Law Reform Commission Report, *Consumer Warranties and Guarantees in the Sale of Goods.* See chapter 5, pp. 65–77 especially.

[14] For discussion of the criteria which determine the efficacy of exemption clauses in non-consumer sales, see below, pp. 152–158.

[15] For limitation periods, see below, pp. 296–299.

[16] Working Paper No. 64, para. 127.

[17] *Op. cit.,* para. 122. The distinction still has important ramifications where exemption clauses are concerned: see below, pp. 142–143.

would be difficult to justify. At least where the plaintiff has suffered personal injuries there is much to be said for adopting a uniform principle of recovery as between consumer and non-consumer sales, and as between sales and the supply of services.[18] Finally, non-purchasers would not be able to recover on the original sales contract, unless there was a corresponding relaxation of horizontal privity limitations as well. Mrs Daniels would not have been able to sue Whites, although she suffered the same injury and inconvenience as her husband.

Dispensing with horizontal privity requirements[19]

There are many situations where the requirement of privity does apparent injustice to persons who are clearly consumers or users, but who cannot recover damages for their injuries because they did not themselves purchase the goods.[20] In some cases the buyer may inform the seller that he is acquiring the goods as a gift, although the identity of the donee may not necessarily be disclosed: alternatively, the point may be made clear implicitly, as where goods are gift-wrapped at Christmas time. In other cases it may be obvious that the purchaser is buying goods for the use of others, as where parents buy toys or children's clothing, or a restaurant or beauty parlour owner takes delivery of food, cosmetics, hair dye or lotions.[1] In yet other cases it may be clear that although the purchaser will use the goods he will not do so exclusively, as where furniture or detergent is purchased for household use, or food is purchased for family consumption. Finally, there are cases in which the product may be purchased for the buyer's own use, but where third parties (whether they are members of the family or not) are likely to be affected by it. A car, for example, will clearly be used to carry passengers, and it is also likely to affect other third parties, whether road users or pedestrians.

A number of devices have been brought into play to confer a remedy on persons who might otherwise have been regarded as strangers to the contract under which the goods were purchased.[2] Thus resort has been had

---

[18] A relaxation of vertical privity which was confined to consumer sales would not, e.g., benefit the small retailer injured by defective goods as in *Barnett* v. *H. and J. Packer & Co., Ltd.*, [1940] 3 All E.R. 575.

[19] For the meaning of "horizontal privity", see above, p. 25.

[20] See, e.g., *Daniels and Daniels* v. *R. White & Sons, Ltd. and Tarbard*, [1938] 4 All E.R. 258; *Preist* v. *Last*, [1903] 2 K.B. 148; *Buckley* v. *La Reserve*, [1959] Crim. L.R. 451.

[1] See, e.g., *Garthwait* v. *Burgio*, 216 A. 2d 189 (Conn., 1965) where, however, the claim succeeded under the strict tort theory.

[2] Gillam, "Products Liability in a Nutshell", 37 Ore. L.R. 119, 153–155 (1957) refers to twenty-nine such devices used to defeat vertical and horizontal privity requirements in the USA. See also Prosser, "The Assault upon the Citadel", 69 Yale L.J. 1099, 1124–1125 (1960).

to agency principles to permit recovery by the third party.[3] On other occasions the injured party has been deemed to be the purchaser whatever may have been the exact position between the purchasers themselves. This has been true of cases in which food has been purchased in a restaurant,[4] and where goods have been purchased for the exclusive use or consumption of the plaintiff, as where lamb patties were bought for a wife subject to special dietary requirements.[5] The opportunities have not been exploited fully in English law. Yet there are clearly limits to what can be done under an approach which recognises the privity limitation whilst seeking to avoid its full implications.

Nowadays, there would be some agreement that it is not only purchasers who should have the benefit of strict liability. The principal difficulty in any reformulation of the law is to decide how far the benefit should be extended and in respect of what types of damage or loss. A relatively modest extension is to be found in Alternative A of art. 2–318 of the Uniform Commercial Code. This provides that:[6]

> "A seller's warranty whether express or implied extends to any natural person who is in the family or household of his buyer or who is a guest in his home if it is reasonable to expect that such person may use, consume or be affected by the goods and who is injured in person by breach of the warranty. A seller may not exclude or limit the operation of this section."

This provision caters for some of the worst anomalies which flow from the privity limitation, but it is obviously limited in scope. The privity requirement is relaxed only for personal injury to a fairly closely defined category of persons and the relaxation is only at the "horizontal" and not at the "vertical" level. An injured donee could not sue on the warranty unless he was "in the family or household of his buyer or ... a guest in his home"[7] and even then he could sue only on the retail vendor's warranty and not on the manufacturer's.[8]

---

[3] See *Vaccarino v. Cozzubo*, 31 A. 2d 316 (Md., 1943) (daughter agent of father); *Bowman v. Great Atlantic and Pacific Tea Co.*, 133 N.Y.S.2d 904 (1954), affd. 125 N.E. 2d 125 (1955) (sister as agent): *Twombley v. Fuller Brush Co.*, 158 A. 2d 110 (Md., 1960) (wife as agent). See also *Heil v. Hedges*, [1951] 1 T.L.R. 512, 513.

[4] *Lockett v. A. and M. Charles Ltd.*, [1938] 4 All E.R. 170. See also *Wallis v. Russell*, [1902] 2 I.R. 585; *Conklin v. Hotel Waldorf Astoria Corporation*, 161 N.Y.S. 2d 205 (1957). Cf. *Buckley v. La Reserve*, [1959] Crim. L.R. 451.

[5] *Russell v. First National Stores*, 79 A. 2d 573 (N.H., 1951).

[6] See 1 *Uniform Laws Annotated* (Master Edition), p. 249.

[7] See, e.g., *Hochgertel v. Canada Dry*, 187 A. 2d 575 (Pa., 1963) (employee who did not qualify); but cf. *Petterson v. Lamb Rubber Co.*, 5 Cal. Rptr. 863 (1960), where the California Supreme Court held an employee to be within the provision. See also *Miller v. Preitz*, 221 A. 2d 320 (Pa., 1966), where a child was regarded as being in the same "family" as an aunt who lived next door; and in general, 2 Frumer & Friedman, *Products Liability*, s. 16.03[5][6][7]; 16.04[3].

[8] This follows from the fact that the seller's warranty only runs in favour of a natural person

Alternative B of art. 2–318 is not so limited. It extends a seller's warranty to benefit "any natural person who may reasonably be expected to use, consume or be affected by the goods and who is injured in person by breach of the warranty". Again, it is only personal injury which is covered, but this time a donee could sue on the seller's warranty and the provision is not so worded as to preclude an action against an intermediate seller or manufacturer. Finally, Alternative C would go further and include property damage by extending a seller's warranty to benefit "any person[9] who may reasonably be expected to use, consume or be affected by the goods and who is injured by breach of the warranty". This approach is closer to that of the *Restatement of Torts*, 2d, s. 402A and, although this latter provision is expressed as benefiting only an "ultimate user or consumer"[10] it has been extended to cover persons such as bystanders who neither use nor consume.[11] None of the Alternatives extends the warranty to a case of economic loss without physical damage and this extension has not been consistently (or even typically) made under the strict tort or implied warranty theories either.[12]

The general tenor of American decisions has clearly been to expand the scope of recovery and, although the response of the various state jurisdiction has been by no means uniform, there has been a gradual move away from Alternative A of the Code. Thus, whatever the theory of recovery adopted,[13] a wide range of plaintiffs has been afforded the benefit of strict liability. These have included members of a purchaser's family,[14] his guests,[15] employees,[16] users and borrowers,[17] lessees,[18] passengers,[19] beauty

---

who is in the family etc. of *his* buyer. An injured member of a retailer's family could no doubt sue the intermediate seller, but such situations are uncommon.

[9] This time a corporation no less than a "natural person" may benefit from the provision.

[10] For the meaning of "user or consumer" in s. 402A, see accompanying comment (l). S. 402A is set out above, p. 17.

[11] See, e.g., *Elmore* v. *American Motors Corporation*, 75 Cal. Rptr. 652 (1969); *Sills* v. *Massey Ferguson Inc.*, 296 F. Supp. 776 (1969). Caveat 1 to s. 402A is neutral on the question whether the rule may not apply "to harm to persons other than users or consumers": see above, p. 18.

[12] *Cf. Seely* v. *White Motor Co.*, 45 Cal. Rptr. 17 (1965) and, in general, below, pp. 338–342.

[13] And this may be (i) a simple relaxation of privity as traditionally understood; (ii) strict tort liability; or (iii) the attributing of implied warranties to the manufacturer.

[14] *Greenberg* v. *Lorenz*, 173 N.E. 2d 773 (N.Y., 1961); *Klein* v. *Duchess Sandwich Co.*, 93 P. 2d 799 (1939).

[15] *Conklin* v. *Hotel Waldorf Astoria Corporation*, 161 N.Y.S. 2d 205 (1957).

[16] *Petterson* v. *Lamb Rubber Co.*, 5 Cal. Rptr. 863 (1960); *Cintrone* v. *Hertz Truck Leasing and Rental Service*, 212 A. 2d 769 (N.J., 1965); *Haragan* v. *Union Oil Co.*, 312 F. Supp. 1392 (1970) (employee of independent contractor).

[17] *Chapman* v. *Brown*, 198 F. Supp. 78 (1961), affd. 304 F. 2d 149 (9th Cir., 1962).

[18] *Simpson* v. *Powered Products of Michigan, Inc.*, 192 A. 2d 555 (Conn., 1963).

[19] *King* v. *Douglas Aircraft Co.*, 159 So. 2d 108 (Fla., 1963); *Henningsen* v. *Bloomfield Motors, Inc.*, 161 A. 2d 69 (N.J., 1960).

parlour patrons,[20] rescuers,[1] bystanders,[2] hospital patients,[3] repairers,[4] and visitors.[5] There is little doubt that the trend is towards imposing liability without fault where any person is injured or suffers property damage through contact with a defective product.

Again, however, it is important to note the limits which may accompany any decision to extend liability through the medium of relaxing horizontal privity requirements. The main limit reflected in art. 2–318 of the Uniform Commercial Code (in all of its three alternatives) is that liability depends on establishing a "sale", although under Alternatives B and C the seller may be a manufacturer as well as a retailer. In recent years, however, a number of states have enacted legislation covering lessors and other suppliers of products as well as sellers.[6] Substantially the same development is to be seen under the strict tort theory where the reference in the *Restatement of Torts*, 2d, s. 402A to one who "sells" any product has been extended to cover persons other than sellers.[7] Apart from this point, the ability of a third party to sue would still be made dependent on the position as between the contracting parties themselves. Admittedly a retailer in a consumer sale cannot now exclude his liability in English law for breach of the implied conditions of merchantable quality and fitness for purpose. But he may still prevent these conditions from accruing, as by drawing attention to specific defects or by encouraging the buyer to examine the goods.[8] Whether the position of a third party should be thus determined by conduct on the part of the buyer which falls short of a supervening cause may be doubted.[9]

---

[20] *Garthwait v. Burgio*, 216 A. 2d 189 (Conn., 1965).

[1] *Guarino v. Mine Safety Appliance Co.*, 255 N.E. 2d 173 (N.Y., 1969).

[2] *Elmore v. American Motors Corporation*, 75 Cal. Rptr. 652 (1969); *Sills v. Massey Ferguson Inc.*, 296 F. Supp. 776 (1969); *Codling v. Paglia*, 298 N.E. 2d 461 (N.Y., 1973); *Mitchell v. Miller*, 214 A. 2d 694 (Conn., 1965).

[3] *Bernstein v. Lily-Tulip Cup Corporation*, 177 So. 2d 362 (Fla. App., 1965).

[4] *Connolly v. Hagi*, 188 A. 2d 884 (Conn., 1963).

[5] *Handrigan v. Apex Warwick, Inc.*, 275 A. 2d 262 (R.I., 1971).

[6] Massachusetts, for example, has repealed Alternative A of art. 2–318 and substituted the following: "Lack of privity between plaintiff and defendant shall be no defense in any action brought against the manufacturer, seller or supplier of goods to recover damages for breach of warranty, express or implied, or for negligence, although the plaintiff did not purchase the goods from the defendant, if the plaintiff was a person whom the manufacturer, seller or supplier might reasonably have expected to use, consume or be affected by the goods. The manufacturer, seller, lessor or supplier may not exclude or limit the operation of this section." See 1 *Uniform Laws Annotated*, Cumulative Supp. 1976, p. 226, where further examples are cited.

[7] Including, e.g., lessors of products (*Cintrone v. Hertz Truck Leasing and Rental Service*, 212 A. 2d 769 (N.J., 1965)). See further above, p. 18, note 12 and below, chapter 15.

[8] See, respectively, Sale of Goods Act 1893, s. 14 (2) (*a*), s. 14 (2) (*b*), as amended, and below, pp. 144–145.

[9] For discussion of supervening causes, see below, chapter 14, pp. 283–284.

Finally, a relaxation of horizontal privity without further reform may not leave the law in a satisfactory position overall. In Published Working Paper No. 18, the Law Commission originally proposed that:[10]

> "in consumer sales the benefits of the seller's obligations under ss. 12–15 of the Sale of Goods Act 1893 should be extended to any person who may reasonably be expected to use, consume or be affected by the goods".

Had this proposal been enacted within the framework of the existing law one would have reached the somewhat startling position of holding retailers strictly liable to third parties whilst continuing to absolve manufacturers from liability unless negligence could be established. A manufacturer's contract of sale would not come within the category of a consumer sale.

---

[10] Para. 37.

3 Express Warranties and Misrepresentations: I

Before or at the time of entering a contract a buyer's attention will frequently be drawn to statements which relate to the quality and potential of the goods. Such statements may take any one of a number of forms and the way they are classified will have an important effect on the remedies available should they ultimately be found to be false or unsubstantiated. Thus a statement may be no more than a mere "puff" or a matter of opinion and, as such, it will usually give rise to no liability whatsoever.[1] Alternatively it may constitute a misrepresentation of fact inducing the representee to enter into the contract. The traditional remedy would then be rescission of the contract and an indemnity in equity,[2] damages in the tort of deceit if the statement was made fraudulently[3] and, more recently, damages under the *Hedley Byrne*[4] doctrine if it was made negligently.[5] Within English law the Misrepresentation Act 1967 is now of considerable importance in such cases. Such a statement may also give rise to an estoppel, thus precluding its maker from asserting its falsity as against a person who was intended to rely on it and did rely on it to his detriment.[6] Finally, the statement may be classified as a contractual term. Where this is so the maker will be taken to have warranted or guaranteed the truth of the statement and a remedy will be available without the need to prove

---

[1] Liability might exceptionally be incurred under the *Hedley Byrne* doctrine: see below, p. 45.
[2] See *Newbigging* v. *Adam* (1886), 34 Ch.D. 582, C.A., and below, pp. 49–53.
[3] See *Derry* v. *Peek* (1889), 14 App. Cas. 337, H.L., below, pp. 300–302.
[4] *Hedley Byrne & Co., Ltd.* v. *Heller & Partners, Ltd.*, [1964] A.C. 465; [1961] 1 All E.R. 82, H.L.
[5] As in *Esso Petroleum Co., Ltd.* v. *Mardon*, [1976] 2 Q.B. 801; [1976] 2 All E.R. 5 below, p. 40, where damages were also awarded for breach of contract. There has been some doubt as to the application of this principle as between contracting parties. But *Esso Petroleum Co., Ltd.* v. *Mardon* appears to have removed the doubts: see below, p. 44.
[6] See Spencer Bower and Turner, *Estoppel by Representation* (2nd edn., 1966), chapter II: Cross, *Evidence* (4th edn., 1974), chapter XIII, pp. 302–306 especially; Atiyah, "Misrepresentation, Warranty and Estoppel" (1971), 9 Alberta Law Rev. 347, 368–385.

deceit or negligence. The precise nature of this remedy (whether repudiation or damages) will depend on the status or importance of the term to the contract.[7] This classification and its legal consequences will now be examined in more detail in so far as it affects the relationship of vendor and purchaser. Thereafter it is proposed to discuss the possible application of some of the principles to manufacturers. In this latter context particular reference will be made to the express warranty theory of American law and to the collateral contract doctrine of English and Commonwealth law.

Liability as between vendors and purchasers

Puffs and statements of opinion[8]

A statement which constitutes a mere puff has no legal effect. *Simplex commendatio non obligat.* Such a statement is invariably vague and impressionistic, part of the accepted licence accorded to salesmen and the advertising industry, and its truth or falsity cannot be assessed by reference to any identifiable standard. Examples from Anglo-American jurisprudence are legion. Thus statements that land was "uncommonly rich water meadow" or "fertile and improvable"[9] have been regarded as mere puffs, as have statements that a reaper was "a very good second-hand reaper";[10] the defendant would serve a "good" sandwich;[11] a ladder would "last a lifetime" or was of "good quality";[12] a fingernail kit was "wonderful";[13] an abrasive disc was better than any other available anywhere;[14] and that a stove was "fool proof".[15] Such statements add nothing to the seller's obligations under the general law and reliance on them is clearly unjustifiable.

But the licence to puff cannot be taken too far and both English and American courts have shown a willingness to attribute legal effect to statements of commendation. This is true of statements such as those in *Carlill*

---

[7] See further below, pp. 41–43.

[8] See *Benjamin's Sale of Goods* (1974), paras. 733–735; *Williston on Sales* (3rd edn., revd., 1948), ss. 202–204; (4th edn., 1974), ss. 15–8, 17–6.

[9] See *Scott* v. *Hanson* (1829), 1 Russ. & M. 128; *Dimmock* v. *Hallett* (1866), 2 Ch. App. 21.

[10] *Chalmers* v. *Harding* (1868), 17 L.T. 571. See also *Walker* v. *Milner* (1866), 4 F. & F. 745 ("strong, holdfast, thiefproof" safe: not a warranty).

[11] *Albrecht* v. *Rubenstein,* 63 A. 2d 158 (Conn., 1948), 7 A.L.R. 2d 1022 (1949).

[12] *Lambert* v. *Sistrunk,* 58 So. 2d 434 (Fla., 1952); *Carney* v. *Sears Roebuck & Co.,* 309 F. 2d 300 (4th Cir., 1962).

[13] *Jacquot* v. *William Filene's Sons Co.,* 149 N.E. 2d 635 (Mass., 1958).

[14] *Jakubowski* v. *Minnesota Mining and Manufacturing Co.,* 193 A. 2d 275 (N.J., 1963).

[15] *Camden Fire Insurance Co.* v. *Peterman,* 270 N.W. 807 (Mich., 1937). For an extensive list of examples, see *Williston on Sales* (revised edn.), s. 203, footnote 16.

v. *Carbolic Smoke Ball Co.*[16] where fairly specific claims have been made for the product. It is also true of statements which induce reliance whilst being less specific. Thus representations of safety have frequently been held to counteract the effect of an accompanying warning[17] and, as will be seen later, American courts have been willing to base a manufacturer's express warranty on general advertising claims.[18] In *Osborn* v. *Hart*[19] it was held that the words "superior old port wine" were capable of constituting a warranty which was broken on delivery of wine which was almost undrinkable. In more recent years McNair, J. treated a dealer's assurances that a car was "a good little bus. I will stake my life on it" as forming the basis of a collateral contract whereby the car was warranted reasonably safe for use.[20] Similarly in *Admiral Oasis Hotel Corporation* v. *Home Gas Industries Inc.*[1] the Appellate Court of Illinois held that a warranty might be founded on statements claiming that an air conditioning unit was well constructed and would cool rooms as well or better than any other on the market. Obviously there might be room for disagreement over how cold was "cool", and as to when a unit was "well constructed". But the accuracy of the statements could nonetheless be gauged by reference to meaningful standards of ordinary commercial usage. Where such standards exist the statement is unlikely to be regarded as a mere puff.

There is a similar difficulty in distinguishing between statements of opinion and statements of fact when the words do not take the form of a commendation or puff. The distinction has proved troublesome in a number of cases involving paintings attributed to a particular artist,[2] and horses which were claimed to be sound.[3] The whole area is one in which generalisations are unhelpful since much will depend on the precise words

---

[16] [1893] 1 Q.B. 256, C.A. (£100 "reward" to anyone who contracted influenza after using Smoke Ball three times daily for two weeks according to printed instructions).

[17] See, e.g., *Maize* v. *Atlantic Refining Co.*, 41 A. 2d 850 (Pa., 1945); *McLaughlin* v. *Mine Safety Appliances Co.*, 181 N.E. 2d 430 (N.Y.C.A., 1962), and below, pp. 243–244.

[18] See *Baxter* v. *Ford Motor Co.*, 12 P. 2d 409, 88 A.L.R. 521 (1932), and below, pp. 58–62.

[19] (1871), 23 L.T. 851. See also *Anthony* v. *Halstead* (1877), 37 L.T. 433.

[20] *Andrews* v. *Hopkinson*, [1957] 1 Q.B. 229; [1956] 3 All E.R. 422. For collateral contracts, see below, p. 38, and pp. 64–65.

[1] 216 N.E. 2d 282 (Ill. App., 1965).

[2] Compare *Jendwine* v. *Slade* (1797), 2 Esp. 572 (no warranty as to paintings said to be by Loraine and Teniers) with *Power* v. *Barham* (1836), 4 Ad. & El. 473 (warranty as to painting being a Canaletto); *Lomi* v. *Tucker* (1829), 4 C. & P. 15 ("a couple of Poussin's"); *De Sewhangerg* v. *Buchanan* (1832), 5 C. & P. 343 (Rembrandt: "I am an *ancien militaire*, and would not deceive you"); *Leaf* v. *International Galleries*, [1950] 2 K.B. 86; [1950] 1 All E.R. 693 (Salisbury Cathedral by Constable).

[3] Compare *Hopkins* v. *Tanqueray* (1854), 15 C.B. 130 with *Schawel* v. *Reade*, [1913] 2 Ir. Rep. 81; *Couchman* v. *Hill*, [1947] K.B. 554; [1947] 1 All E.R. 103. See also *Gee* v. *Lucas* (1867), 16 L.T. 357 ("In foal to Warlock" held to be a warranty) and, in general, *Benjamin's Sale of Goods*, para. 734.

used and the context in which they were uttered. The following points may, however, be noted. Firstly, statements of opinion will, at the very least, embody an implied representation of fact that the opinion or belief is honestly held.[4] If a private seller of a car informs the buyer that he believes the car to be in good order he may have expressed no more than an opinion about the state of the car but he will have made an affirmation of fact as to the genuineness of his belief.[5] The same reasoning might be applied to statements concerning the value of goods which would themselves normally be treated as expressions of opinion.[6] Secondly, importance will be attached to the parties' relative expertise and access to the facts. Where the representor is an expert, the courts may find an implied affirmation of fact that he has reasonable grounds for his belief.[7] Such a finding is unlikely where the parties were dealing at arm's length or where the representee appreciated that the matter was one of speculation, the representor having no experience in the field.[8] Estimates as to potential performance may, however, amount to actionable misrepresentations of fact or even embody a promise that care has been taken in making an estimate.[9] The distinction between opinion and fact can usually be subsumed within a wider inquiry into whether there was reasonable reliance on the part of the representee.[10]

---

[4] See *Smith* v. *Land and House Property Corporation* (1884), 28 Ch.D. 7, C.A.; *Brown* v. *Raphael*, [1958] Ch. 636; [1958] 2 All E.R. 79.

[5] 2 *Williston on Sales*, (4th edn., 1974), s. 15–8, pp. 357–358. The distinction is far from clear cut. In *Oscar Chess, Ltd.* v. *Williams*, [1957] 1 All E.R. 325; [1957] 1 W.L.R. 370 below, p. 39 the private vendor's statement as to the age of her second-hand car appears to have been treated as a statement of fact. Yet it is doubtful whether she was doing more than expressing an opinion. See also *Ecay* v. *Godfrey* (1947), 80 LL.L Rep. 286.

[6] See *Haygarth* v. *Wearing* (1871), L.R. 12 Eq. 320, 327–328 (Wickens, V.C.). U.C.C. s. 2–313 (2) states, *inter alia*, that "an affirmation merely of the value of the goods...does not create a warranty".

[7] See *Smith* v. *Land and House Property Corporation* (1884), 28 Ch.D. 7, 15 *per* Bowen, L. J. In *United States Pipe and Foundry Co.* v. *City of Waco*, 108 S.W. 2d 43 (Tex. 1937) it was said: "Superior knowledge of seller and relative ignorance of buyer converts slightest divergence from mere praise into representations of fact". See also *Ruberoid Co., Inc.* v. *Briscoe*, 293 F. 2d 712 (5th Cir., 1961).

[8] *Bisset* v. *Wilkinson*, [1927] A.C. 177, P.C.; *Anderson* v. *Pacific Fire and Marine Insurance Co.* (1872), L.R. 7 C.P. 65.

[9] *Esso Petroleum Co., Ltd.* v. *Mardon*, [1976] 2 Q.B. 801; [1976] 2 All E.R. 5 below, p. 40; see also *Cullinane* v. *British "Rema" Manufacturing Co., Ltd.*, [1954] 1 Q.B. 292; [1953] 2 All E.R. 1257, C.A., and *cf. Savage & Sons Pty., Ltd.* v. *Blakney* (1970), 119 C.L.R. 435 (High Ct. Australia).

[10] See below, pp. 46–47.

Warranties and "mere" representations[11]

English law has experienced considerable difficulty in dealing with liability between contracting parties in respect of affirmations of fact which prove to be false. Part of this difficulty has been self-imposed. However, much of it is inherent in the need to determine the circumstances in which relief will be granted to the representee and the type of relief or remedy which will be afforded.

Representation or term: promissory intent, reliance, or basis of bargain

Affirmations of fact which are made before or at the time of entering a contract might be classified in a number of ways. In the United States of America the Uniform Sales Act classifies according to whether the buyer had purchased the goods in reliance on the affirmation.[12] The present Uniform Commercial Code emphasises the importance of the affirmation within the bargain. Article 2–313 provides that:[13]

> "(1) Express warranties by the seller are created as follows: (a) Any affirmation of fact or promise made by the seller to the buyer which relates to the goods and becomes part of the basis of the bargain creates an express warranty that the goods shall conform to the affirmation or promise. . . .
>
> (2) It is not necessary to the creation of an express warranty that the seller use formal words such as 'warrant' or 'guarantee' or that he have a specific intention to make a warranty . . ."

The change of emphasis from "reliance" to "basis of the bargain" does not seem to have made much difference in practice. What is important, rather, is the equivalence of affirmations of fact and promises and the ability of either to constitute an express warranty.

Within English law the emphasis is, at least in theory, different. The effect of the decision of the House of Lords in *Heilbut, Symons and Co. v. Buckleton*[14] is that an affirmation of fact is a warranty only where, in words

---

[11] See *Benjamin's Sale of Goods* (1974), paras. 743–751; 1 *Williston on Sales*, revised edn., chapter VIII, ss. 194–202 especially; *Williston on Sales*, 4th edn., 1974, chapter 15; chapter 17; Greig, "Misrepresentations and Sales of Goods" (1971), 87 L.Q.R. 179; Atiyah, "Misrepresentation, Warranty and Estoppel" (1971), 9 Alberta L. Rev. 347; Allan, "Affirmations or Promises Made in the Course of Contract Negotiations" (1967), 41 A.L.J. 274.

[12] The Uniform Sales Act, s. 12, provides in part: "Any affirmation of fact or a promise by the seller relating to the goods is an express warranty if the natural tendency of such affirmation or promise is to induce the buyer to purchase the goods, and if the buyer purchases the goods relying thereon."

[13] See 1 *Uniform Laws Annotated*, p. 172. See also 3 *Williston on Sales*, 4th edn., 1974, Ch. 17.

[14] [1913] A.C. 30, H.L.

which Lord Moulton attributed to Holt, C. J., "it appear on evidence to be so intended".[15] The classification depends, in other words, on the affirmation having been made with an intent to warrant or promissory intent. It is not sufficient to constitute a warranty that the statement, being more than a matter of mere opinion, induced entry into the contract or even that it formed part of the basis of it. It must have been made *animo contrahendi*.[16]

Although the actual decision in the *Heilbut, Symons* case is perfectly satisfactory it is now generally accepted that this insistence on promissory intent was neither true to the historical origins of the warranty[17] nor a fair reflection of the judgments of Lord Holt.[18] Moreover there are good reasons for holding that if a seller intends to affirm something as a fact and the affirmation is of sufficient importance reasonably to induce entry into the contract that should, of itself, entitle the buyer to a remedy in damages if it proves to be false. In practice this result seems to have been achieved even before the enactment of the Misrepresentation Act 1967 by a willingness on the part of the courts to construe such statements as contractual terms. Thus in *Dick Bentley Productions, Ltd.* v. *Harold Smith, Ltd.*[19] a dealer was taken to have given a warranty when he affirmed that a Bentley car had done only twenty thousand miles since being refitted with a replacement engine and gearbox. Similarly in *Beale* v. *Taylor*[20] a newspaper advertisement reading "Herald convertible, white, 1961" was treated as part of the contract description without there being any apparent preliminary inquiry whether it was made with promissory intent.

Further examples of express warranties have included affirmations that

---

[15] *Ibid.*, at p. 49. See also *ibid.*, at p. 38 (Viscount Haldane, L.C.), p. 43 (Lord Atkinson).

[16] The requirement of promissory intent has been affirmed in modern Australian cases: see, e.g., *Savage & Sons Pty., Ltd.* v. *Blakney* (1970), 119 C.L.R. 435 (High Ct. Australia) and the helpful judgment of Gillard, J., in the Supreme Court of Victoria, [1973] V.R. 385; *Mihaljevic* v. *Eiffel Tower Motors Pty., Ltd. and General Credits, Ltd.*, [1973] V.R. 545 (Vict. Sup. Ct.). See also Sutton, *Sale of Goods*, 2nd edn., 1974, pp. 110–113.

[17] See Williston, "Representation and Warranty in Sales—*Heilbut* v. *Buckleton*", 27 Harv. L. Rev. 1 (1913). For further discussion of the historical background, see Ames, "The History of Assumpsit", 2 Harv. L. Rev. 1 (1888); Williston, "What Constitutes an Express Warranty in the Law of Sales" 21 Harv. L. Rev. 555 (1908); Williston, "Liability for Honest Misrepresentation" 24 Harv. L. Rev. 415 (1911); Stoljar, "Conditions, Warranties and Descriptions of Quality in Sale 'of Goods' " (1952), 15 M.L.R. 425, 425–430; Greig, 87 L.Q.R. 179.

[18] The background is somewhat complicated. In *Pasley* v. *Freeman* (1789), 3 Term. Rep. 51, 56–57, Buller, J., had said that it had been rightly held by Holt, C.J., in *Crosse* v. *Gardner* (1689), Carth. 90; Holt K.B. 5 and in *Medina* v. *Stoughton* (1699), Salk 210; Holt, K.B. 208, that "an affirmation at the time of sale is a warranty, provided it appear on evidence to have been so intended". As had been frequently pointed out none of the reports of these cases says anything about intent (let alone an intent to warrant): see Williston, 27 Harv. L. Rev. 1, 3–4 (1913). See also, however, *Chandelor* v. *Lopus* (1603), Cro. Jac. 4 (bezoar stone).

[19] [1965] 2 All E.R. 65; [1965] 1 W.L.R. 623, C.A.

[20] [1967] 3 All E.R. 253; [1967] 1 W.L.R. 1193, C.A.

hops had not been treated with sulphur,[1] a heifer was "unserved",[2] a horse was "perfectly sound",[3] sand had a low iron oxide content,[4] machinery would roll half-inch plate,[5] the firebox and tubes in a locomotive were made of copper,[6] and that certain vessels were, respectively, "copper fastened" and "absolutely sound and seaworthy".[7] The warranty will sometimes be regarded as forming the basis of a collateral contract in order, perhaps, to avoid the parol evidence rule[8] or the effect of a disclaimer of liability[9] or in order to construct a contract between persons who are not parties to a contract of sale.[10] Here again, however, the affirmation must be shown to have been made with promissory intent.[11]

The translation from representation to promise is assisted by the fact that the inquiry is not directed towards ascertaining the subjective intentions of the representor. Denning, L.J. emphasised the point in *Oscar Chess, Ltd.* v. *Williams* when he said:[12]

"The question whether a warranty was intended depends on the conduct of the parties, on their words and behaviour, rather than on their thoughts. If an intelligent bystander would reasonably infer that a warranty was intended, that will suffice."[13]

In applying this objective approach a court will be especially influenced

---

[1] *Bannerman* v. *White* (1861), 10 C.B.N.S. 844.

[2] *Couchman* v. *Hill*, [1947] K.B. 554; [1947] 1 All E.R. 103, C.A.

[3] *Schawel* v. *Reade*, [1913] 2 Ir. Rep. 81. *Cf. Hopkins* v. *Tanqueray* (1854), 15 C.B. 130.

[4] *Wells (Merstham), Ltd.* v. *Buckland Sand and Silica, Ltd.*, [1965] 2 Q.B. 170; [1964] 1 All E.R. 41.

[5] *F. Jones & Co., Pty. Ltd.* v. *C. G. Grais & Sons Pty., Ltd.* (1962), 62 S.R. (N.S.W.) 410 (N.S.W. District C.A.).

[6] *Cowdy* v. *Thomas* (1877), 36 L.T. 22.

[7] *Shepherd* v. *Kain* (1821), 5 B. & Ald. 240; *Sullivan* v. *Constable* (1932), 48 T.L.R. 267.

[8] *Cf. City and Westminster Properties (1934), Ltd.* v. *Mudd*, [1959] Ch. 129; [1958] 2 All E.R. 733; *Birch* v. *Paramount Estates, Ltd.* (1956), 168 Estates Gazette 396. See also *Stuart* v. *Dundon*, [1963] S.A.S.R. 134 (S.A. Sup. Ct.) where the attempt to establish a collateral warranty failed.

[9] *Cf. Webster* v. *Higgin*, [1948] 2 All E.R. 127; *Couchman* v. *Hill*, [1947] K.B. 554; [1947] 1 All E.R. 103.

[10] *Cf. Yeoman Credit, Ltd.*, v. *Odgers*, [1962] 1 All E.R. 789, [1962] 1 W.L.R. 215, C.A.; *Andrews* v. *Hopkinson*, [1957] 1 Q.B. 229; [1956] 3 All E.R. 422; *Brown* v. *Sheen and Richmond Car Sales*, [1950] 1 All E.R. 1102; *Mihaljevic* v. *Eiffel Tower Motors Pty., Ltd.*, [1973] V.R. 545 (Vict. Sup. Ct.) (purchaser and dealer in hire-purchase transactions). See also below, pp. 64–65.

[11] *Heilbut Symons & Co.* v. *Buckleton*, [1913] A.C. 30. See also *Blakney* v. *Savage & Sons Pty., Ltd.*, [1973] V.R. 385; affd. (1970) 119 C.L.R. 435; *Cutts* v. *Buckley* (1933), 49 C.L.R. 189 (High Ct. Australia). A non-promissory representation may, however, override an exemption clause: see *Curtis* v. *Chemical Cleaning and Dyeing Co.*, [1951] 1 K.B. 805; [1951] 1 All E.R. 631 and below, p. 126.

[12] [1957] 1 All E.R. 325, 328, C.A.

[13] See also *Hornal* v. *Neuberger Products, Ltd.*, [1956] 3 All E.R. 970, 972–973 *per* Denning, L.J.; *Blakney* v. *J. J. Savage and Sons Pty., Ltd.*, [1973] V.R. 385, 388 *per* Gillard, J. (Vict. Sup. Ct.) affd. (1970) 119 C.L.R. 435 (High Ct. Australia).

by the relative knowledge and expertise of the parties. This may not be a decisive test.[14] Indeed other factors may be important, such as the time when the statement was made,[15] the importance to the buyer of its being correct,[16] its effect in inducing him to refrain from an independent examination,[17] and the presence or absence of a later written document incorporating or failing to incorporate the statement.[18] But the relative expertise of the parties is certainly of the utmost importance. Thus in *Oscar Chess, Ltd.* v. *Williams* Denning, L.J. said:[19]

> "When the seller states a fact which is or should be within his own knowledge and of which the buyer is ignorant, intending that the buyer should act on it and he does so, it is easy to infer a warranty.... If, however, the seller, when he states a fact, makes it clear that he has no knowledge of his own but has got his information elsewhere, and is merely passing it on, it is not so easy to imply a warranty."

On the facts of the case the Court of Appeal declined to imply a warranty when a private vendor of a second-hand Morris car informed the plaintiff motor dealers that it was a 1948 model whereas it was in fact a 1939 model, the logbook having been altered by an earlier owner. The same conclusion was reached in *Routledge* v. *McKay*[20] where there was a similar discrepancy in dates on the sale of a motorcycle combination between two private parties.

The willingness of the courts to imply a warranty where the representor

---

[14] The suggestion to the contrary in *De Lassalle* v. *Guildford*, [1901] 2 K.B. 215, 221, C.A., was castigated by Lord Moulton in *Heilbut's* case, [1913] A.C. 30, 50 as a "serious deviation from the correct principle".

[15] Other things being equal the statement is less likely to be regarded as a term of the contract if it is made well before the contract is concluded: see *Routledge* v. *McKay*, [1954] 1 All E.R. 855; [1954] 1 W.L.R. 615 (no warranty when statement as to the age of a motor-cycle was made seven days before the contract of sale). Discussion of the distinction between representations and terms is to be found in standard books on contract law. See, e.g., Cheshire and Fifoot, *Law of Contract*, 9th edn., 1976, pp. 116–121: Treitel, *Law of Contract*, 4th edn., 1975, pp. 228–233.

[16] See, e.g., *Bannerman* v. *White* (1861), 10 C.B.N.S. 844; *F. Jones and Co.* v. *C. G. Grais and Sons Pty., Ltd.* (1962), 62 S.R. (N.S.W.) 410.

[17] As in *Schawel* v. *Reade*, [1913] 2 I.R. 81. Where the seller suggests that the buyer should have an independent survey a warranty is unlikely to be inferred: *Ecay* v. *Godfrey* (1947), 80 Lloyd's Rep. 286.

[18] If a later written document fails to incorporate the statement this may suggest that the statement was not intended to be a term. The inference is, however, less than compelling: see *Birch* v. *Paramount Estates Ltd.* (1956), 168 Estates Gazette 396.

[19] [1957] 1 All E.R. 325, 329.

[20] [1954] 1 All E.R. 855. See also *Leaf* v. *International Galleries*, [1950] 2 K.B. 86; [1950] 1 All E.R. 693, below, p. 51, where, however, there was no claim for damages for breach of warranty on the sale of a painting "Salisbury Cathedral by J. Constable". Rescission for innocent misrepresentation was also the only remedy claimed in *Long* v. *Lloyd*, [1958] 2 All E.R. 402, C.A., on the private sale of a lorry said to be in "exceptional condition".

is an expert or otherwise knowledgeable is also to be seen in *Esso Petroleum Co., Ltd. v. Mardon.*[1] Here the Court of Appeal treated Esso's assertion to a prospective tenant that annual sales of petrol from a particular garage would rise to an estimated 200,000 gallons after two years as a warranty as well as a representation.[2] The field was one in which Esso had special skill and expertise and whilst such a prediction could not be taken as a guarantee that this "throughput" would be achieved it could nonetheless be taken as embodying a promise that reasonable care had been exercised in making the estimate. The tenant would not have entered the agreement but for Esso's assurances that his lower estimate of 100,000 to 150,000 gallons was unduly pessimistic.[3]

Cases such as *Esso Petroleum Co., Ltd. v. Mardon*[4] suggest that whilst the distinction between representations and terms is formally enshrined in English law the requirement of an *animus contrahendi* as the basis of a warranty creates little difficulty in practice. In any future reform of the law of contract a case could be made out for adopting the approach of the Uniform Commercial Code[5] and so treating affirmations of fact and promises as equivalent. But the need is hardly pressing. The central problem is to determine whether the representor can fairly be required to assume responsibility for the truth of his statement and there is sufficient flexibility within English law to achieve this. This is not to say that the formal distinction between representations and terms does not carry practical consequences. Certainly it does. An affirmation of fact which is reasonably believed to be true will give rise to a remedy in damages only if it can be classified as a contractual term.[6] As a misrepresentation inducing reliance it may attract the relief of rescission in equity together with an indemnity,[7] but it will not provide a basis for a claim for damages whether under the Misrepresentation Act 1967 or under the *Hedley Byrne* principle.[8] Secondly, a promise as to the future may embody representations as to a number of existing facts[9] but, as a promise, it will attract liability in contract if it is to

---

[1] [1976] 2 Q.B. 801; [1976] 2 All E.R. 5, C.A.

[2] At first instance Lawson, J., had held that Esso's statement was a representation but not a warranty: [1975] Q.B. 819; [1975] 1 All E.R. 203.

[3] Damages were subsequently agreed between the parties but the terms of settlement were not disclosed: see *The Times*, 4 March 1976.

[4] [1976] 2 All E.R. 5; [1976] 2 Q.B. 801.

[5] Art. 2–313: see above, p. 36.

[6] The strict nature of contractual liability is discussed below, pp. 107–110.

[7] See below, pp. 49–53.

[8] Discussed below, at pp. 45–48, 56–58 and pp. 43–45, 337–338, respectively.

[9] Notably as to the present intentions of the promisor: see *Edgington v. Fitzmaurice* (1885), 29 Ch. D. 459, 482 *per* Bowen, L.J. The distinction between statements of fact and promises has recently been discussed in the context of the Trade Descriptions Act 1968, s. 14(1); see *British Airways Board v. Taylor*, [1976] 1 All E.R. 65; [1976] 1 W.L.R. 13, H.L.; *R. v. Sunair Holidays Ltd.*, [1973] 2 All E.R. 1233; [1973] 1 W.L.R. 1105 C.A.; *Beckett v. Cohen*, [1973] 1 All E.R. 120; [1972] 1 W.L.R. 1593 D.C.

attract liability at all. Thirdly, there are important remedial consequences which flow from the distinction and these are noted below.[10]

Classification of terms: conditions, warranties and innominate terms

Stipulations forming part of a contract are traditionally divided into conditions and warranties. The consequences of this distinction are stated in the Sale of Goods Act 1893, s. 11 (1) (*b*) in the following terms:

"Whether a stipulation in a contract of sale is a condition, the breach of which may give rise to a right to treat the contract as repudiated, or a warranty, the breach of which may give rise to a claim for damages but not to a right to reject the goods and treat the contract as repudiated, depends in each case on the construction of the contract. A stipulation may be a condition, though called a warranty in the contract."

This usage of the word "condition" may be inaccurate historically[11] and its juxtaposition with the word "warranty" is unfortunate. But the terminology is now firmly ensconced in the law of sale of goods and it has the advantage of familiarity. In recent years it has been joined by the so-called "fundamental" term the meaning and significance of which is discussed in a later chapter.[12]

The general rule is that classification of terms into conditions and warranties depends on whether the intentions of the parties "will best be carried out by treating the promise as a warranty sounding only in damages, or as a condition precedent by the failure to perform which the other party is relieved of his liability."[13] This process of construction can, however, operate only within fairly narrow limits. The 1893 Act designates correspondence with description, merchantable quality and reasonable fitness for purpose implied conditions.[14] Hence breach of a term which, for example, identifies, as opposed to merely describes, the goods will

---

[10] See below, at p. 53 *et seq.*

[11] For discussion of the various meanings and uses of the word "condition" see *Benjamin's Sale of Goods* (1974), paras. 753–757; Sutton, *Sale of Goods*, 2nd edn., 1974, pp. 113–116; Stoljar, "The Contractual Concept of Condition" (1953), 69 L.Q.R. 485; Greig, "Condition or Warranty?" (1973), 89 L.Q.R. 93

[12] See below, ch. 7, pp. 132–133.

[13] *Bentsen* v. *Taylor, Sons & Co.* (No. 2), [1893] 2 Q.B. 274, 281 *per* Bowen, L.J. This usage of the word "condition" approximates to its true historical meaning. See also *Bannerman* v. *White* (1861), 10 C.B.N.S. 844, 860 *per* Erle, C.J.; *Tramways Advertising Pty., Ltd.* v. *Luna Park (N.S.W.) Ltd.* (1938), 38 S.R. (N.S.W.) 632, 641–643 *per* Jordan, C.J.

[14] See, respectively, ss. 13, 14 (2), 14 (3) of the 1893 Act as amended by the Supply of Goods (Implied Terms) Act 1973, ss. 2, 3. These implied conditions are discussed below, chs. 5 and 6.

42   *Express warranties and misrepresentations: I*

entitle the buyer to reject although he has suffered no loss.[15] Where such constraints do not apply there is room for more flexibility in determining the status of the term in the light of matters such as the importance to the buyer of compliance.[16]

A recent and interesting development is to be seen in *Cehave N.V.* v. *Bremer Handelsgesellschaft m.b.H.*[17] The contract was for the sale of a quantity of citrus pulp pellets to be "shipped in good condition" from Florida to Rotterdam. On arrival of one shipment at Rotterdam it was found that part of the cargo was damaged through overheating. The market price of citrus pellets had fallen and the buyers purported to reject the goods. They later made the pellets up into cattle feed in almost the same manner and quantity as they would have done with sound pellets. In subsequent proceedings the Court of Appeal held that (i) the pellets were of merchantable quality within the Sale of Goods Act,[18] and (ii) the buyers were not entitled to reject for breach of the express stipulation that the pellets be "shipped in good condition".

It is the reasoning behind this latter conclusion which is of interest in the present context. In the judgment of the court s. 11 (1) (*b*) of the Act did not necessitate a rigid classification whereby breach of any given stipulation must either invariably (if it were a condition) or never (if it were a warranty) entitle the buyer to reject. The common law rules had been preserved by s. 61 (2) of the Act[19] and, leaving aside the special case of the statutory implied conditions, there was room for the more flexible approach associated with the decision in *Hong Kong Fir Shipping Co., Ltd.* v. *Kawasaki Kisen Kaisha, Ltd.*[20] Hence entitlement to reject did not depend on an *a priori* classification. It depended on whether the consequences of the breach had struck at the root of he bargain, thus depriving the buyer of substantially the whole benefit of the contract.[1] The application of this principle to contracts for the sale of goods is not entirely novel and indeed seems to be supported by cases holding an exemption clause ineffective to

---

[15] See *Arcos, Ltd.* v. *E. A. Ronaasen & Son*, [1933] A.C. 470, H.L. and below, p. 74.

[16] See, e.g., *Harling* v. *Eddy*, [1951] 2 K.B. 739; [1951] 2 All E.R. 212, *Bannerman* v. *White* (1861), 10 C.B.N.S. 844; and *Benjamin's Sale of Goods* (1974), para. 757.

[17] [1976] Q.B. 44; [1975] 3 All E.R. 739, C.A., reversing [1974] 2 Lloyd's Rep. 216 (Mocatta, J.). See Reynolds, (1976) 92 L.Q.R. 17.

[18] Section 14 (2). See below, p. 78 *et seq.*

[19] Section 61 (2) provides in part: "The rules of the common law, including the law merchant, save in so far as they are inconsistent with the express provisions of this Act . . . shall continue to apply to contracts for the sale of goods".

[20] [1962] 2 Q.B. 26; [1962] 1 All E.R. 474, C.A. Designation of other express stipulations "conditions" would not necessarily be conclusive. See *Wickman Machine Tool Sales, Ltd.* v. *A Schuler AG*, [1974] A.C. 325; [1973] 2 All E.R. 39, H.L., and *cf. The Mihalis Angelos*, [1971] 1 Q.B. 164; [1970] 3 All E.R. 135, C.A.

[1] *Cf.* the observations of Diplock, L.J., in the *Hong Kong Fir* case, [1962] 1 All E.R. 474, 487. See also *Cehave N.V.* v. *Bremer*, [1975] 3 All E.R. 739, 757 *per* Roskill, L.J.

protect against the consequences of a fundamental breach of contract.[2] Such stipulations may be called "intermediate" or "innominate" terms,[3] but this is perhaps an unnecessary complication. Thus in the *Cehave* case Ormrod, L.J. doubted whether the decision "involves the creation of a third category of stipulations; rather it recognises another ground for holding that a buyer is entitled to reject, namely that, *de facto*, the consideration for his promise has been wholly destroyed".[4]

Liability for misrepresentations

For many years there was no remedy in damages in English law for misrepresentations causing economic loss unless the plaintiff could satisfy the stringent requirements of the tort of deceit.[5] The only remedy available to the representee induced to enter a contract with the representor was rescission in equity and an indemnity against costs necessarily incurred.[6] In many cases rescission might be barred through lapse of time, inability to make *restitutio in integrum*, or for some other reason.[7] Moreover, it was far from clear that the remedy extended to a contract for the sale of goods.[8] The position has now been modified both through the development of the common law and through the Misrepresentation Act 1967 so as to enable the representee to claim damages where the misrepresentation was made negligently. As between contracting parties the statutory development is the more important. It is convenient, however, to refer to the common law development initially.

The Hedley Byrne case

The decision of the House of Lords in *Hedley Byrne & Co., Ltd.* v. *Heller*

---

[2] See, e.g., *Harbutt's Plasticine, Ltd.* v. *Wayne Tank and Pump Co., Ltd.*, [1970] 1 Q.B. 447; [1970] 1 All E.R. 225, C.A., below, pp. 135–137: *semble* that the actual contract was for work and materials.

[3] *Cf.* the approach of Lord Denning, M.R., in the *Cehave* case [1975] 3 All E.R. 739, 748.

[4] *Ibid.*, at p. 766. One advantage of the "intermediate term" approach is that it sidesteps any difficulty which might be occasioned by s. 62(1) of the Act which defines a warranty as an agreement "the breach of which gives rise to a claim for damages but not to a right to reject the goods and treat the contract as repudiated." Alternatively, s. 62(1) can be read as being subject to the rules of the common law preserved by s. 61(2).

[5] See *Derry* v. *Peek* (1889), 14 App. Cas. 337 and, in general, Winfield and Jolowicz, *The Law of Tort*, 10th edn., 1975, pp. 212–221. See also below, pp. 300–302.

[6] See *Redgrave* v. *Hurd* (1881), 20 Ch.D. 1; *Newbigging* v. *Adam* (1886), 34 Ch.D. 582, C.A.; *Whittington* v. *Seale-Hayne* (1900), 82 L.T. 49; see further below, pp. 49–53.

[7] See e.g., *Leaf* v. *International Galleries*, [1950] 2 K.B. 86; [1950] 1 All E.R. 693; *Long* v. *Lloyd*, [1958] 2 All E.R. 402. The bars to rescission are noted below, p. 51.

[8] See below, p. 49 and the cases there cited.

& *Partners, Ltd.*[9] imposes liability at common law for loss caused by negligent misstatements where there is a "special relationship" between the parties and the defendant has assumed responsibility for taking care. An attempt to apply this principle within the general framework of product liability would, however, have to surmount two substantial obstacles. Firstly, it is unclear whether the principle applies where the representor is neither in the business of giving information or advice nor holds himself out as possessing an equivalent skill and competence.[10] Vendors of goods would not typically satisfy any such requirement.[11] Secondly, there is doubt as to whether the principle applies to pre-contractual statements.[12]

Presumably it would not be argued that either of these restrictions was applicable in a case of physical injury where the possibility of a more general and concurrent liability has long been clear.[13] In *Esso Petroleum Co., Ltd.* v. *Mardon*,[14] moreover, the Court of Appeal has recently held that the

---

[9] [1964] A.C. 465; [1963] 2 All E.R. 575. See Honore (1965), 8 J.S.P.T.L. (N.S.) 284.

[10] The doubt stems from *Mutual Life and Citizens' Assurance Co., Ltd.* v. *Evatt*, [1971] A.C. 793; [1971] 1 All E.R. 150 where a bare majority of the Privy Council held that the principle was thus limited. The majority recognised that there might be exceptions to the rule, as, perhaps where the advisor had a financial interest in the transaction: see *W. B. Anderson & Sons, Ltd.* v. *Rhodes (Liverpool) Ltd.*, [1967] 2 All E.R. 850. An alternative limit of general (if not universal) application might be that the advice should be "sought and given in a business or professional context". This was the view of the dissenting minority (Lords Reid and Morris) in *Evatt's* case: [1971] A.C. 793, 811. Or the principle might be limited to persons possessing some specialised skill or knowledge: see *Jones* v. *Still*, [1965] N.Z.L.R. 1071 (N.Z. Sup. Ct.); but *cf. Barrett* v. *J. R. West, Ltd.*, [1970] N.Z.L.R. 789 (N.Z. Sup. Ct.).

[11] Although, as is pointed out in *Benjamin's Sale of Goods* (1974) para. 912, note 57, "the seller of specialised articles such as computers or aircraft might do so". For a case applying the principle in the context of product liability, see *Sealand of the Pacific Ltd.* v. *Ocean Cement Ltd.* (1973), 33 D.L.R. (3d) 625; affd. (1975) 51 D.L.R. (3d) 702 (B.C.C.A.); *cf. J. Nunes Diamonds Ltd.* v. *Dominion Electric Protection Co.* (1972), 26 D.L.R. (3d) 699 (Sup. Ct. Canada). See also below, pp. 337–338.

[12] In favour of the view that there may be concurrent liability in contract and tort in respect of such statements see *Dillingham Constructions Pty., Ltd.* v. *Downs*, [1972] 2 N.S.W.L.R. 49 (N.S.W. Sup. Ct.); *Ellul* v. *Oakes*, [1972] 3 S.A.S.R. 377 (S.A. Sup. Ct.); *Capital Motor Co., Ltd.* v. *Beecham*, [1975] 1 N.Z.L.R. 576 (N.Z. Sup. Ct.). *Contra*, see *Clark* v. *Kirby Smith*, [1964] Ch. 506; [1964] 2 All E.R. 835; *Oleificio Zucchi ASP* v. *Northern Sales Ltd.*, [1965] 2 Lloyd's Rep. 496, 519 *per* McNair, J. See also *Presser* v. *Caldwell Estates Pty., Ltd.*, [1971] 2 N.S.W.L.R. 471 (N.S.W.C.A.); *Morrison-Knudson* v. *The Commonwealth* (1972), 46 A.L.J.R. 265 (High Ct. Australia) and the *Sealand of the Pacific* and *Nunes Diamonds* cases, above, note 11. For recent discussions, see Greig, "Misrepresentations and Sales of Goods" (1971), 87 L.Q.R. 179, 190–206; Symmons, "The Problems of the Applicability of Tort Liability to Negligent Mis-statements in Contractual Situations" (1975), 21 McGill L.J. 79.

[13] See, e.g., *Andrews* v. *Hopkinson*, [1957] 1 Q.B. 229; [1956] 3 All E.R. 422; *Clarke* v. *Army and Navy Cooperative Society*, [1903] 1 K.B. 155. The same should be true of damage to property: see *Fillmore's Valley Nurseries, Ltd.* v. *North American Cyanamid, Ltd.* (1958), 14 D.L.R. (2d) 297, below, p. 56. The liability in tort of vendors is discussed below, ch. 15, pp. 304–307. See also below, pp. 243–244 (Warnings and Directions for Use: Representation of Safety).

[14] [1976] 2 Q.B. 801; [1976] 2 All E.R. 5, above, p. 40.

Hedley Byrne principle is not thus restricted in a case of purely economic loss. It is submitted that this is correct. Within English law, however, the point will rarely have practical significance. There would be few cases in which a contracting party would be taken to have assumed responsibility in relation to the accuracy of the statement and yet not have made it *animo contrahendi*. Where both remedies are available an action on the warranty would normally, although not invariably, be the more attractive.[15] Moreover, a claim would usually lie under the Misrepresentation Act and this would have the added attraction of placing the onus on the representor to establish a reasonable belief in the truth of the statement.[16] However, the prediction as to the "throughput" of the garage in the *Esso Petroleum* case[14] was made well before the 1967 Act came into force and this serves as a timely reminder that there may still be further cases to be decided on the basis of the pre-1967 law. Similarly the *Hedley Byrne* doctrine may be attractive where one is dealing with a matter of opinion. The 1967 Act applies only to representations of fact[17] whereas at common law responsibility may have been assumed for taking care in giving advice or expressing an opinion.[18] This may be important where there is doubt whether the statement is one of fact or opinion or where the statements of fact are correct and the fault lies in the inferences which are drawn.

The Misrepresentation Act 1967[19]

The Misrepresentation Act 1967 makes the following provisions for awarding damages for misrepresentation. By s. 2 of the Act:

> "(1) Where a person has entered into a contract after a misrepresentation has been made to him by another party thereto and as a result thereof he has suffered loss, then, if the person making the misrepresentation would be liable to damages in respect thereof had the misrepresentation been made fraudulently, that person shall be so liable notwithstanding that the misrepresentation was not made fraudulently, unless he proves that he had reasonable ground to believe and did believe up to the time the contract was made that the facts represented were true.

---

[15] For discussion of the differing approaches to quantifying damages in contract and tort, see below, pp. 53–56.

[16] Misrepresentation Act 1967, s. 2 (1), below.

[17] The Act does not state that this is so but presumably it is to be inferred from the ordinary legal usage of the word "misrepresentation". See below, p. 46.

[18] *Cf.* the statement of Taylor, J., in the High Court of Australia in the *Evatt* case (1968), 42 A.L.J.R. 316, 330, cited by Greig, *Sale of Goods* (1974), p. 154, note 5.

[19] The Act implements, with some modifications, the recommendations in the Law Reform Committee's Tenth Report, Cmnd. 1782 (1962). For general commentary, see Atiyah and Treitel, "Misrepresentation Act 1967" (1967) 30 M.L.R. 369.

(2) Where a person has entered into a contract after a misrepresentation has been made to him otherwise than fraudulently, and he would be entitled, by reason of the misrepresentation, to rescind the contract, then, if it is claimed, in any proceedings arising out of the contract, that the contract ought to be or has been rescinded, the court or arbitrator may declare the contract subsisting and award damages in lieu of rescission, if of opinion that it would be equitable to do so, having regard to the nature of the misrepresentation and the loss that would be caused by it if the contract were upheld, as well as to the loss that rescission would cause to the other party.

(3) Damages may be awarded against a person under subsection (2) of this section whether or not he is liable to damages under subsection (1) thereof, but where he is so liable any award under the said subsection (2) shall be taken into account in assessing his liability under the said subsection (1)."

The following points may be noted about the scope of this statutory remedy. Firstly, it is available only where the representee is complaining that he has suffered loss as a result of entering into a contract with the representor. It has no application where the representee has entered a contract with a third party or acted to his detriment in some other way.[20] Secondly, a misrepresentation, being undefined in the Act, would no doubt bear the same meaning as under the general law. Hence a representation of fact would be required and statements of law or of opinion or of intention would be insufficient.[1] Thirdly, the representee must have relied on the representation as an inducement to contract on the agreed terms.[2] It is probably also the case that his reliance must have been justifiable in the eyes of a reasonable man,[3] but doubtful whether an otherwise operative inducement would cease to be actionable simply because the representee

---

[20] In such circumstances it may be possible to construct a collateral contract if the representation is promissory (see *Shanklin Pier, Ltd.* v. *Detel Products, Ltd.*, [1951] 2 K.B. 854; [1951] 2 All E.R. 471, and below, pp. 64–65) or liability may be incurred in tort, as under the *Hedley Byrne* principle, discussed above, pp. 43–45.

[1] For the distinction between statements of fact and of opinion, see above, pp. 33–35. See also above, p. 40, note 9 (statements of fact and intention of promises) and, in general, Treitel, *The Law of Contract*, 4th edn., 1975, pp. 213–218; Winfield and Jolowicz, *The Law of Tort*, 10th edn., 1975, pp. 213–215.

[2] The requirement would not be satisfied where the representee did not know of the statement or did not believe it to be true: *Re Northumberland and Durham District Banking Co.*, *Ex parte Bigge* (1858), 28 L.J. Ch. 50, 54. Nor would it be satisfied where he relied on his own judgment: *Attwood* v. *Small* (1838), 6 Cl. & Finn. 232; *Jennings* v. *Broughton* (1854), 5 De G. M. & G. 126; or where the falsity of the representation was obvious: see *Southern* v. *Howe* (1617), 2 Roll Rep. 5. "El la difference est prise lou jeo vend chivall que ad nulli oculus, la nul action gist. auterment lou il ad un counterfeit faux and bright eye".

[3] The provisions in the Marine Insurance Act 1906, ss. 18, 20, requiring disclosure of circumstances which are "material" would seem to be of general application in a case of misrepresentation. See Treitel, *The Law of Contract*, 4th edn., 1975, pp. 219–220.

had an opportunity to discover its falsity.[4] The position is well summarised in *Williston on Sales* in the following terms:[5]

"There is danger of giving greater effect to the requirement of reliance than it is entitled to. Doubtless the burden of proof is on the buyer to establish this as one of the elements of his case.[6] But the warranty need not be the sole inducement to the buyer to purchase the goods;[7] and as a general rule no evidence of reliance by the buyer is necessary other than the seller's statements were of a kind which naturally would induce the buyer to purchase the goods and that he did purchase the goods."

Fourthly, the basic scheme of the Act is to place the onus on the representor to establish that "he had reasonable ground to believe and did believe up to the time the contract was made that the facts represented were true".[8] If he fails to discharge this onus the representee will be entitled to damages under s. 2 (1) of the Act. If he succeeds the representee will not be entitled to damages although he may, in the result, be awarded damages in lieu of rescission under s 2 (2).[9] A variety of factors might affect the issue of whether the statutory onus has been discharged. The most important, no doubt, would be whether the representor had access to information to enable him to determine the truth of the matter.[10]

Fifthly, there may be difficulty in deciding to what extent silence can constitute a misrepresentation for the purposes of the Act.[11] A half-truth may clearly amount to a misrepresentation[12] and so may a statement which

---

[4] An opportunity to verify the accuracy of the statement does not defeat rescission in equity: *Redgrave* v. *Hurd* (1881), 20 Ch.D. 1. An opportunity to inspect does not defeat a claim that the goods are not of merchantable quality under the Sale of Goods Act 1893, s. 14 (2), below, p. 95. Nor should it preclude a claim for damages in deceit (see *Dobell* v. *Stevens* (1825), 3 B. & C. 623). *Pearson* v. *Dublin Corporation*, [1907] A.C. 351, but *cf. Horsfall* v. *Thomas* (1862), 1 H. & C. 90 where deceit was unsuccessfully raised as a defence to an action on a bill—or under the 1967 Act. It is possible, however, that it might lead to a dimunition in damages under the Law Reform (Contributory Negligence) Act 1945. The position of the representee under the 1967 Act would seem to be strengthened by the fiction of fraud on which s. 2 is based.

[5] Vol. 1, revised edn., s. 208.

[6] *Smith* v. *Chadwick* (1884), 9 App. Cas. 187, H.L.

[7] *Edgington* v. *Fitzmaurice* (1885), 29 Ch.D. 459, C.A.

[8] Section 2 (1). Presumably the representor may be liable under the Act although in no way culpable in failing to communicate with the representee before the contract was made. A contract may have been concluded by, e.g., the representee posting a letter of acceptance: *Adams* v. *Lindsell* (1818), 1 B. & Ald. 681.

[9] See further, below, pp. 49–53.

[10] Hence, presumably, damages would not be awarded on the facts of a case such as *Oscar Chess, Ltd.* v. *Williams*, [1957] 1 All E.R. 325; [1957] 1 W.L.R. 370 above, p. 39.

[11] See Winfield and Jolowicz, *The Law of Tort*, 10th edn., 1975, pp. 215–217; Hudson, "Making Misrepresentations" (1969), 85 L.Q.R. 524.

[12] See *Peek* v. *Gurney* (1873), L.R. 6 H.L. 377, 403 *per* Lord Cairns; *Arkwright* v. *Newbold* (1881), 17 Ch.D. 301, 318 *per* James, L.J. Active concealment of a defect should also be sufficient

is true when it is made but which is falsified by later events.[13] Hence it is submitted that the representor who knew or ought to have known of the falsification will be liable in damages under s. 2(1) of the Act unless he informs the representee before the contract is concluded. On the other hand, the wording of the Act, being couched in positive terms,[14] does not seem apt to cover a simple case of non-disclosure where there has been no anterior statement. This would seem to be the case even though the relationship between the parties is such as to impose a duty of disclosure if rescission is to be avoided.[15] Two matters require further discussion, namely (i) the availability of rescission in contracts for the sale of goods, and (ii) the assessment of damages under the Act and its relationship to the assessment of damages in contract and in tort generally. These points are discussed in the following chapter.

(*Schneider* v. *Heath* (1813), 3 Camp. 506: Street, *The Law of Torts*, 6th edn., 1976, p. 379) provided, at least, that the other party has been misled by it. *Horsfall* v. *Thomas* (1862), 1 H. & C. 90 (sale of gun with concealed defect) seems to turn on the fact that the buyer had not examined the gun and was not misled. *Sed quaere?*

[13] *With* v. *O'Flanagan*, [1936] Ch. 575; 584, *per* Lord Wright, M.R.; *Traill* v. *Baring* (1864), 4 De G. J. & S. 318, 329 *per* Turner, L.J.

[14] Thus s. 2(1) of the Act refers to a person who has entered into a contract "*after a misrepresentation has been made to him* . . .": emphasis supplied. See also ss. 1 and 3 of the Act where the same terminology is adopted.

[15] The main example is a contract *uberrimae fidei* such as a contract of insurance or a contract for family settlement. See also Companies Act 1948, s. 38 (company prospectus). For general discussion of the point, see Hudson, *op. cit.*, at pp. 526–529. Where there is an existing relationship between the parties it is arguable that the *Hedley Byrne* principle, above, pp. 43–45, might cover an assumption of responsibility to *inform* no less than an assumption of responsibility to take care in making statements.

4 Express Warranties and Misrepresentations: II

Liability as between vendors and purchasers—Rescission and damages

Rescission

Although there are dicta[1] and authority[2] to the contrary, the balance of English authority supports the view that rescission for innocent misrepresentation may be obtained in contracts for the sale of goods.[3] The Misrepresentation Act 1967 does not itself confer the remedy[4] but its availability has been assumed by the Court of Appeal on at least two occasions.[5] Moreover in *Goldsmith* v. *Rodger*[6] the court went somewhat further and held that a seller was entitled to rescind when the purchaser of a certain motor vessel had innocently misrepresented that it had rot and worm in the keel. In this case rescission was being used in a defensive role whereas in others a purchaser may be rescinding to recover the contract price. There is also authority for the view that, irrespective of any question of misrepresentation,[7]

"A contract is also liable to be set aside if the parties were under a common

---

[1] *Riddiford* v. *Warren* (1901), 20 N.Z.L.R. 572 (N.Z.C.A.); *Re Wait*, [1927] 1 Ch. 606, 635–636, C.A., *per* Atkin, L.J.

[2] *Watt* v. *Westhoven*, [1933] V.L.R. 458 (Vict. Sup. Ct.).

[3] For general discussion of the point, see Sutton, *Sale of Goods*, 2nd edn., 1974, pp. 5–8; Greig, *Sale of Goods* (1974), pp. 258–261; Gower (1950), 13 M.L.R. 362; Atiyah (1959), 22 M.L.R. 76.

[4] Section 1 allows the representee to rescind "if otherwise he would be entitled to rescind".

[5] In *Leaf* v. *International Galleries*, [1950] 2 K.B. 86; [1950] 1 All E.R. 693, below, p. 51, and *Long* v. *Lloyd*, [1958] 2 All E.R. 402; [1958] 1 W.L.R. 753.

[6] [1962] 2 Lloyd's Rep. 249.

[7] *Solle* v. *Butcher*, [1950] 1 K.B. 671, 693 *per* Lord Denning, M.R.

misapprehension either as to facts or as to their relative and respective rights, provided that the misapprehension was fundamental and that the party seeking to set it aside was not himself at fault."[8]

The status of this doctrine is, however, uncertain and there are those who doubt whether there is any such equitable jurisdiction to rescind a contract on the ground of common mistake.[9] In any event the doctrine would rarely apply to a contract for the sale of goods.[10]

A matter which has received considerable attention is the inter-relation of the equitable remedy of rescission and the common law remedies for breach of contract. One view is that where the representation has been incorporated as a term of the contract, the entitlement to rescind does not, statutory provisions apart,[11] survive the incorporation. The representee's remedies are for breach of contract alone. This view is supported by the argument that the function of equity was to supplement the lack of a remedy at common law where the misrepresentation was neither promissory nor deceitful.[12] Hence the availability of the contractual remedy is said to remove the reason which justifies the intervention of equity. Moreover to deny that this is so would obliterate the distinction between conditions and warranties since even though the term was incorporated as a warranty the buyer might nonetheless rescind on account of the representation.[13] These arguments are highly persuasive. Yet from the standpoint of the representee there is also force in the argument that, whether or not he is entitled to damages, he should be free to rescind a contract entered into through reliance on a false and material affirmation of fact. The representation was, *ex hypothesi*, a material inducement to

---

[8] See also *Magee* v. *Pennine Insurance Co., Ltd.*, [1969] 2 Q.B. 507, 514 *per* Lord Denning, M.R.; *Grist* v. *Bailey*, [1967] Ch. 532; [1966] 2 All E.R. 875.

[9] The existence of the jurisdiction is difficult to reconcile with cases such as *Bell* v. *Lever Brothers, Ltd.*, [1932] A.C. 161, H.L., and *Smith* v. *Hughes* (1871), L.R. 6 Q.B. 597. *Cf.* the observations in *Amalgamated Investment and Property Co., Ltd.* v. *John Walker & Sons, Ltd.*, [1976] 3 All E.R. @ 509, C.A. If the jurisdiction exists in a case of common mistake it must *a fortiori* exist where A is under no such misapprehension and appreciates that B is.

[10] Thus the contract was not rescinded in *Harrison and Jones* v. *Bunten and Lancaster*, [1953] 1 Q.B. 646; [1953] 1 All E.R. 903 where both parties believed that a commodity was pure Kapok when it contained a proportion of cotton. See also *F. E. Rose (London), Ltd.* v. *Wm. Pim Jnr. & Co., Ltd.*, [1953] 2 Q.B. 450; [1953] 2 All E.R. 739. *Cf.*, however, the dicta of Denning, L.J. in *Oscar Chess, Ltd.* v. *Williams*, [1957] 1 All E.R. 325, 327, and of Hallett, J. in *Nicholson and Venn* v. *Smith Marriott* (1947), 177 L.T. 189. It is of course possible for parties to contract (whether expressly or impliedly) on the basis that the accrual of rights and obligations depends on the correctness of a given assumption. But this has nothing to do with rescission in equity. See, in general, Atiyah, *Sale of Goods*, 5th edn., 1975, pp. 105–109.

[11] Notably the Misrepresentation Act 1967, s. 1 (*a*), discussed below.

[12] See, respectively, *Heilbut Symons & Co.* v. *Buckleton*, [1913] A.C. 30, H.L. and *Derry* v. *Peek* (1889), 14 App. Cas. 337.

[13] *Cf.* Atiyah, (1959) 22 M.L.R. 76, 78.

enter the contract and equity regards it as a moral fraud to seek to retain an advantage from a statement which is admittedly false.[14] The point is still important in a number of common law jurisdictions.[15] Within English law the position has now been affected by the Misrepresentation Act 1967, s. 1 (*a*). This provides that the representee, if otherwise entitled to rescind the contract, shall be so entitled, subject to the provisions of the Act, notwithstanding that the misrepresentation has become a term of the contract.[16] However, unless the misrepresentation was fraudulent, it is open to the court to declare the contract subsisting and to award damages in lieu of rescission.[17] If the representation is incorporated as a warranty this might be regarded as a reason for denying rescission. Where the representee seeks to rescind and so to disown the contract he cannot at the same time claim damages for breach.[18] It is arguable, however, that his entitlement to damages for breach might be revived by a s. 2 (2) declaration that the contract is subsisting.

Related problems arise when one turns to consider the circumstances in which an entitlement to rescind for misrepresentation may be lost. Apart from the statutory discretion to declare a contract subsisting under the Misrepresentation Act 1967, s. 2 (2) an entitlement to rescind may be lost through (i) an inability to effect a substantial *restitutio in integrum*; (ii) the intervention of third party rights; (iii) affirmation and (iv) lapse of time.[19] In *Leaf* v. *International Galleries*[20] the plaintiff bought from the defendant an oil painting of Salisbury Cathedral. The picture was exhibited as a work by J. Constable and a representation that it was, "a Constable" was

---

[14] See *Redgrave* v. *Hurd* (1881), 20 Ch.D. 1, 12–13, *per* Jessel, M.R. Carried to its logical conclusion this means, admittedly, that all representations inducing have the same rescissory force as conditions precedent.

[15] See, e.g., *Academy of Health and Fitness Pty., Ltd.* v. *Power,* [1973] V.R. 254 (Vict. Sup. Ct.); *Mihaljevic* v. *Eiffel Tower Motors Pty., Ltd.,* [1973] V.R. 545; *O'Flaherty* v. *McKinlay,* [1953] 2 D.L.R. 514 (Newfoundland Sup. Ct.)—all permitting rescission.

[16] The position before the Act was the subject of conflicting dicta. See *Pennsylvania Shipping Co.* v. *Compagnie Nationale de Navigation,* [1936] 2 All E.R. 1167, 1171 (Branson, J.) holding rescission to be unavailable. *Contra Compagnie Française des Chemins de Fer Paris-Orléans* v. *Leeston Shipping Co., Ltd.* (1919), 1 Ll.L.R. 235, 237–238 (Roche, J.). Section 1 (*b*) of the Act provides that rescission is not barred because "the contract has been performed", thus abrogating the rule in *Seddon* v. *North-Eastern Salt Co., Ltd.,* [1905] 1 Ch. 326 and *Angel* v. *Jay,* [1911] 1 K.B. 666.

[17] Section 2 (2). Section 2 (3) of the Act seeks to ensure that there is no element of double compensation where the representee is awarded damages under s. 2 (1).

[18] His remedy is an indemnity and it depends *inter alia* on his being able to make substantial *restitutio in integrum*. For a recent discussion in the context of land law, see Michael Albery, "Mr Cyprian Williams' Great Heresy" (1975), 91 L.Q.R. 337.

[19] For these limits to the right to rescind, see Cheshire and Fifoot, *The Law of Contract*, 9th edn., 1976, pp. 268–273; Treitel, *The Law of Contract*, 4th edn., 1974, pp. 249–257; *Benjamin's Sale of Goods,* (1974), paras. 902–907.

[20] [1950] 2 K.B. 86; [1950] 1 All E.R. 693.

incorporated as a term of the contract. Some five years later the plaintiff was informed by Christie's, the art dealers, that the painting was not by John Constable. He then sought to rescind the contract and recover the contract price.[1] In the circumstances it is hardly surprising that the claim failed. An entitlement to rescind must be exercised within a reasonable time. As Jenkins, L.J. put it:[2]

> "[It] behoves the purchaser either to verify or, as the case may be, to disprove the representation within a reasonable time, or else stand or fall by it. If he is allowed to wait five, ten, or twenty years and then reopen the bargain, there can be no finality at all."

Denning, L.J. gave a somewhat different reason for dismissing the claim, saying:[3]

> "Although rescission may in some cases be a proper remedy, it is to be remembered that an innocent misrepresentation is much less potent than a breach of condition; and a claim to rescission for innocent misrepresentation must at any rate be barred when a right to reject for breach of condition is barred. A condition is a term of the contract of a most material character, and if a claim to reject on that account is barred, it seems to me a fortiori that a claim to rescission on the ground of innocent misrepresentation is also barred. So, assuming that a contract for the sale of goods may be rescinded in a proper case for innocent misrepresentation, the claim is barred in this case for the self-same reason as a right to reject is barred. The buyer has accepted the picture. He had ample opportunity for examination in the first few days after he had bought it. Then was the time to see if the condition or representation was fulfilled. Yet he has kept it all this time. Five years have elapsed without any notice of rejection. In my judgment he cannot now claim to rescind."[4]

The circumstances in which the buyer will lose his right to reject for breach of condition or for breach of a warranty going to the root of the contract[5] will be examined in a later chapter.[6] Here, however, it may be

---

[1] Atiyah and Treitel have noted that it is only in the statement of facts in the official Law Reports that it is said that the defendants represented that the picture was painted by *John* Constable: see (1967), 30 M.L.R. 369, 376, note 21. Given that the contract price was £85 the existence of such a representation seems doubtful.

[2] [1950] 2 K.B. 86, 92. See also *ibid.,* at p. 94 (Lord Evershed, M.R.).

[3] [1950] 2 K.B. 86, 90–91.

[4] Jenkins, L.J. prefaced his judgment which followed that of Denning, L.J. by saying: "I agree" but did not otherwise refer to the significance of acceptance: *ibid.,* at p. 91. He also noted that the picture had been delivered and the contract executed but left open the question of whether this would have prevented rescission: *ibid.,* at p. 92. See also *ibid.,* at p. 95 (Lord Evershed, M.R.) and at p. 90 (Denning, L.J.). On this point, see now Misrepresentation Act 1967, s. 1 (*b*).

[5] *Cf. Cehave N.V.* v. *Bremer Handelsgesellschaft m.b.H.,* [1976] Q.B. 44; [1975] 3 All E.R. 739, C.A., above, p. 42.

[6] See below, at pp. 110–115.

said that Denning, L.J. was, with respect, surely right in adopting this approach. There is no reason why an entitlement to rescind should survive where the right to reject has been lost through acceptance.[7] Where the representation has not been incorporated as a term it would again seem right to bar rescission if the right to reject would have been lost had it been incorporated as a condition.[8] In both instances an exception might be made for representations which are fraudulent. Nowadays the adoption of such rules is unlikely to lead to injustice. The Misrepresentation Act 1967, s. 4, has curtailed the circumstances in which rejection is unavailable[9] and resort may be had also to devices such as total failure of consideration[10] and fundamental breach.[11] Neither the loss of right to rescind nor of the right to reject will affect the entitlement of the buyer to damages for breach of contract or for negligent misrepresentation under the Misrepresentation Act 1967 s. 2(1). Loss of the right to rescind would, however, seem to preclude an award of damages under s. 2(2) of the Act since damages may be awarded only "in lieu of rescission" and this presumably means that rescission must be otherwise available. Hence where the representation is neither promissory nor negligent damages could not be awarded where rescission is barred through lapse of time, affirmation or some other reason.[12]

Damages

Assessment of damages in contract and tort

A book on product liability is not the place for a detailed discussion of the

---

[7] It is difficult to appreciate how an entitlement to reject could have survived the conclusion of the contract of sale in *Leaf's* case. Property presumably passed to the buyer at that time under s. 18, rule 1 of the 1893 Act and the unamended s. 11(1)(c) of the Act would then have precluded rejection: see J. C. Smith (1951), 14 M.L.R. 173. For the amendment to s. 11(1)(c), see below, p. 112, note 11.
[8] See *Long* v. *Lloyd*, [1958] 2 All E.R. 402, 407, C.A., where the buyer could not rescind a contract to purchase a lorry which he had accepted. The contract had, however, been "affirmed".
[9] See below, p. 111 *et seq.*
[10] *Rowland* v. *Divall*, [1923] 2 K.B. 500. See also *Kennedy* v. *Panama Mail Co., Ltd.* (1867), L.R. 2 Q.B. 580, 587 *per* Blackburn, J.; *O'Flaherty* v. *McKinlay*, [1953] 2 D.L.R. 514.
[11] *Farnworth Finance Facilities, Ltd.* v. *Attryde*, [1970] 2 All E.R. 774; [1970] 1 W.L.R. 1053, and below, p. 114 and pp. 133–137.
[12] As in *Leaf* v. *International Galleries*, [1950] 2 K.B. 86; [1950] 1 All E.R. 693; *Oscar Chess, Ltd.* v. *Williams*, [1957] 1 All E.R. 325; [1957] 1 W.L.R. 370 (lapse of time); *Long* v. *Lloyd*, [1958] 2 All E.R. 402; [1958] 1 W.L.R. 753 (affirmation).

assessment of damages in contract and tort.[13] Generally, however, it will be recalled that within English law affirmations of fact may partake of the nature of both contractual terms and representations depending on whether they are made with promissory intent.[14] On breach of a contractual promise the buyer will be *prima facie* entitled to recover the difference between the value of the goods at the time of delivery and the value they would have had if they had answered to the warranty.[15] In tort compensation will be based on the loss actually incurred through reliance on the representation. The distinction is often expressed as being between "expectation" and "reliance" interests but this is something of an over-simplification.[16]

The difference between the contractual and the tortious measure of damages may be illustrated by taking a simple standard example.

A agrees to buy and B agrees to sell a painting which B represents as an original Picasso. It is in fact a copy. The contract price paid by A is £500 and the painting would have been worth £5,000 had it been a Picasso. As a copy it is worth only £50. On such facts the contractual measure of damages would *prima facie* entitle A to £4,950, that is, to £5,000 (the value as promised) less £50 (the value as delivered).[17] The tortious measure of damages would entitle him to £450, that is, to £500 (the contract price) less £50 (the value as delivered). Equity would allow him to rescind and recover the contract price of £500. Had A made a bad bargain agreeing to pay more for the painting than it was worth, he might have been better off suing in tort on the representation rather than in contract on the promise.

The above example is admittedly somewhat stylised although it is not entirely unrealistic. If the defendants in *Leaf* v. *International Galleries*[18] had been successfully sued on a contractual promise that the painting was by John Constable, the difference between the value as warranted and the value as delivered would have been considerable. In the typical case, however, the

---

[13] See Ogus, *The Law of Damages* (1973), pp. 286–288; *McGregor on Damages*, 13 edn., 1972, chs. 18, 19 especially; *Benjamin's Sale of Goods* (1974), paras. 1261–1361; Treitel, *Law of Contract*, 4th edn., 1975, ch. 21; Sutton, *Sale of Goods*, 2nd edn., 1974, ch. 21; Atiyah, *Sale of Goods*, 5th edn., 1975, ch. 28.

[14] See *Heilbut, Symons & Co.* v. *Buckleton*, [1913] A.C. 30, above, pp. 36–41.

[15] Sale of Goods Act 1893, s. 53 (3).

[16] "Reliance" damages may sometimes be recovered in contract. See *McRae* v. *Commonwealth Disposals Commission* (1950), 84 C.L.R. 377; *Anglia Television* v. *Reed*, [1972] 1 Q.B. 60; [1971] 3 All E.R. 690; Fuller and Perdue, "The Reliance Interest in Contract Damages", 46 Yale L. Jo. 52; 373 (1936); Ogus, *op. cit.,* pp. 346–354. See also *Esso Petroleum Co., Ltd.* v. *Mardon,* [1976] Q.B. 801; [1976] 2 All E.R. 5, C.A.

[17] This was not always the case. In *Watson* v. *Denton* (1835), 7 C. & P. 85, at p. 91; Tindall, C.J. directed the jury that if they found a breach of warranty that a horse was sound they should "give as damages the difference between the price paid and the real value of the horse". See also Waddams, "Strict Liability, Warranties and the Sale of Goods" (1969), 19 Univ. Toronto Law Jo. 157, 160, note 17.

[18] [1950] 2 K.B. 86; [1950] 1 All E.R. 693, above, p. 51.

contract price will itself provide the only evidence of the value of the goods as warranted.[19] This will tend to lead to an approximation of the measure of damages in contract and tort. The *prima facie* measure of damages in contract may, moreover, be displaced and the buyer awarded the cost of remedying the defect.[20] He may be expected to take reasonable steps to this end but need not engage in speculative attempts to minimise his loss.[1] The value of the defective goods as delivered will be assessed by reference to their market price at the time of the delivery which may well be nil.[2]

A product which is defective or which does not perform as warranted may cause physical injury to the buyer or damage to his property or it may lead to a loss of profits where it is being used in a business venture. The general principle is that the seller's strict contractual liability will extend to such consequential losses provided that they would have been within the reasonable contemplation of the parties at the time of the sale.[3] Thus recovery has been granted where, for example, a defective catapult put out an eye;[4] an excess of bisulphite soda in undergarments caused contact dermatitis;[5] industrial chemicals caused an explosion;[6] and where toxic animal feed caused the death of mink.[7] In such cases the application of the

---

[19] See, e.g., *Minster Trust, Ltd.* v. *Traps Tractors, Ltd.*, [1954] 3 All E.R. 136, 156.

[20] See the dicta of Upjohn, L.J., in *Charterhouse Credit Co., Ltd.* v. *Tolly*, [1963] 2 Q.B. 683, 711–712, C.A., a hire-purchase case. See also *Sykes* v. *Drummond and Dvoretsky* (1925), 27 W.A.L.R. 126 (W.A. Sup. Ct.) (agricultural machinery); *Bowman Steel Corporation* v. *Lumbermen's Mutual Cas. Co.*, 364 F. 2d 246 (3d Cir., 1966) (asbestos felt). The approach is associated with building and similar contracts as in *Hoenig* v. *Isaacs*, [1952] 2 All E.R. 176, C.A., and it may be especially appropriate where a defective product is incorporated into realty.

[1] See *Hammer and Barrow* v. *Coca Cola*, [1962] N.Z.L.R. 723, 725 (defective yoyos) where the point is helpfully discussed by Richmond, J., sitting in the New Zealand Supreme Court.

[2] In which case the market value as warranted will be the *prima facie* measure of damages. See *F. Jones & Co.* v. *C. G. Grais and Sons* (1962), 62 S.R. (N.S.W.) 410, 416–417; *Ford Motot Co. of Canada, Ltd.* v. *Haley* (1967), 62 D.L.R. (2d) 329 (Canada Sup. Ct.). See also *Biggin & Co. Ltd.* v. *Permanite, Ltd.*, [1950] 2 All E.R. 859, 870–871 per Devlin, J.; *Pagnan and Fratelli* v. *Corbisa Industrial Agropacuaria* [1971] 1 All E.R. 165; [1970] 1 W.L.R. 1306.

[3] Under the twin rule in *Hadley* v. *Baxendale* (1854), 9 Exch. 341 the "reasonable contemplation" test may be satisfied if (i) the loss is of a type which would arise "according to the usual course of things"; or (ii) the seller knew of the special circumstances rendering the loss likely on the facts of the case. See also *Victoria Laundry (Windsor), Ltd.* v. *Newman Industries, Ltd.*, [1949] 2 K.B. 528; [1949] 1 All E.R. 997.

[4] *Godley* v. *Perry*, [1960] 1 All E.R. 36; [1960] 1 W.L.R. 9

[5] *Grant* v. *Australian Knitting Mills, Ltd.*, [1936] A.C. 85, P.C. See also *Wilson* v. *Rickett, Cockerell & Co. Ltd.*, [1954] 1 Q.B. 598; [1954] 1 All E.R. 868; *Andrews* v. *Hopkinson*, [1957] 1 Q.B. 229; [1956] 3 All E.R. 422.

[6] *Vacwell Engineering Co., Ltd.* v. *B.D.H. Chemicals, Ltd.*, [1971] 1 Q.B. 88; [1969] 3 All E.R. 1681.

[7] *Ashington Piggeries, Ltd.* v. *Christopher Hill, Ltd.*, [1972] A.C. 441; [1971] 1 All E.R. 847, H.L. See also *Harbutt's Plasticine, Ltd.* v. *Wayne Tank and Pump Co., Ltd.*, [1970] 1 Q.B. 447; [1970] 1 All E.R. 225, C.A., below, p. 135. For compensation for loss of profits through inability to use

rules for assessing damages in contract and tort will normally lead to the same result. Occasionally, however, there may be advantages in suing in tort where the rules governing remoteness of damage are more favourable.[8] This latter point is well illustrated by the Canadian case of *Fillmore's Valley Nurseries, Ltd. v. North American Cyanamid, Ltd.*[9] The plaintiff nursery was a large-scale grower of pansy plants and the defendants manufactured and sold fertilisers and herbicides. The defendant's senior agriculturalist informed the plaintiffs that a certain chemical fertiliser and herbicide, amino triazole, would not leave any harmful residue in the soil beyond twelve to fourteen days of application. The statement was untrue or, at least, misleading in the absence of a warning. In fact a residue remained in the soil some two months after application when pansies were planted and the plaintiffs lost some 175,000 plants which was virtually the entire stock for the year. In an action in contract on the warranty the plaintiffs recovered the value of the pansies which had been lost, this being regarded as the "natural and probable consequences" of the breach. But in an action in tort on the representation they recovered ancillary profit losses under three further heads to cover (i) loss of sales on other nursery products in the same year; (ii) loss of pansy sales in future years through lack of continuity in the business; and (iii) loss of sales of other nursery products in future years.

Damages under the Misrepresentation Act 1967

The proper approach to the assessment of damages under the Misrepresentation Act 1967 is not entirely clear. Since the action is founded on a misrepresentation, the tortious measure of damage ought in principle to apply in the same way as it applies where the claim is under the *Hedley Byrne* decision.[10] Certain complications might, however, result from the curious way in which the Act was drafted. Section 2(1) does not say that a person shall be liable in respect of a negligent misrepresentation which causes loss to a person induced to enter a contract. It says rather that

"if the person making the misrepresentation would be liable to damages in

the chattel or where it does not perform as warranted, see *Benjamin's Sale of Goods* (1974), paras. 1321–1325.
[8] See *Koufos* v. *C. Czarnikow Ltd.: The Heron II*, [1969] 1 A.C. 350, 385; [1967] 3 All E.R. 686, 691, H.L., *per* Lord Reid.
[9] (1958), 14 D.L.R. (2d) 297 (Nova Scotia Sup. Ct.).
[10] *Hedley Byrne & Co. Ltd.* v. *Heller & Partners, Ltd.*, [1964] A.C. 465; [1963] 2 All E.R. 575, H.L., above, p. 43. See also *Esso Petroleum Co., Ltd.* v. *Mardon*, [1976] Q.B. 801; [1976] 2 All E.R. 5, above, p. 40.

respect thereof had the misrepresentation been made fraudulently, that person shall be so liable notwithstanding that the misrepresentation was not made fraudulently"

unless he can establish that he reasonably believed the representation to be true.

The introduction of this fiction of fraud might affect the statutory remedy in a number of ways. The *prima facie* measure of damages in the tort of deceit is the loss incurred through reliance on the misrepresentation. This would normally be purely financial but may include physical damage as well.[11] The representee is, however, neither entitled to nor limited by the contractual measure of damages the object of which is to place the plaintiff in the position he would have enjoyed had the promise been performed. It may be that English law is open to criticism in adopting this approach[12] but the point seems to be clearly established.[13] Hence it is submitted that a recent decision is wrong in so far as it awards damages for loss of bargain under the Act.[14] Lord Denning, M.R., has also said *obiter* that in deceit all losses flowing directly from the fraudulent inducement are recoverable and "it does not lie in the mouth of the fraudulent person to say that they could not reasonably have been foreseen".[15] If this is correct consequential losses may be recoverable more readily in deceit than in contract or in the tort of negligence. It would be curious indeed if a person who was not in fact fraudulent was subjected to a similar liability under the Act.[16]

Finally reference may be made to the decision of Judge Fay in *Davis & Co. (Wines), Ltd.* v. *AFA-Minerva (E.M.I.), Ltd.*[17] Here the plaintiff owners of

---

[11] See, e.g., *Langridge* v. *Levy* (1837), 2 M. & W. 519; affd. (1838), 4 M. & W. 337, (gun which exploded); *Mullett* v. *Mason* (1866), L.R. 1 C.P. 559 (infected cows). The word "loss" in s. 2 (1) of the 1967 Act would no doubt cover such damage.

[12] The approach may, e.g., lead to the deceitful defendant paying less damages than the defendant who innocently made a false affirmation with promissory intent. U.C.C., art. 2–721 avoids this result by providing: "Remedies for material misrepresentation or fraud include all remedies available under this Article for non-fraudulent breach".

[13] See *McConnel* v. *Wright*, [1903] 1 Ch. 546, 554 *per* Lord Collins, M.R.; *Doyle* v. *Olby (Ironmongers), Ltd.*, [1969] 2 Q.B. 158; [1969] 2 All E.R. 119, C.A.; Treitel (1969), 32 M.L.R. 556; *McGregor on Damages,* 13th edn., 1972, para. 538.

[14] See *Watts* v. *Spence*, [1975] 2 All E.R. 528; [1975] 2 W.L.R. 1039, where Graham, J. awarded the plaintiff his loss of bargain after the defendant had claimed to be entitled to sell a certain house. See also *Gosling* v. *Anderson* (1972), 223 Estates Gazette 1743, C.A.

[15] *Doyle* v. *Olby (Ironmongers), Ltd.*, [1969] 2 Q.B. 158, at p. 167. Winn, L.J. also appears to have favoured a "direct consequences" test: *ibid.*, at p. 168. See also *ibid.*, at p. 171 *per* Sachs, L.J.

[16] There is also the possibility that exemplary damages might be awarded though it is still unclear whether they are available in deceit: see *Mafo* v. *Adams*, [1970] 1 Q.B. 548; [1969] 3 All E.R. 1404, C.A., where the point was left open; *McGregor on Damages,* 13th edn., 1972, para. 1376.

[17] [1974] 2 Lloyd's Rep. 27.

a small retail liquor shop were suing in respect of damage to their property and loss of stock following the breakdown of their burglar alarm system which had been installed by the defendants. The system had become inoperative when the control panel was wrenched off. The claim failed in so far as it was based on an alleged breach of contract but succeeded in part under the Misrepresentation Act 1967, s. 2 (1). The defendants were found to have represented that the alarm bell would ring continuously if the wires were broken which was misleading since the system could be overridden. They were liable to compensate for the loss of stock but not for the damage caused in the initial breaking-in since this would have occurred anyway even if the representation had been true. The case serves as a useful reminder that whatever the theory of liability there must be a causative link between the misconduct and the damage or loss in respect of which compensation is claimed.[18]

Liability as between manufacturers and remote consumers

Express warranties in American law[19]

At a relatively early stage American product liability law developed the concept of the express warranty[20] as a means of imposing obligations on manufacturers in respect of statements made on labels and brochures or in the course of advertising. The basis and scope of this liability appears strange to the English lawyer. The express warranty has the contractual characteristic of being independent of any requirement of deceit or negligence and yet, being grounded in tort, the true historical basis of the warranty, it is not limited by any requirement of privity or of consideration. In essence it is a strict liability for misrepresentations which induce reliance with consequent harm. The principle is set out in the *Restatement of Torts*, 2d, s. 402B in the following terms:

> "One engaged in the business of selling chattels who, by advertising, labels, or otherwise, makes to the public a misrepresentation of a material fact concerning the character or quality of a chattel sold by him is subject to liability for

---

[18] See further, below, pp. 273–290.
[19] See 2 Frumer and Friedman, *Products Liability*, s. 16.04 [4]; Prosser, *Law of Torts*, 4th edn., 1971, pp. 651–653; Legh-Jones, "Products Liability: Consumer Protection in America" (1969), C.L.J. 54, pp. 57–61.
[20] For the definition of a warranty in United States jurisdictions, see U.C.C., art. 2–313, above, p. 36.

physical harm to a consumer of the chattel caused by justifiable reliance upon the misrepresentation, even though

(*a*) it is not made fraudulently or negligently, and

(*b*) the consumer has not bought the chattel from or entered into any contractual relation with the seller."[1]

Baxter v. *Ford Motor Co.*[2] was an important early case which came before the Washington Supreme Court in 1932. The plaintiff had bought a Ford sedan car from a dealer and had lost an eye when the windshield shattered as a stone was thrown up by a passing car. In an action against the manufacturer of the car the trial court judge had refused to admit in evidence catalogues which Ford had distributed to its dealers. One such catalogue stated that "all of the new Ford cars have a Triplex shatterproof glass windshield so that it will not fly or shatter under the hardest impact". The catalogue continued by stressing that "this is an important safety factor because it eliminates the danger of flying glass—the cause of most of the injuries in automobile accidents". Reversing with directions for a new trial, the Washington Supreme Court dealt with the objection that there was no privity of contract between the parties by saying:[3]

> "It would be unjust to recognize a rule that would permit manufacturers of goods to create a demand for their products by representing that they possess qualities which they, in fact, do not possess, and then, because there is no privity of contract existing between the consumer and the manufacturer, denying the consumer the right to recover if damages result from the absence of those qualities, when such absence is not readily noticeable."

Similar reasoning has been adopted in many other cases, as where a Toni Home Permanent set was advertised as being safe, harmless and "very gentle";[4] a tin of boned chicken was advertised as containing "no bones";[5] a detergent was labelled "kind to hands";[6] and where the defendants claimed that fabrics treated by their chemical resin were "shrink-proof".[7]

---

[1] A caveat is added stating that no opinion is expressed as to whether the principle may apply (1) where the representation is not made to the public, but to an individual, or (2) where physical harm is caused to one who is not a consumer of the chattel.

[2] 12 P. 2d 409, 88 A.L.R. 521 (1932); 15 P. 2d 1118 (1932) (rehearing); 35 P. 2d 1090 (1934) (second appeal). See also *Bahlman* v. *Hudson Motor Car Co.*, 288 N.W. 309 (Mich., 1939).

[3] 88 A.L.R. 521, 526 (1932).

[4] *Rogers* v. *Toni Home Permanent Co.*, 147 N.E. 2d 612 (Ohio, 1958); see also *Markovich* v. *McKesson and Robbins*, 149 N.E. 2d 181 (Ohio, 1958) (permanent); *Perma-Strate Co.* v. *Gemus*, 430 S.W. 2d 665 (Tenn., 1967) (hair straightener).

[5] *Lane* v. *Swanson & Sons*, 278 P. 2d 723 (Cal. App., 1955). See also *Bonker* v. *Ingersoll Products Corporation*, 132 F. Supp. 5 (1955).

[6] *Worley* v. *Proctor and Gamble Manufacturing Co.*, 253 S.W. 2d 532 (Mo. App., 1952). See also *Hamon* v. *Digliani*, 174 A. 2d 294 (Conn., 1961).

[7] *Randy Knitwear Inc.* v. *American Cyanamid Co.*, 181 N.E. 2d 399 (N.Y., 1962). See also *Santor* v. *A. and M. Karagheusian Inc.*, 207 A. 2d 305 (N.J., 1965); *Ford Motor Co.* v. *Lonon*, 398 S.W. 2d 240 (Tenn., 1966); *Restatement of Torts*, 2d, s. 552D (tentative draft).

The latter case is of particular interest as suggesting that economic losses no less than physical damage may be compensated. The plaintiff accordingly benefits from the contractual as well as the tortious associations of warranty liability.

The contents of such statements may come to the plaintiff's attention through a wide range of sources, including labels attached to the product or its container,[8] accompanying brochures,[9] trade journals, newspapers, and radio or television commercials.[10] However, it is in the sphere of mass advertising that the doctrine finds its main justification. In many such cases the statement will be construed as a mere "puff" or sales talk rather than as a positive assertion of fact. Alternatively, it may simply describe or provide information about the goods,[11] or be genuinely qualified, as where an oral contraceptive was advertised as conferring "virtually 100 per cent protection".[12] Yet the overriding impression is of a willingness to spell out a warranty whenever possible.[13] Manufacturers can hardly complain if a serious intent is attributed to the output of the advertising industry operating on their behalf.

The distinction between an express warranty and an advertising "puff" may be viewed as illustrative of a requirement of reasonable reliance as a cornerstone of liability. That there is a general requirement of reliance is clear. Its full implications are, however, less certain. In the typical case the plaintiff will have purchased the goods in reliance on an assertion which he associates with the manufacturer and then suffered injury as a consequence of using them. Yet not all these elements are necessary. Certainly, knowledge of the assurance must be established, since statements which are unread cannot constitute either operative representations inducing reliance or contractual offers capable of acceptance.[14] On the other hand, it is not

---

[8] See, e.g., *Bonker* v. *Ingersoll Products Corp.*, 132 F. Supp. 5 (1955); *Worley* v. *Proctor and Gamble Manufacturing Co.*, 253 S.W. 2d 532 (Mo. App., 1952).

[9] See, e.g., *Mannsz* v. *MacWhyte Co.*, 155 F. 2d 445 (3rd Cir., 1946) (tensile strength of wire rope).

[10] See, e.g., *Pritchard* v. *Liggett and Myers Tobacco Co.*, 295 F. 2d 292 (3rd Cir., 1961) (cigarettes); *Markovich* v. *McKesson and Robbins*, 149 N.E. 2d 181 (Ohio, 1958) (permanent).

[11] See, e.g., *Denna* v. *Chrysler Corporation*, 206 N.E. 2d 221 (Ohio, 1964) ("full-time constant control power steering" on car); *Braniff Airways Inc.* v. *Curtiss-Wright Corporation*, 411 F. 2d 451 (2nd Cir., 1969); *Brown* v. *General Motors Corporation*, 355 F. 2d 814 (4th Cir., 1966).

[12] *Whittington* v. *Eli Lilly & Co.*, 333 F. Supp. 98 (1971)—the plaintiff had, of course, become pregnant.

[13] See, e.g., *Worley* v. *Proctor and Gamble Manufacturing Co.*, 253 S.W. 2d 532 (Mo App., 1952) (detergent "kind to the hands"); *Ireland* v. *Louis Liggett Co.*, 137 N.E. 371 (Mass., 1922) (cold cream "pure and healthful"); *Greenman* v. *Yuba Power Products Inc.*, 27 Cal. Rptr. 697 (1963) (power-tool described as "rugged"). See further, above, pp. 33–34 for discussion in the context of the vendor's liability.

[14] See, respectively, *Horsfall* v. *Thomas* (1862), 1 H. & C. 90; *R.* v. *Clarke* (1927), 40 C.L.R. 227. In *Arrow Transport Co.* v. *A. O. Smith Co.*, 454 P. 2d 387 (Wash., 1969) an express warranty claim failed when knowledge was not established. See also *Borowicz* v. *Chicago Mastic Co.*, 355 F. 2d 751 (7th Cir., 1966).

necessary to show that the warranty was known to have emanated from the defendant.[15] To this extent the requirement of reliance is diluted. Again, it is not wholly clear whether knowledge before purchase is essential, or whether knowledge before use is sufficient.[16] The latter should be sufficient since liability is founded on the representation and not on the furnishing of consideration through purchasing the goods from a third party. The same reasoning would permit recovery by a non-purchasing user who knew of the assurance. In *Bonker* v. *Ingersoll Products Corporation*[17] the point was conceded when the plaintiff suffered injury on swallowing a bone from a tin of "boneless chicken fricassée" manufactured by the defendants and bought by her mother from a retail shop.[18] The result is not only consistent with the fact that the action is founded in tort; it also accords with common sense. To limit recovery to purchasers would simply lead to the adoption of agency fictions to circumvent the limitation.[19]

The California case of *Corporation of Presiding Bishop of the Church of Jesus Christ of Latter Day Saints* v. *Cavanaugh and Plastic Process Co.*[20] is also in point. Here the engineer of the plaintiff church had relied on assurances in the defendant's sales literature that plastic piping might be used in preference to copper in a central heating system. The piping was subsequently purchased and installed in the church by a third party contractor and it proved to be unsatisfactory. Recovery was again granted although the plaintiff had not purchased the piping but had specified its use on the recommendation of the engineer, who had himself been influenced by the defendant's brochures and advertising.[1] The same result could no doubt be achieved under the traditional English approach of the collateral warranty.[2] It remains to be seen whether the principle will be extended to benefit a plaintiff who has suffered injury or damage following reliance and use by an independent third party, such as a hairdresser or someone providing a similar service.

In relatively recent years the express warranty theory of *Baxter* v. *Ford*

---

[15] *Seely* v. *White Motor Co.*, 45 Cal. Rptr. 17 (1965).

[16] In *Perma-Strate Co.* v. *Gemus*, 430 S.W. 2d 665 (Tenn., 1967) a requirement of knowledge before *use* was stressed. *Cf.*, however, *Randall* v. *Goodrich Gamble Co.*, 54 N.W. 2d 769 (Minn., 1952). See also *Kepling* v. *Schlueter Manufacturing Co.*, 378 F. 2d 5 (6th Cir., 1967).

[17] 132 F. Supp. 5 (1955).

[18] See also *Connolly* v. *Hagi*, 188 A. 2d 884 (Conn., 1963) (reliance by filling station attendant who was not a purchaser; recovery granted). See also *Mannsz* v. *MacWhyte Co.*, 155 F. 2d 445 (3rd Cir., 1946). But *cf. Speed Fastners Inc.* v. *Newsom*, 382 F. 2d 395 (10th Cir., 1967).

[19] See above, pp. 27–28, where the point is discussed in the context of "horizontal privity".

[20] 32 Cal. Rptr. 144 (Cal. App., 1963).

[1] *Restatement of Torts*, 2d, s. 402B, comment (j) would also permit recovery by a third party "consumer" injured as a consequence of the purchaser's reliance, as where a wife is driving her husband's car and knows nothing of the manufacturer's advertising claims.

[2] See below, pp. 64–65.

Motor Co.[3] has been largely supplanted by the implied warranty and strict tort theories.[4] Both of these theories have a potentially wider range of application since liability follows from the simple presence of the product on the market and not from positive assurances as to its safety or suitability. Hence the plaintiff who has doubts as to whether the statement is sufficiently specific to constitute a warranty may well fall back on alternative theories. But there are equally cases in which the product is neither unmerchantable nor unreasonably dangerous and where the plaintiff may yet recover on proof of an express warranty. Here the doctrine retains its full importance. Thus the defendant may expressly warrant that a dress is not injurious to wear,[5] or that a cosmetic is completely safe,[6] and the plaintiff may recover in respect of an allergic reaction which would not be compensated under any other theory.[7] A victim of lung cancer might recover against a cigarette manufacturer who had advertised his product as being safe;[8] and in *Seely v. White Motor Co.*,[9] the Supreme Court of California denied liability under the strict tort theory but still upheld a judgment for the plaintiff because the motor vehicle had been warranted free from defects.[10]

English and Commonwealth developments[11]

Neither English nor Commonwealth jurisdictions have developed a body of case law equivalent to the express warranty of American law. Substantially similar results might, however, be achieved in a number of ways. Thus liability may be imposed in tort where a product is marketed without adequate warnings and directions for use and physical injury or property damage results.[12] Where the packaging or labelling of the product or its

---

[3] 12 P. 2d 409, 88 A.L.R. 521 (Wash., 1932); 15 P. 2d 1118 (1932) (rehearing); 35 P. 2d 1090 (1934) (second appeal).
[4] See, respectively, *Henningsen* v. *Bloomfield Motors Inc.*, 161 A. 2d 69 (N.J., 1960), and *Greenman* v. *Yuba Power Products*, 27 Cal. Rptr. 697 (Cal. Sup. Ct. 1963).
[5] *McLachlan* v. *Wilmington Dry Goods*, 22 A. 2d 851 (Del., 1941).
[6] *Drake* v. *Charles of Fifth Avenue Inc.*, 307 N.Y.S. 2d 310 (1970).
[7] For discussion of allergies, see below, pp. 106–107, 324–326.
[8] *Pritchard* v. *Liggett and Myers Tobacco Co.*, 350 F. 2d 479 (3rd Cir., 1965) (new trial ordered, where the advertisements included statements such as, "Nose, Throat And Accessory Organs Not Adversely Affected By Smoking Chesterfields").
[9] 45 Cal. Rptr. 17 (1965) below, p. 341.
[10] Recovery for economic loss under the strict tort theory is discussed below, pp. 338–342.
[11] See Tobin, "Products Liability: a United States Commonwealth comparative survey", (1969) 3 N.Z.U.L.R. 377, 390–399; Fricke, "Manufacturer's Liability for Breach of Warranty" (1959), 33 A.L.J. 35.
[12] See, e.g., *Vacwell Engineering Co., Ltd.* v. *B.D.H. Chemicals, Ltd.*, [1971] 1 Q.B. 88; [1969] 3 All E.R. 1681 (explosive chemicals), and, in general, below, ch. 12.

supporting advertising contains representations of safety the plaintiff is likely to have an even stronger case.[13] Admittedly liability will be incurred only where the manufacturer knew or ought to have known of the danger. In practice, however, there would be few cases where the product was in fact unreasonably dangerous as marketed without this requirement being met.[14] The position with respect to tortious liability is discussed in the second part of the book. Here it is convenient to confine discussion to contractual liability.

Contracts of sale

Although most manufacturers market their products through independent retailers, some deal directly with their consumers, thus cutting out all intermediate parties. A farmer may, for example, sell his produce at the farm gate and a manufacturer may sell through his own retail outlets or through mail order. Transactions of this nature are by no means uncommon and in such cases the normal sales warranties will attach to the contract of sale.[15] The same would be true of a case in which a manufacturer sells through an agent. This latter situation would, however, seem to be rare. Dealers who hold stocks of a product would almost invariably be regarded as independent operators buying and selling in their own right. This is so even though they are described as sole or exclusive "agents" to sell within a particular area. The consumer's contract of sale would then be with the dealer rather than with the manufacturer. The consequences are to be seen in a leading Australian case, *International Harvester Co. of Australia Pty., Ltd. v. Carrigan's Hazeldene Pastoral Co.*[16] The plaintiff farmer had attended an agricultural show in Sydney where he visited a stand run by the defendant company. He was given a pamphlet describing one of the defendant's automatic hay balers which he later acquired from local dealers who carried on business as machinery and general agents. The baler did not work properly and since the dealers were insolvent it was sought to establish that the defendant manufacturer was a party to the contract of sale. The High Court of Australia held that there was no evidence to support such a conclusion. The dealers were no doubt "agents" in a general business sense in that they formed part of the distribution

---

[13] See, e.g., *Christ* v. *Art Metal Works*, 243 N.Y.S. 496 (1930) (toy gun advertised as "absolutely harmless"), and below, pp. 243–244.

[14] Pharmaceutical products might be exceptional in this respect. But even then there would be a duty to warn of subsequently discovered dangers: see below, pp. 247–251. For proof of negligence, see below, ch. 13.

[15] See below, chs. 5 and 6.

[16] (1958), 100 C.L.R. 644. See Stoljar, "The International Harvester Case: a manufacturer's liability for defective chattels" (1959), 32 A.L.J. 307.

network for the product. But they were not agents in the sense of being empowered to create a legal relationship between the manufacturer as principal and a third party purchaser.[17] The claim accordingly failed.

Collateral contracts [18]

Where there is no contract of sale between manufacturer and consumer as in the *International Harvester* case,[19] it may still be possible to hold the manufacturer liable on a collateral contract. In *Shanklin Pier, Ltd.* v. *Detel Products, Ltd.*[20] the plaintiffs were the owners of the Shanklin pier on the Isle of Wight. They alleged that, in consideration of an express warranty as to the qualities of a paint "D.M.U." manufactured by the defendants, they had specified that this paint should be used by contractors under a contract to repaint the pier. The paint proved to be unsuitable and additional expenses were incurred. Holding the defendants liable for breach of contract Mcnair, J. said:[1]

> "If, as is elementary, the consideration for the warranty in the usual case is the entering into of the main contract in relation to which the warranty is given, I see no reason why there may not be an enforceable warranty between A and B supported by the consideration that B should cause C to enter into a contract with A or that B should do some other act for the benefit of A."

The collateral contract has not been exploited fully as a device for holding a manufacturer strictly liable and it is uncertain how far the principle may be taken. The following points or limitations may be noted. Firstly, the affirmation must have been made *animo contrahendi*. It is not sufficient that it induce reliance on the part of the representee without having been made with promissory intent.[2] Secondly, English cases have been concerned mainly with direct interpersonal communications. It is no doubt in such cases that a promissory intent can be most readily established. However,

---

[17] *Cf.* (1958), 100 C.L.R. 644, 652–653 especially. For the position of the dealer as an agent in instalment credit transactions, see *Branwhite* v. *Worcester Works Finance, Ltd.*, [1969] 1 A.C. 552; [1968] 3 All E.R. 104; Consumer Credit Act 1974, ss. 56 (2), 57 (3), 69 (6), 102 (1).

[18] See Wedderburn, "Collateral Contracts", [1959] C.L.J. 58; see also above, p. 38. (vendor's liability) and below, pp. 160–165 (manufacturers' guarantees).

[19] (1958) 100 C.L.R. 644, above, p. 63.

[20] [1951] 2 K.B. 854; [1951] 2 All E.R. 471. See also *Wells (Merstham), Ltd.* v. *Buckland Sand and Silica, Ltd.*, [1965] 2 Q.B. 170; [1964] 1 All E.R. 41; *Brown* v. *Sheen and Richmond Car Sales, Ltd.*, [1950] 1 All E.R. 1102; *Andrews* v. *Hopkinson*, [1957] 1 Q.B. 229; [1956] 3 All E.R. 422; *Yeoman Credit, Ltd.* v. *Odgers*, [1962] 2 Q.B. 508; [1962] 1 All E.R. 789; *Webster* v. *Higgin*, [1948] 2 All E.R. 127.

[1] [1951] 2 All E.R. 471, 472.

[2] *Heilbut Symons & Co.* v. *Buckleton*, [1913] A.C. 30 H.L.; *Savage & Sons Pty., Ltd.* v. *Blakney* (1970), 119 C.L.R. 435 (High Court of Australia); and above, p. 36 *et seq.*

an offer of a unilateral contract may be made to the world at large[3] and hence there is scope for movement towards a liability based on general advertising claims as in American law.[4] This would be especially important where the loss is purely financial, as where material is advertised as "shrinkproof" or "waterproof" when it is not.[5] Such losses are unlikely to be compensated as non-promissory representations in the law of tort[6] but they may clearly be compensated if a contract can be established.[7]

Thirdly, there is room for argument over the ways in which the contractual requirement of consideration may be satisfied. Purchase of the goods from a third party such as a dealer will be sufficient[8] as will their specification to one who subsequently purchases from the manufacturer[9] or, no doubt, from a third party. Whether anything less than this is sufficient is unclear. English cases have assumed that the consideration will take the form of entry into a subsequent contract, but it is arguable that use of the goods by the plaintiff will suffice.[10] This is especially so where the goods are consumed out of an existing stock which will thereafter need to be replenished. Mere use by a third party without any prior specification by the plaintiff could not be accommodated within a contract paradigm although the plaintiff who suffers personal injury or property damage might recover in tort if negligence can be established. Finally, English cases have not extended the collateral contract approach beyond express warranties. It would be theoretically possible to imply warranties of merchantibility and reasonable fitness for purpose from the mere presence of goods on the market.[11] But this would be tantamount to imposing general liability without fault and any such development is likely to come through legislation rather than case law.[12]

---

[3] *Carlill* v. *Carbolic Smoke Ball Co.*, [1893] 1 Q.B. 256, C.A.

[4] *Baxter* v. *Ford Motor Co.*, 12 P. 2d 409, 88 A.L.R. 521 (1932), 35 P. 2d 1090 (1934), above, pp. 58–62.

[5] *Cf. Randy Knitwear Inc.* v. *American Cyanamid Co.*, 181 N.E. 2d 399 (N.Y., 1962).

[6] For the position with respect to compensation for economic loss in the law of tort, see below, ch. 16, pp. 328–344.

[7] *Cf. Shanklin Pier, Ltd.* v. *Detel Products, Ltd.*, [1951] 2 K.B. 854; [1951] 2 All E.R. 471, above; *Brown* v. *Sheen and Richmond Car Sales Ltd.*, [1950] 1 All E.R. 1102. Where physical injury or property damage is involved an action in negligence is also likely to be available: see *Andrews* v. *Hopkinson*, [1957] 1 Q.B. 229; [1956] 3 All E.R. 422.

[8] *Wells (Merstham), Ltd.* v. *Buckland Sand and Silica, Ltd.*, [1965] 2 Q.B. 170; [1964] 1 All E.R. 41.

[9] *Shanklin Pier, Ltd.* v. *Detel Products, Ltd.*, [1951] 2 K.B. 854; [1951] 2 All E.R. 471.

[10] Support for this view is to be found in *Carlill* v. *Carbolic Smoke Ball Co.*, [1893] 1 Q.B. 256. See also *Wood* v. *Lectrik, Ltd.*, (1932), *Times*, 13 January (electric comb); *Goldthorpe* v. *Logan*, [1943] 2 D.L.R. 519 (Ont. C.A.) (hair removed by electrolysis, "results guaranteed").

[11] This was effectively the step taken in *Henningsen* v. *Bloomfield Motors Inc.*, 161 A. 2d 69 (N.J., 1960), above, p. 16.

[12] See, however, the dicta of Riddell J.A. in *Shandloff* v. *City Dairy*, [1936] 4 D.L.R. 712

Manufacturers' guarantees

A further possibility is that it may be open to the consumer to sue the manufacturer on a manufacturers' guarantee. Since such "guarantees" have frequently contained exemption clauses purporting to take away far more than they confer it is convenient to postpone discussion of their legal effect until a later chapter.[13]

(Ont. C.A.) and *Arendale* v. *Canada Bread Co.*, [1941] 2 D.L.R. 41 (Ont. C.A.) cited by Tobin, (1969) 3 N.Z.U.L.R. 377, 392–393.
[13] See below, ch. 8, pp. 160–165.

5 Implied Terms Governing Correspondence with Description, Merchantability and Fitness for Purpose: I

Introduction[1]

In addition to imposing liability for any express warranties and misrepresentations,[2] English law imposes a further measure of contractual liability on vendors of goods through the medium of the implied term. From at least the early nineteenth century, contracts for the sale of goods have been taken to require that the vendor supply goods which correspond with the contract description and which are of merchantable quality and reasonably fit for their purpose.[3] The common law developments were enacted in the Sale of Goods Act 1893 which was amended by the Supply of Goods (Implied Terms) Act 1973.[4] Similar terms now cover contracts for the sale of goods and hire purchase agreements and hence references to contracts

---

[1] See *Benjamin's Sale of Goods* (1974), ch. 11; 3 *Williston on Sales*, 4th edn., 1974, chs. 16, 17, 18, 19; Atiyah, *Sale of Goods*, 5th edn., 1975, ch. 12; Greig, *Sale of Goods* (1974), pp. 174–207; Sutton *Sale of Goods*, 2nd edn., 1974, chs. 8, 9, 10. Excellent if somewhat outdated treatment is also to be found in *Benjamin on Sale*, 8th edn., 1950, p. 599 *et seq*; *Williston on Sales* (revd. edn., 1948), ch. 8, ss. 223–226; ch. 9.

[2] See above, chs. 3, 40.

[3] Leading nineteenth-century cases include *Chanter* v. *Hopkins* (1838), 4 M. & W. 399; *Gardiner* v. *Gray* (1815), 4 Camp. 144; *Jones* v. *Just* (1868), L.R. 3 Q.B. 197; *Bigge* v. *Parkinson* (1862), 7 H. & N. 955; *Randall* v. *Newson* (1877), 2 Q.B.D. 102.

[4] The Act was based on the recommendations in the Law Commission report *Exemption Clauses in Contracts, First Report: Amendments to the Sale of Goods Act 1893*, Law Com. No. 24, July 1969.

for the former may be taken generally to apply *mutatis mutandis* to the latter.[5]

Where defective goods are supplied under a transaction which does not fall under the Sale of Goods Act 1893, as amended, resort must be had to the common law. The goods may, for example, be supplied as free gifts or as prizes in competitions, or under a contract of exchange or barter, of hire, for work and materials, or a contract involving the rendering of a service to which the use of goods is incidental. In some transactions of this nature the common law has developed implied terms similar to those now enacted in sales legislation. There are, however, differences between the exact nature of the terms implied. Moreover, the statutory control of exemption clauses introduced by the 1973 Act has not yet been extended to cases falling outside the Act although the Law Commission has recommended that such an extension be made.[6] Hence it remains necessary to distinguish contracts for the sale or hire purchase of goods from other transactions.[7]

Sale of goods and hire purchase agreements

The Sale of Goods Act 1893 imposes a number of progressively circumscribed duties on sellers of goods. Subject to the limitations imposed the goods supplied under the contract must correspond with the contract description[8] and be of merchantable quality[9] and reasonably fit for any particular purpose for which the buyer has indicated he requires them.[10]

---

[5] The provisions for hire purchase agreements were subsequently reproduced with minor textual amendments in the Consumer Credit Act 1974, s. 192, Sch. 4, para. 35.

[6] See the Law Commission's *Second Report on Exemption Clauses in Contracts,* Law Com. No. 69, 1975. For discussion of the control of exemption clauses under the 1973 Act, see below, ch. 8, pp. 142–158.

[7] Contractual liability in cases not involving a sale or hire-purchase agreement is discussed below pp. 115–122. For discussion of liability in tort in such cases, see below, ch 15.

[8] Section 13, as renumbered and expanded by the Supply of Goods (Implied Terms) Act 1973, s. 2. For the equivalent provision in hire purchase agreements see s. 9 of the 1973 Act and the Consumer Credit Act 1974, s. 192, Sch. 4, para. 35.

[9] Section 14 (2), as amended by the Supply of Goods (Implied Terms) Act 1973, s. 3. For the equivalent provision in hire purchase agreements see s. 10 (2) of the 1973 Act and the Consumer Credit Act 1974, s. 192, Sch. 4, para. 35.

[10] This implied condition was originally contained in s. 14 (1) of the Sale of Goods Act 1893. The Supply of Goods (Implied Terms) Act 1973 s. 3 renumbers the 1893 Act so that the provision is now contained in s. 14 (3) and amends its scope in certain important respects. For the equivalent provision in hire purchase agreements see s. 10 (3) of the 1973 Act and the Consumer Credit Act 1974, s. 192, Sch. 4, para. 35. Further implied conditions relate to title and freedom from encumberances: see Sale of Goods Act 1893, s. 12, as amended by the Supply of Goods (Implied Terms) Act 1973, s. 1, and for hire purchase agreements s. 8 of the

Similar terms are implied in Australasian and Canadian legislation[11] and in the Uniform Commercial Code of the United States of America.[12] Hence reference to cases from these jurisdictions is frequently instructive for purpose of comparison.

The implied condition of correspondence with description[13]

The Sale of Goods Act 1893, s. 13(1) provides that:

> "Where there is a contract for the sale of goods by description, there is an implied condition that the goods shall correspond with the description; and if the sale be by sample, as well as by description, it is not sufficient that the bulk of the goods correspond with the sample if the goods do not also correspond with the description."

This provision is fundamental and the general reasoning which lies behind it is clear. If a seller has contracted to sell goods of a certain description, then he must plainly deliver goods which correspond with it. The buyer should not be required to accept a substitute. This is as true of a private seller who has placed an advertisement on a notice board in a shop as of a seller who operates a nationwide mail order business. Indeed the only surprising feature of s. 13 in a straightforward case is that the obligation to deliver the contract goods should be described as implied rather than express.[14] There are, however, difficulties in ascertaining the full implications of the section.

1973 Act and the Consumer Credit Act 1974, s. 192, Sch. 4, para. 35; and to correspondence with sample: see Sale of Goods Act 1893, s. 15, and for hire purchase agreements s. 11 of the 1973 Act and the Consumer Credit Act 1974 s. 192, Sch. 4, para. 35. These latter obligations are not discussed other than incidentally in this book.

[11] For discussion which is linked to these jurisdictions see respectively Sutton, *Sale of Goods in Australia and New Zealand,* 2nd edn., 1974, chs. 8, 9, 10; Waddams, *Products Liability* (1974), ch. 3.

[12] See U.C.C. art. 2–313(1)(b) (correspondence with description); 2–314 (merchantability); 2–315 (fitness for purpose). For general comparison of the English and Commonwealth provisions with the U.C.C. provisions see Sutton, "Sales Warranties under the Sale of Goods Act and the Uniform Commercial Code" (1967), 6 Melbourne Univ. L.R. 150; Sutton "Reform of the Law of Sales" (1969), 7 Alberta L.R. 130, 173.

[13] See Coote, "Correspondence with Description in the Law of Sale of Goods" (1976) 50 A.L.J. 17; Stoljar, "Conditions, Warranties and Descriptions of Quality in Sale of Goods II" (1953), 16 M.L.R. 174; Feltham, "The Sale by Description of Specific Goods" [1969], J.B.L. 16.

[14] *Cf.* U.C.C. art. 2–313(1)(b) which provides that: "Any description of the goods which is made part of the basis of the bargain creates an express warranty that the goods shall conform to the description".

Representations, warranties and description

A preliminary issue is whether the effect of s. 13 is to designate all descriptive words in a sale by description implied conditions, thus riding roughshod over the distinctions between representations and terms and between conditions and warranties. It would be strange if the section had dispensed with the need for an initial inquiry into whether an affirmation of fact had been made with promissory intent[15] and more curious still if it had had the effect of making contractual conditions out of statements of opinion.[16] The balance of the meagre authority in point suggests that s. 13 should not be interpreted in this way. Thus in the frequently cited New Zealand case of *Taylor* v. *Combined Buyers, Ltd.*,[17] where the contract was for the sale of a Calthorpe motor car, Salmond, J. was clear that:

> "A description not forming part of the contract still remains a mere representation, and has not as such and in general any operation on the rights of the parties unless fraudulent."[18]

Similarly in *T. and J. Harrison* v. *Knowles and Foster*[19] the Court of Appeal treated the defendant's statement that certain steamships had a deadweight capacity of 460 tons as a representation having no contractual effect. The need for this preliminary classification might have been overlooked in *Beale* v. *Taylor*.[20] Here a private seller had advertised a secondhand car as a "Herald convertible, white, 1961" whereas, unbeknown to him, it was made up from two cars welded together and the front end came from an earlier and less powerful model. The buyer was awarded damages for breach of s. 13, but it is doubtful whether the disinterested observer would have concluded that the seller was warranting the truth of the description.[1]

A related question is whether descriptive words which are incorporated as terms in a contract for the sale of goods by description must necessarily be classified as conditions rather than warranties. The wording of the section might suggest that this is so. In *Taylor* v. *Combined Buyers*,

---

[15] See *Heilbut, Symons & Co.* v. *Buckleton*, [1913] A.C. 30, H.L., above, pp. 36–41.

[16] For the distinction between opinions and affirmations of fact see above, pp. 33–35.

[17] [1924] N.Z. Gazette L.R. 51, [1924] N.Z.L.R. 627.

[18] *Ibid.*, p. 57. In English law the statement may now be actionable under the Misrepresentation Act 1967 or the *Hedley Byrne* decision (see above, pp. 45–48 and pp. 43–45, respectively), but this does not affect the substance of the argument.

[19] [1918]1 K.B. 608.

[20] [1967] 3 All E.R. 253, C.A.

[1] *Cf. Oscar Chess, Ltd.* v. *Williams*, [1957] 1 All E.R. 325, C.A., above, pp. 38–39. See also *Routledge* v. *Mckay*, [1954] 1 W.L.R. 615; *Marks* v. *Hunt Brothers (Sydney) Pty., Ltd.* (1958), 58 S.R. (N.S.W.) 380.

Ltd.,[2] however, Salmond, J. held that statements descriptive of specific goods were not invariably to be treated as conditions the breach of which would entitle the buyer to reject the goods. In his judgment:[3]

> "The description, within the meaning of the Act, means a statement of the kind, class or species to which the article belongs. Any descriptive statement so far as it goes beyond this indication of kind, class or species is not the kind of description which is the subject of an implied statutory condition in the case of specific articles."

A similar conclusion had been reached by Bailhache, J. at first instance in *T. and J. Harrison* v. *Knowles and Foster*,[4] where he held that the statement as to the deadweight capacity of the ships was a warranty rather than a condition.[5] It might be argued that the approach of Salmond, J. is unnecessarily restrictive, albeit that it has recently received the imprimatur of the House of Lords.[6] But it would be inconvenient if one were required to treat all descriptive terms as conditions.

When is a sale by description?

The benefit of the implied condition imposed by s. 13 of the 1893 Act attaches only to contracts for the sale of goods by description. It seems that the original intention was to distinguish sales of unascertained and future goods from sales of specific goods and that the sale would be by description only where the descriptive words were used to *identify* the subject matter of the sale and not simply as an inducement to the buyer to purchase.[7] There were, however, considerable pressures working towards an extended meaning. In particular, the requirement that the sale be by description also attached to the implied condition of merchantable quality under s. 14 (2) of the Act,[8] and it has been suggested that the courts in practice tended to interpret s. 13 with half an eye to s. 14.[9] The buyer would otherwise have been denied a remedy unless the seller had expressly warranted the goods or had been informed of the particular purpose for which the buyer required them.

---

[2] [1924] N.Z. Gazette L.R. 51.

[3] *Ibid.*, at p. 57.

[4] [1917] 2 K.B. 606, 610.

[5] The Court of Appeal did not find it necessary to decide whether it would have reached the same conclusion since the statement was not regarded as a term of the contract: see above, note 19 and corresponding text.

[6] In *Ashington Piggeries, Ltd.* v. *Christopher Hill, Ltd.*, [1972] A.C. 441; [1971] 1 All E.R. 847, H.L., below, p. 75 *et seq.*

[7] See *Benjamin on Sale*, 8th edn., 1950, pp. 609–613; 1 *Williston on Sales*, revd. edn., ss. 224–225.

[8] The requirement was dispensed with by the Supply of Goods (Implied Terms) Act 1973, s. 3.

[9] See Atiyah, *Sale of Goods*, 5th edn., 1975, p. 76.

Varley v. *Whipp*[10] was a significant case. The plaintiff had agreed to sell and the defendant to buy a "self-binder" reaping machine which the plaintiff said was then at Upton and which the defendant had never seen. The plaintiff also said that the machine had been new the previous year and that it had cut no more than fifty or sixty acres. The defendant, having discovered that these statements were untrue, returned the machine and the plaintiff sued for the contract price. The claim failed, it being held that the reaper had been sold "by description" and that property had not passed to the buyer.[11] In the judgment of Channell, J.: "The term 'sale of goods by description' must apply to all cases where the purchaser has not seen the goods, but is relying on the description alone".[12] The truth of the matter was that the machine had been sufficiently identified through the statement that it was at Upton. The additional statements went to its quality or attributes alone.

Subsequent decisions indicate that specific goods may be sold by description even though the buyer has seen and examined them.[13] The same is true of an ordinary sale in a shop. In the words of Lord Wright in *Grant* v. *Australian Knitting Mills, Ltd*:[14]

> "There is a sale by description even though the buyer is buying something displayed before him on the counter: a thing is sold by description, though it is specific, so long as it is sold not merely as the specific thing but as a thing corresponding to a description, e.g., woollen under-garments, a hot water bottle, a second-hand reaping machine, to select a few obvious illustrations."[15]

Doubts were expressed in the Molony Committee report whether a sale could be by description where goods were sold in a self-service store or its equivalent, rather than across the counter.[16] The new s. 13 (2) of the Sale of Goods Act attempts to clarify the point by providing that:

> "A sale of goods shall not be prevented from being a sale by description by

---

[10] [1900] 1 Q.B. 513. See Stoljar (1953), 16 M.L.R. 174, 177–180.

[11] As it would have done if there had been an unconditional contract for the sale of specific goods: see Sale of Goods Act 1893, ss. 17, 18, rule 1.

[12] [1900] 1 Q.B. 513, at p. 516.

[13] See *Beale* v. *Taylor*, [1967] 3 All E.R. 253, C.A., above, p. 70; *H. Beecham & Co., Pty. Ltd.* v. *Francis Howard & Co. Pty., Ltd.*, [1921] V.L.R. 428 (Vict. Sup. Ct.) (timber with dry rot); *David Jones, Ltd.* v. *Willis* (1934), 52 C.L.R. 110 (High Ct. Australia) (walking shoes). That examination may be consistent with the sale being by description was implicit in the proviso relating to examination in s. 14 (2) of the unamended Sale of Goods Act, see below, pp. 95–97.

[14] [1936] A.C. 85, 100, P.C.

[15] See also the judgement of Dixon, J. in the Australian High Court: (1933), 50 C.L.R. 387, 417–418; *Morelli* v. *Fitch and Gibbons*, [1928] 2 K.B. 636, C.A.; *Wren* v. *Holt*, [1903] 1 K.B. 610, C.A.; *Godley* v. *Perry*, [1960] 1 All E.R. 36; [1960] 1 W.L.R. 9.

[16] Report of the Committee on Consumer Protection (1962) Cmnd. 1781, para. 441. See also the Law Commission report on *Exemption Clauses in Contracts*, Law Com. No. 24, 1969, paras. 21–25.

reason only that, being exposed for sale or hire, they are selected by the buyer."[17]

Unfortunately the negative terms in which this provision is couched leave room for argument that it might not have achieved its apparent objective. Subject to this point it would seem that although goods may occasionally be sold as specific objects—especially when they are secondhand[18]—the vast majority of consumer transactions would involve sales by description. This would be true of contracts to buy goods whose identity is revealed to the purchaser through the labelling on their containers or packaging (as with tinned fruit or packets of washing powder) or through inscriptions or lettering attached to or embossed on branded products. Other cases might continue to present difficulties. Thus it is doubtful whether goods are sold by description where they are unlabelled and their full identity is immediately apparent to even the most uninformed buyer. Fresh fruit, vegetables or game would normally be left to describe itself and it would be unrealistic to regard such sales as falling into this category.[19] Close distinctions might arise in such cases,[20] but they are rarely likely to carry practical consequences now that the requirement that the sale be by description no longer attaches to the implied condition of merchantable quality under s. 14 (2) of the Act.[1] The commercial seller of specific goods would rarely be in breach of s. 13 without being in breach of s. 14 as well.

Description, quality, fitness for purpose and the effect of non-compliance

Related difficulties occur when determining the breadth of the contract description against which the goods are to be judged for the purposes of s. 13. The short, if unhelpful, answer is that this depends on the terms of the individual contract and the specificity with which the parties define the subject matter of the sale. A number of general points may, however, be noted.

---

[17] Section 13 (2) was added to the 1893 Act by the Supply of Goods (Implied Terms) Act 1973, s. 2.

[18] See, e.g., *Barr* v. *Gibson* (1838), 3 M. & W. 390 (ship); *Parsons* v. *Sexton* (1847), 4 C.B. 899 (fourteen-horse engine); *Taylor* v. *Bullen* (1850), 5 Exch. 779 (teak-built barque); *Hopkins* v. *Hitchcock* (1863), 14 C.B. N.S. 65 (iron); *Legett* v. *Taylor* (1965), 50 D.L.R. 2d 516 (B.C. Sup. Ct.) (power cruiser).

[19] In *Wallis* v. *Russell*, [1902] 2 I.R. 585, 615, Fitzgibbon, L.J. was of the opinion that the sale of two fresh crabs displayed by the defendant fishmonger in the normal manner was "by description", but Holmes, L.J. observed: "If the crabs in this case were sold by description, no sale otherwise than by description would be possible": *ibid.*, p. 631.

[20] As when a chicken or a hot water bottle is wrapped in cellophane carrying an appropriate, if superfluous, description; or when the labelling on the shelves (bread, apples, etc.) is more for the benefit of the sales staff replenishing stock than for the information of the customer.

[1] See the Supply of Goods (Implied Terms) Act 1973, s. 3.

Firstly, in determining the breadth of the contract description, regard must be had to the consequences of non-compliance with it. Here English law has adopted a strict approach. The buyer is entitled, *de minimis* deviations apart, to insist on precise compliance before accepting the goods. There is no room for a doctrine of substantial performance. The decision of the House of Lords in *Arcos, Ltd.* v. *E. A. Ronaason & Son*[2] is frequently cited in this context. The contract was for the sale of a quantity of staves $\frac{1}{2}$ inch thick which the buyer required for making cement barrels. A high proportion of the staves was found on delivery to measure between $\frac{1}{2}$ inch and $\frac{9}{16}$ inch, but only five per cent measured $\frac{1}{2}$ inch precisely. Holding that the buyer was entitled to reject the entire consignment although it was of merchantable quality and fit for his purpose, Lord Atkin said:[3]

> "If the written contract specifies conditions of weight, measurement and the like, those conditions must be complied with. A ton does not mean about a ton, or a yard about a yard. Still less when you descend to minute measurements does $\frac{1}{2}$ inch mean about $\frac{1}{2}$ inch. If the seller wants a margin he must and in my experience does stipulate for it."[4]

Such an approach suggests that there are advantages in adopting a narrow definition of the contract description with which there must be precise compliance. It would then remain open to a court to designate a particular stipulation an express condition if, in the circumstances, non-compliance deprived the buyer of the substance of his bargain.[5]

Secondly, it is convenient to adopt a structured approach to the conditions implied by the 1893 Act, so holding in so far as possible that the contract description ends where statements as to qualities or suitability for a particular purpose begin. A clear-cut division along these lines is admittedly neither possible nor desirable. As Professor Coote has observed,[6] the courts have long tended even with sales of specific goods, to discover some measure of description by which the goods had been sold.[7] Buyers might otherwise have been unprotected against both exemption clauses and the *caveat emptor* doctrine. Where the goods are unascertained the likelihood of

---

[2] [1933] A.C. 470, H.L.

[3] *Ibid.*, at p. 479.

[4] See also *Bowes* v. *Shand* (1877), 2 App. Cas. 455, at p. 480 *per* Lord Blackburn; *Re Moore & Co., Ltd. and Landauer & Co.*, [1921] 2 K.B. 519. A doctrine of substantial performance has been adopted in some American cases (see 1 *Williston on Sales* (revd. edn.), para. 225a) and in English cases involving building contracts (see *Hoenig* v. *Isaacs*, [1952] 2 All E.R. 176).

[5] See the Sale of Goods Act 1893, s. 14(4) and see also *Cehave N.V.* v. *Bremer Handelsgesellschaft m.b.H.*, [1976] Q.B. 44; [1975] 3 All E.R. 739, C.A., above pp. 41–43.

[6] (1976) 50 A.L.J., 17, 20.

[7] See, e.g., *Shepherd* v. *Kain* (1821), 5 B. & Ald. 240 (copper-fastened vessel); *Allan* v. *Lake* (1852), 18 Q.B. 560 (Skirving's swedes).

an overlap between description and purpose or quality is increased considerably. Description and purpose may be inextricably interwoven[1] and descriptive words may be indicative of the quality to be expected.[2] Similarly there will be cases where the goods as delivered are so completely out of line with legitimate functional or qualitative expectations that they no longer correspond with the contract description.

However, when due allowance has been made for these points the line between description and attributes has frequently been blurred. A wide range of attributes has been regarded as forming part of the contract description including the way the goods were packed,[3] the nature of previous usage[4] and their dimensions.[5] The New Zealand case of *Cotter* v. *Luckie*[6] is one of the more extreme examples. The defendant had bought a particular purebred Polled Angus bull from the plaintiff farmer, it being understood that the animal was required for stud purposes. It had a physical deficiency which prevented copulation and the buyer was held to be entitled to reject on the ground that it was not a stud bull and so did not correspond with the contract description. Yet it is doubtful whether the capacity to copulate really formed part of the animal's description as opposed to its attributes.

A more restrictive approach may follow from the decision of the House of Lords in *Ashington Piggeries, Ltd.* v. *Christopher Hill, Ltd.*,[7] a case which is of considerable importance in delimiting the scope of both ss. 13 and 14 of the 1893 Act.

---

[1] See *Teheran-Europe Co., Ltd.* v. *S. T. Belton (Tractors), Ltd.*, [1968] 2 Q.B. 545, at p. 559 *per* Diplock, L.J.; *Chanter* v. *Hopkins* (1838), 4 M. & W. 399, 405 *per* Lord Abinger, C.B. In *Benjamin's Sale of Goods* (1974), para. 778 "baby-food", "cough mixture" and "cold cure" are given as examples. One might add "football boots", "washing powder", "racing car", "dish-washer", "cigarette vending-machine", etc.

[2] See *Re North Western Rubber Co., Ltd. and Hüttenbach & Co.*, [1908] 2 K.B. 907 ("fair usual quality Jelutong Rubber"); *Simond* v. *Braddon* (1857), 2 C.B. N.S. 324 ("fair average Nicranzi rice"); *Jones* v. *Clarke* (1858), 2 H. & N. 725 ("fair average Savannah pitch pine timber"); *Wimble, Sons & Co.* v. *Lillico & Son (London)* (1922), 38 T.L.R. 296 (percentage ingredients of cotton cake); *Toepfer* v. *Continental Grain Co.*, [1973] 1 Lloyd's Rep. 289, 294, *per* Cooke, J., ("No. 3 Hard Amber" wheat). But see *Ashington Piggeries, Ltd.* v. *Christopher Hill, Ltd.*, [1972] A.C. 441; [1971] 1 All E.R. 847, H.L., below.

[3] *Re Moore & Co., Ltd. and Landauer & Co.*, [1921] 2 K.B. 519 (fruit packed in cases of 24 rather than 30 tins); *Manbre Saccharine Co., Ltd.* v. *Corn Products Co., Ltd.*, [1919] 1 K.B. 198 (starch in bags of wrong size); *Ballantine & Co.* v. *Camp and Bosman* (1923), 129 L.T. 502. See also *Smith Brothers, Ltd.* v. *Gosta Jacobsson & Co.*, [1961] 2 Lloyd's Rep. 522.

[4] *Armaghdown Motors, Ltd.* v. *Gray Motors, Ltd.*, [1963] N.Z.L.R. 5 (statement that no previous usage as taxi or hire car).

[5] *Arcos, Ltd.* v. *E. A. Ronaasen & Son*, [1933] A.C. 470, H.L., above p. 74; *Rapalli* v. *K.L. Take, Ltd.*, [1958] 2 Lloyd's Rep. 469 (undersized and sprouting onions). See further, Coote (1976), 50 A.L.J. 17, 19.

[6] [1918] N.Z.L.R. 811.

[7] [1972] A.C. 441; [1971] 1 All E.R. 847.

In 1960 the respondents, a well-known firm of animal feeding stuff compounders, had been approached by a Mr Udall who controlled the appellant company and who was a leading expert on mink nutrition. The proposition was that they should compound a mink food to be called "King Size" in accordance with a formula prepared by U. One of the ingredients was to be herring meal. A contract was concluded on these terms and over several months King Size was fed to mink in some one hundred farms without their suffering any harm. Thereafter the respondents began to prepare King Size from a consignment of Norwegian herring meal supplied by a third party, Norsildmel, under a separate and more detailed contract with a "fair average quality of the season" clause. This herring meal contained a preservative, sodium nitrate, which produced dimethylnitrosamine (DMNA) and this proved to be highly toxic to mink. An outbreak of severe liver disease followed and many mink were lost both on the appellant's farm and elsewhere. There was evidence that all animals were sensitive to DMNA to a greater or lesser extent, but no evidence that animals other than mink had suffered any ill effects from eating food made up from the relevant consignment.[8] The respondents sued for the price of the King Size sold and delivered to the appellants. The latter counter-claimed for damages in respect of the losses incurred through the death and injury to the mink, alleging breaches of the conditions implied by ss. 13, 14 (1) and (2) of the Sale of Goods Act. The respondents in turn sued the third party for an indemnity and alleged breaches of ss. 13 and 14 (1).

For reasons which will be discussed later the House of Lords held that the respondent compounders were liable to the appellants under s. 14 (1) and (2) of the Act and the third party was liable to the respondents under s. 14 (1).[9] However, neither the respondents nor the third party were in breach of the condition implied by s. 13. In reaching this conclusion the House of Lords adopted a narrower approach to s. 13 than is to be found in many other cases. In their Lordships' judgment the contamination of the herring meal affected its quality but not its essential identity, and it was with identity that the section was concerned.[10] Rejection was permissible under s. 13 only where the goods were of a different kind, class or species from that contracted for[11] and, in the words of Lord Wilberforce, "buyers and

---

[8] The matter is dealt with fully in the speech of Lord Diplock: [1972] A.C. 441, 498–500.
[9] See below, pp. 100–101 for discussion of s. 14 (1) (now s. 14 (3)), and p. 80 for discussion of s. 14 (2).
[10] *Cf.* [1972] A.C. 441, 466–467, 470 (Lord Hodson), 472–473, 475 (Lord Guest), 489 (Lord Wilberforce), 503–504 (Lord Diplock). Viscount Dilhorne held that there had been a breach of s. 13, but he agreed that "Where a sale is by description the description identifies the goods": *ibid.*, at p. 486.
[11] A similar view had been expressed by Salmond, J. in *Taylor v. Combined Buyers, Ltd.*, [1924] N.Z. Gazette L.R. 51, 57; [1924] N.Z.L.R. 627, cited above, p. 71.

sellers and arbitrators in the market, asked what this was, could only have said that the relevant ingredient was herring meal and, therefore, that there was no failure to correspond with description".[12]

Although this decision has its critics[13] it is submitted, with respect, that it represents the most satisfactory approach to s. 13. Whether it will have much effect in practice, especially in sales of unascertained goods, remains to be seen. It is probable, however, that goods will continue to be identified at a relatively low level of abstraction.[14] A contract to sell a quantity of vintage Krug would not be fulfilled by delivering a lesser champagne, and a contract for the sale of a "new Singer car" would surely require the delivery of precisely that.[15] Features such as brand names, models, and the year or period of manufacture will no doubt continue to affect the "kind" of goods sold[16] thus entitling the buyer to reject if they are not complied with. So also will distinctive varieties and places of origin, such as common English sainfoin seed, Skirving's swedes, Calcutta linseed, Lincoln ewes and Buckingham Down cattle.[17] Where goods are adulterated through the presence of some extraneous ingredient they may

---

[12] [1972] A.C. 441, 489. But, as has been noted by Patient (1971), 34 M.L.R. 557, it is less clear that they would have concluded that the toxic substance was "King Size", which was the true contract description.

[13] See Patient (1971), 34 M.L.R. 557. See also Coote (1976), 50 A.L.J. 17 who notes that the return to the "kind" or "class" analysis parallels the distinctions taken in cases of "fundamental breach" in order to protect the buyer against exemption clauses: see below, pp. 132–133. Samuel Williston would no doubt have approved of the decision: see 1 *Williston on Sales* (revd. edn.), s. 224.

[14] The decision may have a greater effect where the sale is of specific goods which can be physically identified other than by the use of a description: see, e.g., *Beale v. Taylor*, [1967] 3 All E.R. 253; *Varley v. Whipp*, [1900] 1 Q.B. 513. But even here most significant attributes in a sale of specific goods are still likely to receive the protection of s. 13. Examples might include a sale over the counter of a "silk" tie, a "pure wool" suit, a shirt with a "size 15 collar", a "colour" television set, etc.

[15] Cf. *Andrews Brothers (Bournemouth), Ltd. v. Singer & Co., Ltd.*, [1934] 1 K.B. 17, discussed in *Benjamin on Sale*, 8th edn., 1950, pp. 622–623.

[16] See, e.g., *Scaliaris v. E. Ofverberg & Co.* (1921), 37 T.L.R. 307 (saccharine "Monsanto brand"); *Nicholson and Venn v. Smith Marriott* (1947), 177 L.T. 189 (linen of the reign of Charles I); *Beale v. Taylor*, [1967] 3 All E.R. 253 (Triumph Herald Convertible 1200); *Taylor v. Combined Buyers, Ltd.* [1924] N. Z. Gazette L.R. 51 (Calthorpe motor car); *Bristol Tramways Carriage Co., Ltd. v. Fiat Motors, Ltd.*, [1910] 2 K.B. 831 (Fiat omnibus); *Clarke v. McMahon*, [1939] S.A.S.R. 64 (Kelvinator refrigerator); *F. and B. Transport, Ltd. v. White Truck Sales Manitoba, Ltd.* (1965), 49 D.L.R. (2d) 670 (Man. C.A.) (different year); *Hall v. Queensland Truck Centre Pty., Ltd.*, [1970] Qd. Rep. 231 (different model).

[17] See *Wallis, Son and Wells v. Pratt and Haynes*, [1911] A.C. 394 (common English sainfoin seed); *Allan v. Lake* (1852), 18 Q.B. 560 (Skirving's swedes); *Wieler v. Schilizzi* (1856), 17 C.B. 619 (Calcutta linseed, *tale quale*); *Boys v. Rice* (1908), 27 N.Z.L.R. 1038 (N.Z. Sup. Ct.) (Lincoln ewes); *Kidman v. Fisken*, [1907] S.A.L.R. 101 (Buckingham Down cattle).

differ in kind from that which was contracted for[18] but where it is the use of a normal ingredient which produces untoward results, as in *Ashington Piggeries, Ltd.* v. *Christopher Hill, Ltd.,*[19] the complaint would generally be confined to their quality or fitness for purpose. The position would be different if the ingredient were itself so grossly contaminated (or if it produced such a reaction) as to affect the essential identity or characteristics of the substance into which it was incorporated.

Private sales

The implied condition of correspondence with description applies to private no less than to business sellers. This is acceptable enough when the case concerns the entitlement of a buyer to reject goods or to recover the contract price. Breach of s. 13 might, however, lead to a private vendor incurring contractual liability for damage caused through the purchaser's use of the goods and this even though he has made no representations as to their safety and has not been negligent. This would be unfortunate. In most cases the result could be avoided by holding that the damage was caused by a qualitative defect rather than by misdescription. If in *Beale* v. *Taylor*,[20] for example, the buyer had been involved in an accident when using the car he would probably not have recovered in contract in respect of his physical injury. The car would have been equally unsafe if it had been made up from two Triumph 1200s welded together (rather than from one 1200 and an earlier model), but it is doubtful whether it would then have been misdescribed.

The implied condition of merchantable quality[1]

Introduction

The common law rule *caveat emptor* which enjoins the purchaser of goods to

---

[18] See, e.g., *Pinnock Brothers* v. *Lewis and Peat, Ltd.,* [1923] 1 K.B. 690 (copra cake adulterated by castor beans); *Robert A. Munro & Co., Ltd.* v. *Meyer,* [1930] 2 K.B. 312 (bone meal with cocoa husks); *Nichol* v. *Godts* (1854), 10 Exch. 191 (rape oil with hemp oil); *Josling* v. *Kingsford* (1863), 13 C.B. N.S. 447 (oxalic acid with sulphate of magnesia).

[19] [1972] A.C. 441; [1971] 1 All E.R. 847, above.

[20] [1967] 3 All E.R. 253, C.A., above, p. 70.

[1] See Prosser, "The Implied condition of Merchantable Quality" 27 Minn. L.R. 117 (1943), reprinted in (1943), 21 Can. Bar Rev. 446; Davies "Merchantability and Fitness for Purpose" (1969), 85 L.Q.R. 74.

take care of his own interests has been tempered from the early nineteenth century by an implied condition that goods sold by description shall be of merchantable quality. In *Gardiner* v. *Gray*,[2] decided at *nisi prius* in 1815, the contract was for the sale of twelve bags of waste silk which, on arrival from the continent, were found to be of inferior quality and not saleable under their contract description. In the words of Lord Ellenborough:[3]

> "[The] purchaser has a right to expect a saleable article answering the description in the contract. Without any particular warranty, this is an implied term in every such contract. . . . He cannot without a warranty insist that it shall be of any particular quality or fineness, but the intention of both parties must be taken to be, that it shall be saleable in the market under the denomination mentioned in the contract between them. The purchaser cannot be supposed to buy goods to lay them on a dunghill."

Where the contract was for the sale of specific goods the purchaser did not have the benefit of this implied term. However, if he was known to have required the goods for a particular purpose and the circumstances indicated that he had relied on the judgment or skill of the vendor, he might yet benefit from a further implied condition that the goods be reasonably fit for that purpose.[4]

These common law developments were enacted in the Sale of Goods Act 1893 and the Supply of Goods (Implied Terms) Act 1973, s. 3 removed some of the limitations to which they were originally subject.[5] The residual *caveat emptor* doctrine is restated in s. 14 (1) of the 1893 Act[6] and the implied condition of merchantable quality is set out in s. 14 (2) in the following terms:

> "Where the seller sells goods in the course of a business, there is an implied condition that the goods supplied under the contract are of merchantable quality, except that there is no such condition—

---

[2] (1815), 4 Camp. 144. See also *Laing* v. *Fidgeon* (1815), 4 Camp. 169 (saddles).

[3] (1815), 4 Camp. 144, 145.

[4] See *Brown* v. *Edgington* (1841), 2 Man. & G. 279 (rope made to order for wine merchant); *Jones* v. *Bright* (1829), 5 Bing. 533 (copper sheathing for ship). *Cf. Chanter* v. *Hopkins* (1838), 4 M. & W. 399. The position was well summarised by Mellor, J. in *Jones* v. *Just* (1868), L.R. 3 Q.B. 197, 201–203. This implied condition is discussed below, at p. 98 *et seq.*

[5] The amendments were based on the recommendation of the Law Commission in its report, "Exemption Clauses in Contracts, First Report: Amendments to the Sale of Goods Act 1893", Law Com. No. 24, July 1969, paras. 27–55 especially. Section 3 inserts an amended and renumbered s. 14 into the principal Act of 1893.

[6] Section 14 (1) states: "Except as provided by this section, and section 15 of this Act and subject to the provisions of any other enactment there is no implied condition or warranty as to the quality or fitness for any particular purpose of goods supplied under a contract of sale". Section 15 covers sales by sample.

(a) as regards defects specifically drawn to the buyer's attention before the contract is made; or

(b) if the buyer examines the goods before the contract is made, as regards defects which that examination ought to reveal."[7]

The amendments introduced by the 1973 Act do not apply to contracts entered into before the commencement date, 18 May 1973, and cases arising out of such contracts will no doubt be before the courts for many years to come.[8] Here, however, it is proposed to concentrate on the present law.

Sale in the course of a business

There are sound reasons for distinguishing between business and private sellers when implying terms demanding merchantability and reasonable fitness for purpose. In its unamended version s. 14 (2) of the 1893 Act applied only where goods were "bought by description from a seller who deals in goods of that description". In *Ashington Piggeries, Ltd.* v. *Christopher Hill, Ltd.*[9] the Court of Appeal interpreted this requirement very narrowly as demanding that the seller deal in goods of the precise contract description (King Size mink food) as opposed to goods of that general type or kind (animal feeding stuffs). This approach did not, however, receive the support of the House of Lords[10] and a much more general provision is now to be found in the amended version of s. 14 (2). This imposes an implied condition of merchantable quality where the seller "sells goods in the course of a business".[11] The word "business" is defined to include "a profession and the activities of any government department . . . local authority or statutory undertaker".[12]

There will no doubt be difficulties in deciding whether certain non-profit making organisations are businesses[13] and when the isolated trans-

---

[7] See also s. 15 (2) (c) which provides that in a sale by sample: "There is an implied condition that the goods shall be free from any defect rendering them unmerchantable which would not be apparent on reasonable examination of the sample".

[8] See, e.g., *Cehave N.V.* v. *Bremer Hendelsgesellschaft m.b.H.*, [1976] Q.B. 44; [1975] 3 All E.R. 739, C.A., below, p. 90; *McDonald* v. *Empire Garage (Blackburn), Ltd.*, (1975), *Times*, 8 October, below p. 94.

[9] [1969] 3 All E.R. 1496.

[10] [1972] A.C. 441; [1971] 1 All E.R. 847 (Lord Hodson and Lord Diplock dissenting on this point). It was conceded that the goods were unmerchantable.

[11] The amendment was introduced by the Supply of Goods (Implied Terms) Act 1973, s. 3. By s. 14 (5) of the principal Act, as amended, sales by business agents acting for private vendors are also included unless the purchaser knows it is a private sale or reasonable steps have been taken to inform him. See *Benjamin's Sale of Goods* (1974), para. 791.

[12] See the Sale of Goods Act 1893, s. 62 (1), as amended by the Supply of Goods (Implied Terms) Act 1973, s. 7 (1).

[13] For example, universities, colleges, etc.: see *Benjamin's Sale of Goods* (1974) para. 789.

actions of private individuals have a sufficient continuity of operation to constitute a business.[14] Problems are also likely to be caused by the subsidiary or incidental activities of established businesses. Under the Uniform Commercial Code the sales warranty arises only where the seller is "a merchant with respect to goods of that kind".[15] This requirement is intended to exclude an isolated transaction by someone who is not in the business of selling goods of the relevant kind.[16] The concept of selling "in the course of a business" is obviously wider than this. It would, for example, cover the case of a car-hire business which periodically renews its fleet[17] and the Law Commission has suggested that it would cover the sale by a coal merchant of his delivery lorry.[18] It would be regrettable, however, if s. 14 (2) were regarded as extending to literally all sales of second-hand goods by businesses. For example, the sale by a professional man of the partnership car is essentially a private transaction and there is no reason why it should attract the strict liability of s. 14 (2), expecially where the complaint is of physical injury through use as opposed to financial loss through purchase. Perhaps the wording of the Act is flexible enough to exclude purely incidental or ancillary sales which are in no sense an integral part of the business.[19]

---

[14] The business aspect may, moreover, be successfully hidden where the seller operates from a home address and sells through the classified advertisement columns of newspapers. The Director-General of Fair Trading has proposed that this practice be controlled under the Fair Trading Act 1973 and has referred the matter to the Consumer Protection Advisory Committee. See the supporting dossier (17/3) "Seeking to Sell Goods Without Revealing that they are being Sold in the Course of a Business" and the C.P.A.C. report *Disguised Business Sales*, May 1976.

[15] Art. 2–314 (1). For the definition of "merchant", see art. 2–104 (1). See, in general, 3 *Williston on Sales*, 4th edn., 1974, s. 18–6. Like the unamended English Sale of Goods Act 1893 the Uniform Sales Act, s. 15 (2), refers to a seller "who deals in goods of that description".

[16] See Official Comment 3 to art. 2–314. See also *Prince* v. *Le Van*, 486 P. 2d 959 (Alaska, 1971); *Mutual Services of Highland Park Inc.* v. *S.O.S. Plumbing and Sewerage Co.*, 93 Ill. App. 2d 257 (1968). The overall position seems to be substantially the same as in English law after *Ashington Piggeries, Ltd.* v. *Christopher Hill, Ltd.*, [1972] A.C. 441; [1971] 1 All E.R. 847, H.L., but before the amendments introduced by the 1973 Act.

[17] As in *Havering London Borough* v. *Stevenson*, [1970] 3 All E.R. 609; [1970] 1 W.L.R. 1375, D.C. The case was concerned with the application of the Trade Descriptions Act 1968, s. 1 (1) (*b*) which applies to "Any person who, *in the course of a trade or business,* . . . supplies or offers to supply any goods to which a false trade description is applied": emphasis supplied. Cases decided under the 1968 Act may be relevant in the interpretation of s. 14 (2).

[18] "Exemption Clauses in Contracts, First Report", Law Com. No. 24, July 1969, para. 31, note 30.

[19] The main purpose of the Law Commission was "to insure that the conditions implied by section 14 are imposed on every trade seller, no matter whether he is or is not habitually dealing in goods of the type sold": *op. cit.* para. 31, note 29. The Molony Committee in its Final Report used the expression "sells by way of trade" (see Cmnd. 1781, July 1962, para. 443), but the Law Commission chose not to adopt this expression which is perhaps regrettable.

Goods supplied under the contract

In United States jurisdictions there has been an "astonishing little argument"[20] as to whether a seller's warranty extends to the container in which goods are sold as well as to its contents. Most modern authorities have held that it does[1] and the Uniform Commercial Code predictably adopts the same position.[2] English law has not experienced the same difficulties and liability may clearly be imposed where the defective condition is in the container rather than its contents[3] and this, it is submitted, irrespective of whether the contents are themselves affected.[4] Similarly goods may be unmerchantable through deficiencies in labelling, as when a label infringes a trade mark.[5] Again, it is clear that "foreign elements" no less than the goods themselves would be "supplied under the contract" for the purposes of s. 14 (2).[6]

Merchantable quality

The key concept in s. 14 (2) of the 1893 Act is the standard of merchantable quality by which the goods are judged. The meaning of this term is by no means self-evident and until recent years it was not defined in the Act. A number of frequently cited tests had, however, been advanced and their

---

[20] Prosser, *Law of Torts*, 4th edn., 1971, p. 637.

[1] See Prosser, *op. cit.*, p. 637 and cases there cited; 2 Frumer and Friedman, *Products Liability*, ss. 19.03 [4] [*d*], 26.03 [1] [*b*]. For decisions to the contrary, see, e.g., *Stubblefield* v. *Johnson-Fagg Inc.*, 379 F. 2d 270 (10th cir., 1967) (steel strap around cardboard box which flew up and damaged plaintiff's eye); *Foley* v. *Weaver Drugs Inc.*, 177 So. 2d 221 (Fla., 1965) (defective bottle).

[2] See U.C.C. art 2–314 (2) which requires that the goods "(e) are adequately contained, packaged, and labelled as the agreement may require; and (*f*) conform to the promises or affirmations of fact made on the container or label if any". For discussion of these requirements, see Nordstrom, *Handbook on the Law of Sales*, pp. 236–238.

[3] See, e.g., *Morelli* v. *Fitch and Gibbons*, [1928] 2 K.B. 636, (bottle which broke at neck injuring plaintiff). Neither does it affect the position if the container remains the property of the vendor: see *Geddling* v. *Marsh*, [1920] 1 K.B. 668 (bottle of mineral water to be returned when empty).

[4] See *Gilbert Sharp and Bishop Ltd.* v. *George Wills & Co., Ltd.*, [1919] S.A.L.R. 114 (canned pears: some tins being dented with soiled labels). *Cf.*, however, *Gower* v. *Von Dedalzen* (1837), 3 Bing N.C. 717.

[5] *Niblett*, Ltd. v. *Confectioners' Materials Co., Ltd.*, [1921] 3 K.B. 387. But merchantability does not import a requirement that goods be saleable in a particular foreign market: *Sumner Permain & Co.* v. *Webb & Co.*, [1922] 1 K.B. 55 (tonic water containing salicylic acid rendering it unsaleable in the Argentine).

[6] As in *Wilson* v. *Rickett, Cockerell & Co., Ltd.*, [1954] 1 Q.B. 598; [1954] 1 All E.R. 868, C.A. (Coalite containing an explosive substance).

main strands were recently summarised by Ormrod, L.J., in the following terms:[7]

"In *Kendall* v. *Lillico*[8] Lord Reid, said that "merchantable" must mean "commercially saleable", but, as he went on to demonstrate, there is more to it than that. It is a composite quality comprising elements of description, purpose, condition and price. The relative significance of each of these elements will vary from case to case according to the nature of the goods in question and the characteristics of the market which exists for them. This may explain why the formulations of the test of merchantable quality vary so much from case to case. For example, the price element was irrevelant in *Kendall* v. *Lillico* because experts in the market for ground-nuts gave evidence that ground-nuts contaminated by the poison, aflatoxin, could be sold at the normal market price since the poison did not affect cattle, so long as the concentration was less than a given amount. Consequently, little consideration was given to the price element in that case. In contrast, in *B. S. Brown & Son, Ltd.* v. *Craiks Ltd.*[9] the price element was important because the material involved in that case could be used for making dresses or for industrial purposes. The defects which rendered it unsuitable for making dresses did not affect its use in industry, although for such purposes it commanded a lower price in the market. Attention was, therefore, concentrated on the price element, obliging Lord Guest to modify considerably the formulation which he had adopted in *Kendall* v. *Lillico*,[10] and to disagree with Dixon, J.'s definition in *Australian Knitting Mills, Ltd.* v. *Grant*[11] under which goods would be unmerchantable unless they could be resold 'without abatement of price'. In *Cammell Laird & Co., Ltd.* v. *Manganese Bronze and Brass Co., Ltd.,*[12] on the other hand, the element of purpose was dominant."[13]

Following the recommendations of the Law Commission[14] a statutory definition was included in the Supply of Goods (Implied Terms) Act 1973.[15]

---

[7] *Cehave N.V.* v. *Bremer Handelsgesellschaft m.b.H.,* [1975] 3 All E.R. 739, 763–764, below, p. 90.

[8] [1969] 2 A.C. 31, 75; [1968] 2 All E.R. 444, 449, H.L. See further below, pp. 86–88.

[9] [1970] 1 All E.R. 823; [1970] 1 W.L.R. 752, H.L., below, p. 89.

[10] [1969] 2 A.C. 31, 108.

[11] *Cf.* (1933) 50 C.L.R. 387, 408 (High Ct. Australia), cited below, p. 89.

[12] [1934] A.C. 402.

[13] This led Lord Wright to say: "What subsection (2) now means by 'merchantable quality' is that the goods in the form in which they were tendered were of no use for any purpose for which such goods would normally be used and hence were not saleable under that description": *ibid.,* at p. 430. In another frequently cited test Farwell, L.J. said: "The phrase in section 14 (2) is, in my opinion, used as meaning that the article is of such quality and in such condition that a reasonable man acting reasonably would after a full examination accept it under the circumstances of the case in performance of his offer to buy that article whether he buys it for his own use or to sell again." *Bristol Tramways etc. Carriage Co., Ltd.* v. *Fiat Motors, Ltd.,* [1910] 2 K.B. 831, 841.

[14] See "Exemption Clauses in Contracts, First Report: Amendments to the Sale of Goods Act 1893", Law Com. No. 24, July 1969.

[15] Section 7 (2).

The definition which builds on the common law is now enacted as a new s. 62 (1A) in the 1893 Act. It provides as follows:

"Goods of any kind are of merchantable quality within the meaning of this Act if they are as fit for the purpose or purposes for which goods of that kind are commonly bought as it is reasonable to expect having regard to any description applied to them, the price (if relevant) and all the other relevant circumstances; and any reference in this Act to unmerchantable goods shall be construed accordingly."

Merchantability and description

Although the application of s. 14 (2) no longer depends on the sale being by description,[16] the question of merchantability cannot be divorced from the description under which the goods were sold. Indeed this must be the starting point in any inquiry since the issue cannot be determined in the abstract.[17] Goods may be unmerchantable if sold as "new" or as corresponding with a particular grade, but quite acceptable if sold as "secondhand" or as "seconds".[18] The point is reinforced by the wording of s. 62(1A) of the 1893 Act which requires one to have regard to any description applied to the goods. A similar provision is to be found in art 2–314 (2) of the Uniform Commercial Code which states that for goods to be merchantable they must be at least such as "(a) pass without objection in the trade under the contract description". The departure from the requisite standard may occasionally be such that the goods are not of the kind contracted for (in which case there would be a breach of s. 13 of the 1893 Act),[19] but qualitative defects of a lesser order may render the goods unmerchantable.

Merchantability, saleability and purpose

A significant feature of the new statutory definition is that it links

---

[16] The former requirement of the unamended Act rarely caused difficulty since most sales were regarded as being "by description". For discussion of the point in the context of s. 13 see above, pp. 71–73.

[17] See *Taylor* v. *Combined Buyers, Ltd.,* [1924] N.Z. Gazette L.R. 51, 61; [1924] N.Z.I.R. 627, *per* Salmond, J.

[18] *Cf. Cehave N.V.* v. *Bremer Handelsgesellschaft m.b.H.,* [1975] 3 All E.R. 739, 749 *per* Lord Denning, M.R. For the application of s. 14 (2) to sales of secondhand goods, see below, pp. 94–95.

[19] An analogy might be found in *Asfar & Co.* v. *Blundell,* [1896] 1 Q.B. 123, a shipping case in which dates had been contaminated with sewage. See also *Duthie* v. *Hilton* (1838), L.R. 4 C.P. 138 (wet cement) and the comments of Davies, L.J., in *Christopher Hill, Ltd.* v. *Ashington Piggeries, Ltd.,* [1969] 3 All E.R. 1496, 1512, on the status of oysters which were unfit for human consumption.

merchantability to fitness for purpose rather than to commercial saleability.[20] This may constitute little more than a recognition that a once mercantile concept is now frequently associated with consumer transactions where the complaint is of unsuitability for use rather than of unsuitability for resale. On the other hand, the functional overtones of the definition are not well suited to the fact that goods may perform their allotted task to perfection and yet be unmerchantable at common law. The legitimate expectations of the consumer relate to aesthetic as well as to functional considerations. If he were paying the full price he would not, for example, accept a washing machine which was badly chipped but which worked adequately, or some other article which was dented or scratched. Similarly, goods may be quite fit for their purpose and yet not of the grade or quality which would be expected having regard to the contract price.[21] It is substantially certain that the statutory definition will be construed broadly so as not to restrict the scope of the entitlement to reject.[22]

The association of merchantability with fitness for purpose prompts inquiry as to the respective scope of the conditions implied by s. 14 (2) and (3)[1] of the Act. The broad relationship between the two implied conditions is both rational and readily understandable. The former contemplates fitness for the common or ordinary purpose for which goods of that type are bought whereas the latter protects the buyer who had a particular or special purpose in mind which he communicated or made known to the seller. However, a wide range of goods admits only of one normal use and once it had been decided that a "particular" purpose might at the same

---

[20] As Lord Reid had done in *Henry Kendall & Sons* v. *William Lillico & Sons, Ltd.*, [1969] 2 A.C. 31, 75. But he goes on to discuss the standard in terms of fitness for purpose: *ibid.*, at pp. 77–79. See also the test advanced by Lord Wright in *Cammell Laird & Co., Ltd* v. *Manganese Bronze and Brass Co., Ltd.*, [1934] A.C. 402, 430 cited above, p. 83, note 13. Section 62 (1A) is in line with the modern tendency. Under U.C.C., art. 2–314 (2) (*c*) goods to be merchantable must be at least such as "are fit for the ordinary purposes for which such goods are used". In *Hemmingsen* v. *Bloomfield Motors Inc.*, 161 A 2d 69, 76 (N.J., 1960), above, p. 16, the manufacturers' warranty of merchantability was defined as requiring that the product be "reasonably fit for the general purpose for which it is manufactured and sold." See also the South Australian Consumer Transactions Act 1972, s. 8 (5) which states, *inter alia*, that "goods are of merchantable quality if they are as fit for the purpose for which goods of that description are ordinarily used as is reasonable to expect..."

[21] For the relevance of price, see below, pp. 89–90.

[22] For examples of goods being unmerchantable through being dented, etc., see *Jackson* v. *Rotax Motor and Cycle Co.*, [1910] 2 K.B. 937 (motor horns which were dented and scratched); *International Business Machines Co.* v. *Shcherban*, [1925] 1 D.L.R. 964 (Sask. C.A.) (computing scale with broken glass dial); *Winsley Brothers* v. *Woodfield Importing Co.*, [1929] N.Z. Gazette L.R. 270; [1929] N.Z.L.R. 480 (cracked planing machine). A *de minimis* rule applies, but there is no general principle requiring the buyer to accept goods which can be made merchantable. U.C.C. art. 2–508 (i) states that the seller may cure a non-conforming tender within the time allotted for delivery.

[1] Section 14 (3)—formerly s. 14 (1)—is discussed below, p. 98 *et seq.*

time be a common and singular purpose[2] there was considerable scope for overlap between the two implied conditions. There is no objection to this. Indeed, before the 1893 Act was amended the overlap assisted a number of plaintiffs who might otherwise have been denied recovery because, for example, they had bought under a trade name or without reliance on the vendor's skill or judgment[3] or because the goods had not been sold by description[4] or had not been sold by a seller who dealt in goods of that description.[5]

The difficulty arises with goods which might be used for a variety of purposes. The leading case of *Henry Kendall & Sons* v. *William Lillico & Sons, Ltd.*[6] illustrates the point. The original plaintiffs, Hardwick Game Farm, had lost a substantial number of breeding pheasants which had been fed with a compound supplied by a local firm, SAPPA. The deaths had been caused by a Brazilian groundnut extraction which had been used as an ingredient in the feed and which was contaminated by the poison, aflatoxin. SAPPA settled with the plaintiffs but proceeded against their own suppliers, Grimsdale and Lillico, who in turn brought in their suppliers, Kendall, the importers of the groundnuts. There was, in short, a chain from Kendall to Lillico to SAPPA to the game farm.

Dealing with the issue as between Kendall and Lillico, the House of Lords held that there had been a breach of s. 14 (1) (now s. 14 (3)) of the Act, since the groundnuts were not fit for the purpose for which they were known to be required, namely compounding into food for cattle and poultry generally. However, a majority of the House of Lords held that the groundnuts were of merchantable quality and hence that there had been no breach of s. 14 (2). The reasoning was in essence that it had subsequently become apparent that a degree of contamination would not have affected cattle. Hence, it was said, purchasers who were reselling or compounding only for cattle food and who knew of the contamination would have bought the goods under their contract description at the ordinary market price. The fact that Lillico's particular purpose was known to Kendall had

---

[2] *Preist* v. *Last*, [1903] 2 K.N. 148, C.A. (hot water bottle which burst: liability under s. 14 (1)); *Grant* v. *Australian Knitting Mills, Ltd.*, [1936] A.C. 85, P.C. (woollen underpants).

[3] *Daniels and Daniels* v. *R. White & Sons, Ltd.*, [1938] 4 All E.R. 258 (R. White's lemonade); *Wren* v. *Holt*, [1903] 1 K.B. 610 (Holden's beer) (goods purchased under trade name and inference of non-reliance: liability under s. 14 (2) but not 14 (1)). For purchases under trade names, see below, pp. 104–105.

[4] See, e.g., *Wallis* v. *Russell*, [1902] 2 I.R. 585 (crabs displayed in fishmonger's shop; liability under s. 14 (1), but doubtful whether the sale was by description under s. 14 (2)).

[5] In *Christopher Hill, Ltd.* v. *Ashington Piggeries, Ltd* [1969] 3 All E.R. 1496 the buyers failed in the Court of Appeal under s. 14 (2) on the ground that the seller did not deal in goods of that description. The majority of the House of Lords disagreed with this view: see [1972] A.C. 441 and above, p. 80.

[6] [1969] 2 A.C. 31; [1968] 2 All E.R. 444, H.L.

to be ignored since s. 14 (2) was concerned with quality and not with suitability for purpose. More generally, goods were held to be of merchantable quality provided that they were fit for one purpose for which such goods would commonly be used and this even though they were unfit (and indeed lethal) when used for another common purpose for which the plaintiff was known to require them.

The general conclusion is surprising[7] and the reasoning behind it un-convincing in that it ignores what Lord Pearce called the "trap element".[8] Buyers who are appraised of the true facts might indeed purchase the goods at the contract price, but an informed choice depends on knowledge and where the danger is neither obvious nor well known this may require a warning. It is submitted that Lord Pearce was correct in holding the goods to be unmerchantable and in saying:[9]

> "[The] absence of a warning was in itself a serious defect, which can make goods unmerchantable even though they would have been merchantable if sold with due notice of the hidden defect. On this point it is irrelevant to consider whether, *with* a warning, it would have found buyers at the price. In my opinion, the real question for the court to consider is whether *this* groundnut meal with its particular toxicity but *without any warning to buyers* was merchantable as groundnut meal, which normally was fit for consumption by cattle and poultry without discrimination."[10]

The approach of the majority of the House of Lords may have repercussions in other cases where goods are fit for their purpose in a narrow sense and yet, because of their ingredients or unpredictable side-effects, unsafe in the absence of a warning or directions for use. Thus hair dyes or sprays may set hair but cause dermatitis;[11] a spot remover may remove spots but cause hepatitis;[12] and, as in the thalidomide tragedy, a tranquilliser may calm the nerves but produce serious deformities in the foetus when taken by pregnant women. In many such cases liability might no doubt be

---

[7] Although it derives some support from the judgments of Lord Wright in *Canada Atlantic Grain Export Co., Inc.* v. *Eilers* (1929), 35 Ll.L.Rep. 206, 213; and *Cammell Laird Co., Ltd.* v. *Manganese Bronze and Brass Co., Ltd.,* [1934] A.C. 402, 430.

[8] [1969] 2 A.C. 31, 119; [1968] 2 All E.R. 444, 487.

[9] *Ibid.,* at p. 119 and p. 487 respectively.

[10] Lord Wilberforce agreed with Lord Pearce on this point: see [1969] 2 A.C. 31, 126. The unreality of the majority approach was heightened by the fact that at the time of the sale of the groundnuts in 1960 it would not have been appreciated that they could have been safely compounded into cattle food. This had, however, become clear by the time of the trial. To take account of this subsequently acquired knowledge seems to create a hypothetical market which would not, *ex hypothesi,* have existed at the time of the sale: see [1969] 2 A.C. 31, 119 (Lord Pearce).

[11] *Holmes* v. *Ashford,* [1950] 2 All E.R. 76.

[12] *Twombley* v. *Fuller Brush Co.,* 158 A. 2d 110 (Md., 1960). See also *Clement* v. *Crosby Co.,* 111 N.W. 745 (Mich., 1907) (inflammable stove polish); *Martin* v. *Bengue Inc.,* 136 A. 2d 626 (N.J., 1957) (chest ointment ignited by cigarette when plaintiff was smoking in bed).

imposed under the fitness for purpose provision of s. 14 (3) of the Act, but this will not always be possible where the goods might be used for a variety of narrowly defined purposes and a particular purpose has not been communicated.[13] Warnings and directions for use may clearly be required of the manufacturer by the law of tort.[14] It is submitted that in the law of sale there should similarly be a secondary warranty whereby merchantability is taken to demand reasonable safety in use.[15]

It is not clear whether the new statutory definition of merchantable quality has had the effect of changing the law. Section 62 (1A) refers, in part, to goods being "as fit for the purpose or purposes for which goods of that kind are commonly bought as it is reasonable to expect..."[16] The definition might be interpreted as demanding fitness for *all* such purposes (or an appropriate warning that they are fit only for specific purposes) and not simply fitness for one such purpose.[17] This would have the advantage of helping to assimilate the standards of merchantability in contract and of reasonable safety in tort.[18]

---

[13] As perhaps in Lord Pearce's example in *Henry Kendall & Sons* v. *Lillico*, [1969] 2 A.C. 31, 119, of food which will be consumed by humans generally but which is sold without a warning that it is dangerous to young children. In practice, however, the courts have been willing to impose liability under s. 14 (3) and have defined the relevant "particular" purposes in the most general of terms: see e.g., *Kendall* v. *Lillico*, above, *Ashington Piggeries, Ltd.* v. *Christopher Hill, Ltd.* [1972] A.C. 441, and below, pp. 100–101.

[14] See, e.g., *Vacwell Engineering Co., Ltd.* v. *B.D.H. Chemicals, Ltd.*, [1971] 1 Q.B. 88; [1969] 3 All E.R. 1681, below, p. 179 (no warning of risk of explosion on contact of boron tribromide with water). Warnings and directions for use are discussed below, ch. 12.

[15] American cases do not appear to show a consistent pattern. In *Rumsey* v. *Freeway Manor Minimax*, 423 S.W. 2d 387 (Tex. Civ. App. 1968) liability for breach of warranty was denied where a poison which killed a child who had swallowed it was labelled inadequately whilst being perfectly suitable as an insecticide. But a different approach was adopted in *Twombley* v. *Fuller Brush Co.*, 158 A. 2d 110 (Md., 1960) (spot remover causing hepatitis). See also *Simmons* v. *Rhodes and Jamieson, Ltd.*, 293 P. 2d 26 (Cal., 1956) (cement causing burns) and, in general, 2 Frumer and Friedman, *Products Liability*, s. 19.03[2][a]; Nordstrom, *Law of Sales*, pp. 235–236. The point might have arisen in *Vacwell Engineering Co., Ltd.* v. *B.D.H. Chemicals, Ltd.* above, note 14. But the plaintiffs succeeded under s. 14 (1) (now s. 14 (3)) and in the tort of negligence so there was no need to press an argument under s. 14 (2). Rees, J. saw a number of difficulties in establishing a breach of the subsection: *cf.* [1971] 1 Q.B. 88, 108.

[16] Section 62 (1A) is set out above, p. 84.

[17] The uncertainty on this point is reflected in the different (and tentative) views advanced in standard texts on the law of sale. In *Benjamin's Sale of Goods* (1974), para. 801 it is said that "the new definition is to a large extent declaratory". See also Atiyah, *Sale of Goods*, 5th edn., 1975, p. 85. *Cf.*, however,, Sutton, *Sale of Goods* 2nd edn., 1974, p. 179; Waddams, *Products Liability* (1974), p. 73. There is no suggestion in the Law Commission report on which the definition was based that a change in the law was intended. A reversal of *Kendall* v. *Lillico* is recommended in the Ontario Law Reform Commission, "Report on Consumer Warranties and Guarantees in the Sale of Goods" (1972), pp. 39–40.

[18] See further, below, pp. 186–189.

Merchantability and price

Any complete definition of merchantable quality, whether it is directed towards commercial saleability or the reasonable expectations of the consumer buyer, must include a reference to the contract price. The requirement of merchantability does not mean that the goods must match up to some minimum and universally applicable standard since, as Salmond, J. once observed,

"Goods may be of inferior or even bad quality but yet fulfil the legal requirement of merchantable quality. For goods may be on the market in any grade, good, bad, or indifferent, and yet all equally merchantable."[19]

Unless the contract description provides for the quality to be expected (and most commercial contracts will do so) the appropriate grade is likely to be indicated through the price.

In one of the most widely cited definitions of merchantable quality Dixon, J. laid down the stringent requirement that the goods must be:[20]

"in such an actual state that a buyer fully acquainted with the facts and, therefore, knowing what hidden defects exist and not being limited to their apparent condition would buy them without abatement of the price obtainable for such goods if in reasonable sound order and condition and without special terms."

This test received the support of several members of the House of Lords in *Kendall* v. *Lillico*,[1] but it soon became apparent that it could not be taken literally. In *B.S. Brown & Son, Ltd.* v. *Craiks, Ltd.*[2] the contract was for the sale of a quantity of cloth which the seller assumed was required for industrial purposes but which the buyer in fact required for making up into dresses. The contract price was 36.25d per yard, which was high for industrial fabric but not exorbitant, and some of the cloth was eventually sold off at 30d per yard to be used for industrial purposes. The House of Lords held that the cloth was of merchantable quality, Lord Guest saying of Dixon, J.'s test:[3]

"The expression he used—'without abatement of the price obtainable'—cannot be construed strictly. It cannot be a necessary requirement of merchantability that there should be no abatement of price. If the difference in price is substantial

[19] *Taylor* v. *Combined Buyers, Ltd.*, [1924] N.Z. Gazette L.R. 51, 60. Some qualification to this statement would be needed where the goods are unsafe; see below, p. 93.
[20] *Australian Knitting Mills, Ltd.* v. *Grant* (1933), 50 C.L.R. 387, 418 (High Ct. Australia).
[1] *Cf.* [1969] 2 A.C. 31, 79 (Lord Reid with qualifications), p. 108 (Lord Guest), p. 118 (Lord Pearce).
[2] [1970] 1 All E.R. 823, H.L.
[3] *Ibid.*, at p. 828.

so as to indicate that the goods would only be sold at a 'throw-away-price', then that may indicate that the goods were not of merchantable quality."

Although it would be wrong to fasten on literally *any* diminution in price, a reference to a "throw-away-price" would go too far in the opposite direction. Most goods could be disposed of at something better than a "throw-away-price" but this would not necessarily make them merchantable.[4] A significant or marked price differential is, however, required before one can say that goods of the contract description would not ordinarily be put to the alternative uses which are suggested.

A number of examples might be cited in which this requirement was met.[5] But *Cehave N.V.* v. *Bremer Handelsgesellschaft*[6] serves as a recent and timely reminder that the conclusion cannot be expressed in terms of a general percentage reduction since everything will depend on the facts of the individual case and the reasons for the discrepancy in price. The contract price on the sale of a quantity of citrus pulp pellets for delivery in Rotterdam was approximately £100,000 and on arrival it was found that part of the cargo had been severely damaged by overheating. The cargo was eventually disposed of in a forced sale for £30,000. Such facts suggest a simple case of unmerchantability, but the Court of Appeal was unanimous in allowing the seller's appeal and it is submitted, with respect, that it was right to do so. After the forced sale the respondents had repurchased the self-same pellets for £30,000 and had used them in accordance with their original intentions as a base for cattle feed and in substantially the same manner and quantity. Had they succeeded in their contention that the pellets were unmerchantable, they would not only have insulated themselves from the effect of a bad bargain (the price in Rotterdam having fallen to £86,000 between the contract and the arrival of the vessel), they would have made a very considerable profit. The case is also of more general significance because of Lord Denning, M.R.'s suggestion that goods would be unmerchantable only when a commercial man would

---

[4] In *Asfar & Co.* v. *Blundell*, [1896] 1 Q.B. 123 the cargo of dates, though contaminated with sewage, was still of "considerable value" and was used for the purpose of distillation into spirit.

[5] See, e.g., *H. Beecham & Co. Pty., Ltd.* v. *Francis Howard & Co. Pty., Ltd.*, [1921] V.L.R. 428 (Vict. Sup. Ct.) (spruce timber intended for making pianos but containing dry rot was unmerchantable though suitable for box making at a much lower price); *Jones* v. *Just* (1868), L.R. 3 Q.B.D. 197 (manilla hemp found by the jury to be unmerchantable though re-sold at 75 per cent of the price). *Cf. Colyer Watson Pty., Ltd.* v. *Riverstone Meat Co. Pty., Ltd.* (1944), 46 S.R. (N.S.W.) 32.

[6] [1976] Q.B. 44; [1975] 3 All E.R. 739, C.A. The case is discussed in the context of the classification of express terms, above, p. 42.

agree that the buyer should be entitled to reject them and not be content with a remedy in damages. The standard is thus defined by reference to the consequences which accompany its breach.[7]

Merchantibility, durability and safety

In principle, the time at which the goods must be merchantable is when property passes or, in CIF and FOB sales, the time of shipment.[8] If they are merchantable at this time, the risk of subsequent deterioration will fall on the buyer. However, the very quality of being merchantable will itself typically demand that goods last for at least a minimum period of time. This has caused some difficulty when perishable goods such as vegetables, fish or game deteriorate in the course of transit after property has passed to the buyer.[9] Here the courts have in effect required that the contract goods possess the usual capacity of goods of that type to survive a normal transit in which all appropriate precautions have been taken.[10] The buyer is thereafter accorded a reasonable opportunity to deal with them in the course of business on arrival. If appropriate precautions, such as refrigeration or ventilation, have not been taken and this has caused the goods to deteriorate the seller will not be liable under the contract of sale[11] although there may be liability under a contract of carriage.

These cases apart, there is a singular lack of decisions providing any firm indication of the durability and standards demanded. Certainly s. 14 (2) is neither designed nor apt to prevent the proliferation of cheap and shoddy goods: still less does it demand the production and sale of goods which

---

[7] [1975] 3 All E.R. 739, 749. *Quaere* on what basis damages would then be awarded unless there were an express term governing quality as in the *Cehave* case itself?: see Weir, [1976] C.L.J. 33, 38.

[8] For the rules governing the passing of property see the Sale of Goods Act 1893, ss. 17, 18.

[9] See, in general, *Benjamin's Sale of Goods* (1974), paras. 829–830, 1429–1444; Sutton, *Sale of Goods*, 2nd edn., 1974, pp. 179–180. If property does not pass until the goods arrive the risk will fall on the seller (see *Winnipeg Fish Co.* v. *Whitman Fish Co.* (1909), 41 S.C.R. 453 (Can.)) unless the risk of deterioration is *necessarily* incident to the course of transit (see the Sale of Goods Act 1893, s. 33 and *Bull* v. *Robison* (1854), 10 Exch. 342 (hoop iron)).

[10] See *Mash and Murrell, Ltd.* v. *Joseph I. Emanuel, Ltd.,* [1961] 1 All E.R. 485; [1961] 1 W.L.R. 862 (potatoes) (Diplock, J.); reversed on the facts: [1962] 1 All E.R. 77 note, *Beer* v. *Walker* (1877), 46 L.J.Q.B. 677 (rabbits); *A. B. Kemp, Ltd.* v. *Tolland,* [1956] 2 Lloyd's Rep. 681 (peaches).

[11] See *Wardar's (Import and Export) Co., Ltd.* v. *W. Norwood & Sons, Ltd.,* [1968] 2 Q.B. 663; [1968] 2 All E.R. 602 (kidneys: inadequate refrigeration); *Mash and Murrell, Ltd.* v. *Joseph I. Emanuel, Ltd.,* [1962] 1 All E.R. 77, n., C.A. (potatoes: inadequate ventilation).

will not wear out or which are as long lasting as they can be made to be.[12] The Australian case of *George Wills & Co., Ltd. v. Davids Pty., Ltd.*[13] is frequently cited in this context. The defendants manufactured and sold tins of beetroot which they pickled in vinegar rather than the customary brine. The product was found to have a shorter life than the average for canned vegetables (one year as against a minimum of three) and a shorter life than beetroot canned in brine. The plaintiffs, a firm of wholesale grocers, had purchased three hundred and sixty cases of "tinned beetroot" which became unfit for human consumption within some fourteen or so months. They claimed damages for breach of contract maintaining that the goods were not of merchantable quality. Allowing the defendant vendor's appeal the High Court of Australia said:[14]

> "... if the contract called for the supply of beetroot canned in vinegar, the parties were bound to deliver and accept goods of this description and, if the condition and quality of the goods were normal for goods of this description, the purchaser could have no complaint on the ground of their merchantability. It would be nothing to the point, on any such complaint, to show that beetroot canned in vinegar would not keep for as long a period as canned peas or canned beans or, indeed, beetroot canned in brine ..."

The decision may be questioned on its facts[15] and it cannot in any event be taken too far. With some goods there may be a general understanding that it is all a matter of luck and that the goods may wear out immediately. Light bulbs and nylon stockings may fall into this category. A minimum period of relatively trouble-free usage will, however, normally be expected although its length will depend on factors such as the nature of the goods and the price paid.

As for quality, article 2–314 (2) (*b*) of the Uniform Commercial Code requires in the case of fungible goods that they be "of fair average quality within the description", and Official Comment 7 elaborates by saying that this means "goods centering around the middle belt of quality, not the least or the worst that can be understood in the particular trade by the

---

[12] The Ontario Law Reform Commission "Report on Consumer Warranties and Guarantees in the Sale of Goods" (1972) recommends the enactment of "an implied warranty that the goods (including, where appropriate, the individual components of the goods) shall be durable for a reasonable period of time, having regard to all the surrounding circumstances of the sale" and "an implied warranty that spare parts and reasonable repair facilities will be available for a reasonable period of time with respect to goods that normally require repairs": see p. 45, Recommendations 5 (d) (*e*) of the report.

[13] (1957), 98 C.L.R. 77 (High Ct. Australia); See also *Cordova Land Co., Ltd. v. Victor Brothers Inc.,* [1966] 1 W.L.R. 793 (skins); *Jakubowski v. Minnesota Mining and Manufacturing Co.,* 199 A. 2d 826 (N.J., 1964) (abrasive disk).

[14] *Ibid.,* at p. 89.

[15] See Greig, *Sale of Goods* (1974), pp. 201–202.

designation, but such as can pass 'without objection' ". The English standard is, on the face of it, less demanding. In any event, Lord Reid said in *Kendall* v. *Lillico* that it was not disputed that where various qualities of goods were commonly sold under a description "the *lowest* quality commonly so sold is what is meant by merchantable quality".[16] The difference may, however, be more apparent than real. As Lord Reid was later to agree in *B. S. Brown & Son, Ltd.* v. *Craiks, Ltd.*[17] questions of price may be all important and they may surely affect the reasonable expectations of the consumer buyer no less than those of the commercial purchaser. The purchaser may, in other words, have to put up with the "lowest" rather than the "middle belt" of quality for goods sold at a given price, but if he pays a higher price he is entitled to expect a better quality.

If the requirements of merchantability play no more than a modest role in imposing standards of durability and quality they may be somewhat more demanding where goods are unsafe and cause physical injury. Thus there is little doubt that the presence of extraneous or toxic substances in consumable or fungible goods, such as stones in buns, typhoid germs in milk and arsenic in beer, will render the goods both unmerchantable in contract and unreasonably dangerous in tort.[18] The same would be true of a failure to eliminate a natural object where this was reasonably to be expected.[19] In other cases goods may be unsafe and unmerchantable because of a miscarriage in the production process or because of the unsuitability of the materials or ingredients used in their composition.[20] Here much less attention is likely to be given to the price factor than where the complaint is that the goods are simply shoddy.[1] In *Godley* v. *Perry*,[2] for example, the catapult which broke after a few days' use, putting out a child's eye, was made by injection moulding from polystyrene, the cheapest kind of injection moulding material. The fact that it cost only sixpence did not prevent recovery under s. 14 (2) for breach of the implied condition of merchantable quality. This suggests that, at least with

---

[16] [1969] 2 A.C. 31, 75; [1968] 2 All E.R. 444, 450; emphasis supplied.

[17] [1970] 1 All E.R. 823, 825, H.L.

[18] See *Chaproniere* v. *Mason* (1905), 21 T.L.R. 633 (stone in bun); *Frost* v. *Aylesbury Dairy Co.*, [1905] 1 K.B. 608 (typhoid in milk); *Wren* v. *Holt*, [1903] 1 K.B. 610 (arsenic in beer). See also *Daniels and Daniels* v. *White & Sons. Ltd.*, [1938] 4 All E.R. 258 (lemonade containing carbolic acid); *Wilson* v. *Rickett, Cockerell & Co., Ltd.*, [1954] 1 Q.B. 598; [1954] 1 All E.R. 868 (explosive substance in a delivery of coalite); *Wallis* v. *Russell*, [1902] 2 I.R. 585 (crabs: food poisoning).

[19] See, e.g., *Tarling* v. *Nobel*, [1966] A.L.R. 189 (A.C.T. Sup. Ct.) (bone in chicken sandwich) and, in general, below, p. 193.

[20] See, e.g., *Bristol Tramways Carriage Co., Ltd.* v. *Fiat Motors, Ltd.*, [1910] 2 K.B. 831; *Randall* v. *Newson* (1877), 2 Q.B.D. 102; *Preist* v. *Last*, [1903] 2 K.B. 148.

[1] Section 62 (1A) of the 1893 Act recognises that price will not always be relevant.

[2] [1960] 1 All E.R. 36; [1960] 1 W.L.R. 9. See also *Buckley* v. *Lever Brothers*, [1953] 4 D.L.R. 16.

goods which have only one common use, certain minimum standards of design and construction must be observed if the goods would otherwise be unsafe.[3]

Secondhand goods[4]

There is likely to be difficulty in applying the standard of merchantable quality to the sale of secondhand goods. As with goods which are described as "shop-soiled" or as "seconds" the purchaser cannot reasonably expect the same standard as for goods which are new and sold at the full price. The point arose in a recent New Zealand case[5] where the contract was for the sale of a secondhand Leyland 600 engine which the purchaser required to fit into a road compaction roller. The contract price was 750 dollars and the price of a new engine would have been of the order of 4,000 dollars. After some forty-eight hours' use over a period of four days the engine broke down and the connecting rod and crank-shaft were found to be damaged beyond repair. Mahon, J. dismissed the purchaser's appeal, saying that he had "failed to establish on the evidence that the engine as delivered was not commercially saleable as a secondhand engine with a limited operating life."[6]

In other cases plaintiffs have suceeded in establishing that secondhand goods were not of merchantable quality. Many such cases have, predictably, involved secondhand cars.[7] *Crowther* v. *Shannon Motor Co.*[8] is a recent example. The plaintiff had bought from the defendants, a firm of reputable dealers in Southampton, a Jaguar car with a mileometer reading of some 82,000 miles. Three weeks and 2,000 miles later, the engine seized up and needed to be replaced. The Court of Appeal upheld a judgment in the plaintiff's favour, Lord Denning saying that the evidence showed that at the time of the sale the car was not reasonably fit for the purpose of

---

[3] This is presumably the case even though physical damage does not in fact result. The child would, in other words, have recovered the cost of the catapult. The problems of multi-purpose goods and of goods which are fit for their purpose but dangerous in the absence of a warning are discussed in the light of the decision in *Henry Kendall & Sons* v. *Lillico & Sons,* [1969] 2 A.C. 31, [1968] 2 All E.R. 444, H.L. above, pp. 86–88.

[4] See Greig, *Sale of Goods* (1974), pp. 185–187. For a collection of American cases decided under the strict tort theory, see Annotation 53 A.L.R. (3d) 338. See also 2 Frumer and Friedman, *Products Liability*, s. 19.03[5].

[5] *Feast Contractors, Ltd.* v. *Ray Vincent, Ltd.,* [1974] 1 N.Z.L.R. 212 (N.Z. Sup. Ct.).

[6] *Ibid.*, at p. 218.

[7] The cases are discussed by Whincup, "Reasonable Fitness of Cars" (1975), 38 M.L.R. 660, 665–671 especially.

[8] [1975] 1 All E.R. 139; [1975] 1 W.L.R. 30, C.A. See also *Frank* v. *Grosvenor Motors Auctions Pty., Ltd.,* [1960] V.R. 607 (Vict. Sup. Ct.) (split gear box and differential).

being driven on the road.[9] Merchantability will not, however, always import such a requirement since regard must be had to the terms of the contract under which the goods were sold. As James, L.J. is reported as saying in a recent case involving a secondhand Renault car with faulty brakes: "Many cars were sold as secondhand cars which needed something to be done to them before they were fit for the road."[10] If the agreed price assumes that the buyer will rectify the fault, the goods may well be merchantable under the contract,[11] although this should not preclude liability in negligence to a third party if the seller acted unreasonably in looking to the buyer to carry out the necessary repairs.[12]

Notification of defects and inspection

By the amended s. 14 (2) of the Sale of Goods Act the implied condition of merchantable quality does not apply.

> "(a) as regard defects specifically drawn to the buyer's attention before the contract is made; or
> (b) if the buyer examines the goods before the contract is made, as regards defects which that examination ought to reveal."

Proviso (a) had no counterpart in the original Sale of Goods Act 1893 and it might be argued that it is superfluous. If a defect has been drawn specifically to the buyer's attention the goods would rarely, if ever, be unmerchantable under the contract. However, the Law Commission took the view that it was desirable to give the seller a clear-cut defence in law[13]

---

[9] *Ibid.*, at p. 141. The claim was under s. 14 (1) (now s. 14 (3)) of the 1893 Act, but the same standard would be demanded under s. 14 (2).

[10] *McDonald* v. *Empire Garage (Blackburn), Ltd.,* (1975), *Times*, 8 October, C.A. Bridge L.J. concurred in holding that a breach of s. 14 (2) had not been established but Lord Denning, M.R., dissented. The case was decided on the pre-1973 law and hence under s. 14 (2) the sale had to be "by description". The majority of the court was not satisfied that this requirement had been met.

[11] As in *Bartlett* v. *Sidney Marcus, Ltd.,* [1965] 2 All E.R. 753; [1965] 1 W.L.R. 1013, C.A. (defective clutch). *Semble* that the position will not be affected by the fact that the fault proves to be more serious than expected.

[12] *N.B.*, however, that some English cases assume that such an opportunity for intermediate action will preclude recovery against the original defendant. For general discussion of the point, see below, ch. 14, pp. 284–290.

[13] See "Exemption Clauses in Contracts, First Report: Amendments to the Sale of Goods Act 1893", Law Com. No. 24, July 1969, paras. 49–50.

and there is no objection to this. There will inevitably be borderline cases in which it is unclear whether the true extent of the defect has been drawn to the buyer's attention or whether the buyer is simply complaining that the defect is more expensive to rectify than he had envisaged.[14]

Proviso (*b*) is similar to the proviso contained in the unamended Act and the wording is more favourable to the buyer than the equivalent provision in the Uniform Commercial Code. In particular, s. 14 (2) (*b*) applies only if the buyer has actually examined the goods[15] whereas art 2–316 (3) (*b*) of the Code equally excludes the warranty in the case of a buyer who has refused a specific demand that he examine.[16] On the face of it the Code provision seems fairer as between the parties especially in the light of Official Comment 8 which makes it clear that a demand is needed and a reasonable opportunity to examine insufficient.[17]

There is also a difference between the Sale of Goods Act 1893 and the Uniform Commercial Code in terms of what is expected of the buyer who does examine. The unamended version of s. 14 (2) negatived the implied condition with respect to defects which "such examination ought to have revealed" and in *Thornett and Fehr* v. *Beers & Son*[18] this phrase was interpreted objectively. A reasonably careful examination of certain barrels of vegetable glue would have revealed their unmerchantable condition and it was held that the buyer was no better off because his nominees, being pressed for time, had conducted an examination carelessly and so had not discovered it. The result seems eminently sensible[19] and it is similar to the position adopted in the Uniform Commercial Code under which "there is no implied warranty with regard to defects which an examination ought in the circumstances to have revealed".[20] The decision was, however, criticised and the re-worded version of s. 14 (2) (*b*) with

---

[14] As in *Bartlett* v. *Sidney Marcus, Ltd.*, [1965] 2 All E.R. 753; [1965] 1 W.L.R. 1013, C.A., above, note 11.

[15] Or, no doubt, if he is stopped from denying that he has examined them: *Thornett and Fehr* v. *Beers & Son*, [1919] 1 K.B. 486, 489 *per* Bray, J. Section 15 (2) (*c*) (sale by sample) is not so limited since the implied condition of merchantable quality applies only to defects "which would not be apparent on reasonable examination of the sample".

[16] Article 2–316 (3) (*b*) provides: "when the buyer before entering into the contract has examined the goods or the sample or model as fully as he desired or has refused to examine the goods there is no implied warranty with regard to defects which an examination ought in the circumstances to have revealed to him".

[17] Such an opportunity was sufficient to exclude the warranty at common law: *Jones* v. *Just* (1868), L.R. 3 Q.B. 197.

[18] [1919] 1 K.B. 486 (Bray, J.).

[19] *Cf.*, however, *Frank* v. *Grosvenor Motor Auctions Pty., Ltd.*, [1960] V.R. 607 (Vict. Sup. Ct.).

[20] See art. 2–316 (3) (*b*), above, note 16. This is of course without prejudice to any liability in deceit or in respect of a breach of the duty to warn of *known* dangers. These minimum duties common to all suppliers are discussed below, pp. 300–304.

its reference to *that* examination (as opposed to *such* examination) is generally taken to have been intended to reverse it.[1] The assumption that it has done so seems unwarranted, but if it is correct the full advice to the purchaser intent on avoiding the proviso is accordingly, "Do not examine. But if you must then make sure that it is a thoroughly cursory examination of a type which would not be apt to reveal any defect."[2] Accepting always that there are many defects which would not be revealed by a reasonable examination[3] this seems a strange conclusion. The purchaser who acted on such advice might yet find that he was denied recovery on grounds of causation, or perhaps contributory negligence, if he suffered consequent physical injury in using defective goods.[4] Similarly it might be argued that the goods had thereby been rendered merchantable since under s. 62 (1A) of the Act merchantability is linked to the reasonable expectations of the purchaser and regard must be had to all the circumstances of the case.

---

[1] See, e.g., *Benjamin on Sale* (1974), para. 807; Atiyah, *Sale of Goods* 5th edn., 1975, p. 83. There is no suggestion in the Law Commission report that this was intended.

[2] It would be uncharitable to suggest that this is what the Code of Practice for the Motor Industry has in mind when stating in para. 3.11: "Under the Sale of Goods Acts, if the buyer examines the goods before the contract is made there is no condition of merchantable quality as regards defects which that examination ought to reveal. Dealers should therefore provide all reasonable facilities to enable prospective customers or their nominees to carry out an examination of the car prior to sale, in order that any defects which ought to be revealed at the time of sale are made known to both parties".

[3] Standard examples from the cases include arsenic in beer: *Wren* v. *Holt*, [1903] 1 K.B. 610; a catapult made from insufficiently strong material: *Godley* v. *Perry*, [1960] 1 All E.R. 36; [1960] 1 W.L.R. 9; and an excess of free sulphites in undergarments: *Grant* v. *Australian Knitting Mills, Ltd.*, [1936] A.C. 85, P.C.

[4] There is some difficulty on this point. *Mowbray* v. *Merryweather*, [1895] 2 Q.B. 640, C.A., is sometimes regarded as having decided that contributory fault could not bar recovery where the claim is in contract. See, however, *Hadley* v. *Droitwitch Construction Co., Ltd.*, [1967] 3 All E.R. 911, C.A., and Glanville Williams, *Joint Torts and Contributory Negligence* (1951), pp. 220–221. For a recent Commonwealth example of contributory negligence being successfully pleaded see *Hunnerup* v. *Goodyear Tyre and Rubber Co. (Australia), Ltd.*, (1974) 7 S.A.S.R. 215 (S.A. Sup. Ct.) (deflating tyre followed by road accident). The better reasoned American cases similarly suggest that recovery may be denied on this basis: see, e.g., *Dallison* v. *Sears Roebuck and Co.*, 313 F. 2d 343 (10th cir., 1962) (nightgown catching fire: plaintiff smoking in bed after taking sleeping pill); *Erdman* v. *Johnson Bros. Radio and Television Co.*, 271 A 2d 744 (Md., 1970) (continuing use of television after sparks and smoke were seen coming from set). There has, however, been considerable difficulty and confusion as to the place of contributory negligence under both warranty and strict tort theories. See 2 Frumer and Friedman, *Products Liability*, s. 16A [5] [*f*], and below pp. 295–296. Apportionment under the Law Reform (Contributory Negligence) Act 1945 is possible only where the breach of contract also constitutes a tort: see *Sole* v. *W. J. Hallt, Ltd.*, [1973] 1 Q.B. 574; [1973] 1 All E.R. 1032; *cf. Driver* v. *William Willett (Contractors), Ltd.*, [1969] 1 All E.R. 665, and see, in general, Glanville Williams, *op. cit.*, pp. 328–332; Treitel, *Law of Contract*, 4th edn., 1975, pp. 656–658.

6 Implied Terms Governing Correspondence with Description, Merchantability and Fitness for Purpose: II

The implied condition of reasonable fitness for purpose

Apart from the implied condition of merchantable quality, the nineteenth century saw the development of a further implied condition whereby goods were taken to be reasonably fit for any particular purpose for which the buyer was known to require them. *Jones* v. *Bright*[1] was an important early case. The contract was for the sale of one thousand sheets of copper which the seller knew was required for sheathing the bottom of a vessel, the *Isabella*. Such sheathing would normally last for four to five years but after four to five months the copper had corroded badly and was full of holes. The defendant's witnesses attributed this to the "singular inveteracy of the barnacles in the river at Sierra Leone" where the ship had been lying, but the jury was unconvinced and found that the decay had been caused by an intrinsic defect. Judgment for the plaintiff was affirmed, Best, C.J. saying:[2]

> "[I] wish to put the case on a broad principle:—If a man sells an article, he thereby warrants that it is merchantable,—that it is fit for some purpose.... If he sells it for a particular purpose, he thereby warrants it fit for that purpose; and no case has decided otherwise, although there are, doubtless, some dicta to the contrary."

---

[1] (1829), 5 Bing. 533. See also *Brown* v. *Edgington* (1841), 2 Man. & G. 279; *Bigge* v. *Parkinson* (1862), 7 H. & N. 955; *Jones* v. *Just* (1868), L.R. 3 Q.B. 197, 202–203 *per* Mellor, J.
[2] (1829), 5 Bing. 533, 544.

The latter proposition was enacted as s. 14(1) of the Sale of Goods Act 1893, now renumbered and amended as s. 14(3).[3] Section 14(3) provides as follows:

"Where the seller sells goods in the course of a business and the buyer, expressly or by implication, makes known to the seller any particular purpose for which the goods are being bought, there is an implied condition that the goods supplied under the contract are reasonably fit for that purpose, whether or not that is a purpose for which such goods are commonly supplied, except where the circumstances show that the buyer does not rely, or that it is unreasonable for him to rely, on the seller's skill or judgment."

A number of the general points made when discussing the implied condition of merchantable quality apply equally to s. 14(3). For example, both implied conditions require that the sale be "in the course of a business",[4] and both extend to "goods supplied under the contract"—a phrase which seems apt to cover containers and extraneous materials as well as the immediate subject matter of the sale.[5] These points do not need further discussion. Section 14(3) has, however, certain preconditions and provisos of its own.

Making known a particular purpose

In the first place the subsection applies only where the buyer "expressly or by implication, makes known to the seller any particular purpose for which the goods are being bought." The word "particular" is used in the sense of "specified", "defined" or "stated" and not as being the opposite of a general purpose.[6] Section 14(3) accordingly applies even though the goods are bought for their common or even for their singular purpose, as where there is a purchase of food, a hot-water bottle, woollen undergarments or clothes pegs.[7] A singular purpose will, moreover, be made known "by implication" through the simple act of buying the goods. It does not have to be communicated expressly.[8] Here and in all cases where the purpose

---

[3] The change was effected by the Supply of Goods (Implied Terms) Act 1973, s. 3.
[4] See above, pp. 80–81.
[5] See above, p. 82.
[6] See *Henry Kendall & Sons* v. *Lillico & Sons*, [1969] 2 A.C. 31, 83 (Lord Reid), 123 (Lord Wilberforce); *Ashington Piggeries, Ltd.* v. *Christopher Hill, Ltd.*, [1972] A.C. 441; *Wallis* v. *Russell*, [1902] 2 I.R. 585, 598–599 (Palles, C.B.).
[7] See, respectively, *Wallis* v. *Russell*, [1902] 2 I.R. 585 (unwholesome crab); *Preist* v. *Last*, [1903] 2 K.B. 148 (hot-water bottle); *Grant* v. *Australian Knitting Mills, Ltd.*, [1936] A.C. 85, P.C. (undergarments); *Buckley* v. *Lever Brothers, Ltd.*, [1953] 4 D.L.R. 16 (clothes pegs).
[8] *Preist* v. *Last*, [1903] 2 K.B. 148, 153 (Collins, M.R.); *Wallis* v. *Russell* [1902] 2 I.R. 585, 634 (Holmes, L.J.).

is implicit in the contract description[9] there is considerable overlap between s. 14(2) and (3). Indeed Williston has said that in such cases "fitness for a particular purpose may be merely the equivalent of merchantability".[10] In English law the tendency of the subsections to provide cumulative remedies is enhanced by the fact that merchantable quality is now defined in terms of reasonable fitness for purpose rather than commercial saleability.[11]

In other cases the buyer's purpose must be made known to the seller[12] either by express communication or by an indication of the object which he expects to achieve. This would be necessary when, for example, the buyer requires a propeller to fit a particular ship, a rope to raise barrels of wine from a cellar, a car which is suitable for touring purposes, a tractor for road construction work, or a bus capable of operating in heavy traffic in a hilly district.[13] Where a specialised or secondary purpose is not made known all duties are likely to be discharged by supplying goods which are of merchantable quality. Hence in *B. S. Brown & Son, Ltd.* v. *Craiks, Ltd.*[14] the buyers failed under the present heading since they had not informed the sellers that they required the cloth for making up into dresses.

Some recent cases have defined the relevant "particular purpose" extremely broadly. For example, in *Kendall* v. *Lillico*[15] both sub-buyers (SAPPA and Lillico) recovered under s. 14(1) (now s. 14(3)) because they were known to have required the goods for compounding into feed for animals and poultry *generally*. The contaminated groundnut extraction was

---

[9] Examples would include an oil storage tank, a potato digger and a milk pump: see *Williston on Sales* (revd. ed.), para. 235, note 6 and cases there cited. See also above, p. 75, note 1.

[10] *Op. cit.*, para. 235, p. 605.

[11] See above, pp. 84–88.

[12] It would presumably be sufficient that the seller knew that the goods were required for a given specialised purpose and that the buyer was relying on him even though this purpose had not been *made known* in any positive sense. However, in the *Ashington Piggeries* case [1972] A.C. 441, 513, Lord Diplock required that the source of the knowledge be the buyer himself. The wording of the equivalent provision in U.C.C., art. 2–315 is more satisfactory in this respect. It provides: "Where the seller at the time of contracting *has reason to know* any particular purpose for which the goods are required and that the buyer is relying on the seller's skill or judgment to select or furnish suitable goods, there is unless excluded or modified under the next section, an implied warranty that the goods shall be fit for such purpose": emphasis supplied.

[13] See, respectively, *Cammel Laird & Co., Ltd.* v. *Manganese Bronze and Brass, Ltd.*, [1934] A.C. 402 (propeller); *Brown* v. *Edgington* (1841), 2 Man. & G. 279 (rope); *Baldry* v. *Marshall*, [1925] 1 K.B. 260 C.A. (car); *Ashford Shire Council* v. *Dependable Motors Pty., Ltd.*, [1961] A.C. 336; [1961] 1 All E.R. 96, P.C. (tractor); *Bristol Tramways Carriage Co., Ltd.* v. *Fiat Motors, Ltd.*, [1910] 2 K.B. 831 (bus to operate in Bristol). See also *Manchester Liners, Ltd.* v. *Rea., Ltd.*, [1922] 2 A.C. 74 (coal for burning in a particular steam ship).

[14] [1970] 1 All E.R. 823; [1970] 1 W.L.R. 752, H.L., above, p. 89. See also *Jones* v. *Padgett* (1890), 24 Q.B.D. 650, C.A.

[15] [1969] 2 A.C. 31; [1968] 2 All E.R. 444, H.L., above, p. 86.

unfit for this general purpose although it would have been fit for the more limited purpose of feeding to cattle. The particular purpose was even wider in the *Ashington Piggeries*[16] case, where both the respondents and the third party were also held liable under the present heading. The herring meal would have had an alternative use as a fertiliser and the House of Lords agreed that compounding into animal feeding-stuffs was a sufficiently particularised purpose without further subdivision according to the different types of animals to which it might have been fed. Indeed Viscount Dilhorne regarded it as:[1]

> "... almost unarguable that a person who goes into a shop and asks for a food for feeding to animals has not made known the particular purpose for which he is requiring the food and that he has only made known the particular purpose if he specifies the variety or varieties of animals he wants to feed."[2]

If a range of narrowly defined purposes is subsumed within a broader unifying purpose the likelihood of the "particular purpose" being made known to the seller is correspondingly increased. No doubt it should then follow that the range of goods which is reasonably fit for this broader purpose is itself similarly extended.[3] There is no reason in principle why s. 14 (3) should demand reasonable fitness with respect to the unifying purpose and to all of its constituent narrower purposes when the standard of merchantable quality under s. 14 (2) seems to make no such demands, it being sufficient that the goods are fit for *one* purpose.[4] Yet cases such as *Kendall* v. *Lillico*[5] nonetheless suggest that the buyer may be well advised to invoke s. 14 (3) in preference to s. 14 (2) where goods might have been put to a variety of different uses only some of which would have occasioned damage or loss. Section 14 (3) may be especially attractive where the goods are fit for their purpose in an immediate and narrow sense and yet unsafe in the absence of a warning or directions for use.[6]

---

[16] [1972] A.C. 441; [1971] 1 All E.R. 847, H.L., above, p. 75.

[1] [1972] A.C. 441, 487.

[2] *Cf.* the view of Lord Diplock who held that the third parties were not in breach of s. 14 (1) since they did not know that the meal was to be used as an ingredient in the diet of mink and were still operating on a "range of purposes" basis; *ibid.*, at pp. 512–513.

[3] "The less circumscribed the purpose, the less circumscribed will be, as a rule, the range of goods which are reasonably fit for such purpose": *per* Lord Pearce in *Henry Kendall & Sons* v. *Lillico & Sons,* [1969] 2 A.C. 31, 115. See also Sutton, *Sale of Goods*, 2nd edn., 1974, p. 152.

[4] This was certainly so under the unamended 1893 Act: see *Kendall* v. *Lillico,* [1969] 2 A.C. 31 and above, p. 86–88. *Quaere* whether the new statutory definition in s. 62 (1A) of the Sale of Goods Act 1893 has affected the position: see above, p. 88.

[5] [1969] 2 A.C. 31; [1968] 2 All E.R. 444.

[6] Because, e.g., of the "trap element" in *Kendall* v. *Lillico* itself. See *Vacwell Engineering Co., Ltd.* v. *B.D.H. Chemicals, Ltd.,* [1971] 1 Q.B. 88; [1969] 3 All E.R. 1681 (no warning of risk of explosion on contact of boron tribromide with water). The possibility of implying a secondary warranty demanding reasonable safety in use is discussed above, pp. 87–88.

Reasonable reliance

Section 14 (3) has no application "where the circumstances show that the buyer does not rely, or that it is unreasonable for him to rely, on the seller's skill or judgment". Reasonable reliance is indeed the cornerstone of the subsection for without it there is no basis on which one can fairly impute to the seller a promise that the goods will be fit for the buyer's purpose.[7] Conversely, knowledge of this purpose is essential if the seller is to exercise skill or judgment in the selection of goods appropriate to the buyer's needs. Moreover, such knowledge must obviously exist at the time of the contract[8] although subsequently acquired knowledge may give rise to a duty to warn of hidden dangers. Breach of this duty is actionable in tort.[9]

The fact that the requirement is stated by way of an exception or proviso suggests that the seller must prove that there are circumstances establishing a lack of reasonable reliance and that it is not for the buyer to establish the contrary.[10] It is doubtful whether the same was true of the equivalent provision in the original and unamended Act.[11] But in any event there would be few cases in which the evidence was so evenly balanced that the court was unable to reach a conclusion one way or the other.

The comparative skill and expertise of the parties is likely to be the most important single factor in determining the issue of reasonable reliance.[12] Thus reliance has been readily assumed in ordinary consumer sales and in respect of matters on which the seller has specialised knowledge.[13] Occasionally no doubt the proper inference in such cases will

---

[7] Since *unreasonable* reliance will prevent liability from accruing considerations of contributory negligence cannot arise on this issue. *Aliter* where damage is incurred through subsequent use of the goods once their unsuitability has been discovered. See also above, p. 97, note 4.

[8] The requirement is stated expressly in U.C.C., art. 2–315, cited above, p. 100, note 12.

[9] See below, ch. 12, pp. 247–251.

[10] *Cf. The Glendaroch*, [1894] P. 226 and the cases discussed in Cross, *Evidence*, 4th edn., 1974, p. 92. This was the intention of the Law Commission: see "Exemption Clauses in Contracts, First Report: Amendments to the Sale of Goods Act 1893", Law. Com. No. 24, July 1969, para. 37.

[11] The unamended Act used the phrase "so as to show that the buyer relies" and the balance of authority suggests that there was no general presumption of reliance: see *Henry Kendall & Sons* v. *Lillico & Sons,* [1969] 2 A.C. 31, 81–82 (Lord Reid), 106–107 (Lord Guest); *Ashington Piggeries, Ltd.* v. *Christopher Hill, Ltd.*, [1972] A.C. 441, 476–477 (Lord Guest); but *cf.* the view of Lord Pearce in *Henry Kendall & Sons* v. *Lillico & Sons* [1969] 2 A.C. 31, 115. See, in general, Sutton, *Sale of Goods*, 2nd edn., 1974, pp. 145–147.

[12] As it is on determining the question of whether an express affirmation is a representation or warranty: see *Esso Petroleum Co., Ltd.* v. *Mardon*, [1976] Q.B. 801; [1976] 2 All E.R. 5, C.A., above, pp. 36–41.

[13] See, e.g., *Grant* v. *Australian Knitting Mills, Ltd.*, [1936] A.C. 85, 99 (Lord Wright) (retail sale of undergarments); *Godley* v. *Perry*, [1960] 1 All E.R. 36 (catapult); *David Jones, Ltd.* v.

be that the parties are merely expecting that the goods will be fit for the buyer's purpose but that the seller has made no implied promise to this effect.[14] If goods are sold "with all faults" or "as is", it might sometimes be right to draw the same inference.[15] Where the parties are equally knowledgeable, the inference of reliance is less likely to be drawn. Yet reliance was established in *Kendall* v. *Lillico*[16] in spite of the fact that the buyer and seller were both members of the same commodity market and the goods were afloat at the time of the sale. At the other extreme the condition would rarely be implied in respect of matters on which it was the buyer who had the expertise. *Teheran Europe Co., Ltd.* v. *S. T. Belton (Tractors), Ltd.*[17] is illustrative. Here the contract was for the sale of a number of mobile air compressors which the buyers, a Persian company, required for resale in Persia. The sellers knew nothing of the special characteristics of the Persian market and the Court of Appeal rightly held that the buyers had relied on their own skill and judgment. Indeed, as Diplock, L.J. observed, a contrary conclusion would have smacked of "nonsense".[18]

Partial reliance

Although reliance on the seller's skill or judgment is essential it does not have to be total and exclusive. It is sufficient that it is "a substantial and effective inducement which leads the buyer to agree to the purchase".[19] In *Cammell Laird & Co., Ltd.* v. *Manganese Bronze and Brass Co., Ltd.*[20] the plaintiff shipbuilders had contracted with the defendants for the supply of two manganese bronze propellers to be fitted to ships which were under construction in the plaintiffs' yard on the River Mersey. The propellers were to be manufactured in accordance with a blueprint supplied by the plaintiffs, but details of matters such as the thickness of the blades were left to the discretion of the defendants. One of the propellers proved to

---

Willis (1934), 52 C.L.R. 110 (shoes); *Cammel Laird & Co., Ltd.* v. *Manganese Bronze and Brass Co., Ltd.*, [1932] A.C. 402, H.L. below (specialist seller of propellers).

[14] See, e.g., *Chanter* v. *Hopkins* (1838), 4 M. & W. 339 (smoke consuming furnace), below, p. 105; *Dixon Kerly, Ltd.* v. *Robinson*, [1965] 2 Lloyd's L.R. 404 (yacht built to new design).

[15] A point which has obvious implications to the protection accorded to purchasers in consumer sales. The implied condition cannot be excluded. But it may be prevented from accruing. See further below, p. 144.

[16] [1969] 2 A.C. 31; [1968] 2 All E.R. 444.

[17] [1968] 2 Q.B. 545; [1968] 2 All E.R. 886, C.A.

[18] [1968] 2 All E.R. 886, 894. See also *Sumner Permain & Co.* v. *Webb & Co.*, [1922] 1 K.B. 55 (tonic water for resale in Argentine).

[19] *Medway Oil and Storage Co., Ltd.* v. *Silica Gel Corporation* (1928), 33 Com. Cas. 195, 196, H.L., *per* Lord Sumner.

[20] [1932] A.C. 402.

be noisy and unsatisfactory and the inference was that the problem did not stem from the plaintiffs' specifications. The House of Lords held that the plaintiffs were entitled to recover for breach of s. 14(1) (now s. 14(3)), Lord Wright saying:[1]

> "I do not find in the section anything inconsistent with a division of reliance, the buyer relying in part on himself and in part on the seller; there will then be the implied condition of fitness in regard to that latter part, so that the seller will be responsible for a breach of that condition."

The same point was made in the *Ashington Piggeries*[2] case where Lord Diplock commented that this correspondence of the scope of the implied condition with the sphere of the seller's expertise was "consistent with common sense and business honesty".[3] Here the respondents had compounded the mink food "King Size" to a formula supplied by the appellant's controlling director who was himself a leading expert on mink nutrition. Had the contaminated herring meal been harmful only to mink the respondents would not have been liable for breach of s. 14(1) since the idiosyncrasies of mink fell outside their sphere of expertise. Similarly no liability would have been incurred under s. 14(1) had the danger to mink stemmed from the formula itself. But once the unsuitability of the food for mink had been established the onus seems to have been placed on the respondents to prove that it was suitable for feeding to animals and poultry generally and the onus was not discharged.[4]

Purchases under patent or trade names

Under the original Sale of Goods Act the implied condition of fitness for purpose did not apply where there was a contract for the sale of a specified article under its patent or other trade name. This proviso was deleted when the Act was amended in 1973[5] but it had in any event been construed so narrowly as to add nothing to the overall requirement of reliance. In the leading case of *Baldry* v. *Marshall*[6] where the contract was for the sale of an eight cylinder Bugatti car, Bankes, L.J. said that the test for the application of the proviso was:[7]

---

[1] *Ibid.,* at p. 428.
[2] [1972] A.C. 441, H.L.
[3] *Ibid.,* at p. 508.
[4] *Cf.* [1972] A.C. 441, 508–509 *per* Lord Diplock who would have preferred to see this onus placed on the appellant buyers. For discussion of this point, see Greig, *Sale of Goods,* pp. 194–197.
[5] By the Supply of Goods (Implied Terms) Act 1973, s. 3. A similar step was taken in U.C.C. art. 2–315 in relation to the Uniform Sales Act, s. 15.
[6] [1925] 1 K.B. 260, C.A. See also *Bristol Tramways Carriage Co., Ltd.* v. *Fiat Motors, Ltd.,* [1910] 2 K.B. 831.
[7] [1925] 1 K.B. 260, 267.

"Did the buyer specify it under its trade name in such a way as to indicate that he is satisfied, rightly or wrongly, that it will answer his purpose, and that he is not relying on the skill or judgment of the seller."

The test was not satisfied since the plaintiff buyer had relied on the seller's skill or judgment to provide him with a car which was suitable for touring purposes. The position had been different in *Chanter* v. *Hopkins*[8] where the defendant had sent a written order to the plaintiff patentee: "Send me your patent hopper and apparatus, to fit up my brewing copper with your smoke-consuming furnace". The apparatus did not consume smoke in the expected manner but the Court of Exchequer held that the vendor was nonetheless entitled to recover the contract price. In the judgment of Lord Abinger, C.B., "this is the ordinary case of a man who has had the misfortune to order a particular chattel on the supposition that it will answer a particular purpose, but who finds it will not."[9]

Although the proviso is no longer in the Act, the fact that the goods have been purchased under a trade or brand name should continue to be relevant on the issue of reasonable reliance.[10] Indeed the reality of the situation is surely that in the vast majority of consumer sales of branded goods, the buyer relies on the skill or judgment of the manufacturer rather than on that of the retail vendor.[11] Reliance on the vendor may be inferred more realistically where he has selected or recommended a particular brand as being suitable for the buyer's purpose. It is in such situations that s. 14 (3) appears most apposite.

Inspection and examination

Unlike s. 14 (2), s. 14 (3) does not make express provision for the buyer who has examined the goods.[12] The rule at common law was that as regards defects which were discoverable such a buyer bought at his own risk whenever the goods were *in esse* and open to inspection.[13] Under the 1893 Act a test or examination may be similarly relevant as indicating that the buyer is relying on his own judgment and is not buying in reliance

---

[8] (1838), 4 M. & W. 399.
[9] *Ibid.*, at 405. See also *Dixon Kerly, Ltd.* v. *Robinson*, [1965] 2 Lloyd's Rep. 404 (yacht built to new design).
[10] See U.C.C. art 2–315, Official Comment 5.
[11] See *Daniels and Daniels* v. *R. White & Sons, Ltd.*, [1938] 4 All E.R. 258, 263, *per* Lewis, J.; *Wren* v. *Holt*, [1903] 1 K.B. 610; *Harris & Sons* v. *Plymouth Varnish and Colour Co., Ltd.* (1933), 49 T.L.R. 521.
[12] For the position under s. 14 (2) see above, pp. 95–97.
[13] See *Jones* v. *Just* (1868), L.R. 3 Q.B. 197, 202 *per* Mellor, J.; *Emmerton* v. *Mathews* (1862), 7 H. & N. 586; *Smith* v. *Baker* (1878), 40 L.T. 261. *Aliter* where the defect was not discoverable: *Drummond* v. *Van Ingen* (1877), 12 App. Cas. 284, H.L.; *Jones* v. *Bright* (1829), 5 Bing. 533.

on the skill or judgment of the seller.[14] The same might be true of cases where a certificate has been issued by some agency[15] or where there has been an inspection by a third party specialist. In the latter situation there may be need for a close inquiry into whether the third party was an employee of the buyer at the time (in which case the buyer may be said to have relied vicariously through him) or an independent contractor operating on his own behalf.[16]

The standard demanded

Where s. 14 (3) applies, the seller is not obliged to supply goods which are absolutely fit in all respects for the buyer's purpose. It is sufficient that the goods are "reasonably fit". In determining whether this standard has been met regard must be had to substantially the same considerations as are relevant to establish whether goods are of merchantable quality for the purposes of s. 14 (2) of the Act. For example, the standard will vary according to the price paid and to whether the allegation is that the goods are unsafe or simply shoddy and to whether they are new or secondhand.[17]

Difficulty has been experienced in cases where it is claimed that the plaintiff's loss or damage was attributable to an abnormal susceptibility or idiosyncrasy. The point arose in the *Ashington Piggeries*[18] case where the evidence suggested that mink were unusually susceptible to the toxicity of D.M.N.A. Had the sellers established that other than in an exceptionally high concentration D.M.N.A. was harmful only to mink,[19] the goods would have been reasonably fit for compounding into a general feeding-stuff for animals which was the communicated purpose. Liability would not then have been incurred under the fitness for purpose provision.

---

[14] Similarly where the buyer has himself selected from stock: see *H. Beecham & Co., Pty., Ltd.* v. *Francis Howard & Co. Pty., Ltd.*, [1921] V.L.R. 428 (Vict. Sup. Ct.) (timber with dry rot), although the buyer might still argue that he relied on the seller's selection of his stock; see *Kurriss* v. *Conrad and Co.*, 46 NE 2d 12 (Mass., 1942). For general discussion see *Wallis* v. *Russell*, [1902] 2 I.R. 585. See also *Smart* v. *Preston*, [1937] N.Z.L.R. 467.

[15] See *Phoenix Distributors, Ltd.* v. *L. B. Clarke (London), Ltd.*, [1967] 1 Lloyd's Rep. 518, C.A. (potatoes: N. Ireland Ministry of Agriculture Health Certificate). *Cf. Henry Kendall & Sons* v. *William Lillico & Sons*, [1969] 2 A.C. 31, 95, *per* Lord Morris.

[16] The point caused difficulty in *Ashford Shire Council* v. *Dependable Motors Pty., Ltd.*, [1961] A.C. 336; [1961] 1 All E.R. 96, P.C. where the contract was for the purchase of a tractor for use in road construction work and the purchasers were held to have relied vicariously through their engineer designate.

[17] See above, pp. 89–90 (merchantability and price); pp. 91–93 (merchantability and safety); pp. 94–95 (secondhand goods).

[18] [1972] A.C. 441; [1971] 1 All E.R. 847, H.L.

[19] And the onus of proof was, it seems, on them: *cf.* [1972] A.C. 441, 508–509 (Lord Diplock).

Griffiths v. *Peter Conway, Ltd.*[20] was such a case although the context was somewhat different. The claim was in respect of dermatitis which had developed after the plaintiff had begun to wear a Harris Tweed coat which she had purchased from the defendant retailer. The coat did not contain a primary irritant likely to affect a normal person[1] and the plaintiff's reaction was found to have been wholly idiosyncratic. The Court of Appeal upheld the trial court judge's dismissal of her claim on the ground that "the particular purpose for which the goods were required was the purpose of being worn by a woman suffering from an abnormality" and this had not been communicated to the defendants. It was irrelevant that the plaintiff had not appreciated her condition.[2] Allergies and peculiar susceptibilities are discussed further in a later chapter.[3]

The strict nature of contractual liability

Where the goods supplied under the contract are found to be unmerchantable or unfit for their purpose it will not avail the defendant to plead that he has exercised all reasonable care. The strict nature of contractual liability was pointed to by Blackburn, J. in *Randall* v. *Newson*[4] where he said, commenting on an earlier judgment:[5]

> "My own opinion was...that [the suppliers'] warranty was that the thing supplied was reasonably fit in fact; and if there was a defect in fact, even though that defect was one which no reasonable skill or care could discover, the person supplying the article should nevertheless be responsible, the policy of the law being that in a case in which neither were to blame, he, and not the person to whom they were supplied, should be liable for the defect."

This view has been vindicated in a series of cases so that it is now clear that

---

[20] [1939] 1 All E.R. 685. See also *Ingham* v. *Emes*, [1955] 2 Q.B. 366; [1955] 2 All E.R. 740.

[1] As the underwear had done in *Grant* v. *Australian Knitting Mills, Ltd.*, [1936] A.C. 85, P.C. See also *Mayne* v. *Silvermere Cleaners, Ltd.*, [1939] 1 All E.R. 693.

[2] [1939] 1 All E.R. 685, 691. This would suggest that the sellers would not have been liable in the *Ashington Piggeries* case if D.M.N.A. had been harmful only to mink and this even though it was known that the feed was required specifically for mink. Their unknown and abnormally high susceptibility to D.M.N.A. would not have been communicated and this would have formed part of the particular purpose. Contrast *Manchester Liners, Ltd.* v. *Rea, Ltd.*, [1922] 2 A.C. 74, H.L. (coal to be suitable for the steamship *Manchester Importer*, there being no standard type of ship); *Greaves & Co., Contractors, Ltd.* v. *Baynham Meikle & Partners*, [1975] 3 All E.R. 99 (warehouse designed as a store for oil drums to be moved by fork-lift trucks).

[3] See below, pp. 324–326.

[4] (1876), 45 L.J.Q.B. 364.

[5] *Ibid.*, at p. 365. The earlier judgment was delivered in the Court of Queen's Bench in *Readhead* v. *The Midland Rail. Co.* (1867), L.R. 2 Q.B. 412. Blackburn, J.'s view was not supported on appeal to the Exchequer Chamber (1869), L.R. 4 Q.B. 379, though he was ultimately vindicated in the Court of Appeal in *Randall* v. *Newson* (1877), L.R. 2 Q.B. 102.

the vendor may be liable although the goods were sold in a container or pre-packed and though the defect was discoverable only by a minute chemical analysis.[6] Recent decisions of the House of Lords confirm the point. Thus in *Henry Kendall & Sons* v. *William Lillico & Sons*, Lord Reid said that s. 14 (1) (now 14 (3)) covers "defects which are latent in the sense that even the utmost skill and judgment on the part of the seller would not have detected them".[7] Similarly, liability was imposed in the *Ashington Piggeries* case even though, in the words of Lord Diplock, "in the then state of knowledge, scientific and commercial, no deliberate exercise of human skill or judgment could have prevented the meal from having its toxic effect upon mink. It was sheer bad luck".[8]

In the light of such forthright statements there would be little point in seeking to reopen the issue in an English court. Reference may nonetheless be made to a series of interesting American cases which have explored the boundaries of strict liability. The cases have been concerned for the most part with blood plasma, drugs and cigarettes and actions have been brought against hospitals, blood banks and manufacturers under the implied warranty and strict tort theories. A variety of issues may be raised. Some products may be quite safe in the vast majority of cases and yet involve a risk of harm which is known but which is scientifically undiscovered in any particular case. The risk may stem from some impurity or extraneous matter or from a reaction between the product and other substances to be found, for example, in the body's chemistry. Alternatively, the problem may arise when an advance in scientific knowledge establishes a long-term causal connection between the product and the incidence of a particular disease.

In the frequently cited case of *Perlmutter* v. *Beth David Hospital*,[9] where hepatitis was alleged to have been caused by a transfusion of impure blood, the New York Court of Appeals denied liability on the technical ground that the transfusion involved the supply of a service rather than a sale.[10] This hardly seems a sufficient reason for dismissing a claim, but an underlying problem of policy lies behind the court's supporting observation "that there is today neither a means of detecting the presence of the jaundice-producing agent in the donor's blood nor a practical method of

---

[6] See, e.g., *Jackson* v. *Watson & Sons,* [1909] 2 K.B. 193, C.A. (tinned salmon); *Frost* v. *Aylesbury Dairy Co.,* [1905] 1 K.B. 608, C.A. (milk containing typhoid germs); *Grant* v. *Australian Knitting Mills, Ltd.,* [1936] A.C. 85, 100, P.C. (excess of free sulphites in underpants); *Wren* v. *Holt,* [1903] 1 K.B. 610 (arsenic in beer).

[7] [1969] 2 A.C. 31, 84, H.L. For the facts of the case see above, p. 86.

[8] [1972] A.C. 441, 498, H.L. For the facts of the case see above, p. 75.

[9] 123 N.E. 2d 792 (N.Y., 1954).

[10] For a discussion of the distinction between "sales" and "services" and the warranties implied in the latter, see below, pp. 119–121.

treating the blood . . . so that the danger may be eliminated".[11] The danger was, in other words, scientifically undiscoverable. This consideration did not, however, prevent the Supreme Court of Illinois from imposing liability under the strict tort theory in a later hepatitis case.[12] In the judgment of the court:[13]

> "To allow a defense to strict liability on the ground that there is no way, either practical or theoretical, for a defendant to ascertain the existence of impurities in his product would be to emasculate the doctrine and in a very real sense would signal a return to a negligence theory."

Although there is support for this view,[14] many states decline to impose liability under strict tort or warranty theories in blood transfusion cases.[15] There is also widespread statutory protection operating in favour of hospitals and blood banks.[16]

Whilst it seems difficult to argue that contaminated blood is neither unfit for its purpose nor defective,[17] drug cases add a further dimension to the problem in that, without being contaminated, drugs may combine with some other factor to produce a reaction which is predictable in general terms though not in the individual case. The risk of brain damage from the whooping cough vaccine (pertussis) seems to fall into this category. Here

---

[11] 123 N.E. 2d 792, 795, (N.Y., 1954).

[12] *Cunningham* v. *MacNeal Memorial Hospital*, 266 N.E. 2d 897 (Ill., 1970).

[13] *Ibid.*, at p. 902.

[14] See, e.g., *Rostocki* v. *Southwest Fla. Blood Bank Inc.*, 276 So. 2d 475 (Fla., 1973).

[15] The result may be acceptable but the reasoning is sometimes strained. Thus in *Shepard* v. *Alexian Brothers Hospital Inc.*, 109 Cal Rptr. 132 (1973), a California Court of Appeal fell back on the "service" rather than a "sale" argument, holding both the strict tort theory and the sales warranties to be inapplicable. See also *Brody* v. *Overlook Hospital*, 317 A. 2d 392 (N.J. 1974) (unavoidably unsafe product under Restatement, *Torts*, 2d, s. 402A, Comment (k)); *Hines* v. *St Joseph's Hospital*, 527 P. 2d 1075 (N.M., 1974); *Balkowitsch* v. *Minneapolis War Memorial Blood Bank*, 132 N.W. 2d 805 (Minn., 1965). For more general discussion see Nordstrom, *Sales*, s. 80, Byrne, 57 Marquette Law Rev. 660 (1974).

[16] In the aftermath of the *Cunningham* case, above, note 12, the Illinois State legislature adopted a statute exempting from liability in the absence of negligence or wilful misconduct. By 1972 similar statutes had been passed in some forty-one states: see *McDaniel* v. *Baptist Memorial Hospital*, 469 F. 2d 230, 234 (6th Cir., 1972). Trichinosis-infected pork has given rise to similar problems of scientifically undiscoverable dangers. The problem can be partly avoided on the ground that pork should not be eaten raw. But this should not theoretically affect the breach of warranty issue if, e.g., a commercial buyer were rejecting a consignment: see *Williston on Sales*, revd. edn., para. 243a and cases there cited. For discussion of abnormal use see below, pp. 294–295.

[17] Although the "unavoidably unsafe" exception of Restatement, *Torts, s. 402A, Comment (k) has been called in aid it hardly seems apt to cover such unintended conditions which are akin to miscarriages in the production process. For the meaning of a "defect" see Traynor, "The Ways and Meanings of Defective Products and Strict Liability", 32 Tenn. L.R. 363 (1965); Keeton, "Products Liability: liability without fault and the requirement of a defect", 41 Tex. L.R. 855 (1963) and below, pp. 186–189.

the product is more likely to be regarded as satisfying the standards demanded by sales legislation and the law of tort provided, at least, that any appropriate warning has been issued.[18] Further control factors may be called in aid. For example, the plaintiff may be regarded as an allergic user.[19]

Somewhat different problems are likely to be caused by products with carcinogenic properties or which otherwise carry a long-term health hazard. With cigarettes, for example, the retail sources and the brands smoked are likely to be many and varied. Hence there will be problems of causation and of pinpointing a particular defendant in addition to the problem of establishing that the product is unmerchantable or defective.[20] More fundamental, however, is the question of whether liability should, in any event, be imposed in respect of risks which may well have been scientifically unforeseeable at the time the product was marketed. Such risks, unlike those which are statistically predictable though random in their incidence, cannot be covered by insurance. Nor can a fund be accumulated to guard against their financial consequences. Hence compensation can be justified only under a theory of enterprise liability which "shifts" yet does not "spread" the loss.[1] It is a curious paradox of English law that any such liability is likely to be contractual and thus visited, at least in the first instance, on the retail vendor rather than the manufacturer.

The right to reject

Rejection, rescission and repudiation

An important characteristic of the terms implied by ss. 13 and 14 of the Sale of Goods Act 1893 is that being conditions their breach will *prima facie* entitle the buyer to reject the goods.[2] Rejection for breach of condition or

---

[18] Warnings and directions for use are discussed below, ch. 12.
[19] See above, pp. 106–107, below, pp. 324–326.
[20] Cigarettes are discussed below, pp. 216–217. Leading cases include *Pritchard* v. *Liggett and Myers Tobacco Co.,* 350 F. 2d 479 (3rd Cir., 1965); *Green* v. *American Tobacco Co.,* 304, F. 2d 70 (5th Cir., 1962), 154 So. 2d 169 (Fla., 1963), 325 F. 2d 673 (1963), 391 F. 2d 97 (1968), 409 F. 2d 1166 (1969); *Lartique* v. *R. J. Reynolds Tobacco Co.,* 317 F. 2d 19 (5th Cir., 1963); *Ross* v. *Phillip Morris & Co.,* 328 F. 2d 3 (8th Cir., 1964).
[1] For discussion of this and related points see Blum and Kalven, *Public Law Perspectives on a Private Law Problem* (1965); Calabresi, *The Costs of Accidents: a legal and economic analysis* (1970); Fleming, James, "The Untoward Effects of Cigarettes and Drugs: some reflections on enterprise liability", 54 Cal. L.R. 1550 (1966); Calabresi, "Some Thoughts on Risk Distribution and the Law of Torts", 70 Yale L.J. 499 (1961); "The Decision for Accidents: an approach to non-fault allocation of costs", 78 Harv. L. Rev. 713 (1965); Morris, "Enterprise Liability and the Actuarial Process: the insignificance of foresight", 70 Yale L.J. 554 (1961).
[2] The same is of course true of express conditions: see, e.g., *Bannerman* v. *White* (1861), 10 C.B.N.S. 844.

for breach of some other stipulation going to the root of the contract[3] has much in common with the equitable remedy of rescission for misrepresentation discussed in an earlier chapter.[4] The two remedies should, however, be kept distinct. Rescission for misrepresentation presupposes the disowning of the contract and an accompanying claim for damages for breach of contract is inapposite.[5] Rejection for breach of condition is a different matter since the buyer is not disowning the contract but is simply rejecting the performance as tendered. Hence rejection may be accompanied by a claim for damages for breach of contract. Alternatively the buyer may pursue a restitutionary or quasi-contractual remedy and recover the contract price if this has been paid in advance.[6] Some authorities suggest that rejection of the tendered performance does not constitute such a repudiation of the contract as would preclude the seller from substituting a conforming tender or curing the defect within the contract period.[7] The point is, however, far from clear. Unlike the Uniform Commercial Code,[8] the Sale of Goods Act 1893 does not grant this right expressly. Indeed it seems, rather, tacitly to assume that there is no such right.[9]

The loss of the right to reject

By s. 11 (1) (c) of the Sale of Goods Act 1893 the right to reject is lost once the buyer has accepted the goods unless there is a term of the contract to the contrary effect.[10] The former provision whereby the right was also lost through the passing of title where there was an unconditional contract for

---

[3] *Hong Kong Fir Shipping Co., Ltd.* v. *Kawasaki Kisen Kaisha, Ltd.*, [1962] 2 Q.B. 26; [1962] 1 All E.R. 474; *Cehave N.V.* v. *Bremer Handelsgesellschaft m.b.H.*, [1976] Q.B. 44; [1975] 3 All E.R. 739, C.A.

[4] See above, pp. 49–53.

[5] Equity will, however, grant an indemnity in respect of losses necessarily incurred: see *Newbigging* v. *Adam* (1886), 34 Ch. D. 582; *Whittington* v. *Seale-Hayne* (1900), 82 L.T. 49. And damages may be granted under the Misrepresentation Act 1967, s. 2.

[6] See *Benjamin's Sale of Goods* (1974), para. 895; Cheshire and Fifoot, *Law of Contract*, 9th edn., 1976, pp. 648–650.

[7] See *Borrowman, Phillips & Co.* v. *Free and Hollis* (1878), 4 Q.B.D. 500, C.A.; *Ashmore & Son* v. *C. S. Cox & Co.*, [1899] 1 Q.B. 436, 440 (Lord Russell, C.J.); *E. E. and Brian Smith (1928), Ltd.* v. *Wheatsheaf Mills, Ltd.*, [1939] 2 K.B. 302, 314–315 (Branson, J.). See also Devlin [1966] C.L.J. 192, 194; *Benjamin's Sale of Goods* (1974), para. 877.

[8] See U.C.C. art. 2–508.

[9] Thus s. 11 (1) (b) (c) equates rejection with repudiation.

[10] Section 11 (1) (c) provides as follows: "Where a contract of sale is not severable, and the buyer has accepted the goods, or part thereof, the breach of any condition to be fulfilled by the seller can only be treated as a breach of warranty, and not as a ground for rejecting the goods and treating the contract as repudiated, unless there be a term of the contract, express or implied, to that effect". For the position where the contract of sale is severable, see Atiyah, *Sale of Goods*, 5th edn., 1975, pp. 285–286, 297–300.

the sale of specific goods in a deliverable state has been repealed.[11] The crucial concept is now that of acceptance and here s. 35 of the 1893 Act, as amended by the Misrepresentation Act 1967, s. 4(2), provides that:

> "The buyer is deemed to have accepted the goods when he intimates to the seller that he has accepted them, or (except when section 34 of this Act otherwise provides) when the goods have been delivered to him, and he does any act in relation to them which is inconsistent with the ownership of the seller, or when after the lapse of a reasonable time, he retains the goods without intimating to the seller that he has rejected them."

Acceptance may accordingly occur in any one of three ways. Firstly, there may be an express and unequivocal intimation that the goods have been accepted.[12] Secondly, the buyer may indicate acceptance through acting in a way which is consistent only with there having been an unconditional transfer of title to him. For example, he might resell and deliver the goods to a sub-buyer[13] or register a car in his own name.[14] Here the effect of the paranthetic reference to s. 34 of the Act is that such acts will be deemed to constitute acceptance only if the buyer has had a reasonable opportunity of examining the goods for the purpose of ascertaining whether they are in conformity with the contract.[15] Thirdly, acceptance may occur through the buyer failing to reject the goods after the lapse of a reasonable period of time. It is unclear whether the reference to s. 34 applies to the third limb of s. 35 as well as to the second.[16] The point would rarely be of practical importance since the buyer who fails to reject timeously would normally have had a reasonable opportunity of examining the goods.

These rules are not easy to apply to latent defects and it is in such cases that an entitlement to reject is most likely to accrue. The place of delivery is *prima facie* the place for examination,[17] but where mer-

---

[11] This part of s. 11 (1) (*c*) was repealed by the Misrepresentation Act 1967, s. 4(1).

[12] See *Mechans, Ltd.* v. *Highland Marine Charters, Ltd.*, 1964 S.C. 48. *Varley* v. *Whipp*, [1900] 1 Q.B. 513, above, p. 72 was a case in which a communication constituted neither a rejection nor an acceptance.

[13] See *Chapmsn* v. *Morton* (1843), 11 M. & W. 534; *Hardy* v. *Hillerns and Fowler*, [1923] 2 K.B. 490, C.A.; *E. and S. Ruben* v. *Faire Brothers & Co., Ltd.*, [1949] 1 K.B. 254; [1949] 1 All E.R. 215.

[14] *Armaghdown Motors, Ltd.* v. *Gray Motors, Ltd.*, [1963] N.Z.L.R. 5.

[15] Thus reversing the decision in *Hardy* v. *Hillerns and Fowler*, [1923] 2 K.B. 490, C.A., where it was held that s. 35 was not limited by s. 34.

[16] *Cf.* Atiyah and Treitel (1967), 30 M.L.R. 369, 385–387, where it is suggested that it might do so.

[17] See *Perkins* v. *Bell* [1893] 1 Q.B. 193; *Taylor* v. *Combined Buyers, Ltd.*, [1924] N.Z. Gazette L.R. 51, 64 (Salmond, J.); *Heilbutt* v. *Hickson* (1872), L.R. 7 C.P. 438 (shoes for the French army: *prima facie* rule displaced); and, in general, *Benjamin's Sale of Goods* (1974), para. 874.

chantability (or representations as to performance or suitability) can be verified only by using the goods such use should not, of itself, preclude rejection.[18] Rejection is, however, unlikely to be permitted where goods have been used over an extended period, or where there has been a significant deterioration in their condition whether through wear and tear or for some other reason not immediately attributable to their defective condition.[19] Hence to the extent that merchantability imports a requirement of durability it is likely to be vindicated only by a claim for damages.[20] Similar considerations apply to the implied condition of reasonable fitness for purpose.[1] This will not normally lead to injustice since a benefit will have been received (albeit at the expense of inconvenience) and it will be impossible to return the goods in their original condition.[2] Where there is no deterioration in use the advantages to be gained from finalising transactions may still dictate that the defect or deficiency be discovered expeditiously if the right of rejection is not to lapse. In *Leaf* v. *International Galleries*[3] five years was certainly far too long a period to discover the falsity of an alleged representation or condition that a painting *Salisbury Cathedral* was attributable to Constable. Indeed Denning, L.J. suggested that this should have been done within the first few days of the sale.[4] Yet much will depend on the circumstances of the individual case. A buyer of cases of vintage wine may well retain the right of rejection if the bottles prove to be unmerchantable when opened five years later.

There must be many cases in which buyers delay rejection by seeking or acquiescing in the attempted repair of defective goods, whether by the seller or by the manufacturer. Indeed they may be persuaded to do so by the seller's assurances that faults will be eradicated and teething troubles overcome. The effect on the right of rejection is not entirely clear. On one

---

[18] Neither should consumption of the goods in so far as it is directed to testing for merchantability or suitability: see *Lucy* v. *Mouflet* (1860), 5 H. & N. 229 (cider); *cf. Harnor* v. *Groves* (1855), 15 C.B. 667 (flour: excessive use). See also *Long* v. *Lloyd*, [1958] 2 All E.R. 402, 407, C.A. where it was noted that this might have been true of representations that a lorry could do 40 m.p.h. and 11 m.p.g.

[19] See, e.g., *Long* v. *Lloyd*, [1958] 2 All E.R. 402; [1958] 1 W.L.R. 753; *Taylor* v. *Combined Buyers, Ltd.*, [1924] N.Z. Gazette L.R. 51 (car); *Diamond* v. *British Columbia Thoroughbred Breeders' Society* (1966), 52 D.L.R. (2d) 146 (B.C. Sup. Ct.) (racehorse).

[20] See above, pp. 91–93.

[1] As in *Jones* v. *Bright* (1829), 5 Bing, 533, above, p. 98 (implied term that copper was fit for sheathing a ship). See also the observations of Salmond, J. in *Taylor* v. *Combined Buyers, Ltd.*, [1924] N.Z. Gazette L.R. 51, 64; [1924] N.Z.L.R. 627.

[2] The point is linked to the quasi-contractual nature of the action to recover the contract price and the requirement that there be a total failure of consideration. *Cf.*, however, *Rowland* v. *Divall*, [1923] 2 K.B. 500, C.A., for the position where the seller is in breach of the implied condition as to title under s. 12 of the Act.

[3] [1950] 2 K.B. 86; [1950] 1 All E.R. 693, C.A.

[4] *Ibid.*, at pp. 90–91.

view it might be said that this is tantamount to an election to accept the goods and to be content with a claim for damages should the repair prove ineffective. Thus in *Long* v. *Lloyd*[5] the Court of Appeal found the buyer's agreement to a proposal that the seller should pay half the cost of a replacement dynamo for the defective lorry "difficult to reconcile with the continuance of any right of rescission".[6] In the result it was unnecessary to decide the point. The lorry was used the following day with full knowledge of its deficiencies to take a four ton load from Sevenoaks to Middlesborough and this was held to be a final acceptance.

A different view was taken in *Farnworth Finance Facilities* v. *Attryde*[7] where the Court of Appeal permitted the repudiation of a contract for the hire purchase of a new motor cycle although it had been used for some four months to travel four thousand miles. The machine had been sent back to the manufacturers for repair and the defendant had complained persistently about an accumulation of defects which was held to constitute a fundamental breach of contract. In the circumstances he was taken not to have affirmed the contract. The decision cannot be applied directly to cases of sale although there is clearly a close parallel between affirmation of hire purchase contracts and the acceptance of goods.[8] As a matter of policy there is no reason why a buyer should lose his right to reject by giving the seller an opportunity to repair. The arrangement is often convenient to both parties and acceptance may be viewed as conditional on such repairs or adjustments being effective. This approach has been adopted in a number of Canadian decisions involving so-called fundamental breaches of contract.[9]

The Uniform Commercial Code reaches the same conclusion through a different approach. Under art. 2–608 (1) of the Code the buyer may revoke his acceptance where non-conformity substantially impairs the value of the goods and he has accepted,

"(*a*) on the reasonable assumption that its non-conformity would be cured and it has not been seasonably cured: or

(*b*) without discovery of such non-conformity if his acceptance was reasonably

---

[5] [1958] 2 All E.R. 402, C.A.

[6] *Ibid.,* at p. 408.

[7] [1970] 2 All E.R. 774; [1970] 1 W.L.R. 1053, C.A.

[8] Hire purchase legislation does not have an equivalent of ss. 11, 34 and 35 of the 1893 Act and the Supply of Goods (Implied Terms) Act 1973, s. 14, states expressly that s. 11 (1) (*c*) of the 1893 Act does not apply to conditional consumer sales. For the effect of continuing to pay instalments see *Yeoman Credit, Ltd.* v. *Apps,* [1962] 2 Q.B. 508; [1961] 2 All E.R. 281.

[9] See, e.g., *Burroughs Business Machines, Ltd.* v. *Feed-Rite Mills (1962), Ltd.* (1973), 42 D.L.R. (3d) 303 (Man. C.A.) (computer system); *Barker* v. *Inland Truck Sales* (1970), 11 D.L.R. (3d) 469 (B.C. Sup. Ct.) (truck with defective brakes); *Lightburn* v. *Belmont Sales, Ltd.* (1969), 6 D.L.R. (3d) 692 (B.C. Sup. Ct.) (car needing constant repair and servicing).

induced either by the difficulty of discovery before acceptance or by the seller's assurances."[10]

Such revocation must occur within a reasonable time of acquiring actual or constructive knowledge of the deficiency and before there has been any substantial change in the condition of the goods.[11] Whether the difficulty of discovering latent defects should be a sufficient reason for postponing the finality of acceptance may be doubted. The other provisions represent a sensible balance between the need to finalise transactions and the need to protect a buyer who wishes to reject defective goods.

Transactions other than contracts of sale and hire purchase[12]

Goods are frequently supplied on a commercial or quasi-commercial basis under transactions which are not covered by the provisions of the Sale of Goods Act 1893, as amended.[13] For example, they may be supplied as "free" samples or as prizes in competitions, or under a contract of exchange, for work and materials, a contract involving the rendering of a service, or of hire. In such circumstances the supplier will be subject to obligations under the law of tort and these will be examined later.[14] Basically, however, the English law of tort demands only that reasonable care be exercised, though in a growing number of American states commercial suppliers of goods have been subjected to strict tort liability.[15] Stipulations similar to ss. 13 and 14 of the Sale of Goods Act may also be implied under any relevant contract and in such cases liability may be strict.

Near sales transactions and promotional gifts

When an intending purchaser of goods is injured before the conclusion of

---

[10] Cases of general importance include *Zabriskie Chevrolet Inc.* v. *Smith* 240 A. 2d 195 (N.J., 1968); *Rozmus* v. *Thompson's Lincoln Mercury Co.,* 224 A. 2d 782 (Pa., 1966). For commentary, see Peters, "Right to Discontinue Contracts under the Code", 73 Yale L.J. 199 (1968). In *Mechan & Sons, Ltd.* v. *Bow*, 1910 S.C. 758, 763. Lord Salvensen suggested *obiter* that acceptance might be revoked where the defect was undiscoverable on delivery.

[11] Article 2–608 (2).

[12] See *Benjamin's Sale of Goods* (1974), paras. 24 *et. seq.;* Atiyah, *Sale of Goods*, 5th edn., 1975, pp. 3–17; Greig, *Sale of Goods*, pp. 5–12; Waddams, "Strict Liability, Warranties and the Sale of Goods" (1969), 19 Univ. Toronto L.J. 157.

[13] The Act as amended by the Supply of Goods (Implied Terms) Act 1973, s. 16 also covers goods supplied on the redemption of trading stamps.

[14] See below, ch. 15.

[15] See, e.g., *Vandermark* v. *Ford Motor Co.,* 37 Cal. Rptr. 896 (Sup. Ct. California, 1964) (retailer); *Cintrone* v. *Hertz Truck Leasing and Rental Service,* 212 A. 2d 769 (N.J., 1965) (hirer-out).

the contract of sale his remedy will be in tort alone. This would be true, for example, of a customer who is injured by an exploding bottle which he is taking off a supermarket shelf.[16] There is no obvious reason why such a customer should be treated differently according to whether he has taken the goods through the check out point. The result stems from a combination of the rules for the formation of contracts in English law,[17] the extension of strict contractual liability to include consequential losses[18] and the present requirement of proof of negligence in tort.[19]

In other situations it may be possible to construct a contract between the parties. However, this will be a contract of sale attracting the implied conditions of the 1893 Act only where the buyer has furnished a *monetary* consideration.[20] Such consideration may be nominal but it must exist. There should be little difficulty where a contract of sale exists and additional goods of the same type have been supplied as part of a "bargain offer". On a "three for the price of two" arrangement the third unit (no less than the second) would constitute goods supplied under the contract of sale for the purpose of s. 14 of the 1893 Act.[1] Where goods of a different type are supplied as part of a linked arrangement (for example, a World Cup coin for every four gallons of petrol purchased) any contract in relation to them is unlikely to be a contract of sale.[2] The same would seem to be true of cases where drugs are supplied by a chemist under the National Health Service[3] or where goods are supplied in return for coupons or wrappers,[4] as prizes in competitions, or against a credit card such as

---

[16] As in *Lasky* v. *Economy Grocery Stores*, 65 N.E. 2d 305 (Mass., 1946). See also *Hart* v. *Dominion Stores* (1968), 67 D.L.R. (2d) 675 (Ont. High Ct.) where there was a successful action in tort against the bottler.

[17] See *Pharmaceutical Society of Great Britain* v. *Boots*, [1953] 1 Q.B. 401; [1953] 1 All E.R. 482. *Cf. Gillespie* v. *Great Atlantic and Pacific Tea Co.*, 187 S.E. (2d) 441 (N.C., 1972) (exploding bottle: sale had occurred although plaintiff had not reached the check-out point).

[18] *Randall* v. *Newson* (1877), 2 Q.B.D. 102 above, p. 5, was an early case.

[19] See below, ch. 13.

[20] Sale of Goods Act 1893, s. 1 (1). The equivalent provision in U.C.C. art. 2–304 (1) does not contain the same limitation.

[1] See *Fillmore's Valley Nurseries, Ltd.* v. *North American Cyanamid, Ltd.* (1958), 14 D.L.R. (2d) 297, 304 (Nova Scotia S.C.), above, p. 56, where Ilsley, C.J. found that "this arrangement was that the defendant would supply 33 lbs. [of herbicide] for the price of 25" and no distinction was taken as to the additional 8 lbs. For the Sale of Goods Act 1893, s. 14, see above, pp. 78–107, at p. 82 especially.

[2] See *Esso Petroleum, Ltd.* v. *Customs and Excise Commissioner*, [1976] 1 All E.R. 117, H.L.

[3] *Appleby* v. *Sleep*, [1968] 2 All E.R. 265, 269 *per* Lord Parker, C.J. See also *Pfizer Corporation* v. *Ministry of Health*, [1965] A.C. 512; [1965] 1 All E.R. 450.

[4] As in *Chappell & Co., Ltd.* v. *Nestle Co., Ltd.*, [1960] A.C. 87; [1959] 2 All E.R. 701, H.L. The position is different where there is *some* monetary consideration: see, e.g., *Buckley* v. *Lever Brothers*, [1953] 4 D.L.R. 16 (Ont. High Ct.) (apron and twelve plastic clothes-pegs in return for two soap-box tops and fifty cents. A peg broke, putting out the plaintiff's eye).

Access or Barclaycard.[5] In such cases qualitative stipulations analogous to those contained in the Sale of Goods Act 1893 might readily be implied. But the transaction would not seem to fall under the 1893 Act as such since the buyer would not have acquired the goods "for a money consideration, called the price".[6] Consequently any such stipulations might be excluded.[7] Where goods are available in retail outlets as "free" promotional samples or where they are supplied directly to householders without any prior request there can be no contractual liability at all. Any liability would be in tort and in English law this would require proof, at least, of negligence.[8]

Contracts of exchange

Similar difficulties might arise in distinguishing between contracts of sale and contracts of exchange. A simple agreement to exchange one product for another would not be a contract of sale in English law but relatively few commercial transactions would take this form.[9] In the typical transaction, involving perhaps the "trading-in" of a car, a value is placed on the goods and an appropriate monetary adjustment made. There is no difficulty in regarding such transactions as reciprocal contracts of sale and it seems clear that they are so regarded in practice.[10] As such they would attract the implied conditions of the 1893 Act. It is unclear whether similar conditions might be implied in a contract of exchange, but there is no reason in principle why they should not. The point might be important when, for example, a manufacturer agrees to replace defective goods "free of charge".

Contracts for work and materials

There is no hard and fast distinction between a contract for the sale of goods and a contract for work and materials. An agreement between a

---

[5] Notwithstanding the Consumer Credit Act 1974, s. 75. I am grateful to my colleague Michael Bridge for drawing my attention to some of the difficulties caused by these tripartite arrangements.

[6] Sale of Goods Act 1893, s. 1 (1).

[7] Proposals for reform are contained in the Law Commission's "Second Report on Exemption Clauses", Law Com. No. 69, August 1975. See also Hansard, H.C. Debs. Vol. 914, col. 377 (W.A.), 5 July 1976.

[8] It seems clear that a duty of care would be owed with respect to the safety of such goods: see *Hawkins* v. *Coulsdon and Purley U.D.C.*, [1954] 1 All E.R. 97, 104, *per* Denning, L.J.; *Levi* v. *Colgate Palmolive Pty., Ltd.* (1941), 41 S.R. (N.S.W.) 48; and below, pp. 308–309.

[9] See, however, the Law Commission's, "Second Report on Exemption Clauses", Law Com. No. 69, paras. 16–17, suggesting that such transactions may become more common. A number of recent Scottish cases is cited: see, e.g., *Widenmeyer* v. *Burn Stewart & Co.*, 1967 S.C. 85.

[10] See G. J. *Dawson (Clapham), Ltd.* v. *H. and G. Dutfield*, [1936] 2 All E.R. 232; *Commission Car Sales (Hastings), Ltd.* v. *Saul*, [1957] N.Z.L.R. 144; *Aldridge* v. *Johnson* (1857), 7 E. & B. 885; Atiyah, *Sale of Goods*, 8th edn., 1975, pp. 5–6. There is more difficulty where the price allowed on the "trade-in" is the same as the price "paid" for the replacement: but see *Davey* v. *Paine Brothers, Ltd.*, [1954] N.Z.L.R. 1122.

dentist and a patient for the supply of two sets of false teeth has been held to be a contract of sale[11] and there is no doubt that contracts for tailor-made suits and shirts are so classified.[12] On the other hand, a commission to paint a portrait has been held to be a contract for work and materials on the ground that the materials used were of no importance when compared with the skill of the artist.[13] Similar difficulties occur when a contractor supplies goods and then installs or fits them. Such an agreement may be regarded as a contract for work and materials or as a sale coupled with a contract to install. Much is likely to depend on the relative importance and difficulty of the element of installation. So agreements to fit brake linings and connecting rods to cars,[14] and to install a built-in cocktail cabinet,[15] lift,[16] central heating system[17] and burglar-proof doors[18] on premises have all been regarded as contracts for work and materials. Yet the supply and fitting of carpets and of a domestic oil heater have been regarded as contracts of sale[19] as has the making of propellers to order for a particular ship.[20]

The distinction between contracts for work and materials and contracts of sale is rendered less important by the willingness of the courts to imply qualitative terms in the former contracts.[1] Such terms would not be implied in all cases and need not necessarily be identical to the implied terms of the Sale of Goods Act 1893.[2] But it has been said that "the larger the element of supply of particular goods in the contract, the closer should be the

---

[11] *Lee* v. *Griffin* (1861), 1 B. & S. 272. See also *Samuels* v. *Davis*, [1943] 2 All E.R. 3, C.A. The classification is perhaps surprising. *Cf. Texas State Optical Inc.* v. *Barbee*, 417 S.W. 2d 750 (Tex. Civ. App., 1967) (contact lenses); *Cox* v. *Cartwright*, 121 N.E. 2d 673 (Ohio, 1953) (denture) and, in general, Waddams (1969) 19 Univ. Toronto L.J. 157, 176–177.

[12] See *Grafton* v. *Armitage* (1845), 2 C.B. 336, 341 *per* Coltman, J.

[13] *Robinson* v. *Graves*, [1935] 1 K.B. 579.

[14] *Stewart* v. *Reavell's Garage*, [1952] 2 Q.B. 545 (brake linings); *G. H. Myers and Co.* v. *Brent Cross Service Co.*, [1934] 1 K.B. 46 (connecting rods).

[15] *Brooks Robinson Pty., Ltd.* v. *Rothfield*, [1951] V.L.R. 405 (Vict. Sup. Ct.).

[16] *Sydney Hydraulic and General Engineering Co.* v. *Blackwood and Son* (1908), 8 S.R. N.S.W. 10 (N.S.W. District C.A.).

[17] *Aced* v. *Hobbs-Sesack Plumbing Co.*, 360 P. 2d 897 (Cal. Sup. Ct., 1961).

[18] *Reg. Glass Pty., Ltd.* v. *Rivers Locking Systems Pty., Ltd.* (1968), 42 A.L.J.R. 254 (High Ct. Australia).

[19] *Philip Head and Sons Ltd.* v. *Showfronts Ltd.*, [1970] 1 Lloyd's L.R. 140 (carpets); *Collins Trading Co. Pty., Ltd.* v. *Maher*, [1969] V.R. 20. (Vict. Sup. Ct.) (oil heater).

[20] See *Cammell Laird and Co., Ltd.* v. *Manganese Bronze and Brass Co., Ltd.*, [1934] A.C. 402. See also *J. Marcel (Furriers) Ltd.* v. *Tapper*, [1953] 1 All E.R. 15 (mink jacket made to order).

[1] It is also less important since the Law Reform (Enforcement of Contracts) Act 1954, s. 1, repealed the old Statute of Frauds requirement that contracts for the sale of goods above a certain sum be evidenced in writing etc. In later years this requirement appeared as s. 4 of the Sale of Goods Act 1893.

[2] Especially s. 14 (2) (merchantable quality), above, pp. 78–97; s. 14 (3) (reasonable fitness for purpose), above, pp. 98–107.

similarity of warranties to be implied with those arising on a sale".[3] The exclusion of such terms is not yet subject to statutory control.[4] In the leading English case of *Young and Marten, Ltd.* v. *McManus Childs, Ltd.*[5] a firm of builders had subcontracted the roofing of certain dwelling houses, stipulating that a particular make of tiles be used. A batch supplied by the sole manufacturers was defective and reroofing was necessary. The House of Lords held that a term should be implied in the contract for work and materials whereby the appellants warranted that the tiles were of good quality and not subject to latent defects. On the facts of the case they were liable for its breach. The analogy here is with the implied condition of merchantable quality of sales legislation.[6] In other cases the term implied may be one of reasonable fitness for a particular purpose.[7] Such a term was implied in an Australian case[8] involving the supplying and fitting of a steel-sheeted door intended to provide protection against burglary.[9]

Contracts for services

There may also be difficulties in distinguishing between contracts for the sale of goods and contracts for the supply of services involving the use of a product.[1] In English law the provision of food in a restaurant has been regarded as a contract of sale[2] though the point has caused some difficulty in American cases.[3] On the other hand, persons such as hairdressers or beauticians are normally thought of as providing a service to which the use

---

[3] *Young and Marten, Ltd.* v. *McManus Childs, Ltd.*, [1969] 1 A.C. 454, 476–477; [1968] 2 All E.R. 1169, 1178–1179, *per* Lord Wilberforce.

[4] For the control of exemption clauses in contracts for the sale of goods, see Sale of Goods Act 1893, s. 55, as amended by the Supply of Goods (Implied Terms) Act 1973, s. 4, below, pp. 142–158. For recommendations for controlling the exclusion of liability, see the Law Commission "Exemption Clauses: Second Report", Law Com. No. 69.

[5] [1969] 1 A.C. 454; [1968] 2 All E.R. 1169, H.L. *Cf. Gloucestershire County Council* v. *Richardson*, [1969] 1 A.C. 480; [1968] 2 All E.R. 1181.

[6] Sale of Goods Act 1893, s. 14(2), as amended, above, 78–97. See also *G. H. Myers & Co.* v. *Brent Cross Service Co.*, [1934] 1 K.B. 46.

[7] See the Sale of Goods Act 1893, s. 14(3), as amended, above, p. 98–107.

[8] *Reg. Glass Pty., Ltd.* v. *Rivers Locking Systems Pty., Ltd.* (1968), 42 A.L.J.R. 254 (High Ct. Australia). See also *Samuels* v. *Davis*, [1943] 2 All E.R. 3, C.A. (denture).

[9] *Cf. Helicopter Sales (Australia) Pty., Ltd.* v. *Rotor-Work Pty., Ltd.* (1974), 48 A.L.J.R. 390 (High Ct. of Australia) (no implied term in contract for the supply of a bolt bought in from the manufacturer. The bolt had a latent defect and this caused a helicopter to crash).

[1] See Waddams (1969), 19 Univ. Toronto L. Jo. 157, 166–180.

[2] See *Lockett* v. *A. & M. Charles Ltd.*, [1938] 4 All E.R. 170.

[3] See, e.g., *Nisky* v. *Childs Co.*, 50 A.L.R. 227 (N.J., 1927); *Dickens* v. *Horn Baking Co.* 209 A. 2d 169 (Del., 1965). U.C.C. art. 2–314(1) now provides that for the purposes of the code "the serving for value of food or drink to be consumed either on the premises or elsewhere is a sale".

of a product such as a hair dye or permanent wave solution would be incidental. They are nonetheless frequently subject to implied warranties similar to those of sales legislation. So in *Watson* v. *Buckley, Osborne, Garrett and Co. Ltd.*,[4] for example, where a hairdresser had applied a dye to the plaintiff's hair, Stable, J. held that the implied warranty of merchantability was "no less than it would be in the case of the sale of goods simply".[5] Some American cases have invoked similar warranties where goods have been repaired or processed.[6]

The courts have typically been more reluctant to imply warranties imposing strict liability in contracts for medical and other professional services. Here the standard obligation has been to exercise reasonable care.[7] This reluctance was seen in the American case of *Perlmutter* v. *Beth David Hospital*[8] involving the supply of contaminated blood to a private patient. Although the blood was charged separately, the New York Court of Appeals held that it had not been "sold" and further that the contract for its supply did not contain an implied warranty of fitness. More recently the New Jersey courts have declined to impose strict liability on a dentist when a hypodermic needle broke in the plaintiff's jaw.[9] These cases may be contrasted with the decision of Hallett, J. in *Dodd* v. *Wilson*.[10] The plaintiffs had engaged the services of the defendant veterinary surgeons to inoculate their cattle. The serum used was defective and the cattle became ill. The defendants were held liable for breach of an implied warranty that the serum should be reasonably fit for the purpose for which it was required. The result might, however, have been influenced by the fact that the defendants' own suppliers and manufacturers had been joined in third and fourth party proceedings, so enabling the loss to be passed down the line.[11]

Greaves and Co. (Contractors), Ltd. v. *Baynham Meikle and Partners*[12] is also in point. The plaintiff building contractors had engaged the services of the defendant consultant structural engineers to design a warehouse and had

---

[4] [1940] 1 All E.R. 174.

[5] *Ibid.*, at p. 180. See also *Newmark* v. *Gimbel's Inc.*, 258 A. 2d 697 (N.J., 1969); *cf. Epstein* v. *Giannattasio*, 197 A. 2d 342 (Conn., 1963).

[6] See, e.g., *Texas Metal Fabricating Co.* v. *Northern Gas Products Corp.*, 404 F. 2d 921 (10th Cir., 1968) (repair); *Vitromat Piece Dye Works* v. *Lawrence of London, Ltd.*, 256 N.E. 2d 135 (Ill., 1970) (processing).

[7] See *Bolam* v. *Friern Hospital Management Committee*, [1957] 2 All E.R. 118, 121 *per* McNair, J.

[8] 123 N.E. 2d 792 (N.Y., 1954), above, p. 108.

[9] *Magrine* v. *Krasnica*, 227 A. 2d 539 (1967), affd. 241 A. 2d 637 (N.J., 1968). See, in general, Note, "Liability of Design Professionals", 58 Iowa L.R. 1221 (1973).

[10] [1946] 2 All E.R. 691.

[11] See also *Samuels* v. *Davis*, [1943] 2 All E.R. 3 (warranty that dentures should be reasonably fit for their purpose).

[12] [1975] 3 All E.R. 99, C.A.

informed them that it was required for storing oil drums to be moved by fork-lift trucks. The design was not suitable for this purpose and the vibrations set up by the trucks caused serious structural damage to the premises. The defendants were held liable both in negligence and for breach of an implied warranty that the design should be fit for its intended purpose. The Court of Appeal emphasised, however, that the decision did no more than give effect to the common intention of the parties. It did not lay down any general principle whereby a professional man was taken to guarantee a satisfactory result.

Contracts of hire[13]

Products are frequently the subject of hiring agreements. These may be short term, as when a car is hired for the day, or, as often happens with television sets, they may last for the useful lifetime of the product. Goods ranging from the most simple household equipment to the most complex industrial machinery may be involved. Such contracts clearly embody implied terms broadly similar to those now enacted in sales legislation but there is some doubt as to the precise nature of the terms implied. A number of earlier cases involved the hiring of a carriage and horses[14] and of equipment to unload ships.[15] More recently in *Reed* v. *Dean*[16] the contract was for the hire of the defendant's motor launch *Golden Age* which the plaintiffs were to use for a holiday on the Thames. Some two hours after their departure a fire broke out. The fire extinguisher was out of order and the plaintiffs lost their belongings and suffered personal injuries. Holding the defendants liable for breach of contract, Lewis, J. agreed with the plaintiff's contention that:[17]

> "Where a vessel or other thing is hired there is an implied term that the vessel or thing hired shall be as fit for the purpose as reasonable care and skill can make it."

Doubts as to the application and incidence of the implied term ought strictly speaking to be resolved by reference to the common law governing contracts of hire with assistance from the common law of sale and hire

---

[13] See Turner, "Common Law Implied Terms of Fitness in Contracts of Simple Hire and Hire Purchase" (1972), 46 A.L.J. 560, 619; Davies, "Implied Conditions as to Fitness in a Contract of Hire" (1964), 38 A.L.J. 277.

[14] *Fowler* v. *Lock* (1872), L.R.7 C.P. 272; *Hyman* v. *Nye* (1881), 6 Q.B.D. 685.

[15] *Mowbray* v. *Merryweather*, [1895] 2 Q.B. 640, C.A.

[16] [1949] 1 K.B. 188.

[17] *Ibid.*, at p. 193.

purchase.[18] In practice, however, the courts may assimilate the various contracts by looking to the statutory developments of the law of sale and hire-purchase.[19] Terms may clearly be implied in contracts for the hire of specific goods[20] but it is less clear whether they will be implied only where the defendant has hired the goods out in the ordinary course of his business.[1] Again there is some doubt as to the necessity of establishing reliance on the part of the hirer[2] and it is unsettled whether the term implied is that the goods are in fact fit for the hirer's purpose or simply that they are as fit as reasonable care and skill can make them.[3] The point would be important where the defects were latent and undiscoverable. Whatever the precise scope and nature of the term the ability to exclude it by an appropriate exemption clause is not presently subject to statutory control.[4]

---

[18] See *Becker* v. *Derbyshire Building Co. Pty. Ltd.* (1961), 78 W.N. (N.S.W.) 813 (N.S.W. Full Sup. Ct.); affd. (1962), 107 C.L.R. 633 (High Ct. Australia). See Turner (1972) 46 A.L.J. 619, 620–624.

[19] In particular ss. 13, 14 of the Sale of Goods Act 1893, as amended by the Supply of Goods (Implied Terms) Act 1973, ss. 2, 3 and the equivalent provisions for hire purchase agreements in ss. 9 and 10 of the 1973 Act and the Consumer Credit Act 1974, s. 192, Sch. 4, para. 35.

[20] *Reed* v. *Dean*, [1949] 1 K.B. 188; *Jones* v. *Page* (1867), 15 L.T. (N.S.) 619.

[1] The older cases such as *Hyman* v. *Nye* (1881), 6 Q.B.D. 685 involved defendants who would have satisfied such a requirement. See also *Star Express Merchandising Co. Pty. Ltd.* v. *V. G. McGrath Pty. Ltd.*, [1959] V.R. 443 (Vict. Sup. Ct.); *Pampris* v. *Thanos* (1967), 69 S.R. (N.S.W.) 226 (N.S.W.C.A.). See also above, pp. 80–81 for the position in contracts of sale.

[2] *Semble* that the onus may be on the supplier to negative a reasonable inference of reliance: see *Star Express Merchandising Co. Pty. Ltd.* v. *V. G. McGrath Pty. Ltd.*, [1959] V.R. 443, 446 *per* Dean, J.

[3] The English cases seem to favour the latter: see, e.g., *Reed* v. *Dean*, [1949] 1 K.B. 188, 193, *per* Lewis, J., above, p. 121; *Hyman* v. *Nye* (1881), 6 Q.B.D. 685, 687–688 *per* Lindley, J. *Hadley* v. *Droitwich Construction Co. Ltd.* (1967) 3 K.I.R. 578, 585 *per* Sellers, L.J. But see *White* v. *John Warrick & Co., Ltd.*, [1953] 2 All E.R. 1021, 1025 *per* Denning, L.J. For contrasting Australian authority, see *Gemmell Power Farming Co., Ltd.* v. *Nies* (1935), 35 S.R. (N.S.W.) 469, 475, *per* Jordan, C.J.; and cases cited by Turner (1972) 46 A.L.J. 560, 564. See also *Astley Industrial Trust Ltd.* v. *Grimley*, [1963] 2 All E.R. 33, C.A.

[4] The Law Commission has published proposals recommending statutory control: see "Exemption Clauses, Second Report", Law Com. No. 69 (1975). For exemption clauses generally, see below, chs. 7 and 8.

7 Exemption Clauses: I

Introduction[1]

Parties to contracts frequently seek to exclude or modify the liabilities and remedies which would otherwise arise through breach of the express and implied terms discussed in earlier chapters. Such exemption or exclusion clauses may take a variety of forms. For example, there may be a simple statement that the goods are sold as is, or with all faults; or the clause may be exhaustively comprehensive. Similarly there may be an attempt to place a time limit on claims, to circumscribe the ability to reject defective goods, or to substitute lesser obligations for those which would arise under the general law. There is nothing inherently objectionable in this where the parties are bargaining on an equal footing and the contract is the result of a genuine agreement between them. In principle commercial men ought to be free to decide on the allocation of risks (and so of insurance cover) under their contract. They are unlikely to approve of well-meaning attempts to override the effect of their bargain.[2]

In many cases, however, there will be no semblance of genuine agreement or of equality of bargaining power between the parties. The terms of the contract will be in standard form and the consumer will have no meaningful opportunity to modify them or to obtain more favourable conditions elsewhere. The main targets for exemption clauses in standard form contracts are the duties created by the courts through the medium

---

[1] Coote, *Exception Clauses* (1964); Waddams, *Products Liability* (1974) ch. 7; *Benjamin's Sale of Goods* (1974) ch. 13; Atiyah, *Sale of Goods*, 5th edn. 1975 ch. 14; Sutton, *Sale of Goods* 2nd edn. (1974) ch. 23; Greig, *Sale of Goods*, pp. 224–246; Law Commission, *Exemption Clauses in Contracts, First Report*, Law Com. No. 24 (1969); Law Commission, *Exemption Clauses, Second Report*, Law Com. No. 69 (1975); Ontario Law Reform Commission, *Report on Consumer Warranties and Guarantees in the Sale of Goods* (1972), ch. 3.
[2] Thus it is well known that the decision in *Harbutt's Plasticine, Ltd.* v. *Wayne Tank and Pump Co., Ltd.*, [1970] 1 Q.B. 447; [1970] 1 All E.R. 225 was met with widespread disapproval by insurers.

of the implied term. Hence it is hardly surprising that the courts have themselves developed a number of techniques to control the effectiveness of such clauses. In particular the clause must be shown to have been properly incorporated into the contract and to be applicable when construed *contra proferentem* and on the assumption that it was intended to be consistent with the contract's fundamental obligations. Thus far English courts have stopped short of striking down an exemption clause on the broad ground that it was unconscionable at common law.[3] A general doctrine of unconscionability has however been developed in the United States of America[4] and it is also appearing in other areas of English law.[5]

All these common law techniques retain their general importance. Indeed they are still of crucial importance in some product liability cases, as where defective goods have been supplied under a contract of hire or a contract for work and materials.[6] Further reference will be made to them below.[7] But the modern tendency is undoubtedly to supplement common law controls by statutory provisions. These may take a number of forms. Some sanction the continued use of exemption clauses but require compliance with a general standard of reasonableness or its equivalent. The standard may be applied *ex post facto* by the courts,[8] or through the prior vetting of some agency.[9] The legislature may or may not spell out the factors to be taken into account in determining whether it has been met. Alternatively exemption clauses may be banned altogether in circumstances which are defined by reference to the status of the parties or some other criterion.[10] Finally, statutory provisions might take a somewhat more positive line and extend the traditional implied conditions of merchan-

---

[3] See, however, the suggestions of Lord Denning, M.R. in *Gillespie Brothers Ltd.* v. *Roy Bowles Ltd.*, [1973] 1 All E.R. 193, 200, C.A.

[4] Both at common law or in equity (see *Campbell Soup Co.* v. *Wentz*, 172 F. 2d 80 (3rd Cir., 1948) and now under U.C.C., Art. 2–302.

[5] See, e.g., *A. Schroeder Music Publishing Co., Ltd.* v. *Macaulay*, [1974] 3 All E.R. 616; [1974] 1 W.L.R. 1308 and below, pp. 137–140.

[6] For the Law Commission proposals for dealing with contracts falling outside the Sale of Goods Act 1893 and the Supply of Goods (Implied Terms) Act, 1973, see *Exemption Clauses, Second Report*, Law Com. No. 69 (1975). Early implementation of these proposals is likely: see Hansard, H.C. Deb. Vol. 914, col. 377 (W.A.), 5 July 1976.

[7] At pp. 125–137.

[8] See, e.g., the Misrepresentation Act 1967, s. 3 and the provisions for non-consumer sales in the Sale of Goods Act 1893, s. 55 as amended by the Supply of Goods (Implied Terms) Act 1973, s. 4.

[9] As under the Israeli Standard Contracts Law 1964, s. 10. For discussion of the advantages and disadvantages of such a system, see Law Com. No. 69 (1975), paras. 290–314. See also the Housing Act 1961, s. 33 (6) (7) (covenants to repair).

[10] As with implied terms in contracts for the sale of goods which constitute "consumer sales": see the Sale of Goods Act 1893, s. 55 (4) as amended. See also the Road Traffic Act 1960, s. 151 (passengers in public vehicles); Road Traffic Act 1972, ss. 143, 148 (3) (passengers in other vehicles).

tability and fitness for purpose to include a minimum period of durability and after sales service.[11]

The discussion of the common law and statutory controls which follows is mainly concerned with a vendor's attempts to exclude his contractual obligations. Many of the points made in the former part of the chapter are, however, applicable *mutatis mutandis* to other suppliers. Neither the vendor nor any other supplier may exempt himself from liability in tort to a person with whom he has no contractual relationship, although the claim may be defeated by a plea of *volenti non fit injuria* or on the ground that the plaintiff was the sole effective cause of his own misfortune.[12] Similarly, where the claim is based on the *Hedley Byrne* principle[13] the presence of a disclaimer may negative the assumption of responsibility on which the duty of care depends. These points are of particular importance in the case of manufacturers' guarantees since manufacturers and consumers are rarely parties to the same contract. Manufacturers' guarantees are discussed in the following chapter, together with the position with respect to exemption clauses under the strict tort theory and under a régime which permits a third party to sue on the contract itself, the requirements of "vertical" and "horizontal" privity having been relaxed.[14]

Control through the requirements of incorporation and the common law rules of construction

Incorporation[15]

A seller of goods cannot rely on an exemption clause unless he can establish that the clause was incorporated in the contract from which he seeks protection. This requirement of incorporation will be most readily satisfied where the purchaser has signed the document containing the clause. A person is normally bound by the terms of a document he has signed

---

[11] See Ontario Law Reform Commission *Report on Consumer Warranties and Guarantees in the Sale of Goods* (1972), pp. 37, 40. See also the Second Hand Motor Vehicles Act 1971 (South Australia), s. 24; Motor Dealers Act 1974 (N.S.W.), s. 27 both imposing obligations on the sale of secondhand motor vehicles.

[12] *Volenti non fit injuria* and causation are discussed below, ch. 14, at pp. 283–284 and pp. 291–296 especially.

[13] *Hedley Byrne & Co.* v. *Heller & Partners*, [1964] A.C. 465; [1963] 2 All E.R. 575.

[14] See below, at pp. 160–165 (manufacturers' guarantees); pp. 166–168 (strict tort); pp. 165–166 (third parties suing on the contract).

[15] Treitel, *The Law of Contract*, 4th edn., 1975, pp. 137–141; *Benjamin's Sale of Goods*, paras. 924–926; Greig, *Sale of Goods*, pp. 232–236; Clarke, "Notice of Contractual Terms", [1976] C.L.J. 51.

even though he has neither understood nor read it,[16] assuming always that the document is a contractual document and not a mere receipt[17] or delivery note[18] which came too late to form a part of the bargain.[19] Similarly, such an exemption clause may fail if its effect has been misrepresented,[20] or if it is inconsistent with other express assurances given by or on behalf of the defendant.[1] The tendency nowadays is to give priority to such assurances. And in this area the distinction between contractual promises, mere representations, and statements operating by way of estoppel[2] is of little importance.[3] Nor, for that matter is the parol evidence rule. The essential point is that, through inducing reliance, the assurance will nullify an otherwise effective exemption clause whilst leaving express or implied contractual obligations intact.

Where there is no signed contractual document exempting provisions may still be incorporated into the contract provided that the purchaser has received reasonable notice.[4] The sufficiency of the notice will depend on a number of factors. Thus it may be necessary to consider the nature of the document, invoice or label which contains the clause, the size and intensity of the print[5] and the type of damage or loss against which protection is sought.[6] Some documents would be more readily assumed

---

[16] *L'Estrange* v. *F. Graucob, Ltd.*, [1934] 2 K.B. 394; Spencer, [1973] C.L.J. 104.

[17] *Chapelton* v. *Barry U.D.C.*, [1940] 1 K.B. 532; [1940] 1 All E.R. 356.

[18] *Lowe* v. *Lombank, Ltd.*, [1960] 1 All E.R. 611; [1960] 1 W.L.R. 196. See also *Olley* v. *Marlborough Court*, [1949] 1 K.B. 532; [1949] 1 All E.R. 127; *Thornton* v. *Shoe Lane Parking, Ltd.*, [1971] 2 Q.B. 163; [1971] 1 All E.R. 686.

[19] For the circumstances in which *non est factum* may be pleaded see *Saunders* v. *Anglia Building Society*, [1971] A.C. 1039; [1971] 1 All E.R. 243.

[20] *Curtis* v. *Chemical Cleaning and Dyeing Co.*, [1951] 1 K.B. 805; [1951] 1 All E.R. 631; *Jaques* v. *Lloyd George & Partners, Ltd.*, [1968] 2 All E.R. 187; [1968] 1 W.L.R. 625.

[1] The assurance may form part of the main contract or form the basis for a collateral contract: see *Mendelssohn* v. *Normand*, [1970] 1 Q.B. 177; [1969] 2 All E.R. 1215; *Couchman* v. *Hill*, [1947] K.B. 554; [1947] 1 All E.R. 103; *Gallaher* v. *British Road Services and Container and Roadferry, Ltd.*, [1974] 2 Lloyds' Rep. 440; *J. Evans & Son (Portsmouth), Ltd.* v. *Andrea Merzario, Ltd.* [1975], 1 Lloyd's Rep. 162; Wedderburn, [1959] C.L.J. 58.

[2] As in *City and Westminster Properties (1934), Ltd.* v. *Mudd*, [1959] Ch. 129; [1958] 2 All E.R. 733, though the case was not concerned with an exemption clause.

[3] *Mendelssohn* v. *Normand*, [1969] 2 All E.R. 1215, 1218 *per* Lord Denning M.R. The distinction remains important, of course, where the plaintiff is seeking to sue on the statement itself: see above, pp. 36–41.

[4] *Parker* v. *South Eastern Rail. Co.* (1877), 2 C.P.D. 416. Reasonable notice is also important to the issue of "fair or reasonable reliance" on exemption clauses in non-consumer sales. See Sale of Goods Act 1893, s. 55 (5) (c), as amended, and below, pp. 155–156.

[5] *Cf. J. Spurling, Ltd.* v. *Bradshaw*, [1956] 1 W.L.R. 461, 466 *per* Denning L.J. See also *Boeing Airplane Co.* v. *O'Malley*, 329 F. 2d 585 (8th Cir., 1964). U.C.C., Art. 2–316 (2) requires the disclaimer to be "conspicuous".

[6] *Cf. Thornton* v. *Shoe Lane Parking, Ltd.*, [1971] 1 All E.R. 686, 692 *per* Megaw, L.J., where a requirement of reasonable notice of *the* exempting *condition* (in the singular) is stressed. See also *ibid.*, at pp. 689–690 *per* Lord Denning, M.R.

to contain exempting provisions than others,[7] whilst the exclusion of liability for personal injury would often need to be more explicit than in the case of property damage.[8]

In many cases the parties will have dealt together in the past. Where there is a consistent course of earlier dealings, the present contract may be viewed as having been concluded on the same terms even though notice has not been given afresh.[9] This is only a matter of common sense. If A and B have contracted consistently on identical terms in the past it is reasonable to assume that their present contract will have been concluded on the same terms unless there is anything to suggest the contrary.[10] Yet the area is obviously one in which there is ample scope for applying a broad test of reasonableness or conscionability even if this is done only covertly. Indeed, in a recent plant-hire case Lord Denning, M.R. did this quite openly[11] in explaining and distinguishing another case[12] on the ground that incorporation through a course of consistent dealing depended on equality of bargaining power between the parties. He was, in effect, applying at the preliminary level of incorporation the statutory guideline which would have been available to him on the issue of "fair or reasonable reliance" in a case of sale.[13]

A simple oral contract may also contain exempting provisions which are incorporated directly, as where goods are sold under an oral bargain with all faults, or indirectly, as where incorporation is by reference to written conditions containing the clause. It would seem unlikely that protection could be obtained from a general notice in a shop or office, unless attention has been specifically drawn to it or there is a relevant course of earlier dealing.[14] Hence notices proclaiming, for example, that com-

---

[7] See, e.g., *Walls* v. *Centaur Co., Ltd.* (1921), 122 L.T. 242 (catalogue ineffective).

[8] *Thornton* v. *Shoe Lane Parking, Ltd.*, [1971] 1 All E.R. 686, 692 *per* Megaw, L.J. See also *Henningsen* v. *Bloomfield Motors Inc.*, 161 A. 2d 69 (N.J., 1960).

[9] See *Henry Kendall & Sons* v. *William Lillico & Sons, Ltd.*, [1969] 2 A.C. 31; [1968] 2 All E.R. 444.

[10] In *McCutcheon* v. *David MacBrayne, Ltd.*, [1964] 1 All E.R. 430, 437 Lord Devlin stated that, "Previous dealings are relevant only if they prove knowledge of the terms, actual and not constructive, and assent to them". See also *D. J. Hill & Co. Pty., Ltd.* v. *Walter H. Wright Pty., Ltd.*, [1971] V.R. 749 (Vict. Sup. Ct.). But an objective approach was adopted in *Henry Kendall & Sons* v. *William Lillico & Sons*, [1969] 2 A.C. 31, 90, 104, 105, 113, 130, H.L. See also *British Crane Hire Corporation, Ltd.* v. *Ipswich Plant Hire, Ltd.*, [1974] 1 All E.R. 1059, 1062–1063, C.A., *per* Lord Denning, M.R.

[11] *British Crane Hire Corporation, Ltd.* v. *Ipswich Plant Hire, Ltd.*, [1974] 1 All E.R. 1059, 1061–1062.

[12] *Hollier* v. *Rambler Motors (A.M.C.), Ltd.*, [1972] 2 Q.B. 71; [1972] 1 All E.R. 399.

[13] See Sale of Goods Act 1893, s. 55 (5) (*a*) and below, pp. 153–154.

[14] See *McCutcheon* v. *David MacBrayne, Ltd.*, [1964] 1 All E.R. 430, H.L., where the exempting provisions were not incorporated through being displayed in the defendant's office. *Cf.*, however, *Ashdown* v. *Samuel Williams & Sons, Ltd.*, [1957] 1 Q.B. 409; [1957] 1 All E.R. 35.

plaints cannot be entertained once the customer has left the shop would generally be ineffective through lack of incorporation into the contract whatever their position under the Supply of Goods (Implied Terms) Act 1973. The point might be important to a retailer buying in a trade warehouse since he would not have the benefit of the same protection against exemption clauses as is accorded in the case of consumer sales.[15]

The contra proferentem rule[16]

Assuming that the exemption clause has been effectively incorporated into the contract it will be construed *contra proferentem* and thus against the party who seeks to rely on it. Indeed this basic hostility is to be seen in an initial process of classification since the prevalent view is still that exemption clauses operate as shields to accrued rights, that is, in derogation of obligations, rather than as means of delimiting the extent of the obligation undertaken. As Denning, L.J. put it in *Karsales (Harrow), Ltd. v. Wallis*, "it is necessary to look at the contract apart from the exempting clauses to see what are the terms express or implied, which impose an obligation on the party."[17] This approach has been criticised persuasively.[18] But there seems little doubt that the philosophy underlying it provided a measure of protection for the consumer during a period in which legislative reform was decidedly incomplete.

With the widening scope of statutory protection the *contra proferentem* rule is less important than was once the case. The same is true of the related doctrine of fundamental breach to which reference is made below.[19] Admittedly, being rules of construction designed (in theory) to ascertain the intentions of the parties,[20] both operate at a stage which is logically anterior to any statutory prohibition or guideline. The latter apply only to clauses which have survived the process of construction and have been found *prima facie* to be applicable. Similarly, there are areas of product liability which still await statutory reform, notably the law governing product hire, contracts for work and materials and manufacturers' guar-

---

[15] See Sale of Goods Act 1893, s. 55 (4), as amended, and below p. 142 *et seq.* For regulations banning such notices in the case of a consumer sale, see below, p. 145.

[16] *Benjamin's Sale of Goods*, paras. 928–944.

[17] [1956] 2 All E.R. 866, 869, C.A. See also *S.S. Istros (Owners) v. F. W. Dahlstroem & Co.*, [1931] 1 K.B. 247, 252–253 *per* Wright, J. *Cf. G. H. Renton & Co., Ltd. v. Palmyra Trading Corporation*, [1957] A.C. 149; [1956] 3 All E.R. 957.

[18] See Coote, *Exception Clauses* (1964), Ch. 1.

[19] At p. 131 *et seq.*

[20] The status of fundamental breach as a rule of construction as opposed to substantive law is discussed below, pp. 134–137.

antees. But it is likely that most of these gaps will soon be filled.[1] Where statute has intervened and invalidated exemption clauses (as in the case of consumer sales)[2] there is little point in inquiring whether they would have failed in any event as a matter of construction. Where it has subjected them to a test of reasonableness[3] there would be few cases in which this requirement would be satisfied but in which the clause would still fail on a point of construction.

The essential feature of a construction *contra proferentem* is that the clause is given the narrowest possible scope consistent with the intention of the parties. All ambiguities will be resolved against the party seeking to rely on it. This has a number of well-established implications. One is that an express warranty will be considered to have been given in addition to (and not in lieu of) the implied warranties unless there are clear indications to the contrary. This was true at common law[4] and the principle has since been enacted in the Sale of Goods Act. Section 55 (2) of the Act now provides that:

"An express condition or warranty does not negative a condition or warranty implied by this Act unless inconsistent herewith."[5]

On this basis a guarantee or undertaking in a factory warranty would not oust the implied conditions of merchantability and fitness for purpose otherwise applicable. As Brownridge, J.A. noted in *Western Tractor, Ltd.* v. *Dyck*,[6] a guarantee that a tractor will last for 1500 hours coupled with a promise to replace defective parts within this period does not carry the implication that the tractor will not last any longer. This is especially so when it is set alongside statements claiming that "thousands of profit-making hours have been built into this equipment". Typically, however, the factory warranty will stipulate that it is given in lieu of any other undertakings.[7]

---

[1] See the Law Commission *Exemption Clauses, Second Report,* Law Com. No. 69 (1975); Hansard, H.C. Deb. Vol. 914, col. 377 (W.A.), 5 July 1976.

[2] See the Sale of Goods Act 1893, s. 55 (4), as amended by the Supply of Goods (Implied Terms) Act 1973, s. 4.

[3] As in the case of a contract for the sale of goods which is not a consumer sale: see Sale of Goods Act 1893, s. 55 (4), as amended by the Supply of Goods (Implied Terms) Act 1973, s. 4.

[4] See *Bigge* v. *Parkinson* (1862), 7 H. & N. 955.

[5] U.C.C., Art. 2–317 contains a broadly similar provision. See also *L. and N. Sales Co.* v. *Stuski,* 146 A. 2d 154 (Pa., 1958); *Crotty* v. *Shartenberg's New Haven Inc.,* 162 A. 2d 513 (Conn., 1960).

[6] (1969), 7 D.L.R. (3d) 535, 543–544 (Sask. C.A.). See also *Sutter* v. *St. Clair Motors Inc.,* 194 N.E. 2d 674 (Ill., 1963).

[7] See, e.g., *Henningsen* v. *Bloomfield Motors Inc.,* 161 A. 2d 69 (N.J., 1960). See also *Eimco Corporation* v. *Tutt Bryant, Ltd.,* [1970] 2 N.S.W.R. 249.

A further well-established principle of construction is that legal terms will be construed in the light of their technical meanings even though it might seem that they were being used in a general colloquial sense. There are many well-known cases in point of which *Wallis, Son and Wells* v. *Pratt and Haynes*[8] is one of the most important. Here it was held that a provision in a contract for the sale of common English sainfoin that "sellers give no warranty, express or implied, as to growth, description or any other matters" was ineffective where breach of an implied *condition* was in issue,[9] the seller having delivered giant sainfoin, a different and inferior seed. The same approach is to be seen in *Andrews Brothers (Bournemouth), Ltd.* v. *Singer & Co., Ltd.*[10] The contract was for sale of "new Singer cars" and the clause more comprehensive in that it purported to exclude "all conditions, warranties and liabilities implied by common law, statute or otherwise". Yet it provided no defence to an action based on the delivery of a car which was not "new", since this was an *express*, rather than an implied, term of the contract.[11] Similarly, the sale of goods "with all faults and imperfections", or "as is", may affect qualitative requirements of merchantability. But it will not affect the requirement that the goods correspond with the contract description.[12] Nor, indeed is it likely to affect any requirement that the goods shall be reasonably fit for their intended purpose. Exemption clauses purporting to govern the remedies available or the time within which they may be exercised will be subjected to the same treatment.[13]

A further feature of the *contra proferentem* rule is to be seen in situations

---

[8] [1910] 2 K.B. 1003, C.A.; [1911] A.C. 394, H.L.

[9] No doubt of s. 13 of the 1893 Act. But the same reasoning applies to the other implied conditions of the Act, e.g. those imposed by ss. 14 and 15. See *Henry Kendall & Sons* v. *William Lillico & Sons, Ltd.*, [1969] 2 A.C. 31; [1968] 2 All E.R. 444, H.L.; *Cammell Laird & Co., Ltd.* v. *The Manganese Bronze and Brass Co., Ltd.*, [1934] A.C. 402, 431–432. For the various meanings which may be attributed to phrases such as "no warranty is given", see *Benjamin's Sale of Goods*, para. 930.

[10] [1934] 1 K.B. 17.

[11] Some cases have also reasoned that since the implied sales warranties arise independently and by operation of law they cannot be excluded by general provisions stating that the written contract of sale represents the entire agreement between the parties. Express exclusion is necessary: see *Frigidinners Inc.* v. *Branchtown Gun Club*, 109 A. 2d 202 (Pa., 1954); *Bekkevold* v. *Potts*, 216 N.W. 790 (Minn., 1927). But *cf. Mechanical Horse (Australia) Pty., Ltd.* v. *City of Broken Hill* (1941), 41 S.R. N.S.W. 135, 138–139 *per* Jordan, C.J. (N.S.W. Sup. Ct.).

[12] *Robert A. Munro & Co., Ltd.* v. *Meyer*, [1930] 2 K.B. 312; *Shepherd* v. *Kain* (1821), 5 B. & Ald. 240. Or with the sample: *Champanhac & Co., Ltd.* v. *Waller & Co., Ltd.*, [1948] 2 All E.R. 724.

[13] *Szymonowski & Co.* v. *Beck & Co.*, [1923] 1 K.B. 457, C.A., affd. *sub nom. Beck & Co., Ltd.* v. *Szymanowski & Co., Ltd.*, [1924] A.C. 43 H.L., is the leading case. See also *Vigers Brothers* v. *Sanderson Brothers*, [1901] 1 Q.B. 608; *Minister of Materials* v. *Steel Brothers & Co., Ltd.*, [1952] 1 All E.R. 522; *Lamson* v. *Spicers (Australia), Ltd.*, [1953] S.A.S.R. 297; *Benjamin's Sale of Goods*, paras. 937–944; Coote, *Exception Clauses*, pp. 150–156.

in which there is a potentially concurrent liability in negligence and on some further basis not requiring proof of negligence. Here it is well established that it is only the latter (strict) liability which will be excluded[14] unless, in the circumstances of the case, the parties are to be presumed to have intended the contrary.[15] Hence in contracts for the sale or hire of goods general words of exemption will normally be taken to refer to the defendant's obligations as a warrantor that the goods conform to expressly guaranteed or implied standards, thus leaving intact a potential liability in tort for negligence.[16] Moreover even where the sole obligation is to exercise reasonable care the clause should, if it is to be effective, clearly indicate that it is intended to exclude liability in all circumstances including negligence. Otherwise it may be understood as a simple warning that the defendant would not be liable in the *absence* of negligence. This was one of the grounds on which the exemption clause failed in *Hollier* v. *Rambler Motors (A.M.C.), Ltd.*,[17] where the plaintiff's car had been damaged by fire when left at the defendant's garage for repair.

Fundamental terms and fundamental breach[18]

Although the *contra proferentem* rule is important, its demands can be satisfied by the use of an appropriate formula, the wording of which should not pose any real problems for the modern draftsman. So it proved and, as Professor Atiyah has observed,[19] the courts began to see a steady stream of hard cases in the 1950s and 1960s. Most of them involved the supply of grossly defective motor vehicles under contracts of sale and hire

---

[14] See *White* v. *John Warrick & Co., Ltd.*, [1953] 2 All E.R. 1021; [1953] 1 W.L.R. 1285 C.A., and, in general, Treitel, *Law of Contract*, 4th edn., pp. 142–144, Coote, *op. cit.*, pp. 33–36; Gower (1954), 17 M.L.R. 155.

[15] As in *Gillespie Brothers & Co., Ltd.* v. *Roy Bowles Transport, Ltd.*, [1973] 1 Q.B. 400; [1973] 1 All E.R. 193 ("all claims or demands whatsoever"). See also *Hair and Skin Trading Co., Ltd.* v. *Norman Airfreight Carriers, Ltd.*, [1974] 1 Lloyd's Rep. 443, where the "magic word" 'whatsoever' was omitted but the clause was still regarded as operative.

[16] See *White* v. *John Warrick and Co., Ltd.*, [1953] 2 All E.R. 1021; [1953] 1 W.L.R. 1285, C.A., above, note 14. See also *Hawkes Bay and East Coast Aero Club* v. *McLeod*, [1972] N.Z.L.R. 289, 308 (N.Z.C.A.).

[17] [1972] 2 Q.B. 71; [1972] 1 All E.R. 399. *Cf. Alderslade* v. *Hendon Laundry Ltd.*, [1945] K.B. 189; [1945] 1 All E.R. 244.

[18] The subject has attracted a voluminous amount of literature. See *Benjamin's Sale of Goods*, paras. 945–960; Coote, *Exception Clauses*, ch. 8; Guest (1961), 77 L.Q.R. 98; Reynolds (1963), 79 L.Q.R. 534; Montrose, [1964] C.L.J. 60, 254; Lord Devlin, [1966] C.L.J. 192; Drake (1967), 30 M.L.R. 531; Legh-Jones and Pickering (1970), 86 L.Q.R. 513; (1971), 87 L.Q.R. 515; Coote, [1970] C.L.J. 221; Dawson (1975) 91 L.Q.R. 380.

[19] *Sale of Goods*, 5th edn., p. 126.

purchase with comprehensive exemption clauses.[20] Pending legislative reform, the response was to develop the doctrines of the fundamental term and the fundamental breach. The essential feature of this development was that even the most widely drafted exemption clause came to be read on the understanding that it did not affect the central obligations of the contract. But the circumstances in which it is permissible to regard a term or breach as "fundamental" remains unclear as does the precise effect of so classifying a given term or breach.

Fundamental terms

Parties may contract on the basis that something may or may not exist: in which case the buyer will take the risk that they do not and so cannot complain if they are not forthcoming.[1] Similarly, if the requirements of certainty are observed, they may agree that the seller will have the option to determine what he is to supply in performance of the contract.[2] But what the seller cannot do is to promise to deliver one thing and then deliver something else. In such a case, no exemption clause will protect him, since he will have acted outside the terms of the contract as the parties have defined it. To this extent, at least, there are certain "fundamental terms" within every contract of which it can be said that liability for non-compliance cannot be excluded.

The distinction between non-performance and a lesser breach of contract was noted by Lord Abinger, C.B. in *Chanter* v. *Hopkins* when he said:[3]

> "If a man offers to buy peas of another, and he sends him beans, he does not perform his contract; but that is not a warranty; there is no warranty that he should sell him peas; the contract is to sell peas, and if he sends him anything else in their stead, it is a non-performance of it."

Basically the distinction is between the supply of goods different in kind from that which the seller had contracted to sell and the supply of goods which are defective in quality alone. This is of course the dividing line

---

[20] See, e.g., *Karsales (Harrow), Ltd.* v. *Wallis*, [1956] 2 All E.R. 866; [1956] 1 W.L.R. 936; *Yeoman Credit, Ltd.* v. *Apps*, [1962] 2 Q.B. 508; [1961] 2 All E.R. 281; *Charterhouse Credit Co., Ltd.* v. *Tolly*, [1963] 2 Q.B. 683; [1963] 2 All E.R. 432.
[1] See, e.g., *Marquis of Bute* v. *Thompson* (1844), 13 M. & W. 487; *Smith* v. *Harrison* (1857), 26 L.J.Ch. 412 (sale of my title, if any, to land) where, however, the sale was set aside on the facts. The general principles are well stated in *McRae* v. *The Commonwealth Disposals Commission* (1950), 84 C.L.R. 377 (High Ct. Australia).
[2] *Cf.* Lord Devlin, [1966] C.L.J. 192, 212.
[3] (1838), 4 M. & W. 399, 404. See also *U.G.S. Finance, Ltd.* v. *National Mortgage Bank of Greece*, [1964] 1 Lloyd's Rep. 446, 453 *per* Pearson, L.J. (chalk and cheese).

between ss. 13 and 14 of the Sale of Goods 1893. In the past it was doubtful whether all breaches of s. 13 could be equated with the breach of a fundamental term.[4] Indeed Devlin, J. once observed that a fundamental term was "narrower than a condition of the contract".[5] But any such distinction is likely to prove illusory in the aftermath of the restrictive approach to s. 13 which was adopted in the *Ashington Piggeries* case.[6] In insisting that the section was concerned only with attributes which *identified* the goods the House of Lords effectively equated "descriptive" and "fundamental" terms in contracts for the sale of goods.[7]

Fundamental breach

Goods may occasionally contain such a veritable "congerie of defects" as will affect their very identity.[8] Yet an argument along these lines is rarely realistic. An alternative approach has looked to the consequences of breach, rather than the nature of the term broken, arguing that they were such as to deprive the contracting party of substantially the whole benefit of the contract. In a contract of sale, the concern would be with s. 14 of the 1893 Act, but not all breaches of the implied conditions of merchantability and reasonable fitness for purpose can be treated as "fundamental" in this sense.[9] Nor is there any clear dividing line between those which can and those which cannot. An otherwise minor breach may, it seems, become fundamental if the consequences which flow from it are sufficiently grave as to strike at the root of the bargain.[10] In practice most of the cases have involved the hire-purchase, sale or leasing of motor vehicles which were unsafe to drive or of industrial equipment which was in need of constant

---

[4] For example, it is doubtful whether the breach in *Arcos, Ltd.* v. *Ronaasen*, [1933] A.C. 470, above, p. 74, would have been so equated.

[5] *Smeaton Hanscomb & Co., Ltd.* v. *Setty (Sassoon), Sons & Co.*, [1953] 2 All E.R. 1471, 1473. On the difficulties of defining the unexcludable core of the contract, see Coote, *Exception Clauses*, chs. 3 and 8; Melville (1956), 19 M.L.R. 26.

[6] [1972] A.C. 441; [1971] 1 All E.R. 847, above, p. 75 *et seq.*

[7] See Coote (1976), 50 A.L.J. 17.

[8] The phrase is associated with the speech of Lord Dunedin in *Pollock and Co.* v. *MacRae*, 1922 S.C. (H.L.) 192, 200. *Karsales (Harrow), Ltd.* v. *Wallis*, [1956] 2 All E.R. 866; [1956] 1 W.L.R. 936. C.A. might possibly fall into this category. A vandalised object incapable of self-propulsion is not aptly described as a "car".

[9] Indeed, if they could there would be little scope for the limited ability to rely on exemption clauses in non-consumer sales or hire-purchase agreements under the Sale of Goods Act 1893, s. 55 (4), as amended, and the Supply of Goods (Implied Terms) Act 1973, s. 12 (3), as amended by the Consumer Credit Act 1974, s. 192 (3) (a) and Sch. 4, para. 35.

[10] See *Harbutt's Plasticine, Ltd.* v. *Wayne Tank & Pump Co., Ltd.*, [1970] 1 Q.B. 447; [1970] 1 All E.R. 225. The approach coincides with the test for discharge by frustration: *Davis Contractors, Ltd.* v. *Fareham Urban District Council*, [1956] A.C. 696.

repair. Their results indicate a reluctance to hold that the plaintiff has accepted goods which are virtually worthless or incapable of performing their normal function, thus leaving him with, at best, a remedy in damages, and at worst, no remedy at all.[11] There should be less reluctance to conclude that he has taken the risk that defective parts will need replacing or repairing,[12] especially when this is to be done under a standard factory warranty.

The legal consequences of breach

There has been much controversy over the precise effect of a fundamental breach or of the breach of a fundamental term and the matter is still unresolved.[13] No doubt there is a principle or rule of law that the vendor must honour his basic obligation to deliver the contract goods although the practical consequences of this obligation depend on the generality with which one chooses to define the subject matter of the sale.[14] Similarly it would be accepted that an exemption clause cannot protect a person against the consequences of deceit.[15] Some of the earlier cases also assumed that disentitlement to rely on the clause followed in all cases,[16] but there was support for the view that the overriding concern was the intention

---

[11] See, e.g., *Farnworth Finance Facilities, Ltd.* v. *Attryde*, [1970] 2 All E.R. 774; [1970] 1 W.L.R. 1053 C.A.; *Karsales (Harrow), Ltd.* v. *Wallis*, [1956] 2 All E.R. 866; [1956] 1 W.L.R. 936 C.A.; *Lightburn* v. *Belmont Sales, Ltd.* (1969), 6 D.L.R. (3d) 692 (B.C. Sup. Ct.); *Gibbons* v. *Trapp Motors, Ltd.* (1970), 9 D.L.R. (3d) 742 (B.C. Sup. Ct.); *Burroughs Business Machines, Ltd.* v. *Feed-Rite Mills, Ltd.* (1973), 42 D.L.R. (3d) 303 (Man. C.A.), and Reynolds (1963), 79 L.Q.R. 534, 544. See also *Charterhouse Credit Co.* v. *Tolly*, [1963] 2 Q.B. 683; [1963] 2 All E.R. 432, C.A., *Yeoman Credit, Ltd.* v. *Apps*, [1962] 2 Q.B. 508; [1961] 2 All E.R. 281; C.A.; *R. G. McLean, Ltd.* v. *Canadian Vickers, Ltd.* (1970), 15 D.L.R. (3d) 15 (Ont. C.A.) and *Western Tractor, Ltd.* v. *Dyck* (1969), 7 D.L.R. (3d) 535 (Sask. C.A.) where there were successful claims for damages.

[12] See, e.g., *Astley Industrial Trust, Ltd.* v. *Grimley*, [1963] 2 All E.R. 33; [1963] 1 W.L.R. 584 C.A.

[13] See Coote, "The Effect of Discharge by Breach on Exception Clauses", [1970] C.L.J. 221.

[14] For example, in *Andrews Brothers (Bournemouth), Ltd.* v. *Singer & Co., Ltd.*, [1934] 1 K.B. 17 the essential core of the contract might, in theory, have been defined as a "car" or a "Singer car" or, preferably, a "new Singer car". See above, pp. 73–78.

[15] See *S. Pearson & Son, Ltd.* v. *Dublin Corporation*, [1907] A.C. 351, 353–354, 362; *Hall* v. *Queensland Truck Pty., Ltd.*, [1970] Qd. Rep. 231. Or, presumably, where he has failed to act with "common humanity", see Coote (1975) 125 N.L.J. 752. For the relevance of the fact that a given breach is deliberate, see the *Suisse Atlantique Société D'Armement Maritime S.A.* v. *N.V. Rotterdamsche Kolen Centrale*, [1967] 1 A.C. 361, 435; [1966] 2 All E.R. 61, 94 (Lord Wilberforce).

[16] See, e.g., *Karsales (Harrow), Ltd.*, v. *Wallis*, [1956] 2 All E.R. 866, 868–869 (Lord Denning), 871 (Parker, L.J.).

of the contracting parties.[17] Exemption clauses would not normally be construed as covering a fundamental breach though it remained open to the parties to make it clear that this was indeed what was intended. This view was generally taken to have been adopted by the House of Lords in the *Suisse Atlantique* case[18] in 1966. Thus in a passage which may be cited as representative of their Lordships' opinions, Lord Wilberforce said:[19]

> "The conception, therefore, of 'fundamental breach' as one which, through ascertainment of the parties' contractual intention, falls outside an exceptions clause is well recognised and comprehensible. Is there any need, or authority, in relation to exceptions clauses, for extension of it beyond this? In my opinion there is not. The principle that the contractual intention is to be ascertained — not just grammatically from words used, but by consideration of those words in relation to commercial purpose ... is surely flexible enough ..."[20]

It is unfortunate that the *Suisse Atlantique* case was one in which the innocent party, a charterer, had elected to affirm the contract in the face of the breach. Where this occurs the contract must clearly be taken to have been affirmed in its entirety[1] so that the meaning and effect of an exemption clause falls to be determined as a matter of construction thereafter.[2] This feature was not present in the later case of *Harbutt's Plasticine Ltd.* v. *Wayne Tank and Pump Co., Ltd.*[3] Here the plaintiff's factory had been destroyed by fire following the defendant's specification and installation of a plastic piping which had overheated. The piping was wholly unsuitable for the purpose for which it had been installed, namely the dispensing of molten stearine, and the breach was taken to be "fundamental". Damages assessed at some £146,000 were awarded. On appeal both Widgery and Cross, LL.J. were of the opinion that a clause in the contract limiting liability to £2,300 was, as a matter of construction, apt to cover the events which had occurred.[4] Yet the Court of Appeal

---

[17] See *U.G.S. Finance, Ltd.* v. *National Mortgage Bank of Greece*, [1964] 1 Lloyd's Rep. 446, 453 (Pearson, L.J.).

[18] *Suisse Atlantique Société d'Armement Maritime S.A.* v. *N.V. Rotterdamsche Kolen Centrale*, [1967] 1 A.C. 361; [1966] 2 All E.R. 61.

[19] [1967] 1 A.C. 361, 434.

[20] See also *ibid.*, at p. 392 (Viscount Dilhorne), pp. 405–406 (Lord Reid), p. 410 (Lord Hodson), pp. 425–426 (Lord Upjohn).

[1] See *ibid.*, at p. 398 (Lord Reid).

[2] Yet even in such cases the plainest possible language will be needed to make it clear that the clause is intended to cover the consequences of a fundamental breach: see *Wathers (Western), Ltd.* v. *Austins (Menswear), Ltd.*, [1976] 1 Lloyd's Rep. 14, C.A.; Reynolds (1976), 92 L.Q.R. 172. Perhaps contracts should now use the phrase "whether fundamental or otherwise".

[3] [1970] 1 All E.R. 225.

[4] *Cf.* [1970] 1 All E.R. 225, 238 (Widgery, L.J.), p. 241 (Cross, L.J.). Lord Denning thought that the clause was ambiguous: *ibid.*, at p. 233.

was unanimous in holding that the defendants were not entitled to rely on it. According to Lord Denning, M.R., an innocent party faced with a fundamental breach of contract, the consequences of which have deprived him of the opportunity to elect to affirm,[5]

> "is entitled to sue for damages for the breach and the guilty party cannot rely on the exclusion or limitation clause: for the simple reason that he, by his own breach, has brought the contract to an end; with the result that he cannot rely on the clause to exempt or limit his liability for that breach."

This conclusion appears to be stated as a rule of law of general application which is in no way dependent on the contracting parties' intentions. The same reasoning would no doubt apply where there had been an opportunity for election and the innocent party had "brought the contract to an end" by opting to disaffirm and so to treat the contract as terminated.[6] The doctrine of fundamental breach is apparently seen as operating at the level of construction only where there has been an election to affirm, as in the *Suisse Atlantique* case itself.[7] Moreover, such an election will not readily be implied. Indeed, in *Farnworth Finance Facilities, Ltd.* v. *Attryde*, Lord Denning said that "a man only affirms a contract when he knows of the defects and by his conduct elects to go on with the contract despite them."[8]

The *Harbutt's Plasticine* case raises many problems[9] and is, with respect, almost certainly wrong. The notion that a contract is brought to an end when it has not been affirmed after a breach is misleading. The "innocent" party is no doubt excused from future performance and may recover what he has furnished under the contract if there has been a total failure of consideration. But this does not mean that the provisions of the contract are nullified retrospectively subject to his entitlement to sue for breach. Neither frustration nor, it seems, breach of a condition carries this consequence.[10] The same must surely be true of a fundamental breach. A

---

[5] *Ibid.*, at p. 234.

[6] Some support for this view may be found in the speeches of Lord Reid and Lord Upjohn in the *Suisse Atlantique* case: [1967] 1 A.C. 361, 398, 425.

[7] Unless one can legitimately regard the *Harbutt* case as involving (and being limited in application to) instances of "deviation", as where a carrier takes the wrong route or a bailee stores goods in the wrong place, or some other total non-performance, as where beans are delivered instead of peas: see *Kenyon, Son and Craven, Ltd.* v. *Baxter Hoare & Co., Ltd.*, [1971] 2 All E.R. 708, 718–719 (Donaldson, J.).

[8] [1970] 2 All E.R. 774, 778, C.A. The case involved a hire-purchase agreement for a new motor cycle. Such agreements are not governed by statutory rules for acceptance which parallel those applicable to a contract of sale: see above, pp. 111–115. See also above, p. 114, note 8.

[9] See Coote, [1970] C.L.J. 221; Weir, [1970] C.L.J. 189; Legh-Jones and Pickering (1970), 86 L.Q.R. 513 (1971), 87 L.Q.R. 515; Sutton, *Sale of Goods*, 2nd edn., pp. 404–406.

[10] See *Heyman* v. *Darwin's, Ltd.*, [1942] A.C. 356; [1942] 1 All E.R. 337, H.L. See also Coote, [1970] C.L.J. 221, at pp. 224–229 especially.

party who has committed a "fundamental" breach can hardly be thereby disentitled from (say) suing on the contract in a counterclaim in respect of earlier minor breaches by the "innocent" party. More generally, it is wrong in principle to deprive the parties of the ability to provide for the consequences of a fundamental breach when they have made their intentions perfectly clear.

Unconscionability[11]

Failure to satisfy the demands of conscionability has been invoked in a number of different contexts over the years as a means of relieving a promisor of the obligation to fulfil his promise. In a recent restraint of trade case Lord Diplock has placed the matter in historical perspective and formulated the justification underlying such protection in the following terms:[12]

"It is, in my view, salutory to acknowledge that in refusing to enforce provisions of a contract whereby one party agrees for the benefit of the other party to exploit or to refrain from exploiting his own earning-power, the public policy which the court is implementing is not some 19th-century economic theory about the benefit to the general public of freedom of trade, but the protection of those whose bargaining power is weak against being forced by those whose bargaining power is stronger to enter into bargains that are unconscionable. Under the influence of Bentham and of laissez-faire the courts in the 19th century abandoned the practice of applying the public policy against unconscionable bargains to contracts generally, as they had formerly done to any contract considered to be usurious; but the policy survived in its application to penalty clauses and to relief against forfeiture and also to the special category of contracts in restraint of trade. If one looks at the reasoning of 19th-century judges in cases about contracts in restraint of trade one finds lip service paid to current economic theories but if one looks at what they said in the light of what they did, one finds that they struck down a bargain if they thought it was unconscionable as between the parties to it, and upheld it if they thought that it was not."

Unconscionability is not, therefore, a new term in the law of contract. Many of the earlier cases involved expectant heirs who had borrowed

---

[11] See Waddams, "Unconscionability in Contracts" (1976), 39 M.L.R. 369; Leff, "Unconscionability and the Code" 115 Univ. Pa. L.R. 485 (1967); Ellinghaus, "In Defense of Unconscionability" 78 Yale L.J. 757 (1969). In writing on unconscionability we have benefited from discussions with Stephen Furst Esq., B.A., Ll.B., Barrister-at-law.

[12] *A. Schroeder Music Publishing Co., Ltd.* v. *Macaulay*, [1974] 3 All E.R. 616, 623, H.L.

money on the strength of their inheritance at exorbitant rates of interest.[13] But the Chancellor's protection was also given to others who were susceptible to exploitation or pressure including the needy, the ignorant and the sick.[14] Indeed, as Professor Leff has observed,[15] certain whole classes of "presumptive sillies" such as sailors, farmers and women were taken under the Chancellor's wing.[16] Unconscionability has also been invoked in land law. But cases involving an application for specific performance should be treated with caution since they frequently do no more than indicate the terms on which equitable (and thus discretionary) remedies will be granted.[17]

In recent years, a test of conscionability has also been applied to contracts between young composers of popular music and their publishers. In the leading case of *A. Schroeder Music Publishing Co., Ltd.* v. *Macaulay*,[18] the publishers had obtained the composer's signature to an agreement which was one-sided in the extreme. It required him as a young man of twenty-one to assign the copyright of his works to them for a period which was likely to run to ten years. There was no corresponding undertaking to publish or, indeed, to release for distribution through other channels in the event of a decision not to publish. The publisher had the right to assign or terminate the agreement but the composer did not. Similar terms were not imposed on established composers. Generally the contract, which was in standard form, had neither been "made freely by parties bargaining on equal terms", nor had it been "moulded under the pressures of negotiation, competition and public opinion".[19] Superior bargaining power and the ability to adopt a take-it-or-leave-it attitude

---

[13] See, e.g., *Earl of Chesterfield* v. *Janssen* (1750), 2 Ves. Sen. 125; *Earl of Aylesford* v. *Morris* (1873), 8 Ch. App. 484. A modern and more general counterpart is to be found in the Consumer Credit Act 1974, ss. 137–140, giving the courts power to reopen extortionate credit bargains so as to do justice between the parties.

[14] See, e.g., *Blackwilder* v. *Loveless*, 21 Ala. 371 (1852) (needy); *Banaghan* v. *Malaney*, 85 N.E. 839 (Mass., 1908) (ignorant); *Fitzpatrick* v. *Dorland*, 27 Hun. 291 (N.Y., 1882) (sick).

[15] 115 Univ. Pa.L.R. 485, 532 (1967).

[16] *Cf. How* v. *Weldon* (1754), 2 Ves. Sen. 516, 518 (sailors—"a race of men loose and unthinking"); *Koch* v. *Streuter*, 83 N.E. 1072 (Ill., 1908) (farmers); *Friend* v. *Lamb*, 152 Pa. 529 (1893) (women). All benefited from what Leff has termed the "pore-ole-widder-lady" syndrome; 115 Univ. Pa.L.R. 485, 527.

[17] For a recent example see *Mountford* v. *Scott*, [1974] 1 All E.R. 248, 252, where in a successful action for specific performance of an option to purchase land, Brightman, J. asked whether "as a matter of discretion, ought this court to grant the equitable remedy of specific performance in the present circumstances, having regard to the illiteracy of the defendant, the nature of the option agreement and the absence of any legal advice for the assistance of the defendant", Affd., [1975] 1 All E.R. 198, C.A.

[18] [1974] 3 All E.R. 616; [1974] 1 W.L.R. 1308, H.L.

[19] *Ibid.*, at p. 622 *per* Lord Reid quoting from the speeches of Lord Pearce and Lord Wilberforce in *Esso Petroleum Co., Ltd.* v. *Harper's Garage (Stourport), Ltd.*, [1967] 1 All E.R. 699, 723, 729.

did not, in the view of Lord Diplock, raise a presumption that the publishers had used such power to drive an unconscionable bargain.[20] It did, however, call for vigilance on the part of the courts where restraint of trade was involved. In the result the House of Lords agreed that the contract was unenforceable as being in unreasonable restraint of trade.

Clifford Davis Management, Ltd. v. *W.E.A. Records, Ltd.*[1] was a similar case. The manager of a "pop group" had been granted an interim injunction restraining the publication of a record album of which he claimed to be entitled to the copyright. Because of the nature of the action it was unnecessary for the Court of Appeal to reach a firm conclusion as to whether the contract between the manager and the group was enforceable. It was sufficient for the appellants to show that they had an arguable case and that the balance of convenience was in favour of publishing. This they succeeded in establishing. Lord Denning pointed to a number of features which might have been said to indicate or reflect such an inequality of bargaining power as would have made the contract unenforceable. There was, for example, a ten-year tie without a retaining fee or a firm undertaking to publish; a consideration which was arguably grossly inadequate; a relationship of dependence founded on a desire to see the compositions published and a lack of experience in business matters; and the possibility that undue influence or pressure had been brought to bear. Above all, the contract form was long and full of legal terminology and the composer had not taken legal advice.[2] Lord Denning concluded by suggesting that, "if the publisher wished to exact such onerous terms or to drive so unconscionable a bargain. he ought to have seen that the composer had independent advice".[3]

Contracts in restraint of trade fall into an area of the law where the ability of the courts to demand compliance with a broad requirement of reasonableness or conscionability is well established. They provide no direct support for the existence of a similar common law power in other cases. Yet it is also true that the standard-form contracts of the recent "pop group" cases have much in common with the comprehensive exemption clauses which have appeared in cases discussed earlier in the chapter. The superior bargaining power and expertise which underlies them is common to both.

Under the existing law there are a number of ways in which this imbalance might be reflected in a judgment in a product liability case. It has been suggested, for example, that equality of bargaining power may

---

[20] *Cf.* [1974] 3 All E.R. 616, 624.
[1] [1975] 1 All E.R. 237, C.A.
[2] *Ibid.*, at p. 239.
[3] *Ibid.*, at p. 241. See also *Lloyd's Bank, Ltd.* v. *Bundy*, [1974] 3 All E.R. 757, C.A.

be crucial on the preliminary issue of incorporation.[4] And there are statements suggesting that the status of the parties and their relative bargaining power may colour a court's attitude to the construction of an exemption clause.[5] But there are obviously limits to the protection which can be afforded through screening at the point of incorporation and through construing the contract *contra proferentem* and on the assumption that it was not intended to exempt from liability for fundamental breaches. The question then arises whether there is a residual common law power to strike out the clause on the ground of public policy. Lord Denning, in *Gillespie Brothers & Co., Ltd.* v. *Roy Bowles Transport, Ltd.*, concluded that such a power existed when the clause was "so unreasonable, or applied so unreasonably, as to be unconscionable".[6] The statement was, however, *obiter* and Buckley, L.J. expressly denied that any such power exists.[7] There seems little doubt that this is the predominant English view.[8] It finds support, for example, in the judgment of Donaldson, J., in *Kenyon, Son and Craven, Ltd.* v. *Baxter Hoare & Co., Ltd.*, where he said: "The redress of such imbalance and relief from its consequences are matters for Parliament rather than the courts".[9] The point is less important than it used to be now that Parliament has legislated for contracts of sale and hire purchase.[10] Legislation covering other areas, such as contracts of hire and contracts for work and materials, should not be long delayed.[11]

---

[4] See *British Crane Hire Corporation, Ltd.* v. *Ipswich Plant Hire, Ltd.*, [1974] 1 All E.R. 1059, 1062–1063, C.A., *per* Lord Denning, M.R.

[5] See, e.g., *Hawkes Bay and East Coast Aero Club Inc.* v. *Mcleod*, [1972] N.Z.L.R. 289, 295 *per* North, P.; *H. and E. Van der Sterren* v. *Cibernetics (Holdings) Pty., Ltd.* (1970), 44 A.L.J.R. 157, 158 *per* Walsh, J. Superior skill and knowledge may also affect the issue of whether a statement is a representation or a contractual promise: see *Oscar Chess, Ltd.* v. *Williams*, [1957] 1 All E.R. 325; [1957] 1 W.L.R. 370 above, p. 39.

[6] [1973] 1 All E.R. 193, 200, C.A.

[7] *Ibid.*, at p. 205.

[8] Though not the American: see *Henningsen* v. *Bloomfield Motors Inc.*, 161 A. 2d 69 (N.J., 1960). See also *Foley Motors, Ltd.* v. *McGhee*, [1970] N.Z.L.R. 649, discussed by Coote (1971) 4 N.Z.U.L.R. 293.

[9] [1971] 2 All E.R. 708, 720. See also the speech of Lord Reid in the *Suisse Antlantique* case, [1967] 1 A.C. 361, 406, H.L.

[10] See below, pp. 142–158.

[11] See the Law Commission *Exemption Clauses in Contracts, Second Report*, Law Com. No. 69, 1975; Hansard, H.C. Deb., Vol. 914, col. 377 (W.A.), 5 July 1976.

8 Exemption Clauses: II

Statutory control of exemption clauses

Statutory control of exemption clauses in English product liability law currently stems from two main sources,[1] the Misrepresentation Act 1967 and the Supply of Goods (Implied Terms) Act 1973. The 1973 Act is the more important and will be examined initially. Reference will also be made to art. 2–302 of the Uniform Commercial Code which provides as follows:[2]

> "(1) If the court as a matter of law finds the contract or any clause of the contract to have been unconscionable at the time it was made the court may refuse to enforce the contract, or it may enforce the remainder of the contract without the unconscionable clause, or it may so limit the application of any unconscionable clause as to avoid any unconscionable result.
>
> (2) When it is claimed or appears to the court that the contract or any clause thereof may be unconscionable the parties shall be afforded a reasonable opportunity to present evidence as to its commercial setting, purpose and effect to aid the court in making the determination."

---

[1] Other sources include the Agriculture Act 1970, ss. 68 (6), 71 (4), 72 (3) (sale of fertilisers and feeding stuffs); Plant Varieties and Seeds Act 1964, s. 17 (1) (sale of seeds).

[2] See 1 *Uniform Laws Annotated*, p. 137. For comment see Leff, "Unconscionability and the Code: the Emperor's new clause" 115 U. Pa. L. Rev. 485, (1967); Ellinghaus, "In Defense of Unconscionability", 78 Yale Law Jo. 757 (1969); Spanogle, "Analyzing Unconscionability Problems", 117 U. Pa. L. Rev. 931 (1969). For general comparative discussion, see 1 *Williston on Sales* 4th edn., 1973, ch. 11; Eorsi, "Exemption Clauses" (1975), 23 A.J. Comp. L. 215.

The Supply of Goods (Implied Terms) Act 1973

Introduction

This Act is based on the Law Commission's *First Report on Exemption Clauses*.[3] It applies to contracts of sale or hire purchase of goods other than those entered into before the commencement date, 18 May 1973.[4] In the case of contracts of sale s. 4 of the 1973 Act amends s. 55 of the principal Act of 1893. The central provision is to be found in the new s. 55 (4) which states that:

"In the case of a contract of sale of goods, any term of that or any other contract exepting from all or any of the provisions of ss. 13, 14 or 15 of this Act shall be void in the case of a consumer sale and shall, in any other case, not be enforceable to the extent that it is shown that it would not be fair or reasonable to allow reliance on the term."[5]

Parallel provisions for hire purchase agreements are to be found in s. 12 of the 1973 Act[6] and subsequent references to contracts of sale may generally be taken to apply *mutatis mutandis* to such agreements. By s. 16 of the 1973 Act, it is further provided that on the redemption of trading stamps for goods the appropriate warranties will be implied "notwithstanding any terms to the contrary".[7] Before discussing the definition of a "consumer sale" and the statutory guidelines on the issue of fair or reasonable reliance several points of a more general nature may be noted.

The scope of control

Firstly, s. 55 applies only to a "contract of sale of goods". It has no application to other contracts, such as contracts of hire, of exchange, for work and materials, or contracts involving the rendering of a service to which the use of a product is necessarily incidental.[8] The Law Commission has recently recommended that provision be made for the statutory

---

[3] See Law Com. No. 24, Scot. Law Com. No. 12, July 1969. For general discussion of the Act, see *Benjamin's Sale of Goods* (1974), paras. 969–991; Greig, *Sale of goods* (1974), pp. 225–232; Atiyah, *The Sale of Goods* 5th edn., 1975, pp. 131–135; Yates, [1973] J.B.L. 135, 141–145, (1973) 123 N.L.J. 529.

[4] Supply of Goods (Implied Terms) Act 1973, s. 18 (3), (5).

[5] Terms purporting to exempt from the provisions of s. 12 of the Act (implied undertakings as to title, etc.) are also void: see s. 55 (3), as amended.

[6] As amended by the Consumer Credit Act 1974, s. 192 (3) (*a*) and Sch. 4 para. 35.

[7] Section 16 replaces s. 4 of the Trading Stamps Act 1964.

[8] Hire purchase agreements and contracts involving the redemption of trading stamps for goods are, however, covered: see above, notes 6 and 7 and corresponding text.

control of exemption clauses in such contracts and it seems likely that the recommendations will be implemented.[9] Meanwhile they remain subject to control through the common law rules of construction[10] and a source of attraction to dealers intent on avoiding the constraints of the 1973 Act.[11]

Secondly, it is necessary to decide what constitutes a term "exempting from all or any of the provisions" of the relevant sections of the Act. Section 55 (4) is given some further content by s. 55 (9) which provides that:

> "Any reference in this section to a term exempting from all or any of the provisions of any section of this Act is a reference to a term which purports to exclude or restrict, or has the effect of excluding or restricting, the operation of all or any of the provisions of that section, or the exercise of a right conferred by any provision of that section, or any liability of the seller for breach of a condition or warranty implied by any provision of that section."

The wording of s. 55 (4) with its reference to "any terms of that or any other contract" is also important in this context. This extends the statutory control to cover terms in collateral contracts, contracts with third parties, or contracts of indemnity no less than terms in the contract of sale itself. Section 5 (1) of the 1973 Act is also designed to prevent avoidance of the statutory controls through choice of law clauses or through adopting the Uniform Law on International Sales in contracts which do not involve the international sale of goods.[12]

The definition of an exemption provision in s. 55 (9) of the 1893 Act, as amended, would cover all typical exemption clauses including those which purport to circumscribe the right to reject goods or to place a time limit on claims. Genuine liquidated damages clauses and arbitration clauses are not normally thought of as exemption clauses,[13] although technically the wording of s. 55 (9) would seem to be wide enough to cover both. Similarly a clause which designates the seller as the sole arbiter of defectiveness would be a term which has the effect of

---

[9] See the *Second Report on Exemption Clauses*, Law Com. No. 69, Scot. Law Com. No. 39, August 1975; Hansard, H.C. Deb., vol. 914, col. 377. For the distinction between contracts of sale and other contracts and for the implied conditions attaching to the latter, see above, pp. 115–122.

[10] See above, pp. 125–137.

[11] See Greig, "A Distinction Recreated" (1972), 122 N.L.J. 884 where the point is made in relation to contracts for work and materials.

[12] However exclusion of the conditions and warranties implied by ss. 12–15 of the 1893 Act, as amended, is permitted to the same extent as at common law where the contract is for the international sale of goods: see s. 61 (6) of the 1893 Act, as amended by the Supply of Goods (Implied Terms) Act 1973, s. 6. For discussion of choice of law issues, see below, pp. 351–355.

[13] Thus in the *Suisse Atlantique* case, [1967] 1 A.C. 361; [1966] 2 All E.R. 61 the demurrage clause was not viewed as an exemption clause. For arbitration clauses, see *Woolf* v. *Collis Removal Service*, [1948] 1 K.B. 11; [1947] 2 All E.R. 260, C.A. See also the *Second Report on Exemption Clauses*, Law Com. No. 69, paras. 160–168.

excluding or restricting the operation of the statutory implied terms. Doubts have been expressed as to whether the section covers clauses excluding or limiting liability for consequential loss. But the doubts appear to be ill founded. To the extent that losses of this nature are otherwise recoverable,[14] such a clause would purport "to exclude or restrict ... any liability of the seller for breach of a condition" implied by the relevant sections of the Act. The issue would typically arise in a non-consumer sale where the goods are being used in a commercial venture.

Thirdly, there may be problems in distinguishing between an exemption clause strictly so-called and an attempt by the seller to ensure that the implied conditions do not attach to the contract. Within limits the seller will clearly be able to prevent an obligation from accruing even though he cannot exempt himself from liability for breach. The implied condition of reasonable fitness for purpose does not arise "where the circumstances show that the buyer does not rely, or that it is unreasonable for him to rely, on the seller's skill or judgment.[15] Similarly, the implied condition of merchantable quality does not arise "(*a*) as regards defects specifically drawn to the buyer's attention before the contract is made; or (*b*) if the buyer examines the goods before the contract is made, as regards defects which that examination ought to reveal".[16] A simple recital in the contract that the buyer is relying on his own judgment (or an acknowledgment that his attention has been drawn to specific defects or that he has examined the goods) may possibly be of some evidential value. But it can hardly be conclusive since the court must clearly determine the truth of the matter.[17] Indeed the recital or acknowledgment would not even operate as an estoppel where the seller knows it to be untrue.[18] On the other hand, the seller should not be prejudiced by the new s. 55 where he has genuinely done something which would prevent the implied condition from applying. Otherwise there would be no point in having the various preconditions built into the substantive obligations themselves. The distinction between the two situations may be difficult to draw where one has an expression such as "with all faults" or "as is" which could be viewed either as a genuine attempt to delimit the substantive obligations undertaken or as an exempting provision.

---

[14] As to which, see *Hadley* v. *Baxendale* (1854), 9 Ex. 341; *Victoria Laundry (Windsor), Ltd.* v. *Newman Industries, Ltd.,* [1949] 2 K.B. 528; [1949] 1 All E.R. 997, and, in general, Treitel, *The Law of Contract,* 4th edn., 1975, pp. 642–650.

[15] Section 14 (3) of the 1893 Act, as amended: see above, p. 102 *et seq.*

[16] Section 14 (2) of the 1893 Act, as amended: see above, pp. 95–97.

[17] Exemption clauses strictly so called are, however, incorporated by signature although they have not been read: see *L'Estrange* v. *F. Graucob, Ltd.,* [1934] 2 K.B. 394, above, pp. 125–128.

[18] This would seem to follow by analogy with *Lowe* v. *Lombank, Ltd.,* [1960] 1 All E.R. 611; [1960] 1 W.L.R. 196, where the buyer had signed a delivery note.

Similar considerations arise under s. 13 of the Act where the implied condition that the goods shall correspond with the contract description must be viewed against the background of what the seller has contracted to sell.[19] The breadth or narrowness of the contract description may affect the content of the seller's obligations under ss. 13–15 of the Act. But the seller who otherwise avoids the Scylla of uncertainty and the Charybdis of breach should not fail thereafter on the ground that the contract description "has the effect of excluding" the operation of the provisions of the Act. The short answer is that it has not. The amendments to s. 55 of the 1893 Act were not intended to prevent a person from contracting to sell a lorry-load of assorted junk provided that the goods are so described.

Fourthly, s. 55 (4) does not *prohibit* the use of exemption clauses designed to deprive the buyer of the benefits of the implied conditions laid down by ss. 13–15 of the Act. It merely provides that such clauses shall be void in the case of a consumer sale and otherwise unenforceable to the extent that reliance on them is not fair or reasonable. Hence the full benefits of the 1973 Act depend on there being a general understanding of the law and a willingness on the part of the consumer to enforce his rights. It was always predictable that such understanding and willingness could not be safely assumed. The Director-General of Fair Trading accordingly sought to take matters a stage further. Acting under the Fair Trading Act 1973[20] he proposed that it be made unlawful in the case of a consumer transaction to purport to exclude the rights safeguarded by s. 55 (4) of the 1893 Act, or to fail to explain the existence of these rights when issuing written statements concerning the obligations of the supplier or a third party such as a manufacturer. The Consumer Protection Advisory Committee reported its general agreement with these proposals.[1] An order implementing the proposals and taking account of the Committee's modifications has recently been laid before Parliament and approved by the House of Commons and the House of Lords.[2]

Finally, it is important to note that the new provisions of s. 55 (4) of the Act only control exemption clauses which strike at the terms implied by

---

[19] Section 13 (1) of the 1893 Act as amended is discussed above, pp. 69–78. See also Coote (1970), 34 Conv. (N.S.) 224 for discussion of the technique of shrinking the core of the contract.

[20] Sections 14, 17 and 19.

[1] See *A Report on Practices Relating to the Purported Exclusion of Inalienable Rights of Consumers and Failure to Explain their Existence*, December 1974. The practices are referred to in para. 2 of the report; the proposals in paras. 4–6; and the C.P.A.C.'s conclusions and suggested modifications in paras. 93–98. See also the Director-General's supporting dossier 17/1 (April 1974).

[2] See the Consumer Transactions (Restrictions on Statements) Order 1976; Hansard, H.C. Deb. vol. 916, cols. 1161–1171, 30 July 1976, H.L. Deb. vol. 375, cols. 97–118, 11 October 1976.

ss. 13–15 of the Act. The implied conditions as to title in s. 12 of the 1893 Act are safeguarded by the new s. 55(3).[3] But there is no statutory control safeguarding other implied conditions, such as the seller's duty to deliver the goods at the right time and in the right quantity.[4] Still less does the Act protect a buyer whose sole complaint is that he has paid a grossly excessive price for shoddy goods. Nor indeed does it protect a seller who may be just as open to gross exploitation as a buyer. In this it is narrower in scope than art. 2–302 of the Uniform Commercial Code.[5] Indeed it may appear somewhat paradoxical to an English lawyer that the leading pre-Code case on unconscionability in the United States was concerned with the protection of a seller.[6] The Campbell Soup Company was seeking a decree of specific performance for the delivery of certain Chantenay carrots grown for the company under contract on the defendant's farm. The contract price was some thirty dollars per ton and the market price at least ninety dollars per ton. The Court of Appeals declined to grant the order, saying of the contract "that the sum total of its provisions drives too hard a bargain for a court of conscience to assist".[7] Specific performance might of course be declined in an English court on similar facts, but the case serves as a reminder that a seller may deserve protection no less than a buyer.

Consumer sales[8]

Any attempt to distinguish between different types of transactions according to the status of the parties and the nature of the goods involved must inevitably lead to problems in marginal cases. This is true of the provision in the new s. 55 of the Sale of Goods Act 1893 whereby terms exempting from liability in respect of the conditions implied by ss. 13–15 of the Act are void in the case of a "consumer sale". Some of these problems are noted below. It is important, however, that the problems be kept in perspective. In the vast majority of cases it will be quite clear into which

---

[3] And by the Supply of Goods (Implied Terms) Act 1973, s. 12(2) in the case of a hire purchase agreement. See also the Consumer Credit Act 1974, s. 192, Sch. 4, para. 35.

[4] See Sale of Goods Act 1893, ss. 10(1), 29 30. See also *Benjamin's Sale of Goods*, paras. 659–665, for discussion of clauses excusing non-delivery.

[5] Article 2–302 is set out above, p. 141.

[6] See *Campbell Soup Co. v. Wentz*, 172 F. 2d 80 (3rd Cir., 1948).

[7] *Ibid.*, at p. 84. For example, para. 9 of the contract excused Campbell from taking carrots in certain circumstances but did not allow the grower to dispose of them elsewhere unless Campbell agreed. For other American cases stressing price as an element in unconscionability, see 1 *Williston on Sales*, 4th edn., pp. 487–490 and below, p. 158.

[8] See *Benjamin's Sale of Goods*, paras. 975–986; Law Commission, *First Report on Exemption Clauses in Contracts*, Law Com. No. 24, July 1969, paras. 85–95.

category a particular sale falls, and in borderline cases reliance on the clause is, in any event, unlikely to be regarded as fair or reasonable in the circumstances.

Section 55 (7) of the Sale of Goods Act 1893, as amended, defines a "consumer sale" as:

> "a sale of goods (other than a sale by auction or by competitive tender) by a seller in the course of a business where the goods—
> (a) are of a type ordinarily bought for private use or consumption; and
> (b) are sold to a person who does not buy or hold himself out as buying them in the course of a business."

By s. 55 (8) of the Act it is further provided that:

> "The onus of proving that a sale falls to be treated for the purposes of this section as not being a consumer sale shall lie on the party so contending."

Sales by auction or by competitive tender can accordingly never rank as consumer sales for the purposes of the section. In other cases the classification is determined by reference to the following three elements: (i) the status of the seller; (ii) the status or apparent status of the buyer; and (iii) the type of goods forming the subject matter of the sale.

Sale in the course of a business

The requirement that the seller should act "in the course of a business" is intended to exclude the private seller of secondhand goods. Section 62 (1) of the 1893 Act, as amended,[9] defines a "business" as including "a profession and the activities of any government department ... local authority or statutory undertaker". The words "in the course of a business" will no doubt be construed in the same way as in s. 14 of the Act.[10] Accordingly it would cover both those who deal in the goods sold and those who are selling off surplus stock or equipment but who are not otherwise engaged in selling. As with s. 14, there will be difficulty in determining when a limited number of similar transactions by a private individual constitutes a "business".[11] And there is also the point that the business element may be successfully disguised by the seller who operates from a home address making his contacts through the advertisement sections of local newspapers.[12]

---

[9] By the Supply of Goods (Implied Terms) Act 1973, s. 7 (1).
[10] Subject, perhaps, to an agency point discussed in *Benjamin's Sale of Goods*, para. 976.
[11] See above, pp. 80–81.
[12] A practice which the Director-General of Fair Trading has referred to the Consumer Protection Advisory Committee: see the supporting dossier 17/3 (March, 1975), and the C.P.A.C. report *Disguised Business Sales* (May 1976).

Buying or appearing to buy in the course of a business

By s. 55 (7) (*b*) of the 1893 Act, as amended, a sale of goods will not be a consumer sale if the buyer either buys, or holds himself out as buying, in the course of a business. A person may no doubt hold himself out as buying in the course of a business if he asks for trade terms, or buys with a trade card or from a trade source.[13] The more difficult (and important) question is when a purchase is "in the course of a business" for the purposes of the subsection.

Certain points are clear. A person will buy in the course of a business if he buys to process, resell, or hire out, whether to the trade or to private individuals. The same will be true of the person who uses or consumes the goods when providing a service, as when the owner of a launderette buys soap powder or the owner of a supermarket buys shelving. Hence the supplier may be protected by an exemption clause if reliance on the clause is fair or reasonable.

What is less clear is whether all acquisitions by business buyers are necessarily made "in the course of a business". A trader might, for example, buy a van, or a farmer a piece of agricultural machinery; a solicitor, intent on maximising his deductible expenses, might buy a gallon of anti-freeze or oil for a partnership car, charging the bill to the partnership account at the local garage. All are clearly as much at risk as any private purchaser buying in similar circumstances. Hence it is tempting to argue that a person buys goods in the course of a business only when he makes a business of buying goods of the relevant type.[14] Such an interpretation would exclude a buyer from the full protection of the Act only if he deals in or with the goods, or uses them in a way which is more than purely incidental to the business. An argument along these lines is not, however, likely to succeed. It might be seen as a persuasive (though hardly a fatal) objection that it is contrary to the assumptions contained in the Law Commission report on which the amendments to the 1893 Act were based.[15] The real difficulty, however, is that when the phrase "in the course of a business" is used in relation to *sellers* it is certainly not intended to be limited to sellers who deal

---

[13] *Benjamin's Sale of Goods*, para. 980 suggests that assistance may be derived from the Partnership Act 1890, s. 14.

[14] *Cf.* Atiyah, *Sale of Goods*, 5th edn., 1975, p. 134.

[15] Indeed the different interpretations reflect the distinction between the two definitions of a "consumer sale" advanced in the report as Alternatives A and B. Alternative A (which was to operate if it were decided *not* to impose statutory controls over non-consumer sales) would have enabled acquisitions by business buyers of the type mentioned in the text to qualify as consumer sales. But Alternative B was adopted by the legislature and the assumption was clearly that under this Alternative such acquisitions would not be consumer sales: see *First Report on Exemption Clauses*, Law Com. No. 24, paras. 90–95 and pp. 56–58.

in goods of that type.[16] It would be strange if the same phrase were to bear a different meaning when used in relation to buyers. On the other hand, the solicitor in the above example would have the full protection of the Act if he required the anti-freeze or oil privately and then proceeded to use it in the partnership car. It is the mode of acquisition (actual or apparent) which is important and not the use to which the goods are put.[17]

Goods of a type ordinarily bought for private use or consumption

By s. 55 (7) (*a*) of the 1893 Act, as amended, a sale of goods will not be a consumer sale where the goods are not "of a type ordinarily bought for private use or consumption". A number of difficulties may be envisaged when applying this limitation.

Firstly, it is not clear whether the subsection requires that the goods be of a type ordinarily bought for the buyer's *own* private use or consumption. Such a limitation is not stated expressly and it is arguable that it should not be implied. The point might be important to, say, the private buyer of a large domestic central heating boiler who had not held himself out as being in the trade. Goods of this type would ordinarily be purchased by heating engineers for a trade use (installation in a dwelling house), the benefit of which would accrue to a private user or consumer. Whether the transaction is a consumer sale accordingly depends on whether it is the buyer's own private use or consumption which is the controlling factor.

Assuming that the concern is specifically with the buyer's own use, many goods are, in any event, increasingly sold to both trade and private customers. In a "do it yourself" age, handymen frequently act as their own plumbers, electricians and mechanics. They buy guttering, bathroom tiles, electric cable and spare parts for cars, as well as the traditional chisels, hammers and nails. This may lead to difficulty in deciding when acquisition for private use has become "ordinary". Statistical evidence as to the proportion of private to trade sales (and of private to trade outlets) would no doubt be relevant and admissible. Purchases for private use or consumption must presumably form a significant proportion of the market,

---

[16] This is certainly true of ss. 14 (2), (3) of the 1893 Act, as amended (see above, pp. 80–81). As was submitted above it would also appear to be true of s. 55 (7) itself.

[17] There may also be difficulty where goods are bought partly for business purposes and partly for private purposes. It has been suggested in the Ontario Law Reform Commission *Report on Consumer Warranties and Guarantees in the Sale of Goods,* 1972, p, 57, that in such a case "the primary purpose of the purchase should govern its characterisation". For difficulties where a private purchaser buys through a commercial agent, see *Benjamin's Sale of Goods,* para. 983.

and even though they fall well short of a majority they may certainly be within the subsection.

There is also scope for argument over when goods are of the same type as goods which are ordinarily bought for private use or consumption.[18] The categorisation of the various "types" of goods can be drawn ultimately only on grounds of convenience and common sense. Account must presumably be taken of the size of the unit which is being purchased where there are distinct commercial and domestic markets for different sizes. An amplifier and loudspeakers may be designed for use in a small flat or for a building such as the Albert Hall. But it would not be realistic to regard the sale of the latter equipment to a private buyer as a consumer sale simply because the majority of amplifiers and loudspeakers are bought for private use. A more difficult question is whether account must also be taken of the size or nature of the container in which goods are packaged. Private buyers increasingly buy from discount warehouses, hypermarkets and superstores with the result that there is often no clear dividing line between the purchasing habits of the small retailer and those of the private bulk-buyer. But where there is a distinct container for the trade it is arguable that goods would not be within the definition of a consumer sale if they are bought in it. On this basis the private purchaser of a full-sized barrel of beer from a brewery might be outside the subsection since a barrel is different in kind from the bottle or keg in which beer would ordinarily be bought for private use. Yet it is doubtful whether quantity, as such, can be said to affect the "type" of goods which are sold. The man who buys chickens for his deep-freezer would buy goods "of a *type* ordinarily bought for private use or consumption" whether he buys two or two-hundred.

Non-consumer sales

Where a contract of sale of goods in not a consumer sale an exemption clause may still be unenforceable under s. 55 (4) of the Act "to the extent that it is shown that it would not be fair or reasonable to allow reliance on the term". By s. 55 (5) it is further provided that "In determining for the purpose of subsection (4) above whether or not reliance on any such term would be fair or reasonable regard shall be had to all the circumstances of the case and in particular to the [matters listed in guidelines (a)–(e)]".[19]

The new s. 55 gives the courts considerable discretion when dealing with exemption clauses in non-consumer sales. The wording of s. 55 (4)

---

[18] See also above, pp. 73–78, where the point is discussed in relation to s. 13 of the 1893 Act, and above, pp. 132–133, where it is discussed in the context of the breach of fundamental terms.

[19] The statutory guidelines are discussed below, pp. 152–158.

suggests that a clause need not be struck down or upheld in its entirety but may be held partly enforceable and partly unenforceable. A term might, for example, be regarded as unreasonable to the extent that it purports to exempt from *all* liability for breach of the implied condition of merchantable quality, but fair in so far as it places a time limit on the ability to reject. This characteristic is shared by both the Misrepresentation Act 1967, s. 3,[20] and art. 2–302(1) of the Uniform Commercial Code.[1] The onus of proof on the issue of fair or reasonable reliance is on the party who is challenging the term.

It is not clear whether the fairness or reasonableness of reliance is to be determined by reference to the position at the time of contracting (as in art. 2–302 of the Uniform Commercial Code)[2] or by reference to the overall position at the time of the hearing. Support for the former view is to be found in the wording of statutory guideline (*d*) which refers to the time of the contract.[3] This choice of words was, moreover, deliberate since the Law Commission's original suggested guideline was amended as a matter of policy to omit an element of retrospection.[4] In the words of Lord Hailsham, L.C. during the Bill's report stage in the House of Lords:[5]

> "We continue to take the view that whether it is reasonable to allow reliance on a term of the contract should be decided in the light of the circumstances at the time of formation of the contract. To take account of later events for this purpose could be equivalent to changing the rules in the middle of the game."

The guidelines, generally, all seem to refer to the time of formation of the contract. However, the opening words of s. 55(5) require that regard be had "to all the circumstances of the case" and it might be argued that this includes post-contractual developments. The general tenor of the section provides support for this view. The court is called on to decide whether *reliance* on the clause is fair or reasonable not whether the clause was fair or reasonable as drafted.

To the extent that the overall position is in doubt, it would seem

---

[20] See below, pp. 158–160.

[1] Article 2–302 is set out above, p. 141 and it provides in part that: "the court may refuse to enforce the contract, or it may enforce the remainder of the contract without the unconscionable clause, or it may so limit the application of any unconscionable clause as to avoid any unconscionable result".

[2] See above p. 141. See also *Sinkoff Beverage Co.* v. *Schlitz Brewing Co.*, 273 N.Y.S. (2d) 364 (1966).

[3] See below, p. 156.

[4] This appeared as guideline (*e*) in the Law Commission report and it read: "Where the provision excludes or restricts liability unless certain conditions are complied with ... *whether it was, in the events that have occurred, reasonably practicable to comply with those conditions*": see the Law Commission's *First Report on Exemption Clauses in Contracts*, Law Com. No. 24, para. 113.

[5] See Hansard, H.L.Deb., Vol. 338, cols. 802–803, 11 February 1973.

preferable to clarify the law by a suitable amendment at some opportune time. At the very least the uncertainty should not be repeated when reforming the law on exemption clauses in contracts for the supply of goods other than by way of sale or hire purchase.[6] There will be few cases in which a different result is reached according to which point of time is considered appropriate. It is submitted, however, that the position should be determined in the light of the circumstances at the date of the contract[7] without taking account of subsequent developments which make reliance on the clause more or less reasonable.[8]

The statutory guidelines[9]

One of the major criticisms of the Misrepresentation Act 1967, s. 3, is that it gives no indication of the factors which a court is to take into account when determining whether reliance on an exemption clause is fair or reasonable.[10] The same criticism has been voiced of art. 2–302 of the Uniform Commercial Code.[11] The validity of this criticism is by no means uniformly accepted and there are those who consider that Parliament's function is sufficiently discharged by legislating in general terms.[12] In their *First Report on Exemption Clauses* the Law Commission indicated certain guidelines which might feature among the considerations to be taken into account when passing on the issue of fair or reasonable reliance.[13] It was not intended that these should be incorporated into legislation implementing the Report. In the result, however, the guidelines were enacted with a number of modifications and they now appear as s. 55 (5) (a)–(e) of the 1893 Act.

---

[6] See the Law Commission's *Second Report on Exemption Clauses,* Law Com. No. 69, Scot. Law Com. No. 39. The Law Commission favours a test which would result in the uncertainty being repeated: see para. 183. The Scottish Law Commission recommends that regard should be had to the position "at the time when the contract was made or the notice given": see para. 177.

[7] The arguments for and against this view are discussed in the Law Commission's *Second Report on Exemption Clauses,* above note 6, paras. 169–183. *Quaere* to what extent proponents of the opposite view would allow a party to point to developments after the original hearing? Might a change of circumstances lead to a term being regarded as enforceable at the time of the hearing and invalid at the time of the appeal, or vice versa?

[8] This is the approach of U.C.C., art. 2–302: see above, p. 141.

[9] See Greig, *Sale of Goods,* pp. 229–232; *Benjamin's Sale of Goods,* para. 987.

[10] *Cf.* Atiyah and Treitel (1967), 30 M.L.R. 369, 384–385.

[11] *Cf.* Leff, 115 U. Pa. L. Rev. 485, 558 (1967).

[12] See, e.g., the views of the Scottish Law Commission as expressed in the *Second Report on Exemption Clauses in Contracts,* Scot. Law Com. No. 39, 1975, paras. 193–196.

[13] See Law Com. No. 24, 1969, paras. 98–113, expecially para. 113.

The bargaining position of the parties

By s. 55 (5) (a) of the Act a court is required to have regard to:

"the strength of the bargaining position of the seller and buyer relative to each other, taking into account, among other things, the availability of suitable alternative products and sources of supply."

In some cases it has been possible to apply general theories of contract law in a way which takes account of the relative strength of the parties' bargaining positions.[14] However this has been done only to a limited extent. Indeed in the *Suisse Atlantique* case Lord Reid criticised the developing case law on fundamental breach for the generality of its application. In his view it did not appear to distinguish between the person who had no choice or room for bargaining and the person who had bargained on terms of equality.[15]

The extent to which a court should be willing to hold an exemption clause unenforceable by virtue of the factors listed in s. 55 (5) (a) is a matter for debate. On one view it might be suggested that wholesale interference with exemption clauses which reflect the bargaining power of the parties is neither more nor less warranted than a general rendering of assistance to a person who has been on the receiving end of a hard bargain. Small retailers typically pay more for their goods than large multiples which buy in bulk. But there is no power in English law to protect them from this hard fact of commercial life. Article 2–302 of the Uniform Commercial Code is couched in wider terms than the provisions of s. 55 of the 1893 Act. But it is significant that the Official Commentary states that: "The principle (*sc.* of unconscionability) is one of the prevention of oppression and unfair surprise and not of disturbance of allocation of risks because of superior bargaining power."[16] Hence the use of superior bargaining power is not *per se* unconscionable under the Code. Such power may, however, be used unconscionably where there is an element of oppression or economic duress or unfair surprise and the terms of the contract bear no reasonable relation to the business risks. A broadly similar approach is likely to be used when considering the relevance of the strength of the parties' bargaining positions under the 1893 Act.[17]

---

[14] As, e.g., on the issue of incorporation: see *British Crane Hire Corporation, Ltd.* v. *Ipswich Plant Hire, Ltd.,* [1974] 1 All E.R. 1059, 1061–1062, C.A., *per* Lord Denning, M.R., and above, p. 127.

[15] See *Suisse Atlantique Société d'Armement Maritime S.A.* v. *N.V. Rotterdamsche Kolen Centrale,* [1967] 1 A.C. 361, 406, H.L.

[16] See 1 *Uniform Laws Annotated,* p. 137.

[17] Assistance may also be derived from cases such as *A. Schroeder Music Publishing Co., Ltd.* v. *Macaulay,* [1974] 3 All E.R. 616, H.L., discussed above, pp. 137–140.

The leading and most instructive American case is *Henningsen* v. *Bloomfield Motors Inc.*[18] Here the buyer of a Chrysler car had received a factory warranty expressed to be in lieu of all other warranties. The warranty was a uniform one issued by the Automobile Manufacturers' Association to which all major car manufacturers belonged. Its terms were harsh and one-sided and, in the words of the Supreme Court of New Jersey, "a sad commentary upon the automobile manufacturers' marketing practices".[19] The dealer, who was bound to the manufacturer by a franchise agreement, had not drawn the buyer's attention to the terms of the "warranty". But even if he had it is unlikely that the buyer would have understood it. In any event there was no scope for negotiation and no opportunity to buy on different terms elsewhere. Although the Uniform Commercial Code provision was not in force in New Jersey, the disclaimer was held void on the broad ground that it was contrary to public policy.[20] Were similar terms to appear in a contract of sale of goods in English law it is likely that they would be regarded as, at best, unenforceable under the 1893 Act.[1] Indeed guideline (*a*) refers specifically to "the availability of suitable alternative products and sources of supply". An alternative source of supply is unlikely to be regarded as "suitable" where the supplier contracts on the self-same oppressive terms.[2]

Inducement to agree to the term

Section 55 (5) (*b*) requires a court to have regard to the question:

> "whether the buyer received an inducement to agree to the term or in accepting it had an opportunity of buying the goods or suitable alternatives without it from any source of supply."

The latter part of the clause again emphasises the importance of meaningful choice. Presumably the presence of an inducement may make reliance on the exempting term more or less reasonable according to the circumstances

---

[18] 161 A. 2d 69 (N.J., 1960), above, p. 16. See also *Central Ohio Co-op Milk Producers Inc.* v. *Rowland*, 281 N.E. 2d 42 (Ohio, 1972); *American Home Improvement Inc.* v. *MacIver*, 201 A. 2d 886 (N.H. 1964); *Vlases* v. *Montgomery Ward & Co.*, 377 F. 2d 846 (3rd Cir., 1967); *Bill Stremmel Motors Inc.* v. *I.D.S. Leasing Corporation*, 514 P. 2d 654 (1974). Note, "Bargaining Power and Unconscionability", 114 U. Pa. L. Rev. 998 (1966).

[19] 161 A. 2d 69, 78.

[20] *Ibid.*, at p. 95. Contrast the approach of a Virginia Court in *Marshall* v. *Murray Oldsmobile Co.*, 154 S.E. 2d 140 (Va., 1967).

[1] The problems of spelling out a contract in the case of a manufacturer's "guarantee' are discussed below, pp. 160–165, at p. 163 especially.

[2] Lack of meaningful choice has also been emphasised in other American cases such as *Williams* v. *Walker-Thomas Furniture Co.*, 350 F. 2d 445 (D.C., 1965); *Morris* v. *Capitol Furniture and Appliance Co.*, 280 A. 2d 775 (D.C., 1971).

of the case. The buyer who is offered a substantial discount or a guaranteed source of supply as a *quid pro quo* for accepting the term may well find that it is enforceable against him. This is especially so where he was bargaining from a position of strength and active in extracting the favourable terms.[3] On the other hand, there may equally be cases in which a term will be unfair precisely because the buyer has been lulled into a false sense of security by the presence of an inducement. An inducement may be as indicative of unfair surprise as of a fair bargain.

Knowledge of the existence and extent of the term

By s. 55 (5) (*c*) of the Act account must also be taken of:

> "whether the buyer knew or ought reasonably to have known of the existence and extent of the term (having regard, among other things, to any custom of the trade and any previous course of dealing between the parties)."

There is clearly a substantial overlap here between the issue of whether a term has been incorporated into a contract[4] and the issue of whether reliance on it is fair or reasonable on the assumption that it has. The statutory guidelines do not prevent a court from holding that a given provision is not a term of the contract.[5] Hence there will be cases in which its efficacy might be denied on either ground. Section 55 (5) (*c*) will be important, however, where incorporation is through signature and hence operates independently of any requirement of notice.[6] The parallel provision in the Uniform Commercial Code requires that a written disclaimer be "conspicuous".[7] In a representative cross-section of cases it has been held that this requirement will not be met where the disclaimer is in small print,[8] in the same size and colour of print as the remainder of the

---

[3] See Hansard, H.L. Deb., Vol. 855, col. 802, 1 February 1973 (Lord Hailsham). The parallel guideline (*d*) in the original Law Commission report envisaged a buyer who adopted a passive role: see Law Com. No. 24, para. 113.

[4] See above, pp. 125–128.

[5] See s. 55 (6) of the 1893 Act, as amended.

[6] See *L'Estrange* v. *F. Graucob, Ltd.*, [1934] 2 K.B. 394.

[7] "Conspicuous" is defined (in part) in art. 1–201 (10) as follows: "A term or clause is conspicuous when it is so written that a reasonable person against whom it is to operate ought to have noticed it". Disclaimer of the warranty of fitness must (subject to the provisions of art. 2–316 (3) (*a*) for "as is" sales) be in writing and be conspicuous: see U.C.C., art. 2–316 (2). Under the same provision the warranty of merchantability may, it seems, be disclaimed orally but any written disclaimer must be conspicuous. The U.C.C. provisions on limitation of remedies in art. 2–719 do not require the limitation to be conspicuous. See 2 Frumer and Friedman, *Products Liability*, s. 19–07 [6].

[8] *Minikes* v. *Admiral Corporation*, 266 N.Y.S. (2d) 461 (1966); *Holcomb* v. *Cessna Aircraft Co.*, 438 F. 2d 1150 (5th Cir., 1971).

contractual document,[9] on the reverse side of the contractual document with nothing further to indicate its presence,[10] and where it is incorporated in paragraphs and clauses suggesting that a warranty is being given.[11] Assistance may also be obtained from English cases under the Trade Descriptions Act 1968, where a false trade description may apparently be neutralised by a disclaimer which is "as bold, precise and compelling as the trade description itself".[12]

There is some English authority suggesting that a clause may fail at the point of incorporation where it is unusual or unreasonable in scope.[13] Whether incorporation really depends on notice of the extent (rather than simply of the existence) of the term may be doubted. In any event it is clear that both elements may affect the issue of reasonable reliance under s. 55 (5) (c). This might be important in a case where the seller has simply procured the buyer's signature on a contract form without taking steps to explain the extent of an exempting provision,[14] Similar considerations underly the unconscionability clause of the Uniform Commercial Code which, it has been noted, is designed to prevent unfair surprise.[15]

Non-compliance with a specified condition

By s. 55 (5) (d) of the Act provision is made for terms which exempt from all or any of the requirements of ss. 13, 14 or 15 of the Act "if some condition is not complied with". In such a case regard must be had to:

> "whether it was reasonable at the time of the contract to expect that compliance with that condition would be practicable".

This guideline is aimed primarily at clauses which require that the seller be notified of defects within a specified time of the buyer taking delivery. Such time clauses are frequently unobjectionable where there are good

---

[9] *Boeing Airplane Co.* v. *O'Malley*, 329 F. 2d 585 (8th Cir., 1964). U.C.C. art. 1–201 (10) refers to the importance of contrasting type or colour.

[10] *Hunt* v. *Perkins Machinery Co. Inc.*, 226 N.E. 2d 228 (Mass., 1967). See also *Zabriskie Chevrolet Inc.* v. *Smith*, 240 A. 2d 195 (N.J., 1968); *Koellmer* v. *Chrysler Motors Corp.*, 276 A. 2d 807 (Conn., 1970).

[11] *Massey Ferguson Inc.* v. *Utley*, 439 S.W. 2d 57 (Ky., 1969).

[12] See *Norman* v. *Bennett*, [1974] 3 All E.R. 351, 354 *per* Lord Widgery, C.J.

[13] *Cf. J. Spurling, Ltd.* v. *Bradshaw*, [1956] 2 All E.R. 121, 125, *per* Denning, L.J.; *Thornton* v. *Shoe Lane Parking, Ltd.*, [1971] 1 All E.R. 686, 692 (Megaw, L.J.), pp. 689–690 (Lord Denning, M.R.).

[14] Such cases may border on fraud or duress. See *Knupp* v. *Bell* (1968), 67 D.L.R. (2d) 256 (Sask. C.A.).

[15] See the Official Commentary cited above, p. 153.

commercial reasons for finalising the risks of a venture.[16] But they may also work oppressively and it is right that the likelihood of the condition being met should affect the issue of reasonable reliance. The fact that the position is to be judged "at the time of contract" will mean that the guideline may sometimes be of little assistance to the buyer who has taken delivery of goods which develop unexpected defects. The courts have, however, been astute at construing time clauses restrictively. Hence the seller may yet find that the clause is interpreted as referring only to defects ascertainable at the time of delivery,[17] or as circumscribing the right to reject but not the right to claim damages.[18] In such cases the *contra proferentem* principle of construction may prove to be a useful supplement to the statutory protection.[19]

Goods manufactured to the buyer's order

Section 55 (5) (*e*) of the Act requires the court to have regard to the question of:

> "whether the goods were manufactured, processed, or adapted to the special order of the buyer."

This requires little comment. The buyer who specifies his requirements and for whom the goods are made or adapted to special order is likely to find that he does not benefit from an implied condition that the goods be reasonably fit for his particular purpose.[20] By guideline (*e*) the same circumstances may equally help to validate an exemption clause which excludes liability for any breach of this condition. On the other hand, there seems no reason why the factors mentioned in guideline (*e*) should affect the implied condition of merchantable quality or make reliance on an exemption clause any more (or less) reasonable where qualitative defects are concerned.

Residual matters

The statutory guidelines noted above are not the only factors to be taken

---

[16] See, e.g., *H. and E. Van der Sterren* v. *Cibernetics (Holdings) Pty., Ltd.* (1970), 44 A.L.J.R. 157 (High Ct. Australia).

[17] *Cameron* v. *Hillier*, [1941] Q.S.R. 298.

[18] *Beck & Co., Ltd.* v. *Szymanowsky & Co., Ltd.*, [1923] 1 K.B. 457, C.A., affd. on a further ground, [1924] A.C. 43, H.L.

[19] See above, pp. 128–131.

[20] See above, pp. 98–107.

into account on the issue of fair or reasonable reliance. Indeed s. 55 (5) requires the court to have regard to "all the circumstances of the case". Such circumstances may be extremely diverse and they may be indicative of either procedural or substantive abuse. American cases have emphasised the importance of the personal characteristics of the buyer. A buyer who has a poor command of the English language[1] or who is otherwise open to exploitation is more likely to receive protection than is, say, a practising lawyer who should be able to protect his own interests.[2] Similarly there is a substantial body of American case law holding that gross overpricing may assist in a finding of unconscionability even if it does not itself make the contract unconscionable.[3] An English court might take the same view in spite of our traditional reluctance to inquire into the adequacy of the consideration furnished.

Article 2–719 (3) of the Uniform Commercial Code provides that:

"Limitation of consequential damages for injury to the person in the case of consumer goods is prima facie unconscionable but limitation of damages where the loss is commercial is not."[4]

A broadly similar distinction might be taken in English law.[5] There would be few cases in which the buyer in a non-consumer sale would have suffered injury to his own person.[6] But the principle might be extended in favour of a retailer seeking an indemnity from a manufacturer whose defective goods had injured a consumer.[7]

The Misrepresentation Act 1967

The Misrepresentation Act 1967, s. 3, provides as follows:

---

[1] See, e.g., *Frostifresh Corporation* v. *Reynoso*, 281 N.Y.S. (2d) 964 (1967) (native language Spanish); *Jefferson Credit Corporation* v. *Marcano*, 302 N.Y.S. (2d) 390 (1969).

[2] *K. and C. Inc.* v. *Westinghouse Electric Corporation*, 263 A. 2d 390 (Pa., 1970).

[3] See, e.g., *Patterson* v. *Walker-Thomas Furniture Co.*, 277 A. 2d 111 (D.C., 1971); *Jones* v. *Star Credit Corporation*, 298 N.Y.S. (2d) 264 (1969); *Toker* v. *Perl*, 247 A. 2d 701 (N.J., 1968), affd. 260 A. 2d 244; 1 *Williston on Sales*, 4th edn., 1973, pp. 487–490.

[4] The same must presumably be true of a *disclaimer* of liability, although art. 2–316 (Exclusion or Modification of Warranties) has no equivalent provision. See *Walsh* v. *Ford Motor Co.*, 298 N.Y.S. (2d) 538 (1969); *Matthews* v. *Ford Motor Co.*, 479 F. 2d 399 (4th Cir., 1973).

[5] Indirect support might be derived from *Thornton* v. *Shoe Lane Parking, Ltd.*, [1971] 2 Q.B. 163; [1971] 1 All E.R. 686 C.A.

[6] See, however, *Barnett* v. *H. and J. Packer & Co., Ltd.*, [1940] 3 All E.R. 575; *Geddling* v. *Marsh*, [1920] 1 K.B. 668.

[7] *Cf. Ford Motor Co.* v. *Tritt*, 430 S.W. 2d 778 (Ark., 1968); *Sarfati* v. *M. A. Hittner & Sons Inc.*, 318 N.Y.S. (2d) 352 (1970); 2 Frumer and Friedman, *Products Liability*, s. 19.07 [2], and below, p. 167.

"If any agreement (whether made before or after the commencement of this Act) contains a provision which would exclude or restrict—

(*a*) any liability to which a party to a contract may be subject by reason of any misrepresentation made by him before the contract was made; or
(*b*) any remedy available to another party to the contract by reason of such a misrepresentation;
   that provision shall be of no effect except to the extent (if any) that, in any proceedings arising out of the contract, the court or arbitrator may allow reliance on it as being fair and reasonable in the circumstances of the case."

This section creates a number of problems. Its broad effect is to subject to statutory control agreements which purport to exclude or restrict liabilities or remedies in respect of misrepresentations inducing a contract. Such remedies include damages under s. 2 of the 1967 Act, claims to rescind the contract and, no doubt, the setting up of the misrepresentation as a defence to an action brought by the representor.[1] Misrepresentations actionable only under the *Hedley Byrne*[2] principle are not included. In all such cases the agreement is valid only to the extent that the court or arbitrator "may allow reliance on it as being fair and reasonable in the circumstances of the case".[3] No indication is given of the factors to be taken into account in reaching a decision on this point, an omission which two distinguished commentators have described as "little short of scandalous"[4] but which is in line with the approach of the Scottish Law Commission in a recent report.[5]

The 1967 Act does not define the words "exclude or restrict" and it is likely that they will be construed broadly.[6] A genuine attempt to prevent an obligation from arising should not, however, be regarded as falling within the section. A principal does not bring himself within s. 3 by limiting his agent's ostensible authority[7] and neither should a representor if he insists that the representee verify the truth of an affirmation for himself. There is also difficulty in deciding to what extent the section

---

[1] As in *Goldsmith* v. *Rodger*, [1962] 2 Lloyd's Rep. 249. For general discussion of rescission and damages, see above, pp. 49–58.
[2] *Hedley Byrne & Co., Ltd.* v. *Heller & Partners, Ltd.*, [1964] A.C. 465; [1963] 2 All E.R. 575, H.L., above, pp. 43–45, below, pp. 337–338.
[3] The new s. 55 (4) of the Sale of Goods Act 1893, above, p. 142, uses the disjunctive "fair or reasonable" as opposed to the "fair *and* reasonable" of s. 3 of the 1967 Act but presumably nothing should be made of the difference of terminology.
[4] Atiyah and Treitel (1967), 30 M.L.R. 369, 385.
[5] *Exemption Clauses: Second Report*, Scot. Law Com. No. 39, paras. 193–196. *Cf.* the views of the English Law Commission in paras. 185–192 of the report.
[6] *Cf.* the Sale of Goods Act 1893, s. 55 (9), above, p. 143.
[7] See *Overbrooke Estates, Ltd.* v. *Glencombe Properties, Ltd.*, [1974] 3 All E.R. 511; [1974] 1 W.L.R. 1335.

applies to misrepresentations which are or which become terms of the contract. Where a misrepresentation is incorporated as a contractual term the entitlement to rescind is preserved[8] and since this remedy is available by reason of the misrepresentation it would be protected by s. 3. On the other hand, express warranties containing promises as to the future would give rise only to remedies for breach of contract. Such remedies do not arise by reason of a misrepresentation and hence the 1967 Act would *prima facie* be inapplicable. However, it is arguable that an exempting provision which purports to cover both misrepresentations and terms may be controlled as to the latter no less than the former. Such a provision would presumably be "of no effect" except to the extent (if any) that the court allows reliance on it.[9]

Manufacturers and consumers

Manufacturers' guarantees[1]

In English law the relationship between a manufacturer and a consumer of his product is usually discussed in terms of the scope and application of the tort of negligence. Where a producer or manufacturer sells directly to a consumer the normal sales conditions will attach to the contract of sale. Occasionally it may be possible to spell out a collateral contract where the manufacturer has given assurances about the suitability or potential of his product and the plaintiff has purchased the product from a third party or stipulated that it be used.[2] A more widespread strict liability might be imposed in respect of the breach of express warranties[3] or under a strict tort or implied warranty theory.[4] These features of American

---

[8] Misrepresentation Act 1967, s. 1 (*a*). Rescission is subject to the discretion of the court to declare the certain subsisting under s. 2 (2) of the Act.

[9] See Atiyah and Treitel (1967), 30 M.L.R. 369, 383.

[1] *Benjamin's Sale of Goods*, paras. 998, 1005–1011; *Final Report of the Committee on Consumer Protection* (Moloney Committee), Cmnd. 1781 (1962) pp. 131–137; 155–157, paras. 410–426, 474–478; Atiyah, *Sale of Goods*, 5th edn., 1975, pp. 114–117; Ontario Law Reform Commission *Report on Consumer Warranties and Guarantees in the Sale of Goods* (1972), chs. 6, 7, especially Treblicock (1972), 18 McGill, L.J. 1; Ziegel (1973), 22 I.C.L.Q. 363; Moore (1972), 4 Adelaide, L.R. 423; Law Commission's *Second Report on Exemption Clauses*, Law Com. No. 69 (1975), paras. 99–105; Hansard, H.C. Debs. Vol. 809, cols, 475–486, 15 January 1971; Vol. 815, cols. 1183–1187, 21 April 1971.

[2] See, e.g., *Wells (Merstham), Ltd.* v. *Buckland Sand and Silica, Ltd.,* [1965] 2 Q.B. 170; [1964] 1 All E.R. 41; *Shanklin Pier, Ltd.* v. *Detel Products, Ltd.,* [1951] 2 K.B. 854; [1951] 2 All E.R. 471, and above, pp. 64–65.

[3] See *Baxter* v. *Ford Motor Co.*, 12 P. 2d 409, 88 A.L.R. 521 (1932); 15 P. 2d 1118 (1932) (rehearing); 35 P. 2d 1090 (1934) (second appeal), above, pp. 58–62.

[4] See *Greenman* v. *Yuba Power Products Inc.*, 27 Cal. Rptr. 697 (Cal. Sup. Ct., 1963); *Henningsen* v. *Bloomfield Motors Inc.*, 161 A. 2d 67 (N.J., 1960), above, pp. 15–17.

product liability law have not, however, made any progress in English or Commonwealth jurisdictions. Whilst the above possibilities are familiar enough to lawyers none of them corresponds with the first thoughts of an ordinary purchaser of a consumer durable which proves to be defective. His reaction will typically be to turn to any manufacturers' guarantee which may have accompanied the goods. In view of the prevalence of such guarantees it is strange that there is a paucity of litigation in this area whether by a purchaser seeking to enforce a promise under the guarantee or by a manufacturer seeking protection from it.

Claims on guarantees

A manufacturers' guarantee will typically contain an undertaking to repair or replace defective parts within a limited period of time or to refund the purchase price if the goods "fail to please" or do not give "entire satisfaction". The good features of such guarantees were fairly summarised by the Molony Committee in 1962 when it noted:[5]

"No one suggests that there is anything undesirable in the concept of the manufacturer's guarantee. It is accepted as an inevitable consequence of modern trading methods. If the manufacturer undertakes full responsibility for replacing unsatisfactory goods or for rectifying manufacturing defects which come to light within a reasonable time; if he makes arrangements which bring his accumulated experience and technical resources to bear upon the individual consumer's troubles; if he honours his undertaking quickly and without quibble or formality—in such circumstances the manufacturer is providing a service which could not be surpassed, and which it would be difficult to equal, by other means."

The person seeking to enforce such an undertaking might do so on the ground that it formed either a unilateral or a bilateral contract. In both instances it would be necessary to establish that consideration had been furnished and where the contract is bilateral the general view is that communication of acceptance would also be required.[6] Purchase of the goods covered by the guarantee can realistically be viewed as the consideration necessary to support a unilateral contract. The buyer need not show that it was the guarantee which prompted him to buy the goods[7] although he must, strictly speaking, establish that he knew before he

---

[5] Cmnd. 1781, para. 414.
[6] See *Felthouse* v. *Bindley* (1862), 11 C.B. N.S. 869, affd. (1863), 1 New Rep. 401; *cf.* Miller (1972) 35 M.L.R. 489. There would be no such requirement in a unilateral contract: *Carlill* v. *Carbolic Smoke Ball Co.,* [1893] 1 Q.B. 256, 270 *per* Bowen, L.J.
[7] *Williams* v. *Carwardine* (1833), 4 B. & Ad. 621; *Thomas* v. *Thomas* (1842), 2 Q.B. 851.

bought them that a guarantee existed.[8] Since many guarantees are only taken out and read once the goods are unpacked, this might prove a stumbling block. In practice, however, it is likely that the transaction would be taken as a whole.[9] In any event it would probably be sufficient that the goods were of a type which was typically guaranteed, such as watches or electrical equipment. It is unlikely that a court would insist on prior knowledge of the terms of the guarantee in question.[10]

Many guarantees require that the owner of the goods complete and post off a slip to have the guarantee registered. Such conduct might serve a dual purpose. Where it is argued that the contract is bilateral it would constitute a communication of acceptance. In the case of a potentially unilateral contract it might be viewed as sufficient consideration to support the manufacturer's undertakings. A similar significance might be attached to the act of returning the defective goods to the manufacturer.[11] In all such cases it remains important to ascertain precisely what the manufacturer has undertaken. A simple statement that the goods are "guaranteed" probably has no greater content than the manufacturer chooses to give it.[12] Moreover, the typical "guarantee" does not warrant that the goods are free from defects as such. It merely undertakes to replace defective parts within a limited period if certain conditions are satisfied. Hence claims for consequential losses are unlikely to be covered.[13]

Exclusion of liability

Although manufacturers' guarantees frequently confer valuable rights their primary function over the years has been to seek to exclude liabilities which might otherwise have been incurred.[1] Thus documents mas-

---

[8] *Roscorla* v. *Thomas* (1842), 3 Q.B. 234.

[9] *Cf.* Treitel, *Law of Contract*, 4th edn., 1975, p. 54. A similar indulgence might not be shown where a manufacturer is relying on the "guarantee" as an exemption clause.

[10] The U.C.C., art. 2–313, Official Comment 7, seems to avoid the "past consideration" problem, at least in contracts of sale. It provides: "The precise time when words of description or affirmation are made...is not material...If language is used after the closing of the deal (as when the buyer when taking delivery asks and receives an additional assurance), the warranty becomes a modification and need not be supported by consideration...".

[11] *Chappell & Co., Ltd.* v. *Nestlé Co., Ltd.*, [1960] A.C. 87; [1959] 2 All E.R. 701 might be cited in support of such a submission. The point might also be important to a person who had received the goods as a donee or to one who had only found the guarantee after the conclusion of the contract of sale.

[12] See the Molony Committee report, Cmnd. 1781 (1962), para. 418. It might sometimes be possible to imply terms similar to those which are implied in contracts of sale: see above, p. 115 *et seq.*

[13] *Cf. Adams* v. *Richardson and Starling, Ltd.*, [1969] 2 All E.R. 1221; [1969] 1 W.L.R. 1645, C.A.

[1] Examples are to be found in Hansard, H.C. Debs. Vol. 809, cols. 475–486, 15 January 1971 (Greville Janner, M.P.).

querading as "guarantees" may do no more than undertake to replace a defective part which has not been "misused", leaving the customer to despatch the goods at his own expense and to pay the labour costs. Moreover the manufacturer may be designated the sole arbiter of defectiveness.[2] In return for this strictly limited undertaking, the purchaser has often been required to relinquish the extensive statutory and common law rights he would otherwise have possessed. It was always doubtful whether such "guarantees" were effective to protect the retailer although they typically purported to do so. The retailer would not be a party to the contract and could not be protected by its terms.[3] It would seem that the point is no longer important since exemption clauses in contracts for the sale of goods are now controlled by legislation whether the term be in the contract of sale or in "any other contract".[4] In particular it would seem that if the exemption clause in the contract of sale was otherwise inoperative, the purchaser would not be prejudiced by any undertaking he may have given to the manufacturer not to sue the vendor.[5]

At present there is no statutory restriction in English law on the entitlement of a manufacturer to exempt his own liability for negligence by a suitably worded "guarantee". Such a "guarantee" can, however, operate as an exemption clause only where a contract can be established and then only as between the parties to the contract of "guarantee".[6] A manufacturer's typical undertaking to repair or replace defective parts would, in principle, constitute sufficient consideration to support a promise not to sue in negligence in respect of personal injury or property damage. Such an undertaking goes beyond a manufacturer's obligations under the general law[7] and English law does not inquire into the adequacy of the

---

[2] As in *Henningsen* v. *Bloomfield Motors Inc.*, 161 A. 2d 67, 78–79 (N.J. 1960).

[3] *Scruttons, Ltd.* v. *Midland Silicones, Ltd.*, [1962] A.C. 446; [1962] 1 All E.R. 1, H.L. It is of course possible to argue that the guarantee had been incorporated into the contract of sale itself, in which case its effectiveness would be determined by sales legislation: see the following text.

[4] Sale of Goods Act 1893, s. 55 (4), as amended by the Supply of Goods (Implied Terms) Act 1973, s. 4, above pp. 142–158.

[5] But for the 1893 Act, as amended, the manufacturer might presumably intervene to stay the proceedings, or sue for damages for breach of the contract of "guarantee" where he has undertaken to indemnify the retailer: see *Gore* v. *Van der Lann*, [1967] 2 Q.B. 31; [1967] 1 All E.R. 360; *Snelling* v. *John G. Snelling, Ltd.*, [1973] 1 Q.B. 87; [1972] 1 All E.R. 79. An attempt by the manufacturer to stay proceedings brought by the buyer in respect of a breach of ss. 12–15 of the 1893 Act would now be caught by s. 55 (4), (9), as amended. *Semble* that a manufacturer's claim for damages under the contract of "guarantee" would also be caught by the provisions of s. 55. The problem would rarely arise since such contracts do not typically contain positive undertakings by the purchaser not to sue.

[6] In the absence of a contract the clause might occasionally operate to discharge the manufacturer's duty through adequate warning or directions for use: see above, ch. 12.

[7] For the position with respect to purely economic loss, see below, ch. 16.

consideration furnished. There may be more difficulty in establishing a communication of acceptance of the offer containing the exempting clause. A manufacturer could not impose such a contract by stating that silence will be deemed to constitute acceptance.[8] But the filling in and returning of the guarantee for registration would appear to be sufficient.

Where a contract can be established it will be construed *contra proferentem* and thus against the party seeking to rely on the exempting provision.[9] It is doubtful whether English law would strike down a "guarantee" on the ground that it was unconscionable or contrary to public policy to enforce it;[10] but it would certainly hold that it was inapplicable as a matter of construction. The language of exempting provisions in such "guarantees" frequently refers to the statutory implied warranties of fitness and merchantability. Since these do not apply in English law as between a manufacturer and a remote consumer they do not require to be excluded. It is liability in tort for negligence which requires to be excluded and it is doubtful whether such terminology is apt to achieve this.[11]

Finally, it may be noted that there are currently a number of proposals for the reform of the law in this area. The Law Commission has recently recommended that:[12]

> "(P)rovisions excluding or restricting liability for loss or damage arising while goods are in consumer use, due to the negligence of a person concerned in the manufacture or distribution of goods, should be made void if they are contained in a guarantee of the goods."

Although this recommendation is to be welcomed it is doubtful whether it goes far enough. Void provisions would probably continue to thrive on public ignorance, although perhaps to a lesser extent than in the parallel area of consumer sales where the Director-General of Fair Trading has already found it necessary to recommend that such provisions be made *unlawful*. As part of this latter proposal, which has been accepted (subject to modifications) by the Consumer Protection Advisory Committee,[13] the Director-General has also recommended that guarantees and other written statements relating to rights against third parties such as the manufacturer must also indicate that the buyer has rights against the seller if the goods

---

[8] *Felthouse* v. *Bindley* (1862), 11 C.B.N.S. 869, affd. (1863), 1 New Rep. 401. An example of such an attempt might read: "The guarantee is automatically effective . . . you do not have to return the form": see Hansard, H.C. Debs. Vol. 809, col. 478.

[9] For discussion of this principle of construction, see above, pp. 128–131.

[10] As in *Henningsen* v. *Bloomfield Motors Inc.*, 161 A. 2d 67 (N.J., 1960); *Walsh* v. *Ford Motor Co.*, 298 N.Y.S. (2d) 538 (1969). For discussion of unconscionability, see above, pp. 137–140.

[11] See Atiyah, *Sale of Goods*, 5th edn., 1975, p. 116.

[12] See *Exemption Clauses: Second Report*, Law Com. No. 69 (1975), para. 105.

[13] See *Rights of Consumers: A Report on Practices Relating to the Purported Exclusion of Inalienable Rights of Consumers and Failure to Explain their Existence* (1974), above, p. 145.

are faulty. An order implementing these proposals has since been laid before Parliament and approved by the House of Commons and the House of Lords.[14]

Neither of these proposals goes as far as the recommendations in the Ontario Law Reform Commission Report *Consumer Warranties and Guarantees in the Sale of Goods*. These envisage that manufacturers should be required where appropriate to give express performance warranties backed up by adequate spare parts and servicing facilities.[15] The Molony Committee in its report in 1962 was not "attracted by the idea of writing a statutory contract for each trade",[16] and had no positive suggestions to offer beyond enjoining the consumer to secure protection by his own vigilance.[17] But it is likely that developments along these lines will represent the pattern for the future. Australian legislation is also notable for imposing certain obligations on dealers to repair new and secondhand motor vehicles for a period after the purchaser takes delivery.[18]

Exemption clauses under the strict tort and other theories of liability

If a further measure of strict liability were to be introduced into English product liability law, it would be necessary to decide on the place of exemption and limitation clauses within the new system. This raises a number of difficult questions the answers to which may depend on both the theory of liability chosen and the nature of the claim.

Where the requirements of privity are relaxed so as to enable a third party to sue on a contract of sale[1] it would seem right that the third party should be bound by the terms of any disclaimer to the same extent as the contracting party. This is the approach of Official Comment 1 to art. 2–318 of the Uniform Commercial Code which states that:[2]

> "To the extent that the contract of sale contains provisions under which warranties are excluded or modified, or remedies for breach are limited, such provisions are equally operative against beneficiaries of warranties under this section."

---

[14] Consumer Transactions (Restrictions on Statements) Order 1976, Hansard, H.C. Deb., Vol. 916, col. 1161–1171, 30 July 1976, H.L. Deb. Vol. 375, cols. 97–118, 11 October 1976.

[15] See chs. 2, 6, 7 of the report, at pp. 40–41, 45, 90–91, 96, 100, 102.

[16] Cmnd. 1781, para. 417.

[17] *Ibid.,* para. 425.

[18] See Second-Hand Motor Vehicles Act 1971 (S.A.), s. 24; Motor Dealers Act 1974 (N.S.W.), s. 27. In the United Kingdom there is a growing tendency for manufacturers to undertake such obligations voluntarily: e.g., the British Leyland "Supercover" system.

[1] The implications of this approach are discussed above, p. 27 *et seq.*

[2] See 1 *Uniform Laws Annotated* (1968), p. 251.

This would not of course prevent the third party from suing in tort and thus quite independently of the contract of sale.

Different considerations arise where the rights are not derivative but stem from obligations directly imposed whether on the manufacturer or on some other person in the chain of distribution. The contractual associations of the implied warranty theory might lend weight to an argument that a disclaimer could be effective against a third party as under art. 2–318 of the Code. In the leading case of *Henningsen* v. *Bloomfield Motors Inc.*[3] it was unnecessary to deal with the point. The disclaimer was held to be void as against the husband-purchaser[4] and as such it could hardly have been effective as against the wife to whom the car had been given as a gift and who was injured when the steering failed.

A number of possibilities might be envisaged in the event of a strict tort theory of liability being adopted in English law. A plaintiff claiming against a manufacturer in respect of physical injury or property damage would not be prejudiced by an exemption clause in a contract to which he was not a party.[5] He might, however, fail on the quite distinct ground that he had assumed the risk of injury[6] or that he was the sole effective cause of his own injury or damage. The same would be true of a case in which a person other than a purchaser was suing a retailer under a strict tort theory. In *Vandermark* v. *Ford Motor Co.*,[7] for example, the plaintiff passenger was not affected by a contractual disclaimer when suing the dealer who had sold a car to her brother. The car had later crashed because of a defect in the brake system.

The position as between a purchaser and a vendor of goods might cause more difficulty. In a non-consumer sale the vendor would presumably retain his limited ability to exclude liability for breaches of the implied

---

[3] 161 A. 2d 69 (N.J., 1960). See also *Haley* v. *Merit Chevrolet Inc.*, 214 N.E. 2d 347 (Ill., 1966); *Suvada* v. *White Motor Co.*, 201 N.E. 2d 313 (Ill., 1964). For discussion in this context see 2 *Frumer and Friedman*, s. 19.07 [4] where it is noted: "If the injured third party chooses to take the benefit of a warranty, the argument is available that the limitations on the warranty or its total disclaimer should also be the burden of the claimant".

[4] See above, p. 154.

[5] See *Scruttons, Ltd.* v. *Midland Silicones, Ltd.*, [1962] A.C. 446; [1962] 1 All E.R. 1. *Cf.*, however, *New Zealand Shipping Co., Ltd.* v. *A. M. Satterthwaite & Co., Ltd.*, [1975] A.C. 154; [1974] 1 All E.R. 1015, P.C.

[6] For discussion of *volenti non fit injuria*, see below, p. 291. *Quaere* whether he would be any better off if his assent happened to be expressed in the terms of a contract to which he was not a party? See further *Scruttons, Ltd.* v. *Midland Silicones, Ltd.*, [1962] A.C. 446, 488–489, *per* Lord Denning; *White* v. *John Warrick & Co., Ltd.*, [1953] 2 All E.R. 1021, 1026, *per* Lord Denning; *Wilson* v. *Darling Island Stevedoring and Lighterage Co., Ltd.* (1956), 95 C.L.R. 43, 82–83, *per* Kitto, J.

[7] 37 Cal. Rptr. 896 (Cal. Sup. Ct., 1964). See also *Velez* v. *Craine and Clark Lumber Corporation*, 305 N.E. 2d 750 (N.Y.C.A., 1973).

conditions of merchantable quality and reasonable fitness for purpose.[8] In principle it should also be possible to exclude a strict tort liability unless there are specific statutory provisions prohibiting this.[9] Where personal injury is concerned, reliance on an exemption clause would rarely be fair or reasonable for the purpose of s. 55 (4) of the 1893 Act. Nor would a clause normally be construed as extending to such injury for the purpose of the strict tort theory.[10] Commercial purchasers would rarely suffer such injury in person.[11] But a similar approach might be adopted where a retailer had been sued by a consumer purchaser and where he was claiming to be indemnified by the manufacturer under his own contract to purchase the goods.[12] Where the claim is in respect of property damage there is no reason why there should be the same reluctance to allow reliance on the clause in a non-consumer sale.[13]

If recovery were to be permitted in tort in respect of purely economic losses[14] it would be necessary to re-examine the rule whereby exemption clauses are capable of being effective only as between the parties to the contract in which they are embodied. A simple combination of tort liability for economic loss and a privity limitation on the effectiveness of disclaimers would produce absurd consequences. The point may be illustrated with a simple example. If A, a business purchaser, has bought a product from B which B had earlier acquired from C and both contracts were subject to exemption clauses reliance on which was reasonable in the circumstances one could not justify permitting A to sue C directly for

---

[8] See above, pp. 150–158.

[9] Such provisions may be expected. See the proposed EEC directive, art. 10; Strasbourg Convention, art. 8. See also *Restatement of Torts*, 2d, s. 402A, Comment m, which states that strict tort liability "is not affected by limitations on the scope and content of warranties"; s. 402B, Comment d (public misrepresentation). See also *Vandermark* v. *Ford Motor Co.*, 37 Cal. Rptr. 896 (1964) where the dealer's liability to the purchaser was not excluded.

[10] In *Henningsen* v. *Bloomfield Motors Inc.*, 161 A. 2d 69 (N.J., 1960) such a clause was held to be void as being contrary to public policy. See also *Thornton* v. *Shoe Lane Parking, Ltd.*, [1971] 2 Q.B. 163; [1971] 1 All E.R. 686, C.A.

[11] See, however, *Barnett* v. *H. and J. Packer & Co., Ltd.*, [1940] 3 All E.R. 575; *Geddling* v. *Marsh*, [1920] 1 K.B. 668.

[12] The general position has caused difficulty in the USA. Some courts are unwilling to uphold a manufacturer's disclaimer, viewing the retail vendor as a mere conduit: see *Ford Motor Co.* v. *Tent*, 430 S.W. 2d 778 (Ark., 1968); *Sarfati* v. *M. A. Hittner & Sons Inc.*, 318 N.Y.S. 2d 352 (1970); and *cf. Williams* v. *Chrysler Corporation*, 137 S.E. 2d 225 (Va., 1964). Yet this view of the retailers' role is difficult to reconcile with cases such as *Vandermark* v. *Ford Motor Co.*, above, which impose strict tort liability on a retailer precisely because he is not a "mere conduit".

[13] See *Delta Airlines* v. *McDonnell Douglas Corporation*, [1975] 1 Lloyds Rep. 205 (5th Cir., 1974). See also *Keystone Aeronautics Corporation* v. *R.J. Enstrom Corporation*, 364 F. Supp. 1063 (1973); *Arrow Transportation Co.* v. *Freuhauf Corporation*, 289 F. Supp. 170 (1968).

[14] The scope of liability for economic loss is discussed below, ch. 16, pp. 328–344.

purely economic losses without being affected by a disclaimer.[15] The present authors do not favour an extended liability for economic losses whether under a strict tort or negligence theory or, indeed, any other theory which does not depend on express warranties having been made.[16] But if a different view were to prevail then it is submitted that an action should in any event fail if either (i) the plaintiff was bound by an exempting provision in his own contract, or (ii) the defendant was protected by such a provision in his contract of sale. Similar provisions should apply *mutatis mutandis* to other contracts such as contracts of hire.

---

[15] See *T.W.A.* v. *Curtiss-Wright Corporation*, 148 N.Y.S. 2d 284, 290 (1955) and below, p. 339. In the USA there is ample scope for conflict between U.C.C., art. 2–316 which envisages that disclaimers may be effective and the strict tort theory which denies their effectiveness at least where personal injury is concerned. For general discussion, see Note, "Economic Loss in Products Liability Jurisprudence", 66 Col. L.R. 917 (1966); Speidel, "Products Liability, Economic Loss and the UCC", 40 Tenn. L.R. 309 (1973); Franklin, "When Worlds Collide: liability theories and disclaimers in defective products cases", 18 Stan. L.R. 974 (1966).

[16] See *Baxter* v. *Ford Motor Co.*, 12 P. 2d 409 (1932); 15 P. 2d 1118 (1932) (rehearing); 35 P. 2d 1090 (1934) (second appeal), and, in general, above, pp. 58–62.

Part II
Liability in Tort

9 The Manufacturers' Liability: Some Preliminary Considerations

Introduction

The broad framework of product liability in the English law of tort was outlined in an earlier chapter[1] where it was noted that until the decision in *Donoghue* v. *Stevenson*[2] in 1932 the general rule was one of non-liability. This rule was associated with *Winterbottom* v. *Wright*,[3] a case decided in the Court of Exchequer in 1842, and a number of exceptions were developed. But it was still generally understood that there was no liability in tort where damage was caused by a latent and unknown defect in goods which were not inherently dangerous as a class.[4]

The result is to be seen in cases such as *Blacker* v. *Lake and Elliot, Ltd.*[5] The plaintiff was a bicycle maker and repairer who had acquired a brazing lamp from an intermediate party and suffered injury when it burst. The jury found that the lamp was designed defectively and that the defendant manufacturers ought to have known that it was dangerous. Yet in the judgment of the Divisional Court this was not a sufficient reason for imposing liability. The manufacturers owed a duty to the person to whom they had sold the lamp but they did not owe a duty to third parties such as the plaintiff.

A similar conclusion had been reached in *Earl* v. *Lubbock*[6] where the

---

[1] See above, ch. 1, pp. 5–11 especially.
[2] [1932] A.C. 562, H.L.
[3] (1842), 10 M. & W. 109.
[4] For "inherently dangerous" goods, see above, pp. 10–11 and below, pp. 253–255.
[5] (1912), 106 L.T. 533, D.C.
[6] [1905] 1 K.B. 253. See also *Bates* v. *Batey & Co., Ltd.*, [1913] 3 K.B. 351.

Court of Appeal held that the plaintiff van driver had no cause of action against the defendant, a master wheelwright, whose alleged carelessness in repairing a van under contract with the plaintiff's employer was said to have caused the accident which was the subject of the claim. In dismissing the claim Collins, M.R. noted that the circumstances of the case were indistinguishable from those of *Winterbottom* v. *Wright*,[7] and that "that decision, since the year of 1842 in which it was given, has stood the test of repeated discussion".[8] Mathew, L.J. purported to justify the denial of liability in more general terms by saying of the plaintiff's contention that "it is difficult to see how, if it were the law, trade could be carried on". "No prudent man," he added, "would contract to make or repair what the employer intended to permit others to use in the way of his trade."[9] These sentiments and assumptions were, of course, an echo of those advanced in *Winterbottom* v. *Wright*[7] some sixty years earlier.

George v. *Skivington*[10] was one of the few cases which did not fit readily into the recognised pattern of exceptions.[11] Here the declaration stated that the defendant chemist negligently compounded a hair wash to a secret formula and sold it to G, knowing that it was intended for the use of his wife and representing that it was "fit and proper to be used for washing the hair". G's wife suffered personal injury as a result of using the compound and brought the action joining her husband as a co-plaintiff "for conformity". The defendant having entered a demurrer on which issue was joined, the Court of Exchequer gave judgment for the plaintiff. In concluding that the declaration disclosed a cause of action, the court viewed the case as being on all fours with *Langridge* v. *Levy*,[12] except that the allegation was one of negligence rather than fraud. Thus emphasis was placed on the fact that the defendant knew the purpose for which the compound was required and the person who was going to use it,[13] as had the vendor of the gun in the earlier case. Whilst the willingness to extend liability on such facts from a case of fraud to one of negligence had considerable potential for development, *George* v. *Skivington* was not generally regarded as a case to be followed[14] until it was finally approved in *Donoghue* v. *Stevenson*[15] itself.

---

[7] (1842), 10 M. & W. 109.
[8] [1905] 1 K.B. 253, 255.
[9] *Ibid.*, at p. 259.
[10] (1869), L.R. 5 Exch. 1.
[11] See also *Anglo-Celtic Shipping Co.* v. *Elliott and Jeffrey* (1926), 42 T.L.R. 297, discussed by Bohlen, "Liability of Manufacturers to Persons other than their Immediate Vendees" (1929), 45 L.Q.R. 343, 350–353.
[12] (1837), 2 M. & W. 519, below, p. 301.
[13] *Cf.* (1869) L.R. 5 Exch. 1, at p. 4 (Kelly, C.B.), *ibid.* (Pigott, B.), and at p. 5 (Cleasby, B.).
[14] See the discussion of the case and of the authorities which have considered it in *Blacker* v. *Lake & Elliot, Ltd.* (1912), 106 L.T. 533, 537–539, D.C. (Hamilton, J.).
[15] [1932] A.C. 562, H.L.

Donoghue *v.* Stevenson

In *Donoghue* v. *Stevenson*[15] the appellant was a shop assistant who averred that she had accompanied a friend to the cafe of one Minchella in Paisley where the friend had purchased some ice cream and a bottle of ginger beer. She further averred that the bottle was made of dark opaque glass; that Minchella had poured some of the ginger beer into a tumbler and over the ice cream which she had then consumed; that when the friend was pouring out the remainder of the ginger beer a decomposed snail had floated out of the bottle; and that as a result of the nauseating sight of the snail and of the impurities in the ginger beer consumed she had suffered shock and severe gastro-enteritis. As for the respondents, it was averred that they were the manufacturers and bottlers of the ginger beer; that they had sent the bottles out sealed with a metal cap and labelled with their name to be drunk by members of the public; and that it was their duty to ensure that snails did not get into the bottles and to inspect the bottles before filling them.

The respondent's objection that the averments disclosed no cause of action was dismissed by the Lord Ordinary but sustained on appeal by the Second Division of the Court of Session following an earlier decision of the same court the facts of which were indistinguishable except that they involved a mouse rather than a snail.[16] The case then proceeded to the House of Lords where it was held that the averments, *pro veritate*, disclosed a cause of action entitling the appellant to have them remitted for proof. The case was accordingly remitted to the Court of Session "to do therein as shall be just and consistent with this judgment". It was not disputed that the law of Scotland and the law of England were as one on the issues raised.

Whether the celebrated snail was ever in the bottle was never determined since it seems that the manufacturer died before proof and that the claim was settled out of court by the payment of £100.[17] The point is of some interest as an historical vignette but not important to the development of the law of product liability. What was important, rather, was the recognition by the House of Lords that on proof of such facts a manufacturer would owe a duty of care to the remote consumer of his product. Unlike the equivalent American decision in *Macpherson* v. *Buick Motor Co.*,[18] this conclusion was not reached through an extension of the recognised exception for "inherently dangerous" goods. It envisaged, rather, a reversal of the general rule of non-liability or more precisely a denial that any such rule existed. Thus having formulated his celebrated "neighbour

---

[16] *Mullen* v. *Barr & Co., Ltd.*, 1929 S.C. 461.
[17] See Heuston, "*Donoghue* v. *Stevenson* in Retrospect" (1957), 20 M.L.R. 1, 2.
[18] 217 N.Y. 382, 111 N.E. 1050 (1916), above, p. 13.

principle" requiring the exercise of reasonable care towards all who are foreseeably likely to be injured in person or property by one's conduct,[19] Lord Atkin outlined the scope of the manufacturers' liability in the following terms:[20]

> "My Lords . . . a manufacturer of products, which he sells in such a form as to show that he intends them to reach the ultimate consumer in the form in which they left him with no reasonable possibility of intermediate examination, and with the knowledge that the absence of reasonable care in the preparation or putting up of the products will result in an injury to the consumer's life or property, owes a duty to the consumer to take reasonable care."

In retrospect, the only surprising thing about the decision is that it commended itself to no more than a bare majority of the House of Lords. As Lord Atkin noted, only a lawyer would have doubted that the principle which he had formulated represented the law.[1] Marketing conditions had changed considerably since the days when *Winterbottom* v. *Wright*[2] was decided in 1842, as had the capacity of industry to absorb and to distribute the cost of meeting such claims. The direct sale from producer to user was no longer the norm. It had given way increasingly to distribution through a network of middlemen who often acted as little more than conduit pipes but whose very existence was sufficient to deny the consumer a contractual remedy against the producer. Moreover the establishment of the principle was undoubtedly aided by the particular facts of the case itself.

As Lord Macmillan pointed out, acceptance of the defendant's submissions would have meant that a baker would have been immune from civil liability to a remote consumer if he had allowed a quantity of arsenic to be mixed with a batch of his bread.[3] Similarly it was important to the success of the appeal that the offending bottle was both sealed and opaque, since this effectively ruled out any question of intervening tampering by a third party.[4]

This is not to suggest that the speeches of the majority, Lords Atkin, Macmillan and Thankerton, are especially convincing in their treatment of the earlier cases. Indeed from this strictly legalistic point of view there is much to be said for the conclusions of the dissenting minority, Lords Buckmaster and Tomlin. At this distance of time, and having regard to subsequent developments, it is not intended to examine the matter in

---

[19] [1932] A.C. 562, 580.
[20] *Ibid.*, at p. 599.
[1] *Ibid.*
[2] (1842), 10 M. & W. 109.
[3] [1932] A.C. 562, 620–621.
[4] Issues of causation and intermediate examination are discussed below, pp. 273–290.

detail. It is sufficient to say that of the main obstacles to recovery *Winterbottom* v. *Wright*[5] was construed narrowly as having decided no more than that A's carelessness in the performance of a contractual obligation owed to B did not of itself furnish a cause of action to a third party, C.[6] As for *Longmeid* v. *Holiday*,[7] it was noted that in this case there was no averment of negligence but only an unsubstantiated allegation of fraud.[8] Finally, Lord Atkin confessed to having found difficulty in deciding on what grounds the judgment in *Blacker* v. *Lake and Elliot, Ltd.*[9] was based before concluding that the Divisional Court had held that there was no evidence of negligence to go to the jury. All observations thereafter could consequently be relegated to the status of a "series of important dicta".[10]

Products

Once the decision had been taken there was no real suggestion that it would be construed narrowly whether in terms of the range of products to which it might be applied, or of plaintiffs who might benefit from it or defendants who might be held liable. In this, at least, Lord Buckmaster has been proved to have been correct when he asked, echoing the words of Alderson, B. before him,[11] "If one step, why not fifty?"[12] *Grant* v. *Australian Knitting Mills, Ltd.*[13] was significant in this respect. Here the Privy Council held in favour of a medical practitioner who had contracted dermatitis after an excess of bisulphite soda had been allowed to remain in woollen undergarments manufactured by the defendant company. A distinction between food and drink for internal consumption and articles for external wear was advanced by counsel for the defendants but without success. Later cases have confirmed the application of the principle to suppliers of articles such as hair dye and bath salts which are intended for use on or application to the body.[14] Such cases may create problems

---

[5] (1842), 10 M. & W. 109, above, p. 7.
[6] *Cf.* [1932] A.C. 562, 589 (Lord Atkin), and at p. 610 and p. 613 (Lord Macmillan). Lord Macmillan adopted the conclusion advanced in Pollock, *Law of Torts*, 13th edn., p. 570.
[7] (1851), 6 Exch. 761, above, p. 10.
[8] *Cf.* [1932] A.C. 562, 590 (Lord Atkin).
[9] (1912), 106 L.T. 533, above, p. 171.
[10] *Cf.* [1932] A.C. 562, 593. See also *ibid.*, at pp. 615–616 (Lord Macmillan).
[11] In *Winterbottom* v. *Wright* (1842), 10 M. & W. 109, 115.
[12] [1932] A.C. 562, 577.
[13] [1936] A.C. 85, P.C.
[14] *Watson* v. *Buckley, Osborne, Garrett & Co., Ltd.*, [1940] 1 All E.R. 174 (hair dye); *Levi* v. *Colgate Palmolive Pty., Ltd.* (1941), 41 S.R.N.S.W. 48 (N.S.W. Sup. Ct.) (bath salts: no liability on facts).

where it is contended that the plaintiff is an abnormally sensitive user or is allergic to the product in question.[15]

The duty to exercise reasonable care also extends to defects in products such as vehicles or lifts;[16] chisels brittle through excessive hardening;[17] inflammable, explosive, or poisonous substances supplied without adequate warning or directions for use;[18] substances which contain a latent health hazard such as a carcinogen;[19] or indeed any other product in domestic or commercial use. The position is the same whether the complaint relates to the product itself or to the container or packaging[20] and whether it charges the addition of a foreign element to the product or a failure to eliminate something which is an intrinsic part of the product in its natural state.[1] Equally, there is no doubt that liability may be incurred where the sole foreseeable risk is one of physical damage to property such as crops, animals or fruit trees.[2] Defects in houses have, however, been seen as creating their own problems requiring separate discussion.[3] The same is true of cases where the complaint is that the product is substandard in terms of normal commercial expectations although physical damage has not occurred (as where a dangerously defective crane is repaired before it collapses)[4] and of cases where the product is substandard without there being any potential for harm (as where a garment shrinks or a carpet is disfigured).[5] Here the problem is one of liability for economic loss and the position of the manufacturer in such cases is discussed in a later chapter.[6]

---

[15] See below, pp. 324–326.

[16] *Herschtal* v. *Stewart and Ardern, Ltd.*, [1940] 1 K.B. 155; [1939] 4 All E.R. 123 (reconditioned car); *Haseldine* v. *Daw & Son, Ltd.*, [1941] 2 K.B. 343; [1941] 3 All E.R. 156 (lift).

[17] *Mason* v. *Williams and Williams, Ltd.*, [1955] 1 All E.R. 808.

[18] See, e.g., *Vacwell Engineering Co., Ltd.* v. *B.D.H. Chemicals, Ltd.*, [1971] 1 Q.B. 88; [1969] 3 All E.R. 1681 (explosive industrial chemicals); *Norton Australia Pty., Ltd.* v. *Streets Ice Cream Pty., Ltd.* (1968), 120 C.L.R. 635 (High Ct. of Australia) (highly inflammable adhesive substance: no liability on facts). For warnings and directions for use generally, see below, ch. 12.

[19] *Wright* v. *Dunlop Rubber Co., Ltd.* (1972), 13 K.I.R. 255, C.A.

[20] See, e.g., *Fisher* v. *Harrods, Ltd.*, [1966] 1 Lloyd's Rep. 500 (container of jewellery cleaning fluid); *O'Dwyer* v. *Leo Buring Pty., Ltd.*, [1966] W.A.R. 67 (W.A. Sup. Ct.) (stopper on bottle of sparkling wine).

[1] As in *Tarling* v. *Nobel*, [1966] A. L.R. 189 (A.C.T. Sup. Ct.) (bone in chicken sandwich). See further below, pp. 191–193.

[2] See, e.g. *Ruegger* v. *Shell Oil Co. of Canada, Ltd.* (1964), 41 D.L.R. (2d) 183 (Ont. H. Ct.) (crop spray); *Grant* v. *Cooper*, [1940] N.Z.L.R. 947 (N.Z. Sup. Ct.) (sheep dip); *Kolberg* v. *Sherwin Williams Co.*, 269 P. 975 (Cal. App., 1928) (fruit spray).

[3] For the liability of building contractors and builder-vendors, see below, pp. 313–315.

[4] As in *Rivtow Marine, Ltd.* v. *Washington Iron Works* (1974), 40 D.L.R. (3d) 533 (Sup. Ct. of Canada).

[5] As in *Santor* v. *A. & M. Karaghension Inc.*, 207 A. 2d 305 (N.J., 1965).

[6] See below, ch. 16, pp. 328–344.

Plaintiffs

As for potential plaintiffs, liability has been extended beyond purchasers and other immediate recipients[7] to benefit domestic and commercial users and other persons likely to be endangered by the product if it is defective or otherwise dangerous. These include passengers in a vehicle,[8] employees who handle or service the product,[9] persons who borrow it,[10] and retailers who stock it.[11] The most significant step was the inclusion of bystanders and this was taken at a relatively early date when *Stennett* v. *Hancock and Peters*[12] came before Branson, J. in 1939. Here the plaintiff was walking along the pavement when she was struck on the leg by a flange which had come off the wheel of the defendant's lorry. The lorry had been recently collected from the second defendant, a motor repairer, who had been instructed to repair and re-assemble the wheel in question and who had returned it little more than an hour earlier. Holding the repairer liable Branson, J. regarded the case as falling squarely within the decision in *Donoghue* v. *Stevenson*, saying:[13]

> "He knew that, if it was not repaired with due care, with this wheel so assembled as to make it keep together and not fly apart upon the road, in all probability somebody would be injured as the result of his not having done that which he should have done."

No liability was incurred by the first defendant who had exercised reasonable care in relying upon an independent contractor to repair the vehicle.

A similar, if somewhat more extreme, example is provided by the Canadian case of *Martin* v. *T. W. Hand Fireworks Co., Ltd.*[14] Here the plaintiff was attending a fireworks' display in a public park when she was seriously injured by a Roman Candle which came out of the ground

---

[7] As in *Donoghue* v. *Stevenson*, [1932] A.C. 562, and *Grant* v. *Australian Knitting Mills, Ltd.*, [1936] A.C. 85.

[8] *Malfroot* v. *Noxal, Ltd.* (1935), 51 T.L.R. 551.

[9] *Vacwell Engineering Co., Ltd.* v. *B.D.H. Chemicals, Ltd.*, [1971] 1 Q.B. 88; [1969] 3 All E.R. 1681; *Mason* v. *Williams and Williams, Ltd.*, [1955] 1 All E.R. 808; [1955] 1 W.L.R. 549; *Shields* v. *Hobbs Manufacturing Co.* (1962), 34 D.L.R. (2d) 307 (Sup. Ct. of Canada). See also the Health and Safety at Work Act 1974, s. 6, which imposes certain duties on "any person who designs, manufactures, imports or supplies any article for use at work". Breach of such a duty is a criminal offence (s. 33 (1) (*a*)), but does not itself confer a right of action in civil proceedings (s. 47 (1) (*a*)).

[10] *Griffiths* v. *Arch Engineering Co., Ltd.*, [1968] 3 All E.R. 217.

[11] *Barnett* v. *H. and J. Packer and Co., Ltd.*, [1940] 3 All E.R. 575 (confectioner injured by wire protruding from sweet).

[12] [1939] 2 All E.R. 578.

[13] *Ibid.*, at p. 83.

[14] (1962), 37 D.L.R. (2d) 455 (Ont. High Ct.).

where it had been properly placed in accordance with the accompanying instructions. The offending firework had travelled some two hundred feet at an ever-increasing speed pursuing an erratic course as it expelled fireballs before striking the plaintiff on the leg and exploding. The defendant manufacturers were held liable on the ground that they had either included a defective firework within the batch or, alternatively, had sent out the fireworks with inappropriate directions for use.

Defendants

Liability has also been extended beyond manufacturers to cover wholesalers, retailers, assemblers, repairers, and those who hire products out to domestic or business users.[15] The nature of the duties owed by such persons will be discussed in a later chapter as will be the minimum duties owed by all who supply or control the use of products.[16]

Product liability and the general negligence action

Apart from its importance to the law of product liability *Donoghue* v. *Stevenson*[17] is of more general importance as establishing the existence of an independent tort of negligence. There may be certain respects in which the rules for product liability in the English law of tort differ from those which apply to the general law of negligence,[18] but to a large extent the subject involves the application of general principles to a specific area of activity. Thus the standard of care demanded of the manufacturer or supplier of a product is that of the reasonable man in the circumstances. In applying this formula, account must be taken of the likelihood of the product causing injury or damage, the probable gravity of such damage and the cost and practicability of taking measures to eliminate or reduce the risk.[19] Subject to the possibility of *res ipsa loquitur* shifting the onus

---

[15] See, e.g., *Watson* v. *Buckley, Osborne, Garrett & Co., Ltd.*, [1940] 1 All E.R. 174 (wholesale distributor); *Fisher* v. *Harrods, Ltd.*, [1966] 1 Lloyd's Rep. 500 (retailer); *Malfroot* v. *Noxal, Ltd.* (1935), 51 T.L.R. 551 (assemblers); *Haseldine* v. *Daw & Son, Ltd.*, [1941] 2 K.B. 343; [1941] 3 All E.R. 156 (repairer); *Griffiths* v. *Arch Engineering Co., Ltd.*, [1968] 3 All E.R. 217 (hirer-out).

[16] See below, ch. 15.

[17] [1932] A.C. 562, H.L.

[18] Notably, with respect to the effect of opportunities for intermediate examination of the product (see below, pp. 284–290) and of the plaintiff knowing of the defect or danger (see below, pp. 292–293).

[19] See, in general, Street, *The Law of Torts*, 6th edn., 1976, pp. 117–130; Winfield and Jolowicz, *The Law of Tort*, 10th edn., 1975, pp. 61–69; Salmond, *The Law of Torts*, 16th edn.,

of proof,[20] the plaintiff must establish a lack of reasonable care on the part of the defendant and that this caused the damage which is the subject of the claim. Liability will be incurred only in respect of damage which is of a type or kind which ought reasonably to have been foreseen,[1] but if this requirement is met, it is irrelevant that the extent of the damage was unforeseeable.[2] Defences of contributory negligence and assumption of the risk will be available.[3]

The application of general principles within the context of product liability is well illustrated in the case of *Vacwell Engineering Co., Ltd. v. B.D.H. Chemicals, Ltd.*[4] The defendants manufactured a chemical, boron tribromide, which they marketed for industrial use in glass ampoules bearing a warning label "harmful vapour". Following discussion with the defendants, the plaintiffs used the chemical in their business of manufacturing transistor materials. In order to prepare the chemical the labels were washed off the ampoules in sinks containing water and a detergent. In April 1966 a visiting Russian physicist was engaged in this task when there was a violent explosion resulting in his death and in extensive damage to the plaintiff's premises. In all probability one of the ampoules had been dropped into the sink where it had shattered, releasing the chemical into the water. The ensuing reaction had broken the glass of the other ampoules, causing a major explosion. At the time the explosive properties of boron tribromide on contact with water were unknown to the defendants; neither were they referred to in a standard work on the industrial hazards of chemicals, nor in three other modern works which the defendants had apparently consulted. Nonetheless the dangers had been detailed in scientific literature dating from 1878.

In the resultant action founded on both the tort of negligence and on breach of s. 14 (1) (now s. 14 (3)) of the Sale of Goods Act 1893,[5] Rees, J. held that the defendant manufacturers were liable in respect of the damage suffered. In his judgment they had failed to carry out adequate and proper research into the scientific literature and so to give a full warning of the dangers accompanying the use of the product. Research consistent with the exercising of reasonable care would have revealed the hazard.

1973, pp. 222–231; Fleming, *The Law of Torts*, 4th edn., 1971, pp. 113–120. The standard of care and proof of negligence is discussed further below, pp. 252–272.

[20] Technically, it seems that the maxim does not apply to a case of product liability: see below, p. 257.

[1] *Cf. Overseas Tankship (U.K.), Ltd. v. Morts Dock and Engineering Co., Ltd. (The Wagon Mound)*, [1961] A.C. 388; [1961] 1 All E.R. 404, P.C.

[2] *Cf. Smith v. Leech Brain & Co., Ltd.*, [1962] 2 Q.B. 405; [1961] 3 All E.R. 1159; *Robinson v. Post Office*, [1974] 2 All E.R. 737; [1974] 1 W.L.R. 1176.

[3] See below, pp. 291–296.

[4] [1971] 1 Q.B. 88; [1969] 3 All E.R. 1681.

[5] The implied condition of reasonable fitness for purpose, see above, pp. 98–107.

Dealing with the point that the extent of the damage might not have been foreseeable his Lordship added:[6]

> "Here it was a foreseeable consequence of the supply of boron tribromide without a warning—and a fortiori with an irrelevant warning about harmful vapour—that in the ordinary course of industrial use it could come into contact with water and cause a violent reaction and possibly an explosion. It would also be foreseeable that some damage to property would or might result. In my judgment the explosion and the type of damage being foreseeable, it matters not in the law that the magnitude of the former and the extent of the latter were not."

The Court of Appeal subsequently approved the terms of a settlement on the basis that Rees, J. had been correct in adopting this approach to the question of remoteness of damage in tort. A reduction of twenty per cent in the damages to be assessed by an Official Referee was, however, agreed to take account of the possibility of contributory negligence.[7]

Difficulties in deciding who is a manufacturer of a finished product

It may sometimes be important to determine whether a particular defendant is a manufacturer of a finished product. Indeed, this might happen quite frequently if we were to introduce a system of strict liability which was applicable only to such manufacturers.[8] The notion of manufacturing a finished product is, however, a flexible one which may create problems in borderline cases. It clearly covers enterprises which have an exclusive responsibility for producing a particular artifact or which grow or rear a natural product such as vegetables or meat for subsequent distribution in an unaltered form. It has been suggested that the word "producer" is more apt to include the latter cases[9] and the Strasbourg Convention and the proposed EEC directive both refer to "producers" rather than to "manufacturers".[10] Beyond this there is room for debate. One readily

---

[6] [1971] 1 Q.B. 88, 109–110.

[7] *Ibid.*, at pp. 111–112.

[8] The point would be less important if strict liability were extended to retailers, wholesalers, and producers of component parts. California has made the extension to retailers and wholesalers: see, respectively, *Vandermark* v. *Ford Motor Co.*, 37 Cal. Rptr. 896 (Cal. Sup. Ct., 1964); *Canifax* v. *Hercules Powder Co.*, 46 Cal. Rptr. 552 (Cal. App., 1965), but the position of the producer of components is not settled.

[9] Law Commission Working Paper No. 64, "Liability for Defective Products", para. 48.

[10] Article 2(*b*) of the Strasbourg Convention provides: "the term 'producer' indicates the manufacturers of finished products or of component parts and the producers of natural products". See also art. 3(2), cited below, p. 182. The proposed EEC directive, art. 2, is similarly worded.

thinks of enterprises concerned with canning or bottling vegetables, fruit or drink as "manufacturers" even though they may buy in both containers and contents from a third party. The same is true of those who process natural products such as animal furs and skins. Yet not all processors are manufacturers. For example, one would not describe a person whose function was to harden chisels in these terms.

Manufacturers and assemblers

Related problems arise when distinguishing between manufacturers and assemblers. The distinction may sometimes be clear cut. The building contractor who erects scaffolding from tubular steel parts is an assembler whilst companies such as British Leyland are manufacturers even though their products contain a substantial number of components bought in from third party specialists. In other cases the distinction would be more difficult to draw. Again, many products will require to be assembled or adjusted after leaving the manufacturer and before they are finally marketed. This may involve complete construction from a kit or minor attention to detail. The possible variations suggest that there would be formidable problems in confining a régime of strict liability to manufacturers of finished products, defined, perhaps, as persons who put products into circulation in the form in which they are offered to the public.[11] Under the present law a person may of course incur liability as a producer of a component part[12] or as an assembler or erector.[13]

In an attempt to meet some of these difficulties some modern American cases have applied a principle expressed in the *Restatement of Torts*[14] so as to hold producers subject to a non-delegable duty with respect to latent defects in components such as a car dimmer switch[15] or brakes.[16] Some cases have gone further and held producers liable when the defective condition was created during pre-delivery adjustments by an authorised

---

[11] Under art. 2 (*d*) of the Strasbourg Convention a product has been put into circulation "when the producer has delivered it to another person". See also para. 43 of the accompanying commentary.

[12] See *Evans* v. *Triplex Safety Glass Co., Ltd.*, [1936] 1 All E.R. 283 where the claim against the manufacturer of a car windscreen failed on the facts. See further below, pp. 197–198, 227–228.

[13] See *Brown* v. *Cotterill* (1934), 51 T.L.R. 21 and, in general, below, pp. 311–313.

[14] See *Restatement of Torts*, 2d, s. 400, below, p. 182.

[15] *Ford Motor Co.* v. *Mathis*, 322 F. 2d 267 (5th Cir., 1963).

[16] *Standard Motor Co.* v. *Blood*, 380 S.W. 2d 651 (Tex. Civ. App., 1964). See also *Markel* v. *Spencer*, 171 N.Y.S. 2d 770 (N.Y., 1958) affd. 157 N.E. 2d 713 (1959); *Gittelson* v. *Gotham Pressed Steel Corporation*, 42 N.Y.S. 2d 341 (N.Y., 1943); *Boeing Airplane Co.* v. *Brown*, 291 F. 2d 310 (9th Cir., 1961). The principle has not, however, been accepted in all cases: *cf. Pabon* v. *Hackensack Auto Sales and Ford Motor Co.*, 164 A. 2d 773 (N.J. Sup. Ct., 1960); *Smith* v. *Peerless Glass Co.*, 181 N.E. 576 (N.Y.C.A., 1932).

dealer.[17] It is submitted that this is sound in principle and reflects the true marketing condition.

Products marketed under trade or brand names

It also seems right to require a firm to undertake responsibility as a manufacturer if it markets a commodity under its own trade or brand name and this even though the commodity was produced entirely by a third party. This marketing policy is adopted by a number of well-known retail establishments and mail order firms and the reliance placed by the consumer on their reputation should be reflected in the responsibility undertaken. It is not clear that English law has committed itself to this position[18] but the *Restatement of Torts* 2d, s. 400, contains the following provision:

> "One who puts out as his own product a chattel manufactured by another is subject to the same liability as though he were its manufacturer."[19]

A similar approach is to be found in the Strasbourg Convention, art. 3 (2) which provides:

> "Any person who has imported a product for putting it into circulation in the course of a business[20] and any person who has presented a product as his product by causing his name, trademark or other distinguishing feature to appear on the product, shall be deemed to be producers for the purposes of this Convention and shall be liable as such."[1]

There is no clear-cut distinction between one who incurs liability in respect of a product "as though he were its manufacturer" and one whose liability can be grounded on distribution alone. American cases suggest, however, that liability as a manufacturer will not be avoided simply because the label attached to the product specifies in small print that it was "made for" or "distributed by" the firm in question. This is especially

[17] *Sabloff* v. *Yamaha Motor Co.*, 273 A. 2d 606, affd. 283 A. 2d 321 (N.J., 1971). See also *Vandermark* v. *Ford Motor Co.*, 37 Cal. Rptr. 896 (Cal. Sup. Ct., 1964) and, in general, below, pp. 202–207.
[18] *Cf.*, however, *Goodchild* v. *Vaclight, Ltd.* (1965), *Times*, 22 May.
[19] Some leading cases include *Carney* v. *Sears, Roebuck & Co.*, 309 F. 2d 300 (4th Cir., 1962); *Penn* v. *Inferno Manufacturing Corporation*, 199 So. 2d 210 (La. App., 1967) affd. 202 So. 2d 649 (1967); *Forry* v. *Gulf Oil Corporation*, 237 A. 2d 593 (Pa., 1968); *Smith* v. *Regina Manufacturing Corporation*, 396 F. 2d 826 (4th Cir., 1968); *Wagner* v. *Larson*, 136 N.W. 2d 312 (Iowa, 1965); *Burkhardt* v. *Armour & Co.*, 115 Conn. 249, 90 A.L.R. 1260 (Conn., 1932). See, in general, 2 Harper & James, *The Law of Torts* (1956) and Supplement, s. 28.28; 1 Frumer & Friedman, *Products Liability*, s. 10.02.
[20] See further below, pp. 310–311.
[1] See also the proposed EEC directive, art. 2, which provides, in part: "'Producer' means... any person who, by putting his name, trademark or other distinguishing feature on the article, represents himself as its producer".

so if the name of the actual manufacturer is either omitted or virtually unknown. In *Swift & Co.* v. *Blackwell*,[2] for example, the defendant wholesalers incurred liability as manufacturers when their name was repeated on the label of a tin of condensed milk some eight times and despite the fact that the label also used the word "distributors". A similar view was taken in *Slavin* v. *Francis H. Leggett & Co.*,[3] where the plaintiff was injured biting on a stone in a tin of peas sold under the trade name of the defendant company but with the word "distributor" on the tin.[4] In such cases questions of degree are inevitably involved[5] and it may be thought that nothing should turn on the way one describes the defendant's function. Yet the terminology may prove crucial where latent defects are concerned. The company which buys in a tin of produce containing a foreign object from a reputable supplier and distributes it under its own trade name would be unlikely to incur liability as a retailer or wholesaler.[6] But it might incur liability if it were treated as the manufacturer of the tin and negligence in the canning process could be inferred.

With products such as golf clubs or other sporting equipment the wording or inscription is that of an endorser or sponsor who lends his name to the product in return for a fee. Such a person could not be said to incur liability "as a manufacturer" although it is possible that he might do so as an endorser.[7]

Production on a non-commercial basis

The word "manufacturer" is associated typically with persons or companies making products for sale on a commercial basis. Persons who make products for their own use or for the use of their friends or family would not normally be discussed in terms of the rules for product liability although they do of course owe the normal duty of care.[8] The point is likely to be important only if manufacturers or producers are subjected to a special régime of strict liability.

The distinction between the two cases is made expressly in the Strasbourg Convention on Products Liability, art. 5 (1) (*c*), which provides that the

---

[2] 84 F. 2d 130 (4th Cir., 1936).
[3] 114 N.J.L. 421, 177 Atl. 120 (N.J.Sup.Ct., 1935).
[4] The cases are not, however, all one way. See, e.g., *Degouveia* v. *H.D. Lee Mercantile Co.*, 100 S.W. 2d 336 (Mo., 1936) — "packed for" inconsistent with defendant being the packer.
[5] *Cf.* the position where wine is "shipped by" a well-known English company, such as Grants of St. James, but produced and bottled abroad.
[6] See below, ch. 15, p. 304 *et seq.*
[7] For liability as an endorser or sponsor, see below, p. 317.
[8] As in *Swanson* v. *Hanneson* (1972), 26 D.L.R. (3d) 201 (Man. Q.B.), affd. (1974), 42 D.L.R. (3d) 688 (Man. C.A.) (racing car with accelerator which jammed).

producer shall not be liable under the Convention if he proves "that the product was neither manufactured for sale, hire or any other form of distribution for the economic purposes of the producer nor manufactured or distributed in the course of his business". There is no similar provision in the EEC draft directive though it is arguable that the same position is reached through a defence whereby the producer "shall not be liable if he proves that he did not put the article into circulation".[9]

Types of defects and deficiencies in products

There are a number of different respects in which it may be claimed that a product is defective. These will be examined in the following chapters. A few general observations may, however, be helpful at this stage.

In some cases the plaintiff may contend that a product is defective in the sense that there has been a miscarriage in the production process. Foreign objects or impurities in food or drink, the use of weak materials, and incorrect assembly are common examples. Here the essence of the complaint is that the product was not produced as intended whether through an inadequate system of screening, inspection and testing or through the failure of an individual employee properly to operate an adequate system. It is in such cases that there is likely to be most scope for the contention that the manufacturer was acting reasonably in looking to an intermediate examination to eliminate the defect.[10] The plaintiff's main difficulty may be the lack of any direct evidence as to how the defective condition occurred. Any evidence is likely to be circumstantial.

In other cases the plaintiff may contend that a particular product is so designed as to be unsafe when used for its intended purpose.[11] Here the suggestion is not that there has been a miscarriage in the production process. On the contrary the product will have been produced precisely as intended. The complaint relates rather to the very form in which it was conceived, or to the adequacy or suitability of the materials or ingredients used. Thus an agricultural machine may be so designed as to expose its operator to contact with moving parts;[12] a cocktail dress may be highly inflammable;[13] a feeding compound may contain ingredients

---

[9] Article 5. The accompanying memorandum states that it was considered unnecessary to define the words "put into circulation" since they are self-explanatory. But does a handyman put a product into circulation if he gives it to a friend?

[10] Intermediate examination is discussed below, pp. 284–290.

[11] Design deficiencies are discussed below, ch. 11.

[12] *Huset* v. *J.I. Case Threshing Machine Co.*, 120 F. 865 (8th. Cir., 1903). See also *Griffiths* v. *Arch Engineering Co., Ltd.*, [1968] 3 All E.R. 217.

[13] *Noone* v. *Fred Perlberg Inc.*, 49 N.Y.S. 2d 460 (1944), affd. 60 N.E. 2d 839 (1945).

fatal to the animals for whose use it is intended;[14] and a drug or cosmetic may produce serious side effects whether on persons generally, or on those who are allergic to it.[15] In all such cases the manufacturer is likely to view an adverse decision with particular concern. At best the inference is that the product should be withdrawn in its present form and appropriate warnings issued:[16] at worst irreparable long-term damage may already have been inflicted on persons who have consumed or otherwise been in contact with the product.[17]

At the other end of the line running from drawing-board through to distribution the allegation of defectiveness may refer, rather, to the manner in which the product has been marketed. The suggestion may be that the product is unsafe because it was marketed without sufficiently clear warning labels or directions for use.[18] Alternatively, the complaint may specify the somewhat more positive claims made by the manufacturer in his promotion or labelling of the product.[19] Warnings or directions for use may serve a dual function. They may either enable the user to handle the product without danger to himself or others or they may appraise him of an unavoidable risk which he may thereafter choose to run.

Finally, there are cases in which safety and physical damage are not in issue and where the plaintiff's sole complaint is that he has incurred financial loss through his purchase or use of the product. The suggestion may be that the product was unmerchantable, that is, unfit for the purpose or purposes for which such goods are commonly bought, or that it was unfit for the particular purpose for which the plaintiff was known to require it.[20] In either case the problem may stem from a miscarriage in the production process or from the product's basic conception or design. Consequential business losses may be involved or the loss may be confined to the difference between the price paid and the value (if any) of the defective product. English law has barely been troubled with such problems where claims by consumers against manufacturers are concerned.

---

[14] *Henry Kendall & Sons* v. *William Lillico & Sons, Ltd.*, [1969] 2 A.C. 31; [1968] 2 All E.R. 444, H.L., and *Ashington Piggeries, Ltd.* v. *Christopher Hill, Ltd.*, [1972] A.C. 441; [1971] 1 All E.R. 847, H.L., although in both cases the actions were in contract against the immediate vendor.

[15] For discussion of product liability for drugs, see below, pp. 214–215. Allergies are discussed, below, pp. 324–326.

[16] The duty to warn of subsequently discovered dangers is discussed below, pp. 247–251.

[17] As in *Wright* v. *Dunlop Rubber Co., Ltd.* (1972), 13 K.I.R. 255; C.A., below, p. 248.

[18] Inadequate warnings and directions for use are discussed below, ch. 12.

[19] See below, pp. 243–244. See also, above, pp. 58–62 for discussion of the express warranty theory of liability in American law.

[20] For discussion in the contractual context, see above, pp. 78–97 (merchantable quality), pp. 98–107 (fitness for a particular purpose). See also above, pp. 15–16 for a reference to the American implied warranty theory of *Henningsen* v. *Bloomfield Motors*, 161 A. 2d 69 (N.J., 1960).

Considerable difficulties have, however, arisen in American case law and the subject is discussed in a separate chapter.[1]

The definition of a defect and the standard demanded

There is some difficulty in establishing a satisfactory overall test of liability for defective or deficient products. The difficulty is admittedly largely one of terminology whilst much depends on the types of damage or loss for which one wishes to cater. If economic losses are included the test of liability is likely to be framed in terms of merchantable quality and reasonable fitness for purpose as in sales legislation.[2] If the concern is solely with physical injury and property damage the test is likely to emphasise a requirement of reasonable safety.

Within the latter category, the best-known model is to be found in the *Restatement of Torts*, 2d, s. 402A, which imposes strict liability on one who "sells any product in a defective condition unreasonably dangerous to the user or consumer or to his property".[3] Although the *Restatement* formula has a substantial following, some courts have refused to apply it. Thus it has been held that the reference to an "unreasonably dangerous" condition is more restrictive than the test laid down in the leading case of *Greenman* v. *Yuba Power Products Inc.*[4] This position was adopted by the Californian Supreme Court in *Cronin* v. *J.B.E. Olson Corporation*.[5] The plaintiff was driving a bread delivery van which collided with another vehicle when the force of the collision broke an aluminium safety hasp, releasing bread trays which, in turn, propelled him through the windscreen. There was evidence that the safety hasp was porous and defective with a low tolerance to force but the defendants contended that they had been prejudiced by the lack of a finding that it was unreasonably dangerous. Dismissing the objection the court said:[6]

> "We believe the *Greenman* formulation is consonant with the rationale and development of products liability law in California because it provides a clear and simple test for determining whether the injured plaintiff is entitled to recovery. We are not persuaded to the contrary by the formulation of s. 402A which inserts the factor of an 'unreasonably dangerous' condition into the equation."

---

[1] See below, ch. 16, pp. 328–344.

[2] See above, pp. 78–97 (implied condition of merchantable quality), pp. 98–107 (implied condition of reasonable fitness for purpose).

[3] Section 402A is set out above, p. 17.

[4] 27 Cal. Rptr. 697 (1963), above , p. 17.

[5] 104 Cal. Rptr. 433 (1972). See also *Glass* v. *Ford Motor Co.*, 304 A. 2d 562 (N.J., 1973); *Berkebile* v. *Brantly Helicopter Corporation*, 337 A. 2d 893 (Pa., 1975). *Cf. Kirkland* v. *General Motors Corporation*, 521 P. 2d 1353 (Okla., 1974) and 2 Frumer and Friedman, *Products Liability*, s. 16A [4][e]; Note, 42 Fordham L.R. 943 (1974).

[6] 104 Cal. Rptr. 433, 443 (1972).

Other courts have adopted a diametrically opposite position, requiring the product to be unreasonably dangerous and eschewing the use of the word defective.[7] The difference between the two approaches is, however, essentially one of terminology rather than substance. In rejecting the *Restatement* formula in favour of a simple requirement that the product be defective, the California court was obviously not demanding absolute safety. Some writers prefer to reserve the word "defective" for cases involving miscarriages in the production process as opposed to design deficiencies or inadequate warnings.[8] This may correspond more closely with its normal usage. On the other hand, it may be objected that continued emphasis on a requirement that the product be unreasonably dangerous is apt to lead to an element of fault infiltrating a strict liability system. This, at least, was one of the considerations behind the judgment in the *Cronin* case.

Alternative formulations are to be found in recent European developments. The Strasbourg Convention[9] states that a product has a defect:

"when it does not provide the safety which a person is entitled to expect, having regard to all the circumstances including the presentation of the product."

The proposed EEC directive on product liability uses similar terms. By art. 4 of the proposed directive,

"A product is defective when it does not provide for persons or property the safety which a person is entitled to expect."

A common feature of these various definitions is that the standard demanded is a qualified one. Even a system of strict liability does not demand that products be absolutely safe. The manufacturer will incur liability only if the product is "unreasonably dangerous" or, to put in more positively, if it does not meet the safety standards which can legitimately be expected by the ordinary user. "Danger" and "safety" are relative terms and a variety of considerations must be taken into account when determining whether the appropriate standard has been met. Some of the more important considerations include the following.

Firstly, it is difficult to think of a product which is totally incapable of causing harm when it is misused. A hair pin would no doubt constitute a serviceable murder weapon whilst a feather pillow might suffocate a child. Furthermore some products would be quite useless for their

---

[7] See *Reyes* v. *Wyeth Laboratories*, 498 F. 2d 1264 (5th Cir., 1974). See also *Pyatt* v. *Engel Equipment Inc.*, 309 N.E. 2d 225 (Ill. App., 1974).
[8] See, in general, Keeton, "Products Liability: liability without fault and the requirement of a defect", 41 Texas L.R. 855 (1963); Traynor, "The Ways and Meanings of Defective Products and Strict Liability", 32 Tenn. L.R. 363 (1965).
[9] Article 2 (c).

normal legitimate purpose if they did not have the potential for serious abuse. A razor blade must cut as must a knife or an axe; explosives must be capable of shifting rock; and whisky must contain alcohol.[10] This does not mean that such products are unreasonably dangerous although liability may be incurred if they are individually defective or impure or if they are supplied into the wrong hands. A defence of "misuse" should not, however, be taken too far. To some extent the possibility of misuse must be catered for at the design stage.[11]

Secondly, some products such as cosmetics and even strawberries and shell-fish may be perfectly safe for the vast majority of users, whilst producing an allergic reaction in others. The effect on the individual may be extremely serious and incapacitating and indeed lead to death; but this does not mean that the product is unreasonably dangerous. Whether it is in any given case will depend on matters such as the seriousness of the reaction and the percentage of users similarly affected.[12] With other products the probability of an adverse reaction may be wholly predictable; yet the beneficial effect may far outweigh the disadvantages. The Pasteur vaccine against rabies is frequently cited in this context.[13] Such products are not unreasonably dangerous. Similar difficulties may accompany drugs with known side-effects and here reasonable safety may demand an issuing of a warning to users or to responsible intermediaries such as doctors.[14] Yet other products such as cigarettes may be unavoidably dangerous in the state of current scientific knowledge whilst affording pleasures to those who use them. Notwithstanding the high, if unpredictable, risk involved, it is doubtful whether cigarettes can be regarded as unreasonably dangerous.[15]

Thirdly, account must be taken of a host of more general factors such as the practicability of safety measures, cost, style, and the question of whether the danger is obvious or concealed. Indeed there is weighty English and Commonwealth authority for the view that the plaintiff must fail if he knows of the danger and that this is not simply a matter which goes to causation, assumption of the risk and contributory negligence.[16]

---

[10] *Cf.* Prosser, *Law of Torts,* 4th edn., 1971, p. 659; 2 Harper and James, *Torts,* p. 1542; *Restatement of Torts,* 2d, s. 402A, comment i. See also *Pritchard* v. *Liggett and Myers Tobacco Co.,* 295 F. 2d 292, 303 (3rd Cir., 1961) (butter and cholesterol).

[11] Misuse is discussed below, pp. 294–296.

[12] Allergies are discussed below, pp. 324–326.

[13] *Restatement of Torts,* 2d, s. 402A, comment k.

[14] For discussion of drugs, see below, pp. 214–215. See also below, pp. 245–247 (warnings to responsible intermediaries).

[15] See below, pp. 216–217.

[16] See, e.g., *Farr* v. *Butters Brothers & Co.,* [1932] 2 K.B. 606; *Daley* v. *Gypsy Caravan Pty., Ltd.,* [1966] 2 N.S.W.R. 22; *Cathcart* v. *Hull,* [1963] N.Z.L.R. 333. For criticism and further analysis, see below, p. 292.

The same distinction between "patent" and "latent" dangers has be-
devilled American cases where it was rightly castigated by Justice Clarke
as a "sterile definitional quibble".[17]

Fourthly, the test of reasonable safety must be judged in the light of the
standards which were generally acceptable when the product was originally
marketed. Safety features which are commonplace in the mid-1970s would
not have been expected a decade earlier and this is very noticeable in
areas such as car design.[18] The point was made in *Balido* v. *Improved
Machinery Inc.*,[19] a decision of a California Court of Appeal. The case
involved a plastic injection moulding press which crushed the plaintiff's
hand in 1965 and which had been manufactured in 1950. Dealing with
the standard of safety which was demanded the court said:[20]

> "Strict liability for deficient design of a product (as differentiated from de-
> fective manufacture or defective composition) is premised on a finding that the
> product was unreasonably dangerous for its intended use, and in turn, the
> unreasonableness of the danger must necessarily be derived from the state of the
> art at the time of design."

If this is true of a system of strict liability it must *a fortiori* be true of a
system which requires proof of negligence. This is not to say that
"development risks", as such, are excluded. Where liability is strict the
manufacturer may be held liable although he could not reasonably have
discovered the facts which rendered the product unreasonably dangerous
in the light of the prevailing standards.[1]

In the chapters which follow it is proposed to discuss the manufacturers'
liability for physical injury and property damage under three main headings: (i) miscarriages in the production process; (ii) design deficiencies; and
(iii) inadequate warnings and directions for use. Proof of negligence which
is still required under English and Commonwealth law will be discussed
later as will issues of causation and the availability of certain defences. Here
it is convenient to note that there are far more points of similarity than
differences between systems imposing strict liability and those which
require proof of negligence. The problems of causation are essentially
the same as is the standard of safety demanded. Defences of contributory
negligence and assumption of the risk are normally available under either
system. Certainly it is true that it is only where negligence is required

---

[17] In *Messina* v. *Clark Equipment Co.*, 263 F. 2d 291, 293 (2nd Cir., 1959).
[18] See below, pp. 223–227.
[19] 105 Cal. Rptr. 890 (Cal. App., 1973). See also *Gray* v. *General Motors Corporation*, 434
F. 2d 110, 113–114 (8th Cir., 1970); *Schneider* v. *Chrysler Motors Corporation*, 401 F. 2d 549
(1968).
[20] *Ibid.*, p. 895. See Murray, "The State of the Art Defence" 57 Marquette L.R. 649 (1974).
[1] For a possible qualification where the danger is scientifically undiscoverable, see above,
pp. 107–110.

that the manufacturer can excuse himself by pleading that a miscarriage in the production process was consistent with reasonable care. But the willingness of the courts to act on circumstantial evidence has gone a long way towards making this distinction theoretical.[2] The same is true of claims by a manufacturer that he has failed reasonably to appreciate the dangers associated with the product he was marketing. In both respects, however, it may be that the need to prove negligence acts as a considerable disincentive against litigation even if it has little effect on cases which actually get to court.

---

[2] See *Grant* v. *Australian Knitting Mills, Ltd.*, [1936] A.C. 85, P.C., below, p. 256.

10 The Manufacturers' Liability: Miscarriages in the Production Process

Alleged miscarriages in the production process may take a variety of forms. Some of the most typical are examined below. The common contention in all such cases is that the product was not produced as intended so that the consequent defect,[1] impurity or construction flaw caused damage to the person or property of the plaintiff. Where liability depends on proof of negligence it is further contended that the presence of the defect was attributable to a lack of reasonable care.[2]

Foreign objects and substances

There are many cases in which injury has allegedly been suffered through the presence of a foreign object or substance in food or drink. A cross-section might range from the famous snail of *Donoghue* v. *Stevenson*[3] itself to cases in which carbolic acid was found in lemonade and a stone in a bath bun.[4] Examples from the North American continent where workmen would seem to have a more warped sense of humour have included a chlorine solution in beer; caustic soda, tobacco, cigarette stubs and match

---

[1] For discussion of the meaning of the word "defect", see above, pp. 186–189.
[2] For proof of negligence, see below, pp. 252–272. A lack of reasonable care is not of course required where liability is strict whether under a warranty or strict tort theory.
[3] [1932] A.C. 562, H.L.
[4] See, respectively, *Daniels* v. *R. White & Sons, Ltd.*, [1938] 4 All E.R. 258, above, p. 23; *Chaproniere* v. *Mason* (1905), 21 T.L.R. 633. See also *Barnett* v. *Packer and Co.*, [1940] 3 All E.R. 575 (wire protruding from sweet).

sticks, an unpackaged prophylactic, an open safety pin, a cigar butt, a carcass of a mouse or a rat, and a decomposed worm—all in (different) soft drink bottles;[5] and a tack in blueberry pie.[6]

Impurities and natural substances

In other cases the defect may be an impurity, rather than a "foreign object", or something which, though natural to the product, ought nonetheless to have been eliminated in the production process. Thus in *Read v. Croydon Corporation*,[7] for example, liability was incurred when the typhoid bacillus contaminated a public water supply. There is also a host of American cases in which actions have been brought against manufacturers, restaurateurs and others, alleging negligence in the supply of meat, fish, baked goods and other products containing impurities rendering them unfit for human consumption. Thus one manufacturer was held liable where illness was suffered through eating contaminated corned beef.[8] Other cases have involved death or illness resulting from eating pork infected with trichinae but these have mainly denied recovery.[9] Similarly there have been cases in which hair dyes, cosmetics and clothing have allegedly contained impurities causing illness or severe discomfort.[10]

---

[5] See, respectively, *Varga* v. *John Labett, Ltd.*, *Highgate and Hurst* (1956), 6 D.L.R. 2d 336 (Ont. H. Ct.) (chlorine solution); *Willis* v. *Coca-Cola Co. of Canada, Ltd.*, [1934] 2 D.L.R. 173 (B.C.C.A.) (caustic soda); *Jasper Coca-Cola Bottling Co.* v. *Roberts*, 252 So. 2d 428 (Ala., 1971) (tobacco etc.); *Wallace* v. *Coca-Cola Bottling Plants Inc.*, 269 A. 2d 117 (Maine, 1970) (prophylactic); *Coca-Cola Bottling Co.* v. *McBride*, 20 S.W. 2d 862 (Ark., 1929) (safety-pin); *Keller* v. *Coca-Cola Bottling Co.*, 330 P. 2d 346 (Or., 1958) (cigar butt); *Tate* v. *Mauldin*, 154 S.E. 431 (S.C., 1930) (mouse or rat); *Norfolk Coca-Cola Bottling Works* v. *Land*, 52 S.E. 2d 85 (Va., 1949) (worm).

[6] *Ash* v. *Childs Dining Hall Co.*, 120 N.E. 396 (Mass., 1918). See also *Saddlemire* v. *Coca-Cola Co. of Canada, Ltd.*, [1941] 4 D.L.R. 614 (Ont. H. Ct.); *Mathews* v. *Coca-Cola Co. of Canada, Ltd.*, [1944] 2 D.L.R. 355 (Ont. C.A.); *Curll* v. *Robin Hood Multifoods, Ltd.* (1974), 56 D.L.R. (3d) 129 (Nova Scotia Sup. Ct.). An exhaustive annotation of American cases is to be found in 77 A.L.R. 2d 7 (food) and p. 215 (beverages). See also 2 *Frumer and Friedman*, ch. 7.

[7] [1938] 4 All E.R. 631. See also *Barnes* v. *Irwell Valley Water Board*, [1939] 1 K.B. 21; [1938] 2 All E.R. 650, C.A.

[8] *Armour & Co.* v. *Leasure*, 9 A. 2d 572 (Md., 1939). Comprehensive coverage is to be found in 2 *Frumer and Friedman*, ss. 21, 22, 24, 25. More recent cases have typically proceeded on a breach of warranty or strict tort theory of liability. For an English case in which contractual liability was established following the supply of food in an hotel, see *Lockett* v. *A. M. Charles, Ltd.*, [1938] 4 All E.R. 170.

[9] *Ketterer* v. *Armour and Co.*, 247 F.921 (2nd Cir., 1917) is a leading case. For further discussion of American cases see 2 *Frumer and Friedman*, s. 21.04, 25.04 [2]; Annotation 77 A.L.R. 2d, s. 42. See also *Yachetti* v. *John Duff and Sons, Ltd.*, [1943] 1 D.L.R. 194 (Ont. H. Ct.).

[10] See, e.g., *Watson* v. *Buckley, Osborne, Garrett & Co., Ltd.*, [1940] 1 All E.R. 174; *Parker* v. *Oxolo, Ltd. and Senior*, [1937] 3 All E.R. 524 (hair dye); *Levi* v. *Colgate-Palmolive Pty., Ltd.*

Tarling v. *Nobel*[11] provides a modern Commonwealth example of liability being incurred on failure to eliminate a "natural" object. Damages were awarded against the preparer of a chicken sandwich when the plaintiff had been injured by a chicken bone sticking in his throat on eating the sandwich at a snack bar. That liability might be incurred on such facts cannot be sensibly denied.[12] Yet the decision itself is not wholly convincing. In all such cases liability should depend on what is reasonably to be expected by the consumer and the common understanding is surely that chicken sandwiches may contain bones.[13] The same might be true of other cases, as where a shell is found in a dish of oysters, a fish bone in a New England fish chowder, or a bone in a turkey dish or in a chicken pie.[14] The position might be different where the product was advertised as "boneless"[15] or where this was the common understanding.[16]

Unwholesomeness

Difficulties may sometimes arise in determining whether a "foreign object" is unwholesome or injurious to health. How, for example, should one react to a complaint of nausea when a customer in a restaurant discovers a live caterpillar in a bowl of fresh salad or when a housewife discovers a dead caterpillar at the bottom of a tin of partly consumed peas? In *Smedleys, Ltd.* v. *Breed*,[1] a case decided under the Food and Drugs Act, Lord Hailsham, L.C. observed that the complainant could have consumed such a caterpillar "without injury to herself, and even, perhaps, with

---

(1941), 41 S.R. N.S.W. 48 (bath salts); *Grant* v. *Australian Knitting Mills, Ltd.*, [1936] A.C. 85, P.C. (underpants).

[11] [1966] A.L.R. 189 (A.C.T. Sup. Ct.).

[12] Some American cases have, however, adopted a rigid system of classifying into "foreign objects" and "natural substances", denying recovery in the latter case: see 2 *Frumer and Friedman*, s. 25.04[1]; Prosser, *Law of Torts*, 4th edn., 1971, p. 660; 2 *Harper and James*, s. 28.13, n. 13.

[13] In *Betehia* v. *Cape Cod Corporation*, 103 N.W. 2d 64 (1960), however, a Wisconsin court refused to rule that as a matter of law the consumer must so expect.

[14] See *Allen* v. *Grafton*, 164 N.E. 2d 167 (Ohio, 1960) (oysters); *Webster* v. *Blue Chip Tea Room*, 198 N.E. 2d 309 (Mass., 1964) (fish chowder); *Silva* v. *F. W. Woolworth Co.*, 83 P. 2d 76 (Cal. App., 1938) (turkey dish); *Mix* v. *Ingersoll Candy Co.*, 59 P. 2d 144 (Cal., 1936) (chicken pie). See also *Brown* v. *Nebiker*, 296 N.W. 366, 371 (1931), where an Iowa court observed: "One who eats pork chops or ... spare ribs ... ought to anticipate and be on his guard against the presence of bones."

[15] As in *Bryer* v. *Rath Packing Co.*, 156 A. 2d 442 (Md., 1959) (ready to serve boned chicken).

[16] Presumably the ubiquitous fish-finger would provide an example. As to a bone in chicken soup "ingested more by drinking or direct swallowing without mastication", see *Wood* v. *Waldorf System Inc.*, 83 A. 2d 90 (R.I., 1951).

[1] [1974] 2 All E.R. 21, H.L.

benefit".[2] But this is not to say that he would have denied liability had she been claiming compensation in tort for discomfort actually suffered. A warning against too sophisticated or robust an attitude in such cases was issued by a Florida court in *Food Fair Stores of Florida* v. *Macurda*.[3] Here the court admitted that they were "not connoisseurs of cuisine that qualifies us to view as delicacies some foodstuffs that might be indigestible to others", but had no difficulty in holding worms in a tin of spinach to be unfit for human consumption.

Physical and psychological responses

Related problems arise in deciding what types of injury or reaction warrant compensation. Internal bleeding or abrasion from the swallowing of a foreign object clearly qualifies as does an identifiable form of food poisoning. There is perhaps more difficulty where nausea, vomiting and illness occur as a purely psychological response to the ingestion of the foreign object or even to the sight of it. Here some American cases have denied recovery, demanding a specifically physical reaction as a peg on which to hang the claim.[4] The balance of authority does not, however, favour this limitation.[5] Similarly, in a recent Canadian case a plaintiff recovered in respect of an aggravation of a nervous condition brought on by seeing the remains of a decomposed mouse in a bag of flour.[6] It is thought that English law would adopt the same view provided that a physical reaction akin to nervous shock could be established.[7] This would seem to be the right policy, since a genuine psychological response may be much more serious than a mild case of food poisoning and difficult to distinguish from it.

---

[2] *Ibid.*, at p. 24.
[3] 93 So. 2d 860, 861 (Fla., 1957), cited in 2 *Frumer and Friedman*, s. 25.01[1], p. 655 where there is a general discussion of "unwholesomeness".
[4] See, e.g., *Cushing Coca-Cola Bottling Co.* v. *Francis*, 245 P. 2d 84 (Okla., 1952).
[5] *Medeiros* v. *Coca-Cola Bottling Co.*, 135 P. 2d 676 (Cal. App. 1943) is a leading case. See also *Wallace* v. *Coca-Cola Bottling Plants Inc.*, 269 A. 2d 117 (Maine, 1970) and, in general, 2 *Frumer and Friedman*, s. 25.01[2], note 6 especially. *Finocchiaro* v. *Ward Baking Co.*, 241. A 2d 619 (R.I., 1968) is an unusual case. The plaintiff was granted a new trial following summary judgment for the manufacturer when it appeared that she was suffering from a phobic fear of rats after having mistakenly assumed that dried dough in bread was rat fecal.
[6] *Curll* v. *Robin Hood Multifoods, Ltd.* (1974), 56 D.L.R. (3d) 129 (Nova Scotia Sup. Ct.).
[7] Indeed it is not clear that the plaintiff's condition in *Donoghue* v. *Stevenson*, [1932] A.C. 562, H.L., above, p. 173 was not predominantly psychological in origin. A passing feeling of fear or revulsion would not be sufficient: see *Hinz* v. *Berry*, [1970] 1 All E.R. 1074, 1075, *per* Lord Denning, M.R. See also below, p. 321.

Weak or defective materials

Another common contention is that injury or damage has resulted from the use of weak or defective materials. English cases have involved chisels brittle through excessive hardening,[1] a "bull ring" forming part of a trolley bus system which gave way because of a defective weld,[2] a car with defective steering,[3] and a water bottle which burst after some three months, scalding the user.[4] From other jurisdictions one may cite instances of a defective coil in an engine which led to an explosion and the subsequent loss of a vessel,[5] an aeroplane which developed metal fatigue in a wing joint,[6] and a car tyre which exploded and injured a garage employee.[7] In all such cases negligence in failing to detect and eliminate the defect may lead to liability on the part of the manufacturer responsible for the defective condition.

Assembly and construction

In other cases the emphasis has been on negligence in the assembly or construction of the product. Thus the valve of a boiler may have been fitted incorrectly, so causing an explosion or an escape of gas,[8] electrical busbars within a kiosk may be said to have been unprotected by insulating material,[9] a bicycle saddle may pitch forward,[10] a car wheel may come off[11] or a sidecar depart from a motor cycle.[12] Elsewhere the fuse mechan-

---

[1] *Taylor* v. *Rover Co., Ltd.*, [1966] 2 All E.R. 181; [1966] 1 W.L.R. 1491; *Mason* v. *Williams & Williams, Ltd.*, [1955] 1 All E.R. 808; [1955] 1 W.L.R. 549. See also *Davie* v. *New Merton Board Mills, Ltd.*, [1959] A.C. 604; [1959] 1 All E.R. 346, H.L., where the action was against an employer.

[2] *Dransfield* v. *British Insulated Cables, Ltd.*, [1937] 4 All E.R. 382.

[3] *Andrews* v. *Hopkinson*, [1957] 1 Q.B. 229; [1956] 3 All E.R. 422. See also *Phillips* v. *Chrysler Corporation of Canada, Ltd.* (1962), 32 D.L.R. 2d 347 (Ont. H. Ct.); *Markel* v. *Spencer*, 171 NYS 2d 770, affd. 157 N.E. 2d 713 (1958) (brakes).

[4] *Steer* v. *Durable Rubber Manufacturing Co.*, (1958), *Times*, 20 November.

[5] *McKee* v. *Brunswick Corp.*, 354 F. 2d 577 (7th Cir., 1965).

[6] *Northwest Airlines Inc.* v. *Glenn L. Martin Co.*, 224 F. 2d 120 (6th Cir., 1955).

[7] *Tralli* v. *Triplex X Stores Inc.*, 112 A. 2d 507 (1954); *Ewer* v. *Goodyear Tire & Rubber Co.*, 480 P. 2d 260 (1971).

[8] *Howard* v. *Furness Houlder Argentine Lines, Ltd.*, [1936] 2 All E.R. 781; *Willey* v. *Fyrogas Co.*, 251 S.W. 2d 635 (Mo., 1952); *Dominion Natural Gas Co., Ltd.* v. *Collins & Perkins*, [1909] A.C. 640, P.C.

[9] *Paine* v. *Colne Valley Electricity Supply Co., Ltd. and British Insulated Cables, Ltd.*, [1938] 4 All E.R. 803.

[10] *White* v. *John Warrick & Co., Ltd.*, [1953] 2 All E.R. 1021; [1953] 1 W.L.R. 1285 C.A.

[11] *Herschthal* v. *Stewart and Ardern, Ltd.*, [1940] 1 K.B. 155; [1939] 4 All E.R. 123. See also *Stennett* v. *Hancock and Peters*, [1939] 2 All E.R. 578; *General Motors Corporation* v. *Johnson*, 137 F. 2d 320 (4th Cir., 1943).

[12] *Malfroot* v. *Noxal, Ltd.*, (1935) 51 T.L.R. 551.

ism on a firework may be fitted incorrectly[13] or a mason may leave a tombstone in a dangerous position.[14] Responsibility in such cases may be incurred by one who has subsequently installed, serviced or repaired the product[15] but the manufacturer may also be held liable where the fault lies in the original production process.

Containers and packaging

The defective condition may sometimes be in the container or packaging as opposed to the product itself. Here, too, it is clear that a duty is owed to the ultimate consumer, user or bystander.[1] The suggestion of Horridge, J. in *Pattendon* v. *Beney*[2] that an early decision to the contrary[3] had survived *Donoghue* v. *Stevenson* can hardly be correct.[4] Typically it has been the manufacturer of the end product who has been sued but there is no doubt that the manufacturer of the container or packaging may be held liable as well.[5] Questions may also arise as to the general suitability of the container or packaging[6] and as to the adequacy of warnings or directions for use on the label or in accompanying literature.[7]

The range of cases is almost as wide as the number of products requiring containers or packaging, and injury may result from either the container or packaging itself, the contents which are released when it fails, or from both.[8] Typical instances include explosions within bottles, tins, kegs and

---

[13] *Callahan* v. *Keystone Fireworks Manufacturing Co.*, 435 P. 2d 626 (Wash., 1967). See also *Martin* v. *T. W. Hand Fireworks Co., Ltd.* (1962), 37 D.L.R. 2d 455, above, p. 177.

[14] *Brown* v. *Cotterill* (1934), 51 T.L.R. 21.

[15] As in *Haseldine* v. *C. A. Daw & Son, Ltd.*, [1941] 2 K.B. 343; [1941] 3 All E.R. 156 (lift); *Stennett* v. *Hancock & Peters*, [1939] 2 All E.R. 578 (car). See, in general, below, pp. 311–313.

[1] See also above, p. 82 where it is noted that the implied conditions of merchantable quality and reasonable fitness for purpose also extend to the container and packaging.

[2] (1933) 50 T.L.R. 10.

[3] *Bates* v. *Batey & Co., Ltd.*, [1913] 3 K.B. 351.

[4] See the comments of Lord Atkin in *Donoghue* v. *Stevenson*, [1932] A.C. 562, 595 H.L.

[5] See, e.g., *Smith* v. *Peerless Glass Co.*, 181 N.E. 576 (N.Y., 1932) (exploding soda water bottle); *Trani* v. *Anchor Hocking Glass Corporation*, 116 A. 2d 167 (Conn., 1955) (glass jar); Annotation 81 A.L.R. 2d 350.

[6] See, e.g., *Adelaide Chemical and Fertiliser Co., Ltd.* v. *Carlyle* (1940), 64 C.L.R. 514 (High Ct. Australia). The point was important because evidence of the defective condition of the *particular* bottle might have been inadmissible as hearsay. See, in general, below p. 208, *et seq.*

[7] See, e.g., *Fisher* v. *Harrods, Ltd.*, [1966] 1 Lloyd's L.R. 500, and, in general, below, p. 229. *et seq.*

[8] Comprehensive annotation of American cases is to be found in 81 A.L.R. 2d 229, 350.

drums containing carbonated beverages,[9] cosmetics,[10] cleaning fluids,[11] oxygen,[12] chemicals,[13] or food requiring heating;[14] glass containers which break, either cutting the handler[15] or injuring one who later consumes the product;[16] metal, wooden, or earthenware drums with defects in the plug, handle, or elsewhere;[17] cartons which collapse and shed their contents on their handler;[18] and metal boxes with jagged edges or dangerous protrusions.[19] The extent of the duty owed by the producer of the end product (and, in particular, whether it is confined to buying in from a reputable supplier and carrying out any reasonable inspections and tests) is considered below.[20]

Manufacturers of components and materials

In *Macpherson* v. *Buick Motor Co.*[1] the New York Court of Appeals left open the question of whether liability might be imposed on the manufacturer of a defective component part such as the car wheel in the case itself. Later cases have predictably made the extension. Actions have, for

---

[9] See, e.g., *Hart* v. *Dominion Stores, Ltd.* (1968), 67 D.L.R. 2d 675 (Ont. H. Ct.); *Cohen* v. *Coca-Cola, Ltd.* (1967), 62 D.L.R. 2d 285 (Sup. Ct. Canada) (soft drink bottles); *Fehr Brewing Co.* v. *Corley*, 96 S.W. 2d 860 (Ky., 1936) (beer keg); *O'Dwyer* v. *Leo Buring, Pty., Ltd.*, [1966] W.A.R. 67 (cork from wine bottle). See also 2 *Frumer and Friedman*, s. 26 for discussion of the legal and scientific issues raised by cases of exploding bottles.

[10] *Revlon Inc.* v. *Buchanan*, 271 F. 2d 795 (5th Cir., 1959) (deodorant); *Armour* v. *Wanamaker*, 202 F. 423 (3rd Cir., 1913) (hair tonic). See also *Fisher* v. *Harrods, Ltd.*, [1966] 1 Lloyd's Rep. 500, where the action was against the retailer, and the bottle contained a corn solvent.

[11] *Licari* v. *Markotos*, 180 N.Y.S. 278 (1920).

[12] *Liberatore* v. *National Cylinder Gas Co.*, 193 F. 2d 429 (2nd Cir., 1952).

[13] *Vacwell Engineering Co., Ltd.* v. *B.D.H. Chemicals, Ltd.*, [1971] 1 Q.B. 88; [1969] 3 All E.R. 1681, above, p. 179.

[14] *Healey* v. *Trodd*, 7 A. 2d 640 (N.J., 1939) (can of spaghetti).

[15] *Mead* v. *Coca-Cola Bottling Co.*, 108 N.E. 2d 757 (Mass., 1952). See also *Morelli* v. *Fitch and Gibbons*, [1928] 2 K.B. 636, D.C., where liability was based on breach of warranty.

[16] *Kraft-Phenix Cheese Corporation* v. *Spelce*, 113 S.W. 2d 476 (Ark., 1938).

[17] See, e.g., *Fisher* v. *Harrods, Ltd.*, [1966] 1 Lloyd's Rep. 500 (jewellery cleaning fluid); *Devilez* v. *Boots Drug Co., Ltd.* (1962) 106 Sol. Jo. 552 (corn solvent); *Marshall* v. *Russian Oil Products, Ltd.*, 1938 S.C. 773 (petrol barrel); *Adelaide Chemical and Fertiliser Co., Ltd.* v. *Carlyle* (1940), 64 C.L.R. 514 (High Ct. of Australia) (sulphuric acid in unsuitable earthenware jar). See also *Salt* v. *Imperial Chemical Co.* (1958), *Times*, 1 February, C.A. (caustic soda in drum; no liability on facts).

[18] *Behringer* v. *William Gretz Brewing Co.*, 169 A. 2d 249 (Del., 1961); *Waller* v. *Coca Cola Bottlers Association*, 523 S.W. 2d 306 (Tex. Civ. App., 1975).

[19] *Stubblefield* v. *Johnson-Fagg Inc.*, 379 F. 2d 270 (10th Cir., 1967) (no liability on facts).

[20] At p. 199 *et seq.*

[1] 217 N.Y. 382, 111 N.E. 1050, 1053 (1916).

example, been brought against the manufacturers of a cable for a lift,[2] controls for a water heater,[3] a valve for a gas powered generator,[4] a part for a safety belt,[5] and against the manufacturers of a hull of a boat.[6] There are few English cases in point but there is no doubt that we proceed on the same basis. So in *Evans* v. *Triplex Safety Glass Co., Ltd.*[7] the manufacturers of a car windscreen which shattered, injuring passengers in the car, might clearly have been liable in principle though liability was not incurred on the facts.[8] The same is true of the manufacturer of defective materials[9] and of processors who leave a product in a dangerous condition.[10]

In any such case the plaintiff may have to deal with a number of difficulties. The supplier of the component or raw materials may, for example, claim that he acted reasonably in looking to an intermediate examination by the manufacturer of the end product to eliminate the defect.[11] Indeed this objection was raised successfully in the *Triplex* case.[12] Even more fundamental is the point that many basic materials such as planks of wood, nuts and bolts and industrial fasteners are capable of being used for a wide variety of purposes.[13] For this reason there has been considerable debate both in America and Europe over whether strict liability should extend to producers of component parts.[14] The point is discussed in later chapters.[15]

---

[2] *Carson* v. *Weston Hotel Corporation*, 97 N.E. 2d 620 (Ill., 1951).

[3] *Deveny* v. *Rheem Manufacturing Co.*, 319 F. 2d 124 (2nd Cir., 1963). See also *American Radiator and Standard Corporation* v. *Titan Valve and Manufacturing Co.*, 246 F. 2d 947 (6th Cir., 1957).

[4] *B. K. Sweeney Co.* v. *Mcquay-Norris Manufacturing Co.*, 489 P. 2d 356 (Colo., 1971).

[5] *Edison* v. *Lewis Manufacturing Co.*, 336, P. 2d 286 (Cal. App. 1959).

[6] *Maryland* v. *Garzell Plastics Industries*, 152 F. Supp. 483 (1957). See also *Noel* v. *United Aircraft Corporation*, 219 F. Supp. 556 (1963) (propeller manufacturer); *Starkey* v. *Miami Aviation Corporation*, 214 So. 2d 738 (Fla. App., 1968) (fuel tanks), and, in general, 1 *Frumer and Friedman*, s. 9 and cases there cited.

[7] [1936] 1 All E.R. 283.

[8] See also *Dransfield* v. *British Insulated Cables, Ltd.*, [1937] 4 All E.R. 382 ("bull-ring" carrying overhead trolley-bus wire: no liability on facts).

[9] *Restatement, Torts*, 2d, s. 395, comment m; 1 *Frumer and Friedman*, s. 9.01.

[10] Cf. *Block* v. *Urban*, 166 F. Supp. 19 (1958) (where D had coated with aluminium oxide a bow manufactured by T). Hence liability should be incurred by a chisel hardener in cases such as *Taylor* v. *Rover Co., Ltd.*, [1966] 2 All E.R. 181; [1966] 1 W.L.R. 1491 below, p. 200.

[11] Intermediate examination is discussed below, pp. 284–290.

[12] [1936] 1 All E.R. 283.

[13] See the Law Commission Working Paper No. 64, "Liability for Defective Products", paras. 68–73.

[14] The *Restatement of Torts*, 2d, s. 402A, enters a specific caveat on the question. The Strasbourg Convention, art. 2(*b*), defines a "producer" as including manufacturers of component parts as does the EEC draft directive, art. 2.

[15] See below, at pp. 227–228; 359–360.

Liability of the manufacturer of the end product for components, containers and processing

The duty to exercise reasonable care

The tendency towards specialisation within developed economies means that a number of different organisations are frequently involved in the production of any given product. Components, containers or materials may, for example, be bought in from a third party, or an outside specialist may be employed to process the product. It has been seen that such suppliers or specialists may themselves be held liable in tort for negligence[16] but the manufacturer of the end product also owes a duty with respect to such matters. In *Taylor* v. *Rover Co., Ltd.* Baker, J. approved the following passage in *Charlesworth on Negligence* where it is said:[17]

> "A manufacturer's duty is not limited to those parts of his product which he makes himself. It extends to component parts, supplied by his sub-manufacturers or others, which he uses in the manufacture of his products. He must take reasonable care, by inspection or otherwise, to see that those parts can properly be used to put his product in a condition in which it can be safely used or consumed in the contemplated manner by the ultimate user or consumer."

The measures required of the manufacturer of the end product will vary according to the risk involved and the cost and practicability of avoiding it. In some cases he will have to establish a system for testing and inspecting the component, container or materials. Simple reliance on a reputable third party will not be sufficient.[18] *Macpherson* v. *Buick Motor Co.*[19] was such a case. Here it was held that the defendant car manufacturers were under a duty to test the dangerously defective wheel bought in from a third party supplier. In the words of Justice Cardozo: "[The] defendant was not absolved from a duty of inspection because it bought the wheels from a reputable manufacturer. It was not merely a dealer in automobiles. It was responsible for the finished product".[20] A similar view has been taken in other leading American cases, as when a bakery failed to discover a dead mouse in a pie filling bought in from a third party[1] and a shipbuilder to carry out proper tests on a defective

---

[16] See above, pp. 196–198. See also below, pp. 311–313.
[17] [1966] 2 All E.R. 181, 186. The statement is now in the 5th edn., para. 632. Baker, J. was citing an identical passage in the 4th edn., para. 797.
[18] See 1 *Frumer and Friedman*, s. 10.01; 3 A.L.R. 3d 1016.
[19] 217 N.Y. 382, 111 N.E. 1050 (N.Y.C.A., 1916).
[20] 111 N.E. 1050, 1055 (1916).
[1] *Sullivan* v. *Manhattan Market Co.*, 146 N.E. 673 (Mass. 1925).

shackle.[2] The same duty to test and inspect has been recognised in a series of cases against bottlers of carbonated drinks who have allegedly used defective containers.[3]

In other cases reasonable care would not demand the carrying out of independent tests and inspections. This would be true when, for example, the component comes in a sealed casing so that its usefulness would be destroyed if it were opened.[4] Baker, J. reached the same conclusion in *Taylor v. Rover Co., Ltd.*[5] The plaintiff had been blinded by the splintering of a chisel which had been fashioned and supplied by the second defendants and which was excessively brittle because of negligence on the part of a third party to whom it had been put out for hardening. Holding that the second defendants had exercised reasonable care although they had not tested the chisel for conformity with British Standard Specifications, the learned judge said:[6]

> "[They] were entitled to assume, in my view, having got competent hardeners to do the hardening of this guilty chisel for them, that the work was properly done, and it was no part of their duty in law or in good sense to set about the chisel when they received it from the hardeners and to examine it and to test it by hardness test..."[7]

If the manufacturer's responsibility is limited to carrying out such tests and inspections on components, containers and materials as would be consistent with reasonable care an injured plaintiff may be at a serious disadvantage. In any given case it may be difficult to trace the precise reason for an accident. For example, a bottle may have exploded but it may be unclear whether there was a fault in the bottle or whether the problem lay in the excessive pressure of the contents. Again, a component may fail but it may be uncertain whether it was defective as supplied or whether it was incorrectly assembled into the end product. In *Evans v. Triplex Safety Glass Co.*,[8] for example, one of the reasons for the failure of a claim against the manufacturers of the component windscreen was precisely because it could not be established that the windscreen had

---

[2] *Sieracki v. Seas Shipping Co.*, 149 F. 2d 98 (3rd Cir., 1945). See also *O'Donnell v. Asplundh Tree Expert Co.*, 99 A. 2d 577 (New Jersey S.C., 1953); *McKee v. Brunswick Corporation*, 354 F. 2d 577 (7th Cir., 1965); *Willey v. Fyrogas Co.*, 251 S.W. 2d 635 (Mo., 1952); *Tromza v. Tecumseh Products Co.*, 378 F. 2d 601 (3rd Cir., 1967); *Rauch v. American Radiator & Standard Sanitary Corporation*, 104 N.W. 2d 607 (Iowa, 1960).

[3] *Smith v. Peerless Glass Co.*, 181 N.E. 576 (N.Y.C.A., 1932) is a leading case. A series of cases is collected in 81 A.L.R. 2d 229.

[4] *Cf. O'Rourke v. Day and Night Water Heater Co.*, 88 P. 2d 191 (Cal. App., 1939). See also *Pabon v. Hackensack Auto Sales and Ford Motor Co.*, 164 A. 2d 773 (New Jersey S.C., 1960).

[5] [1966] 2 All E.R. 181.

[6] *Ibid.*, at p. 186.

[7] For further discussion of this case, see below, p. 283.

[8] [1936] 1 All E.R. 283.

shattered because it was defective, and not because it had been strained when it was screwed into the frame. Had the plaintiff sued the manufacturer of the Vauxhall saloon car in which the windscreen had been incorporated, she would have had the same difficulty. In yet other cases there may be the further complication of a possible failure in any one of a number of different components bought in from separate third parties. Alternatively the component itself may be made up from a number of parts, as where brakes manufactured by A, incorporate rubber supplied by B and are, in turn, incorporated into a car marketed by C.[9]

The drawbacks of requiring proof of personal fault in any such case are obvious. Even in jurisdictions in which *res ipsa loquitur* may be invoked[10] it would seem that, whilst an exclusive control over the immediate instrument of harm will not be demanded, the rule is still that "the plaintiff does not make out a preponderant case against either of two defendants by showing merely that he has been injured by the negligence of one or the other".[11] Certainly there are cases in which the evidence will permit or require the inference that the negligence of both D1 and D2 has contributed to an accident in equal degree.[12] But where the evidence indicates only that either D1 or D2 was responsible and there is nothing to suggest that both were there is no logical basis for singling out the one rather than the other or, indeed, for holding both equally responsible.[13] American product liability cases appear to have accepted that this is so, although *res ipsa* has been applied in isolated decisions against the bottler and retailer of a carbonated drink[14] and against the manufacturer of a component part and the manufacturer and operator of the end product.[15]

---

[9] This appears to have occurred in October 1975 when British Leyland announced that some 300,000 recently manufactured cars ran the risk of having faulty brakes: see *Guardian*, 3 October 1975.

[10] *Semble* that it cannot be invoked in an English product liability case although circumstantial evidence may be acted on with similar effect: see below, at pp. 257–258.

[11] *Cf.* Prosser, *The Law of Torts*, 4th edn., 1971, p. 221. For further discussion of the problem of *res ipsa* and multiple defendants in a product liability case, see 1 *Frumer and Friedman*, s. 12.03 [3].

[12] As where vehicles collide in the centre of the road or at cross-roads where there is no priority: see, e.g., *Baker* v. *Market Harborough Industrial Co-operative Society, Ltd.*, [1953] 1 W.L.R. 1472, C.A.; *France* v. *Parkinson*, [1954] 1 All E.R. 739; [1954] 1 W.L.R. 581.

[13] *Cf. Nesterczuk* v. *Mortimore* (1965), 115 C.L.R. 140 (High Ct. Australia); *Maher-Smith* v. *Gaw*, [1969] V.R. 371 (Vict. Sup. Ct.). An exception might be made for cases in which it is clear that both D1 and D2 were acting negligently and the issue is who as between the two of them caused the damage: see *Cook* v. *Lewis*, [1951] S.C.R. 830 (Sup. Ct. Canada).

[14] *Loch* v. *Confair*, 93 A. 2d 451 (Pa., 1953). *Cf. Huggins* v. *Morrell*, 198 N.E. 2d 448 (Ohio, 1964).

[15] *Becker* v. *American Airlines*, 200 F. Supp. 839 (1961) (altimeter); *Dement* v. *Olin Mathison Chemical Corporation*, 282 F. 2d 76 (5th Cir., 1960) (dynamite and cap). The theory is one of successive control and it is far from convincing.

Non-delegable duties

In cases such as those outlined above the position of the injured party would be eased substantially if the manufacturer of the end product were subject to a non-delegable duty with respect to the overall condition of the finished product at the time it was marketed. Even within a legal system requiring proof of negligence liability might then be incurred for carelessness on the part of independent suppliers of components or processors. Without prejudice to other possibilities (including the adoption of an avowedly strict liability) it is submitted that the manufacturer should be subjected to such a duty. The result would correspond with commercial reality. After all, the consumer buys the finished product (the car manufactured by X or the industrial machinery by Y) and not an "assembled collection of component parts". Admittedly there will be cases in which it will be extremely difficult to say whether a particular defendant is the manufacturer of the end product for present purposes. A watertight definition is probably impossible. There will also be cases in which the plaintiff might still fall within two stools, as where the defect might have originated in the poor storage conditions of an independent wholesaler, or in the installation of the product by an independent electrician or plumber, or in repair.[16] And there may be cases where apparent injustice might be worked, as where the manufacturer is a small concern buying in parts from an organisation which supplies the trade. The latter case could, however, normally be taken care of by a claim over, whether in contract or in third party proceedings.[17] It remains to be seen whether the present law corresponds with the position preferred above. The issues have been discussed much more fully in American cases than in this country.

The earlier American cases generally went no further than holding the manufacturer of the finished product liable for his own failure to carry out such tests and inspections as were reasonably necessary.[18] In *Smith* v.

---

[16] Representative examples from American cases include *Koktavy* v. *United Fireworks Manufacturing Co.*, 117 N.E. 2d 16 (Ohio, 1954) (fireworks subsequently stored in third party's warehouse); *Lutheran Church* v. *Canfield*, 233 So. 2d 331 (La. App., 1970) (air heating unit installed by third party); *Warren* v. *General Motors Corporation*, 329 F. Supp. 240 (1971) (repair by third party). There are obvious advantages in such cases in having the product installed by the manufacturer. Issues of causation are discussed below, pp. 273–290.

[17] *Tromza* v. *Tecumseh Products Co.*, 378 F. 2d 601 (3rd Cir., 1967) affords an example of a successful claim for an indemnity by the manufacturer of a refrigerator against the manufacturer of the component compressor unit which exploded, injuring the plaintiff.

[18] See, in general, 1 *Frumer and Friedman*, s. 10.02; Annotation 3 A.L.R. 1016, 1035 *et seq.*

Peerless Glass Co.,[19] for example, the New York Court of Appeals treated a bottle of soda water as "an assembled product of which the bottle itself was a component part" and proceeded to hold the bottle manufacturer liable whilst absolving the bottler. The latter had carried out such independent tests and inspections as were reasonably necessary and no more was demanded. The same position has been adopted in some of the more recent cases in which a negligence-based liability has been in issue. A notable example is to be found in the New Jersey case of *Pabon* v. *Hackensack Auto Sales and Ford Motor Co.*[20] Here an action was brought against the manufacturers of a Ford motor car which had gone out of control when the steering mechanism locked as a result of a defect in the ball-bearing assembly. Ford had bought in the bearings, fully assembled, from a third party which, as one of the largest ball-bearing manufacturers in the world, supplied most of the trade. Upholding the trial judge's dismissal of the plaintiff's case against Ford (in so far as it was based on negligence) the Superior Court of New Jersey said: "It is undoubtedly the law of this State that latent defects, not discoverable by reasonable inspection methods, will not result in the liability of the assembler or supplier."[1]

There is, however, a growing body of case law which refuses to limit the manufacturer's liability in this way. Thus in the New York case of *Markel* v. *Spencer*,[2] where a defective bolt had been incorporated into the brake mechanism of a car, the court cited the *Restatement of Torts*, 2d, s. 400,[3] saying:[4]

> "The defendant represented to the public that the car as a whole was manufactured by it. One who puts out a complete product, as being of his manufacture, is liable for any defect in a component part as if he had manufactured it, even though, in fact, he had purchased the part from others ... It is not

---

[19] 181 N.E. 576 (N.Y.C.A., 1932). See also *Martin* v. *Studebaker Corporation*, 133 A. 384 (N.J., 1926); *Willey* v. *Fyrogas Co.*, 251 S.W. 2d 635 (Mo., 1952).

[20] 164 A. 2d 773 (Sup. Ct. N.J., 1960).

[1] *Ibid.*, at p. 782. But the court also held that the assembler-manufacturer might be held liable on a breach of warranty theory. For further cases supporting the approach favoured in *Pabon's* case (whether expressly or implicitly), see *O'Rourke* v. *Day and Night Water Heater Co.*, 88 P. 2d 191 (Cal. App., 1939); *Taylor* v. *Reo Motors Inc.*, 275 F 2d 699 (10th Cir., 1960); *Defore* v. *Bourjois Inc.*, 105 So. 2d 846 (Ala., 1958).

[2] 171 N.Y.S. 2d 770 (1958).

[3] This provides that, "One who puts out as his own product a chattel manufactured by another is subject to the same liability as though he were its manufacturer". Section 400 is also called in aid to impose liability on a distributor who might otherwise have been regarded as subject to the less extensive liability of a retailer or wholesaler, see above, pp. 182–183. For the liability of retailers and wholesalers, see below, pp. 304–307 and pp. 310–311 respectively.

[4] 171 N.Y.S. 2d 770, 780.

material in such a case whether the defect could have been discovered by inspection at the time of assembly."

A similar view was taken in *Ford Motor Co. v. Mathis*,[5] where the issue was clearly presented in that the jury had found that the defendants could not have discovered the defect in the headlight dimmer switch by reasonable inspection. Holding that the defendant company was nonetheless liable under Texas law, the United States Court of Appeals for the Fifth Circuit said:[6]

"In effect, the purchaser does not distinguish between the assembler and the manufacturer. Nor does the manufacturer-assembler wish him to do so. Although he may realise that the assembler actually does not design and manufacture every component part, the purchaser assumes that the manufacturer-assembler will procure non-defective parts from reputable firms without the ultimate customer having to ascertain the manufacturer of each part ... Thus the assembler bears the liability of his manufacturer-supplier."

This case is of particular interest to English law in that the court made it quite clear that it was discussing a liability which depended on proof of negligence. Substantially similar reasoning and results are to be found in a number of other cases including a California case in which a defective alternator drive had been incorporated into a Boeing aeroplane,[7] and a New York case in which the manufacturer of a children's game had bought in a defective top from a third party.[8]

Similar issues may be raised at the opposite end of the manufacturing and distribution process and there is some authority suggesting that they will attract the same solution. In *Vandermark* v. *Ford Motor Co.*[9] the Supreme Court of California reversed a judgment in favour of a car manufacturer when an authorised dealer had failed to eliminate a defect in a brake master cylinder during a pre-delivery inspection and the car later crashed. *Vandermark's* case was cited by the New Jersey Superior Court in *Sabloff* v. *Yamaha Motor Co.*,[10] where the plaintiff had been injured when the front wheel of a motor-cycle suddenly locked, causing it to skid and crash into a parked car. This time the dealer played a somewhat more positive role in that he was required to attach the wheel of the

[5] 322 F. 2d 267 (5th Cir., 1963).
[6] *Ibid.*, at p. 274. Section 400 of the *Restatement* was again cited.
[7] *Boeing Airplane Co.* v. *Brown*, 291 F. 2d 310 (9th Cir., 1961).
[8] *Gittelson* v. *Gotham Pressed Steel Corporation*, 42 N.Y.S. 2d 341 (1943). See also *Poplar* v. *Bourjois*, 80 N.E. 2d 334 (N.Y., 1948); *Dow* v. *Holly Manufacturing Co.*, 321 P. 2d 736 (Cal., 1958); *Standard Motor Co.* v. *Blood*, 380 S.W. 2d 651 (Tex., 1964); *Sieracki* v. *Seas Shipping Co.*, 149 F. 2d 98 (3rd Cir., 1945): *King* v. *Douglas Aircraft Co.*, 159 So. 2d 108 (Fla. App., 1963); *A.E. Finley & Associates Inc.* v. *Medley*, 141 So. 2d 613 (Fla. App., 1962).
[9] 37 Cal. Rptr. 896 (Cal. Sup. Ct., 1964).
[10] 273 A. 2d 606, affd. 283 A. 2d 321 (1971).

motor-cycle to the front fork with a nut and bolt. The product was not, in other words, completely assembled when it reached him. A summary judgment in favour of the manufacturer was reversed by the New Jersey court on the ground that:[11]

"If the jury should find the dealer's lack of a sufficient tightening of the particular nut was the cause of the front wheel's failure to rotate, then the jury might also visit responsibility upon defendant manufacturer for the function delegated by it to be performed by the dealer and not properly performed."[12]

In neither of these cases was negligence pleaded as the sole basis of liability. Nonetheless both provide further support for the view that under the American law of negligence the manufacturer is subject to a non-delegable duty with respect to the marketing of a carefully constructed product.[13]

The issues raised by such cases have received little or no attention in English courts. In *Taylor* v. *Rover Co., Ltd.*,[14] however, the dismissal of the claim against the second defendants who had fashioned the chisel presupposed that they were not liable for the negligence of the third party hardeners.[15] In reaching this conclusion Baker, J. relied on *Davie* v. *New Merton Board Mills, Ltd.*,[16] another case involving facial injuries from a defective tool. Here the House of Lords had held that an employer was not liable to an injured employee when he had acquired the tool from a reputable source and otherwise exercised reasonable care.[17] This

---

[11] 273 A. 2d 606, 612.

[12] See also *Alvarez* v. *Felker Manufacturing Co.*, 41 Cal. Rptr. 514 (Cal. App., 1964); *Williams* v. *Ford Motor Co.*, 411 S.W. 2d 443 (Mo. App., 1966); *Malinak* v. *Firestone Tire and Rubber Co.*, 436 S.W. 2d 210 (Tex. Civ. App., 1969).

[13] In *Vandermark's* case *Greenman* v. *Yuba Power Products Inc.*, 27 Cal. Rptr. 697 (1962) was cited, but the court also noted that "even before such strict liability was recognised, the manufacturer of a completed product was subject to vicarious liability for the negligence of his suppliers or subcontractors that resulted in defects in the completed product": 37 Cal. Rptr. 896, 898. The judgment was reversed as to the non-suit of the negligence action. Another view, however, is that this approach may only be adopted in a negligence (as opposed to a strict tort or warranty) action where the dealer is the agent of the manufacturer: see *Alvarez* v. *Felker Manufacturing Co.*, 41 Cal. Rptr. 514 (Cal. App., 1964); *Malinak* v. *Firestone Tire and Rubber Co.*, 436 S.W. 2d 210 (Tex. Civ. App., 1969).

[14] [1966] 2 All E.R. 181; [1966] 1 W.L.R. 1491, above, p. 200.

[15] The claim also failed on the ground that the employer's failure to withdraw the chisel after its dangerous condition was appreciated was the sole effective cause of the accident. For discussion of this point see below, p. 283.

[16] [1959] A.C. 604; [1959] 1 All E.R. 346, approving *Mason* v. *Williams and Williams, Ltd.*, [1955] 1 All E.R. 808; [1955] 1 W.L.R. 549. See also *Sumner* v. *William Henderson, Ltd.*, [1964] 1 Q.B. 450; [1963] 1 All E.R. 408 reversing [1963] 2 All E.R. 712, C.A.

[17] In *Davie's* case the employer had in fact bought the chisel from an intermediate supplier rather than from the manufacturer. But it is clear that this did not affect the reasoning or the result; *cf.* [1959] A.C. 604, 629 (Lord Morton); *ibid.*, at p. 648 (Lord Tucker). The liability of the employer for defective equipment is now governed by the Employers' Liability (Defective Equipment) Act 1969.

was so, moreover, even if the employer's duty was non-delegable[18] since:[19]

> "[The] manufacturer could not by any legitimate use of language be considered the servant or agent of, or an independent contractor with, the employer who buys his manufactures in the market."

Nor could the manufacturer be said to be a person to whom the employer "delegated" a duty which it was for him to perform.

Although *Davie's* case was concerned with the liability of an employer rather than a manufacturer, it is of general importance on the issue of what constitutes a purported "delegation" of a duty where the duty is such as to be non-delegable. The inference is clearly that even if the duty of the manufacturer could be so described, still he would not have "delegated" its discharge by buying components, containers or materials on the open market or by putting the product out to a reputable processor.[20] It might be argued that there had been a purported "delegation" when the components, containers or materials had been made up to the manufacturer's special order or design. In *Davie's* case Viscount Simonds left the point open.[1] Any such distinction would, however, be unsatisfactory. The consumer injured by flying glass from an exploding bottle might appreciate why he should fail in a claim against the bottlers where the fault lies in the construction of the bottle. He should be forgiven for failing to understand the further subtlety whereby the success of the claim would turn on whether the bottles had been made up to special order or purchased in the market as a standard size. It would seem preferable to hold the manufacturer of the end product liable in all such cases[2]—including those

---

[18] See *Wilsons and Clyde Coal Co.* v. *English*, [1938] A.C. 57; [1937] 3 All E.R. 628, H.L.

[19] [1959] A.C. 604, 624–625 *per* Viscount Simonds. See also *ibid.*, p. 648 (Lord Keith).

[20] Examples of a far-reaching liability for the negligence of others are to be found in the common law liability of an occupier to a visitor under contract, and that of a carrier to a fare-paying passenger: see *Francis* v. *Cockrell* (1870), L.R. 5 Q.B. 501; *Maclenan* v. *Segar*, [1917] 2 K.B. 325, and North, *Occupiers' Liability* (1971), pp. 155–156. On the liability of a carrier under the Hague Rules to exercise due diligence to make the ship seaworthy, see *Riverstone Meat Co. Pty., Ltd.* v. *Lancashire Shipping Co., Ltd.*, [1961] A.C. 807; [1961] 1 All E.R. 495; *Scrutton on Charterparties*, 18th edn., p. 422 *et seq.* W. *Angliss & Co.* v. *P. and O. Steam Navigation Co.*, [1927] 2 K.B. 456 suggests that the carrier will not be liable for latent defects caused by negligence in construction which are not subsequently discoverable by reasonable care. This view was not dissented from in the *Riverstone* case.

[1] *Cf.* [1959] A.C. 604, 626. Where the design is *itself* dangerous liability may clearly be incurred (see below, p. 208 *et seq.*) The present concern is with defects in workmanship.

[2] An exception might be made for components widely advertised in their own right—e.g. car tyres. For American cases discussing the liability of the manufacturer of the end product for the condition of replacement parts, see *Rauch* v. *American Radiator and Standard Sanitary Corporation*, 104 N.W. 2d 607 (Iowa, 1960); 1 *Frumer and Friedman*, s. 10.03.

in which the defect stems from pre-delivery adjustments by authorised dealers.[3] Such liability would, of course, be without prejudice to any claim over which the manufacturer might have against the supplier, dealer or processor immediately responsible.

---

[3] As in the *Sabloff* case, 273 A. 2d 606, affd. 283 A. 2d 321 (N.J., 1971), above, p. 204.

11 The Manufacturers' Liability: Product Design and Specifications

Introduction[1]

In the last chapter, we discussed products which are alleged to be defective in the sense that they were not produced as intended. This is the standard complaint in an English product liability case. But it is clear that liability may equally be incurred where the product, although produced precisely in accordance with specifications and functioning as well (or as badly) after the accident as before, is nonetheless unreasonably dangerous to person or property.[2] The danger may stem from the choice of inappropriate materials, from the product's formula ingredients or specifications, or from failure to build in sufficient safety features. The category of cases reflects the once favoured distinction between chattels which are "inherently dangerous" or dangerous *per se*, and those which are dangerous only when constructed carelessly.[3] In many such cases the danger may stem solely from a failure to give adequate warnings or directions for safe use. In others the problem may be more deep rooted. There is no clear-cut distinction between "design" and "inadequate warning" cases although convenience in exposition justifies their being treated separately. Warnings and directions for use are accordingly discussed in the next chapter.

---

[1] See Noel, "Negligence of Design or Directions for Use of a Product", 71 Yale, L.J. 816 (1962); Noel, "Recent Trends in Manufacturers' Negligence as to Design, Instructions or Warnings", 19 Sw. L.J. 43 (1965); "Manufacturer's Negligence of Design or Directions for use of a Product", 42 Tenn. L.R. 11 (1974); Prosser, *Law of Torts*, 4th edn., 1971, pp. 644–646; 2 Harper & James, *Torts*, pp. 1541–1557; 1 Frumer and Friedman, *Products Liability*, s. 7; Annotation 76 ALR 2d 91, 54 ALR 3d 352.

[2] The requirement that the design be "unreasonably dangerous" before liability will be incurred is discussed above, pp. 186–189.

[3] See above, pp. 10–11 and for the current position, see below, pp. 253–255.

From the point of view of the plaintiff the problem of proving that the product was unreasonably dangerous may be formidable, especially where the complaint relates to the absence of safety features. The American power mower and car design cases bear witness to this.[4] Similarly, within a system requiring proof of negligence, there is the additional problem of establishing that the manufacturer ought to have appreciated the danger.[5] This may be particularly difficult in the case of pharmaceutical or other products carrying a long-term health hazard. But at least the plaintiff will be spared the problem of tracing any unreasonable danger to the manufacturer since it will not be disputed that any such danger existed from the time of production and marketing. The position is frequently different where there has been an alleged miscarriage in the production process, since there may then be room for an argument that the defect was caused by an intermediary.[6]

The implications for the defendant of an adverse judgment are likely to be far reaching since the judgment will relate to the entire output of the product rather than to an individual unit or batch.[7] The number of potential plaintiffs is accordingly increased and the availability of insurance cover problematic. Indeed, the standard products liability policy excludes liability arising from "any error or defect in or the unsuitability of any plan drawing specification or formula prepared and used as intended by the insured".[8] Cover may, of course, be available under an extension to the standard policy, or otherwise, but it has been said that "it is doubtful whether there is any aspect in the field of public liability insurance which calls for more underwriting judgment and discretion than the consideration of these risks".[9] Beyond this an adverse judgment in a design case may effectively require the manufacturer to lay out considerable sums in modifying the design with consequent interruption in production schedules. The expense and interruption would admittedly be less serious where the danger can be removed by a fuller warning. Generally, it may be suggested that such considerations, coupled with the undesirability of having different judgments as to the same design at the trial court level, are not, of themselves, a sufficient reason for denying recovery. They do, however, emphasise the need for careful consideration of the respective roles of the judicial process and government agencies in promoting safer products.[10]

---

[4] The power mower and car design cases are discussed below, at pp. 222–223 and 223–227, respectively.
[5] For proof of negligence, see below, ch. 13.
[6] See further, below, ch. 14, at pp. 279–281 especially.
[7] See above, pp. 184–185.
[8] *Cf.* Heppell, *Products Liability Insurance* (1967), p. 93.
[9] Heppell, *op cit.*, p. 62.
[10] See further below, pp. 270–272.

In this chapter it is proposed to consider cases of product design and specifications under four main headings: (i) materials and ingredients; (ii) specifications and concealed dangers; (iii) absence of safety features and devices; and (iv) components. The general position under a system of liability requiring proof of negligence is summarised in the *Restatement of Torts*, 2d, s. 398 as follows:

> "A manufacturer of a chattel made under a plan or design which makes it dangerous for the uses for which it is manufactured is subject to liability to others whom he should expect to use the chattel or to be endangered by its probable use for physical harm caused by his failure to exercise reasonable care in the adoption of a safe plan or design."

Materials and ingredients

Materials of insufficient strength or durability

The decision of the High Court of Australia in *Adelaide Chemical and Fertiliser Co., Ltd.* v. *Carlyle*[11] provides a neat example of the distinction between incurring liability through the defective condition of a particular item and through the general choice of materials of insufficient strength. The deceased had been injured when an earthenware jar broke, spilling sulphuric acid over his legs and shortly after the incident he had told his wife that the jar must have been faulty or cracked. He subsequently died when streptococcal septicaemia developed from the burns. In an action against the manufacturer and supplier of the acid, the High Court held that irrespective of whether there was admissible evidence establishing that the *particular* jar was defective,[12] the general brittleness of jars of that type rendered them unsuitable as containers for such a heavy and dangerous liquid. The judgment of the court below in favour of the deceased's widow was accordingly upheld.[13] Liability was similarly incurred in a leading American case[14] when the Ford Motor Company designed a tractor with a rubber steering wheel which broke in the hands of an operator, causing him to fall to the ground where he was run over by the machine. Other manufacturers used wooden or metal wheels and tests showed that the defendant's wheels were likely to break when subjected to normal pressure. In other American cases, design issues were

---

[11] (1940), 64 C.L.R. 514.

[12] The problem was whether the hearsay statement was admissible as part of the *res gestae*.

[13] See also *Steele* v. *Rapp*, 327 P. 2d 1053 (Kan, 1958) (explosive fingernail polish supplied in one-gallon glass bottle).

[14] *Goullon* v. *Ford Motor Co.*, 44 F. 2d 310 (6th Cir., 1930).

raised where ladders,[15] a safety-harness,[16] a surgical pin,[17] and the cover over the moving parts of a harvesting machine[18] were all claimed to lack reasonable safety because of the choice of materials of inadequate strength.[19] In such cases the manufacturer is not obliged to use the safest possible materials. Reasonable safety is all that is required. So in *Watts v. Bacon and Van Buskirk Glass Co.*,[20] where a plate glass door had broken injuring the plaintiff, the Supreme Court of Illinois upheld a directed verdict in favour of the supplier and installer, saying:[1]

> "It is true that tempered glass would be safer, and presumably doors of stronger materials would be still safer. But a supplier of chattels should not be compelled to sell only the ultimate in materials."

The standard required is essentially the same as that which is demanded. by the implied condition of merchantable quality in sales legislation.[2]

Reasonable safety may also require the use of materials which are durable. In *Mickle v. Blackmon*[3] the plaintiff had been involved in a motor accident in which he was impaled on the gear lever of a Ford car, the protective knob of which had deteriorated after some thirteen years of exposure to sunlight. Recovery was granted in a South Carolina court on the ground that there had been negligence in the choice of a material which would create an unexpected and unreasonable risk of harm during the lifetime of the vehicle.[4] Ford should have appreciated the likelihood of deterioration when the car was manufactured, as is necessary in a

---

[15] *Heise v. J. R. Clark Co.*, 71 N.W. 2d 818 (Minn., 1955); *Wilson v. Loe's Asheboro Hardware Inc.*, 131 S.E. 2d 501 (N.C., 1963); *Jimenez v. Sears, Roebuck & Co.*, 93 Cal. Rptr. 769 (Cal. S.C., 1971).

[16] *O'Donnell v. Asplundh Tree Expert Co.*, 99 A 2d 577 (N.J., 1953).

[17] *Bowles v. Zimmer Manufacturing Co.*, 277 F. 2d 868 (7th Cir., 1960). See also *Putensen v. Clay Adams Inc.*, 91 Cal. Rptr. 319 (Cal., 1970) (catheter).

[18] *Huset v. J.I. Case Threshing Machine Co.*, 120 F. 865 (8th Cir., 1903).

[19] See also *Northwest Airlines Inc. v. Glen L. Martin Co.*, 224 F. 2d 120 (6th Cir., 1955) (metal fatigue in aeroplane wing); *Gittelson v. Gotham Pressed Steel Corporation*, 42 N.Y.S. 2d 341 (1943) (child's top); *McGrath v. White Motor Corporation*, 484 P. 2d 838 (Or., 1971) (alloy used in lorry frame); *Filler v. Raytex Corporation*, 435 F. 2d 336 (7th Cir., 1970) (sunglasses).

[20] 163 N.E. 2d 425 (Ill., 1960).

[1] *Ibid.*, at p. 428. See also *Brizendine v. Visador Co.*, 305 F. Supp. 157 (1970). *Reffell v. Surrey County Council*, [1964] 1 All E.R. 743; [1964] 1 W.L.R. 358 illustrates the liability of an occupier who chooses insufficiently strong glass for a school door.

[2] See the Sale of Goods Act 1893, s. 14 (2), and above, p. 82 *et seq.* *Godley v. Perry*, [1960] 1 All E.R. 36; [1960] 1 W.L.R. 9 above, p. 93 (defective catapult) was, in essence, a design case.

[3] 166 S.E. 2d 173 (1969).

[4] See also *Auld v. Sears, Roebuck & Co.*, 25 N.Y.S. 2d 491 (1941) (pin in washing machine); *Noto v. Pico Peak Corporation*, 469 F. 2d 358 (2nd Cir., 1972) (bearings on ski lift).

negligence action[5] unless liability is to be grounded on the breach of a duty to warn of a subsequently discovered danger.[6]

Inflammable, explosive and corrosive materials

Reasonable safety may also require the use of materials which are not unduly inflammable, explosive or corrosive. The leading English and Commonwealth cases have emphasised the need for an adequate warning of such dangers and these will be discussed in the next chapter.[7] Here reference may be made to a number of leading American cases. In *LaGorga* v. *Kroger Co.*,[8] for example, a child had suffered extensive third-degree burns after a spark had ignited his jacket which had not been treated with a flame retardant substance costing no more than a few cents. The seller was held liable and in a persuasive judgment Justice Marsh noted:[9]

> "To an ever-increasing extent in this day of synthetic living, the population is dependent on mass producers for its wearing apparel. The composition and qualities of combined fabrics are not generally known. Greater care and integrity is required by society from sellers, as well as increased caution for the safety and well-being of all users, especially the child consumer. Where experiment or research is necessary to determine the presence or the degree of unusual danger in a child's jacket, the product should not be tried out on those who wear it."

Raymond v. *Riegel Textile Corporation*[10] was a similar case involving a twelve-year-old child who was burned when a flannelette nightgown burst into flames after contact with a grill on an electric stove. The material had a short ignition rate and no effective fire retardant and it was found to be unreasonably dangerous despite the fact that it complied with the requirements of the Federal Flammable Fabrics Act. As will be seen later, compliance with such standards is not conclusive on the issues of reasonable safety and reasonable care.[11] Other American cases have

---

[5] See further, below, pp. 255–260.
[6] As in *Rivtow Marine, Ltd.* v. *Washington Iron Works* (1974) 40 D.L.R. (3d) 530. (Canadian Sup. Ct.) (design of crane). The scope of the duty to warn of subsequently discovered dangers is discussed below, pp. 247–251.
[7] See, e.g., *Anglo-Celtic Shipping Co., Ltd.* v. *Elliott and Jeffrey* (1926), 42 T.L.R. 297; *Norton Australia Pty., Ltd.* v. *Streets Ice Cream Pty., Ltd.* (1968), 120 C.L.R. 635 (High Ct., Australia), and below, pp. 212–213.
[8] 275 F. Supp. 373 (W.D.Pa., 1967).
[9] *Ibid.*, at p. 379.
[10] 484 F. 2d 1025 (1st Cir., 1973).
[11] See below, pp. 265–266.

involved inflammable dresses,[12] a hula skirt,[13] pyroxoloid combs,[14] and a chest ointment, the vapours from which were ignited by a cigarette which the plaintiff was smoking in bed.[15]

In English law the sale of certain products such as nightdresses and electric blankets must comply with regulations made under the Consumer Protection Act 1961[16] and an injured party may sue in respect of the breach of the statutory duty if they do not.[17] For example, a child's nightdress must satisfy the British Standard Specification for fabrics of "low flammability". This approach has much to commend it. The regulations are, however, inevitably piecemeal in their coverage and there is no doubt that manufacturers no less than employers may be held liable at common law.[18] Indeed it is unthinkable that the claim in the *LaGorga* case[19] would have been dismissed summarily in an English court.

Materials carrying long-term health hazards

Other cases have involved materials or ingredients carrying a long-term health hazard for those in contact with them. *Wright* v. *Dunlop Rubber Co., Ltd.*[20] is a leading English case. Here the Court of Appeal upheld a judgment in favour of Dunlop employees suffering from cancer of the bladder caused by their exposure to the chemical substance Nonox S. The second defendants, I.C.I., were held liable for continuing to market the product when they knew that it constituted a serious health hazard.[1]

---

[12] *Dayton* v. *Harlene Frocks Inc.*, 86 N.Y.S. 2d 614 (1948), affd. 86 N.E. 2d 176 (1949); *Noone* v. *Fred Perlberg Inc.*, 49 N.Y.S. 2d 460 (1944), affd. 60 N.E. 2d 839 (1945).

[13] *Chapman* v. *Brown*, 198 F. Supp. 78 (1961) affd. 304 F. 2d 149 (9th Cir., 1962).

[14] *Farley* v. *Edward E. Tower & Co.*, 171 N.E. 639 (Mass., 1930).

[15] *Martin* v. *Benque Inc.*, 136 A. 2d 626 (N.J., 1957). See also *Hentschel* v. *Baby Bathinette Corporation*, 215 F. 2d 102 (2nd Cir., 1954) below, p. 233, n. 17 and, in general, Noel, 71 Yale L.J. 816, 862–866 (1962).

[16] See, respectively, the Nightdresses (Safety) Regulations, S.I. 1967 No. 839; the Electric Blankets (Safety) Regulations, S.I. 1971 No. 1961. A list of the small number of regulations made under the 1961 Act is set out below, at p. 269.

[17] See s. 3 (1) of the 1961 Act.

[18] For an example of a claim against an employer by a film extra required to wear highly inflammable material, see *Naismith* v. *London Film Productions, Ltd.*, [1939] 1 All E.R. 794, C.A.

[19] 275 F. Supp. 373 (1967), above.

[20] (1972), 13 K.I.R. 255. The case is discussed in more detail below, p. 248.

[1] The Health and Safety at Work Act 1974 provides, *inter alia*, that "It shall be the duty of any person who manufactures, imports, or supplies any substance for use at work to ensure, so far as is reasonably practicable, that the substance is safe and without risks to health when properly used": s. 6 (4) (*a*). The Act imposes criminal sanctions but does not provide for civil remedies.

Borel v. *Fibreboard Paper Products Corporation*[2] is a similar American case in which the defendant manufacturers of insulating materials containing asbestos were held liable to the plaintiff who contracted the lung cancer mesothelioma after working with the materials for some thirty-three years. With the increasing publicity now accorded to the dangers of asbestos, it would be surprising if there were not a number of similar English cases in the future. All such cases are likely to cause considerable difficulty, not least with respect to the operation of limitation periods.[3]

Drugs[4]

Similar problems may arise where death or disability has allegedly been caused by the taking of drugs for medicinal purposes. Many such cases have involved negligence in mislabelling,[5] or in putting out an impure or adulterated product[6] or in marketing a drug without adequate warning or directions for use.[7] But liability may equally be incurred where a new and unreasonably dangerous drug is put out without sufficient testing for toxicity or other side-effects. *Parke-Davis & Co.* v. *Stromsodt*[8] is a case in point. Here the defendants were held liable in negligence and for breach of warranty when damage to the brain and central nervous system of the infant plaintiff followed innoculation with their multiple antigen Quadrigen. In another case involving Quadrigen, a Federal District Court judge said that it was clearly established that:[9]

"the manufacturer is liable in negligence where it appears that the drug in fact

---

[2] 493 F. 2d 1076 (5th Cir., 1973). See also *Olgers* v. *Sika Chemical Corporation*, 437 F. 2d 90 (4th Cir., 1971).
[3] See *Central Asbestos Co., Ltd.* v. *Dodd*, [1973] A.C. 518; [1972] 2 All E.R. 1135, H.L. In the *Wright* case (above, note 20) the plaintiffs were employed by Dunlops in the late 1940s and exposed to Nonox S in this period. Cancer was diagnosed in 1966 and actions commenced in 1968. For discussion of limitation periods, see below, pp. 296–299.
[4] See Teff, "Products Liability in the Pharmaceutical Industry at Common Law" (1974), 20 McGill L.J. 102; Rheingold, "Products Liability: the ethical drug manufacturers liability", 18 Rutgers L.R. 947 (1964); James, "The Untoward Effects of Cigarettes and Drugs", 54 Cal. L.R. 1550 (1966); Rheingold, "The Mer/29 Story: an instance of successful mass disaster litigation", 56 Cal. L.R. 116 (1968); 3 *Frumer and Friedman*, s. 32 *et seq.*; Annotation, 79 A.L.R. 2d 301. Teff and Munro, *Thalidomide* (1976), chs. 4, 5, especially.
[5] *Thomas* v. *Winchester*, 6 N.Y. 397, 57 Am. Dec. 455 (1852), above, p. 12.
[6] *Gottsdanker* v. *Cutter Laboratories*, 6 Cal. Rptr. 320 (Cal. App., 1960) (Salk polio vaccine containing live virus: no liability in negligence on facts but liability on a breach of warranty theory).
[7] See 3 *Frumer and Friedman*, s. 33.01 [3], and below, ch. 12, pp. 233–234 especially.
[8] 411 F. 2d 1390 (8th Cir., 1969).
[9] *Tinnerholm* v. *Parke-Davis & Co.*, 285 F. Supp. 432, 446 (N.Y., 1968).

was inadequately tested or that [it] failed to exercise due care in the development of the product prior to its release on the market for commercial distribution."[10]

The position is no doubt the same in English law. In the thalidomide case, for example, Distillers (Biochemicals) Ltd., the English distributors of the drug, might clearly have been held liable if the plaintiffs had established that phocomelia had resulted from the taking of the drug, that Distillers had been careless, and that a duty of care was owed with respect to pre-natal injuries.[11] Generally, it would seem that the teratogenic effect of the drug might have been more readily established than the negligence of the distributor and that any such negligence would have lain in continuing to market the drug without adequate warnings when the dangers should have been appreciated. Cases involving drugs are apt to create problems which are as difficult as any in the whole field of product liability. New drugs are no doubt beneficial to the community in the vast majority of cases and they are typically subject to screening by an official licensing agency before they are marketed.[12] A testing or licensing agency might be held liable for passing a drug which was unreasonably dangerous[13] and it is questionable whether the manufacturer should be required to carry the development risks under a régime which imposes strict liability.[14]

---

[10] See also *Toole* v. *Richardson-Merrell Inc.*, 60 Cal. Rptr. 398 (Cal. App., 1967) (MER/29-triparanol—once used for treatment of arteriosclerosis); *Roginsky* v. *Richardson-Merrell Inc.*, 378 F. 2d 832 (2nd Cir., 1967), and, in general, 3 *Frumer and Friedman*, s. 33.01 [2]; Rheingold, 18 Rutgers L.R. 947, 997–999 especially.

[11] A settlement covering some of the children was approved by Hinchcliffe, J. in *S.* v. *Distillers Co. (Biochemicals), Ltd.*, [1969] 3 All E.R. 1412; [1970] 1 W.L.R. 114. For discussion of some of the jurisdictional problems, see *Distillers Co. (Biochemicals), Ltd.* v. *Thompson*, [1971] A.C. 458; [1971] 1 All E.R. 694, P.C. In general, see Lovell and Griffiths-Jones, "The Sins of the Fathers: tort liability for pre-natal injuries (1974), 90 L.Q.R. 531; Bennett, "The Liability of the Manufacturers of Thalidomide to the Affected Children" (1965), 39 A.L.J. 256; Sjostrom and Nilsson, *Thalidomide and the Power of the Drug Companies* (Penguin, 1972).

[12] In the United Kingdom, for example, one has the Committee on Safety of Medicines constituted under the Medicines Act 1968, s. 4.

[13] *Cf. Griffin* v. *United States*, 351 F. Supp. 10 (Pa., 1972). For further discussion of the position of testing agencies and certifiers of quality, see below, pp. 316–318. The meaning of the term "unreasonably dangerous" is discussed above, pp. 186–189.

[14] See also above, p. 108 for a reference to the question of whether strict liability extends to dangers which were scientifically undiscoverable at the time the product was marketed. In England the Medicines Act 1968, s. 62, empowers the Minister to prohibit the sale or supply of medicinal products in the interests of safety. For regulations made under s. 62, see The Medicines (Hexachlorophane Prohibition) Order 1973, S.I. 1973 No. 1120, as amended by S.I. 1974 No. 2167; the Medicines (Interim Prescription Only) (No. 1) Order 1974, S.I. 1974 No. 711, as amended by S.I. 1974 No. 2167; the Medicines (Phenacetin Prohibition) Order 1974, S.I. 1974 No. 1082, as amended by S.I. 1974 No. 2167.

Cigarettes and tobacco products

Another series of cases of general interest, if not of immediate practical importance to English law, has involved harm associated with cigarettes and other tobacco products. Here it has long been clear that liability may be imposed for harm caused by impurities and extraneous substances in tobacco.[15] More recently, however, it has been sought to hold manufacturers liable for the long-term health hazards of smoking, especially cancer.[16] The cases have been pleaded under strict tort or breach of warranty theories of liability but the issues raised would be substantially similar in a negligence action.[17]

Green v. *American Tobacco Co.*[18] is a leading case. The litigation was protracted and centred on the death of one Edwin Green whom a jury had found to have died from lung cancer caused by smoking Lucky Strike cigarettes. The claim eventually failed when the United States Court of Appeals for the Fifth Circuit affirmed the jury verdict that, in spite of their harmful properties, the cigarettes were reasonably wholesome and fit for use. There was accordingly no breach of the manufacturer's implied warranty on which the claim was founded.[19] On one view it might be thought surprising that the case should have been left to the jury at all.[20] But Justice Coleman would have gone further and directed a verdict for the plaintiff once it appeared that the cigarettes had caused cancer. In his view:[1]

"As to cancer-causing cigarettes, one must ask, how can anything, as a matter of fact, be reasonably fit for use by the general public when it is known to kill and no one knows whom it will kill. . . . Any product for personal use, of

---

[15] *Foley* v. *Liggett and Myers Tobacco Co.*, 241 N.Y.S. 233, affd. 249 N.Y.S. 924 (1930) (fragments of dead mouse); *Liggett and Myers Tobacco Co.* v. *De Lape*, 109 F. 2d 598 (9th Cir., 1940) (explosive substance). See also 80 A.L.R. 2d 681.

[16] See, in general, James, "The Untoward Effects of Cigarettes and Drugs", 54 Cal. L.R. 1550 (1966); Rossi, "The Cigarette-Cancer Problem", 34 South Cal. L.R. 399 (1961); Keeton, "Products Liability: liability without fault and the requirement of a defect", 41 Tex. L.R. 855, 868–873 (1963); 2 *Harper and James*, s. 28.8 (1968 Supp.), pp. 225–226, and above, p. 110.

[17] Especially since some cases have held that strict liability does not extend to dangers which were scientifically undiscoverable when the product was marketed: see *Ross* v. *Phillip Morris & Co.*, 328 F. 2d 3 (8th Cir., 1964); *Lartigue* v. *R.J. Reynolds Tobacco Co.*, 317 F. 2d 19 (5th Cir., 1963).

[18] 304 F. 2d 70 (5th Cir., 1962); 154 So. 2d 169 (Fla., 1963); 325 F. 2d 673 (1963); 391 F. 2d 97 (1968); 409 F. 2d 1166 (5th Cir., 1969).

[19] For a reference to this theory of liability, see above, p. 15.

[20] For supporting cases, see *Pritchard* v. *Liggett and Myers Tobacco Co.*, 295 F. 2d 292 (3rd Cir., 1961) (reversal of directed verdict for defendant); *Cooper* v. *R.J. Reynolds Tobacco Co.*, 234 F. 2d 170 (1st Cir., 1956).

[1] 409 F. 2d 1166, 1167.

whatever name or content, which causes cancer has no better claim to fitness as a fact than that accorded a poison."

Claims in cigarette-cancer cases may also fail through inability to establish a causal link or to identify any particular defendant (as when several brands are smoked) or through failure to show that the health hazard should have been appreciated when the product was marketed. A defence of *volenti non fit injuria* would be difficult to establish given the addictive qualities of nicotine and the relatively recent understanding of the risks involved.[2] Contributory negligence might, however, be pleaded on the basis that the problem is essentially one of excessive smoking or misuse. It would be surprising if an English court applying common law principles were to hold that there was evidence on which a plaintiff might succeed on facts such as those in the *Green* case. The general understanding seems to be that adherence to the Government Health Warning is sufficient to discharge the manufacturers' duty. Beyond that, the individual consumer runs the risk, whether voluntarily or otherwise, until such time, if any, as legislation intervenes or the safe cigarette is developed.

Animal feeding compounds and medicines

There are many American and Canadian cases holding manufacturers of animal feeding compounds and medicines liable for damage to the health of animals.[3] English law would similarly require the manufacturers of such products to adhere to the standards of reasonable safety. An original supplier of a feeding compound in a case such as *Henry Kendall & Sons* v. *William Lillico & Sons, Ltd.*[4] would accordingly be subject to a potential liability in tort to a remote consumer as well as to a potential liability in contract to an immediate purchaser. This would be so whether the fault lay in the use of contaminated ingredients, in the general choice of unsuitable ingredients, or in failure to give adequate warnings or directions for use.[5] The same would be true of a manufacturer of drugs, medicines or vaccines or indeed any other product likely to constitute a danger to the health of animals. For example, in the New Zealand case of *Grant* v.

---

[2] See *Pritchard* v. *Liggett and Myers Tobacco Co.*, 350 F. 2d 479 (3rd Cir., 1965) (subsequent proceedings).
[3] A comprehensive annotation of American cases is to be found in 81 A.L.R. 2d 138. See also 1 *Frumer and Friedman*, s. 5.03[1] n. 19; Note, "Product Liability for Animal Food and Drugs", 48 Iowa L.R. 630 (1963).
[4] [1971] 2 A.C. 441; [1971] 1 All E.R. 847, H.L., above p. 86.
[5] See, e.g., *British Chartered Co. of South Africa* v. *Lennon* (1915), 113 L.T. 935, below, p. 240 (mislabelling of arsenite cattle dip).

Cooper,[6] damages were awarded against the manufacturer of a sheep dip which caused absorptive poisoning in the plaintiff's rams.[7]

Fertilisers, herbicides, insecticides, etc.

A similar requirement of reasonable safety is imposed on those who market products such as fertilisers, herbicides, insecticides or rodenticides which may cause damage to crops, vegetables, fruit, flowers or animals.[8] The typical plaintiff in such a case would be a commercial grower and he is likely to allege that there has been a failure to give adequate warnings or directions for use. A number of Canadian cases are mentioned in the following chapter.[9] Leading American cases have involved damage to an orange crop which had been sprayed with the defendant's product citromulsion[10] and damage to peach trees which had been sprayed with the insecticide E-D-E.[11] Recovery might also be granted on appropriate facts where personal injury results from contact with such products.[12]

Design specifications and concealed dangers

Products may also lack reasonable safety because of their general design specifications rather than because of dangers associated with the materials

---

[6] [1940] N.Z.L.R. 947.

[7] See, also *Bernd Co.* v. *Rahn*, 96 S.E. 2d 185 (Ga., 1956) (animal feed causing anthrax in cows); *Midwest Game Co.* v. *M.F.A. Mill Co.*, 320 S.W. 2d 547 (Mo., 1959) (trout dying through malnutrition: failure to warn that not a "complete" food); *Boehm* v. *Fox*, 473 F. 2d 445 (10th Cir., 1973) (cattle feed); *American Cyanamid Co.* v. *Fields*, 204 F. 2d 151 (4th Cir., 1953) (poultry medicine); *Alman Brothers Farms and Feed Mill Inc.* v. *Diamond Laboratories Inc.*, 437 F. 2d 1295 (5th Cir., 1971), and, in general, 81 A.L.R. 2d 138, ss. 23, 27 especially.

[8] Some of the implications for liability insurers are noted by Heppell, *Products Liability Insurance* (1967), p. 29 and p. 41.

[9] See, e.g., *Ruegger* v. *Shell Oil Co. of Canada, Ltd.* (1964) 41 D.L.R. (2d) 183 (Ont. High Ct.); *Fillmore's Valley Nurseries, Ltd.* v. *North American Cyanamid, Ltd.* (1958), 14 D.L.R. (2d) 297; *Pack* v. *County of Warner* (1964), 44 D.L.R. (2d) 215 (Alberta Sup. Ct.), and below, pp. 234–235.

[10] *Kolberg* v. *Sherwin-Williams Co.*, 269 P. 975 (Cal., 1928).

[11] *Ebers* v. *General Chemical Co.*, 17 N.W. 2d 176 (Mich., 1944). See also *Chapman Chemical Co.* v. *Taylor*, 222 S.W. 2d 820 (Ark., 1949) (drifting insecticide); *La Plant* v. *E.I. Du Pont De Nemours & Co.*, 346 S.W. 2d 231 (Mo., 1961) (herbicides killing plaintiff's cattle); *McClanahan* v. *California Spray-Chemical Corporation*, 75 S.E. 2d 712 (Va., 1953), and, in general, 81 A.L.R. 2d 138, ss. 29, 31, 32, 33; 37 A.L.R. 3d 833.

[12] As in *Skogen* v. *Dow Chemical Co.*, 375 F. 2d 692 (8th Cir., 1967) (insecticide causing brain damage). Such cases are likely to turn on the adequacy of warnings and directions for use. Recovery on the basis of the long-term health hazards of insecticides is quite conceivable, but would be more difficult to establish.

or ingredients from which they are constructed. Many such cases will involve an alleged lack of safety features or devices and these are discussed in the following section. *Hindustan S.S. Co. v. Siemens*[13] is a case involving a somewhat different problem. The plaintiff company was suing the defendant manufacturers of electrical equipment and maintaining that a collision had been caused by their negligence in designing the electric telegraph system linking the wheelhouse and engine-room of a ship. This had resulted in a "full-astern" order being interpreted as "full-ahead". The claim failed on the facts since it was held that the defendants could not have foreseen the train of events leading to the collision, whilst the plaintiffs had had ample opportunity for intermediate examination. Willmer, J. was nonetheless prepared to approach the case on the basis that the decision in *Donoghue v. Stevenson* was "properly applicable to a case where the only complaint made is one of faulty design".[14] This is clearly correct.

A further and more recent example is provided by the decision of the Court of Appeal in *Williams v. Trimm Rock Quarries, Ltd.*[15] where the manufacturers of a new type of drilling machine were held liable for the death of an employee who was killed when the machine toppled over the edge of a quarry. Having said that the worker had not received sufficient instructions in the use of the machine, Lord Denning is reported as adding:[16]

> "Further, before sending a machine like this out for demonstration and putting it on the market, the toolmakers should have guarded against the possibility of its rising up and toppling over, and should have investigated those possible sources of danger. Since this accident they had taken steps to that end and all was now well; but reasonable foresight would have discovered it before the machine was issued."

In other cases similar design issues have been raised when an imported German vacuum cleaner administered a shock to its user;[17] a bubble-car overturned when a tyre burst;[18] a drum of caustic soda sprayed out its contents when the bung was loosened;[19] and when a crane which was disintegrating internally needed urgent repair.[20] Equivalent American cases

---

[13] [1955] 1 Lloyd's L.R. 167.
[14] *Ibid.*, at p. 177.
[15] (1965), 109 Sol. Jo. 454.
[16] *Ibid.*
[17] *Goodchild v. Vaclight*, (1965), *Times*, 22 May.
[18] *Sutcliffe v. Trojan* (1967), (unreported) C.A. 143.
[19] *Broomhall v. British Railways Board* (1963), (unreported) C.A. 110.
[20] *Rivtow Marine, Ltd. v. Washington Iron Works* (1974), 40 D.L.R. (3d) 530 discussed below, pp. 248–249 (duty to warn) and pp. 333–337 (compensation for economic loss). See also *McAlpine & Sons, Ltd. v. Minimax, Ltd.*, [1970] 1 Lloyds Rep. 397; *The Diamantis Pateras*,

have involved an aluminium lounge chair which amputated the finger of a person who sat on it;[1] a milk cooler which electrocuted a person using it;[2] a 1955 Volkswagen car, the inadequate locking mechanism of which caused a child to fall out as the car was rounding a corner;[3] a baseball pitching machine which was activated by a slight vibration, causing severe facial injury to a high school student;[4] and an aircraft which was so designed as to let carbon monoxide enter the cockpit, causing the pilot to lose consciousness and crash.[5] An action in an English court alleging negligence in a product's general design specifications might also find support in modern decisions holding builders, architects and surveyors liable for dangerous structures.[6]

Absence of safety features and devices

The marketing of products without appropriate safety features and devices provides a further aspect of negligence in design. There are few English cases in point[7] but the potential for liability is borne out by a substantial number of American decisions.[8] These have typically involved household, industrial and agricultural equipment with unguarded moving parts and, in recent years, power mowers and motor vehicles. In some cases it is contended that the damage would not have occurred at all had a particular safety device been incorporated whilst in others it is claimed that the absence of the safety feature has enhanced the seriousness of the damage. In American cases the issue for the appellate court is normally that of whether there is evidence on which a jury could properly find for the

[1966] 1 Lloyds L.R. 179; *Martin* v. *T.W. Hand Fireworks Co., Ltd.* (1963), 37 D.L.R. (2d) 455 (Ont. High Ct.).

[1] *Matthews* v. *Lawnlite Co.*, 88 So. 2d 299 (Fla., 1956). See also *Hood* v. *Formatron Corporation*, 448 P. 2d 1281 (Okla., 1971) (hairdryer hood which fell like a guillotine).

[2] *Steele* v. *Westinghouse Electric Corporation*, 159 N.E. 2d 469 (Ohio, 1958).

[3] *McKinney* v. *Frodsham*, 356 P. 2d 100 (Wash., 1960).

[4] *Dudley Sports Co. Inc.* v. *Schmitt*, 279 N.E. 2d 266 (Ind., 1972).

[5] *DeVito* v. *United Air Lines*, 98 F. Supp. 88 (N.Y., 1951). See also *Noel* v. *United Aircraft Corporation*, 219 F. Supp. 556 (Del., 1963); *Berkebile* v. *Brantly Helicopter Corporation*, 337 A. 2d 893 (Pa., 1975).

[6] See, e.g., *Sharpe* v. *E. T. Sweeting & Son, Ltd.*, [1963] 2 All E.R. 455; [1963] 1 W.L.R. 665; *Clay* v. *A. J. Crump & Sons, Ltd.*, [1964] 1 Q.B. 533; [1963] 3 All E.R. 687; *Dutton* v. *Bognor Regis Urban District Council*, [1972] 1 Q.B. 373; [1972] 1 All E.R. 462 and, in general, below, pp. 331–333.

[7] See, e.g., *Griffiths* v. *Arch Engineering Co., Ltd.*, [1968] 3 All E.R. 217 (portable grinding machine with inadequate guard: action against hirer-out).

[8] See Noel, "Negligence of Design or Directions for Use of a Product", 71 Yale L.J. 816, 822–827 (1962); Noel, "Recent Trends in Manufacturers' Negligence as to Design, Instructions or Warnings", 19 Sw. L.J. 43, 56–59 (1965); 1 *Frumer and Friedman*, s. 7.02.

plaintiff so entitling him to avoid a directed verdict. A frequently recurring question is whether recovery is permissible where the danger is "obvious" or "patent".[9]

Household, industrial and agricultural equipment

Reasonable safety may sometimes demand that household, industrial and agricultural equipment be produced with appropriate built-in safety devices. Leading American cases have involved vaporisers and similar products marketed without adequate devices to prevent overheating[10] or with loose-fitting lids.[11] The principle might be extended to a wide range of items including cleansing products and medicines sold in containers which are attractive to children and opened easily by them.[12] Appropriate safety devices or guards may also be required for industrial and agricultural equipment such as punch presses,[13] paper balers,[14] bottle labelling machines,[15] potato harvesters,[16] corn pickers[17] and hay balers.[18] Whether a device is needed in any given case will depend on factors such as its cost and practicability and the extent of the danger created.[19]

Although no equivalent case law has been developed in this country a manufacturer might clearly be held liable according to similar principles. Support for this view is to be found in cases recognising that failure to

---

[9] The leading American case denying liability for "obvious" dangers is *Campo* v. *Scofield*, 95 N.E. 2d 802 (N.Y., 1950). But see *Micallef* v. *Miehle Co.* (N.Y., 1976) and below, p. 292.

[10] *Lindroth* v. *Walgreen Co.*, 87 N.E. 2d 307 (1949), affd. 94 N.E. 2d 847 (Ill., 1950); 80 A.L.R. 2d 598, IIIA. See also *Schipper* v. *Levitt & Sons Inc.*, 207 A. 2d 314 (N.J., 1965) (child burned by water from boiler without mixing valve); *Reamer Industries* v. *McQuay Inc.* 344 F. Supp. 540 (1972).

[11] *McCormack* v. *Hankscraft*, 154 N.W. 2d 488 (Minn., 1967). *Cf. Blissenback* v. *Yanko*, 107 N.E. 2d 409 (Ohio App., 1951).

[12] *Boyd* v. *Frenchee Chemical Corporation*, 37 F. Supp. 306 (N.Y., 1941) (child killed through eating shoe cleaner) provides an example of a case in which recovery was denied. For abnormal use, see below, p. 294. For medicine containers, see also below, pp. 271–272.

[13] *Wells* v. *Webb Machinery Co.*, 315 N.E. 2d 301 (Ill., 1974); *Bexiga* v. *Havir Manufacturing Corporation*, 290 A. 2d 281 (N.J., 1972): *Powell* v. *E. W. Bliss Co.*, 346 F. Supp. 819 (Mich., 1972). *Cf. Rios* v. *Niagara Machine and Tool Works*, 299 N.E. 2d 86 (Ill. App., 1973).

[14] *Jennings* v. *Tamaker Corporation*, 201 N.W. 2d 654 (Mich., App., 1972); but *cf. Patten* v. *Logeman Brothers Co.*, 283 A. 2d 567 (Md. App., 1971).

[15] *Byrnes* v. *Economic Machinery Co.*, 200 N.W. 2d 104 (Mich. App., 1972).

[16] *Lindenberg* v. *Folson*, 138 N.W. 2d 573 (N.D., 1965).

[17] *Galvan* v. *Prosser Packers Inc.*, 521 P. 2d 929 (Wash., 1974); *Wright* v. *Massey-Harris Inc.*, 215 N.E. 2d 465 (Ill. App., 1966); but *cf. Walk* v. *J.I. Case Co.*, 318 N.Y.S. 2d 598 (1971).

[18] *Palmer* v. *Massey-Ferguson Inc.*, 476 P. 2d 713 (Wash. App., 1970); but *cf. Yaun* v. *Allis-Chalmers Manufacturing Co.*, 34 N.W. 2d 853 (Wis., 1948); *Gauthier* v. *Sperry Rand Inc.*, 252 So. 2d 129 (La. App., 1971).

[19] See above, pp. 178–180 and below, ch. 13.

fence dangerous machinery may constitute a breach of an employer's common law duty of care to his employees as well as a breach of a statutory duty. As Glynn-Jones, J. said *obiter* in *Quinn* v. *Horsfall and Bickham, Ltd.*, "the common law obligation to fence is concealed or masked by the wider obligations imposed by statute, and, if for any reason the wider statutory obligation disappears, the common law duty once more arises...".[20] So in *Jones* v. *Richards*,[1] for example, the commercial hirer-out of a threshing machine was held liable both under statute and at common law to one of his employees whose foot was injured by moving parts of the machine.[2] He could hardly have been any the less liable if a third party as opposed to an employee had been injured or if he had manufactured the machine.

The potential liability of the manufacturer in such a case may be important to the employer seeking a contribution or indemnity (as well as to an individual employee), an entitlement which, in the case of injury from defective equipment, is expressly preserved by the Employers' Liability (Defective Equipment) Act 1969, s. 1 (1).[3] It should also be noted that the Health and Safety at Work Act 1974, s. 6 (1) provides that:

> "It shall be the duty of any person who designs, manufactures, imports or supplies any article for use at work —
>
> (*a*) to ensure, so far as is reasonably practicable, that the article is so designed and constructed as to be safe and without risks to health when properly used."

Breach of this duty does not, however, confer a right of action in civil proceedings.[4] The same is true of the more limited duty imposed by the Factories Act 1961, s. 17 (2) on the seller or hirer-out of a machine driven by mechanical power.[5]

Power mowers

More difficulty has been experienced in a series of modern American

---

[20] [1956] 1 All E.R. 777, 782.

[1] [1955] 1 All E.R. 463; [1955] 1 W.L.R. 444.

[2] See also Munkman, *Employer's Liability*, 8th edn., 1975, pp. 110 and 141 and cases there cited.

[3] The 1969 Act does not define the word "defect" when used in relation to equipment in s. 1 (1) (*a*) and (*b*) of the Act. It would seem, however, that the word would encompass a deficiency in design as well as a fault in an individual unit. *Cf.*, however, *Jackson* v. *Mumford* (1902), 8 Comm. Cas. 61 where Kennedy, J. suggested that the words "defect in machinery" when used in a business document excluded "the erroneous judgment of the designer".

[4] See s. 47 of the 1974 Act.

[5] The duty to provide an effective guard extends to "every set screw, bolt or key on any revolving shaft etc.". *Biddle* v. *Truvox Engineering Co., Ltd.*, [1952] 1 K.B. 101; [1951] 2 All E.R. 835 established the lack of a civil remedy.

cases involving power mowers[6] which have either injured their operator
or someone in the immediate vicinity[7] or thrown up a solid object which
has caused damage to person or property.[8] In a number of cases it has been
left to the jury to decide whether the mower failed to meet the requirements of reasonable safety.[9] In others directed verdicts have been entered
for the manufacture on the ground that the danger was "obvious".[10]
Sills v. *Massey-Ferguson Inc.*[11] is a case falling into the former category.
Here a rotary mower manufactured by the defendant company was being
towed behind a tractor when it apparently picked up a bolt which it
threw some 150 feet through the air, striking the plaintiff on the jaw.
Denying the manufacturer's motion to dismiss the action, the District
Court in Indiana left it to the jury to decide, *inter alia*, whether the
blade housing of the mower was designed negligently and whether this
was a cause of the injury. In this area (as in many others) it is unclear
why the substantial number of American cases have apparently no reported
English counterpart.[12] The fact that there are more power mowers *per
capita* in the United States can only be part of the answer.

Vehicle design[13]

Vehicle design is one of the most interesting and controversial areas of

---

[6] See Noel & Phillips, *Products Liability* (1974), pp. 151–153; Annotation, 41 A.L.R. 3d 986.
[7] See, e.g., *Wenzell* v. *M.T.D. Products Inc.*, 336 N.E. 2d 125 (Ill., 1975); *Murphy* v. *Cory
Pump and Supply Co.*, 197 N.E. 2d 849 (Ill., 1964) (severe leg injury to child); *Harrison* v.
McDonough Power Equipment Inc., 381 F. Supp. 926 (1974) (same); *Pontifex* v. *Sears, Roebuck
& Co.*, 226 F. 2d 909 (4th Cir., 1955); *Clark* v. *Sears, Roebuck & Co.*, 254 So. 2d 62 (La.
App., 1971); *South Austin Drive-In Theatre* v. *Thomison*, 421 S.W. 2d 933 (Tex. Civ. App.,
1967); *Luque* v. *Mclean*, 104 Cal. Rptr. 443 (Cal. S.C., 1972).
[8] *Sills* v. *Massey Ferguson Inc.*, 296 F. Supp. 776 (D.C. Ind., 1969) (noted below); *Stovall &
Co.* v. *Tate*, 184 S.E. 2d 834 (Ga. App., 1971) (rock thrown through classroom window,
striking child); *Dura Corporation* v. *Wallace*, 297 So. 2d 619 (Fla. App., 1974).
[9] Notably in *South Austin Drive-In Theatre* v. *Thomison*, *Luque* v. *Mclean*; *Sills* v. *Massey-
Ferguson Inc.*, *Harrison* v. *Mcdonough Power Equipment Inc.*, above.
[10] *Cf. Murphy* v. *Cory Pump and Supply Co.*, above (*cf.* critical comments in *Wright* v. *Massey-
Harris Inc.*, 215 N.E. 2d 465 (Ill. App., 1966); *Pontifex* v. *Sears, Roebuck & Co.*, above;
Stovall & Co. v. *Tate*, above.
[11] 296 F. Supp. 776 (D.C. Ind., 1969). The case was argued in negligence, breach of
implied warranty and strict tort liability.
[12] *Crow* v. *Barford* (1963), C.A. 102 is an unreported Court of Appeal decision denying
liability for injury from a rotary grass cutter.
[13] See, in general, Katz, "Liability of Automobile Manufacturers for Unsafe Design of
Passenger Cars", 69 Harv. L.R. 863 (1956); Nader & Page, "Automobile Design and the
Judicial Process", 55 Cal. L.R. 645 (1967); Note, "Manufacturer's Liability for an 'Uncrash-
worthy' Vehicle", 52 Cornell L.Q. 444; Note, 21 S.W.L.J. 332 (1967), 71 Mich. L.R. 1654
(1973); *Frumer and Friedman*, ss. 7.01[3]; 16A4 (3–329); *Prosser, Law of Torts*, 4th edn., 1971,
pp. 645–646; Annotation, 42 A.L.R. 3d 560.

American product liability litigation. A manufacturer may clearly incur liability where damage is caused by a defect in the construction of a particular vehicle.[14] The "one-off" or "rogue" vehicle creates no special difficulties although it may involve the manufacturer in considerable expense where the defect is common to a substantial run of cars coming off the production line. Much more fundamental problems are raised where it is contended that the car is unreasonably dangerous as designed, whether to its driver or passengers, to other road users, or to pedestrians on the highway. The plaintiff may be claiming that a safer design would have prevented an accident altogether or, more typically, that it would have reduced the injury suffered as the result of an accident.[15]

This is again an area which is largely unexplored in English law but it has been observed that this is "probably as much a comment on the unadventurousness of English litigants and their legal advisors as a reflection on the law".[16] Some discussion is to be found in *Wyngrove's Executrix* v. *Scottish Omnibuses, Ltd.*[17] where the Court of Session in Scotland had held the defendant company to be negligent in operating their service with Bristol Lodeka-type buses. This bus was designed and constructed without a central vertical pillar on the platform when such a pillar would probably have prevented the deceased from falling off the bus as it was approaching a stop. On appeal to the House of Lords, however, the decision was reversed on the ground that the evidence did not support a finding of negligence. Any action against the manufacturers of the bus would presumably also have failed on the facts. The Canadian case of *Phillips* v. *Ford Motor Co. of Canada, Ltd.*[18] provides another example. A first instance judge in the Ontario High Court had held the Canadian distributors of a Lincoln Continental liable on the ground, *inter alia*, of negligence in marketing a car with a power-braking system which was likely to fail. On appeal this decision also was reversed because the form of the hearing had been misconceived.[19] The judge had, in effect, acted as a research director conducting a scientific inquiry.[20]

---

[14] As in *Macpherson* v. *Buick Motor Co.*, 111 N.E. 1050 (N.Y., 1916). See also *Cronin* v. *J.B.E. Olson Corporation*, 104 Cal. Rptr. 433 (Cal. Sup. Ct., 1972), above, p. 186 which illustrates that the distinction between problems of design and miscarriages in the production process is by no means clear cut.

[15] See Roda, "Products Liability: the enhanced injury case", 8 The Forum 643 (1973). An analogy is to be found in the seat-belt cases such as *Froom* v. *Butcher*, [1975] 3 All E.R. 520, C.A.

[16] Elliott and Street, *Road Accidents* (1968), p. 202.

[17] 1966 S.C. (H.L.) 47.

[18] (1970) 12 D.L.R. (3d) 28.

[19] (1971) 18 D.L.R. (3d) 641 (Ont.C.A.).

[20] For newspaper reports of suggestions that actions might be brought by disabled drivers injured in accidents involving invalid tricycles claimed to be unstable and otherwise dangerous, see *Sunday Times*, 10 August 1975; *Guardian*, 14 August 1975. For a critical look at progress in car safety, see *Autocar*, 28 February 1976, pp. 8–12.

American case law has developed with noticeable caution in this area. A consistently high percentage of decisions still ends in a summary judgment for the manufacturer thus holding that there is no evidence on which to base a finding that the vehicle was unreasonably dangerous. Some cases have seemed to doubt the propriety of questioning a manufacturer's judgment in matters of design.[1] Another has gone so far as to equate demands for cars better able to withstand collisions with a demand for a car with pontoons to enable it to float on water.[2] Generally, however, there has been an awareness of the far-reaching consequences of an adverse judgment and a feeling that safety standards should be imposed through legislation[3] rather than through the courts. As Prosser observes[4]

> "It may be significant that the cases that have denied recovery have tended to be those in which protection of the plaintiff would have required an extensive, and costly, redesign of the entire automobile, whilst those allowing it would have tended to call for only minor and inexpensive changes in detail. It seems clear that cost cannot be entirely disregarded in considering the problem."

The cases noted below can do little more than indicate the general range of design features which have been called in question.

Evans v. *General Motors Corporation*[5] is one of the leading cases denying recovery. The deceased driver had been killed in a side-impact collision at a junction and it was alleged that his Chevrolet station wagon was designed negligently in that it had an "X" frame instead of a side-rail perimeter frame. The latter type of frame was used by several competitors and it would have afforded greater protection. The United States Court of Appeals for the Seventh Circuit upheld the summary dismissal of the claim saying:[6]

> "A manufacturer is not under a duty to make his automobile accident-proof or fool-proof; nor must he render the vehicle 'more' safe where the danger to be avoided is obvious to all.[7] Perhaps it would be desirable to require manufacturers to construct automobiles in which it would be safe to collide, but that would be a legislative function, not an aspect of judicial interpretation of existing law.... The intended purpose of an automobile does not include its participation in collisions..."

---

[1] *Cf. Dillingham* v. *Chevrolet Motor Co.*, 17 F. Supp. 615, 618 (Okla., 1936).

[2] *Evans* v. *General Motors Corporation*, 359 F. 2d 822, 825 (7th Cir., 1966), below.

[3] As is done by the National Traffic and Motor Vehicle Safety Act 1966.

[4] *Torts*, 4th edn., 1971, p. 646.

[5] 359 F. 2d 822 (7th Cir.), cert. dend. 385 U.S. 836 (1966).

[6] *Ibid.*, at pp. 824–825.

[7] Citing *Campo* v. *Scofield*, 95 N.E. 2d 802, 804 (N.Y., 1950). But see now *Micallef* v. *Miehle Co.* (N.Y., 1976).

The same view has been taken in many other cases, as when a plaintiff claimed that a car was capable of being driven at an "excessive" speed;[8] a passenger struck her face on a dashboard which was neither padded nor recessed;[9] a back-seat passenger alleged that a car gave insufficient protection in a side-on collision;[10] injuries were suffered when a car rolled over on its roof and the supports collapsed;[11] and when the manufacturer of a Greyhound bus had failed to install seat belts on passenger seats.[12] A number of cases have also denied liability where the external design features of a vehicle were claimed to have increased the injury suffered by other road users.[13]

Larsen v. *General Motors Corporation*[14] is one of the most important and frequently cited cases recognising the potential for liability in the field of vehicle design. The complaint here was that a 1963 Chevrolet Corvair was so designed as to give inadequate protection against backward displacement of the steering column in a head-on collision. The plaintiff driver had received severe head injuries. The defendant manufacturers, General Motors, denied any duty with respect to design features not causally related to the accident, but intended only to reduce its effect. This view was accepted by the District Court, but the Court of Appeals for the Eighth Circuit reversed a summary judgment and held that the car manufacturers' duty was not so limited. Involvement in accidents and collisions, though no part of the intended purpose of the vehicle, was clearly quite foreseeable. In the opinion of the court:[15]

"While all risks cannot be eliminated nor can a crash-proof vehicle be designed under the present state of the art, there are many common-sense factors in

---

[8] *Schemel* v. *General Motors Corporation*, 384 F. 2d 802 (7th Cir., 1967), cert. den. 390 U.S. 945 (1968).

[9] *Burkhard* v. *Short*, 275 N.E. 2d 632 (Ohio, 1971).

[10] *Ford* v. *Ruppell*, 504 P. 2d 686 (Mont., 1972).

[11] *Frericks* v. *General Motors Corporation*, 317 A. 2d 494 (Md., 1974); revd. on appeal, 336 A. 2d 118 (Md., 1975).

[12] *Gleich* v. *General Motors Corporation*, 277 N.E. 2d 566 (Ohio, 1971). *Cf. Mortensen* v. *Southern Pacific Co.*, 53 Cal. Rptr. 851 (Cal. App., 1966); *Forse* v. *Turner* 284 N.Y.S. 2d 995 (1967); Nader and Page, 55 Cal. L.R. 645, 657–658 and cases there cited.

[13] See, e.g., *Hatch* v. *Ford Motor Co.*, 329 P. 2d 605 (1958) (radiator ornament: boy blinded in one eye); *Kahn* v. *Chrysler Corporation*, 221 F. Supp., 677 (Tex., 1963) (tail fin: child on bicycle); *Mieher* v. *Brown*, 301 N.E. 2d 307 (Ill., 1973) (car passing beneath lorry in rear-end collision). *Cf.*, however, *Green* v. *Volkswagen of America Inc.*, 485 F. 2d 430 (6th Cir., 1973); *Passwaters* v. *General Motors Corporation*, 454 F. 2d 1270 (8th Cir., 1972) (below, n. 20). See, in general, Note, "The Automobile Manufacturer's Liability to Pedestrians for Exterior Design: new dimensions in 'crashworthiness'", 71 Mich. L.R. 1654 (1973). Other cases withholding the issue from the jury include *General Motors Corporation* v. *Muncey*, 367 F. 2d 493 (5th Cir., 1966) (ignition key could be removed when engine was running); *McNally* v. *Chrysler Motors*, 284 N.Y.S. 2d 761 (N.Y., 1967) (no brake fluid light).

[14] 391 F. 2d 495 (8th Cir., 1968).

[15] *Ibid.*, at p. 503.

design, which are or should be well known to the manufacturer that will minimise or lessen the injurious effects of a collision. The standard of reasonable care is applied in many other negligence situations and should be applied here."[16]

The same view has been taken in a number of other cases, as where the roof of a Buick Electra hard-top collapsed when it overturned;[17] the fuel tank of a 1962 M.G.B. ruptured and caught fire after a rear impact collision;[18] a paydozer was designed without rear-view mirrors and with a blind spot stretching back some forty-eight feet;[19] and where a 1964 Buick had a wheel cover from which protruded four propeller-like blades.[20] These latter cases may now be said to represent the dominant trend and it would be surprising, if the reasoning and philosophy behind the *Larsen* decision did not prevail.

Components

The imposition of liability on manufacturers of component parts is likely to cause considerable difficulty especially where the complaint is of a general design deficiency rather than a miscarriage in the production process. There is no especial problem with components such as car tyres and brake units which have a single identifiable function though even here it remains open to argument whether a system of strict liability should extend to the manufacturers of such components.[1] The real difficulty is

---

[16] Contrast *Yetter* v. *Rajeski*, 364 F. Supp. 105 (N.J., 1973) following *Evans* and holding that there was no duty to install a collapsible steering column. See also *General Motors Corporation* v. *Howard*, 244 So. 2d 726 (Miss., 1971).

[17] *Dyson* v. *General Motors Corporation*, 298 F. Supp. 1064 (Pa., 1969). See also *Spurlin* v. *General Motors Corporation*, 426 F. 2d 295 (5th Cir., 1970); *Brandenburger* v. *Toyota Motor Sales U.S.A. Inc.*, 513 P. 2d 268 (Mont. 1973).

[18] *Grundmanis* v. *British Motor Corporation*, 308 F. Supp. 303 (Wis., 1970). Similarly in *Self* v. *General Motors Corporation*, 116 Cal. Rptr. 575 (Cal. App., 1974); but *cf. Shumard* v. *General Motors Corporation*, 270 F. Supp. 311 (Ohio, 1967).

[19] *Pike* v, *Frank G. Hough Co.*, 85 Cal. Rptr. 629 (Cal. S.C., 1970) (decedent killed when machine reversed). *Cf. Mondshour* v. *General Motors Corporation.*, 298 F. Supp. 111 (Md., 1969) (bus without right rear-view mirror: no liability).

[20] *Passwaters* v. *General Motors Corporation*, 454 F. 2d 1270 (8th Cir., 1972). See also *Mickle* v. *Blackmon*, 166 S.E. 2d 173 (1969) (gearlever knob); *Storey* v. *Exhaust Specialists and Parts Inc.*, 464 P. 2d 831 (Ore., 1970) (aluminium wheel); *Ford Motor Co.* v. *Zahn*, 265 F. 2d 729 (8th Cir., 1959) (jagged ashtray edge); *Blitzstein* v. *Ford Motor Co.*, 288 F. 2d 738 (5th Cir., 1961) (no escape holes for petrol vapour); *Bolm* v. *Triumph Corporation*, 305 N.E. 2d 769 (1973) (positioning of luggage rack on motor-cycle); *Baumgardner* v. *American Motors Corporation*, 522 P. 2d 829 (Wash., 1974) (front seat displacement).

[1] In *Suvada* v. *White Motor Co.*, 201 N.E. 2d 313 (Ill., 1965) (brakes); *Haley* v. *Merit Chevrolet Inc.*, 214 N.E. 2d 347 (Ill., 1966) (tyre); *B.K. Sweeney Co.* v. *McQuay-Norris Manufacturing Co.*, 489 P. 2d 356 (Colo., 1971) (valve for generator); *Cyr* v. *B. Offen & Co.*

with multipurpose components, such as industrial fasteners, or basic materials, such as nuts and bolts or copper or plastic piping.[2] The manufacturer of such components will frequently not know the specific use to which his product has been put and he can hardly be held accountable if it is used for an unsuitable purpose. The same is true of cases where a danger is caused only through the admixture of a product with another product, as when an alkaline base was added to sulphuric acid to produce a dangerously explosive drain cleaner.[3] In cases of this nature the component manufacturer may be required to issue appropriate warnings. Thereafter he can be accorded sufficient protection by holding that the product was not defective[4] or that the danger was caused through misuse.[5] An approach along these lines leaves room for flexibility in other areas where liability might be properly imposed. Plate glass, for example, is used typically in doors and windows and it is reasonable to require that it be sufficiently strong for this known or common purpose.[6]

Inc., 501 F. 2d 1145 (1st Cir., 1974) (part of printing press) it was so extended. *Cf.*, however, *Goldberg* v. *Kollsman Instrument Corporation*, 191 N.E. 2d 81 (1963) (altimeter). See also above, pp. 197–198, below, p. 359.
[2] See the Law Commission Working Paper No. 64, "Liability for Defective Products", paras. 68–73 citing *Harbutt's Plasticine, Ltd.* v. *Wayne Tank and Pump Co., Ltd.*, [1970] 1 Q.B. 447; [1970] 1 All E.R. 225, above, p. 135 as an example. See also *Restatement of Torts* 2d, s. 402A, Comment p. (pig iron made into a bicycle).
[3] See *Walker* v. *Stauffer Chemical Corporation*, 96 Cal. Rptr. 803 (1971). See also *E.I. du Pont de Nemours* v. *McCain*, 414 F. 2d 369 (5th Cir., 1969) (petrol based solvent in water repellent).
[4] See above, pp. 186–189.
[5] See below, pp. 294–295.
[6] See *Brizendine* v. *Visador Co.*, 437 F. 2d 822 (9th Cir., 1970).

12 The Manufacturers' Liability: Warnings and Directions for Use

Another common allegation in a product liability case is that a manufacturer has failed to give an adequate warning of dangers associated with a product and any necessary directions for safe use.[1] Similarly it may be alleged that he has made positive representations of safety, whether express or implied, and whether in the form of personal assurances, advertising, or in the general presentation and labelling of the product. In such cases it is the manufacturer's conduct when marketing the product which is normally in issue. Occasionally, however, the plaintiff may allege that there has been a breach of a duty to warn of subsequently discovered dangers.[2]

Warnings and directions when the product is marketed

The need for adequate warnings and directions

The general existence of a duty to warn that a product may have dangerous

---

[1] See, in general, Dillard and Hart, "Product Liability: directions for use and the duty to warn", 41 Virginia L.R. 145 (1955); Noel, "Negligence of Design or Directions for Use of a Product", 71 Yale L.J. 816 (1962); Noel, "Recent Trends in Manufacturers' Negligence as to Design, Instructions or Warnings", 19 Sw. L.J. 43 (1965); Noel, "Products Defective Because of Inadequate Directions or Warnings", 23 Sw. L.J. 256 (1969); Keeton, "Products Liability: inadequacy of information", 48 Texas L.R. 398 (1970); Noel and Phillips, *Products Liability* (1974) ch. 8; 2 Harper and James, *Torts*, pp. 646–650; 1 Frumer and Friedman, *Products Liability*, s. 8; Annotation, 76 A.L.R. 2d 9; 53 A.L.R. 3d 239. See also below, pp. 302–303 where the duty to disclose known dangers is noted as being a duty common to all suppliers.

[2] As in *Rivtow Marine, Ltd.* v. *Washington Iron Works, Ltd.* (1974), 40 D.L.R. 3d 530 (Sup. Ct. of Canada), below, p. 248.

characteristics has long been recognised in English law. Indeed it was an established exception to the early rule of non-liability associated with *Winterbottom* v. *Wright*.[3] Nowadays liability does not depend on actual knowledge of the danger and the manufacturer may be held liable in negligence when he ought to have discovered its existence and issued an appropriate warning thereafter. The lack of a warning or directions for use may also render an otherwise satisfactory product defective for the purposes of a strict tort theory of liability. Some American cases have held that strict product liability cannot be based on the absence of a warning where the danger was unknown and undiscoverable.[4] However, other cases have insisted that considerations of reasonable foresight and fault are irrelevant and that the sole question is whether the defendant marketed his product with sufficient instructions and warnings to make it safe.[5] Notwithstanding the logical difficulty in requiring a manufacturer to warn of unknown and unknowable dangers it seems likely that this test of objective safety will prevail.

Whether the marketing of a particular product is required to be accompanied by warnings or directions for use will depend on a variety of considerations. Generally, however, the question will arise only where the danger associated with the product is concealed and a warning is practicable. In a typical case the product will be explosive, highly inflammable, toxic, harmful to the skin, or likely to perform in an unpredictable way,[6] and it will be contended that this characteristic should have been indicated on the container, packaging or elsewhere. Dangers which are either obvious or a matter of common knowledge would not normally need to be emphasised further.[7] Similarly, with some products, warnings may be quite impracticable or inadequate and the manufacturer will have to abandon the project or modify the design. This is especially

---

[3] (1842), 10 M. & W. 109, above, p. 7. *Clarke* v. *Army and Navy Cooperative Society*, [1903] 1 K.B. 155, below, p. 302 is a leading case.

[4] See, e.g., *Oakes* v. *Geigy Agricultural Chemicals*, 77 Cal. Rptr. 709 (Cal. App., 1969); *Christofferson* v. *Kaiser Foundations Hospitals*, 92 Cal. Rptr. 825 (Cal. App., 1971). See also *Restatement of Torts*, 2d, s. 402A, comment j.

[5] *Berkebile* v. *Brantly Helicopter Corporation*, 337 A. 2d 893 (Pa., 1975) (warning and instructions as to autorotation of helicopter blades in the event of engine failure). See also *Jackson* v. *Coast Paint and Lacquer Co.*, 499 F. 2d 809 (9th Cir., 1974).

[6] See, respectively, *Vacwell Engineering Co., Ltd.* v. *B.D.H. Chemicals, Ltd.*, [1971] 1 Q.B. 88; [1969] 3 All E.R. 1681 (explosive); *Norton Australia Pty., Ltd.* v. *Streets Ice Cream Pty., Ltd.* (1968), 120 C.L.R. 635 (High Ct. Australia) (inflammable); *Maize* v. *Atlantic Refining Co.*, 41 A. 2d 850 (Pa., 1945) (toxic); *Fisher* v. *Harrods, Ltd.*, [1966] Lloyd's Rep. 500 (harmful to skin); *Ruegger* v. *Shell Oil Co. of Canada, Ltd.* (1963), 41 D.L.R. 2d 183 (Ont. High Ct.) (herbicide which drifted as an invisible spray).

[7] See, e.g., *Yachetti* v. *John Duff & Sons, Ltd.*, [1943] 1 D.L.R. 194 (Ont. High Ct.) (trichinosis from uncooked pork); *Jamieson* v. *Woodward and Lothrop*, 247 F. 2d 23 (D.C., 1957) (injury from rubber when stretched and released). See also Prosser, *Torts*, p. 659; 2 Harper and James, *Torts*, p. 1642 and, in general, below, pp. 239–240.

true of cases in which the absence of a safety device is in issue.[8] Since the implications of such a decision are likely to be far reaching, there is probably a greater reluctance to impose liability than in a case in which the problem can be met by a fuller warning, as by modifying an accompanying label.[9] The discussion which follows assumes that the product is being used in the normal and intended way by a normal user. Problems of abnormal use and unduly sensitive or otherwise abnormal users are discussed later.[10]

Explosive and inflammable substances

A number of cases have discussed the duty to warn in the context of explosive and inflammable substances. In *Anglo-Celtic Shipping Co., Ltd.* v. *Elliott and Jeffery*,[11] the second defendants manufactured a cleaning fluid known as the "pluperfect liquid" which gave off hydrogen when it came into contact with cast iron. The plaintiff shipowners instructed the first defendants, a firm of repairers, to use the liquid when cleaning a condenser on their ship. Neither was aware of the liquid's peculiar properties. An explosion occurred when a workman approached the condenser carrying a naked flame and the ship was damaged. Roche, J. held the manufacturers of the liquid liable saying that "not only was the article dangerous in itself, but the instructions failed to give any adequate warning."[12] A similar conclusion was reached in *Vacwell Engineering Co., Ltd.* v. *B.D.H. Chemicals, Ltd.*[13] where liability in negligence was founded on the breach of a duty adequately to warn of the explosive properties of boron tribromide on contact with water.

Norton Australia Pty., Ltd. v. *Streets Ice Cream Pty., Ltd.*[14] is a leading Australian case in which the duty to warn was held to have been discharged where a product was highly inflammable. The defendants manufactured an adhesive substance, BM 226, which contained a highly inflammable petrol-based solvent. The substance was distributed in five-gallon drums

---

[8] See above, pp. 220–227.
[9] See above, pp. 184–186.
[10] See below, pp. 294–295 and pp. 324–326, respectively.
[11] (1926), 42 T.L.R. 297.
[12] *Ibid.*, at p. 299. *Quaere*: to what extent the *Anglo-Celtic Shipping* case was consistent with the exceptions to the rule of non-liability as conceived in 1926? See Bohlen, "Liability of Manufacturers to Persons Other than their Immediate Vendees" (1929), 45 L.Q.R. 343, 350 *et seq.* For another important case involving explosive substances, see *Kubach* v. *Hollands*, [1937] 3 All E.R. 907, below, p. 245. See also *Hodge & Sons* v. *Anglo-American Oil Co.* (1922), 12 LL. L.Rep. 183.
[13] [1971] 1 Q.B. 88; [1969] 3 All E.R. 1681, above, p. 179.
[14] (1968), 120 C.L.R. 635.

carrying labels which bore the warning "CAUTION: HIGHLY INFLAMMABLE", and the direction, "For further information ask for data sheet". This sheet, in turn, stated that the adhesive was "highly inflammable" and had a flash point below 73°F.

A contractor was employed by the plaintiff company to apply insulating materials to the walls and ceiling of its premises. When dealing with the ceiling the procedure was to fix aluminium foil coated lightly with the adhesive to the original timber and then to attach slabs of cork to the aluminium with the aid of heated bitumen. The two operations were carried out at the same time on a platform some fourteen feet from the floor. The adhesive had been poured into a shallow tray from which it was applied to the aluminium with rollers, and a burner was used to heat the bitumen some twenty feet away. The room was poorly ventilated. As a sheet of aluminium was being held up to the ceiling, it burst into flames and the plaintiff's property was damaged in the resultant fire. There was no doubt, as the first instance judge found, that the fire had been started by vapour from the solvent coming into contact with the flame of the burner. The substantial question was whether the label together with the data sheet (which had been supplied to the contractors) constituted an adequate warning. Reversing the decision of the courts below, the High Court of Australia held that the warning, taken in conjunction with the smell of petrol given off by the product, could not be said to have been inadequate. It was not necessary for the defendants to seek to define the area of danger since this would depend on the surrounding circumstances. Furthermore, in the judgment of Barwick, C.J., even if the warning had been deficient, the intervening negligence of the contractors was the sole effective cause of the damage. The claim accordingly failed.

Lambert v. *Lastoplex Chemicals Co., Ltd.*[15] is a decision of the Supreme Court of Canada which reached an opposite conclusion on broadly similar facts. The defendants manufactured a fast-drying floor sealer, Supremo W20, which was again highly inflammable and volatile. The plaintiff householder was applying the sealer to a basement room, which connected with the furnace and utility room, when a fire was set off by a pilot light and there was an explosion. The one-gallon can holding the product bore three labels the most informative of which read "CAUTION, INFLAMMABLE— Do not use near open flame or while smoking. Ventilate room while using". The Supreme Court held the labels to be inadequate as failing to warn (as did those of a competitor) of the product's volatile quality and the danger from sparks and pilot lights in a confined space. In the words of Laskin, J., delivering the judgment of the court, the manufacturer,[16]

---

[15] (1971), 25 D.L.R. (3d) 121.
[16] *Ibid.*, at p. 125.

"has a duty to specify the attendant dangers, which it must be taken to appreciate in a detail not known to the ordinary consumer or user. A general warning, as for example, that the product is inflammable, will not suffice where the likelihood of fire may be increased according to the surroundings in which it may reasonably be expected that the product will be used. The required explicitness of the warning will, of course, vary with the danger likely to be encountered in the ordinary use of the product."[17]

Poisonous, toxic, pathogenic and other harm-producing agencies

In other cases, liability has been imposed for the marketing of poisonous, toxic, pathogenic or some similar harm-producing agency without adequate warning or directions for use. The damage may be to persons, animals, or crops and the range of cases parallels the earlier discussion of negligence in design and choice of ingredients.[18]

Where poisons and drugs are concerned, most jurisdictions will have enacted minimum labelling requirements. In English law, for example, the Pharmacy and Poisons Act 1933, as supplemented by the Poisons Rules 1972, contains detailed provisions as to the labelling requirements which must be met in the case of listed poisons.[19] Such regulatory provisions are clearly of great importance, but there may also be liability at common law where harm results from the ingestion, inhaling or absorption of substances such as poisons and drugs. Thus in *Kershaw* v. *Sterling Drug Inc.*,[20] a successful action was brought against the defendant manufacturers of the drug chloroquine phosphate after they had failed to give adequate warning of its harmful side-effects on sight when used over

---

[17] Leading American cases include *Martin* v. *Bengue Inc.*, 136 A. 2d 626 (N.J., 1957) (chest ointment igniting as plaintiff was smoking in bed); *Hentschel* v. *Baby Bathinette Corporation*, 215 F. 2d 102 (2nd Cir., 1954) (bath with magnesium alloy supports). See also *Blasing* v. *Hardenberg Co.*, 226 N.W. 2d 110 (Minn., 1975); *Sterner* v. *U.S. Plywood-Champion Paper Inc.*, 519 F. 2d 1352 (8th Cir., 1975); *Simonetti* v. *Rinshed-Mason Co.*, 200 N.W. 2d 354 (Mich. App., 1972); *Murray* v. *Wilson Oak Flooring Co.*, 475 F. 2d 129 (7th Cir., 1973); *Gardner* v. *Q.H.S. Inc.*, 448 F. 2d 238 (4th Cir., 1971); *Raymond* v. *Riegel Textile Corporation*, 484 F. 2d 1025 (1st Cir., 1973); *Stief* v. *J.A. Sexauer Manufacturing Co.*, 380 F. 2d 453 (2nd Cir., 1967).

[18] See above ch. 11 at pp. 213–218.

[19] S.I. 1972 No. 1939. Requirements as to labelling and containers are contained in rules 20–26. See also the Misuse of Drugs Regulations 1973, S.I. 1973 No. 797, reg. 18; Therapeutic Substances (Manufacture and Importation) General Regulations 1963, S.I. 1963 No. 1450, Part III; Medicines Act 1968, s. 85 and the Medicines (Labelling of Medicated Animal Feeding Stuffs) Regulations 1973, S.I. 1973 No. 1530; Medicines Act 1968, ss. 87, 88 and the Medicines (Child Safety) Regulations, S.I. 1975 No. 2000, below, p. 271; Labelling of Food Regulations 1970, S.I. 1970 No. 400, as amended by S.I. 1972 No. 1510, and S.I. 1974 Nos. 1119, 1121.

[20] 415 F. 2d 1009 (5th Cir. 1969).

a long period. The plaintiff had suffered permanent damage to the retina of each eye after taking the drug as treatment for rheumatoid arthritis. Other modern American cases have involved failure to warn of the dangers of aplastic anaemia on using the drug chloromycetin,[1] and a similar failure to warn of the dangers of inhaling carbon tetrachloride[2] and parathion dust.[3]

Inadequate precautions may similarly be taken where there is a risk of personal injury through a more immediate physical contact with a product. In *Fisher* v. *Harrods, Ltd.*,[4] the defendants sold a jewellery cleaning fluid, Couronne, which contained isopropyl alcohol and ammonium oleate and which was purchased by a third party for the use of the plaintiff. The fluid was supplied in a plastic bottle with a plastic bung and a screw top. As the plaintiff was squeezing the bottle the bung shot out and some fluid splashed into and damaged her eye. In resultant proceedings, McNair, J. held the defendants liable for negligence in marketing the product without appropriate instructions and a warning as to the danger if the liquid came into contact with the eyes. *Devilez* v. *Boots Pure Drug Co., Ltd.*[5] is a similar case. Here recovery was based on a failure to provide an adequate stopper and to warn of the dangers of a corn solvent some of which had splashed on to the plaintiff's lower abdomen, injuring his genitals.

The need for adequate warnings and directions for use has also been discussed in cases in which damage to crops or animals has resulted from the application of fertilisers, herbicides and pesticides. In *Ruegger* v. *Shell Oil Co. of Canada, Ltd.*[6] the defendants had marketed a chemical weed-killer, Amine 80 2-4-D-, which was applied by a crop sprayer to the plaintiff's corn. The spray drifted on a windless day and as an invisible mist to destroy an adjoining field of tomatoes. The only warning which had been given cautioned that the spray should not be allowed to contact vegetables, shrubs or other desirable plants. There was no indication that it might travel unseen for substantial distances. Recovery was granted in the Ontario High Court on the ground that this characteristic should have been appreciated and an appropriate warning issued. In other Canadian cases liability in negligence was similarly incurred where a weedkiller destroyed a nurseryman's pansy plants,[7] and where an insecticide

---

[1] *Stevens* v. *Parke, Davis & Co.*, 107 Cal. Rptr. 45 (Cal. Sup. Ct., 1973). See also *Cunningham* v. *Charles Pfizer*, 532 P. 2d 1377 (Okla., 1975).

[2] *Maize* v. *Atlantic Refining Co.*, 41 A. 2d 850 (Pa., 1945).

[3] *Griffin* v. *Planters Chemical Corporation*, 302 F. Supp. 937 (1969). See, in general, 3 Frumer and Friedman, *Products Liability*, s. 33.01[3].

[4] [1966] 1 Lloyds Rep. 500.

[5] (1962), 106 Sol. Jo. 552.

[6] (1963), 41 D.L.R. (2d) 183.

[7] *Fillmore's Valley Nurseries, Ltd.* v. *North American Cyanamid, Ltd.* (1958), 14 D.L.R. (2d) 297, an important case on the quantum of damage in tort and in contract: see above, p. 56.

caused phosphate poisoning in a farmer's bulls.[8] In both instances the negligence took the form of inadequate warnings coupled with representations that the product might be used safely.

A number of similar American cases were mentioned in the previous chapter.[9] Here reference may be made to *McClanahan* v. *California Spray Chemical Corporation*,[10] a well-known decision of the Virginia Supreme Court of Appeals. In this case, the defendants marketed a spray with a phenyl mercury acetate base which was designed to eliminate fungal growth on apple trees. When applied to the plaintiff's trees it led, rather, to the loss of two years' crops. The immediate cause of the damage was that the spray had been applied when the growth was too far advanced. Although this would not have happened if the instructions for use on the container label had been followed, the Virginia appellate court nonetheless held that the plaintiff was entitled to recover. The basis of the decision was, in essence, that directions for use did not necessarily discharge the manufacturer's duty when they failed to warn of the dangers of misuse.[11]

Other products carrying concealed dangers or behaving unpredictably

Although the cases noted above are representative of the type of dangers in respect of which warnings or directions for use will be required, similar precautions may be needed whenever a product carries a concealed danger or is likely to behave in an unpredictable way. *Jamieson* v. *Woodward and Lothrop*[12] is a frequently cited American case. The defendant manufactured a "Lithe Line" rubber exerciser which slipped off the plaintiff's feet as she was doing a recommended abdominal exercise, hitting her across the face and detaching her retina. A bare majority of the Court of Appeals for the District of British Columbia upheld a directed verdict for the manufacturer emphasising that any foreseeable injury was likely to be minor (a cut lip, black eye, or bloody nose), and that it was a matter of common knowledge that stretched rubber contracts. Consequently there was no duty to warn the user of this characteristic.

McLaughlin v. *Mine Safety Appliances Co.*[13] is a contrasting case. The

---

[8] *Pack* v. *County of Warner* (1964), 44 D.L.R. (2d) 215.
[9] See above, p. 218.
[10] 75 S.E. 2d 712 (Va., 1953). The case prompted the frequently cited article of Dillard and Hart, "Products Liability: directions for use and the duty to warn", 41 Virginia L.R. 145 (1955).
[11] See further below, pp. 294–296. Other American decisions of importance in this area include *La Plant* v. *E.I. du Pont de Nemours & Co.*, 346 S.W. 2d 231 (Mo., 1961); *E.I. du Pont de Nemours & Co.* v. *Baridon*, 73 F. 2d 26 (8th Cir., 1934); *Gonzalez* v. *Virginia-Carolina Chemical Co.*, 239 F. Supp. 567 (D.C.S.C., 1965).
[12] 247 F. 2d 23 (D.C., 1957).
[13] 181 N.E. 2d 430 (1962).

defendant marketed magnesium heat blocks which were intended to supply emergency heat to accident victims. The blocks were covered by a red woollen insulating material and when activated they reached a surface temperature of 204° Fahrenheit within two minutes. They were sold in cardboard containers with the words "always ready for use" in capital letters on the face. On the reverse side in smaller lettering were instructions for use which included: "Wrap in insulating medium, such as pouch, towel, blanket or folded cloth". The plaintiff was a child of six who had been carried unconscious from a lake. She suffered third degree burns when the blocks were applied directly to her body by a nurse who had received them from a fireman called to the scene of the accident. Dealing with the present issue, the New York Court of Appeals held that the jury was justified in finding that the instructions on the container were inadequate as a warning. In the result, however, a new trial was ordered, since it appeared that the fireman appreciated the need for insulation and that his supervening negligence might have been the sole effective cause of the injury suffered.

In other cases grounds for imposing liability have been held to exist where a plastic stopper shot out of a bottle of "Sparkling Rhinegold" wine and hit the plaintiff in the eye;[14] an electric range was so designed that it toppled on to the infant plaintiff, a child of four, who was standing on the open oven door to look into a pot of boiling water;[15] and where the application of a hair dye caused severe dermatitis.[16] Such cases frequently raise the question of whether the manufacturer or distributor must warn or guard against the product being put to abnormal and unintended uses or being in contact with abnormally sensitive users.[17]

Similar problems arise where the potential for harm is activated only by the product being brought into contact with another substance or product. That the manufacturer may be under a duty to warn of the dangers of such a combination is clear. Whether a warning is necessary in any given case will depend on matters such as the likelihood of the combination and the gravity of the risk. In *Anglo-Celtic Shipping Co., Ltd.* v. *Elliott and Jeffery*,[18] for example, contact between the "pluperfect" cleaning liquid and cast iron was clearly foreseeable and a warning of the dangers of an explosion ought to have been given. American cases involving chemicals and other substances might be cited on either side of the

---

[14] *O'Dwyer* v. *Leo Buring Pty., Ltd.*, [1966] W.A.R. 67 (W.A. Sup. Ct.).

[15] *Ritter* v. *Narragansett Electric Co.*, 283 A. 2d 255 (R.I., 1971).

[16] *Watson* v. *Buckley, Osborne, Garrett & Co., Ltd.*, [1940] 1 All E.R. 174; *Parker* v. *Oxolo, Ltd.*, [1937] 3 All E.R. 524. For an American case, see *D'Arienzo* v. *Clairol Inc.*, 310 A. 2d 106 (N.J., 1973).

[17] See further below, at pp. 294–296 and pp. 324–326, respectively.

[18] (1926), 42 T.L.R. 297, above, p. 231.

line. *Croteau* v. *Borden Co.*[19] is a case in which the manufacturer of a chemical, sodium azide, was held to be entitled to a directed verdict in an action brought by the plaintiff laboratory technician. The latter had lost a hand following an explosion which occurred when he was producing the chemical, vinylene diisocyanate, from sodium azide and other substances. Sodium azide was not itself explosive, but the plaintiff maintained that the defendants were negligent in failing to distribute it with a warning as to the dangers of combining it with other chemicals. Dismissing the contention the District Court judge said:[20]

> "No jury could be permitted to find that a manufacturer who sells a harmless chemical to a research laboratory engaged in secret research on rocket fuels owed any duty to warn of the possibility that the product supplied could be used to manufacture explosives."[1]

Some factors affecting the need for and adequacy of warnings

The considerations which will determine the need for, and the adequacy of, a warning in any given case cannot be detailed systematically since they will differ from product to product. Generally, it may be said that the greater the likelihood of damage (or of any damage being serious) and the more practicable the measures to guard against it, the more comprehensive is the warning which will be required. A sufficiently comprehensive warning will remove or reduce the element of danger associated with the product or sever the causative link between the marketing of the product and the damage or injury suffered. Beyond this the cases suggest that the following somewhat more specific factors are numbered amongst those which are relevant: (i) the distinction between warnings and directions or instructions for use; (ii) the obviousness of the danger; (iii) the wording, intensity and location of the warning; (iv) representations of safety and promotional activities; and (v) the sufficiency of warnings to responsible intermediaries.

Warnings and directions for use distinguished

As Dillard and Hart pointed out when discussing *McClanahan* v. *California*

---

[19] 277 F. Supp. 945 (1968), affd. 395 F. 2d 771 (3rd Cir., 1968).
[20] *Ibid.*, at p. 947.
[1] A similar conclusion was reached in *Stief* v. *J.A. Sexauer Manufacturing Co.*, 380 F. 2d 453 (2nd Cir., 1967) (drain solvent), and *Walker* v. *Stauffer Chemical Corporation*, 96 Cal. Rptr. 803 (Cal. App., 1971) (drain solvent). Contrast *E.I. du Pont de Nemours and Co.* v. *McCain*, 414 F. 2d 369 (5th Cir., 1969) (water repellent compound); *Butler* v. *L. Sonneborn Inc.*, 296 F. 2d 623 (2nd Cir., 1961) (explosion following contact of liquid hardener with steel).

Spray Chemical Corporation,[2] the Virginia apple grower's case, there is an important distinction between warnings and directions for use. The function of a warning is to acquaint the user or a responsible third party with dangers associated with a product. Directions or instructions for use indicate how the most beneficial results are to be obtained. Where the dangers of failing to follow directions are neither indicated nor obvious such directions, standing alone, may be insufficient to discharge the manufacturer's duty. It would not be open to him to assume that the directions will be followed.

The point is well illustrated by Dillard and Hart's own example of the new brand of toothpaste which, if used more than twice daily, is likely to discolour the teeth permanently. As they say of such a product:[3]

> "Not only would directions such as, 'For Best Results Use Twice Daily,' be clearly inadequate; even such forthright statements as, 'Do Not Use More Than Twice Daily,' would be inadequate unless accompanied by a warning statement cautioning the user that permanent damage was likely to result from more frequent applications. A bold cautionary statement setting forth the exact nature of the dangers involved would be necessary fully to protect the manufacturer. Such factors as the likelihood that the average toothpaste user would not otherwise take more than a cursory glance at the label of an ordinary toothpaste container must be taken into account."

Conversely, a full warning as to the dangers associated with a product may be inadequate unless accompanied by directions as to how it may be used safely. In the example of the toothpaste, the user would need to know the safe rate of application as well as the danger of more frequent use. By the same token, a helicopter pilot would need instructions as to the course to be followed in the event of engine failure.[4]

The distinction between warnings and directions for use and the possible insufficiency of the latter has been recognised in a substantial number of cases. Thus in the *McClanahan* case[5] itself, for example, the plaintiff succeeded in spite of the fact that defoliation would not have occurred if the fungicide had been applied in accordance with the instructions on the container label. The same view has been taken in other cases, as when magnesium heat blocks carried the instruction "Wrap in insulating material" and a child was burned when it was not followed;[6] an industrial vacuum cleaner was marked "Only use on 115 volts AC or DC" and

---

[2] 75 S.E. 2d 712 (1953), above, p. 235, "Product Liability: directions for use and the duty to warn", 41 Virginia L.R. 145 (1955).

[3] See 41 Virginia L.R. 145, 151.

[4] See *Berkebile* v. *Brantly Helicopter Corporation*, 337 A. 2d 893 (Pa., 1975). See also *Martin* v. *T.W. Hand Fireworks Co.* (1963), 37 D.L.R. (2d), 455 (Ont. High Ct.) (fireworks).

[5] 75 S.E. 2d 712 (1953).

[6] *McLaughlin* v. *Mine Safety Appliances Co.*, 181 N.E. 2d 430 (N.Y., 1962), above, pp. 235–236.

injury was sustained on plugging into a 220 DC outlet;[7] and when charcoal briquettes carried the instructions "Cook only in properly ventilated areas" and a child was asphyxiated when briquettes were burnt in an enclosed area.[8]

The obviousness of the danger

A substantial number of English, Commonwealth and American decisions hold that where the dangers associated with a product are known or obvious, recovery will be precluded as a matter of law.[9] The correctness of this approach may be doubted but it is clear that a warning is less likely to be required where the danger is patent or a matter of common knowledge than where it is hidden. As Prosser has said, there is no duty "to warn the purchaser that a knife or an axe will cut, a match will take fire, dynamite will explode, or a hammer may mash a finger".[10] In such cases all relevant duties will be discharged by supplying a sound product into responsible hands. Similarly it has been held that there is no duty to warn a customer of the dangers of eating raw pork sausages[11] or a gymnast of the dangers of injury to the spinal cord when landing on his head on a trampoline.[12]

There are inevitably borderline cases where it might be argued more convincingly that a warning was required. *Jamieson* v. *Woodward and Lothrop*,[13] the case of the contracting rubber exerciser, is cited frequently in this context. Other typical American cases have involved products such

---

[7] *Post* v. *American Cleaning Equipment Corporation*, 437 S.W. 2d 516 (Ky., 1968).
[8] *Hill* v. *Husky Briquetting Inc.*, 220 N.W. 137 (Mich., 1974). See also *Anglo-Celtic Shipping Co., Ltd.* v. *Elliott and Jeffery* (1926), 42 T.L.R. 297, 299 where Roche, J. said of the "pluperfect liquid" that "not only was the article dangerous in itself, but the instructions failed to give any adequate warning". For further American examples, see *Lovejoy* v. *Minneapolis-Moline Power Implement Co.*, 79 N.W. 2d 688 (Minn., 1956) (no warning as to danger of using tractor in excess of recommended speed); *Hartman* v. *National Heater Co.*, 60 N.W. 2d 804 (Minn., 1953) (no warning as to dangers of removing part of a gas heater). Directed verdicts may, however, be appropriate: see, e.g., *Schmeiser* v. *Trus Joint Corporation*, 540 P. 2d 998 (Ore., 1975); *Jenkins* v. *Helgren*, 217 S.E. 2d 120 (N.C., 1975). See also 1 *Frumer and Friedman*, s. 8.05 [1].
[9] See, e.g., *Farr* v. *Butters Brothers and Co.*, [1932] 2 K.B. 606; *Cathcart* v. *Hull*, [1963] N.Z.L.R. 333; *Messina* v. *Clarke Equipment Co.*, 263 F. 2d 291 (2nd Cir., 1959), and below, pp. 292–293.
[10] *Law of Torts*, 4th edn., p. 649.
[11] *Yachetti* v. *John Duff & Sons, Ltd.*, [1943] 1 D.L.R. 194 (Ont. High Ct.). American cases are generally to the same effect: see, e.g., *Adams* v. *Scheib*, 184 A. 2d 700 (Penn., 1962), and cases cited in Prosser, *op cit.*, p. 648, note 72.
[12] *Garrett* v. *Nissen Corporation*, 498 P. 2d 1359 (N.M., 1972). Cf. *Nissen Trampoline Co.* v. *Terre Haute First National Bank*, 332 N.E. 2d 820 (Ind., 1975).
[13] 247 F. 2d 23 (D.C., 1957), above, p. 235.

as power mowers,[14] cleansing fluids which splash into and damage the eye,[15] and ready-mixed concrete containing lime.[16] *Hodge & Sons* v. *Anglo-American Oil Co.*[17] is also in point. Here an oxy-acetylene burner had set off an explosion in a petrol barge when it was standing at a repairer's yard. The Court of Appeal held that the owner of the barge was not required to warn the repairers of the explosive qualities of any petrol which might have remained in the hold of the barge after a reasonably careful cleaning. Professional repairers might reasonably be taken to appreciate the danger. Atkin, L.J. dissented in part. Being satisfied that negligence in cleansing had been established and that this had increased the level of danger, he concluded that even if knowledge of the lesser danger could fairly be imputed to the plaintiff, knowledge of the greater danger could not.

The wording, intensity and location of the warning

The adequacy of any given warning may also depend on its wording, intensity and location. The wording may be inapt for a variety of reasons. For example, it may be positively misleading, as where a product is mislabelled or a claim to a specific attribute is not met. *British Chartered Co. of South Africa* v. *Lennon, Ltd.*[18] is in point. The respondents, a reputable firm of druggists, had sent out an arsenite cattle dip in drums which were labelled as containing $8\frac{1}{2}$ lb of arsenite of soda to be dissolved in 400 gallons of water. The labels were, however, intended for smaller tins and the drums in fact contained 56 lb of arsenite. The appellants made up the dip in the proportions as indicated, believing that the explanation for the greater bulk was that the arsenite had been mixed with another product. The dip was consequently far too strong and some 180 cattle were killed. In resultant proceedings, the Privy Council advised that the trial court judge's decision in favour of the appellants should be restored.

---

[14] See above, pp. 222–223.

[15] Contrast *Sawyer* v. *Pine Oil Sales Co.*, 155 F. 2d 855 (5th Cir., 1946) with *Hardy* v. *Proctor and Gamble Manufacturing Co.*, 209 F. 2d 124 (5th Cir., 1954) (sodium lauryl sulphate) and *Haberley* v. *Reardon*, 319 S.W. 2d 859 (Mo., 1958) (paint containing lime). See also *Fisher* v. *Harrods, Ltd.*, [1966] 1 Lloyds Rep. 500; *Devilez* v. *Boots Pure Drug Co., Ltd.* (1962), 106 Sol. Jo. 552, above, p. 234.

[16] Contrast *Katz* v. *Arundel Brooks Concrete Corporation*, 151 A. 2d 731 (Md., 1959) with *Sams* v. *Englewood Ready-Mix Corporation*, 259 N.E. 2d 507 (Ohio App., 1970). See also 1 *Frumer and Friedman*, s. 8.04, at pp. 184–185.

[17] (1922), 12 LL. L.Rep. 183.

[18] (1915), 31 T.L.R. 585, P.C.

Lord Sumner is reported as saying of the appellant's reaction to the discrepancy between the label and the weight that

> "they could not reasonably be expected either to hit on the true explanation of it, or to hold their hands for fear-that a description proceeding from so respectable a firm might yet be grossly erroneous. If no such idea occurred to them, they could not be stamped as negligent in consequence."[19]

A warning which is not positively misleading may nonetheless fail to point to the true nature or extent of the danger with sufficient clarity. In pointing to one danger it may, for example, suggest that other dangers do not exist. Thus a warning of "harmful vapours" would not indicate the danger of a substantial explosion,[20] and a general caution "not to allow a spray or spray mist to contact flowers, vegetables or other desirable plants" would not indicate that a weedkiller might drift as an invisible mist over considerable distances.[1] Further examples are to be found in American cases, as when it was held that the words "keep in a cool place" might be understood as indicating that a bottle of bleach might deteriorate rather than explode;[2] a reference to a drain solvent's "effervescent" qualities might not suggest a blinding explosion;[3] and a warning that inhaling dust might be harmful would not indicate a risk of asbestosis or lung cancer.[4] In other cases, a warning has been regarded as inadequate because it was couched in technical terms or even in a language which might not be understood by the person to whom it was addressed. Thus in *Haberly* v.

---

[19] *Ibid.*, at p. 586. See also *Kubach* v. *Hollands*, [1937] 3 All E.R. 907, D.C., below, pp. 245–246; *Thomas* v. *Winchester*, 6 N.Y. 397, 57 Am. Dec. 455 (1852), above, p. 12; *Blacker* v. *Lake and Elliott* (1912), 106 L.T. 533, 541 (Lush, J.); *La Plant* v. *E.I. du Pont de Nemours & Co.*, 346 S.W. 2d 231 (Mo. App., 1961); 1 Frumer and Friedman, *Products Liability*, s. 8.05[3][4].

[20] *Vacwell Engineering Co., Ltd.* v. *B.D.H. Chemicals, Ltd.*, [1971] 1 Q.B. 88, 109–110, above, p. 179.

[1] *Ruegger* v. *Shell Oil Co. of Canada, Ltd.* (1963), 41 D.L.R. (2d) 183 (Ont. High Ct.), above, p. 234. See also *Boyl* v. *California Chemical Co.*, 221 F. Supp. 669 (1963) (sodium arsenite weedkiller: no warning as to delayed dangers through contact with residue five days after application).

[2] *Saporito* v. *Purex Corporation*, 255 P. 2d 7 (Cal., 1953). See also *Crane* v. *Sears Roebuck & Co.*, 32 Cal. Rptr. 754 (Cal., 1963) (warning as to danger of inhaling fumes rather than as to combustibility); *Tucson Industries* v. *Schwartz*, 501 P. 2d 936 (Ariz., 1973) (warning as to flammability and against contact with skin but not that fumes might cause blindness); *Blasing* v. *Hardenberg Co.*, 226 N.W. 2d 110 (Minn., 1975).

[3] *Bean* v. *Ross Manufacturing Co.*, 344 S.W. 2d 18 (Mo., 1961).

[4] *Borel* v. *Fiberboard Paper Products, Ltd.*, 493 F. 2d 1076 (5th Cir., 1974). See also *Krug* v. *Sterling Drug Inc.*, 416 S.W. 2d 143 (Mo., 1967) (risk of loss of sight through taking the drug Aralen (chloroquine phosphate): warning of "visual disturbances"); *Hentschel* v. *Baby Bathinette Corporation*, 215 F. 2d 102 (2nd Cir., 1954) (Frank, J. dissenting); *Rumsey* v. *Freeway Manor Minimax*, 423 S.W. 2d 387 (Texas Civ. App., 1968) (no warning that no known antidote to poison); *Kritser* v. *Beech Aircraft Corporation*, 479 F. 2d 1089 (5th Cir., 1974) (warning as to danger of fuel displacement under "low fuel condition" not sufficiently precise).

Reardon Co.,[5] where a child had run into his father's paintbrush, a caution that the paint contained calcium oxide was insufficient since the user could not be taken to appreciate that calcium oxide is lime or that lime is likely to cause blindness.

The prominence and intensity of the warning will also be important in determining its adequacy especially if it falls below the general standards of the industry.[6] Bold red lettering headed "WARNING" is more apt to put the user on guard than is smaller grey lettering enjoining "Caution".[7] Additional symbols may help to drive the message home. The manufacturer who has given such a warning should not be prejudiced because others have devalued its currency by using a similar warning to describe lesser dangers in the past. As Barwick, C.J. observed in the important Australian case of *Norton Australia Pty., Ltd.* v. *Streets Ice Cream Pty., Ltd.*,[8] to say that the warning "HIGHLY INFLAMMABLE" was not apt to inform a contractor of the dangers of introducing a naked flame into the vicinity of the product is "to deny the significance of simple but dramatic words of the English language".

Importance may also be attached to the location of the warning. A warning printed or embossed directly onto the product itself (as with a power-tool or similar electrical equipment) or onto its immediate container (such as a bottle or aerosol can) is generally more likely to alert than is a warning on external packaging or accompanying leaflets[9] which are likely to be discarded. The point was important in *McLaughlin* v. *Mine Safety Appliances Co.*,[10] where the warning, such as it was, was on the cardboard container, rather than on the magnesium heat blocks themselves, and where it was envisaged that the blocks would be recharged for subsequent use. In some circumstances a warning on the packaging may be equally necessary. Thus in *Alcock* v. *Fisher and Ludlow*,[11] manufacturers of washing machines were held liable for their failure to warn carriers that the machines

---

[5] 319 S.W. 2d 859 (Mo., 1958). See also *Hubbard-Hall Chemical Co.* v. *Silverman*, 340 F. 2d 402 (1st Cir., 1965) (parathion dust affecting Puerto Rican farm employees: sufficiency of warning in English—without further symbols such as skull and crossbones—for jury to determine); *West* v. *Broderick and Bascom Rope Co.*, 197 N.W. 2d 202 (Iowa, 1972) (rope's tensile strength rather than maximum tonnage capacity).

[6] For the effect of compliance or non-compliance with the standards of the industry, see below, pp. 264–265.

[7] According to Ferguson, J. in *Ruegger* v. *Shell Oil Co. of Canada, Ltd.* (1963), 41 D.L.R. 2d 183, 193, "'caution' is, I think, a much milder word than 'warning'".

[8] (1968), 120 C.L.R. 635, 647 (High Ct. of Australia), above, p. 231. *Cf. Lambert* v. *Lastoplex Chemicals Co., Ltd.* (1972), 25 D.L.R. (3d) 121 (Sup. Ct. of Canada), above, p. 232.

[9] *Cf. O'Fallon* v. *Inecto Rapid (Canada), Ltd.*, [1939] 1 D.L.R. 805. Contrast *Holmes* v. *Ashford*, [1950] 2 All E.R. 76, discussed further below, p. 245.

[10] 181 N.E. 2d 430 (N.Y., 1962), above, pp. 235–236.

[11] (1951), C.A. 327.

could not be moved safely by the straps attached to them.[12]

A warning may sometimes be regarded as inadequate unless there has been a direct communication with the plaintiff personally or with a responsible intermediary. In *Yarrow* v. *Sterling Drug Co.*,[13] the plaintiff had suffered permanent damage to her eyes through taking the drug chloroquine phosphate for arthritis. Literature had been circulated to doctors warning of side-effects associated with the drug, but this was held to be insufficient. As the District Court explained:[14]

> "The most effective method employed by the drug company in the promotion of new drugs is shown to be the use of detail men (*scil.* sales representatives); thus, the Court feels that this would also present the most effective method of warning the doctor about recent developments in drugs already employed by the doctor, at no great additional expense. The detail men visit the doctors at frequent intervals and could make an effective oral warning, accompanied by literature on the development, that would affirmatively notify the doctor of side effects such as shown in the facts of this case."

This seems an eminently sensible approach in such a case where there is a risk of severe harm. It is well known that a great deal of literature from drug companies and elsewhere is disposed of by doctors unread.[15]

Representations of safety and promotional activities

Attention may also be focussed on any representations of safety made by the manufacturer and on other aspects of promotional activities. Such statements may occasionally constitute a collateral warranty,[16] but they are generally more relevant as going to the need for, and adequacy of, warnings as to accompanying dangers. Faced with such a representation, the user or a responsible third party such as a parent or doctor[17] might overlook or attach insufficient importance to a danger which might otherwise have been apparent. The point was important in *Watson* v. *Buckley*,

---

[12] Warnings that the product is fragile or should not be bent, etc. will, of course, often be important to the carrier's liability.

[13] 263 F. Supp. 159 (D.C. South Dakota, 1967).

[14] *Ibid.*, at p. 163.

[15] See further below, pp. 245–247 (warning responsible intermediaries).

[16] See *Wells (Merstham), Ltd.* v. *Buckland Sand and Silica, Ltd.*, [1965] 2 Q.B. 170; [1964] 1 All E.R. 41; *Shanklin Pier, Ltd.* v. *Detel Products, Ltd.*, [1951] 2 K.B. 854; [1951] 2 All E.R. 471, above, pp. 38, 64–65. In the USA, they may also ground a more general liability under the express warranty theory: see above, pp. 58–62.

[17] *Christ* v. *Art Metal Works*, 243 N.Y.S. 496 (1930) (parent); *Love* v. *Wolf, Parke-Davis & Co.*, 38 Cal. Rptr. 183 (1964); 58 Cal. Rptr. 42 (1967) (doctor).

Osborne, Garrett & Co., Ltd.[18] where a hair dye which caused dermatitis had been advertised as needing no preliminary tests.

In a leading American case, *Maize* v. *Atlantic Refining Co.*,[19] the deceased, a woman aged thirty-three, had been working in a confined space with a carbon tetrachloride carpet cleaner marketed by the defendant company under the trade-name "Safety Kleen". Granting recovery in respect of her death from renal failure, the Supreme Court of Pennsylvania said of the two gallon container in which the cleaner was supplied:[20]

> "The word 'Safety' was so conspicuously displayed on all four sides of this can of dangerous fluid as to make the word 'Caution' and the admonition against inhaling fumes and as to use only in a well ventilated place seem of comparatively minor import."

Similar reasoning has been used in other American cases, as when the plaintiff had immersed her hands in a solution labelled "It's kind to your hands";[1] a toy gun which set fire to a child's clothes was advertised as "absolutely harmless";[2] and magnesium heat blocks which burned a child were described as "always ready for use".[3] Accepting that many such statements could be viewed only as meaningless advertising puffs,[4] the reasoning behind the cases is sound.

Some American cases have also pointed to the high level of promotional activity behind the product as bearing upon the adequacy of the warning. The theory is that a warning which might otherwise have been adequate may lose its effectiveness when set against a campaign to promote the product. In *Love* v. *Wolf, Parke-Davis & Co.*[5] the plaintiff had contracted aplastic anaemia through taking the antibiotic chloromycetin which had been prescribed by the first defendant, a medical practitioner, and manufactured by the second defendants. The second defendants had attached to circulars, packages and labels the warnings specified by the Food and Drug Administration.[6] But a California court nonetheless held that it was open to a jury to find that the effect of these warnings had been cancelled out by aggressive overpromotion of the drug and the policy of company sales representatives to minimise its dangers.

---

[18] [1940] 1 All E.R. 174.
[19] 41 A. 2d 850 (Pa., 1945).
[20] *Ibid.*, at p. 852.
[1] *McCully* v. *Fuller Brush Co.*, 415 P. 2d 7 (Wash., 1966).
[2] *Christ* v. *Art Metal Works*, 243 N.Y.S. 496 (1930).
[3] *McLaughlin* v. *Mine Safety Appliances Co.*, 181 N.E. 2d 430 (N.Y.C.A., 1962), above, p. 235.
[4] As in *Berkebile* v. *Brantly Helicopter Corporation*, 337 A. 2d 893 (Pa., 1975). For the distinction between advertising puffs and representations of fact, see above, pp. 33–34, and p. 60.
[5] 38 Cal. Rptr. 183 (1964); second appeal, 58 Cal. Rptr. 42 (1967).
[6] For the effect of compliance with such standards, see below, pp. 265–266.

Warning responsible intermediaries[7]

Many cases will turn on the question whether the manufacturers' duty has been discharged by warning a responsible intermediary rather than the plaintiff himself. In some cases a personal warning to those likely to be affected is clearly not practicable, as when the plaintiff is a bystander injured by a stone thrown up from a power-mower[8] or by colliding with a protruding part of a car.[9] Here any unreasonable danger could be removed only by a change of design or, in appropriate cases, by warning the operator of the product. Similar considerations would apply where the danger is from side-effects associated with the taking of a particular drug which is available only on prescription. Inquiry would then concentrate on the adequacy of warnings to the medical profession to enable it to achieve an informed balancing of risks.[10]

The decision of the Court of Appeal in *Holmes* v. *Ashford*[11] is also in point. The defendants manufactured a hair dye Inecto which was supplied to hairdressers with a warning on both the bottles and on accompanying brochures that it might be dangerous to certain skins and that a patch test should be carried out. The first defendant, a hairdresser, understood the warning but chose to ignore it. The dye was applied to the plaintiff's hair without a test and the plaintiff contracted dermatitis. Allowing the manufacturer's appeal Tucker, L.J. said, with Somervell and Singleton, LL.J. concurring:[12]

"[If] they give a warning which, if read by a hairdresser, is sufficient to intimate to him the potential dangers of the substance with which he is going to deal, that is all that can be expected of them. I think it would be unreasonable and impossible to expect that they should give warning in such form that it must come to the knowledge of the particular customer who is going to be treated."[13]

The hairdresser was held liable for negligence and for breach of contract. Similar considerations lay behind the decision in *Kubach* v. *Hollands*.[14]

---

[7] See 1 *Frumer and Friedman*, s. 8.03[3]; 2 *Harper and James*, s. 28.7; Noel, 23 Sw. L.J. 256, 281–283.

[8] *Cf. Sills v. Massey Ferguson Inc.*, 296 F. Supp. 776 (D.C. Ind., 1969) and, in general, above, pp. 222–223.

[9] *Cf. Hatch v. Ford Motor Co.*, 329 P. 2d 605 (1958) and, in general, above, pp. 223–227.

[10] See, e.g., *Love* v. *Wolf, Parke-Davis and Co.*, 38 Cal. Rptr. 183 (1964); second appeal 58 Cal. Rptr. 42 (1967); *Yarrow* v. *Sterling Drug Inc.*, 263 F. Supp. 159 (South Dakota, 1967); *Toole* v. *Richardson-Merrell*, 60 Cal. Rptr. 398 (Cal. 1967).

[11] [1950] 2 All E.R. 76.

[12] *Ibid.*, at p. 80.

[13] *Cf. Watson* v. *Buckley, Osborne, Garrett & Co., Ltd.*, [1940] 1 All E.R. 174.

[14] [1937] 3 All E.R. 907, D.C.

Here the second defendants, a firm of wholesale and retail chemists, had supplied a school science mistress with a quantity of black powder labelled manganese dioxide which was in fact a mixture of ten parts of antimony sulphide to one part of manganese dioxide. When heated together with potassium chloride in a simple class-room experiment designed to produce oxygen an explosion occurred as a result of which the plaintiff, a child aged thirteen, sustained serious injury to an eye. The second defendants were held liable, but failed in a claim for contribution against their own supplier who had furnished the potentially explosive mixture. In the opinion of Hewart, L.C.J., the latter was not a person who would have been held liable if sued by the child. Chemical experiments was only one of a variety of purposes for which the mixture might have been used; the goods had been invoiced with a statement that they must be examined and tested before use; and the difference between antimony sulphide and manganese dioxide was not such as to be apparent to visual inspection although it could be ascertained by a simple test. The conclusion is questionable since, as between himself and the child, it is by no means clear why the supplier should have been entitled to look to the intermediary to carry out such a test.[15] On appropriate facts there is, however, no doubt that a bulk supplier of chemicals or any other product will act reasonably in looking to an intermediate distributor to pass on a warning whether by labelling of smaller containers or otherwise.[16]

In other cases the duty to warn may be discharged by alerting an employer or contractor and by looking to him to pass on the warning or otherwise protect his own employees or customers. *Foster* v. *Ford Motor Co.*[17] is a well-known American case. Here it was held that the manufacturer of a tractor had discharged his duty by issuing instructions and warnings in the operational manual as to the course to be adopted if the tractor became stuck in mud. Consequently no liability was incurred to the plaintiff who, having been engaged to drive the tractor and not having seen the manual, was injured when the tractor reared up and fell on him as he tried to free it in a way which the manual indicated was dangerous.[18] Dillard and Hart regard the case as an example of "a common-sense cutoff of liability".[19]

---

[15] The general position with respect to opportunity for intermediate inspection is discussed further below, pp. 284–290.

[16] For American examples, see *Weekes* v. *Michigan Chrome and Chemical Co.*, 352 F. 2d 603 (6th Cir., 1965) (chlorinated wax); *Kapp* v. *E.I. du Pont de Nemours & Co.*, 57 F. Supp. 32 (D.C. Mich., 1944) (acqua ammonia); *McDaniel* v. *Williams*, 257 N.Y.S. 2d 702 (1965) (beauty product).

[17] 246 P. 945, 48 A.L.R. 934 (1926).

[18] The written instructions had also been supplemented by verbal warnings.

[19] "Product Liability: directions for use and the duty to warn", 41 Virginia L.R. 145, 161.

Sometimes, however, the gravity of the risk and the nature of the product may make it both practicable and necessary for the product to carry its own warnings and directions.[20] Anything less than this may be insufficient to protect employees, second-hand purchasers and other casual users. There may be some difficulty in accepting this as a statement of English law because of the artificial importance attributed to opportunities for intermediate examination.[1] The point is, however, clear in principle. In *West v. Broderick and Bascom Rope Co.*,[2] for example, it was held that it was open to a jury to find that a wire rope sling should not have been marketed without a tag indicating the maximum safe load. A warning to the plaintiff's employer might not have been adequate to protect the plaintiff who was injured when the sling broke as it was being used beyond its rated capacity. In another case where a refrigerator was so designed as to produce carbon monoxide gas unless cleaned regularly it was held that the manufacturer was not entitled to a directed verdict against a second-hand purchaser.[3] The latter might, no doubt, have been warned of the danger if a suitable statement had been attached to or embossed on the refrigerator itself. Where this course is not practicable reasonable safety may require that the design be changed. This would seem to have been the position in one recent American case where the fuses on sticks of dynamite gave no indication, whether through smoke or smell, that they had been lit.[4]

Warnings of subsequently discovered dangers

Manufacturers sometimes issue warnings to warn purchasers of dangers which have come to light after the product was originally marketed. This happens quite regularly with cars and there are also recent examples in-

---

For further examples, see *Thomas v. Arvon Products Co.*, 227 A. 2d 897 (Pa., 1967) (toxic varnish product: warning to employer); *West v. Hydro-Test Inc.*, 196 So. 2d 598 (La. App., 1967) (overshot on rigs: warning to purchaser); *Juhnke v. E.I.G. Corporation*, 444 F. 2d 1323 (9th Cir., 1971) (tear gas gun: warning to purchaser); *Bryant v. Hercules Inc.*, 325 F. Supp. 241 (D.C. Kentucky, 1970) (explosives: warning to miners' employers); *Wilson v. E.Z. Flow Chemical Co.*, 186 N.E. 2d 679 (N.C., 1972) (herbicide: warning to supplier). See also *Norton Australia Pty., Ltd. v. Streets Ice Cream Pty., Ltd.* (1968), 120 C.L.R. 635 (High Ct. of Australia) (inflammable adhesive) (contractor warned).

[20] *Restatement of Torts*, 2d, s. 388, comment n; s. 397, comment b.
[1] See below, pp. 284–290.
[2] 197 N.W. 2d 202 (Iowa, 1972).
[3] *Beadles v. Servel Inc.*, 100 N.E. 2d 405 (Ill. App., 1951).
[4] *Cooley v. Quick Supply Co.*, 221 N.W. 2d 763 (Iowa, 1974).

volving products such as drugs[5] and deep fryers.[6] It is uncertain whether English law recognises a duty to issue such warnings. In *Wright* v. *Dunlop Rubber Co., Ltd.*,[7] the second defendants, I.C.I., were sued in respect of their failure to warn of the carcinogenic properties of the anti-oxidant Nonox S which had caused the plaintiff employee to contract cancer of the bladder. Nonox S had been used as an anti-oxidant since the 1920s and it was finally withdrawn in 1949 without a significantly earlier warning. Dunlops had continued to use it until it was withdrawn. The plaintiff began working for Dunlops in 1946 and after a normal twenty-year time lag he contracted cancer in 1966. The Court of Appeal upheld a judgment against I.C.I., being satisfied that the company knew that Nonox S was a serious health hazard well before the end of 1946 and probably by 1943.[8] Against this background the court said of the manufacturer's duty that:[9]

"[It] is not necessarily confined to the period before the product is first produced or put on the market. Thus, if, when a product is first marketed, there is no reason to suppose that it is carcinogenic, but thereafter information shows, or gives reason to suspect, that it may be carcinogenic, the manufacturer has failed in his duty if he if he has failed to do whatever may have been reasonable in the circumstances in keeping up to date with knowledge of such developments and acting with whatever promptness fairly reflects the nature of the information and the seriousness of the possible consequences."

Taken out of context this statement might be read as recognising a duty to warn of subsequently discovered dangers. But Nonox S was being supplied on an ongoing basis and the Court of Appeal might have been saying only that supplies had to be accompanied by a warning once the danger had come to light. If this is correct, the case would not provide support for the view that there is also a much more onerous duty to warn *past* purchasers of subsequently discovered dangers. Such a duty has, however, been recognised in both Canadian and American cases.

Rivtow Marine, Ltd. v. *Washington Iron Works*[10] is the leading Canadian

---

[5] The drug Eraldin (Practolol) used in the treatment of heart patients is in point. For a brief statement of the warnings of subsequently discovered side-effects issued by the I.C.I. Pharmaceuticals Division, see *The Times*, 24 April 1975, p. 1. It is understood that I.C.I. has made *ex gratia* payments totalling £1m to persons who had suffered side-effects: see *The Times*, 14 July 1976, p. 16.

[6] See the warning issued by ITT Consumer Products (UK), Ltd. in respect of a Deep Fryer Model 7587, *The Times*, 3 March 1976.

[7] (1972), 13 K.I.R. 255.

[8] (1972), 13 K.I.R. 255, 271, 273. At first instance O'Connor, J. had held that I.C.I. would have had to have admitted at any time after 1940 that they did not know whether Nonox S was safe.

[9] *Ibid.*, at p. 272.

case. The facts are set out more fully later. Briefly, however, the Supreme Court of Canada held that the manufacturer of a crane was under a duty to warn a known purchaser that it was likely to be dangerous so as to enable him to have it repaired at a time which would minimise his loss of profit. Breach of this duty led to a successful claim for the additional loss of profit attributable to repairing at a disadvantageous time. Had the crane collapsed and caused physical injury or property damage this would, *a fortiori*, have been covered by the duty to warn.

In the leading American case of *Comstock v. General Motors Corporation*[11] the plaintiff was a garage mechanic who had been injured by a 1953 Buick Roadmaster which, in common with thousands of other cars of the same model, had a defective hydraulic braking system. The accident occurred in January 1954. The Supreme Court of Michigan held that General Motors might be liable in negligence as manufacturers of the car even if they had taken all reasonable testing precautions before marketing it. They knew of the problem. Indeed they had instructed dealers to fit replacement kits to 1953 Buicks at the manufacturer's expense whenever a car was brought in. In such a case, the court held, the law imposed on them a duty "to take all reasonable means to convey effective warning to those who had purchased 1953 Buicks with power brakes when the latent defect was discovered".[12] It was open to a jury to find that a warning to dealers, without further attempts to contact individual purchasers, was insufficient to discharge that duty.[13]

Braniff Airways, Inc. v. Curtiss Wright Corporation[14] is another American case recognising the existence of a continuing duty to warn. Here the action was against the manufacturer of an aeroplane engine which developed cylinder barrel failure, causing a Douglas DC-7C to crash. There was evidence to suggest that the defendants knew of instances of cylinder barrel separation well before the date of the crash. Holding that the case should be submitted to the jury on the issue of negligence the

---

10 (1974), 40 D.L.R. 3d 530, below, p. 333.
11 99 N.W. 2d 627, 78 A.L.R. 2d 449 (Mich., 1961). See 1 *Frumer and Friedman*, s. 8.02; Noel, "Products Defective Because of Inadequate Directions or Warnings", 23 Sw. L.J. 256, 288–289 (1969).
12 78 A.L.R. 2d 449, 457. The National Traffic and Motor Vehicle Safety Act of 1966, s. 1402 (*a*), now imposes a statutory obligation in the following terms: "Every manufacturer of motor vehicles or tires shall furnish notification of any defect in any motor vehicle or motor vehicle equipment produced by such manufacturer which he determines, in good faith, relates to motor vehicle safety, to the purchaser (where known to the manufacturer) of such motor vehicle or motor vehicle equipment, within a reasonable time after such manufacturer has discovered such defect."
13 See further below, p. 284, where the case is noted in the context of supervening causes.
14 411 F. 2d 451 (2nd Cir., 1969).

United States Court of Appeals for the Second Circuit said:[15]

> "It is clear that after such a product has been sold and dangerous defects in design have come to the manufacturer's attention, the manufacturer has a duty either to remedy these or, if complete remedy is not feasible, at least to give users adequate warnings and instructions concerning methods for minimizing the danger."

Support for this view is also to be found in other American cases, as when operational experience suggested that an aeroplane propeller could not be feathered to control overspeeds[16] and when the manufacturer of a "hydraulic paratrooper" device for amusement parks appreciated that it was not being operated in accordance with instructions, so placing unforeseen strains on a radial spindle.[17] In the latter case the duty was discharged by warning the operator.

The general principle of these cases is surely sound,[18] although there is ample room for debate over the steps which would be required to discharge the duty once the danger had come to light. Where the danger is substantial and the identity of purchasers is known or readily identifiable, a warning to individual purchasers is likely to be needed. In other cases general publicity, as through advertising or alerting the news media, may be sufficient whilst in others a warning to dealers or intermediaries may be required.[19] The content of the warning which is needed will similarly vary from case to case. Sometimes the danger will be such as to require a clear warning that the product should no longer be used. Nonox S would have fallen into this category once its carcinogenic properties had become apparent.[20] In other cases it will be sufficient to warn of the danger (possibly with accompanying instructions as to how it may be rectified or minimised) and to leave the decision whether to continue using the product to individual purchasers or intermediaries. A drug which is beneficial but which is discovered to have side-effects might fall into this category.

Some American cases suggest that the manufacturer is under a duty to remedy the defect if this is feasible.[1] It is unlikely that an English court would adopt the same view unless, perhaps, the claim were under a

---

[15] *Ibid.*, at p. 453.

[16] *Noel* v. *United Aircraft Corporation*, 219 F. Supp. 556 (1963).

[17] *Rekab Inc.* v. *Frank Hrubetz & Co.*, 274 A. 2d 107 (Md., 1971).

[18] *Goldman* v. *Hargrave*, [1967] 1 A.C. 645; [1966] 2 All E.R. 989, P.C. might provide a useful analogy in an English court.

[19] See, e.g., *Rekab Inc.* v. *Frank Hrubetz*, above note 17, where the amusement park operator was held liable but the supplier of the machine was not.

[20] See *Wright* v. *Dunlop Rubber Co., Ltd.* (1972), 13 K.I.R. 255, above, p. 248.

[1] See, e.g., *Braniff Airways Inc.* v. *Curtiss Wright Corporation*, 411 F. 2d 451, 453 (2nd Cir., 1969), above, p. 249.

manufacturer's guarantee.[2] In the absence of negligence at the time of marketing the product[3] it is difficult to see how an obligation to remedy the defect can be accommodated within a negligence theory of liability.[4] The same is true of a suggestion in another American case that where "human safety" is involved there is a duty to develop effective safety devices in line with those of competitors and to install them on earlier models.[5] Where the product was reasonably believed to be safe when marketed the most that English law is likely to require is an adequate and timely warning of such dangers as have become known to the manufacturer or, perhaps, of dangers of which he should have been aware in the exercise of reasonable care.[6]

---

[2] See above, pp. 161–162.

[3] As to which, see *Dutton* v. *Bognor Regis Urban District Council*, [1972] 1 All E.R. 462, 474 (Lord Denning, M.R.); *Rivtow Marine, Ltd.* v. *Washington Iron Works* (1974), 40 D.L.R. (3d) 530, 552 (Laskin, J.), and below, pp. 335–336.

[4] The *additional* loss caused by a delayed warning as in the *Rivtow Marine* case can clearly be accommodated: see below, pp. 333–335.

[5] *Noel* v. *United Aircraft Corporation*, 219 F. Supp. 556 (1963). The Second Circuit did not find it necessary to adopt this suggestion in *Braniff Airways, Inc.* v. *Curtiss-Wright Corporation*, 411 F. 2d 451, 453 (1969).

[6] An extension to constructive knowledge would envisage a requirement of ongoing research. A possible compromise would be to impose liability where the manufacturer knew of the condition which constituted the danger whilst failing negligently to appreciate that the condition was dangerous.

13 The Manufacturers' Liability: Proof of Negligence, Causation and Defences: I

In a product liability case, it will be necessary to establish that the product caused the damage or loss which is the basis of the claim, that the damage resulted from a defective or unreasonably dangerous condition, and that responsibility for this condition can be traced to the defendant. Similarly, the claim may fail in whole or in part where the product has been put to an abnormal use, or where contributory negligence, assumption of the risk, or, perhaps, knowledge of the defect or danger can be established. Such problems are common to strict liability and liability dependent on proof of negligence. In the latter case, however, the plaintiff will have the additional burden of establishing a lack of reasonable care on the part of the defendant. No liability will be incurred in respect of dangers which could not reasonably have been foreseen (including some development risks), or in respect of defects not attributable to a want of reasonable care in the production process. In the discussion which follows many of the cases might be considered under a variety of headings since the problems are inextricably linked.

Proof of negligence

Before discussing some of the implications of the requirement of proof of negligence reference must be made to two possible instances in which strict tort liability may be imposed on the manufacturer in English law. The possibility of the manufacturer being under a non-delegable duty with respect to the marketing of a finished product which has been carefully constructed has already been examined.[1]

Liability under Rylands v. Fletcher

The liability without fault which is associated with the rule in *Rylands* v. *Fletcher*[2] may occasionally extend to dangerous or defective products. The cases in point are not, however, numerically significant nor particularly convincing.[3] The possibility of a common law doctrine of strict liability for ultra-hazardous activities[4] was forestalled by the decision of the House of Lords in *Read* v. *J. Lyons & Co., Ltd*[5] with its emphasis on the need for an "escape from control". The same case also casts doubt on the proper application of the rule to claims for personal injury.[6] The result is that whilst the doctrine may still be important where a major accident stems from a breakdown in the manufacturing process, or from goods which are being stored in bulk,[7] it has little application to a normal product liability case as such.

Inherently dangerous chattels

It was seen in an earlier chapter[8] that English law recognised a separate category of inherently dangerous chattels, or chattels dangerous *per se*, as an exception to the early rule of non-liability associated with *Winterbottom* v. *Wright*.[9] The category has been held to include objects such as loaded guns,

---

[1] See above, pp. 199–207 (liability for defects in components, materials, and in processing). See also below, pp. 284–290 (intermediate examination).

[2] (1866), L.R. 1 Exch. 265, affd. (1868), L.R. 3 H.L. 330. The rule is discussed in standard works such as Street, *The Law of Torts*, 6th edn., 1976, ch. 12; Fleming, *The Law of Torts*, 4th edn., 1971, ch. 14.

[3] Examples include *Hale* v. *Jennings Brothers*, [1938] 1 All E.R. 579, C.A. (chair-o-plane); *Shiffman* v. *The Venerable Order of the Hospital of St. John of Jerusalem*, [1936] 1 All E.R. 557 (flag-pole); *Perry* v. *Kendricks Transport, Ltd.*, [1956] 1 All E.R. 154; [1956] 1 W.L.R. 85 (petrol tank of motor coach).

[4] See *Restatement, Torts* 2d, s. 519.

[5] [1947] A.C. 156; [1946] 2 All E.R. 471.

[6] *Cf.* [1947] A.C. 156, 173 (Lord Macmillan); p. 169 (Viscount Simon); p. 178 (Lord Porter). See further Street, *op. cit.*, p. 255.

[7] As in *Mason* v. *Levy Auto Parts of England, Ltd.*, [1967] 2 Q.B. 530; [1967] 2 All E.R. 62, although the defendant was not a manufacturer.

[8] See above, ch. 1, pp. 10–11.

[9] (1842), 10 M. & W. 109.

petrol, sulphuric acid, poison and defective gas installations,[10] but not, it seems, air rifles, bows and arrows and catapults.[11] The designation of a particular chattel as being dangerous *per se* fell to be determined as a matter of law.[12] Generally speaking, however, the category comprised products which were viewed as dangerous by their very nature, rather than dangerous in an individual case because they had been produced defectively. With the demise of *Winterbottom* v. *Wright*, a rough classification along these lines is helpful as concentrating attention on the adequacy of the manufacturer's warnings and directions for use, rather than on his production process. Similarly, of course, the negligence equation will itself demand a degree of care in storing and distributing such products which is commensurate with the risk involved. Typically the risk will be a high one, for the product, in the words of a leading American case, will be "imminently dangerous to the life or health of mankind".[13]

Beyond this, the continuation of a formal system of classification is likely to be both misleading and artificial. As Scrutton, L.J. once remarked, the unfavoured category of things dangerous only *sub modo* may be the more dangerous for they constitute "a wolf in sheep's clothing instead of an obvious wolf".[14] Moreover, danger is, in any event, a relative term which cannot sensibly be divorced from circumstances of time and space. A phial of poison is hardly an agent of harm when encased in concrete at the bottom of the sea; a defectively produced chair is substantially certain to cause injury when placed untended in a geriatric ward. Recognition of such considerations has led to judicial statements denying that any such distinction exists. Thus in *Beckett* v. *Newalls Insulation Co., Ltd.*, where a shipworker had been injured by an explosion in a calor gas cylinder, Singleton, L.J. agreed that:[15]

---

[10] See, respectively, *Burfitt* v. *A. E. Kille*, [1939] 2 All E.R. 372, 378 (Atkinson, J.); *Sullivan* v. *Creed*, [1904] 2 I.R. 317, 340 (loaded gun); *Jefferson* v. *Derbyshire Farmers, Ltd.*, [1921] 2 K.B. 281, 289 (Atkin, L.J.) (petrol); *Adelaide Chemical Co., Ltd.* v. *Carlyle* (1940), 64 C.L.R. 514 (High Ct. of Australia) (sulphuric acid); *Thomas* v. *Winchester*, 6 N.Y. 397, 57 Am. Dec. 455 (1852) (poison); *Dominion Natural Gas Co., Ltd.* v. *Collins and Perkins*, [1909] A.C. 640, P.C. (gas installation).

[11] See, respectively, *Donaldson* v. *McNiven*, [1952] 1 All E.R. 1213, 1216 (Pearson, J.) (air rifle); *Ricketts* v. *Erith Borough Council*, [1943] 2 All E.R. 629, 632 (Tucker, J.) (bow and arrow); *Smith* v. *Leurs* (1945) 70 C.L.R. 256 (High Ct. of Australia) (catapult). See further Charlesworth, *Negligence*, 5th edn., 1971, paras. 615–623; Salmond, *Torts*, 16th edn., 1973, pp. 307–308 and cases there cited.

[12] *Blacker* v. *Lake and Elliot, Ltd.* (1912), 106 L.T. 533, 535 (Hamilton, J.).

[13] *Huset* v. *J. I. Case Threshing Machine Co.*, 120 F. 865, 870 (8th Cir., 1903) *per* Sanborn, J. The American exception to the general rule of non-liability which preceded *Macpherson* v. *Buick Motor Co.*, 111 N.E. 1050 (N.Y.C.A., 1916) was somewhat wider than its English counterpart: see above, pp. 12–13.

[14] *Hodge & Sons* v. *Anglo-American Oil Co.* (1922), 12 LL.L. Rep. 183, 187.

[15] [1953] 1 All E.R. 250, 254 adopting a passage from the submissions of Sir Hartley Shawcross, Q.C., A.G. in *Read* v. *J. Lyons & Co., Ltd.*, [1947] A.C. 156; [1946] 2 All E.R. 271.

"The true question is not whether a thing is dangerous in itself but whether, by reason of some extraneous circumstances it may become dangerous. There is really no category of dangerous things; there are only some things which require more and some which require less care."

Whilst this is clearly the better view, the classification has shown a remarkable capacity for survival. It was not until 1957 that the distinction ceased to govern the liability in negligence of one who had installed upon premises an appliance which later injured a third party.[16] It still continues to be used in relation to product liability in practitioners' works[17] and in modern Commonwealth cases which sometimes go so far as to suggest that chattels dangerous *per se* carry an absolute liability.[18] Other Commonwealth cases, however, deny the validity of the distinction.[19] In England, the Court of Appeal in *Wright* v. *Dunlop Rubber Co., Ltd.*,[20] found it unnecessary to determine whether I.C.I. would have been strictly liable for cancer suffered through exposure to their product Nonox S but indicated that compliance with a high standard of care was all that was required.[1] As a statement of the present English law, this is surely correct.[2] Whether we should adopt a régime of strict liability in such cases is, of course, another matter.

The duty to test, inspect and discover

In discharging his duty of care a manufacturer must ensure that his product

---

[16] See *A. C. Billings & Sons, Ltd.* v. *Riden*, [1958] A.C. 240; [1957] 3 All E.R. 1. The earlier decision in *Ball* v. *London County Council*, [1949] 2 K.B. 159; [1949] 1 All E.R. 1056, C.A. was persuasively criticised by Goodhart, "Dangerous Things and the Sedan Chair" (1949), 65 L.Q.R. 518.

[17] As, e.g., Charlesworth, *Negligence*, paras. 615–623; Bingham, *All the Modern Cases on Negligence*, 2nd edn., 1964, p. 77.

[18] *Nordstrom* v. *McBurnie* (1968), 63 W.W.R. 626, 628 (B.C. Sup. Ct.) (loaded gun). See also *Rosetown Service Garage, Ltd.* v. *Canadian Propane, Ltd.* (1966), 56 W.W.R. 45, 47 (Sas. C.A.) (propane tanker); *Ostash* v. *Sonnenberg* (1968), 67 D.L.R. (2d) 311 (Alberta Sup. Ct.) (natural gas installation).

[19] See, e.g., *Dahlberg* v. *Naydiuk* (1970), 72 W.W.R. 210, 214–216 (Man., C.A.). For further references to and discussion of the distinction, see *Imperial Furniture Pty., Ltd.* v. *Automatic Fire Sprinklers Pty., Ltd.*, [1967] 1 N.S.W.R. 29 (N.S.W.C.A.); *Tanner* v. *Atlantic Bridge Co.*, (1966), 56 D.L.R. (2d) 162 (Nova Scotia Sup. Ct.); *Jull* v. *Wilson*, [1968] N.Z.L.R. 88 (N.Z. Sup. Ct.).

[20] (1972), 13 K.I.R. 255, above, p. 248.

[1] *Ibid.*, at p. 273.

[2] See, e.g., the approach of Lord Macmillan in *Read* v. *J. Lyons & Co., Ltd.*, [1947] A.C. 156, 172–173 which was cited by the Court of Appeal in the *Wright* case. See also *Donoghue* v. *Stevenson*, [1932] A.C. 562, 611 where Lord Macmillan emphasises the need for a high degree of care where dangerous chattels are concerned, but does not suggest that liability is absolute. For the contrary view, see Charlesworth, *Negligence*, para. 622, but the cases there cited do not carry the point.

is subjected to a system of quality control commensurate with the risk involved. Similarly he must exercise reasonable care in ensuring that the product is so designed as to be reasonably safe to the user and to others likely to be affected by it. This may entail original research or keeping abreast of current research so as to be in a position to minimise or warn of risks and to give any necessary directions for safe use.

The adequacy of any given system of testing and inspection for latent defects will depend on the nature of the product and the gravity of the risk. Where the risk is high, as with impurities in food, or defects in products such as aeroplanes, cars or their tyres, and safety harnesses, the standard of quality control demanded will be correspondingly stringent. With some products, visual inspection and a system of spot checks or sampling will be sufficient. With others, reasonable care will require that the product be subjected to appropriate physical, chemical or metallurgical tests. In all cases the suggested system must be practicable, economically feasible in relation to the risk, and apt to reduce the likelihood of damage occurring. A defect, unlike a design feature, cannot in the nature of things be justified in terms of its social utility.

Even though an acceptable system of testing and inspection has been established, the manufacturer may still be held liable for the failure of an individual employee to operate it with the necessary care. This places the manufacturer in something of a dilemma, since the weightier the evidence establishing the adequacy of the system, the more is driven to the conclusion that an employee was at fault in operating it.[3] Indeed in deposing to the excellence of his system the manufacturer may come close to providing the plaintiff's case whenever the court is satisfied that the goods were in fact defective when they left the manufacturer's control. *Grant* v. *Australian Knitting Mill, Ltd.*[4] illustrates the point. Here the defendant manufacturer had previously treated some 4.7 million garments by a similar process without complaints of dermatitis. The safety record was accordingly excellent. Yet the Privy Council reasoned:[5]

"According to the evidence, the method of manufacture was correct: the danger of excess sulphites being left was recognised and was guarded against: the process was intended to be fool proof. If excess sulphites were left in the garment, that could only be because someone was at fault."[6]

The same distinction between the general system and the way it was

---

[3] *Cf.* 2 Harper and James, *Law of Torts*, s. 28.14, p. 1569. A collection of American cases is to be found in 6 A.L.R. 3d 91. See also 1 *Frumer and Friedman*, s. 6.01.
[4] [1936] A.C. 85, P.C.
[5] *Ibid.*, at p. 101.
[6] For similar reasoning in an American case, see *Minutilla* v. *Providence Ice Cream Co.*, 144 A. 884 (R.I., 1929).

operated on a particular occasion is also apparent, although in a different context, in the decision of the House of Lords in *Smedley's Ltd.* v. *Breed*.[7] Smedleys were appealing against conviction on a charge under the Food and Drugs Act 1955 in respect of the sale of a tin of peas containing a green caterpillar, the larva of a hawk moth. The justices had found that Smedleys had instituted and maintained a satisfactory system of testing and inspection. But the caterpillar, being of similar size, density, weight and colour to peas had escaped both the mechanical screening process and the system of visual inspection by trained employees to achieve what Lord Hailsham, L.C. termed "a sort of posthumous apotheosis".[8] In dismissing the appeal, the House of Lords held that, even if it were a defence under the 1955 Act to show that the presence of extraneous matter was unavoidable by the exercise of reasonable care, the defence would not assist Smedleys. They had not shown that reasonable care had been exercised by all concerned in the processes of collection and preparation. The system, as such, was quite satisfactory. But the presence of the caterpillar in that particular tin might have been caused by the negligence of an individual employee, and the statutory defence would have required Smedleys to establish the contrary.[9]

In a tort claim based on similar facts it would seem that *res ipsa loquitur* cannot technically be invoked in English law,[10] at least if *res ipsa* is understood as shifting the onus on proof to the defendant and not simply as providing a basis on which the plaintiff may (or must) succeed in the absence of rebutting evidence.[11] Canadian and American cases invoke the

---

[7] [1974] 2 All E.R. 21.

[8] *Ibid.*, at p. 24.

[9] Section 3 (3) of the 1955 Act provides that "In proceedings under section two of this Act in respect of any food...containing some extraneous matter, it shall be a defence for the defendant to prove that the presence of that matter was an unavoidable consequence of the process of collection or preparation".

[10] See *Donoghue* v. *Stevenson*, [1932] A.C. 562, 622, H.L. *per* Lord Macmillan; *Mason* v. *Williams and Williams Ltd.*, [1955] 1 All E.R. 808, 810, *per* Finnemore, J. For discussion of *res ipsa* in the context of product liability, see Waddams, *Products Liability* (1974), pp. 54–58; 1 *Frumer and Friedman*, s. 12.03; Fleming, *Law of Torts*, 4th edn., 1971, pp. 447–449. For general discussion, see Street, *The Law of Torts*, 6th edn., 1976, pp. 134–141; 2 Harper & James, *Law of Torts*, s. 19.5, s. 19.12; Seavey, 63 Harv. L.R. 643 (1950); Paton, (1936) 14 C.B.R. 480; Atiyah, (1972) 35 M.I.R. 337. See also above, p. 201 for reference to the problems posed by multiple defendants.

[11] The predominant English view is that *res ipsa* does operate to place the onus of proof on the defendant: see, e.g., *Henderson* v. *Henry E. Jenkins & Sons*, [1970] A.C. 282; [1969] 3 All E.R. 756, H.L.; *Moore* v. *R. Fox & Sons*, [1956] 1 Q.B. 596; [1956] 1 All E.R. 182, C.A. The predominant Australian view is that it does not: see *Nominal Defendant* v. *Halsbauer* (1967), 117 C.L.R. 448; *Government Insurance Office of New South Wales* v. *Fredrichberg* (1968), 118 C.L.R. 403 (High Ct. of Australia). See further Cross, *Evidence*, (4th edn., 1974), pp. 131–134; Atiyah, (1972) 35 M.I.R. 337.

maxim in name as well as in spirit.[12] In practice, however, there will be a few cases in which the result will differ according to whether *res ipsa* is applied. The important point is that there is a general willingness to act on circumstantial evidence both on the issue of causation[13] and on the issue of negligence. As to the latter, it has been clear since the decision in *Grant* v. *Australian Knitting Mills, Ltd.* that the plaintiff "is not required to lay his finger on the exact person in all the chain who was responsible or to specify what he did wrong. Negligence is found as a matter of inference from the existence of the defects taken in connection with all the known circumstances".[14]

Whether the inference is permissible will depend on the facts of the individual case. When a foreign object or impurity is found on opening food or drink sold in a sealed container the inference that it was there from the date of manufacture is virtually irresistible and an inference of negligence scarcely less strong.[15] American cases also suggest a general willingness to act on circumstantial evidence where bottles have exploded[16] but little willingness to do so where tyres have blown out during the course of driving.[17] In a selection of other cases, it has been held to be a matter of common experience that carefully designed and constructed telephones do not make an explosive sound, impairing the hearing of the user;[18] electric ovens do not ignite when the switch is moved to the "off"

---

[12] See, e.g., *Arendale* v. *Canada Bread*, [1941] 2 D.L.R. 41, 44 (Ont., C.A.); *Zeppa* v. *Coca Cola, Ltd.*, [1955] 5 D.L.R. 187, 193 (Ont., C.A.). *Escola* v. *Coca Cola Bottling Co.*, 150 P. 2d 436 (Cal., 1944) is perhaps the most important of the early American cases.

[13] See below, ch. 14, at pp. 274–275, 276–277.

[14] [1936] A.C. 85, 101, P.C. For a similar approach, see *Donoghue* v. *Concrete Products (Kirkcaldy), Ltd.*, 1976, S.L.T. 58; *Lockhart* v. *Barr*, 1943 S.C. (H.L.) 1; *Chaproniere* v. *Mason* (1905), 21 T.L.R. 633, 634, C.A.; *Mason* v. *Williams and Williams, Ltd.*, [1955] 1 All E.R. 808, 810; *Steer* v. *Durable Rubber Manufacturing Co.* (1958), *Times*, 20 November.

[15] See, e.g., *Lockhart* v. *Barr*, 1943 S.C. (H.L.); *Zeppa* v. *Coca Cola, Ltd.*, [1955] 5 D.L.R. 187 (glass in soft drink); *Shandloff* v. *City Dairy* [1936] 4 D.L.R. 712 (glass in chocolate milk); *Mathews* v. *Coca Cola Co. of Canada, Ltd.*, [1944] 2 D.L.R. 355 (mouse in soft drink); *Varga* v. *John Labatt, Ltd.*, Highgate and Hurse (1957), 6 D.L.R. (2d) 336 (chlorine solution in beer). *Daniels and Daniels* v. *White*, [1938] 4 All E.R. 258 (carbolic acid in lemonade) is one of the few cases in which the claim failed. For criticism, see (1939) 55 L.Q.R. 6, 352.

[16] See 2 *Frumer and Friedman*, s. 26. Any inference may be displaced where there is evidence to suggest improper handling: see, e.g., *Yelland* v. *National Cafe*, [1955] 5 D.L.R. 560 (Sask. C.A.).

[17] See, e.g., *Shramek* v. *General Motors Corporation*, 216 N.E. 2d 244 (Ill. App. 1964); *Markwell* v. *General Tire & Rubber Co.*, 367 F. 2d 748 (7th Cir., 1966). *Cf. Markle* v. *Mulhollands Inc.*, 509 P. 2d 529 (Ore., 1973). *Aliter* where a tyre has exploded when being inflated and fitted: see, e.g., *Ewer* v. *Goodyear Tire and Rubber Co.*, 480 P. 2d 260 (Wash. App., 1971).

[18] *Gandy* v. *Southwestern Bell Telephone Co.*, 341 S.W. 2d 554 (Tex. Civ. App., 1960); *Scott* v. *Diamond State Telephone Co.*, 239 A. 2d 703 (Del., 1968).

position;[19] cigarettes do not explode,[20] and chewing tobacco does not contain the remnants of a moth or worm.[1]

To the extent that a court is willing to act on circumstantial evidence, the distinction between liability which requires proof of negligence and strict liability becomes correspondingly less important. Certainly there is the formal distinction that where liability is strict, the manufacturer cannot adduce evidence of his system of quality control since this will tend only to establish reasonable care and this is irrelevant.[2] Moreover, the basis of liability and the incidence of the onus of proof may have an important psychological effect in determining whether the case gets to court. But under both systems there is a need to trace a defective condition to the defendant and to establish that this caused the damage. Circumstantial evidence is likely to play a prominent role in these issues whatever the basis of liability.[3]

Reasonable care is also demanded in relation to the discovery and warning of risks associated with the product. Thus in *Vacwell Engineering Co., Ltd.* v. *B.D.H. Chemicals, Ltd.*,[4] the defendant manufacturers and distributors of industrial chemicals were held liable for their failure to warn of the highly explosive qualities of boron tribromide on contact with water. In the judgment of Rees, J. they had been negligent in failing to establish a system that would ensure adequate research into scientific literature dealing with the hazards of products they were marketing. Moreover, there had also been negligence on the part of their technical development manager and their chief analyst in failing to carry out proper research into the literature available to them under the existing system. This latter conclusion was reached in spite of the fact that they had referred to four modern books, including a standard work on the industrial hazards of chemicals, none of which noted the danger of an explosion. Similarly, in *Wright* v. *Dunlop Rubber Co., Ltd.*,[5] I.C.I. were held liable for continuing to market Nonox S when, in the view of the Court of Appeal, they knew of its carcinogenic qualities.

Where liability is dependent on proof of negligence, the manufacturer will be judged according to the means of knowledge available when the product was marketed. The fact that the risk was obvious at the time of

---

[19] *Peterson* v. *Minnesota Power and Light Co.*, 291 N.W. 705 (Minn., 1940). But *cf. Godfrey's, Ltd.* v. *Ryles* [1962] S.A.S.R. 33 (S.A. Sup. Ct.) (fire in secondhand kerosene refrigerator).

[20] *Liggett and Myers Tobacco Co.* v. *De Lape*, 109 F. 2d 598 (9th Cir., 1940).

[1] *Webb* v. *Brown and Williamson Tobacco Co.*, 2 S.E. 2d 898 (W. Va., 1939).

[2] *McKasson* v. *Zimmer Manufacturing Co.*, 299 N.E. 2d 38 (Ill. App., 1973) provides an example. The case involved an intramedullary rod which broke when implanted in the plaintiff's femur.

[3] See further below, at pp. 279–282 and pp. 277–279 respectively.

[4] [1971] 1 Q.B. 88; [1969] 3 All E.R. 1681.

[5] (1972), 13 K.I.R. 255.

the action does not mean that it should have been appreciated earlier since the frontiers of knowledge may have been advanced in the meantime.[6] In this respect a system of strict liability is more demanding. Yet the differences can be exaggerated. In a negligence action a high standard of care will typically be demanded, whilst there is a body of American case law which suggests that strict liability will not extend to a failure to warn of dangers which were scientifically undiscoverable at the material time.[7]

Similarly it would seem that, even under a system of strict liability, design specifications and safety standards are to be judged in the light of the standards prevailing when the product was sold. The standard of reasonable safety is not an absolute one and a plaintiff suing in respect of injuries received in 1976 from a product produced and sold in 1966 would fail if he could prove only that the product did not incorporate safety features considered appropriate at the time of the action.[8]

The safety record of the product[9]

Absence of previous accidents

The fact that the defendant's product has a good safety record may be relevant for a variety of reasons. For example, it may suggest that the product did not cause the damage or injury, that it was not unreasonably dangerous as designed, or that the manufacturer was not negligent in failing to appreciate that it was unreasonably dangerous. It will be open to the manufacturer to adduce evidence of safe use to establish such points, but the evidence will rarely be conclusive.

In *Grant* v. *Australian Knitting Mills, Ltd.,*[10] for example, the Privy Council was satisfied that there was a causal connection between the wearing of the underpants and the onset of dermatitis in spite of evidence that the defendants had sold 4.7 million garments treated by a similar process without complaint. Similarly, in *Devilez* v. *Boots Pure Drug Co.,*

---

[6] *Roe* v. *Ministry of Health*, [1954] 2 Q.B. 71; [1954] 2 All E.R. 131, C.A.

[7] See, e.g., *Christofferson* v. *Kaiser Foundation Hospitals*, 92 Cal. Rptr. 825 (Cal. App., 1971) (side-effect from drug); *Oakes* v. *E.I. Dupont de Nemours & Co.*, 77 Cal. Rptr. 709 (Cal. App., (1969), and above, p. 230.

[8] *Cf. Balido* v. *Improved Machinery Inc.*, 105 Cal. Rptr. 890, 895–896 (Cal. App., 1972). See further above, p. 189. There may, however, be a duty to warn of subsequently discovered dangers: see above, pp. 247–251.

[9] See 1 *Frumer and Friedman*, s. 12.01 [2] [3]; Noel, "Manufacturer's Negligence of Design or Directions for use of a Product", 71 Yale L.J. 816, 830–836 (1962); Morris, "Proof of Safety History in Negligence Cases", 61 Harv. L.R. 205 (1948).

[10] [1936] A.C. 85.

Ltd.,[11] Elwes, J. held that the defendants were negligent in marketing their corn solvent without a more secure stopper or a warning even though some twenty million bottles had been sold in that form over thirty years with only eleven complaints and no claim for personal injuries. In a leading American case,[12] it was held that a jury might find negligence in the design of a bus braking system although buses of the same design had travelled millions of miles without mishap. Such evidence was relevant as tending to establish that the design was reasonably safe. But it was in no sense conclusive, especially when set against evidence that a safer design was practicable and evidence of similar problems with lorries. The good safety record might have been attributable simply to good luck.[13]

Previous accidents[14]

Conversely, the plaintiff may wish to adduce evidence of other accidents or damage associated with the product. In principle, such evidence should be admissible subject to satisfying the normal requirements of relevance. Thus a particular product is more likely to lack reasonable safety if other persons have been injured by it under substantially similar circumstances.[15] Similarly, a history of accidents may help to fix the defendant with knowledge of the danger[16] and so to establish negligence at the initial marketing stage or in failing to warn of subsequently discovered dangers.

There is perhaps more difficulty in adducing similar fact evidence to establish that the product actually caused the damage or that a particular unit had been produced defectively. Evidence would rarely be admissible when it shows only that A has suffered the same type of damage as B after

---

[11] (1962), 106 Sol. Jo. 552. See also *Anglo-Celtic Shipping Co., Ltd.* v. *Elliott and Jeffrey* (1926), 42 T.L.R. 297.

[12] *Carpini* v. *Pittsburgh & Weirton Bus Co.,* 216 F. 2d 404 (3rd Cir., 1954).

[13] Contrast *Wyngrove's Executrix* v. *Scottish Omnibuses, Ltd.,* 1966 S.C. (H.L.) 47 (good safety record of Bristol Lodeka bus: operator's appeal allowed). Further American examples include *Hyatt* v. *Hyster Co.,* 106 F. Supp. 676 (N.Y., 1952); 205 F. 2d 421 (2nd Cir., 1953) (crane design); *Hardman* v. *Helene Curtis Industries Inc.,* 198 N.E. 2d 681 (Ill., 1964) (inflammable hair product); *Mobberly* v. *Sears Roebuck & Co.,* 211 N.E. 2d 839 (Ohio, 1965) (grain elevator); *Williams* v. *Laurence David Inc.,* 534 P. 2d 173 (Ore., 1975).

[14] For a summary of American cases, see 42 A.L.R. 3d 780.

[15] See, e.g., *Finnegan* v. *Havir Manufacturing Corporation,* 290 A. 2d 286 (N.J., 1972) (power press without safety device); *Dipangrazio* v. *Salamonsen,* 393 P. 2d 936 (Wash., 1964) (glass doors). Whilst the circumstances must be substantially similar and reasonably proximate in time they need not be identical: see *Carpini* v. *Pittsburgh and Weirton Bus Co.,* 216 F. 2d 404 (3rd Cir., 1954) (damage to lorries in claim involving bus).

[16] *Prashker* v. *Beech Aircraft Corporation,* 258 F. 2d 602 (3rd Cir., 1958). See also *Ewer* v. *Goodyear Tire and Rubber Co.,* 480 P. 2d 260 (Wash., 1971). English cases relevant by analogy include *Moore* v. *Ransomes* (1898), 14 T.L.R. 539 (previous accidents in dock); *Bebee* v. *Sales* (1916), 32 T.L.R. 413 (previous accidents with airgun).

both have used D's product. Such evidence would raise a host of collateral issues whenever other significant common characteristics might be present. Equally the mere fact that A bought one of D's products which was defective will rarely be admissable to establish that the product acquired by B was similarly defective. As Lord Ellenborough, C.J. once said in a slightly different context, the supplier "might deal well with one, and not with the others".[17] Sometimes, however, the points of similarity between the incidents will be such that it would be an affront to common sense to suppose that they were explicable rationally on the basis of coincidence.[18] If, for example, twenty people are found to be suffering from food poisoning both lawyers and food inspectors would regard it as relevant that they had all dined at D's restaurant earlier the same evening.[19] And if nineteen units from a given batch possess a particular defect the odds are strongly in favour of the twentieth and final unit from the same batch containing the same defect.[20] Yet it will be only in an exceptional case that a verdict against the defendant will be warranted in the absence of supporting testimony as to the condition of the product alleged to have caused the damage.

Subsequent accidents and remedial measures

Evidence of subsequent accidents will also be admissible within the same limits to establish that the product was defective or that it caused the damage which is the subject of the claim. The point is clear in principle since (to return to the example of food poisoning) it could hardly matter that the plaintiff dined earlier rather than later than fellow sufferers called to testify on his behalf. There is, moreover, authority in point. In *Board* v. *Thomas Hedley & Co., Ltd.*,[1] the Court of Appeal permitted discovery of complaints in the period both before and after the plaintiff's purchase of the packet of Tide from which she claimed to have contracted dermatitis. Evidence of

---

[17] *Holcombe* v. *Hewson* (1810), 2 Camp. 391.

[18] In English law the question has generally been discussed in the context of criminal proceedings. But there is little doubt that the principles of *Boardman* v. *Director of Public Prosecutions*, [1975] A.C. 421; [1974] 3 All E.R. 887 apply *mutatis mutandis* to civil proceedings: see *Mood Music Publishing Co., Ltd.* v. *De Wolfe, Ltd.*, [1976] Ch. 119; [1976] 1 All E.R. 763, C.A.

[19] See *Savage* v. *Peterson Distribution Co.*, 150 N.W. 2d 804 (Mich., 1967) (mink food) and cases cited below, p. 274.

[20] Support for admissibility of similar fact evidence in such a case is to be found in *Wilkinson* v. *Clark*, [1916] 2 K.B. 636 (quality of milk from same source in prosecution under Food and Drugs Act). See also *Manchester Brewery Co., Ltd.* v. *Coombs* (1900), 82 L.T. 347, 349; *Hales* v. *Kerr*, [1908] 2 K.B. 601. For American cases more directly in point, see *Strauss* v. *Douglas Aircraft Co.*, 404 F. 2d 1152 (2nd Cir., 1968) (frayed cables on seat belts); *Becker* v. *American Airlines, Inc.*, 200 F. Supp. 243 (N.Y., 1961) (defective altimeters); *Gall* v. *Union Ice Co.*, 239 P. 2d 48 (Cal., 1951) (sulphuric acid drums).

[1] [1951] 2 All E.R. 431.

subsequent accidents could not, however, establish that the defendant knew or ought to have known of the danger. He is entitled to be judged on the facts as they appeared when the product was marketed.[2]

The position with respect to subsequent remedial measures is more problematical. In a leading English case, *Hart* v. *Lancashire and Yorkshire Rail Co.*,[3] it was held that evidence that the defendants had altered their method of changing points after an accident was not admissible to establish that the accident had been caused by negligence. As Channell, B. observed:[4]

> "it is not because the defendants have become wiser and done something subsequently to the accident that their doing so is to be evidence of any antecedent negligence on their part in that respect."

American cases also hold that the adoption of new safety devices or additional warnings does not constitute a tacit admission that the earlier precautions were insufficient.[5] This has the advantage of removing what might otherwise be a considerable disincentive against the adoption of safer measures.

On the other hand, there are now a significant number of Commonwealth and American cases holding evidence of subsequent measures to be admissible for the limited purpose of establishing that alternative safety devices or further warnings were practicable, or to show that the defendant was responsible for maintenance or repair. Thus in *Anderson* v. *Morris Wools Pty., Ltd.*,[6] the addition of a guard to a wool washing machine after an injury to the plaintiff employee went to show that such a guard was feasible, although not to establish that the machine was unreasonably dangerous without it. Similarly in *Sutkowski* v. *Universal Marion Corporation*,[7] the Appellate Court of Illinois held that evidence should have been admitted that a safety barrier had been incorporated into a mammoth earth-moving machine. As the court explained:[8]

---

[2] *Roe* v. *Ministry of Health,* [1954] 2 Q.B. 66; [1954] 2 All E.R. 131. For American cases, see *Boykin* v. *Chase Bottling Works*, 222 S.W. 2d 889 (Tenn., 1949); *Ginnis* v. *Mapes Hotel Corporation*, 470 P. 2d 135 (Nev., 1970); and, in general, 1 *Frumer and Friedman*, s. 12.01 [4].

[3] (1869), 21 L.T. 261.

[4] *Ibid.*, at p. 263.

[5] See *Mobberly* v. *Sears Roebuck & Co.*, 211 N.E. 2d 839 (Ohio, 1965) (farm grain elevator); *Otis Elevator Co.* v. *Mclaney*, 406 P. 2d 7 (Alaska, 1965) (change of lubricant) and, in general, 1 *Frumer and Friedman*, s. 1204; Noel and Phillips, *Products Liability* (1974), pp. 265–269; 64 A.L.R. 2d 1296; Note, "Products Liability and Evidence of Subsequent Repairs" (1972), Duke L.J. 837.

[6] [1965] Qd. R. 65 (Queensland Sup. Ct.). See also *Nelson* v. *John Lysaght (Australia), Ltd.* (1975), Australian L.R. 289 (High Ct. Australia).

[7] 281 N.E. 2d 749 (1972).

[8] *Ibid.*, at p. 753.

"If the feasibility of alternative designs may be shown by the opinion of experts or by the existence of safety devices on other products or in the design thereof we conclude that evidence of a post occurrence change is equally relevant and material in determining that a design alternative is feasible."[9]

This would seem to be correct. But such evidence would rarely carry any weight when set alongside expert testimony and the practices of the industry.[10]

Industrial, regulatory and statutory standards

Industrial standards

A test of liability which is built on standards of reasonable safety and reasonable care is necessarily vague. Hence the manufacturer will frequently be judged in the first instance by reference to whether he has carried out such tests and inspections and incorporated such safety features, directions or warnings as are customary in the industry. Evidence of the safeguards generally adopted in the industry and of the manufacturer's compliance or non-compliance with them is relevant and admissible but it is not conclusive.[11] The position has been well summarised in an American product liability case where it was said:[12]

"[The] observance of the custom or a failure to observe it in a particular business, does not necessarily amount to due care or lack of it; but it is such evidence as is admissible as tending to show what a reasonably prudent manufacturer or person would do under same or similar circumstances."[13]

---

[9] See also *Love* v. *Wolf*, 58 Cal. Rptr. 42 (Cal. App., 1967) (warning label for drug chloromycetin); *Boeing Airplane Co.* v. *Brown*, 291 F. 2d 310 (9th Cir., 1961); *Sterner* v. *U.S. Plywood-Champion Paper Inc.*, 519 F. 2d 1352 (8th Cir., 1975); *Biehler* v. *White Metal Rolling Corporation*, 333 N.E. 2d 716 (Ill., 1975). There has been less difficulty about admitting the evidence where the subsequent changes have been carried out by a person other than the defendant manufacturer: see, e.g., *Brown* v. *Quick Mix Co.*, 454 P. 2d 205 (Wash., 1969); *Wallner* v. *Kitchens of Sara Lee Inc.*, 419 F. 2d 1028 (7th Cir., 1970).

[10] See below.

[11] Leading English cases are to be found in the field of employers' liability: see, e.g., *Brown* v. *Rolls Royce, Ltd.*, [1960] 1 All E.R. 577; [1960] 1 W.L.R. 210 H.L.; *Cavanagh* v. *Ulster Weaving Co., Ltd.*, [1960] A.C. 145; [1959] 2 All E.R. 745, H.L.; *General Cleaning Contractors, Ltd.* v. *Christmas*, [1953] A.C. 180; [1953] 2 All E.R. 1110; Munkman, *Employers' Liability at Common Law*, 8th edn., 1975, pp. 42–50. See also Morris, "Custom and Negligence", 42 Col. L.R. 1147 (1942); Fricke (1960), 23 M.L.R. 653. The same principles would clearly apply in a product liability case.

[12] *Witt* v. *Chrysler Corporation*, 167 N.W. 2d 100 (Mich. App., 1969).

[13] See also *Sheward* v. *Virtue*, 126 P. 2d 345 (Cal., 1942); *Marsh Wood Products Co.* v. *Babock and Wilcox Co.*, 240 N.W. 392 (Wis., 1932); 1 *Frumer and Friedman*, ss. 6.01 [1].

Generally, it would be true to say that non-compliance with customary standards is rarely likely to be held consistent with reasonable care and safety. An industry is unlikely to adopt a superabundance of caution although it may occasionally follow a practice which has no proven value.[14] On the other hand, there is perhaps less reluctance to hold that a common practice provides inadequate precautions. A product may certainly fall short of a standard of reasonable safety although the customary safety devices have been incorporated. A quality control system may be inadequate although it is as good as those of major competitors and the same is true of a system of testing and research for latent dangers. As an American judge once noted, if the practices of industry were conclusive as to due care, "one free disaster would be permitted as to each new product before the sanction of civil liability was thrown on the side of high standards of safety".[15]

Regulatory and statutory standards[16]

A product's design or specifications will often be judged in the light of safety codes or standards which are formulated somewhat more precisely than are the general customs of the industry. These may be laid down by official or semi-official agencies such as the British Standards Institute, or in regulations made under statutory authority. Alternatively, a product may have to satisfy a licensing or certification procedure before being marketed. The terms of such codes or regulations are again admissible in evidence to the extent that they are relevant,[17] and the effect of compliance or non-compliance will vary from jurisdiction to jurisdiction and from product to product.

Compliance with regulatory and statutory standards

Compliance with standards and regulations prescribed by official agencies and by statute is no doubt evidence that due care has been exercised and

---

[14] As in *Brown* v. *Rolls Royce, Ltd.*, [1960] 1 All E.R. 577; [1960] 1 W.L.R. 210 H.L.

[15] *Dalehite* v. *United States*, 346 U.S. 15, 55–56 (1953) *per* Jackson, J.

[16] See *Clerk and Lindsell on Torts*, 14th edn., 1975, ch. 21; Fleming, *Law of Torts*, 4th edn., 1971, pp. 121–132; Prosser, *The Law of Torts*, 4th edn., 1971, pp. 190–204; Waddams, *Products Liability* (1974), ch. 4; Williams (1960), 23 M.L.R. 233; Morris, 46 Harv. L.R. 453 (1933); 49 Col. L.R. 21 (1949).

[17] Thus in *Taylor* v. *Rover Co., Ltd.*, [1966] 2 All E.R. 181; [1966] 1 W.L.R. 1491 evidence was admitted of the British Standards Specifications for chisels.

reasonable safety measures or devices adopted.[18] On the other hand, compliance is unlikely to be regarded as conclusive. English cases have mainly involved employers and factory occupiers,[19] but there is little doubt that the same view would be adopted in the case of a manufacturer. Certainly, American cases emphasize constantly that such standards prescribe no more than minimum levels of acceptability and do not foreclose the issues of reasonable safety and reasonable care. *Raymond v. Riegel Textile Corporation*[20] is a recent and representative case holding that the manufacturer of a flannelette nightgown might be held liable to a child who had suffered burns from material which complied with the requirements of the federal Flammable Fabrics Act. Other cases have reached similar conclusions when charcoal briquettes asphyxiated a child,[1] and when the poison thalium was marketed without a warning that there was no specific antidote, thus delaying the use of a stomach pump on a young child who had swallowed it.[2] In both instances the statutory requirements concerning warnings had been met.

Non-compliance with regulatory and statutory standards

Non-compliance with standards produced by a body such as the British Standards Institute is broadly comparable to non-compliance with general industrial standards. The main difference is, that being written and formulated by experts, such standards are more precise and authoritative. Consequently, it is that much less likely that non-compliance will be seen as consistent with reasonable safety.[3]

Non-compliance with standards imposed by legislation is a different matter. It will frequently constitute a criminal offence, and there may also be a civil remedy for breach of the statutory duty or, as it is termed

---

[18] See *Qualcast (Wolverhampton), Ltd.* v. *Haynes*, [1959] A.C. 743, 756; [1959] 2 All E.R. 38, 43 *per* Lord Keith (employers' duty to provide safe system of work).

[19] See, e.g., *Bux* v. *Slough Metals, Ltd.*, [1974] 1 All E.R. 262, 267–268, C.A. (compliance with Non-Ferrous Metals Regulations, but not with duty to provide safe system of work); *Franklin* v. *Gramophone Co., Ltd.*, [1948] 1 K.B. 542; [1948] 1 All E.R. 353 C.A. See also *Wintle* v. *Bristol Tramways and Carriage Co.* (1917), 86 L.J.K.B. 240, 936 (light locomotive).

[20] 484 F. 2d 1025 (1st Cir., 1973).

[1] *Hill* v. *Husky Briquetting Inc.*, 220 N.W. 2d 137 (Mich., 1974).

[2] *Rumsey* v. *Freeway Manor Minimax*, 423 S.W. 2d 387 (Tex. Civ. App., 1968). See also *Blasing* v. *Hardenberg Co.*, 226 N.W. 2d 110 (Minn., 1975); *Salmon* v. *Parke-Davis & Co.*, 520 F. 2d 1359 (4th Cir., 1975); 1 *Frumer and Friedman*, s. 8.07[1]; 3 *Frumer and Friedman*, s. 29.02[4].

[3] The Health and Safety at Work Act 1974, s. 17(2) goes somewhat further. Failure to observe a code of practice approved by the Health and Safety Commission is to be taken as indicative of a contravention of matters to which the code is relevant unless the court is satisfied that the defendant complied otherwise than by observing the provision of the code.

in some jurisdictions, in respect of negligence *per se*. In some statutes the position with respect to civil remedies is stated clearly.[4] Where it is not, one is called on to discover the legislative intent both as to the existence of the remedy and as to the types of damage or loss covered.[5]

In the United States of America the doctrine of negligence *per se* has been applied across a wide spectrum of product liability cases, thus holding that failure to comply with statutory standards is conclusive on issues of reasonable safety.[6] This position has been adopted when, for example, the marketing of a surgical nail failed to comply with regulations imposed by the federal Food, Drugs and Cosmetic Act,[7] when a defoliant did not meet the requirements of the Insecticide, Fungicide and Rodenticide Act,[8] and in a case in which a deodorant did not comply with regulations imposed by the Hazardous Substances Act.[9] English courts have generally been willing to interpret breaches of safety measures in industrial legislation as conferring a right of action on an employee suing his employer.[10] The same willingness has not, however, been shown in areas more closely associated with product liability, as when unsuccessful actions for breach of statutory duty were brought against suppliers of contaminated milk[11]

---

[4] See, e.g., the Health and Safety at Work Act 1974, s. 47 (1) (*a*); (no civil liability for breach of the duties imposed by ss. 2–8 of the Act); Consumer Protection Act 1961, s. 3 (1) (civil liability imposed): see below, p. 268.

[5] See Glanville Williams, "The Effect of Penal Legislation in the Law of Tort" (1960), 23 M.L.R. 233.

[6] See 1 *Frumer and Friedman*, s. 8.07 [1]; Ballway "Products Liability Based upon Violation of Statutory Standards", 64 Mich. L.R. 1388 (1966). For discussion of the position in Canada, see Waddams, *op. cit.*, pp. 102–112; Linden, *Studies in Canadian Tort Law*, ch. 10, pp. 237–240.

[7] *Orthopedic Equipment Co.* v. *Eutsler*, 276 F. 2d 455 (4th Cir., 1960). See also *Gober* v. *Revlon Inc.*, 317 F. 2d 47 (4th Cir., 1963) (nail polish). For the Act, see 21 U.S.C.A., ss. 301–392.

[8] *Gonzalez* v. *Virginia-Carolina Chemical Co.*, 239 F. Supp. 567 (1965). See also *McClanahan* v. *California Spray-Chemical Corporation*, 75 S.E. 2d 712 (Va., 1953) above, p. 235. For the Act, see 7 U.S.C.A., s. 135 *et seq.*

[9] *Cross* v. *Board of Supervisors of San Mateo County*, 326 F. Supp. 634, affd. 442 F. 2d 362 (1968). For the Act, see 15 U.S.C.A., ss. 1261–1274. For further examples of statutory provisions, see the National Traffic and Motor Vehicle Safety Act, 15 U.S.C.A., s. 1381 *et seq.*; Poison Prevention Packaging Act, 15 U.S.C.A., s. 1471 *et seq.*; Flammable Fabrics Act, 15 U.S.C.A. s. 1191 *et seq.* The Consumer Product Safety Commission established under the Consumer Product Safety Act of 1972 has a general mandate to promulgate safety standards where these are "reasonably necessary to prevent or reduce an unreasonable risk of injury".

[10] See, e.g., *Groves* v. *Wimborne*, [1898] 2 Q.B. 402; Williams (1960) 23 M.L.R. 233, 233–244.

[11] *Square* v. *Model Farm Dairy Co.*, [1939] 2 K.B. 365; [1939] 1 All E.R. 259 C.A. The supply was an offence under the Food and Drugs Act 1938, s. 2. See now Food and Drugs Act 1955, s. 2(1). See also *Heimler* v. *Calvert Caterers, Ltd.* (1974), 49 D.L.R. (3d) 36, 42–43, and on appeal (1975), 56 D.L.R. (3d) 643 (Ont. C.A.). *Cf. Read* v. *Croydon Corporation*, [1938] 4 All E.R. 631 (water infected by typhoid: right of action conferred on ratepayer but not his family).

and against the commercial sellers of a car with defective brakes[12] and of factory machinery which was unfenced.[13] This reluctance is not altogether surprising. Liability for breach of statutory duties is typically strict and, as yet, English law has not followed the American path of awarding damages in the absence of fault.

In English law the most important source of statutory control aimed at ensuring consumer safety is the Consumer Protection Act 1961. By s. 1 (1) of the Act:

> "The Secretary of State may by regulations impose as respect any prescribed class of goods—
> (a) any such requirements, whether as to the composition or contents, design, construction, finish or packing of, or otherwise relating to, goods of that class or any component part thereof, as are in his opinion expedient to prevent or reduce risk of death or personal injury;
> (b) any such requirements for securing that goods of that class or any component part thereof are in the prescribed manner marked with or accompanied by any prescribed warnings or instructions, or any prescribed form of warnings or instructions, which in the opinion of the Secretary of State is or are expedient as aforesaid."

It is an offence to sell in the course of a business or to possess for the purpose of sale goods which do not conform to such regulations.[14] Moreover, breach of a regulation is also actionable at the suit of any person "who may be affected by the contravention of or non-compliance with the requirement in question".[15]

---

[12] *Badham* v. *Lambs, Ltd.*, [1946] K.B. 45; [1945] 2 All E.R. 295—an offence under the Road Traffic Act 1934, s. 8 (1); see now Road Traffic Act 1972, s. 60. See also *Phillips* v. *Britannia Hygienic Laundry Co.*, [1923] 2 K.B. 832, C.A. (lorry operated in breach of Motor Cars (Use and Construction) Order: no action at suit of owner of vehicle into which it collided). *Cf. Monk* v. *Warbey*, [1935] 1 K.B. 75 (permitting use of uninsured car: successful action by injured party against owner).

[13] *Biddle* v. *Truvox Engineering Co.*, [1952] 1 K.B. 101; [1951] 2 All E.R. 835—an offence under the Factories Act 1937, s. 17; see now Factories Act 1961, s. 17.

[14] Section 2 (1). Such a sale may be by a manufacturer importer or wholesaler as well as a retailer. By s. 2 (6) the regulation may cover goods supplied under a hire-purchase or hire agreement. The Act does not cover private transactions nor, *semble*, goods sold at jumble sales, sales of work and the like, and goods supplied without payment, e.g., in return for trading stamps or as prizes in competitions: see *Consumer Safety: a consultative document*, Cmnd. 6398, February 1976, paras. 74–75.

[15] Section 3 (1). *Quaere* whether being "affected" by the contravention includes purely economic loss. The point could be important when, e.g., a retailer discovers that goods cannot be resold because they do not comply with a regulation. For further examples of statutes which provide specifically for a civil remedy see the Deposit of Poisonous Waste Act 1972, s. 2; Nuclear Installations Act 1965, s. 12, amending the Nuclear Installations (Licensing and Insurance) Act 1959. For an example of an express provision in the contrary sense see the Health and Safety at Work Act 1974, s. 47 (1) (a). See also the Trade Descriptions Act 1968, s. 35.

According to a recent consultative document on Consumer Safety issued by the Secretary of State for Prices and Consumer Protection:[16]

"In the past, it has been the practice to rely to a considerable extent on voluntary compliance by the trade with British Standards and with Government safety recommendations. Generally, regulations were made only where other means were unlikely to be effective, for example to guard against hazards from imported goods, although manufacturers who comply with British Standards and safety recommendations often welcome recommendations as they afford a safeguard against unfair competition from traders who do not conform to such standards. Relatively few regulations have consequently been made under the Consumer Protection Act . . . ."

Regulations are currently in force governing the following goods: oil heaters, stands for carry-cots, nightdresses, colour codes on electrical appliances, electric blankets, cooking utensils, fireguards on heating appliances, pencils and graphic instruments, toys, glazed ceramic ware, electrical equipment and hood cords on children's clothing.[17]

The 1961 Act is being used more frequently than in the past, but the regulations are still piecemeal in their coverage. For example, a child's nightdress must meet the British Standard Specification for materials of low flammability,[18] but there is no equivalent provision for clothing such as an anorak.[19] Moreover, as the consultative document notes, the Act has serious gaps as an instrument for promoting consumer safety. The formulation of new regulations and standards is a lengthy process which is not apt to deal with latent hazards as they come to light. There is no power to ban outright the sale of dangerous goods nor to require that steps be taken to seize and destroy them. The purpose of the document is to invite comment on whether further powers are necessary and, if so,

---

[16] Cmnd. 6398, February 1976, para. 29.

[17] For the relevant regulations see Oil Heaters, S.I. 1962 No. 884, as amended by S.I. 1966 No. 588; Stands for Carry Cots (Safety), S.I. 1966 No. 1610; Nightdresses (Safety), S.I. 1967 No. 839; Electrical Appliances (Colour Code), S.I. 1969 No. 310; Electrical Appliances (Colour Code) (Amendment), S.I. 1970 No. 811; Electric Blankets (Safety), S.I. 1971 No. 1961; Cooking Utensils (Safety), S.I. 1972 No. 1957; Heating Appliances (Fireguards), S.I. 1973 No. 2106; Pencils and Graphic Instruments (Safety), S.I. 1974 No. 226; Toys (Safety), S.I. 1974 No. 1367; Glazed Ceramic Ware (Safety), S.I. 1975 No. 1241; Electrical Equipment (Safety), S.I. 1975 No. 1366; Children's Clothing (Hood Cords), S.I. 1976 No. 2; Vitreous Enamelware (Safety), S.I. 1976 No. 454. Further regulations are in preparation to cover per-ambulators and pushchairs and oil heaters (revised regulations to amend and replace regulations of 1962 and 1966). Regulations are under consideration to cover aerosols, dummies, lawn mowers, domestic oil lamps and cosmetics.

[18] See the Nightdresses (Safety) Regulations, S.I. 1967 No. 839, reg. 1.

[19] An item of clothing which had caused extensive third-degree burns in *Lagorga* v. *Kroger Co.*, 275 F. Supp. 373 (1967), above, p. 212.

the form which they should take.[20] Meanwhile the trend towards official intervention is further evidenced by the publication of draft regulations providing for the statutory labelling of some eight hundred dangerous chemicals.[21]

The legislative and judicial roles in promoting safer products

The above discussion prompts the more general question as to the proper division of functions between the legislature and the judiciary in promoting safer products. Here there is no doubt that American judges have adopted a much more active role that their English and Commonwealth counterparts. This is evident both in the widespread imposition of strict liability and, perhaps more significantly, in their willingness to question a manufacturer's design choice and to hold it unreasonably dangerous.

There is little point in asking whether it is part of the proper function of the English judiciary to follow the American example of imposing strict liability on manufacturers and others. The basis of liability is currently under discussion by both a Royal Commission and the Law Commission[1] and any foreseeable change will come through Parliament rather than the courts. Assuming the continuation of the present adversary system, it is, however, relevant to ask to what extent it should fall to the judiciary to determine standards of reasonable product safety. The question is one on which generalisations are difficult. No one would maintain that the area should be reserved to regulations made by or under the authority of Parliament. Yet, equally, it cannot be denied that judicial activity in the area of product design is capable of having profound repercussions.[2]

The basic difficulty can be seen in the American motor vehicle and power-mower cases which were discussed in an earlier chapter.[3] Any decision holding such a product to be unreasonably dangerous as designed will inevitably be seen as a test case. By definition, it is not a "one-off" problem. All products of that model will share the same characteristic. Consequently, there is every chance that there will be a substantial number of claims by persons injured in similar circumstances. Moreover, it would be by no means surprising if different judges reached different con-

---

[20] The deficiencies in the present system are set out in paras. 39–46 of the document and possible remedies are canvassed in paras. 47–106.
[21] See *The Times* (1976), 6 July.
[1] See above, pp. 2–3.
[2] See Henderson, "Judicial Review of Manufacturers' Conscious Design Choices: the limits of adjudication", 73 Col. Law Rev. 1531 (1973); Holford, "The Limits of Strict Liability for Product Design and Manufacture", 52 Tex. L.R. 81 (1973).
[3] See above, pp. 222–227.

clusions on the issue of reasonable safety.[4] To the extent that a consistent view emerges, the manufacturer may feel that it is incumbent on him to change the design of the product. If the danger can be removed by a fuller warning this may not be a major operation. In areas such as vehicle design, however, the task would be formidable. This is obviously an argument in favour of control through measures such as the Motor Vehicles Construction and Use Regulations.[5] It is not unreasonable for a manufacturer to take the view that compliance with highly detailed regulations such as these should be conclusive on issues of reasonable safety. A similar view might be taken with certain high risk products such as drugs and aircraft which cannot be marketed without obtaining a product licence or satisfying a certification procedure. With such products adequate insurance cover may be virtually unobtainable. If strict liability were to be introduced in English law there would be a strong case for channelling it to the testing agency rather than the manufacturer.[6]

As an illustration of the differences between the regulatory approach and control through the courts one may take the problem of medicine containers and child safety. Following recommendations in a report from the Medicines Commission on the Presentation of Medical Products in relation to Child Safety, the Department of Health and Social Services undertook to introduce measures to safeguard children against the risk of accidental poisoning from medicines.[7] It was recognised, however, that such measures could not be introduced from one day to the next. The necessary packing machinery to produce dark tinted reclosable child-resistant containers had to be obtained from abroad. Further time had to be allowed to enable it to be installed without undue interruption to output. Hence it was planned to phase in the regulations over a period of years. In late 1975 regulations were made under the Medicines Act 1968 to cover preparations of aspirin and paracetamol for children.[8] It is proposed to regulate the packaging of all tablets, capsules and pills containing aspirin and paracetamol by January 1977 and then to cover tricyclic anti-depressant drugs, barbiturates and phenothiazine derivatives as early as possible thereafter. The practical difficulties involved in introducing such measures are no doubt paralleled in the case of household cleaning products. They are not a reason for denying recovery to children who are killed or injured before the measures are implemented.

---

[4] As occurred, e.g., in the English contributory negligence seat-belt cases before *Froom* v. *Butcher*, [1976] Q.B. 286; [1975] 3 All E.R. 520, C.A.

[5] See S.I. 1973 No. 24.

[6] For the possible liability of testing agencies, see below, p. 316.

[7] See Hansard, H.C. Debs. Vol. 890, Cols. 325–328, 23 April 1975, W.A.

[8] The Medicines (Child Safety) Regulations, S.I. 1975 No. 2000, made under the Medicines Act 1968, ss. 87 (1), 88 (1) (2), 91 (2).

Indeed litigation may provide the spur to action which was otherwise lacking. There are, however, limits to what can be achieved through the judicial process if the object is to promote safer products and not simply to compensate the individual.

14 The Manufacturers' Liability: Proof of Negligence, Causation and Defences: II

Causation[1]

Proof of the association of the product with the damage

The plaintiff in a product liability case must prove on the balance of probabilities that the defendant's product caused or enhanced the damage which is the subject of the claim. This is so whether the claim is in contract or in tort and whether liability is strict or dependent on proof of negligence. Frequently the task will not be an onerous one. There may, for example, be direct evidence that a bottle has exploded: a stopper has ejected, injuring the plaintiff;[2] a chisel or grinding wheel has shattered;[3] or that a crane sling has failed, dropping its load.[4] In such cases the association of the product with the damage will readily be established, although there may be room for argument over responsibility for the defective condition. In other cases the association may be more difficult to establish.

---

[1] See 1 *Frumer and Friedman*, s. 11; Prosser, *Torts*, 4th edn., 1971, p. 671 *et seq*: 2 Harper and James, *Torts*, s. 28.12; Noel, "Manufacturer's Negligence of Design or Directions for Use of a Product", 71 Yale L.J. 816, 866–872 (1962); Keeton, "Products Liability: problems of proof", 19 Sw. L.J. 26, 33–34 (1965); Keeton, "Products Liability: proof of the Manufacturers' negligence", 49 Virginia L.R. 675, 678–679 (1963).

[2] *O'Dwyer* v. *Leo Buring Pty., Ltd.*, [1966] W.A.R. 67 (W.A. Sup. Ct.).

[3] *Taylor* v. *Rover Co., Ltd.*, [1966] 2 All E.R. 181; *Griffiths* v. *Arch Engineering Co., Ltd.*, [1968] 3 All E.R. 217.

[4] *Dooley* v. *Cammell Laird & Co., Ltd.*, [1951] 1 Lloyd's Rep. 271.

For example, any evidence as to the origins of a fire, explosion or physical injury may be purely circumstantial and may not permit of the inference that it was the defendant's product.[5] Difficulties are likely to arise also where it is sought to link a particular medical condition or outbreak of disease in animals or crops to a given product, drug or feeding stuff. The mere fact that the condition followed use of the product or drug will not generally be sufficient since *non constat* that an extraneous source was not responsible. A protracted medical or scientific inquiry into the incidence and common denominators of sufferers may be required to establish the link.[6]

Grant v. Australian Knitting Mills, Ltd.[7] is again important in this context as illustrating the role of circumstantial evidence on the issue of causation in a product liability case. The appellant medical practitioner had un-doubtedly suffered from an extreme form of dermatitis and he had admittedly worn long woollen "Golden Fleece" undergarments manu-factured by the defendants. But his claim could of course succeed only if he were able to establish that the dermatitis had been caused by wearing the undergarments. Once they had been washed it was impossible to prove by direct evidence that they had contained an excessive amount of free sulphites as alleged. Indeed the manufacturers contended that the dermatitis was internal in origin and of the herpetiformis type. In the result, however, the Privy Council was satisfied (reversing a majority judgment of the High Court of Australia) that there was sufficient circum-

---

[5] Examples of cases in which the circumstantial evidence was strong enough to permit of such an inference include *Vacwell Engineering Co., Ltd. v. B.D.H. Chemicals, Ltd.*, [1971] 1 Q.B. 88; [1969] 3 All E.R. 1681 (boron tribromide); *Lindroth v. Walgreen Co.*, 94 N.E. 2d 847 (Ill., 1950) (vaporiser catching fire); *Wojtowicz v. Sarno*, 195 N.E. 2d 218 (Ill. App., 1963) (oil burner). Contrasting cases include *Schwartz v. Macrosse Lumber and Trim Co.*, 248 N.E. 2d 920 (N.Y., 1969); *McBride v. Proctor and Gamble Manufacturing Co.*, 300 F. Supp. 1150 (Tenn., 1969). A comprehensive citation of American cases is to be found in 1 *Frumer and Friedman*, s. 11.01 [2].

[6] See, e.g., *Wright v. Dunlop Rubber Co., Ltd.* (1972), 13 K.I.R. 255 (cancer from industrial chemicals); *Ashington Piggeries, Ltd. v. Christopher Hill, Ltd.*, [1971] 2 A.C. 441; [1971] 1 All E.R. 847, H.L. (toxic substance in mink food); *McMillen Feeds Inc. v. Harlow*, 405 S.W. 2d 123 (Tex. Civ. App., 1966) (turkey feed); *Perry Creek Cranberry Corporation v. Hopkins Chemical Co.*, 139 N.W. 2d 96 (Wis., 1966) (crop dusting); *Smith v. Atco Co.*, 94 N.W. 2d 697 (Wis., 1958) (treatment for mink nesting boxes). Contrast *Scientific Supply Co. v. Zelinger*, 341 P. 2d 897 (Colo., 1959) (no evidence that insecticide caused inflammation of lungs); *Zampino v. Colgate Palmolive Co.*, 187 N.Y.S. 2d 25 (1959) (no evidence that use of deodorant caused skin complaint); *Elliott v. Lachane*, 256 A. 2d 153 (N. Hamp., 1969) (hair loss and use of shampoo). The problem of establishing a causative link has been especially acute in the American cigarette-cancer cases (discussed above, pp. 216–217): see Rossi, "The Cigarette-Cancer Problem" 34 Southern Calif. L.R. 399, 399–400 (1961).

[7] [1936] A.C. 85, P.C.

stantial evidence to warrant the upholding of the trial court's decision in the appellant's favour. As Lord Wright observed:[8]

"Mathematical, or strict logical, demonstration is generally impossible: juries are in practice told that they must act on such reasonable balance of probabilities as would suffice to determine a reasonable man to take a decision in the grave affairs of life. Pieces of evidence, each by itself insufficient, may together constitute a significant whole, and justify by their combined effect a conclusion."

He added with reference to the facts of the case that the coincidence of the time and place at which the infection originated with the wearing of the undergarments, and the absence of other likely explanations, pointed strongly in the appellant's favour. So also did the fact that some sulphites were admittedly present in the garment and there was nothing to exclude the possibility of there being an excessive amount.[9] Everything ultimately depended on the drawing of such inferences as were proper from the facts it had been possible to establish.

Proof of a defective condition

Assuming the association of the product with the damage, the plaintiff must also prove that it was defective or otherwise dangerous. Here the problems are likely to differ according to whether one is dealing with general deficiencies in design or inadequate warning, or with allegedly defective conditions in individual units. In the former case the nature and state of the product is normally readily ascertainable by reference to other units of the same model, or to its plans, specifications or ingredients. Inquiry is likely to concentrate on whether an objective test of reasonable safety has been met. As was noted earlier[10] this will depend on a balancing of the gravity of the risk with the benefit derived from the use of the product. Regard must also be had to the cost and practicability of reducing the risk and to the frequently conflicting demands of safety, durability, economy and style. The position with respect to matters such as the product's safety record and compliance with the standards of the industry and with regulatory requirements has already been examined.[11]

Proof of a miscarriage in the production process may raise different

---

[8] *Ibid.*, at p. 96.
[9] *Ibid.*
[10] See above, ch. 9, pp. 186–189.
[11] At pp. (260–264 (safety record); pp. 264–266 (industrial and regulatory standards).

issues. In many cases there will be direct evidence of the defective condition, be it a foreign object or impurity in food or drink,[12] weak or faulty materials,[13] or incorrect assembly or construction.[14] Sometimes the condition will be apparent to the untutored eye. In other cases the expert testimony of persons such as analysts, metallurgists, engineers or dermatologists will be needed.

Whilst such evidence is likely to be of great weight, its absence need not be fatal to the plaintiff's case. Just as circumstantial evidence may be sufficient to connect the product to the damage or injury,[15] so also may it be sufficient to establish that the product was defective. Whether this inference is permissible will depend entirely on the facts of the individual case. In some cases, the facts will be such as to point almost irresistibly to this conclusion. Thus whether or not *res ipsa loquitur* is technically applicable, a refrigerator door should not, for example, impart an electric shock,[16] and a bottle should not explode when handled properly.[17] In other cases, the facts may be equally consistent with negligence on the part of the user or operator as with the product having been produced defectively. A verdict against the manufacturer should then be set aside on appeal as being based on nothing more substantial than speculation or guesswork. The fact that a new car or aircraft has crashed does not, without more, suggest a defective condition as opposed to careless driving or piloting.[18] Frequently, however, there will be something in the sur-

---

[12] As in *Daniels and Daniels* v. *R. White & Sons, Ltd.*, [1938] 4 All E.R. 258 (carbolic acid in lemonade) and cases cited above, pp. 191–194. It seems that it was never established whether the famous snail was in the bottle in *Donoghue* v. *Stevenson*, [1932] A.C. 562, L.H.: *cf.* above, p. 173.

[13] As in *Dransfield* v. *British Insulated Cables, Ltd.*, [1937] 4 All E.R. 382 (bull ring forming part of a trolley system) and cases cited above, p. 195.

[14] As in *Dominion Natural Gas Co., Ltd.* v. *Collins and Perkins*, [1909] A.C. 640, P.C. (valve of boiler) and cases cited above, pp. 195–196.

[15] *Cf. Grant* v. *Australian Knitting Mills, Ltd.*, [1936] A.C. 85, P.C., above, p. 274.

[16] *Ryan* v. *Zweck-Wollenberg Co.*, 64 N.W. 2d 226 (Wis., 1954). And a television set should not catch fire: *Gast* v. *Sears Roebuck & Co.*, 313 N.E. 2d 831 (Ohio, 1974).

[17] *Zentz* v. *Coca Cola Bottling Co.*, 247 P. 2d 344 (Cal., 1952). See also *Lindroth* v. *Walgreen Co.*, 94 N.E. 2d 847 (Ill., 1950) (vaporiser catching fire); *Grinnell* v. *Charles Pfizer & Co.*, 79 Cal. Rptr. 369 (Cal. App., 1969) (polio vaccine inducing polio); *Culpepper* v. *Volkswagen of America Inc.*, 109 Cal. Rptr. 110 (Cal. App., 1973) (car rolling over on 18° turn at 50 m.p.h.). Comprehensive citation of American cases is to be found in 1 *Frumer and Friedman*, s. 11.01 [3]; 2 *Harper and James*, 28.13; Annotation, "Proof of Defect" 51 A.L.R. 3d 8. The application of *res ipsa loquitur* is discussed above, pp. 257–258. Strictly speaking, *res ipsa* goes to the issue of negligence, rather than causation.

[18] See *Smith* v. *General Motors Corporation*, 227 F. 2d 210 (5th Cir., 1955); *Schramek* v. *General Motors Corporation*, 216 N.E. 2d 244 (Ill. App., 1966) (tyre blow out); *Hurley* v. *Beech Aircraft Corporation*, 355 F. 2d 517 (7th Cir., 1966); *Reidinger* v. *Trans World Airlines*, 329 F. Supp. 487 (Ky., 1971); *Lindsay* v. *McDonnell Douglas Aircraft Corporation*, 352 F. Supp. 633 (Mo., 1972), affd. 485 F. 2d 1288 (8th Cir., 1973).

rounding circumstances to tip the scale against the manufacturer; something to justify a verdict against him. Thus an eye-witness account of the accident,[19] evidence that the product was not functioning properly,[20] or evidence tending to eliminate other possible causes,[1] may all point to the concluson that the product was defective. So also may evidence of similar accidents, damage, or illness associated with the product, or the fact that persons in otherwise identical circumstances who did not use the product suffered no harm.[2]

Proof that the defective condition caused the damage

Where the evidence establishes that the product was defective or otherwise dangerous the plaintiff will still fail unless he can prove that this condition caused the damage. It need not of course be the sole cause. Indeed in many cases there will be joint or concurrent liability as between the supplier and operator or installer or some other responsible intermediary.[3] Similarly, the plaintiff's damages may be reduced on the ground of his own contributory negligence.[4] The defect must, however, be *a* cause of the damage if liability is to be sustained. This requirement would not be satisfied where the damage would have occurred even if the product had been constructed and designed safely. Defective brakes will not ground liability where the driver did not attempt to use them. The absence of a safety device or of warnings or directions for use is irrelevant unless the

---

[19] *Cf. Elmore* v. *American Motors Corporation*, 75 Cal. Rptr. 652 (Cal. Sup. Ct., 1969) (evidence of following driver that drive shaft disconnected immediately before crash). See also *Mamula* v. *Ford Motor Co.*, 275 N.E. 2d 849 (Ill. App., 1971) (tie rod found 40 yards behind car).

[20] As in *Henningsen* v. *Bloomfield Motors Inc.*, 161 A. 2d 69 (N.J., 1960) (evidence by driver that failure of car steering was preceded by loud crack). See also *Bollmeier* v. *Ford Motor Co.*, 265 N.E. 2d 212 (Ill. App., 1970) (car steering); *Ettin* v. *Ava Truck Leasing Co.*, 251 A. 2d 278 (N.J., 1969) (brakes); *McCann* v. *Atlas Supply Co.*, 325 F. Supp. 701 (Pa., 1971) (tyre); *Kuisis* v. *Baldwin Lima Hamilton Corporation*, 301 A. 2d 911 (Pa., 1973).

[1] *Brownell* v. *White Motor Corporation*, 490 P. 2d 184 (Ore., 1971) (negligence of lorry driver); *Bailey* v. *Montgomery Ward & Co.*, 431 P. 2d 108 (Ariz., 1967) (use of pogo stick). See also *Jakubowski* v. *Minneapolis Mining Co.*, 199 A. 2d 826, 830 (N.J., 1964); *Vandermark* v. *Ford Motor Co.*, 37 Cal. Rptr. 896 (Cal., 1964).

[2] See, e.g., *Carter* v. *Joseph Bancroft & Sons Co.*, 360 F. Supp. 1103 (Pa. 1973) (dress worn by plaintiff the only one to go up in flames). The relevance of the product's safety record is discussed further, above, pp. 260–264.

[3] See, e.g., *Dooley* v. *Cammell Laird & Co., Ltd.*, [1951] 1 Lloyd's Rep. 271 (supplier and employer); *Griffiths* v. *Arch Engineering Co., Ltd.*, [1968] 3 All E.R. 217 (supplier and employer); *Post* v. *Manitowoc Engineering Corporation*, 211 A. 2d 386 (N.J., 1965) (manufacturer and operator). See also 1 *Frumer and Friedman*, s. 11.04[4].

[4] See further below, pp. 293–296.

device would have prevented the accident or the warnings would have been heeded.[5]

Furthermore, the condition must be shown to be related causally to the damage in some meaningful sense. A potential for harm may be activated in the most unlikely way and the repercussions of any given accident may be endless. The consequent need for a cut-off point is familiar to tort lawyers and a variety of expressions is available. It may be said, for example, that the damage was "unforeseeable", insufficiently "proximate", too "remote" or not within the risk created by the defective or unreasonably dangerous condition. Subject to the special problems associated with knowledge of the defect and opportunities for intermediate examination,[6] the normal rules for a negligence action apply.[7] Accordingly, damage to the plaintiff's interests of the type or kind which occurred must have been foreseeable and it must have materialised in a way which was foreseeable or a variant of the foreseeable.[8] Where the product has been put to a wholly abnormal use this requirement may not be met.[9] Beyond this, two typically colourful American cases will serve as examples. In one case,[10] the plaintiff had suffered a heart attack allegedly as a result of seeing rusty brownish water coming from a tap when she had drunk coffee made from the same source. The Supreme Court of New Jersey held that even if a water softener manufactured and supplied by the defendants were defective and this had caused the discolouration, a heart attack was not, as a matter of law, a foreseeable or proximate consequence of its supply. In another case[11] it was similarly ruled that the serving of unwholesome food to A was not a proximate cause of injury suffered by the plaintiff who had slipped on A's vomit at a washroom entrance.

---

[5] American cases in point include *Cunningham* v. *Charles Pfizer & Co.*, 532 P. 2d 1377 (Okla., 1975); *Ellis* v. *Finke, Inc.*, 278 F. 2d 54 (6th Cir., 1960); *Love* v. *Wolf*, 38 Cal. Rptr. 183 (1964); *Mathews* v. *Clairol Inc.*, 371 F. 2d 337 (3rd Cir., 1967). See also *Charles Pfizer & Co.* v. *Branch*, 365 S.W. 2d 832, 834 (Tex. Civ. App., 1963) discussed by Keeton in 19 Sw. L.J. 26, 34 (1965); *Braun* v. *Roux Distribution Co.*, 312 S.W. 2d 758 (Mo., 1958) discussed by Keeton in 49 Virginia L.R. 675, 678–679 (1963); *Barnett* v. *Chelsea and Kensington Hospital Management Committee*, [1969] 1 Q.B. 428; [1968] 1 All E.R. 1068 provides a modern English example from outside the field of product liability. See also Hart and Honore, *Causation in the Law* (1959), ch. 5.

[6] See further below, pp. 292–293 (knowledge of defect); pp. 284–290 (intermediate examination).

[7] *Cf. Vacwell Engineering Co., Ltd.* v. *B.D.H. Chemicals, Ltd.*, [1971] 1 Q.B. 88; [1969] 3 All E.R. 1681, and above, pp. 178–180.

[8] See, in general, *Overseas Tankship (U.K.), Ltd.* v. *Morts Dock and Engineering Co., Ltd.*, *The Wagon Mound* [1961] A.C. 388; [1961] 1 All E.R. 404, P.C.; *Hughes* v. *Lord Advocate*, [1963] A.C. 837; [1963] 1 All E.R. 705, H.L.

[9] See further below, pp. 294–296.

[10] *Caputzal* v. *Lindsay Co.*, 222 A. 2d 513 (N.J., 1966).

[11] *Crankshaw* v. *Piedmont Driving Club Inc.*, 156 S.E. 2d 208 (Ga. App., 1967).

The position may be somewhat different under a régime which imposes strict product liability. Issues of due care and foreseeability would then be irrelevant though the plaintiff would nonetheless be required to establish that the damage was suffered as a natural consequence of the defective condition in which the product was marketed.[12]

Tracing the defective condition to the manufacturer[13]

Related problems arise through the need to trace the defective condition to the manufacturer or to a person for whose acts the manufacturer is responsible.[14] The product must be shown to be defective from the time it left the manufacturer's control. Thus liability will not normally be incurred where the danger stems from subsequent unauthorised modification to or tampering with the product,[15] or from repair or misuse.[16] So much was implicit in Lord Atkin's statement in *Donoghue* v. *Stevenson*,[17] envisaging that the product should reach the ultimate consumer in substantially the same form as it left the manufacturer. There is, however, some American authority for the view that changes or modifications designed to correct an existing defect will not relieve the manufacturer from responsibility.[18]

Again it is important to remember that many products, including food, are perishable and an impurity may have developed solely as a result of unsuitable storage by an intermediate wholesaler or retailer. Most products, including the vast majority of consumer durables, are understood to have a strictly limited lifespan so that there comes a point when the developing condition is readily attributable to lack of repair or servicing, or simply old age. Wood rots and metal corrodes even though plastic may be virtually

---

[12] The distinction was taken in *Berkebile* v. *Brantly Helicopter Corporation*, 337 A. 2d 893 (Pa., 1975). See also Hart and Honore, *Causation in the Law* (1959), p. 256 *et seq.*, Winfield and Jolowicz, *Tort*, 10th edn., 1975, p. 379 and cases there cited.

[13] See 1 *Frumer and Friedman*, s. 11.01[4]; 2 *Harper and James*, s. 28.14; *Prosser*, pp. 674–675; Annotation, "Proof that Defect was Present when Product Left Hands of Defendant", 54 A.L.R. 3d 1079.

[14] The scope of the manufacturers' responsibility for the condition of components and for processing etc., is discussed above, pp. 199–207. The manufacturers' responsibility for intermediate examination by dealers and others is discussed below, pp. 284–290. The liability of persons other than manufacturers is discussed in ch. 15, below.

[15] See, e.g., *Tucson General Hospital* v. *Russell*, 437 P. 2d 677 (Ariz., 1968) (X-ray machine): *Putensen* v. *Clay Adams Inc.*, 91 Cal. Rptr. 319 (Cal. App., 1970) (tubing used as catheter in heart surgery); *Humble Oil and Refining Co.* v. *Whitten*, 427 S.W. 2d 313 (Tex., 1968).

[16] Misuse is discussed below, pp. 294–296.

[17] [1932] A.C. 562, 599, H.L.

[18] *Cf. Greco* v. *Bucciconi Engineering Co.*, 407 F. 2d 87 (3rd Cir., 1969) and cases noted in 54 A.L.R. 3d 1079, 1092. See also *Guffie* v. *Erie Streyer Co.*, 350 F. 2d 378 (3rd Cir., 1965).

indestructible. Food is frequently date-stamped, and cars require an annual test three years after the initial registration. The process is accentuated by what is disparagingly termed the "disposable society". As has been frequently pointed out in American cases, there is no duty to furnish a product which will not wear out.[19] On the other hand, deterioration through lapse of time and long use is not always to be expected, especially when one is dealing with static as opposed to moving parts,[20] and regard must be had to the expectations of the normal user. Good wine is not bottled for immediate consumption. The protecting knob on the top of a gear lever should last for the life of the car even if the gear box does not.[1] A weld may be expected to remain intact for as long as the surrounding metal.[2]

Subject to this need to take proper account of the possibility of tampering and of wear and tear, dangers associated with the product's design, specifications or ingredients can be traced readily to the manufacturer since they will have been built into the product as conceived. The same is true of dangers associated with inadequate warning. However, when the concern is with possible miscarriages in the production process, one has the additional possibility that the defective condition may have been brought about by the intervening act of a third party. As was noted when discussing proof of negligence, this is admittedly unlikely when foreign objects are found in tins, corked, capped or even screwtop containers.[3] The same may be true of defects within mechanical units protected by external metal casing[4] or in products which have remained in a sealed container or even in cardboard or cellophane wrapping. Yet even in an apparently clear case the position may not be so straightforward. The child may have had the piece of wire in its mouth when

---

[19] *Cf. Triplett* v. *American Creosote Works Inc.*, 171 So. 2d 342 (Miss., 1965); *Gomez* v. *E.W. Bliss Co.*, 211 N.Y.S. 2d 246 (1961), and cases cited in 1 *Frumer and Friedman*, s. 11.03, note 1; *Prosser*, p. 674, note 19.

[20] *Cf. Darling* v. *Caterpillar Tractor Co.*, 341 P. 2d 23 (Cal., 1959); *Beadles* v. *Servel Inc.*, 100 N.E. 2d 405, 411–412 (Ill., 1951); and cases cited in *Prosser*, p. 674, note 20.

[1] *Mickle* v. *Blackmon*, 166 S.E. 2d 173 (S.C., 1969) discussed above, p. 211.

[2] *Cf. Pryor* v. *Lee C. Moore Corporation*, 262 F. 2d 673 (10th Cir., 1959) (derrick collapsing at point of weld after fifteen years). For general discussion of the effect of lapse of time, see 1 *Frumer and Friedman*, s. 11.03; Keeton, 49 Virginia L.R. 675, 687–689; 54 A.L.R. 3d 1079, s. 2[b]. See also *Balido* v. *Improved Machinery Inc.*, 105 Cal. Rptr. 890 (Cal. App., 1973).

[3] See, e.g., *Lockhart* v. *Barr*, 1943 S.C. (H.L.) 1; *Zeppa* v. *Coca Cola, Ltd.*, [1955] 5 D.L.R. 187 (Ont. C.A.), and above, p. 258. American cases are noted in 2 *Harper and James*, s. 28.14, notes 5–10; 52 A.L.R. 2d 117 (bottled or canned beverage); 52 A.L.R. 2d 159 (food in can or other sealed container). *Dryden* v. *Continental Baking Co.*, 77 P. 2d 833 (Cal., 1938) (glass in bread) is a leading example.

[4] *Cf. Northern* v. *General Motors Corporation*, 268 P. 2d 987 (Utah, 1954); *Deveney* v. *Rheem Manufacturing Co.*, 319 F. 2d 124 (2nd Cir., 1963); and cases cited in 54 A.L.R. 3d 1079, s. 2[d].

it bit into the ice cream;[5] the housewife may have broken a jar and mixe[d] the glass inadvertently into the contents of the tin; and (if a personal recollection is permitted) the fly may have got into the wine bottle after the cork was drawn and is substantially certain to have done so if it is still alive and kicking. In other cases the defective condition may have been brought about by careless handling on the part of an intermediary, poor storage or incorrect installation.

Considerations such as these have influenced decisions in a number of English cases. *Evans* v. *Triplex Safety Glass Co., Ltd.*[6] is illustrative. Here a Triplex Toughened Safety Glass windscreen had been fitted to a Vauxhall car which was subsequently bought by the plaintiff from an intermediate dealer. Some thirteen months later, the windscreen shattered without any immediately obvious cause with resultant injury. Rejecting a claim against the manufacturer of the windscreen, Porter, J. held that, having regard to the lapse of time, opportunities for intermediate examination and the possibility of faulty fitting by the Vauxhall Motor Company, he was not satisfied that the glass was manufactured improperly or of an unsuitable type and that this had caused the injury. By way of contrast the claim succeeded in *Stennett* v. *Hancock and Peters*[7] where a flange came off the wheel of a lorry an hour or so after the wheel had been repaired and reassembled by the defendant garage. The same was true in *Herschthal* v. *Stewart and Ardern, Ltd.*,[8] where a wheel came off a car the morning after it had been delivered and there was nothing to suggest that there had been any intervening tampering. In a recent American case, a Washington appeal court held that once the plaintiff has proved a defect the onus is on the defendant manufacturer to prove that it was not present in the product from the time it left his control.[9] General adoption of this approach would assist the plaintiff's case to a marked degree. Indeed there is little doubt that a reversal of the onus of proof on this issue would be of more practical benefit than a reversal on the issue of negligence.[10]

---

[5] *Ewing* v. *Von Allmen Dairy Co.*, 264 S.W. 2d 862 (Ky., 1954).

[6] [1936] 1 All E.R. 283.

[7] [1939] 2 All E.R. 578.

[8] [1940] 1 K.B. 155; [1939] 4 All E.R. 123. See also *Malfroot* v. *Noxal, Ltd.* (1935), 51 T.L.R. 551.

[9] *Curtiss* v. *Young Men's Christian Association*, 499 P. 2d 915 (Wash. App., 1972), affd. 511 P. 2d 991 (1973).

[10] Article 5 of the proposed EEC directive provides that "The producer shall not be liable if he proves that [the article] was not defective when he put it into circulation". Under art. 5 (1)(*b*) of the Strasbourg Convention a producer is not liable if he proves, "that, having regard to the circumstances, it is probable that the defect which caused the damage did not exist at the time when the product was put into circulation by him or that this defect came into being afterwards". Under both the draft directive and the Convention the onus of proof is accordingly on the producer rather than the plaintiff.

Proving that the defendant is the manufacturer

Even where it is clear that the product was defective or unreasonably dangerous when manufactured, it remains to identify the defendant as its manufacturer. Generally, this will be little more than a formality, since it will be possible to trace back through the chain of distribution with the aid of purchase orders and invoices or to compare the product with other products known to have been manufactured by the defendant. Reference to labels on the product or on accompanying wrappers or containers may also assist. Manufacturers typically do not miss such opportunities for advertising, however much they may economise on warnings and directions for use. In English law, Part I of the Civil Evidence Act 1968 is important in this context as removing hearsay problems which might otherwise have existed. American case law indicates, however, that practical problems may occur, notably with components and products which do not lend themselves to the carrying of labels.

Schmidt v. *Archer Iron Works Inc.*[11] is a representative decision. The plaintiff was suing in respect of personal injuries received when an "eye pin"; which had been welded defectively, broke, causing a tubular concrete pouring tower to collapse. The narrow issue raised before the Supreme Court of Illinois was whether there was sufficient evidence to permit a finding that the defendants had manufactured the pin. They testified that they were not the manufacturers and maintained that the pin was unlike any they had ever produced. An order for the pouring tower and certain accessories had admittedly been placed with them by a construction equipment dealer who was acting for the bridge construction company which later sold the tower to the plaintiff's employer. But the dealer might have procured the pin and the boom spout bridle in which it was incorporated from another source. Matters were hardly advanced by the fact that it was painted a rust colour similar to that of the tower since other manufacturers painted their products with a protective rust-coloured coating. In the result the Supreme Court held that there was insufficient evidence on which to base a finding that the defendants had manufactured the offending pin.[12]

The proposed EEC directive on product liability contains a useful provision which is intended to deal with such problems.[13] By art. 2 of the proposed directive.

---

[11] 256 N.E. 2d 6 (1970), cert. denied 398 U.S. 959.

[12] For further cases and discussion, see 1 *Frumer and Friedman*, s. 11.01 [4], note 16; 51 A.L.R. 3d 1344; *Picker X-Ray Corporation* v. *Frerker*, 405 F. 2d 916 (8th Cir., 1969) (guide wire used with catheter); *O'Donnell* v. *Geneva Metal Wheel Co.*, 183 F. 2d 733 (6th Cir., 1950) (inflatable wheelbarrow wheel); *McDonough* v. *General Motors Corporation*, 148 N.W. 2d 911 (Mich. App., 1967) (derrick); *Hardware Co.* v. *Chrysler Corporation*, 142 N.W. 2d 728 (Minn., 1966) (car part); *Smith* v. *J.C. Penney Co. Inc.*, 525 P. 2d 1301 (Ore., 1974).

[13] See also art. 3(3) of the Strasbourg Convention on Products Liability.

"Where the producer of the article cannot be identified, each supplier of the article shall be treated as its producer unless he informs the injured person, within a reasonable time, of the identity of the producer or of the person who supplied him with the article."

Supervening cause

Although the product is defective as marketed, the manufacturer may yet escape liability if the subsequent conduct of an intermediary[14] is so grossly careless as to be regarded as the sole effective cause of the damage. *Taylor v. Rover Co., Ltd.*[15] is illustrative. Here a foreman knew of the dangerous state of a chisel but he failed to withdraw it. It later splintered, injuring the plaintiff. Baker, J. held that even if the defendant manufacturers were responsible for the state of the chisel,[16] the foreman's subsequent conduct was the sole effective cause of the injury. Similarly in a leading Australian case,[17] Barwick, C.J. was of the opinion that a contractor's negligence in working with a naked flame near an adhesive which he knew to be highly inflammable superseded any possible inadequacy of warning on the part of the manufacturer.

Ford Motor Co. v. Wagoner[18] is perhaps the best-known American case to make the same point. The defendants were held to be entitled to a directed verdict when the initial purchaser of a car declined their offer to replace a defective hood latch free of charge. The plaintiff was injured when the hood flew up, causing the car to crash as he was travelling in it as a guest of the second purchaser. In other cases the supplier has been absolved through the intervening knowledge and conduct of persons such as owners of defective escalators,[19] employers,[20] processors of animal food,[1] parents[2]

---

[14] Intervening conduct of the plaintiff is discussed below, at p. 291 *et seq.*

[15] [1966] 2 All E.R. 181; [1966] 1 W.L.R. 1491.

[16] See further above, pp. 199–207 for a discussion of the responsibility of the manufacturer for processing, etc.

[17] *Norton Australia Pty., Ltd. v. Streets Ice Cream Pty., Ltd.* (1968), 120 C.L.R. 635, 647–649 (High Ct. of Australia), above, p. 231.

[18] 192 S.W. 2d 840 (Tenn., 1946).

[19] *Drazen v. Otis Elevator Co.*, 189 A 2d 693 (R.I., 1963).

[20] *Stultz v. Benson Lumber Co.*, 59 P. 2d 100 (Cal., 1936). For cases considering the current status of this decision denying liability to an employee injured by a plank which his employer had incorporated into scaffolding knowing it to be defective, see 1 *Frumer and Friedman*, s. 11.04[3][a], note 12.

[1] *E.I. du Pont de Nemours & Co. v. Ladner*, 73 So. 2d 249 (Miss., 1954); *Nishida v. E.I. du Pont de Nemours & Co.*, 245 F. 2d 768 (5th cir., 1957).

[2] *Strahlendorf v. Walgreen Co.*, 114 N.W. 2d 823 (Wis., 1962).

and taxi drivers.[3] Any such decision may be criticised on its facts[4] and recent American cases have been reluctant to absolve on the ground of intervening cause.[5] But it is clearly consistent with principle to hold that prior negligence has been rendered inoperative by the subsequent action or inaction of an intermediary. Such a ruling would, however, be appropriate only in an exceptional case. The general rule in English law as in the United States is that he who creates a situation of danger must expect a third party carelessly (though not consciously) to activate its potential for harm.[6]

Intermediate examination[7]

If a tortfeasor remains generally liable in spite of the intervening acts of a third party, he ought not to be exonerated simply because that third party has failed to act in an expected manner which would have prevented damage from occurring. Regrettably, however, English law has not been consistent with principle in such cases.

The problem originated in Lord Atkin's formulation of the rule for product liability in *Donoghue* v. *Stevenson* where he spoke of:[8]

---

[3] *Mull* v. *Ford Motor Co.*, 368 F. 2d 713 (2nd Cir., 1966).

[4] In the *Wagoner* case, e.g., the first purchaser had travelled about 10,000 miles without experiencing any difficulty with the hood. The case and the contrasting case of *Comstock* v. *General Motors Corporation*, 99 N.W. 2d 627 (Mich., 1959) are discussed by Noel, "Manufacturer's Negligence of Design or Directions for use of a Product", 71 Yale L.J. 816, 869–872 (1962). Contrast *Balido* v. *Improved Machinery Co.*, 105 Cal. Rptr. 890 (Cal. App., 1973) where a charge of $500 was made and the matter was left to the jury: see further below, pp. 289–290.

[5] *Cf. Balido* v. *Improved Machinery Co.*, above; *Bexiga* v. *Havir Manufacturing Corporation*, 290 A. 2d 281 (N.J., 1972).

[6] See, e.g., *Haynes* v. *Harwood*, [1935] 1 K.B. 146; *Philco Radio and Television Corporation of Great Britain* v. *J. Spurling, Ltd.*, [1949] 2 All E.R. 882. Hart and Honore, *Causation in the Law* (1959) summarise the position by saying (at p. 143): "In general the negligent act of a third party is not held to negative causal connection unless it does so on the score of its gross abnormality, though some cases have applied the now discredited principle that the last wrongdoer is alone responsible". See also *Restatement, Torts*, 2d, s. 447.

[7] See Salmond, *The Law of Torts*, 16th edn., 1973, pp. 313–316; Street, *The Law of Torts*, 6th edn., 1976, pp. 176–177; Winfield and Jolowicz, *The Law of Tort*, 10th edn., 1975, pp. 208–210; Fleming, *The Law of Torts*, 4th edn., 1971, pp. 445–446; Clerk and Lindsell, *Torts*, 14th edn., 1975, paras. 883–884; Glanville Williams, *Joint Torts and Contributory Negligence* (1951), pp. 250–251, 324–326; Glanville Williams, "Negligent Contractors and Third Parties" (1942), 92 Law Jo. Newspapers 124; Bohlen, "Liability of Manufacturers" (1929), 45 L.Q.R. 343, 364 *et seq.*

[8] [1932] A.C. 562, 599, H.L.

"a manufacturer of products, which he sells in such a form as to show that he intends them to reach the ultimate consumer in the form in which they left him with no reasonable possibility of intermediate examination."[9]

On the facts of the case this formulation would not have created an obstacle to recovery. The bottle from which the snail had allegedly emerged was made of dark opaque glass and sealed with a metal cap. No intermediate examination was possible. Subsequently, however, lack of such opportunity acquired an artificial importance. Indeed at one stage Lord Atkin's words were taken *au pied de la lettre* so that a "reasonable possibility of intermediate examination" precluded recovery even though such an examination was not contemplated by the manufacturer and the intermediary was not negligent in failing to carry it out.[10] Nowadays, at least, intermediate examination must be probable in a business sense and reasonably to be anticipated.[11] In *Griffiths* v. *Arch Engineering Co., Ltd.*[12] Chapman, J. stated the position as follows:[13]

"The proper question is whether [the supplier] should reasonably have expected that the person to whom he had passed the article would use the opportunity for inspection in such a way as to give him an indication of the risk and the means of warning any subsequent user of the article."

No such expectation existed on the facts of the case where a grinding machine had been handed over for immediate use in a dock. Nor is it reasonably to be expected that underpants will be washed before use to avoid the risk of dermatitis;[14] that a reconditioned car will be inspected before it is taken on the road;[15] nor that an examination will be carried out when goods are marketed in a sealed container[16] or in a form which

---

[9] See also Lord Atkin's further reference to the point at p. 582 and the remarks of Lord Macmillan: *ibid.*, at p. 622. *Cf.* the judgment of Brett, M.R. in *Heaven* v. *Pender* (1883), 11 Q.B.D. 503, 510, which is couched in substantially similar terms.

[10] See *Dransfield* v. *British Insulated Cables, Ltd.*, [1937] 4 All E.R. 382 (Hawke, J.). The decision was supported by Chapman, "Liability for Chattels" (1938), 54 L.Q.R. 46, but criticised persuasively by Goodhart, *ibid.*, at p. 59. See also *Otto* v. *Bolton and Norris*, [1936] 2 K.B. 461; [1936] 1 All E.R. 960; *Farr* v. *Butters Brothers*, [1932] 2 K.B. 606, C.A.

[11] See, e.g., *Paine* v. *Colne Valley Electricity Supply Co., Ltd., and British Insulated Cables, Ltd.*, [1938] 4 All E.R. 803, 808 *per* Goddard, L.J. Goddard, L.J. made the same point in *Haseldine* v. *C.A. Daw & Son, Ltd.*, [1941] 3 All E.R. 156, 183–184 and in *Hanson* v. *Wearmouth Coal Co., Ltd.*, [1939] 3 All E.R. 47, 54.

[12] [1968] 3 All E.R. 217.   [13] *Ibid.*, at p. 222.

[14] *Grant* v. *Australian Knitting Mills, Ltd.*, [1936] A.C. 85, P.C.

[15] *Herschthal* v. *Stewart and Ardern, Ltd.*, [1940] 1 K.B. 155; [1939] 4 All E.R. 123. See also *Malfroot* v. *Noxal, Ltd. and British Insulated Cables, Ltd.* (1935), 51 T.L.R. 551 (sidecar fitted to motorcycle).

[16] As in *Donoghue* v. *Stevenson*, [1932] A.C. 562, H.L. See also *Paine* v. *Colne Valley Electricity Supply Co., Ltd.*, [1938] 4 All E.R. 803, 808, *per* Goddard, L.J.; *Zeppa* v. *Coca-Cola, Ltd.*, [1955] 5 D.L.R. 187 (Ont. C.A.); *Shandloff* v. *City Dairy*, [1936] O.R. 579; *Barnett* v. *H. & J. Packer & Co., Ltd.*, [1940] 3 All E.R. 575.

would require them to be disassembled.[17]

The approach of such cases is certainly to be preferred, but the present English law as stated by Chapman, J. is still unsatisfactory. Applied strictly, it means that there can be little or no room for concurrent liability in tort as between the original manufacturer and the intermediary. A reasonable expectation of an examination apt to reveal the defect would be both a sufficient reason for absolving the former and generally a necessary condition for holding liable the latter.[18] Hence instances of concurrent liability may be cited as invalidating the approach or as being inconsistent with it.[19] The main drawback of the English approach is that it places too much emphasis on an expectation that the defect will be discovered and too little on an expectation that it will be cured. Even an intermediary who discovers a danger may fail to do anything about it whether through forgetfulness or irresponsibility.

The better view is that the manufacturer should be absolved from liability only where he has exercised reasonable care in looking to an intermediary to take adequate measures to safeguard the user or consumer. The fact that the intermediary has carried out an examination carelessly or even that he has discovered the defect should not be conclusive.[20] Clearly there would be circumstances in which a manufacturer would be acting reasonably in looking to an intermediary. For an example, one need look no further than the farmer who sells his crop of vegetables to a manufacturer of tinned goods.[1] No doubt there would be other cases in which it would be consistent with reasonable care to supply batches of

---

[17] See, e.g., *Phillips* v. *E. W. Lundberg & Son* (1968), 88 W.N. (N.S.W.) 166 (speedboat propeller). For similar reasons the defect in such cases can readily be traced to the manufacturer: see above, p. 280.

[18] Where the intermediary in fact examines but could not reasonably have been expected to do so he may, no doubt, incur a liability to which he would not otherwise be subject. The manufacturer might be absolved on the ground of supervening cause (discussed above, pp. 283–284). But could he claim the benefit of the apparently more favourable rules for product liability?

[19] *Griffiths* v. *Arch Engineering Co., Ltd.*, [1968] 3 All E.R. 217, was itself such a case since the hirer-out of the grinding machine and the hirer were both held liable to the injured employee. See also *Watson* v. *Buckley, Osborne, Garrett & Co., Ltd.*, [1940] 1 All E.R. 174, 183, where the intermediate distributor of a hair dye was held liable and it was suggested that the manufacturer might have been sued as well.

[20] Under the present law it sometimes seems to be treated as though it were. See *Buckner* v. *Ashby and Horner, Ltd.*, [1941] 1 K.B. 321 (Atkinson, J.). But the Court of Appeal upheld the decision on a narrower ground. It was open to Atkinson, J. to hold on the facts that the defendant contractors were entitled to assume that adequate safeguards would be taken by the intermediary: *ibid.*, at pp. 338–339 (du Parcq. L.J.). Cases such as *Taylor* v. *Rover Co., Ltd.*, [1966] 2 All E.R. 181; [1966] 1 W.L.R. 1491; *Farr* v. *Butters Brothers*, [1932] 2 K.B. 606; *Cathcart* v. *Hull*, [1963] N.Z.L.R. 333 (N.Z. Sup. Ct.) suggest that knowledge will bar recovery.

[1] See Harper and James, *The Law of Torts*, s. 28.11.

untested goods or to look to an intermediary for a final inspection, testing or adjustment before the product is put into circulation.[2] The supplier of component parts or materials may sometimes be justified in looking to the manufacturer of the end product to test for defects.[3] In other cases all relevant duties may be discharged by warning a responsible intermediary such as a doctor and there would be no necessity to warn the plaintiff himself.[4] Apart from such cases, the manufacturer should remain liable unless the failure of the intermediary to conduct or act on an examination is so grossly negligent as to be viewed as the sole effective cause of the damage.[5] The fact that the intermediary was under a duty to the manufacturer to examine should not be decisive, although it may of course bear upon his own liability and affect the level of his contribution as a joint tortfeasor.[6]

In so far as English law is inconsistent with the approach preferred here, this may fairly be viewed as a relic of the days when we were preoccupied with identifying the last opportunity to avoid the harm. The mainstream of English law has moved on since then and it has done so in areas related closely to the present discussion. Thus it is clear that a carrier who mis-delivers a dangerous chattel may be held liable when an intervening party activates its potential to harm.[7] Similarly there are a number of important cases concerned with liability for dangerous structures. In *Clay* v. *A.J. Crump & Sons, Ltd.*,[8] a labourer who had been injured by the collapse of a wall sought to recover damages against an architect and firms of demolition and building contractors. The architect and demolition contractors maintained that even if they had been negligent in allowing the wall to stand they were absolved from liability because the building contractors had had an opportunity to inspect it. The submission was unsuccessful, the Court of Appeal taking the view that Lord Atkin's statement in *Donoghue* v. *Stevenson*[9] had to be seen in the light of the facts of the case and as being subject to the wider "neighbour principle". The subsequent negligence of the building contractors was not the sole effective cause of the collapse and damages were apportioned as between the several

---

[2] The practice in the car industry of looking to a dealer for a pre-delivery inspection might provide an example. But the argument can be circumvented by regarding the dealer as the manufacturer's agent and holding the manufacturer liable for the dealer's negligence: see further, above, p. 204 *et seq.*

[3] For the liability of suppliers of components and materials, see above, at pp. 197–198, 227–228. See also *Restatement, Torts* 2d, s. 396, Comment c.

[4] See above, pp. 245–247.

[5] For supervening cause, see above, pp. 283–284.

[6] The provisions for apportionment are to be found in the Law Reform (Married Women and Tortfeasors) Act 1935.

[7] As in *Philco Radio Co.* v. *J. Spurling, Ltd.*, [1949] 2 All E.R. 882 (inflammable celluloid film).

[8] [1964] 1 Q.B. 533; [1963] 3 All E.R. 687.

[9] [1932] A.C. 562, 599, H.L. cited above, p. 285.

defendants. The same view was taken by the High Court of Australia in *Voli* v. *Inglewood Shire Council*,[10] where the floor of a community hall had collapsed and where the fact that the plans had been passed by a Public Works Department was held not to be a sufficient reason for absolving the defendant architect from liability. Dangerous structures and dangerous products have not always been treated alike but the close similarity between the two situations suggests that the same approach should be adopted in a product liability case.

Further and more direct support for this view is provided by the New Zealand case of *Jull* v. *Wilson and Horton*.[11] Here the driver of a fork-hoist truck had been injured by the collapse of a weld and the vehicle repairers who had done the weld were joined by the defendant employers in third party proceedings. Holding the case to be one of joint responsibility, Richmond, J. did not regard the employer's opportunity for intermediate inspection as being inconsistent with the repairer's continuing liability. Having referred to Professor Goodhart's statement that "It is difficult to see why a person who has created a dangerous situation should be held not liable on the ground that it had not been abated by another whose duty it was to do so",[12] his conclusion was that:[13]

> "such a person cannot shelter behind a reasonable expectation of intermediate inspection unless the expectation was strong enough to justify him in regarding the contemplated inspection as an adequate safeguard to persons who might otherwise suffer harm."[14]

This, it is submitted, is good sense and (in terms of consistency with general principles) good law.

In the USA, the law has developed more in accordance with general principles. Frumer and Friedman summarise the position as follows:[15]

> "The manufacturer is not relieved of liability in negligence to third persons merely because his immediate vendee or some other person has the opportunity, or is even under the duty, to inspect, and such person fails to inspect or to make an adequate inspection. The failure of such vendee or other person to

---

[10] *Cf.* (1963), 110 C.L.R. 74, 87–88, *per* Windeyer, J. See also Dworkin (1964), 27 M.L.R. 216.
[11] [1968] N.Z.L.R. 88 (N.Z. Sup. Ct.). See also *Driver* v. *William Willett (Contractors), Ltd.*, [1969] 1 All E.R. 665 (employers and consultant safety engineers); *Clelland* v. *Berryman*; *Malman Motors, Ltd.* (1975), 56 D.L.R. (3d) 395 (B.C. Sup. Ct.) (car repairer and driver); *Power* v. *Bedford Motor Co., Ltd.*, [1959] I.R. 665.
[12] (1941) 57 L.Q.R. 162, 163. See also Glanville Williams, *Joint Torts and Contributory Negligence*, p. 325.
[13] [1968] N.Z.L.R. 88, 97.
[14] *Cf.*, however, *Cathcart* v. *Hull*, [1963] N.Z.L.R. 333, which is not readily distinguishable, save on the unsatisfactory ground that it was the injured plaintiff who had the opportunity for intermediate inspection. See further below, p. 292.
[15] *Products Liability*, Vol. 1, s. 11.04[2].

adequately inspect is within the foreseeable risk of the manufacturers' negligence."[16]

This statement is supported fully by the cases. Thus in *Maytag Co. v. Arbogast*,[17] for example, the negligence of a dealer in failing to inspect a washing machine did not absolve the manufacturer from liability for carelessly omitting to fit a spring to secure a lever on the machine. The position is the same where the intermediary is an employer,[18] producer of an end product,[19] or one who hires out a chattel for immediate use.[20] There seem to be few cases in which the manufacturer is exonerated,[1] although there is no lack of cases where the original supplier and intermediary are held liable concurrently.[2]

Where the intermediary acquires actual knowledge of the defect, whether through discovery or warning, there has understandably been greater willingness to absolve the original supplier. *Ford Motor Co. v. Wagoner*[3] has already been cited in this context. It is clear, however, that such knowledge does not automatically (or even normally) bar recovery against the supplier. Thus a representative selection of American cases have held that recovery was not barred as a matter of law when employers knew of the defective condition of a fork-lift truck, and of a lorry's brakes;[4] a fellow employee used a car having momentarily forgotten that it had defective brakes;[5] and when a retailer resold as kerosene for starting fires

---

[16] *Restatement, Torts*, 2d, s. 396 provides that: "A manufacturer of a chattel is subject to liability ... although the dangerous character or condition of the chattel is discoverable by an inspection which the seller or any other person is under a duty to the person injured to make".

[17] 157 S.E. 350 (Ga., 1931). Other leading cases include *Pierce* v. *Ford Motor Co.*, 190 F. 2d 910 (4th Cir., 1951) (car dealer's mechanic); *Foley* v. *Pittsburgh-Des Moines Co.*, 63 A. 2d 517 (Pa., 1949) (company purchasing liquid gas tank); *Alexander* v. *Nash-Kelvinator Corporation*, 261 F. 2d 187 (2nd Cir., 1958) (car dealer).

[18] *Fredericks* v. *American Export Lines*, 227 F. 2d 450 (2nd Cir., 1955), cert. den. 350 U.S. 989 (1956). See also illustration 2 of the *Restatement, Torts*, s. 396 based on *Rosebrook* v. *General Electric Co.*, 140 N.E. 571 (N.Y., 1923).

[19] *Willey* v. *Fyrogas Co.*, 251 S.W. 2d 635 (Mo., 1952) (liability of manufacturer of component valve); *Restatement, Torts*, s. 396, Comment c, noting continuing potential liability of supplier of raw materials.

[20] For the scope of the lessor's duty to inspect, see *Restatement, Torts* 2d, s. 408.

[1] For an example of a case in which the original supplier was exonerated, see *Re New York Dock Co.*, 61 F. 2d 777 (2nd Cir., 1932) (charterer to inspect pile driver and rig before use). *Cf. Schipper* v. *Levitt & Sons, Inc.* 207 A. 2d 314 (N.J., 1965) (builder to install mixing valve).

[2] *Cf. Post* v. *Manitowoc Engineering Corporation*, 211 A. 2d 386 (N.J., 1965) (manufacturer and operator of crane) and, in general, 1 *Frumer and Friedman*, s. 11.04 [4].

[3] 192 S.W. 2d 840 (Tenn., 1946) above, p. 283.

[4] See, respectively, *Yale & Towne, Inc.* v. *Sharpe*, 164 S.E. 2d 318 (Ga. App., 1968); *Polovich* v. *Sayers*, 412 S.W. 2d 436 (Mo., 1967). Contrast *Taylor* v. *Rover Co., Ltd.*, [1966] 2 All E.R. 181; [1966] 1 W.L.R. 1491.

[5] *Comstock* v. *General Motors Corporation*, 99 N.W. 2d 627 (Mich., 1959).

a dangerous mixture of petrol and kerosene.[6] There are, of course, cases where the acts of the intermediary are so grossly careless as to demand a ruling that they constitute the sole operative cause of the damage.[7] But such cases are rare. Indeed, recent decisions show a marked reluctance to withdraw the issue from the jury.

In *Balido* v. *Improved Machinery Inc.*,[8] for example, a California Court of Appeal refused to rule that manufacturers should be exonerated when they had warned a purchaser of a secondhand plastic moulding press manufactured some fifteen years earlier that the press did not comply with industrial safety and had offered to rectify it on payment of $500. The warning and offer were ignored and an operator injured. According to the court it was for the trier of fact to decide whether the defendant should have "reasonably anticipated that a purchaser of a second-hand press would ignore its warning of inadequate safety devices and refuse to spend money to purchase additional safety equipment".[9] Although this case does not stand alone,[10] there is force in the dissenting view of Compton, A.J. that the decision hardly encourages the giving of warnings to prevent injury.[11]

The scope of the manufacturers' protection is likely to be further eroded by acceptance of the principles established in cases such as *Vandermark* v. *Ford Motor Co.*[12] and *Sabloff* v. *Yamaha Motor Co.*[13] These cases suggest that even within a negligence theory of liability the manufacturer is subject to a non-delegable duty with respect to the marketing of a carefully constructed product ready for use. Accordingly he will not be excused by anything which the intermediary does or fails to do.[14]

---

[6] *Kentucky Independent Oil Co.* v. *Schnitzler*, 271 S.W. 570 (Ky., 1925).

[7] As in *Ford Motor Co.* v. *Wagoner*, 192 S.W. 2d 840 and cases noted above, pp. 283–284 when discussing supervening cause.

[8] 105 Cal. Rptr. 890 (Cal. App., 1973).

[9] *Ibid.*, at p. 901.

[10] See, e.g., *Rhoads* v. *Service Machine Co.*, 329 F. Supp. 367 (Ark., 1971); *Bexiga* v. *Havir Manufacturing Corporation*, 290 A. 2d 281 (N.J., 1972); *Finnegin* v. *Havir Manufacturing Corporation*, 290 A, 2d 286 (N.J., 1972). *Cf. Restatement, Torts*, 2d, s. 437 which provides that "If the actor's negligent conduct is a substantial factor in bringing about harm to another, the fact that after the risk has been created by his negligence the actor has exercised reasonable care to prevent it from taking effect in harm does not prevent him from being liable for the harm."

[11] *Cf.* 105 Cal. Rptr. 890, 903–904. It is of course open to the jury to find that the inaction of the intermediary was in fact a supervening cause: see, e.g., *Rekab, Inc.* v. *Frank Hrubetz & Co.*, 274 A. 2d 107 (Md., 1971).

[12] 37 Cal. Rptr. 896 (Cal. Sup. Ct., 1964).

[13] 273 A. 2d 606, affd. 283 A. 2d 321 (N.J., 1971).

[14] See further above, pp. 204–207 *Quaere*, however, whether the principle is of general application or whether it depends on the intermediary being a dealer or agent of the manufacturer? See *Alvarez* v. *Felker Manufacturing Co.*, 41 Cal. Rptr. 541 (Cal. App., 1964) and

Defences

Voluntary assumption of the risk and knowledge[15]

Voluntary assumption of the risk

No liability is incurred towards one who has voluntarily assumed the risk of injury: *volenti non fit injuria*. An assumption of the risk may be express[16] or implied, but it will be inferred only where the injured party had full knowledge of the existence and magnitude of the risk and where he acted without the pressures of economic (or perhaps social) constraints. Employees and rescuers have typically been regarded as subject to such constraints[17] but this limit to the defence of *volenti* is of more general application. So in one recent American case[18] a verdict for the plaintiff was upheld when he had persisted in using his virtually new car knowing that the steering and suspension were seriously defective. Use of a car was essential for his work as a travelling salesman; the defendant manufacturers had refused to replace it although some eight unsuccessful attempts had been made to cure the defects over a four-month period; and the plaintiff, who was already spending one sixth of his income to finance the car, could not afford a replacement. The case was argued under the strict tort theory and there is no doubt that a truly voluntary assumption of the risk will be a defence in such actions as well as in negligence.[19] The Law Commission envisages that the defence would be available in English law in the event of our adopting a system of strict liability for defective products.[20]

---

above, p. 205. See also *Ford Motor Co.* v. *Mathis*, 322 F. 2d 267 (5th Cir., 1963) and cases cited above, pp. 202–204 for the position where there has been carelessness on the part of the supplier of components or materials.

[15] See Keeton "Assumption of Risk in Products Liability Cases", 22 Louisiana L.R. 122 (1961); Keeton, "Assumption of Products Risks", 19 S.W.L.Jo. 61 (1965); 2.*Frumer and Friedman*, s. 16[A][5][f].

[16] If embodied in a contract its efficacy will be determined by the common law (and, where appropriate, statutory) rules governing exemption clauses: see above, chs. 7 and 8.

[17] See, e.g., *Smith* v. *Baker & Sons*, [1891] A.C. 325, H.L. (employees): *Haynes* v. *Harwood*, [1935] 1 K.B. 146 (rescuer).

[18] *Messick* v. *General Motors Corporation*, 460 F. 2d 485 (5th Cir., 1972).

[19] *Campbell* v. *Southern Pacific Co.*, 124 Cal. Rptr. 496 (Cal. App., 1975); *Edwards* v. *Sears, Roebuck & Co.*, 512 F. 2d 276 (5th Cir., 1975); *Sperling* v. *Hatch*, 88 Cal. Rptr. 704 (1970); *Fore* v. *Vermeer Manufacturing Co.*, 287 N.E. 2d 526 (Ill., 1972); *Restatement of Torts*, 2d, s. 402A. Comment n.

[20] See "Liability for Defective Products", Working Paper No. 64, para. 79. The defence is available in other areas of strict liability, e.g., liability for dangerous animals: Animals Act 1971, s. 5(2).

Knowledge

Voluntary assumption of the risk has not been discussed frequently
eo nomine in the context of product liability in English law. We have
tended to adopt the view that the plaintiff's knowledge of the defect will
itself preclude recovery. A number of Commonwealth cases have proceeded on the same basis.[1] *Farr* v. *Butters Brothers*[2] is the leading English
case. The defendant crane manufacturers had sold a crane to a firm of
builders, the arrangement being that the parts were to be assembled by
the builders' men. The plaintiff was an experienced crane erector who
discovered certain defects in the crane as he was assembling it. Nonetheless he began to work the crane and he was killed by a falling jib which he
knew to be defective. His widow's claim under the Fatal Accidents Act
1846 failed, the Court of Appeal holding that no duty was owed to the
deceased with respect to the defects which he had discovered. The same
view would no doubt have been taken had the plaintiff's knowledge been
derived from a warning or from the fact that the defect was patent or
obvious.

In most cases it is no doubt right that a person should not knowingly
use a defective product and then be compensated thereafter for injury
suffered. But such a conclusion is better expressed in terms of causation
or assumption of the risk rather than as a rule of general application. It is
also more likely to be valid when applied to miscarriages in the production
process as opposed to design deficiencies. A product such as an industrial
press or a rotary power mower may still be unreasonably dangerous though
it is obvious that it lacks the safety devices which would render it safe.[3] A
full and detailed warning should not necessarily be conclusive where high
risk products containing explosives or carcinogens are concerned.[4] In all
cases the overriding criterion should be that of reasonable safety[5] and this
may require a change of design. These and other considerations have led
American courts to retreat from their earlier position whereby an artificial
importance was attributed to the fact that the danger was known or
obvious.[6] The emphasis nowadays tends to be on whether there has been

---

[1] See, e.g., *Daley* v. *Gypsy Caravan Pty., Ltd.*, [1966] 2 N.S.W.R. 22; *Cathcart* v. *Hull*, [1963]
N.Z.L.R. 333.
[2] [1932] A.C. at 606, C.A. See also *London Graving Dock Co., Ltd.* v. *Horton*, [1951] A.C. 737;
[1951] 2 All E.R. 1, H.L. (occupiers' liability at common law). For the effect of knowledge
on the part of a third party, see *Taylor* v. *Rover Co., Ltd.*, [1966] 2 All E.R. 181; [1966]
1 W.L.R. 1491 and above, pp. 283–284, 289–290.
[3] See above, pp. 221–222 and pp. 222–223 respectively.
[4] See above, pp. 212–213, 231–233 and pp. 213–214, 233–235 respectively.
[5] As under the Occupiers' Liability Act 1957, s. 2(4)(a).
[6] Contrast *Campo* v. *Scofield*, 95 N.E. 2d 802 (N.Y., 1950) and *Messina* v. *Clarke Equipment
Co.*, 263 F. 2d 291 (2nd Cir., 1959) with *Pike* v. *Frank G. Hough Co.*, 85 Cal. Rptr. 629

a conscious and voluntary assumption of the risk.[7] English law may need the intervention of statute or a decision of the House of Lords if it is to follow the same path. Meanwhile recovery should be denied only to a person who has both a full appreciation of the existence and extent of the risk and a meaningful opportunity of avoiding it.[8]

Contributory negligence and abnormal use[9]

Contributory negligence

At common law there were no provisions for apportioning the loss where the fault of both the plaintiff and the defendant had contributed to the damage suffered. Apportionment provisions were enacted in the Law Reform (Contributory Negligence) Act 1945. By s. 1(1) of the Act a reduction in the damages may be made "to such extent as the court thinks just and equitable having regard to the claimant's share in the responsibility for the damage".

In the context of product liability, contributory fault might, in principle, take a number of forms. For example, failure to discover a defect or to appreciate the dangers of a design deficiency might be a ground for reducing damages under the Act.[10] The same would be true of a case where the plaintiff had handled a product carelessly[11] or failed to follow instructions for use[12] or otherwise to exercise reasonable care for his own safety.[13] Failure to respond to a warning is perhaps more difficult to

---

(1970) and *Wright* v. *Massey-Harris Inc.*, 215 N.E. 2d 465 (Ill., 1966). The *Campo* case has now been overruled in New York: see *Micallef* v. *Miehle Co.* (N.Y., 1976). See, in general, 1 *Frumer and Friedman*, ss. 6.04, 7.02, 8.04.

[7] See, e.g., *Kirkland* v. *General Motors Corporation*, 521 P. 2d 1353 (Okla., 1974); *Clarke* v. *Brockway Motor Trucks*, 372 F. Supp. 1342 (1974); *Berkebile* v. *Brantly Helicopter Corporation*, 337 A. 2d 893 (Pa., 1975).

[8] *Cf. Denny* v. *Supplies and Transport Co., Ltd.*, [1950] 2 K.B. 374.

[9] Noel, "Defective Products: Abnormal Use, Contributory Negligence and Assumption of Risk", 25 Vanderbilt Law R. 93 (1972); Prosser, *Law of Torts*, 4th edn., 1971, pp. 667–671; 1 *Frumer and Friedman*, ss. 13, 15.

[10] See, e.g. *Lafarge Cement, Ltd.* v. *Canadian National Rail. Co.* (1962), 34 D.L.R. (2d) 154 (B.C. Sup. Ct.).

[11] *Cf. Vacwell Engineering Co., Ltd.* v. *B.D.H. Chemicals, Ltd.*, [1971] 1 Q.B. 111; [1970] 3 All E.R. 553, n. C.A., above, p. 179 (explosive substance).

[12] *Pierce* v. *Avon Products Inc.*, 423 P. 2d 461 (Okla., 1966) (bath oil); *Matthias* v. *Lehn and Fink Products Corporation*, 424 P. 2d 284 (Wash., 1967) (permanent wave solution).

[13] See, e.g., *Shields* v. *Hobbs Manufacturing Co.* (1962), 34 D.L.R. (2d) 307 (Sup. Ct. Canada) (electrician failing to ground electrical equipment); *Dallison* v. *Sears, Roebuck and Co.*, 313 F. 2d 343 (10th Cir., 1962) (nightgown ignited when smoking in bed after taking sleeping pill). There are many American examples involving defective cars: see Prosser, *op. cit*, p. 671.

accommodate within a comparative negligence framework as is an allegedly unreasonable reliance on express assurances or representations.[14] But there will be cases in which this might be established. A warning might, for example, have been objectively inadequate and yet the plaintiff might have persisted in using the product whilst suspecting that something was wrong. One underlying difficulty should be noted. The prevailing English view is that the manufacturers' duty arises only where there is no reasonable opportunity of intermediate examination.[15] Applied strictly, this approach would leave little room for contributory negligence, or, indeed, for concurrent liability as between two or more tortfeasors.

Abnormal use

A manufacturer may sometimes claim that injury was suffered only because the product was put to an abnormal or unintended use. Most products are capable of causing harm when used improperly and obviously some limit must be placed on the manufacturers' responsibility. So liability has been denied when a child punctured an aerosol container by banging it on a concrete wall;[16] workmen used a ladder as a horizontal platform between two other upright ladders;[17] trichinae infected pork was cooked insufficiently;[18] an internal decorating powder was stirred with a finger;[19] and when a woman persisted in wearing shoes which were two sizes too small.[20] This approach should not, however, be taken too far since a duty which is framed in terms of a product which is properly used for an intended purpose may be too narrow.[1] Furniture polish is not made to be ingested by a child;[2] an oven door and a chair are not intended to be stood on;[3] cleansing liquids and paints are not made for splashing in the eye;[4] and

---

[14] See, e.g., *Bahlman* v. *Hudson Motor Car Co.*, 288 N.W. 309 (1939). For the effect of representations of safety on the adequacy of warnings, see above, pp. 243–244.

[15] See above, pp. 284–288.

[16] *Rae and Rae* v. *T. Eaton Co. (Maritimes), Ltd.* (1961), 23 D.L.R. (2d) 522 (Nova Scotia Sup. Ct.).

[17] *Campbell* v. *O'Donnell*, [1967] I.R. 226. See also *Poole* v. *Crittal Metal Windows (N.Z.), Ltd.*, [1964] N.Z.L.R. 522 (N.Z. Sup. Ct.) (scaffolding).

[18] *Heil* v. *Hedges*, [1951] 1 T.L.R. 512; *Yachetti* v. *John Duff & Sons, Ltd.*, [1943] 1 D.L.R. 194 (Ont. High Ct.).

[19] *Schfranek* v. *Benjamin Moore and Co.*, 54 F. 2d 76 (N.Y., 1931).

[20] *Dubbs* v. *Zak Bros.*, 175 N.E. 626 (1931) (action against retailer).

[1] *Cf.* the Health and Safety at Work Act 1974, s. 6. See also "Consumer Safety: a consultative document", Cmnd. 6398, February 1976, paras. 91–92.

[2] *Spruill* v. *Boyle-Midway Inc.*, 308 F. 2d 79 (4th Cir., 1962).

[3] *Ritter* v. *Narragansett Electric Co.*, 283 A. 2d 255 (R.I., 1971) (oven door); *Phillips* v. *Ogle Aluminum Furniture Inc.*, 235 P. 2d 857 (Cal., 1951) (chair).

[4] *Sawyer* v. *Pine Oil Sales Co.*, 155 F. 2d 855 (5th Cir., 1946); *Haberley* v. *Reardon Co.*, 319 S.W. 2d 859 (Mo., 1958). Of the cases cited in notes 2–4 it was only in *Sawyer* that the issue was withdrawn from the jury and the case has been much criticised.

a car is not made for collisions.[5] Yet all these occurrences are foreseeable and might to a greater or lesser extent be forestalled by a safer design or a fuller warning. Alternative and more flexible control factors exist such as causation, contributory negligence and the requirement that the product be defective.

Contributory fault and strict liability

Where a legal system adopts a régime of strict liability for defective products defences based on causation, contributory negligence and misuse are likely to assume an added importance. The manufacturer who can no longer plead that he has exercised reasonable care will perforce be driven to explore other possibilities. This has happened in the United States of America. In the leading California case of *Greenman* v. *Yuba Power Products*,[6] Justice Traynor spoke of it being sufficient for the plaintiff to prove "that he was injured while using the Shopsmith in a way it was intended to be used as a result of a defect in design and manufacture of which plaintiff was not aware that made the Shopsmith unsafe for its intended use".[7] Subsequent cases have confirmed that recovery may be precluded where the plaintiff uses the product in a way which was unintended[8] though the manufacturer may be required to take steps to guard against foreseeable misuse.[9] Similarly contributory negligence may be established where the plaintiff knows of the defect[10] but not, it seems, through simple carelessness in failing to discover its existence.[11] In effect, this is almost tantamount to a requirement that there be a voluntary assumption of the risk.[12] The American view is, however, often coloured

---

[5] See *Larsen* v. *General Motors Corporation*, 391 F. 2d 495 (8th Cir., 1968); *cf. Evans* v. *General Motors Corporation*, 359 F. 2d 822 (7th Cir., 1966) and, in general, above, pp. 223–227.

[6] 27 Cal. Rptr. 697 (Cal. Sup. Ct., 1962), above, p. 17.

[7] *Ibid.*, at p. 701. See, in general, 2 *Frumer and Friedman*, s. 16A [5][*f*]; Prosser, *Law of Torts*, 4th edn., 1971, pp. 667–671.

[8] See, e.g., *Lewis* v. *Stran Steel Corporation*, 285 N.E. 2d 632 (Ill., 1972).

[9] See, e.g., *Ritter* v. *Narragansett Electric Co.*, 283 A. 2d 255 (R.I., 1971) and cases cited above, p. 294, notes 2–5.

[10] See, e.g., *Cintrone* v. *Hertz Truck Leasing and Rental Service*, 212 A. 2d 769 (N.J., 1965) (defective brakes); *Codling* v. *Paglia*, 298 N.E. 2d 622 (N.Y., 1973) (steering mechanism).

[11] See, e.g., *Shields* v. *Morton Chemical Co.*, 518 P. 2d 857 (Idaho, 1974) (strict tort); *Ettin* v. *Ava Truck Leasing Inc.*, 251 A. 2d 278 (N.J., 1969); *Hansen* v. *Firestone Tire and Rubber Co.*, 276 F. 2d 254 (6th Cir., 1960) (express warranty); *Bahlman* v. *Hudson Motor Co.*, 288 N.W. 309 (Mich., 1939) (express warranty): *Restatement of Torts*, 2d, s. 402A, Comment n; Prosser, *op cit.* pp. 670–671. The purchaser is less favourably treated under U.C.C. art. 2–316 (3) (*b*): see above, pp. 95–96.

[12] See *Kirkland* v. *General Motors Corporation*, 521 P. 2d 1353 (Okla., 1974). For voluntary assumption of the risk, see above, p. 291.

by the unavailability of apportionment provisions so that a finding of contributory negligence will totally preclude recovery. If English law adopts a system of strict liability it seems likely that damages might be reduced under the Law Reform (Contributory Negligence) Act 1945 in any case in which the plaintiff's fault has contributed to the damage suffered.[13]

Limitation periods

Although all the other ingredients of a successful action are present, a claim will nonetheless fail if it is not brought in time. In English law the statutory limitation period is generally six years, whether the action sounds in contract or in tort.[14] Personal injury litigation is, however, singled out for special treatment in that the operative legislation stipulates the shorter period of three years.[15] This is so whether the action is based on breach of a duty arising by virtue of a contract, or statute or in tort. The plaintiff in a product liability action will accordingly benefit from a more favourable period when suing in negligence for property damage or economic loss, or in contract for breach of an express or implied warranty where personal injury is not in issue. In calculating the limitation period, time does not start to run until the cause of action accrues. So in a claim in negligence the period would not commence until the plaintiff had suffered the damage or loss which is essential to liability.[16] A cause of action in contract would accrue at the moment of breach[17] and this in principle is when the defective goods are delivered.[18]

These rules are not always easy to apply to product liability cases and they might either foreclose or prolong the limitation periods undesirably. For example, express assurances might have been given that a product will last for a certain period of time or similar, if less precise, stipulations as to durability might arise impliedly under the merchantable quality provisions of s. 14 (2) of the 1893 Act.[19] If the goods are incapable of achieving their promised performance it would be strange if time were to

---

[13] See the Law Commission Working Paper, "Liability for Defective Products", Law Com. No. 64, para. 78. See also the Strasbourg Convention on Products Liability, art. 4 (1).

[14] Limitation Act 1939 s. 2 (1). Section 26 contains special provisions for cases of fraud.

[15] Limitation Act 1975, s. 1, amending s. 2 of the 1939 Act.

[16] See *Watson* v. *Winget, Ltd.*, 1960 S.C. (H.L.) 100, 102–103, H.L.; *Long* v. *Western Propeller Co.* (1968), 67 D.L.R. (2d) 345 (Man. C.A.); *Buxton* v. *McKenzie, McKenzie*, [1960] N.Z.L.R. 732.

[17] *Bagot* v. *Stevens Scanlan and Co.*, [1966] 1 Q.B. 197; [1964] 3 All E.R. 577. See also *Howell* v. *Young* (1826), 5 B. & C. 259; *Walker* v. *Milner* (1866), 4 F. & F. 745.

[18] See U.C.C. art. 725 (2).

[19] See above, pp. 91–92.

be held to have run against the purchaser whilst he was testing them in use.[20] At the other extreme the limitation period might operate to expose a manufacturer to liability many years after a product was originally marketed. In *Davie* v. *New Merton Board Mills, Ltd.*,[1] the defective chisel had been manufactured some seven years before it splintered, putting out a fitter's eye, but the limitation period did not begin to run until the injury had been suffered.[2] The passage of time will often render it increasingly difficult to establish that the product was defective when it left the manufacturer's control.[3] But products such as chisels and hammers would not normally deteriorate when held in stock and liability might be incurred many years after the event.

Substantial difficulty may also be caused where damage occurs or becomes apparent progressively over a period of time. The common law rule in cases of personal injury is that time runs from the moment the damage occurs and this even though the damage was unknown and undiscoverable.[4] This rule worked extremely harshly where insidious industrial diseases were concerned and as a result of statutory intervention the limitation period now runs only from the time the plaintiff knew or ought to have known of the damage.[5] This has obvious implications for manufacturers of industrial and household substances such as asbestos, of drugs and perhaps even cigarettes.[6]

It was always predictable that similar problems would accompany the conferment of a remedy in tort in respect of progressive deterioration in property. The step was taken in relation to realty in *Dutton* v. *Bognor Regis Urban District Council Co.*[7] where a house had been built on inadequate foundations and the Court of Appeal held that a second purchaser had a cause of action against the local authority which had passed the property as complying with the building byelaws. Lord Denning, M.R. suggested that the limitation period began to run from the time the foundations were completed.[8] A number of first instance judges acted on the sug-

---

[20] U.C.C. art. 725 (2) provides expressly for the postponement of the period in such cases. See, e.g., *Hepp Brothers Inc.* v. *Evans*, 420 P. 2d 477 (Okla., 1966) ("lifetime guarantee" of vinyl tiles). See also *Rempe* v. *General Electric Co.*, 254 A. 2d 577 (Conn., 1969) applying a similar principle at common law.

[1] [1959] A.C. 604; [1959] 1 All E.R. 346, H.L.

[2] The point was noted by Lord Denning, M.R. in *Sparham-Souter* v. *Town and Country Developments, Ltd.*, [1976] 2 All E.R. 65, 68, C.A., below, p. 298.

[3] See above, pp. 279–282.

[4] *Cartledge* v. *E. Jopling and Sons, Ltd.*, [1963] A.C. 758; [1963] 1 All E.R. 341, H.L.

[5] Limitation Act 1975, s. 2A, amending s. 2 of the 1939 Act.

[6] See, e.g., *Wright* v. *Dunlop Rubber Co., Ltd.* (1972), 13 K.I.R. 255; *Borel* v. *Fibreboard Paper Products Corporation*, 493 F. 2d 1076 (5th Cir., 1973).

[7] [1972] 1 Q.B. 373; [1972] 1 All E.R. 462, C.A.

[8] [1972] 1 All E.R. 462, 474. See also *ibid.* at p. 482 (Sachs, L.J.) and *Bagot* v. *Stevens Scanlan and Co., Ltd.*, [1964] 3 All E.R. 577, 579 per Diplock, L.J.

gestion,[9] but the matter has recently been re-examined in the substantially similar case of *Sparham-Souter* v. *Town and Country Developments, Ltd.*[10] Here the Court of Appeal held that the earliest moment from which time can be said to run is when the plaintiff acquires the defective property. This, with respect, must clearly be correct even though the limitation period might thus be postponed indefinitely whenever property passes through a number of hands. There is more difficulty in accepting the court's view that the period would commence only when the plaintiff knew or ought to have known that the foundations were defective.[11] This seems to blur the distinction between the factual existence of the defect and its subsequent manifestation. Until the defect appears the owner might, admittedly, resell the property without making a loss. But this does not mean that he has not suffered the damage which is necessary to found a cause of action.

Similar considerations would apply *mutatis mutandis* if an equivalent extension of liability were to be made for defective products. The Canadian Supreme Court refused to make such an extension in the *Rivtow Marine* case whilst recognising that there was a duty to warn of known defects rendering a product dangerous.[12] Breach of this duty led to the recovery of the additional losses incurred through having to repair the product at an inconvenient time. This may also raise problems for limitation periods since the duty to warn must clearly be a continuing one. Hence, if a product is reasonably believed to be safe when marketed in 1960 and it is discovered in 1970 that it is dangerous the limitation period would not begin to run until the moment immediately preceding the issuing of any necessary warning. If a warning is not issued until 1976, a plaintiff would then have a further six years in which to commence an action.[13]

American case law has had to grapple with the same problems and a clear picture is emerging only gradually. Some cases favoured the contract or sales period even though there was no privity of contract between the parties, so holding that the cause of action arose on delivery of the defective goods.[14] Other have held that the period commences when the

---

[9] See *Higgins* v. *Arfon Borough Council*, [1975] 2 All E.R. 589; *Anns* v. *Walcroft Property Co., Ltd.*, [1976] Q.B. 882; [1976] All E.R. See also the Defective Premises Act 1972, s. 1 (5) which provides that a cause of action for breach of the duty imposed by s. 1 (1) of the Act accrues "at the time when the dwelling was completed". The Act does not, however, derogate from common law duties: see s. 6 (2).

[10] [1976] Q.B. 858; [1976] 2 All E.R. 65, C.A.

[11] *Cf. ibid.*, at p. 69 (Lord Denning, M.R.), p. 76 (Roskill, L.J.), pp. 79–80 (Geoffrey Lane, L.J.).

[12] (1974), 40 D.L.R. (3d) 530, below, pp. 333–337. The duty to warn of such defects is discussed above, pp. 247–251.

[13] Examples from American case law include *Tyler* v. *R. R. Street and Co., Inc.*, 322 F. Supp. 541 (1971); *Boains* v. *Lasar Manufacturing Co.*, 330 F. Supp. 1134 (1971).

[14] See, e.g., *Mendel* v. *Pittsburgh Plate Glass Co.*, 253 N.E. 2d 207 (N.Y., 1969); *Van Decker Packing Co.* v. *Corn Products Sales Co.*, 411 F. 2d 850 (6th Cir., 1969).

plaintiff ought to have discovered the defect.[15] The predominant view now seems to be that under the strict tort theory the statutory period does not run until the damage is suffered.[16]

A reasonable compromise aimed at avoiding the problems of both the hidden defect and the indefinite postponement of liability is to be found in the Strasbourg Convention covering personal injury and death. Article 6 of the Convention provides that:

> "Proceedings for the recovery of damages shall be subject to a limitation period of three years from the day the claimant became aware or should reasonably have been aware of the damage, the defect and the identity of the producer."

A further "long stop" is provided by art. 7 whereby:

> "The right to compensation under this Convention against a producer shall be extinguished if an action is not brought within 10 years from the date on which the producer put into circulation the individual product which caused the damage."[17]

---

[15] *Braniff Airways* v. *Curtiss Wright Corporation*, 424 F. 2d 427 (2d Cir., 1970); *Warrington* v. *Charles Pfizer and Co., Inc.*, 80 Cal. Rptr. 130 (Cal. App., 1969).

[16] *Giglio* v. *Connecticut Light and Power Co.*, 284 A. 2d 308 (Conn., 1971); *International Union of Operating Engineers etc.* v. *Chrysler Motor Corporation*, 258 A. 2d 271 (R.I., 1969); *Arrow Transportation* v. *Freuhauf Corporation Inc.*, 289 F. Supp. 170 (D.C. Ore., 1968); *Kirkland* v. *General Motors Corporation*, 521 P. 2d 1353 (Okla., 1974). See in general, Waddams, *Products Liability*, pp. 199–203.

[17] See also the proposed EEC directive, arts. 8 and 9; Law Commission Working Paper No. 64, paras. 141–143.

15 The Liability in Tort of Persons other than Manufacturers

Although this book is concerned primarily with the contractual liability of vendors of goods and with the tortious liability of manufacturers, we include here reference to other persons who may incur liability for defective products. The contractual liability of persons other than vendors has already been noted.[1] Persons other than manufacturers who may incur tortious liability include retailers and persons who hire out or provide services involving the use of a product; donors and gratuitous bailors; wholesalers and importers; those who repair, service, recondition, assemble, install or carry out work on a product; building contractors and builder-vendors; and probably also persons or bodies such as inspectors, designers, engineers, testing agencies, and endorsers or certifiers of quality. Before discussing the circumstances in which such persons or bodies may incur liability a few preliminary observations will be made about the basic duties common to all who supply or control the use of products. As one would expect, these duties correspond closely to the exceptions to the old rule of non-liability in *Winterbottom* v. *Wright*.[2]

Basic duties common to all who supply or control the use of a product[3]

The duty to refrain from deceit

A supplier of goods must of course refrain from deceit, that is, from

---

[1] See the discussion of implied warranties in non-sales transactions, above, pp. 115–122.
[2] (1842) 10 M. & W. 109, above, pp. 7–11.
[3] See 2 Harper and James, *Torts* s. 28–2, pp. 1536–1540. Clerk and Lindsell on *Torts*, 14th edn., 1975, paras. 930–942.

making false representations about goods either knowing them to be false, or not believing them to be true, and intending that they should be acted on by the plaintiff or by a class of persons which includes the plaintiff.[4] The tort covers personal injury[5] and property damage[6] as well as financial loss and it may be committed by the active concealment of a defect[7] no less than by a misrepresentation provided, at least, that the plaintiff has been deceived.[8] *Langridge* v. *Levy*[9] provides an early example of liability being incurred in deceit in respect of a false statement concerning the provenance and safety of a gun. The gun later exploded damaging the hand of the plaintiff, who was a person for whose use the vendor knew the gun to be intended.[10]

Although an action in deceit may have certain advantages over an action in negligence, especially where the loss is financial in nature,[11] deceit has played no more than a minor role in English product liability law. It is capable, theoretically, of extending beyond inter-personal communications to cover false advertising claims.[12] But the need to show a lack of belief

---

[4] See Winfield and Jolowicz, *Law of Tort*, 10th edn., 1975, pp. 212–221; Street, *The Law of Torts*, 6th edn., 1976, ch. 22; Fleming, *The Law of Torts*, 4th edn., 1971, ch. 25, pp. 553–563. See also the discussion of liability for misrepresentations, above, pp. 43–48.

[5] *Langridge* v. *Levy* (1837), 2 M. & W. 519; affd. (1838), 4 M. & W. 337 below; *Nicholls* v. *Taylor*, [1939] V.L.R. 119.

[6] *Mullett* v. *Mason* (1866), L.R. 1 C.P. 559 (cows infected by cow fraudulently represented as being free from disease).

[7] *Schneider* v. *Heath* (1813), 3 Camp. 506, 508, *per* Lord Mansfield, C.J. (ship with worm-eaten hull taken from stocks to water: but a false statement had also been made). See also *Laczko* v. *Jules Meyers Inc.*, 80 Cal. Rptr. 798 (Cal. App., 1969) (turning back odometer on car).

[8] See *Horsfall* v. *Thomas* (1862), 1 H. & C. 90 where the purchaser had not sought to examine a gun sold with a concealed defect and hence had not been deceived. *Sed quaere?*

[9] (1837), 2 M. & W. 519; affd. (1838), 4 M. & W. 337.

[10] The court left open the question whether the plaintiff might have recovered had the vendor not had this knowledge: see (1837) 2 M. & W. 519. 531. In *Blakemore* v. *Bristol and Exeter Rail. Co.* (1858), 8 E. & B. 1035, 1052, Coleridge, J. commented: "[if] a friend of the father or sons, by their permission, had used the gun and sustained the accident, we apprehend ... no action could have been maintained by him".

[11] It would not, e.g., be necessary to establish the "special relationship" required by the *Hedley Byrne* principle: see above, pp. 43–45. Loss which flows directly from the deceit may, it seems, be compensated even though it is not of a type which is foreseeable: see *Doyle* v. *Olby (Ironmongers), Ltd.*, [1969] 2 Q.B. 158; [1969] 2 All E.R. 119, C.A., above, p. 57; and it is possible that exemplary damages might be awarded: see *Mafo* v. *Adams*, [1970] 1 Q.B. 548; [1969] 3 All E.R. 1404 which raised (but did not decide) the point and the comments of Lord Hailsham, L.C. in *Cassell & Co., Ltd.* v. *Broome*, [1972] A.C. 1027, 1079–1080; [1972] 1 All E.R. 801. 831–832, H.L. It would seem that deceit will not compensate a "loss of bargain" (*McConnel* v. *Wright*, [1903] 1 Ch. 546, 554, *per* Lord Collins, M.R. and cases cited above, p. 57), but the point is open to argument.

[12] *Cf. Richardson* v. *Silvester* (1873), L.R. 9 Q.B. 34 (advertising farm for sale). For statements constituting "puffs" or "sales talk", see above, pp. 33–34.

in the truth of the statement[13] is a major limit to the scope of the tort. A steady stream of cases continue to appear in American reports, as where purchasers were assured that a new heating and cooling system was needed when a replacement compressor would have been sufficient and, in another case, that full inventory control could be achieved only by automating an entire accounting system.[14]

The duty to disclose known dangers[15]

A supplier of goods must take steps to inform the recipient if he knows that the goods are dangerous and has no reason to believe that the recipient appreciates the danger and is competent to deal with it. So in *Farrant* v. *Barnes*,[16] liability was incurred when a carboy of nitric acid was delivered to a carrier without warning and the carboy later burst, injuring one of the carrier's employees. The principle has been extended to cases in which the transferor had reason to know that the product might be dangerous.[17] In *Clarke* v. *Army and Navy Cooperative Society*,[18] the plaintiff had suffered injury on opening a tin of chlorinated lime sold as a disinfectant powder by the defendant store. The defendants presumably did not know that the tin in question was dangerous but they appreciated that the tin was a potential source of danger, similar accidents having been reported in the past. Failure to issue an appropriate warning was held to be a sufficient reason for imposing liability. Whether the basic duties of suppliers go beyond this is unclear. Certainly it is arguable that the "neighbour principle" of *Donoghue* v. *Stevenson*[19] now imposes a general duty to carry out such tests and inspections for defects and danger as are reasonable in the circumstances. The point is discussed later when considering the

---

[13] *Derry* v. *Peek* (1889), 14 App. Cas. 337, H.L.

[14] See, respectively, *General Electric Co.* v. *Dorr*, 218 N.E. 2d 158 (Ind., 1966); *Clements Auto Co.* v. *Service Bureau Corporation*, 298 F. Supp. 115 (Minn., 1969); and, in general, 2 *Frumer and Friedman*, s. 17.01. See also *Restatement of Torts*, 2d, s. 402B, *above*, p. 58 (strict liability for public misrepresentations causing physical harm).

[15] See Eldredge, *Modern Tort Problems* (1941), ch. 10, pp. 249–253; ch. 12.

[16] (1862), 11 C.B. N.S. 553. See also *Anglo-Celtic Shipping Co.* v. *Elliott and Jeffery* (1926), 42 T.L.R. 297; *Chapman (or Oliver)* v. *Saddler & Co.*, [1929] A.C. 584. *Cf. Caledonian Rail Co.* v. *Warwick*, [1898] A.C. 216.

[17] See *Restatement of Torts*, 2d, s. 388. Or that it was unlikely to be made reasonably safe: *Restatement*, 2d, s. 389. *Semble* that a consignor is taken impliedly to warrant that the goods are fit for carriage and not dangerous: *Bamfield* v. *Goole and Sheffield Transport Co.*, [1910] 2 K.B. 94, C.A.

[18] [1903] 1 K.B. 155, C.A.

[19] [1932] A.C. 562, H.L.

position of retailers and gratuitous transferors.[20] There is clearly no such duty to warn that goods are shoddy as opposed to dangerous.

The duty not to supply a dangerous article into irresponsible hands

There is also a general duty not to supply a potentially dangerous article into the hands of a person who one knows or has reason to believe is not competent to handle it safely. *Dixon* v. *Bell*[1] was an early case imposing liability for the supply of a loaded gun into the hands of a young child who discharged it and injured a companion in play. Other more recent cases have involved the supply of a pistol, petrol and matches to children,[2] whilst American cases have followed a similar path and extended the principle to cover the supply of a car to a driver known to be incompetent through inexperience, intoxication or a medical condition such as epilepsy.[3]

Liability may also be incurred through the misdelivery of a potentially dangerous substance[4] or through leaving it in a position where it is accessible to a person who could not be trusted to handle it safely. In *McCarthy* v. *Wellington City*,[5] for example, the defendant council was held

---

[20] See below, at pp. 304–307 and pp. 308–309, respectively. The point is supported by *White* v. *Steadman*, [1913] 3 K.B. 340 (dangerous horse). Alternatively the defendant might become subject to such a basic duty when he knows of the *facts* constituting the danger and the danger would have been apparent to a reasonable man. See *Restatement of Torts*, 2d, s. 388 (a), s. 401. *Cf.* the common law duty of licensors to licensees (*Hawkins* v. *Coulsdon and Purley Urban District Council.*, [1954] 1 Q.B. 319 [1954] 1 All E.R. 97) and, *semble*, to trespassers (*British Railways Board* v. *Herrington* [1972] A.C. 877, 939–940; [1972] 1 All E.R. 749, 794, *per* Lord Diplock). Such conduct may, it seems, constitute a failure to act with common humanity for the purposes of the *Herrington* decision.

[1] (1816), 5 M. & S. S. 198.

[2] See *Burfitt* v. *Kille*, [1939] 2 K.B. 743; [1939] 2 All E.R. 372 (pistol and blank ammunition); *Bebee* v. *Sales* (1916), 32 T.L.R. 413 (airgun); *Yachuk* v. *Oliver Blais Co., Ltd.*, [1949] A.C. 386; [1949] 2 All E.R. 150, P.C. (petrol); *Bowman* v. *Rankin* (1963), 41 W.W.R. 700 (D.C. Sask.) (matches sold to child aged six: plaintiff's building destroyed by fire). In principle, fireworks should be covered, at least when sold to someone below a minimum statutory age: see *Burbee* v. *McFarland*, 157 A. 538 (Conn., 1931).

[3] See, e.g., *Johnson* v. *Casetta*, 17 Cal. Rptr. 81 (Cal. App., 1961) (inexperience); *cf. Setchall* v. *Snowdon*, [1974] R.T.R. 389 (no liability on handing over car keys to learner driver who promised not to drive the car); *Knight* v. *Gosselin*, 12 P. 2d 454 (Cal. App., 1932) (intoxication); *Golembe* v. *Blumberg*, 27 N.Y.S. 2d 692 (1941) (epilepsy); *Restatement of Torts*, 2d s. 390. Might a publican be held liable to compensate a third party for selling alcohol to a known drunken driver, or a petrol pump attendant for selling him petrol? See *Fuller* v. *Standard Stations Inc.*, 58 Cal. Rptr. 792 (Cal. App., 1967) and cases there cited; 2 *Frumer and Friedman*, s. 18.05; 20 A.L.R. 2d 119.

[4] *Philco Radio and Television Corporation of Great Britain Ltd.* v. *J. Spurling, Ltd.*, [1949] 2 K.B. 33; [1949] 2 All E.R. 882 (celluloid film strips).

[5] [1966] N.Z.L.R. 481. See also *Sullivan* v. *Creed*, [1904] 2 I.R. 317 (loaded gun); *Williams* v. *Eady* (1893), 10 T.L.R. 41 (phosphorus); *Marcroft* v. *Inger*, [1936] N.Z.L.R. 121.

liable for its failure to keep detonators in a more secure place after two boys, aged about fourteen, had entered a shed in a quarry and broken open a safe. They had removed the detonators from a box labelled "No. 6 100 detonators for high explosives", tried unsuccessfully to set them off and then passed on to a young brother. He slept with them under his pillow, and later gave them to the plaintiff, aged nine, whose right hand was severely injured when a detonator exploded. The New Zealand Court of Appeal held that this chain of events was a foreseeable consequence of an initial failure to exercise reasonable care.[6] All such cases, whether involving a supply or a failure to secure, may of course create difficulties in determining when liability ceases. The general answer must be when the immediate danger terminates, as when the incapacity ends or the article comes into hands which appreciate the danger and are competent to deal with it.

The liability of particular persons or bodies

Retailers

The precise scope of the retailers' liability in tort is open to debate.[7] Certain propositions would, however, be generally accepted. Firstly, retailers are subject to the basic duties common to all suppliers. They must not supply a dangerous article into irresponsible hands[8] and must warn of defects of which they know or have reason to be aware and which render the product dangerous.[9] Such information would be derived typically from complaints by consumers about products from a common source. Occasionally retailers might be held liable on this basis for what

---

[6] Presumably a trespasser who injures himself would be owed only a duty of common humanity under *British Railways Board* v. *Herrington*, [1972] A.C. 877; [1972] 1 All E.R. 749, unless the trespass is ignored as being purely technical. Trespass to goods (that is, to the product itself) seems typically to be ignored. For cases in which a child trespasser failed in his action, see *Clayton* v. *State of Victoria* [1968] V.R. 562 (Vict. Sup. Ct.); *Sullivan* v. *Lipton* (1955), *Times*, 23 February. Both cases involved sulphuric acid.

[7] For general discussion, see Eldredge, *Modern Tort Problems* (1941), p. 243 *et seq.*; Fleming, *Law of Torts*, pp. 450–452; Baker, "The Liability to Third Persons of the Transferor of Defective Chattels" (1951) 25 A.L.J. 2; *Charlesworth on Negligence*, paras. 646–655; Leidy, "Tort Liability of Suppliers of Defective Chattels", 40 Mich. L.R. 679 (1942); Prosser, *Torts*, p. 631 *et seq.*; 2 *Harper and James*, *Torts*, s. 28.29; 28.30; 2 *Frumer and Friedman*, s. 18: Noel & Phillips, *Products Liability* (1974), pp. 8–11.

[8] See *Burfitt* v. *Kille*, [1939] 2 K.B. 743; [1939] 2 All E.R. 372 (pistol and blank ammunition to child) and above, p. 303.

[9] *Clarke* v. *Army and Navy Cooperative Society*, [1903] 1 K.B. 155, C.A.; *Rivtow Marine, Ltd.* v. *Washington Iron Works* (1974), 40 D.L.R. (3d) 530 (distributor); *Restatement of Torts*, 2d, s. 388 (a); s. 401, and above, p. 302.

are essentially design deficiencies common to all such products.[10] Such cases would, however, be exceptional unless, of course, the product has been designed to the retailer's own specifications.[11] Beyond this retailers may be held liable where they have actively created a source of danger through negligence in repair, assembly, installation or storage[12] or through supplying an incorrect part or a mislabelled product.[13] Again, the plaintiff may succeed on showing reliance on a fraudulent or negligent mis-representation that the product might be used with safety or a failure to pass on a warning.[14]

The question remaining is whether retailers have a duty to carry out independent tests and inspections to discover defects of which they have no specific reason to be aware and, if so, in what circumstances. They are under no such duty in English law in so far as their contractual relations with their own suppliers are concerned. Under the Sale of Goods Act 1893, they are entitled to expect that the goods are of merchantable quality[15] and, except where the sale is by sample, an inspection is not, apparently, called for even if the existence of the defect was reasonably to be contemplated.[16] This should not, however, have any direct bearing on their potential liability in tort to a third party.[17] This latter issue has been much debated and a conclusion can be expressed only in the most general of terms. A retailer is bound to carry out such tests and in-spections as are practicable and reasonably necessary having regard to the size, prestige and facilities of the retail outlet and the nature of the product.

The size of the retail outlet has an obvious importance in determining

---

[10] *Ritter* v. *Narragansett Electric Co.*, 283 A. 2d 255 (R.I., 1971); *Garbutt* v. *Schecter*, 334 P. 2d 225 (Cal. App., 1959) (retailer liable qua occupier for unsafe chair). See also 2 *Frumer and Friedman*, s. 18.04.

[11] *Cf. Davie* v. *New Merton Board Mills*, [1959] 1 All E.R. 346, 354 *per* Viscount Simonds, where the point is noted when discussing employers' liability. Negligence in design is discussed, above, ch. 11 and the liability of the designer is considered below, pp. 316–318. Nowadays it is by no means unusual for goods to be produced to the specifications of large-scale retailers.

[12] See, e.g., *Haseldine* v. *Daw & Son, Ltd.*, [1941] 2 K.B. 343; [1941] 3 All E.R. 156; *Malfroot* v. *Noxal, Ltd.* (1935), 51 T.L.R. 551; and, in general, below, pp. 311–313.

[13] *Kubach* v. *Hollands*, [1937] 3 All E.R. 907; *Thomas* v. *Winchester*, 6 N.Y. 397 (1852).

[14] As in *Langridge* v. *Levy* (1837), 2 M. & W. 519; affd. (1838) 4 M. & W. 337, above, p. 301. *Watson* v. *Buckley, Osborne, Garrett & Co., Ltd.*, [1940] 1 All E.R. 174; *Pack* v. *County of Warner* (No. 5) (1964), 44 D.L.R. (2d) 215 (Alberta Sup. Ct.). See further 2 *Frumer and Friedman*, s. 18.03[5]. For a case involving a failure to pass on a warning, see *Holmes* v. *Ashford*, [1950] 2 All E.R. 76, C.A. (hairdresser).

[15] Section 14(2), as amended by the Supply of Goods (Implied Terms) Act 1973, s. 3: see above, pp. 78–97.

[16] Under s. 15(2)(c) of the 1893 Act, the implied condition on a sale by sample is that the goods "shall be free from any defect, rendering them unmerchantable, which would not be apparent on a reasonable examination of the sample".

[17] The same is true of earlier cases such as *Longmeid* v. *Holliday* (1851), 6 Exch. 761 which must now be read subject to the decision in *Donoghue* v. *Stevenson*, [1932] A.C. 562.

the extent of testing and inspection which can be demanded. Retail outlets which market products under their own trade or brand names can fairly be treated as though they were manufacturers and be required to assume corresponding obligations.[18] Other large scale or reputable retailers such as Harrods of London can be expected to make meaningful inquiries as to the manufacturer's system of quality control and ensure that the product is accompanied by adequate warnings and directions for use.[19] But where goods are bought in from a reputable supplier there can be no general requirement that the retailer make independent tests and inspections for latent defects. Retailers do not typically have the time, equipment or expertise to do this.

The extent of a retailer's obligations will also vary according to the type of product involved. Where the danger is great and easily ascertainable a retailer can fairly be required to carry out an inspection or at least warn that he has not done so. An obvious example is a secondhand car and there is little doubt that dealers will be accounted negligent unless they take some action with respect to safety features such as brakes and steering.[20] There is also American authority holding that dealers are under a similar duty to inspect where new cars are concerned,[1] and this is borne out by the practice of the trade. Other American cases have held that liability might be imposed where a nail protruded from the inner sole of a shoe and where a ladder which lacked a safety hook collapsed beneath a sixty-seven year old woman.[2] At the other extreme a retailer who has no reason to suspect that anything is wrong is not of course bound to open and inspect tinned, bottled or pre-packed goods[3] nor indeed any goods which reach the consumer in the manufacturer's container or

---

[18] See *Restatement of Torts*, 2d, s. 400; Strasbourg Convention, art. 3(2); above, pp. 182–183.

[19] See, e.g., *Fisher v. Harrods, Ltd.*, [1966] 1 Lloyds L.R. 500, above, p. 234; *Devilez v. Boots Pure Drug Co.* (1962), 106 Sol. Jo. 552.

[20] *Cf. Andrews v. Hopkinson*, [1957] 1 Q.B. 229; [1956] 3 All E.R. 422. The contractual requirement of merchantable quality will not necessarily demand that the car be immediately fit for driving on the road: see above, p. 94. But *quaere* whether vis-à-vis a third party it is sufficient for the dealer to warn the purchaser that an examination has not been carried out, or whether he must examine for and perhaps rectify basic defects? American cases involving used cars and other secondhand products are noted in 2 *Frumer and Friedman*, s. 18.03[3].

[1] See *McKinney v. Frodsham*, 356 P. 2d 100 (Wash., 1960) and, in general, 2 *Frumer and Friedman*, s. 18.03[2].

[2] See, respectively, *Santise v. Martins Inc.*, 17 N.Y.S. 2d 741 (1940); *Kirk v. Steinway Drug Store*, 187 N.E. 2d 307 (Ill., 1963) and, in general, 2 *Frumer and Friedman*, s. 18.03[1][b].

[3] See *Gordon v. McHardy* (1903), 6 F. (Ct. of Sess.) 210 (tinned salmon) cited with apparent approval by Lord Thankerton and Lord Macmillan in *Donoghue v. Stevenson*, [1932] A.C. 562, 604, 622. For American cases, see 2 *Frumer and Friedman*, s. 22.02[2]: 23.03[3].

packaging.[4] Here the extent of the obligation is to buy in from a reputable supplier, store under appropriate conditions and sell within the appropriate period of time. American case law lends little support to the view that testing obligations extend to products of any complexity such as electrical appliances or to products which have unexpected explosive or inflammable qualities.[5] Indirect assistance may also be found in cases which have considered whether a manufacturer was acting reasonably in looking to an intermediary to discover any defects[6] or whether defects ought to have been revealed by an examination of a sample.[7] *Godley* v. *Perry, Ltd.*[8] was such a case and it is considered below when discussing the liability of wholesalers.

In the United States of America the strict tort liability of the *Restatement of Torts*, 2d, s. 402A is associated primarily with manufacturers. There has, however, been a growing tendency to extend the liability to retailers who, it is said, are "engaged in the business of distributing goods to the public" and are "an integral part of the overall producing and marketing enterprise".[9] Private vendors and businessmen reselling equipment on a "one-off" basis would not be subject to strict tort liability.[10]

Product hire and lease

Products are frequently hired out or "leased" rather than bought and sold. Cars, caravans, television sets, and industrial equipment are obvious examples, but most products can be hired from specialist agencies should the need arise. The mode of supply may affect the contractual obligations undertaken since, unlike the vendor in a consumer sale or the finance company in an equivalent hire-purchase transaction, the person who hires

---

[4] *Cf. Rae and Rae* v. *T. Eaton Co., Maritimes, Ltd.* (1961), 28 D.L.R. (2d) 522 (Nova Scotia Sup. Ct.) (aerosol container).

[5] See, e.g., *Pound* v. *Popular Dry Goods Inc.*, 139 S.W. 2d 341 (Tex. Civ. App., 1940) (washing machine); *Smith* v. *S.S. Kreske Co.*, 79 F. 2d 361 (8th Cir., 1935) (hair combs) and, in general, 2 *Frumer and Friedman*, s. 18.03[1][a].

[6] See above, pp. 284–290. N.B., however, that the better view is that manufacturer and intermediary may be held concurrently liable unless the latter could have been reasonably expected to eliminate as well as discover the defect: see above, p. 286.

[7] Sale of Goods Act 1893, s. 15 (2) (c).

[8] [1960] 1 All E.R. 36; [1960] 1 W.L.R. 9, below, p. 310

[9] *Vandermark* v. *Ford Motor Co.*, 37 Cal. Rptr. 896, 899 (Cal. Sup. Ct., 1964). See also *Realmuto* v. *Straub Motors Inc.*, 322 A. 2d 440 (N.J. 1974) (used car dealer); *Wells* v. *Webb Machinery Co.*, 315 N.E. 2d 301 (Ill. App., 1974); and cases cited in 2 *Frumer and Friedman*, s. 19A[1]. For a discussion of the advantages and disadvantages of an extension beyond manufacturers, see the Law Commission Working Paper, No. 64, paras. 48–62.

[10] See *Balido* v. *Improved Machinery Co.*, 105 Cal. Rptr. 890 (Cal. App., 1973); *McKenna* v. *Art Pearl Works Inc.*, 310 A. 2d 677 (Pa., 1973); *Restatement*, s. 402 A, comment *f*.

out a chattel may exempt himself from his contractual obligations.[11] His liability in tort to third parties for negligence will, however, remain intact.[12] Similar considerations apply to persons who provide services involving the use of products such as hairdressers or cleaners and dyers.[13]

Subject to this point, liability may be easier to establish in the case of product hire than in the case of a retail sale. Those whose business it is to hire out products will typically be expected to carry out periodical servicing and inspections and a failure to meet these obligations may result in liability being incurred. The most frequently cited English case is *White v. John Warrick and Co., Ltd.*,[14] where the saddle of a tradesman's tricycle had tipped forward, throwing its rider to the ground. Recent American cases have held commercial bailors liable under the strict tort theory, arguing that no sensible distinction can be taken between retail sales and commercial bailments of personal property.[15] Strict liability has been imposed also on those who use a product when providing a service but there has been an understandable reluctance to apply similar principles where the services are of a professional nature.[16]

Donors and gratuitous bailors

The liability of donors and gratuitous bailors has been much discussed over the years[17] and it is not proposed to examine the subject in detail

---

[11] For the contractual warranties implied in a case of product hire see *Reed v. Dean*, [1949] 1 K.B. 188 and above, pp. 121–122. For exemption clauses in consumer sales and hire purchase transactions, see above, pp. 141–158. For proposals for reforming the law in areas including product hire, see the Law Commission's "Second Report on Exemption Clauses", Law Com. No. 69 (1975).

[12] As will his liability in negligence to the other contracting party unless excluded expressly or by necessary implication: see *White v. John Warrick & Co., Ltd.*, [1953] 2 All E.R. 1021, above, p. 131.

[13] See, e.g., *Parker v. Oxolo Ltd.*, [1937] 3 All E.R. 524; *Watson v. Buckley, Osborne, Garrett & Co., Ltd.*, [1940] 1 All E.R. 174. In both cases hairdressers were held liable to customers for breach of contract.

[14] [1953] 2 All E.R. 1021; [1953] 1 W.L.R. 1285. See also *Griffiths v. Arch Engineering Co., Ltd.*, [1968] 3 All E.R. 217; *Hadley v. Droitwich Construction Co., Ltd.*, [1967], 3 All E.R. 911.

[15] *Cintrone v. Hertz Truck Leasing and Rental Service*. 212 A. 2d 769 (N.J., 1965) (motor vehicle); *Galluccio v. Hertz Corporation*, 274 N.E. 2d 178 (Ill., 1971) (van); *McClaflin v. Bayshore Equipment Rental Co.*, 79 Cal. Rptr. 337 (Cal. App., 1969) (stepladder); and, in general, 1 *Frumer and Friedman*, s. 5.03[4], s. 16A[4][b][iii]; Annotation, 52 A.L.R. 3d 121.

[16] See, e.g., *Newmark v. Gimbel's Inc.*, 258 A. 2d 697 (N.J., 1969) (permanent wave solution in beauty parlour). *Cf.*, however, *Perlmutter v. Beth David Hospital*, 123 N.E. 2d 792 (N.Y., 1954) (contaminated blood); *Magrine v. Krasnica*, 227 A. 2d 539 (1967); 241 A. 2d 637 (N.J., 1968) (hypodermic needle breaking in dental patient's jaw).

[17] See, in particular, Marsh, "The Liability of the Gratuitous Transferor: A Comparative Study" (1950), 66 L.Q.R. 39. See also Fleming, *The Law of Torts*, 4th edn., 1971, p. 452; Salmond, *The Law of Torts*, 16th edn., 1973, pp. 305–306.

here. The essential point of contention is whether such persons owe duties going beyond the accepted minimal requirements of refraining from deceit, disclosing known dangers and not supplying dangerous articles to persons who cannot handle them safely.[18] The old cases suggest, predictably, that there is no such duty and, in particular, that there is no duty to inspect the product for latent defects.[19] Although the balance of American authority favours this view,[20] it is open to argument that the standard of reasonable care demanded by *Donoghue* v. *Stevenson*[1] applies here as elsewhere.[2]

In any event, it is likely that a broad approach would be adopted where business suppliers are concerned. No distinction is likely to be taken between promotional activities involving the supply of free samples and goods which are marketed with a view to immediate profit.[3] Nor is it likely that the car dealer or rental agency would be subject to less demanding obligations in tort when a car is being used on a trial run rather than after the conclusion of a contract.[4] Evidence of the same broad approach is to be seen in *Griffiths* v. *Arch Engineering Co., Ltd.*,[5] where Chapman, J. treated the interchange of tools between repairers in a dock as "not really gratuitous, because each has an interest in the mutual prosecution of the common work". The position of private donors or gratuitous bailors is less clear. But it is submitted that they also may owe a general duty of care which requires inspection or testing in an appropriate case. It would be strange if a plaintiff were to be worse off because he had borrowed a defective car for the day than if he were travelling as a passenger of the owner-driver.

---

[18] See further, above, pp. 300–304.

[19] See, e.g., *Coughlin* v. *Gillison*, [1899] 1 Q.B. 145; *Blakemore* v. *Bristol and Exeter Rail Co.* (1858), 8 E. & B. 1035. See also *Chapman* (or *Oliver*) v. *Saddler & Co.*, [1929] A.C. 584.

[20] See, e.g., *Miller* v. *Hand Ford Sales*, 340 P. 2d 181 (Ore., 1959) and cases cited in 1 *Frumer and Friedman*, s. 5.03 [4] [b].

[1] [1932] A.C. 562.

[2] See *Fraser* v. *Jenkins*, [1968] N.Z.L.R. 816, 824 (N.Z.C.A.), where it was unnecessary to decide the point since the danger was obvious to both bailor and bailee.

[3] *Cf.* the observations of Denning, L.J. In *Hawkins* v. *Couldson Urban District Council*, [1954] 1 All E.R. 97, 104, C.A. See also *Levi* v. *Colgate Palmolive Pty., Ltd.* (1941), 41 S.R. N.S.W. 48; *Pease* v. *Sinclair Refining Co.*, 104 F. 2d 183 (2nd Cir., 1939); *Fillmore's Valley Nurseries Ltd.* v. *North American Cyanamid, Ltd.* (1958), 14 D.L.R. (2d) 297; Waddams, *Products Liability* (1974), pp. 87–89; 19 Univ. Toronto Law Jo. 157, 163–166 (1969). On the distinction between sales and gifts generally, see *Esso Petroleum, Ltd.* v. *Customs and Excise Commissioners*, [1976] 1 All E.R. 117, [1976] 1 W.L.R. 1, H.L.; *Chappell & Co., Ltd.* v. *Nestle Co., Ltd.*, [1960] A.C. 87, [1959] 2 All E.R. 701, H.L., and above, pp. 115–117.

[4] Prospective bailment and purchase cases appear to be subject to the rules for bailment and sale in the USA: see 1 *Frumer and Friedman*, s. 5.03 [4], n. 7; 2 *Frumer and Friedman*, s. 18.03 [3], n. 9.1.

[5] [1968] 3 All E.R. 217, 220.

Intermediate distributors and importers

Intermediate distributors or wholesalers would rarely incur liability for negligence. Their typical role is to act as a mere conduit between manufacturer and retailer without their having any direct contact with the public. Reasonable care would not normally require them to carry out independent tests or inspections or to issue warnings though they may need to ensure that their own supplier is reputable and has adequate testing facilities. *Watson* v. *Buckley, Osborne, Garrett & Co., Ltd.*[6] is in point. Here an "old established, important and highly reputable" distributor was held liable to the plaintiff who had contracted dermatitis after a hairdresser had treated him with a dye supplied originally by a 'Spanish gentleman" who had just set up business in London after having been driven out of Spain. In imposing liability on the distributors, Stable, J. noted that they had taken no steps to ascertain under what sort of supervision the dye was manufactured. Nor had they carried out any tests themselves. The case against them was, moreover, strengthened by the fact that they had advertised the dye as being safe and as needing no preliminary tests.

Godley v. *Perry, Ltd.*[7] is also of interest. Here it was pleaded as a defence to fourth party proceedings brought by a wholesaler against an importer that the defective condition of a catapult which had injured a child would have been discoverable on a reasonable examination of the sample. The third party wholesaler had pulled on the elastic in the normal way but had not tested it to destruction. Edmund-Davies, J. held that this was unnecessary and added:[8]

> "He might also, I suppose, have tried biting the catapult, or hitting it with a hammer, or applying a lighted match to ensure its non-inflammability . . . But . . . none of these tests is called for by a process of 'reasonable examination', as that phrase would be understood by the common-sense standards of everyday life."

It would be a mistake to assume that the same view would necessarily have been taken if the injured child had been suing the wholesaler in tort. But there is nonetheless a close correspondence between the two situations.

Where the intermediate distributor is an importer of the product there is much to be said for the approach adopted in the Strasbourg Convention on Products Liability of holding him liable as though he were its producer or manufacturer.[9] Failing such a provision, a person injured by a defective

---

[6] [1940] 1 All E.R. 174. See also *Goodchild* v. *Vaclight* (1965), *Times*, 22 May, *Pack* v. *County of Warner* (1964), 44 D.L.R. (2d) 215 (Alb. Sup. Ct.); *Rivtow Marine, Ltd.* v. *Washington Iron Works* (1974), 40 D.L.R. 3d 530 (Sup. Ct. of Canada).

[7] [1960] 1 All E.R. 36.

[8] *Ibid.*, at p. 40.

[9] Art. 3 (2). See also art. 2 of the proposed EEC directive.

product may be left to fall back on a claim against a foreign manu-facturer which would frequently not be worth pursuing. In *Godley* v. *Perry, Ltd.*,[7] for example, the catapult was manufactured in Hong Kong.

Where the defendant is a multi-national company with an English sub-sidiary, there is little justification for treating a plaintiff differently according to whether the product is manufactured abroad or at the local base. Nor should he be required to become involved in jurisdiction or choice of law problems any more than is absolutely necessary.[10] Some support for this view is to be found in the decision at first instance in *Phillips* v. *Ford Motor Co. of Canada, Ltd.*[11] Here Haines, J. refused to treat the defendants any differently because the Lincoln Continental car happened to have been designed and manufactured by the American parent company rather than by their Canadian subsidiary. The judgment in favour of the plaintiff, who had been injured when the brakes failed, was reversed on other grounds, but the Ontario Court of Appeal does not seem to have disagreed with this approach.

The general approach of American cases is to deny liability in negligence unless the intermediate distributor had reason to know that the product was defective or otherwise dangerous and failed thereafter to issue a warning.[12] Wholesalers have, however, been subjected to liability under the strict tort theory which does not of course require proof of negligence. Indeed in *Canifax* v. *Hercules Powder Co.*[13] a California Court of Appeal held that the strict tort theory was applicable to a wholesaler who did not take physical possession of the goods but merely passed on an order to the manufacturer who supplied the customer directly.

Repairers, servicers, reconditioners, assemblers, installers, contractors

Retailers and intermediate distributors typically incur liability because a product was defective when it was marketed. Liability may, however, be incurred through contact with a product at a later stage, as when persons are called in to repair, service or recondition it. Similarly there

---

[10] See below, ch. 17.
[11] (1970) 12 D.L.R. (3d) 28 (Ont. High Ct.), revd. (1971) 18 D.L.R. (3d) 641 (Ont. C.A.).
[12] See 2 *Frumer and Friedman*, s. 20; *Restatement of Torts*, 2d, s. 402. *Willey* v. *Fyrogas Co.*, 251 S.W. 2d 635 (Mo., 1952) is a leading case denying liability. Examples of cases holding that the distributor was subject to a duty to warn include *Blitzstein* v. *Ford Motor Co.*, 288 F. 2d 738 (5th., 1961) (leaking petrol tank); *Morris* v. *Shell Oil Co.*, 467 S.W. 2d 39 (Mo., 1971) (petroleum solvent).
[13] 46 Cal. Rptr. 552 (Cal. App., 1965). See also *Barth* v. *B.F. Goodrich Tire Co.*, 71 Cal. Rptr. 306 (Cal. App., 1968); *Cottom* v. *McGuire Funeral Service Inc.*, 262 A. 2d 807 (1970), *Seattle First National Bank* v. *Volkswagen of America Inc.*, 525 P. 2d 286 (Wash., 1974) (importers), and, in general, 2 *Frumer and Friedman*, s. 20.04 [2]. *Restatement of Torts*, 2d, s. 402 A, comment *f*.

may be liability for negligence in assembling or installing a product and this is so whether the defendant is the manufacturer, vendor or an independent party.[14] Early cases which are inconsistent with this view have long since been overtaken by the decision in *Donoghue* v. *Stevenson*.[15] So in a representative selection of modern cases, liability has been incurred for negligence in repairing a lift, the steering of a motor car, and a fork lift truck;[16] reconditioning a motor car;[17] repairing and reassembling the wheel of a lorry;[18] fitting a sidecar to a motorcycle, a valve to a ship's boiler, and an outlet pipe to discharge gases from a boiler;[19] and in installing an electric meter in a factory, a gas heating system in a house and a juke box in a restaurant.[20]

The negligence in such cases may take a variety of forms. A source of danger may have been created actively, as through misassembly or the use of a defective replacement part. Alternatively, the defendant may have failed to remedy a defect when this was to be expected whether under a specific contract for repair or under a general service contract which was not fulfilled. There are many American decisions holding maintenance contractors liable to third parties who have been injured when a product fails through lack of repair. A high proportion of the cases has involved lifts.[1] In another much cited case a cause of action was held to have been

---

[14] See further, above, pp. 199–207 for discussion of the manufacturers' liability for defects caused by faulty assembly and construction.

[15] [1932] A.C. 562, H.L. Earlier cases included *Winterbottom* v. *Wright* (1842), 10 M. & W. 109 and *Earl* v. *Lubbock*, [1905] 1 K.B. 253.

[16] *Haseldine* v. *Daw & Son, Ltd.*, [1941] 2 K.B. 343; [1941] 3 All E.R. 156, C.A. (lift); *Power* v. *Bedford Motor Co., Ltd.*, [1959] I.R. 391 (car steering); *Jull* v. *Wilson*, [1968] N.Z.L.R. 88 (N.Z. Sup. Ct.) (truck). See also *The Trecarrell*, [1973] 1 Lloyds L.R. 402; *Godfrey's, Ltd.* v. *Ryles*, [1962] S.A.S.R. 33 (S.A.Sup.Ct.); *Marschler* v. *Masser's Garage* (1956), 2 D.L.R. (2d) 484 (Ont. High Ct.); *Clelland* v. *Berryman* (1975) 56 D.L.R. (3d) 395 (B.C. Sup. Ct.).

[17] *Herschtal* v. *Stewart & Ardern, Ltd.*, [1940] 1 K.B. 155; [1939] 4 All E.R. 123; *Algoma Truck and Tractor Sales, Ltd.* v. *Bert's Auto Supply, Ltd.*, [1968] 68 D.L.R. 2d 363. *Quaere* whether damages were properly awarded in the latter case? See below, p. 333.

[18] *Stennett* v. *Hancock and Peters*, [1939] 2 All E.R. 578.

[19] See, respectively, *Malfroot* v. *Noxal, Ltd.* (1935), 51 T.L.R. 551 (sidecar); *Howard* v. *Furness Houlder Argentine Lines, Ltd.*, [1936] 2 All E.R. 781 (valve); *Dominion Natural Gas Co., Ltd.* v. *Collins and Perkins*, [1909] A.C. 640, P.C. (outlet pipe). See also *Erison* v. *Higgins* (1975), 48 D.L.R. (3d) 687 (Ont. C.A.).

[20] See *Hartley* v. *Mayoh & Co.*, [1954] 1 Q.B. 383; [1953] 2 All E.R. 525 (electric meter); *Ostash* v. *Sonnenberg* (1968), 67 D.L.R. (2d) 311 Alberta Sup. Ct.) (heating system); *Tsakiris* v. *Universal Music Manitoba (1971), Ltd.* (1975), 48 D.L.R. (3d) 56 (Man. Q.B.) (jukebox). See also *Ives* v. *Clare Brothers, Ltd.* (1971), 15 D.L.R. (3d) 519 (Ont. High Ct.). Further Canadian cases are cited by Waddams, *Products Liability*, p. 14, notes 5–6.

[1] See, e.g., *Otis Elevator Co.* v. *Lepore*, 181 A. 2d 659 (Md., 1962); *Hickman* v. *Haughton Elevator Co.*, 519 P. 2d 369 (Ore., 1974) and, in general, 1 *Frumer and Friedman*, s. 5.03[3]; 63 ALR 3d 996. *Cf. Helicopter Sales (Australia) Pty., Ltd.* v. *Rotor-Work Pty., Ltd.* (1974), 48 A.L.J.R. 390 (High Ct., Australia) (contract to service helicopter: no liability in contract or for negligence on facts).

stated when a plaintiff's home was destroyed by fire after a fire hydrant installed by the defendant under contract with a third party had failed to operate.[2] With some products, the service contractor who fails to keep a proper record of the work completed might also be liable to a subsequent purchaser though damage is confined to the product itself and conceivably also for the consequences of his having made a bad bargain.[3]

Building contractors and builder-vendors

There has been some difficulty in applying these general principles to cases where a product has been incorporated into realty and to the construction of realty.[4] This, incidentally, is as true of the law as it has developed in the United States of America[5] as of the law in this country. Nowadays it is clear that contractors and suppliers of goods both owe a duty of care with respect to installations and work on premises.[6] Indeed it would be curious if they did not since there is hardly a meaningful distinction to be taken between the supply of, say, a free-standing electric fire which electrocutes a householder and the installation of a domestic boiler which explodes thereafter and injures him.

It is also clearly established that a duty is owed by builders who build on land owned by a third party.[7] Within English law, doubts as to the position of the builder-vendor seem to have been removed by the Defective Premises Act 1972, s. 3(1), which provides that any duty of care owed "shall not be abated by the subsequent disposal of the premises by the person who owed the duty".[8] However s.3(1) applies only to contracts

---

[2] *Doyle* v. *South Pittsburgh Water Co.*, 199 A. 2d 875 (Pa., 1964). *Cf. Clark* v. *Meigs Equipment Co.*, 226 N.E. 2d 791 (Ohio. App., 1967).

[3] *Cf. Hawke* v. *Waterloo-Wellington Flying Club, Ltd.* (1972), 22 DLR (3d 266—York (Ontario) County Court—(aircraft). The problems raised by cases of economic loss are discussed below, ch. 16, pp. 328–344.

[4] See *Malone* v. *Laskey*, [1907] 2 K.B. 141; *Ball* v. *London County Council*, [1949] 2 K.B. 159; [1949] 1 All E.R. 1056 *Bottomley* v. *Bannister* [1932] 1 K.B. 458.

[5] The early reluctance to apply the principles of *Macpherson* v. *Buick Motor Co.*, 111 N.E. 1050 (N.Y.C.A., 1916) above, p. 13 to real property is traced in 1 *Frumer and Friedman*, s. 5.03[2], s. 5.03[5][*b*] discussing, respectively, building and construction contractors and builder-vendors.

[6] *Cf. A. C. Billings & Sons, Ltd.* v. *Riden*, [1958] A.C. 240; [1957] 3 All E.R. 1; *Miller* v. *South of Scotland Electricity Board*, 1958 S.C. (H.L.) 20; *Pusey* v. *Peters* (1974), 119 Sol. Jo. 85 and see North, *Occupiers' Liability* (1971), pp. 220–221.

[7] *Sharpe* v. *E. T. Sweeting & Son, Ltd.*, [1963] 2 All E.R. 455; [1963] 1 W.L.R. 665; *Gallagher* v. *Mcdowell, Ltd.*, [1961] N.I. 26.

[8] The Act implements with some modifications the proposals in the Law Commission report, "Civil Liability of Vendors and Lessors for Defective Premises", Law Com. No. 40, 1970. *Quaere* whether it was "the subsequent disposal of the premises" which prevented liability from accruing?

entered into and disposals completed on or after 1 January 1974. The position in other cases remains uncertain.[9]

By the Defective Premises Act 1972, s. 1 (1), a duty is also imposed on persons

"taking on work for or in connection with the provision of a dwelling (whether the dwelling is provided by the erection or by the conversion or enlargement of a building)."

Such persons would include professional men such as architects and surveyors, subcontractors such as electricians and plumbers, and suppliers of goods to special order. Whether they would include local authority building inspectors is unclear.[10] All are obliged in the words of the subsection:

"to see that the work which he takes on is done in a workman-like or, as the case may be, professional manner, with proper materials and so that as regards that work the dwelling will be fit for habitation when completed".[11]

Breach of the duty is actionable within the limitation period[12] at the suit of anyone who has or who acquires a legal or equitable interest in the dwelling.[13] Economic loss as well as physical damage is clearly covered.

---

[9] For the commencement date, see s. 7 of the 1972 Act. The position at common law is not wholly clear. *Bottomley* v. *Bannister*, [1932] 1 K.B. 458 is generally considered to confer an immunity on the builder-vendor. But in *Dutton* v. *Bognor Regis Urban District Council*, [1972] 1 Q.B. 373; [1972] 1 All E.R. 462, C.A., Lord Denning, M.R. and Sachs, L.J. stated *obiter* that the builder-vendor enjoyed no such immunity. The point was reiterated in *Sparham-Souter* v. *Town and Country Developments (Essex), Ltd.*, [1976] Q.B. 858; [1976] 2 All E.R. 65, C.A. But the traditional view was reaffirmed by Speight, J. in *Bowen* v. *Paramount Builders, Ltd.*, [1975] 2 N.Z.L.R. 546 (N.Z. Sup. Ct.).

[10] See *Sparham-Souter* v. *Town and Country Developments (Essex), Ltd.*, [1976] 2 All E.R. 65, 70, *per* Lord Denning, M.R. Liability may be incurred at common law: see *Dutton* v. *Bognor Regis Urban District Council* [1972] 1 Q.B. 373; [1972] 1 All E.R. 462 and the *Sparham-Souter* case. See also the Law Commission paper No. 40, "Civil Liability of Vendors and Lessors for Defective Premises" (Explanatory Notes) p. 33; North (1973) 36 M.L.R. 628, 629.

[11] *Semble* that the three requirements of (i) good workmanship; (ii) proper materials and (iii) fitness for habitation are distinct and that all must be satisfied: see *Hancock* v. *B. W. Brazier (Anerley), Ltd.*, [1966] 2 All E.R. 901; [1966] 1 W.L.R. 1317, C.A.

[12] By s. 1 (5) of the Act a cause of action for breach of the duty imposed by s. 1 (1) is deemed to have accrued "at the time when the dwelling was completed". There is a saving for the case where a person does further work to rectify a mistake. Section 1 (1) does not, however, derogate from any other duty which might be owed apart from the Act: see s. 6 (2). Hence, in so far as such duties have limitation periods which are calculated by reference to a different point of time, a person might be better off suing at common law even though he falls within the terms of s. 1. Limitation periods are discussed further, above, pp. 296–299. See also the comments of Lord Denning, M.R. in the *Sparham-Souter* case, [1976] Q.B. 858; [1976] 2 All E.R. 65, 70.

[13] Section 1 (1) (*b*).

Suppliers of general building materials or mass-produced components do not seem to fall within s. 1 (1) of the 1972 Act though they might incur liability for negligence or for breach of contract.[14] The same is true of persons who do fall within the subsection but whose work is done in connection with something other than a "dwelling". Generally there has been a certain reluctance to hold suppliers liable for products which have been incorporated into realty and which are accordingly to a greater or lesser extent "immovable".[15] The loss in such cases is frequently economic or, at least, confined to the building itself.[16] Moreover, the problem may become apparent only after a considerable lapse of time. High Alumina cement provides as good an example as any.[17]

In the United States the early reluctance to impose liability also seems to have disappeared so that the building contractor and the builder-vendor are generally held to owe at least a duty of care.[18] The battleground has now predictably moved on to the application of the strict tort and implied warranty theories and some courts have imposed liability on this basis especially in the case of mass-produced houses.[19] This seems sensible since there is no reason, apart from historical accident, why a developer of a housing estate should be treated differently from a manufacturer of products. A further step was taken by the Supreme Court of California in *Connor* v. *Great Western Savings and Loan Association*[20] where a company which financed a housing development knowing the builder to be under-capitalised was held liable to purchasers of houses built on inadequate foundations. The relationship between the financier and the builder involved something more than the lending of money on the security of real property but the decision is nonetheless highly questionable.

---

[14] As to which, see *Young and Marten, Ltd.* v. *McManus Childs, Ltd.*, [1969] 1 A.C. 454; [1968] 2 All E.R. 1169, H.L.

[15] The Strasbourg convention covers movables incorporated into an immovable even though they have lost their individual identity, but does not cover an immovable such as a building itself: see art. 2 (*a*) and accompanying commentary. Any such distinction must be productive of anomalies.

[16] Some of the difficulties of distinguishing between "physical damage" to the property and simple economic loss are discussed below, pp. 328–330, 331–332. The distinction may be crucial when the action is brought at common law rather than under the 1972 Act.

[17] See Adam Neville, *High Alumina Cement* (1975).

[18] See 1 *Frumer and Friedman*, s. 5.03 [2], s. 503 [5] [*b*] and cases there cited.

[19] See, e.g., *Schipper* v. *Levitt and Sons Inc.*, 207 A. 2d 314 (N.J., 1965) (child of purchaser's lessee scalded by hot water heating system installed by builder-vendor); *Kriegler* v. *Eichler Homes Inc.*, 74 Cal. Rptr. 749 (Cal. App., 1969); *Stuart* v. *Crestview Mutual Water Co.*, 110 Cal. Rptr. 543 (Cal. App., 1973).

[20] 73 Cal. Rptr. 369 (1968). *Cf. Bradler* v. *Craig*, 79 Cal. Rptr. 401 (Cal. App., 1969).

Inspectors, designers, engineers, testing agencies, endorsers, and persons occupying a similar position

It is now clear that a wide range of professional men may incur liability in tort to persons who are foreseeably likely to be affected by their conduct. In recent years a number of English and Commonwealth cases involving negligence on the part of surveyors, architects, and construction engineers has arisen in connection with real property.[1] The principles established in such cases might be applied *mutatis mutandis* to products. Indeed Lord Denning has said in a context which suggests that he had products as well as property in mind, that a professional man who gives advice on the safety of buildings or machines or material, owes a duty to all who may suffer if his advice is bad.[2] In some such cases the potential for liability is clear and the consequences need not be far-reaching. There is, for example, little doubt that a careless lift inspector may be held liable in the same way as a lift repairer,[3] and the same is no doubt true of persons who inspect, report on, or issue certificates in respect of the safety of other machines.[4] In *Buszta* v. *Souther*,[5] the Supreme Court of Rhode Island applied this principle to a motor car and held that an official motor vehicle inspection station might be held liable for personal injury when the brakes of a car failed soon after a test certificate had been issued. An English court would probably reach the same conclusion if it could be established that the defect existed at the date of the test and that the garage was careless in failing to discover it.[6]

In other cases the consequences of imposing liability might be far-

---

[1] See, e.g., *Dutton* v. *Bognor Regis Urban District Council*, [1972] 1 Q.B. 373; [1972] 1 All E.R. 462 (local authority surveyor); *Clay* v. *A. J. Crump & Sons, Ltd.*, [1964] 1 Q.B. 533; [1963] 3 All E.R. 687 (architect); *Voli* v. *Inglewood Shire Council* (1963), 110 C.L.R. 74 (High Ct., Australia) (architect); *Bevan Investments, Ltd.* v. *Blackhall and Struthers*, [1973] 2 N.Z.L.R. 45 (N.Z. Sup. Ct.) (structural engineer). *Cf.* *McCrea* v. *City of White Rock* (1975) 56 D.L.R. (3d) 525 (B.C.C.A.) (building inspector). See also *Greaves and Co. Contractors, Ltd.* v. *Baynham Meikle & Partners*, [1975] 3 All E.R. 99; [1975] 1 W.L.R. 1095, C.A., above, p. 120, where the claim was in contract.

[2] *Cf. Dutton* v. *Bognor Regis Urban District Council*, [1972] 1 Q.B. 373, 395.

[3] See, e.g., *Nelson* v. *Union Wire Rope Corporation*, 199 N.E. 2d 769 (Ill., 1964) cited with approval by Lord Denning in the *Dutton* case: [1972] 1 Q.B. 373, 395. See also above, pp. 311–312 for discussion of liability as a repairer.

[4] See, e.g. *Driver* v. *William Willett (Contractors), Ltd.*, [1969] 1 All E.R. 665 (consultant safety engineers); *Otash* v. *Sonnenberg* (1968), 67 D.L.R. (2d) 311 (Alberta C.A.) (gas burner). See also *Gordon* v. *Moen and Captain W. Dunsford, Ltd.*, [1971] N.Z.L.R. 526 (N.Z. Sup. Ct.) (marine surveyor).

[5] 232 A. 2d 396 (1967). See also *Rutherford* v. *A.-G.*, [1976] 1 N.Z.L.R. 403 (N.Z. Sup. Ct.) (heavy motor vehicle).

[6] The test certificate certifies that at the date of the examination of the vehicle it complied with the requirements prescribed by regulations made under the Road Traffic Act 1972, s. 43. See also Sachs, L.J. in the *Dutton* case, [1972] 1 Q.B. 373, 407.

reaching. This would be especially true of cases in which it was sought to hold persons responsible for deficiencies in a product's design, specifications or ingredients, and only marginally less so where there were defects within a substantial batch.[7] The liability of a manufacturer for deficiencies in design rendering a product unreasonably dangerous has been discussed earlier.[8] Specialist designers of products, together with their equivalents in fields such as drugs, medicines and herbicides, would seem to be subject to a similar liability. The same is true of official agencies which grant licences and certificates without which certain products such as drugs or aeroplanes cannot be marketed.[9]

American cases have proceeded with caution in this area. It seems unlikely that persons providing professional and advisory services, such as designers, engineers and architects, will be subjected to strict liability in the same way as manufacturers, land developers and others.[10] On the other hand, an interesting Californian case has pointed to the potential liability for negligence of bodies which endorse or certify a product by means of seals of approval and the like. In *Hanberry* v. *Hearst Corporation*,[11] the plaintiff had slipped on a vinyl floor when wearing shoes which the defendants had advertised as meeting their "Good Housekeeping's Consumers' Guarantee Seal". In the resultant action claiming compensation for personal injuries, the Court of Appeal for the Fourth District said:

> "one who endorses a product for his own economic gain, and for the purpose of encouraging and inducing the public to buy it, may be liable to a purchaser who, relying on the endorsement, buys the product and is injured because it is defective and not as represented in the endorsement."[12]

The advertisement in this case had stated expressly that the defendants were satisfied that products carrying their "guarantee" were good ones. However, the principle seems capable of being applied to cases where

---

[7] As in Lord Denning's example in *Candler* v. *Crane Christmas and Co.*, [1951] 1 All E.R. 426, 433, of the analyst who certifies to a manufacturer of food that a particular ingredient is harmless when it is in fact poisonous.

[8] See above, ch. 11.

[9] For an American example, see *Griffin* v. *The United States*, 351 F. Supp. 10 (Pa., 1972) where the Biological Standards Division of the National Institute of Health was held liable for negligence in testing polio vaccine for neurovirulence.

[10] See, e.g., *Stuart* v. *Crestview Mutual Water Co.*, 110 Cal. Rptr. 543 (Cal. App., 1973), where the developer was regarded as subject to strict liability but the engineer was not, and, in general, Note, "Liability of Design Professionals", 58 Iowa L.R. 1221 (1973); 2 *Frumer and Friedman*, s. 16A [4] [b] [ii]. See also above, pp. 119–121 where the point is discussed in the context of implied warranties.

[11] 81 Cal. Rptr. 519 (Cal. App., 1969). See also Annotation, 39 A.L.R. 3d 181; 1 *Frumer and Friedman*, s. 2.

[12] 81 Cal. Rptr. 519, 521 (1969), relying on Restatement, *Torts*, 2d s. 311.

there is no express statement, as where a sportsman allows his name to be associated with a product in return for a fee, and to cases where the seal of approval is that of a non-profit making organisation. In an age when products increasingly carry such inscriptions and marks, the development may prove to be significant.[13]

---

[13] See also the consultative document "Consumer Safety", Cmnd. 6398 (1976), paras. 16–18, citing the B.S.I. "Kitemark".

16 The Types of Damage or Loss Compensated

Introduction

There may be major difficulties in determining the types of damage or loss which will be compensated in a product liability action. Where the claim is in respect of personal injury or property damage the plaintiff's losses will be compensated to the same extent as in any similar area of the law of tort. The driver of a car who is injured in a collision with another vehicle will be compensated according to the same principles whether he is suing the manufacturer of a defective car or the driver of a safe one. It is not our concern to discuss the rules governing the quantification of damages in such cases though some indication will be given of the broad types of personal injury and property damage covered.

Other cases raise problems of a different order. For example, the plaintiff may be suing the manufacturer in respect of damage which is confined to the defective product itself, as when the brakes of a car have failed and the car has run into a wall. Alternatively, the product may have been repaired in time to prevent such damage and the plaintiff may be claiming the cost of repair.[1] In other cases the allegation may be that the product, though quite safe, is nevertheless unfit for its ordinary purpose or for some special purpose for which it is known to be required. The plaintiff may then be claiming the difference between the price paid and the value received or, perhaps, the cost of adapting the product to make it fit for its purpose. Additional consequential losses might arise in any of the above cases, especially if the product was to be used in a business venture.

---

[1] As in *Rivtow Marine, Ltd.* v. *Washington Iron Works* (1974), 40 D.L.R. (3d) 530 (Sup. Ct. of Canada), below, p. 333.

At some stage the defendant will raise the objection that the plaintiff is claiming to be compensated for purely economic losses. Here the general rule is that such losses fall within the province of the law of contract and are not compensated by the tort of negligence[2] unless the parties stand in a "special relationship" to each other of the type contemplated by the *Hedley Byrne*[3] decision. Manufacturers and remote purchasers hardly stand in such a relationship to each other. Nor, *a fortiori*, do manufacturers and sub-purchasers of secondhand goods or donees. Hence one must enter what has been described as a "scarcely charted sea"[4] with caution. American cases have occasionally imposed liability on a negligence, strict tort or implied warranty theory in such situations but they show no uniformity of approach.[5]

Death, personal and pre-natal injury

English law may eventually adopt a different basis of liability according to whether the claim is in respect of death or personal injury or in respect of property damage. The likelihood of a division along these lines is increased by the fact that both the Strasbourg Convention and the terms of reference of the Pearson Commission are limited to the former type of case, although the proposed EEC directive is not.[6] There should be no difficulty in distinguishing between the two types of claim, though problems might theoretically be caused by artificial limbs or joints or by medical aids such as pacemakers or tubing inserted permanently in the body.[7]

The determination of what constitutes death or a personal injury is also

---

[2] Authorities establishing the general rule are legion. Two of the more important include *S.C.M. (United Kingdom), Ltd.* v. *W.J. Whittal & Son, Ltd.*, [1971] 1 Q.B. 137; [1970] 3 All E.R. 245; *Spartan Steel, Ltd.* v. *Martin & Co. (Contractors), Ltd.*, [1973] Q.B. 27; [1972] 3 All E.R. 557.

[3] *Hedley Byrne & Co., Ltd.* v. *Heller & Partners, Ltd.*, [1964] A.C. 465; [1963] 2 All E.R. 575, above, pp. 43–45, below, pp. 337–338.

[4] *Young and Marten, Ltd.* v. *McManus Childs, Ltd.*, [1969] 1 A.C. 454, 475; [1968] 2 All E.R. 1169, 1177 *per* Lord Upjohn.

[5] See below, pp. 338–342.

[6] Thus art. 3(1) of the Strasbourg convention provides that "The producer shall be liable to pay compensation for death or personal injuries caused by a defect in his product". Liability is strict though it admits of certain defences. For the status of the convention, see above, pp. 3–4. For the terms of reference of the Pearson Commission, see above, p. 2. The EEC draft directive covers damage to property which the claimant has not acquired or used for trade or business purposes: art. 6.

[7] The artificial limb would no doubt constitute "property belonging to another" for the purposes of the Theft Act 1968, s. 1(1).

unlikely to create practical problems apart from the special cases of pre-natal injury and allergic reactions examined below. A working definition is provided by the Limitation Act 1975 which defines "personal injuries" to include "any disease and any impairment of a person's physical or mental condition".[8] Poisoning, dermatitis and bodily disease[9] are clearly covered as are the more obvious cases of injury through impact or burning. Nervous shock and psychiatric illness should equally qualify[10] as should the more extreme forms of nausea even though their origin is purely psychological rather than physical. There is no reason to suppose that recovery would have been denied in *Donoghue* v. *Stevenson*[11] had the snail emerged at the first pouring and had the plaintiff suffered severe nausea on thinking of what she might have consumed. Indeed it is by no means clear that her response was not primarily psychological since her averment referred to both the nauseating sight of the snail and the impurities already consumed.[12]

Holden v. *Kayser Roth Corporation*[13] is an unusual American case which suggests that acute embarrassment or mental suffering through use of a defective product might also be sufficient. The plaintiff contended that her bathing costume became transparent when wet, thus exposing her "private and personal parts", to her "humiliation, mortification and embarrassment". The claims failed through want of proof, the Appelate Court of Illinois leaving open the question whether the manufacturer might have been held liable had the costume been shown to be defective.

Pre-natal Injuries

The aftermath of the thalidomide tragedy has seen an upsurge of interest in the question of whether a cause of action may be founded on pre-natal damage to the embryo or foetus. As yet, there appears to be no English

---

[8] Section 4 (4), Sch. 1, para. 3, amending the Limitation Act 1939, s. 31 (1).

[9] See, e.g., *Thomas* v. *Winchester*, 6 N.Y. 397, 57 Am. Dec. 455 (1852) (poison); *Grant* v. *Australian Knitting Mills, Ltd.*, [1936] A.C. 85, P.C. (dermatitis); *Wright* v. *Dunlop Rubber Co., Ltd.* (1972), 13 K.I.R. 255 (cancer).

[10] *Dooley* v. *Cammel Laird & Co., Ltd.*, [1951] 1 Lloyd's Rep. 271 and *Mount Isa Mines, Ltd.* v. *Pusey* (1971), 45 A.L.J.R. 88 (High Ct. of Australia) both involved products, but in neither case was the action against the manufacturer.

[11] [1932] A.C. 562, H.L.

[12] The balance of American authority appears to permit recovery on such facts: see 2 *Frumer and Friedman*, s. 21.05; s. 25.01 [2] and cases there cited. See also *Curll* v. *Robin Hood Multifoods, Ltd.* (1974), 56 D.L.R. (3d) 129 (Nova Scotia Sup. Ct.) (aggravation of nervous condition on seeing remains of a decomposed mouse in a bag of flour), and above, p. 194.

[13] 235 N.E. 2d 426 (Ill. App., 1968).

decision directly in point,[14] but the Law Commission has suggested "that it is highly probable that the common law would, in appropriate circumstances, provide a remedy".[15] This seems to be a correct assessment of the position and it is supported by decisions from other common law jurisdictions.[16] A right of action is also established by the Congenital Disabilities (Civil Liability) Act 1976 but the Act applies only to births occurring after its passing.[17] This has obvious implications for manufacturers of products generally, and, more especially, for manufacturers of drugs which are capable of having a teratogenic effect.

The probable limits of liability at common law and the limits under the 1976 Act may be summarised as follows. Firstly, it is unlikely that liability would be incurred unless the child is born alive.[18] Hence pre-natal damage from a product which leads to a child being still-born, as through a traumatic effect on a pregnant woman, is unlikely to ground liability to the "child", though it may of course do so to the mother. Under s 4(?) of the 1976 Act, recovery is limited to a child who is "born alive" and "has a life separate from its mother" and by s. 4(4) the child must live for at least forty-eight hours. Secondly, it is fairly clear that the English common law would not permit of claims for so-called "wrongful life" where the essence of the complaint is that the child would have been better off if it had not been born at all.[19] So the manufacturer of a defective contraceptive device could not be sued by a normal healthy child born into the most disadvantageous circumstances, or, for that matter, born ugly. Section 1(1)

---

[14] Claims have, however, been settled in thalidomide cases: see *S. v. Distillers Co. (Biochemicals), Ltd.*, [1969] 3 All E.R. 1412; [1970] 1 W.L.R. 114. See also (1939) 83 Sol. Jo. 185, where reference is made to the settlement of a claim at Liverpool Assizes brought on behalf of a child born prematurely when a ladder fell on a pregnant woman. The child lived for one hour and £100 was paid in settlement. For general discussion of pre-natal injuries, see Lovell and Griffith-Jones, "The Sins of the Fathers: tort liability for pre-natal injuries", (1974), 90 L.Q.R. 531; Gordon, "The Unborn Plaintiff", 63 Mich. L.R. 579 (1965); Winfield, "The Unborn Child", (1942) 8 C.L.J. 76; Law Commission "Report on Injuries to Unborn Children", Law Com. No. 60, August 1974.

[15] Law Com. No. 60, para. 8.

[16] See, e.g., *Watt v. Rama*, [1972] V.R. 353 (Vict. Sup. Ct.); *Duval v. Sequin* (1974), 40 D.L.R. (3d) 666 (Ont. C.A.). Modern American decisions also support recovery. See 40 A.L.R. 3d 1222; note, 110 Univ. Pa. L.R. 554 (1962).

[17] Section 4(5). The Act gives effect to the Law Commission's recommendations: Law Com. No. 60, August 1974.

[18] American cases such as *White v. Yup*, 458 P. 2d 617 (Nev., 1969) allowing recovery where the still-born child was viable might be cited in support of the contrary view: see Lovell and Griffiths-Jones (1974), 90 L.Q.R. 531, 543–547.

[19] See Tedeschi "On Tort Liability for Wrongful Life" (1966), 1 Israel L.R. 513; Lovell and Griffiths-Jones, *op. cit.*, pp. 549–556. *Zepeda v. Zepeda*, 190 N.E. 2d 849 (Ill. App., 1963) (illegitimacy) and *Williams v. New York*, 223 N.E. 2d 343 (1966) (illegitimate child of mental defective) are well-known American cases. See further 22 A.L.R. 3d 1441. A possible exception might be made for a drug which prevents the spontaneous abortion of a deformed foetus.

of the 1976 Act confirms the position by requiring that the child be "born disabled".

Thirdly, and more positively, liability might be incurred although the child was neither viable, nor indeed conceived, when the potential for harm crystallised.[20] An example is provided by the recent American case of *Jorgensen* v. *Meade Johnson Laboratories Inc.*[1] Here it was alleged that a mother had taken certain Oracon birth control pills manufactured by the defendant pharmaceutical company and that these had altered her chromosome structure and caused a Mongoloid deformity in children conceived immediately after she had stopped taking the pills. Reversing the dismissal of an action brought on behalf of the children, the United States Court of Appeals for the Tenth Circuit regarded the claims as raising normal issues of causation to be determined by competent medical proof. This was so, moreover, even though the mother had stopped taking the pills before the children were conceived. It is thought that an English court would adopt the same approach. The 1976 Act provides manufacturers with a measure of protection in such cases. By s. 1 (4) of the Act the child's claim will fail if either or both of the parents knew the risk of the child being born disabled.

Finally, it must be emphasised that cases of this nature may create the most difficult of problems in determining whether a product lacked reasonable safety when it was marketed.[2] This is especially true of drugs which are known to carry the risk of a teratogenic effect but which are nevertheless beneficial to the woman who takes them. In the Law Commission report on Injuries to Unborn Children, it is said that:[3]

"Examples, which have been mentioned to us, include stilboestrol, which, when prescribed for pregnant women liable to miscarriages in the hope of preserving a pregnancy, has been followed by the development of vaginal cancer in their adolescent daughters; anti-convulsant drugs, causing cleft palates; antibiotics causing mottled teeth; progestogens causing severe virilisation in the female foetus with permanent effect on the genitalia; and some drugs used in the treatment of diabetes."

In most cases of this nature it seems substantially certain that all relevant duties to the unborn child would be discharged by a full warning to the mother or to a responsible intermediary such as a doctor.

---

[20] See the Law Commission report, paras. 75–78; Tedeschi, (1966) 1 Israel L.R. 513, referring to a case in the German Supreme Court where an infant was born with congenital syphilis after a blood transfusion had been given to his mother before conception.

[1] 483 F. 2d 237 (10th Cir., 1973).

[2] See above, pp. 186–189 for a general discussion of the implications of the requirement that the danger be "unreasonable".

[3] Law Com. No. 60, para. 21.

Allergies and peculiar susceptibilities

Many commodities such as detergents, cosmetics, dyes, penicillin and other drugs and shell-fish may cause an allergic reaction in persons who are sensitized to them. The effects of such reactions are often extremely serious. But it does not follow that the product which triggers off the reaction lacks reasonable safety or that it is not in conformity with the standards demanded by sales legislation or, within the United States of America, the manufacturers' warranties. Whether the product is so categorised will depend on a variety of considerations.

At the onset it is important to note the narrow limits to the problem of the allergic reaction. Where the product contains a primary irritant likely to affect a normal person liability may clearly be incurred.[5] So too when the product is likely to be harmful to persons generally albeit to a markedly lesser extent than in the case of the plaintiff [6] In the residue of cases where the product is harmful only to persons of abnormal susceptibility the few reported English decisions in point have denied liability. In particular the benefit of the implied condition of reasonable fitness for purpose has been held to depend on the abnormality or idiosyncrasy being communicated to the other contracting party. This requirement was not met in either *Griffiths* v. *Peter Conway, Ltd.*,[7] where the plaintiff had developed dermatitis after wearing a Harris tweed coat, or in *Ingham* v. *Emes*,[8] where dermatitis resulted from the application of the Inecto Rapid hair dye.[9] A claim in tort against a manufacturer similarly failed in an Australian case where a skin disease had resulted from using bath salts which would not have harmed

---

[4] Noel, "The Duty to Warn Allergic Users of Products", 12 Vanderbilt Law R. 331 (1959); Freedman, "Allergy and Products Liability Today", 24 Ohio State Jo. 479 (1963); Whitmore, "Allergies and Other Reactions due to Drugs and Cosmetics", 19 Sw. L.J. 76 (1965); Noel, "Products Defective Because of Inadequate Directions or Warnings", 23 Sw. L.J. 256, 289 *et seq* (1969); Keeton, "Products Liability—Drugs and Cosmetics", 25 Vanderbilt Law R. 131 (1972); 3 *Frumer and Friedman*, s. 28; Noel and Phillips, *Products Liability* (1974), pp. 183–193; 26 A.L.R. 2d 963; 53 A.L.R. 3d 298.

[5] *Grant* v. *Australian Knitting Mills, Ltd.*, [1936] A.C. 85, P.C., was such a case. See also *Mayne* v. *Silvermere Cleaners, Ltd.*, [1939] 1 All E.R. 693.

[6] See *Levi* v. *Colgate-Palmolive Pty., Ltd.* (1941), 41 S.R. N.S.W. 48, 51–52. See also *Smith* v. *Leech Brain & Co., Ltd.*, [1962] 2 Q.B. 405; [1961] 3 All E.R. 1159.

[7] [1939] 1 All E.R. 685, C.A.

[8] [1955] 2 Q.B. 366; [1955] 2 All E.R. 740, C.A.

[9] See also *Ashington Piggeries, Ltd.* v. *Christopher Hill, Ltd.*, [1972] A.C. 441; [1971] 1 All E.R. 847, H.L., and above, p. 106. The requirement exists although the plaintiff is unaware of the abnormality: see *Griffiths* v. *Peter Conway, Ltd.*, [1939] 1 All E.R. 685, 691. But if the defendant warrants expressly that the product is safe liability may be incurred unless, it seems, the plaintiff fails to disclose a known abnormality: see *Ingham* v. *Emes*, [1955] 2 Q.B. 366, 373. For discussion of express warranties in this context, see above, pp. 61–62.

a normal person.[10] Whether the claim is in contract or tort, the lack of liability in such cases is better explained by saying that the product conforms to the standard demanded, rather than by arguing that the predisposition is the sole cause of the harm.

On appropriate facts a manufacturer may clearly incur liability to the abnormal or susceptible user though much will depend on the number of persons who share the characteristic designated "abnormal".[11] Denning, L.J. has said that a product would be dangerous "if it might affect normal users adversely, or even if it might adversely affect other users who had a higher degree of sensitivity than the normal, so long as they were not altogether exceptional".[12] Similarly American cases have held that liability may be imposed where an "appreciable" or "substantial" number of persons is put at risk.[13] But clearly such words do not translate readily into percentages and, in any event, the unreasonableness of a danger is not to be determined by numbers alone. The gravity of the consequences is also important, as is the benefit to be derived from use of the product and the ease with which an effective warning might be given. Other things being equal, one would expect liability to be established more readily where a reaction follows from use of a cosmetic than where it accompanies the taking of a prescription drug.[14]

Wright v. *Carter Products Inc.*[15] is a leading American case. The plaintiff had suffered a severe outbreak of contact dermatitis through using the defendant's underarm deodorant Arrid. The deodorant contained aluminium sulphate to which she was allergic and the trial court judge had dismissed the claim when it appeared that no more than 373 complaints of skin irritation had been received during a period in which over 82 million jars of Arrid had been marketed. Reversing the decision and remanding for trial, the Court of Appeals for the Second Circuit stressed that "duties to warn are not, in all cases, measured by solely quantitative

---

[10] *Levi* v. *Colgate-Palmolive Pty., Ltd.* (1941), 41 S.R. N.S.W. 48 (N.S.W. Sup. Ct.).

[11] There is no clear borderline between "normality" and "abnormality". But the tribunal of fact would rarely have difficulty in deciding on which side of the line a particular characteristic falls: see *Griffiths* v. *Peter Conway, Ltd.,* [1939] 1 All E.R. 685, 691–692, *per* Sir Wilfrid Greene, M.R.

[12] *Board* v. *Thomas Hedley & Co., Ltd.,* [1951] 2 All E.R. 431, 432, C.A. The admissibility of evidence of the product's safety record is discussed above, pp. 260–264.

[13] See, e.g., *Alberto-Culver Co.* v. *Morgan,* 444 S.W. 2d 770 (Tex. Civ. App., 1969); *Crotty* v. *Shartenberg's New Haven Inc.,* 162 A. 2d 513 (Conn., 1960) ("appreciable"); *Kaempfe* v. *Lehn and Fink Products Corporation.,* 249 N.Y.S. 2d 840 (1964), affd. 231 N.E. 2d 294 (1967) ("substantial"). For cases holding that a warning was not required because the number of persons at risk was statistically insufficient, see Prosser, 4th edn., 1971, p. 648, notes 76–77.

[14] Drugs are discussed above, pp. 214–215. See also above, p. 245 where reference is made to some American cases involving drugs and warnings to responsible intermediaries.

[15] 244 F. 2d 53 (2nd Cir., 1957).

standards".[16] Other cases have admittedly denied that there is such a duty unless a substantial number, or an identifiable class of person, is at risk,[17] but this is itself a flexible requirement.

Assuming that the product fails to meet the required standard, liability in tort for negligence will be incurred only where the manufacturer knew or ought to have known of the danger.[18] Thereafter the adequacy of any warning will depend on factors discussed in an earlier chapter.[19] Directions for a patch test will sometimes be sufficient if this would be apt to reveal the danger,[20] as may warnings against continued use where irritation appears. In other cases it may be necessary to bring the presence of the particular sensitizing agency to the attention of the user or a responsible third party. Where there is no practicable way of ascertaining whether an individual is likely to suffer an allergic reaction cautionary words would rarely serve a useful purpose. It might, however, be argued that the incidence or gravity of the risk was such that the product should not have been marketed at all. Alternatively, a full warning might be needed to enable the plaintiff to make an informed decision whether to expose himself to the risk, however remote.[1]

Damage to property other than the defective product

There is no doubt that a manufacturer may be held liable where a defective or otherwise dangerous product causes damage to the plaintiff's property with consequent economic loss. This is so even though the product is of a type whose potential for harm is limited to property damage, as might be

---

[16] *Ibid.*, at p. 56. See also Prosser, *Torts*, pp. 648–649, notes 78, 81, for citation of cases making the same point. An extreme example is *Braun* v. *Roux Distributing Co.*, 312 S.W. 2d 758 (Mo., 1958). The case involved periarteritis nodosa, a rare and normally fatal systemic infection, and a warning was required although this was the first reported instance of the infection developing from the chemical, paraphenylenediamine, contained in the defendant's hair dye.

[17] See, e.g., *Kaempfe* v. *Lehn and Fink Products Corporation*, 249 N.Y.S. 2d 840 (1964), affd. 231 N.E. 2d 294 (1967) (deodorant).

[18] Some American cases hold that, even under a theory of strict liability, the manufacturer will not be liable where untoward side-effects follow on the taking of a drug unless such side-effects were known or discoverable by the application of reasonable, developed human skill and foresight. See, e.g., *Christofferson* v. *Kaiser Foundation Hospitals*, 92 Cal. Rptr. 825 (Cal. App., 1971); *Restatement, Torts*, 2d, s. 402A, comment j.

[19] See above, ch. 12, pp. 237–247.

[20] English cases such as *Parker* v. *Oxolo, Ltd.*, [1937] 3 All E.R. 524 and *Ingham* v. *Emes*, [1955] 2 Q.B. 366; [1955] 2 All E.R. 740, indicate both the need for (and possible inconclusiveness of) a direction for a patch test with certain hair dyes.

[1] An extreme example is provided by *Davis* v. *Wyeth Laboratories Inc.*, 399 F. 2d 121 (9th Cir., 1968) (risk of contracting poliomyelitis from Sabin oral polio vaccine 1:1,000,000, but warning required to enable choice to be made).

the case with a fruit or vegetable spray, or with an animal food, vaccine or disinfectant.[2] What is less clear is how far a requirement of "damage to property" may be taken before one enters the province of purely economic loss where the scope for recovery has traditionally been severely restricted.

In a straightforward case, property will have been damaged in an immediate and physical sense. A car may have suffered impact damage when a defective lorry swerves and crashes into it. Fruit trees or vegetables may have been killed through the application of an insecticide or herbicide supplied without adequate warnings or directions for use. The notion of damage to property will, however, extend beyond this. It would cover a case where a defective deep-freeze fails, ruining its contents, or a case where a product is incorporated into another product, rendering it useless, but without damaging it in a physical sense. So the manufacturer of a defective neon light strip might be held liable if it were to shatter and fall into a vat of fruit juice or into a quantity of breadcrumbs which had been prepared for coating fishcakes.[3] Liability might be incurred also where property is rendered useless through shrinkage or discoloration.

In other cases a manufacturer might be held liable where the complaint is of a failure to warn, as where a product is generally understood to be a "complete" animal or fish food and the plaintiff's animals or fish die from malnutrition because it is not.[4] Yet a claim would be unlikely to succeed where a product fails to confer an expected advantage, such as weight gain in animals, without causing positive detriment.[5] Finally, recovery would seem to extend also to a case where the complaint is of loss of property rather than of damage as such. A defective burglar alarm may cause a jeweller to lose his stock or a defective aquarium may cause its owner to lose his valued and commercially exploitable collection.[6] It can hardly be

---

[2] See, e.g., *McClanahan* v. *California Spray Chemical Corporation*, 75 S.E. 2d 712 (Va., 1953) (fruit spray); *Ruegger* v. *Shell Oil Co. of Canada, Ltd.* (1963), 41 D.L.R. 2d 183 (Ontario High Ct.) (chemical weedkiller); *Grant* v. *Cooper*, [1940] N.Z.L.R. 947 (sheep dip). See also above, pp. 217–218 and pp. 234–235.

[3] The example is adapted from a case cited by Heppell, *Products Liability Insurance* (1967), p. 5. American cases include *Gladiola Biscuit Co.* v. *Southern Ice Co.*, 267 F. 2d 138 (5th Cir., 1959) (dough rendered useless by glass in ice); *Southern Mill Co.* v. *Vege Fat Inc.*, 248 F. Supp. 482 (Ill., 1965) (toxic fat used in animal feed).

[4] See *Midwest Game Co.* v. *M.F.A. Mill Co.*, 320 S.W. 2d 547 (Mo., 1959) (trout raised on a commercial basis).

[5] *Cf. Texsun Feed Yards Inc.* v. *Ralston Purina Co.*, 447 F. 2d 660 (5th Cir., 1971). See also *Western Tank and Steel Corporation* v. *Gandy*, 385 S.W. 2d 406 (Tex. Civ. App., 1964). The distinction between the two situations is not always clear-cut. Into which category would one place the claim of a farmer who has suffered a loss of crops when a weedkiller fails to perform its job? See *Monsanto Co.* v. *Thrasher*, 463 S.W. 2d 25 (Tex. Civ. App., 1970).

[6] The examples are adapted from the facts of the Canadian cases, *J. Nunes Diamonds, Ltd.* v. *Dominion Electric Protection Co.* (1972), 26 D.L.R. (3d) 699 and *Sealand of the Pacific, Ltd.* v. *Ocean Cement, Ltd.* (1973), 33 D.L.R. (3d) 625; (1975), 51 D.L.R. (3d) 72, noted below, p. 337.

the law that the manufacturer of the aquarium might be held liable if the fish expire, but could not if they swim out to sea.[7]

Damage to the defective product: sub-standard goods and the costs of repair[8]

Instead of damaging other property a defective product may simply damage itself. Indeed, this must be an everyday occurrence. For example, a car with defective steering may run off the road and require extensive repairs. Alternatively the owner may discover and repair the defect in time to prevent an accident.[9] The question then arises whether the manufacturer may be sued in tort to recover the costs of repair, assuming negligence in production or design to have been established. Curiously, this question does not appear to have been explored systematically in English law, but the general assumption is probably that the sole remedy in either case is in contract and hence against the immediate retail vendor.[10] A layman unfamiliar with the issues would no doubt regard it as remarkable that any rational distinction could be taken between the position of one plaintiff, who has lost a crop of vegetables through applying a defective herbicide or fertiliser, and the position of another who has run his new car into a brick wall when the brakes fail. In both instances he would regard the loss as "financial" or "economic" and his reaction would be understandable.

Proponents of the view that the owner of the new car would (or should) recover[11] can fairly be asked whether they would adopt the same view in any case in which a product fails to meet the legitimate expectations of its owner. If not, there needs to be some further indication as to where the line is to be drawn. A requirement of impact or collision is one

---

[7] An argument to the contrary might call in aid the fact that an occupier of property does not apparently owe a duty of care with respect to the loss of goods belonging to lawful visitors: see *Tinsley* v. *Dudley*, [1951] 2 K.B. 18 and, in general, North, *Occupiers' Liability* (1971), p. 105 *et seq.* For a case decided under the Misrepresentation Act 1967, see *Davis & Co. (Wines), Ltd.* v. *AFA-Minerva (E.M.I.), Ltd.*, [1974] 2 Lloyd's Rep. 27, above, p. 57 (loss of stock through failure of burglar alarm).

[8] See the Law Commission Working Paper No. 64, "Liability for Defective Products", paras. 10–12, 94–118.

[9] As did the charterer of the barge with the dangerous crane in *Rivtow Marine, Ltd.* v. *Washington Iron Works* (1974), 40 D.L.R. (3d) 530 (Sup. Ct. of Canada), discussed below, p. 333.

[10] *Cf.*, however, the view of Lord Denning, M.R. as expressed in *Dutton* v. *Bognor Regis Urban District Council*, [1972] 1 Q.B. 373, 396; [1972] 1 All E.R. 462, 474, C.A., and of Laskin, J. in the *Rivtow Marine* case (1974), 40 D.L.R. (3d) 530, 552, below, p. 335.

[11] Or recover at least his "direct" losses, that is the cost of repair or replacement etc., as opposed to further consequential losses through an inability to use the product in a business venture.

possibility and it has been adopted in a number of American cases.[12] To insist on this requirement would, however, rule out similar deserving cases, as when a car with an electrical fault burns itself out,[13] or a crane disintegrates.[14] An alternative possibility is to distinguish according to whether a product is unsafe or simply shoddy.[15] Such a distinction is admittedly not free of anomalies.[16] It would favour the manufacturer who produces an article which will not function at all at the expense of one who produces an article which functions badly and thus dangerously.[17] Similarly, the manufacturer of contaminated ginger beer might be held liable whereas the manufacturer of flat ginger beer would not. This might be justifiable because of the higher value which the law places on protecting personal and property interests as opposed to purely financial interests. But the line between that which is unsafe and that which is simply shoddy would not always be easy to draw.

Those who would hold the manufacturer liable only where the damage is external to the defective product itself are faced with problems which are equally difficult to resolve. On a given set of facts it may be far from clear whether such a requirement has been satisfied. In *G. H. Myers & Co.* v. *Brent Cross Service Co.*,[18] for example, extensive damage had been caused to the engine of the plaintiff's car after it had been fitted with a defective replacement connecting rod supplied by the car manufacturers. A claim in contract was brought against the repairers. On such facts the manufacturers might presumably have been held liable for "damage to property" on the basis that the engine was something quite distinct from the replacement rod which had damaged it. But would the position have been equally clear if the rod had been incorporated into the car from new; or would the car then have been regarded as a unit which had suffered purely "internal" damage? Again, would it make any difference if the rod had been supplied by an independent component producer and he were being sued?

---

[12] *Cf. T.W.A.* v. *Curtiss-Wright Corporation*, 148 N.Y.S. 2d 284 (1955), affd. 153 N.Y.S. 2d 546 (1956); *Fentress* v. *Van Etta Motors*, 323 P. 2d 227 (Cal. App., 1958); *Wyatt* v. *Cadillac Motor Car Division*, 302 P. 2d 665 (Cal. App., 1956); 1 *Frumer and Friedman*, s. 5.03[1], note 20, and cases there cited. *Restatement, Torts,* 2d, s. 395, comment n, imposes liability in negligence in respect of damage to the defective product itself and gives an "impact" case as the illustration.

[13] As in *Gherna* v. *Ford Motor Co.*, 55 Cal. Rptr. 94 (Cal. App., 1966) where recovery was allowed on, *inter alia*, a negligence theory.

[14] As in the *Rivtow Marine* case (1974), 40 D.L.R. (3d) 530, below, p. 333.

[15] See above, pp. 176, 184–186.

[16] See further below, p. 336, note 13 for citation of authorities suggesting that economic losses may be recovered where physical damage is threatened, although it does not materialise.

[17] See Waddams, "The Strict Liability of Suppliers of Goods" (1974), 37 M.L.R. 154, 164.

[18] [1934] 1 K.B. 36.

Similar problems are likely to arise with all but the most simple of products. If a defective adhesive manufactered by A causes tiles manufactured by B to fall off and break as they hit the ground the owner of the tiles has presumably suffered "damage to property" in a claim against A under *Donoghue* v. *Stevenson*.[19] It would be strange if the position were different if the tiles were self-adhesive and it were a defence to an action brought by the owner against B that B had himself produced and applied the adhesive in the course of manufacture. Equally, it would be strange if a plaintiff could recover against C, the manufacturer of a defective primer paint which causes a top coat manufactured by D to peel off within a matter of weeks,[20] but could not recover against D when it is the top coat which is defective and which peels off. This need to decide what precisely has been damaged by what (and, indeed, what constitutes "damage") must exist where a legal system is prepared in principle to compensate in such cases whilst stopping short of compensating whenever a loss is suffered through the acquisition or use of a product which is unfit for its ordinary purpose.[1]

English decisions

The decision of the House of Lords in *Young and Marten, Ltd.* v. *McManus Childs, Ltd.*,[2] although not directly in point, contains references to some of the problems raised by such cases. A firm of building contractors, A, had sub-contracted the roofing of certain dwelling houses to B.[3] B had in turn, sub-contracted the supply and laying of the tiles to C who had obtained the tiles, Somerset 13, from the sole manufacturer. A particular batch contained a latent defect and re-roofing was necessary. A was held liable to the house-purchasers in contract and recovered against B who was in breach of an implied condition that the tiles would be of merchantable

---

[19] [1932] A.C. 562, H.L. The example is taken from *Atlas Aluminum Corporation* v. *Borden Chemical Corporation*, 233 F. Supp. 53 (Pa., 1964) (adhesive failed to hold glass and thousands of windows needed reglazing: recovery granted under negligence and implied warranty theories).

[20] See *Quirici* v. *Freeman*, 219 P. 2d 897 (Cal. App., 1950).

[1] *Anthony* v. *Kelsey-Hayes Co.*, 102 Cal. Rptr. 113 (Cal. App., 1972) discussed below, p. 342. provides a good example of a borderline case. In many cases "damage to property" would clearly not be in issue—as in the examples of the computer and typewriter which do not function properly, cited in the Law Commission Working Paper No 64, para. 116.

[2] [1969] 1 A.C. 454; [1968] 2 All E.R. 1169, H.L.

[3] In fact there was no contract between A and B, but the case proceeded on the footing that there was: see [1969] 1 A.C. 454, 465 (Lord Reid).

quality. Being time-barred, B was unable to pass the loss along the line in the normal manner. Had the purchasers of the houses sued the manufacturers for the cost of replacing the tiles, as might have been necessary if the builder had been bankrupt, the indications are that they would not have recovered. Certainly Lord Upjohn would have viewed any such claim as involving a move into a "scarcely charted sea of the law of torts".[4] Lord Pearce also saw:[5]

> "great difficulty in extending to an ultimate consumer a right to sue the manufacturer in tort in respect of goods which create no peril or accident but simply result in sub-standard work under a contract which is unknown to the original manufacturer".[6]

Apart from any other considerations, such a right might effectively deprive a manufacturer of his entitlement to limit his liability under contract with his immediate commercial purchaser. The houseowner would not be bound by the terms of this contract.[7]

There appear to be two English cases which assume that recovery might be granted on broadly similar facts. However, neither is wholly satisfactory. In the *Diamantis Pateras*,[8] shipowners were claiming to be indemnified for the costs of repairing an oil-burning furnace manufactured by the defendants and alleged to be deficient in design. The claim failed on the merits, but, in the judgment of Lawrence, J. it might have succeeded in principle[9] even though there was no question of the furnace having caused physical damage. It seems fair to say, however, that the point passed *sub silentio* without any real discussion of the issues involved.

The same cannot be said of the more recent decision of the Court of Appeal in *Dutton v. Bognor Regis Urban District Council*,[10] where the second purchaser of a house built on insecure foundations recovered the cost of remedying the effects of subsidence. These included cracks in the walls and ceiling, doors and windows which would not close and a staircase which had slipped. The claim was against the council whose surveyor had passed the property as complying with the building byelaws when it did not, but both Lord Denning, M.R. and Sachs, L.J. were of the opinion that the builder (who had paid some £625 *ex gratia*) might also have been held

---

[4] [1969] 1 A.C. 454, 475; [1968] 2 All E.R. 1169, 1177.
[5] [1969] 1 A.C. 454, 469; [1968] 2 All E.R. 1169, 1174.
[6] On the saving for products which create a "peril or accident", see below, p. 336, note 13.
[7] The same point was emphasised in one of the leading American cases *Trans World Airlines* v. *Curtiss-Wright Corporation*, 148 N.Y.S. (2d) 284, 290, affd. 153 N.Y.S. (2d) 546 (1956). See further, below, pp. 339–340.
[8] [1966] 1 Lloyds Rep. 179.
[9] *Cf., ibid.,* at pp. 187–188.
[10] [1972] 1 Q.B. 373; [1972] 1 All E.R. 462.

liable.[11] Lord Denning saw the claim as being in respect of physical damage to the house, as opposed to purely economic loss represented by the diminution in the value of the premises.[12] It seems doubtful, however, whether the results of settlement, or, for that matter, disintegration within a product, can be classified as "physical damage".[13] Sachs, L.J. was nevertheless of the same opinion, although he thought that to classify into "physical damage" and "economic loss" was to adopt a fallacious approach.[14] Finally, Stamp, L.J. noted that under the *Hedley Byrne*[15] decision even purely economic losses might be compensated on appropriate facts and he regarded the council as undertaking a responsibility of the same order as would have been undertaken by the defendant bank in that case had it not excluded liability. He agreed, however, that, although a manufacturer of products was under a duty "not carelessly to put out a dangerous thing which may cause damage to one who may purchase it", there was no duty to refrain from putting out a "defective or useless or valueless thing".[16] He declined to decide whether a builder was subject to a more demanding duty that a manufacturer.

The *Dutton* case would clearly have been more helpful to a discussion of a manufacturer's liability if the builder had been sued and held liable. It might then have been argued that a manufacturer whose product deteriorates through an internal defect may similarly be held liable, even to a second purchaser, for the cost of repair or reinstatement. But there is, of course, no necessary equivalence between the liability of a builder or contractor and that of a manufacturer of products. Indeed the tendency over the years has been to treat them differently. Thus in English law the manufacturers' liability for personal injury was established well before that of the builder and the contractor.[17] Conversely, some American cases impose liability on a manufacturer for damage to the defective product itself only where this occurs as a result of an impact or collision.[18] No

---

[11] See [1972] 1 Q.B. 373, 394 (Lord Denning, M.R.), 402 (Sachs, L.J.). See also *Sparham-Souter* v. *Town and Country Developments (Essex), Ltd.*, [1976] Q.B. 858; [1976] 2 All E.R. 65; C.A.; Defective Premises Act 1972, s. 3. But as to the position at common law, *cf. Bottomley* v. *Bannister*, [1932] 1 K.B. 458, C.A., *Bowen* v. *Paramount Builders (Hamilton), Ltd.*, [1975] 2 N.Z.L.R. 546 (N.Z. Sup. Ct.) and, in general, above, pp. 313–315.

[12] [1972] 1 Q.B. 373, 396; [1972] 1 All E.R. 462, 474.

[13] *Cf.* the views of the Supreme Court of Canada in the *Rivtow Marine* case (1974), 40 D.L.R. (3d) 530.

[14] *Cf.* [1972] 1 Q.B. 373, 403–404; [1972] 1 All E.R. 462, 480–481.

[15] *Hedley Byrne & Co., Ltd.* v. *Heller & Partners, Ltd.*, [1964] A.C. 465; [1963] 2 All E.R. 575. See further above, pp. 43–45, below, pp. 337–338.

[16] *Cf.* [1972] 1 Q.B. 373, 415; [1972] 1 All E.R. 462, 490.

[17] Important cases include *Sharpe* v. *E. T. Sweeting & Son, Ltd.*, [1963] 2 All E.R. 455; [1963] 1 W.L.R. 665; *A. C. Billings & Sons, Ltd.* v. *Riden*, [1958] A.C. 240; [1957] 3 All E.R. 1.

[18] *Cf. Wyatt* v. *Cadillac Motor Car Division*, 302 P. 2d 665 (Cal. App., 1956); *Fentress* v.

such limit could be applied to contractors who, for example, have been held liable for the cost of repairing or reinstating a swimming pool which cracks and breaks up as the water flows out.[19]

Canadian decisions

In at least two Canadian cases manufacturers have been held liable in tort for losses caused by defective products without there being any element of prior physical damage. Thus in one case the Manitoba Court of Appeal held that the owner of a cold storage plant might recover the costs of repair from the defendant manufacturer of an insulating material which had shrunk, causing excessive ice deposits to form in the plant.[20] In a later case,[1] the owner of a cylinder head similarly recovered the cost of repair and consequential losses from the defendant who had reconditioned it defectively. Neither decision can be reconciled with the views of the majority of the Canadian Supreme Court in the recent *Rivtow Marine* case.

The Rivtow Marine case

In *Rivtow Marine, Ltd.* v. *Washington Iron Works*,[2] the plaintiff was the charterer of a log barge, the Rivtow Carrier, which was equipped with two pintle-type cranes designed and manufactured by the first defendants, Washington. In September 1966, some eighteen months after the commencement of the charter and at a time when the coastal logging business was at its height, the charterers learned that a crane which was virtually identical to their own and which had also been designed and manufactured by Washington had collapsed, killing its operator. As a precautionary measure, they ordered the Rivtow Carrier to return to Vancouver for inspection. This revealed that both cranes had serious structural defects in the legs of the pintle masts, necessitating extensive dismantling, modification, repair and reassembly lasting some thirty days. The plaintiff claimed

---

Van Etta Motors, 323 P. 2d 227 (Cal. App., 1958). See, however, *Gherna* v. *Ford Motor Co.,* 55 Cal. Rptr. 94 (Cal. App., 1966).

[19] As in *Stewart* v. *Cox,* 13 Cal. Rptr. 521 (Sup. Ct. of California, 1961). See also *Sabella* v. *Wisler,* 27 Cal. Rptr. 689 (1963).

[20] *Western Processing and Cold Storage* v. *Hamilton Construction Co.* (1965), 51 D.L.R. (2d) 245.

[1] *Algoma Truck and Tractor Sales, Ltd.* v. *Bert's Auto Supply, Ltd.* (1968), 68 D.L.R. (2d) 363 (District Ct., Ontario).

[2] (1974), 40 D.L.R. (3d) 530.

compensation for the cost of repair and for loss of profits during the period in which the barge was inoperative. Washington admitted that the cracking in the legs of the crane was caused by defects in design attributable to the carelessness of their engineers; that by February 1966 they were aware that other cranes of this type had developed similar structural defects in operation; and that thirty days was a reasonable period in which to carry out the necessary modifications. They denied, however, that they had any liability to compensate in respect of the loss suffered. This view was accepted by the British Columbia Court of Appeal.[3] The charterers then appealed to the Supreme Court of Canada. The court was unanimous in allowing the appeal and in awarding damages, but divided about the extent of the claim. The full amount claimed was not granted and both majority and minority judgments are of general interest.

The duty to warn   The majority judgment was delivered by Ritchie, J. with whom Fauteux, C.J.C., Abbott, Martland, Judson, Spence and Pigeon, JJ, concurred. This proceeded on the basis that the defendants were under a duty to warn of known defects and that the charterers were entitled to recover for the losses consequent on its breach. This was not the cost of repair as such. Nor was it the general consequential loss which would necessarily have accompanied the laying up of the barge during the period of repair. It was rather the *additional* loss attributable to the absence of a prior warning which had deprived the charterers of an opportunity of repairing at an economically advantageous time, rather than at the height of the logging season. This had also been the view of the first instance judge whose figures of $90,000 (earnings in the high season) *less* $30,000 (average monthly earnings), leaving $60,000, were accepted.

American cases have accepted that there is a duty to warn of subsequently discovered dangers which result in personal injury,[4] and, on the facts of the *Rivtow Marine* case, an extension to pecuniary losses seems sensible. As Ritchie, J. noted, the defendants were aware of the defects and knew the identity of the plaintiff as a user of the crane and of the seasonal fluctuations of the trade. Hence the pecuniary loss was clearly a foreseeable and "proximate" result of their failure to issue a warning. If the general principle is accepted the scope of the duty remains open for discussion in future cases. In particular, it might be necessary to decide whether (i) steps have to be taken to trace users of a product when their identity is unknown; (ii) the duty exists where the defendant ought to have appreciated that a known (or even a reasonably discoverable) condition was dangerous but did not in fact

---

[3] (1972), 26 D.L.R. (3d) 559.

[4] See, e.g., *Comstock* v. *General Motors Corporation*, 96 N.W. 2d 627 (Mich., 1961); *Braniff Airways Inc.* v. *Curtis Wright Corporation*, 411 F. 2d 451 (2nd Cir., 1969) and, in general, above, pp. 247–251.

do so;[5] and (iii) whether the duty extends to a case where the product is not dangerous to person or property but simply unfit for its ordinary purpose or for some special purpose for which the plaintiff is known to require it. One important point is, however, clear. Being founded on a failure to warn, liability may be incurred even though the original deficiency in design or miscarriage in the production process is in no way indicative of negligence on the part of the defendant.

The cost of repair Laskin, J. with whom Hall, J. concurred, approached the case differently and, dissenting in part, he would have awarded the full cost of repair. In his judgment, the pragmatic considerations which normally justified the denial of recovery for economic loss[6] had no validity in a case such as the present. As he explained:[7]

> "Here then was a piece of equipment whose use was fraught with danger to person and property because of negligence in its design and manufacture; one death had already resulted from the use of a similar piece of equipment that had been marketed by Washington. I see nothing untoward in holding Washington liable in such circumstances for economic loss resulting from the down time necessary to effect repairs to the crane. The case is not one where a manufactured product proves to be merely defective (in short, where it has not met promised expectations), but rather one where by reason of the defect there is a foreseeable risk of physical harm from its use and where the alert avoidance of such harm gives rise to economic loss. Prevention of threatened harm resulting in economic loss should not be treated differently from post-injury cure."

A similar suggestion is to be found in Lord Denning's judgment in the *Dutton* case. Discussing the position of the manufacturer of an article Lord Denning said *obiter* in a passage cited by Laskin, J.:[8]

> "If he makes it negligently, with a latent defect (so that it breaks to pieces and injures someone), he is undoubtedly liable. Suppose that the defect is discovered in time to prevent the injury. Surely he is liable for the cost of repair."

This is a commonsense approach. In the *Rivtow Marine* case, Washington would not necessarily have been exempt from liability had the crane been

---

[5] An affirmative answer is perhaps suggested by the observations of Lord Diplock in *Herrington* v. *British Railways Board*, [1972] A.C. 877, 939–940; [1972] 1 All E.R. 749, 756, H.L. on the scope of the occupiers' duty to act with common humanity towards a trespasser. A similar issue arises with respect to the retailers' duty to warn of known dangers: see above, p. 303, note 20.
[6] That is, the fear of "liability in an indeterminate amount for an indeterminate time to an indeterminate class", *per* Cardozo, J. in *Ultramares Corporation* v. *Touche*, 255 N.Y. 170, 179 (1931) cited by Laskin, J. (1974), 40 D.L.R. (3d) 530, 549–550.
[7] *Ibid.*, at p. 552.
[8] *Dutton* v. *Bognor Regis Urban District Council*, [1972] 1 Q.B. 373, 396; [1972] 1 All E.R. 462, 474 C.A., above, p. 331.

kept in service and then collapsed and injured a third party or damaged the barge itself.[9] In so far as a manufacturer might be held liable on such facts—subject to a claim against the user of the product as a joint tortfeasor or, as the case may be, a reduction in damages for contributory negligence[10]—it would be strange if he were exempt from liability when the user acts responsibly and carries out a timely repair.[11] Indeed an inability to recover the reasonable costs of repairing an article which is, *ex hypothesi*, dangerous and constructed negligently, can act only as a disincentive to repair.[12] Support for the approach of Laskin, J. and Lord Denning may be found in statements which seem to assume that economic losses are recoverable if physical damage was foreseeable even thought it did not materialise.[13]

If the general principle gains acceptance and the costs of averting threatened physical harm become recoverable, there is again difficulty in knowing where the line should be drawn. In the *Rivtow Marine* case Laskin, J envisaged that the repairer might recover where damage to property other than the defective product was the paramount, or presumably the sole, risk.[14] He left open the wider questions whether recovery might be extended to "claims for economic loss where there is no threat of physical

---

[9] This proposition would be readily accepted in the USA: see, e.g., *Balido* v. *Improved Machinery Inc.*, 105 Cal. Rptr. 890 (Cal. App., 1973); *Pike* v. *Frank G. Hough Co.*, 85 Cal. Rptr. 629 (1970) and, in general, above, p. 283 *et seq.* (knowledge on the part of an intermediary) and at p. 292 *et seq.* (knowledge on the part of the plaintiff). English cases sometimes assume that such knowledge exonerates the manufacturer (see, e.g., *Taylor* v. *Rover Co., Ltd.*, [1966] 2 All E.R. 181; [1966] 1 W.L.R. 1491) but the point has not been explored fully.

[10] Under the Law Reform (Married Women and Tortfeasors) Act 1935 and the Contributory Negligence Act 1945, respectively.

[11] It may be objected that the argument establishes too much in that the manufacturer would (at worst) obtain a substantial contribution for the user, assuming him to be solvent. But the cost of compensation may be substantially more than the cost of repair.

[12] In the *Rivtow Marine* case no question was raised as to the reasonableness of repairing or of the costs incurred: see (1974) 40 D.L.R. (3d) 530, 553 (Laskin, J.). A user may act unreasonably if he does not afford the manufacturer an opportunity to repair, as where there is a guarantee in force.

[13] See, e.g., *Morrison S.S. Co., Ltd.* v. *Greystoke Castle (Cargo Owners)* [1974] A.C. 265, 280 (Lord Roche); *Weller & Co.* v. *Foot and Mouth Disease Research Institute*, [1965] 3 All E.R. 560, 570 (Widgery, J.). *Quaere* whether this approach is consistent with the *Wagon Mound* principle? For further discussion, see Atiyah, "Negligence and Economic Loss' (1967), 83 L.Q.R. 248, 260–262 especially. Two of the most frequently cited statements denying the manufacturers' liability are consistent with the view that liability may be incurred where physical harm is threatened. Thus in *Young and Marten, Ltd.* v. *McManus Childs, Ltd.*, [1969] 1 A.C. 454, 469 Lord Pearce limited his observations to "goods which create no peril or accident", whilst in *Dutton* v. *Bognor Regis Urban District Council*, [1972] 1 Q.B. 373, 415, Stamp, L.J. spoke of "a duty not carelessly to put out a dangerous thing which *may cause damage*", contrasting this with a defective or useless or valueless thing" (emphasis supplied).

[14] *Cf.* (1974), 40 D.L.R. (3d) 530, 550.

harm or to claims for damage, without more, to the defective product".[15]

Finally, the *Rivtow Marine* case provides a good illustration of the general uncertainties in determining what constitutes "damage to property" for present purposes. The Canadian Supreme Court evidently accepted that the gradual internal disintegration of the crane did not constitute physical damage to property. Yet in the *Dutton* case a majority of the English Court of Appeal treated the house as having suffered physical damage through the effects of subsidence.[16] On the whole it seems doubtful whether such disintegration or subsidence can be so described. Similarly, in the *Rivtow Marine* case Laskin, J. regarded the crane as being something quite distinct from the barge which it had threatened to damage.[17] But, one might ask, would he have approached the case in the same way if the barge had been built by Washington and the crane incorporated from new; or would he then have found it necessary to answer the wider questions which he chose to leave open?[18]

The Hedley Byrne principle

As was seen in an earlier chapter, the *Hedley Byrne*[19] principle may also be called in aid to impose liability for economic loss where there is a "special relationship" between the parties. In the Canadian case of *Sealand of the Pacific, Ltd.* v. *Ocean Cement, Ltd.,*[20] for example, the manufacturer of a light-weight concrete was held liable following the negligent assurances of a sales representative that the concrete was suitable for use in an oceanarium when it was not. The concrete absorbed water, causing display tanks to settle towards the sea bed and damages were awarded to compensate for the cost of remedial measures and for loss of profits.[1] A further example is provided by a New Zealand case[2] in which the surveyor of a motor launch with extensive dry rot was held liable to a subsequent purchaser of the

---

[15] *Ibid.*, at p. 552.

[16] *Cf.* [1972] 1 All E.R. 462, 474 (Lord Denning, M.R.), 481 (Sachs, L.J.).

[17] *Cf.* (1974), 40 D.L.R. (3d) 530, 549–550 (Laskin, J.).

[18] *Cf.* the reference to *G. H. Myers & Co.* v. *Brent Cross Services*, [1934] 1 K.B. 36, above, p. 329.

[19] *Hedley Byrne & Co.* v. *Heller & Partners*, [1964] A.C. 465; [1963] 2 All E.R. 575, H.L., above, pp. 43–45.

[20] (1973), 33 D.L.R. (3d) 625 (B.C. Sup. Ct.); (1975), 51 D.L.R. (3d) 702 (B.C.C.A.).

[1] Liability was imposed in tort, and in contract for breach of express and implied warranties. On appeal *sub nom Sealand of the Pacific* v. *Robert C. McHaffie, Ltd.* (1975), 51 D.L.R. (3d) 702 naval architects were also held liable for breach of contract. See also *J. Nunes Diamonds, Ltd.* v. *Dominion Electric Protection, Co.* (1972), 26 D.L.R. (3d) 699 (Sup. Ct. of Canada) where the claim was in respect of the loss of diamonds following the failure of a burglar alarm system and no liability was incurred on the facts.

[2] *Gordon* v. *Moen and Captain W. Dunsford, Ltd.*, [1971] N.Z.L.R. 526. See also *Rutherford* v. *A.-G.*; [1976] 1 N.Z.L.R. 403 (N.Z. Sup. Ct.) (M.O.T. certificate).

vessel. The purchaser had relied on a favourable report shown to him by the vendor and prepared by the surveyor for valuation purposes.

Most cases applying the *Hedley Byrne* principle have been concerned with inter-personal communications and their facts have been far removed from a typical product liability case. No doubt the "special relationship" and "assumption of responsibility", which are generally taken to be the hallmarks of the principle, can be established more readily in such cases. The decision is no doubt capable of more general application as is the collateral warranty. But there has been no indication in English or Commonwealth cases that general advertising claims are to be viewed as promissory or as statements in respect of which a responsibility to the ultimate consumer is assumed. There have, however, been extensive American developments in this area.[3]

American cases

American cases have proceeded with caution in this area and show no uniformity of approach as to the proper bounds of liability in tort.[4] There is general agreement that recovery may be granted under a negligence or strict tort theory where the defective product has suffered impact damage following a collision.[5] The limit is an arbitrary one, but the point might be conceded without any substantial inroads being made into a general principle of non-liability. Beyond this, no clear pattern has emerged either

---

[3] See above, pp. 58–62 for discussion of the express warranty theory of liability. Liability for representations is discussed above, p. 43 *et seq.* and collateral contracts are discussed, above, pp. 64–65.

[4] For general discussion, see Prosser, *Torts* 4th edn., 1971, pp. 666–667; 1 *Frumer and Friedman*, s. 5.03 [1], note 20; 2 *Frumer and Friedman*, s. 16A [4] [*f*]; Note, "Economic Loss in Products Liability Jurisprudence", 66 Col. L.R.917 (1966); Speidel, "Products Liability, Economic Loss and the UCC", 40 Tenn. L.R. 309 (1973); Waddams, "Strict Liability of Suppliers of Goods" (1974), 37 M.L.R. 154, 161–166; Tobin, "Products Liability: Recovery of Economic Loss" (1970), 4 N.Z.U.L.R. 36.

[5] See, e.g., *Dennis* v. *Ford Motor Co.,* 471 F. 2d 733 (3rd Circ., 1973) (front-wheel collapse); *Henningsen* v. *Bloomfield Motors Inc. and Chrysler Corporation,* 161 A. 2d 69 (N.J., 1960) (failure of steering); *Simpson* v. *Logan Motor Co.,* 191 A. 2d 122 (D.C.C.A., 1963) (power brake failure); *International Harvester Co.* v. *Sharoff,* 202 F. 2d 52 (10th Cir., 1953) (torque rod and universal joint failure). In *Gherna* v. *Ford Motor Co.,* 55 Cal. Rptr. 94 (Cal. App., 1966) recovery was considered permissible on establishing that a defective condition caused a car to burn itself out. Other cases would insist on impact damage: see, e.g., *Wyatt* v. *Cadillac Motor Car Division,* 302 P. 2d 665 (Cal. App., 1956) (internal damage within car engine not compensated); *Fentress* v. *Van Etta Motors,* 323 P. 2d 227 (Cal. App., 1958). Other Californian cases have regarded any such limits as being inapplicable to the liability of contractors building property without suggesting that they were incorrect as applied to the conventional manufacturer of goods: see *Sabella* v. *Wisler,* 27 Cal. Rptr. 689 (Cal. Sup. Ct., 1963); *Stewart* v. *Cox,* 13 Cal. Rptr. 521 (Cal. Sup. Ct., 1961) and above, p. 332.

in cases in which the claim can be construed as involving an element of property damage or in cases involving what, on any view, is pure economic loss. Thus recovery has been considered permissible, in spite of the lack of a contract between the parties, where the manufacturer of defective cinder blocks was being sued by the owner of cottages built from the blocks;[6] a defective Chevrolet truck-tractor involved the purchaser in repair costs;[7] and where an adhesive failed to hold glass in windows so that thousands of panes required to be replaced with consequent financial loss.[8] On the other hand, recovery has been denied where the purchaser of a Rambler car was suing in negligence for the difference between the price paid and the true value of the defective car;[9] an air conditioning unit was defective and required to be replaced;[10] and where the manufacturer of defective wheels fitted on to motor vehicles was being sued by a disappointed purchaser intent on recovering his losses.[11] United States courts have also developed a liability based on public advertising or misrepresentation under which pecuniary losses may be recovered.[12]

Trans World Airlines v. *Curtiss-Wright Corporation*[13] is perhaps the leading case to discuss the matter solely in terms of a negligence theory of liability. The plaintiff airline had acquired a number of aircraft from the Lockheed Corporation and incurred costs in repairing latent defects in the engines manufactured by Curtiss-Wright. An aircraft had also been lost when it crashed following engine failure. In subsequent proceedings against Curtiss-Wright, Eder, J. noted that the plaintiffs could have sued Lockheed in contract if exception clauses had permitted and that Lockheed could, in turn, have claimed over. He then asked: "May it sue directly the manufacturer, with whom it has no privity of contract, for damage limited to

---

[6] *Spence* v. *Three Rivers Builders and Masonry Supply Inc.,* 90 N.W. 2d 873 (Mich., 1958). There was evidence that the deterioration was progressive and that it would probably endanger the structure of the property at some future date.

[7] *Lang* v. *General Motors Corporation,* 136 N.W. 2d 805 (N.D., 1965).

[8] *Atlas Aluminum Corporation* v. *Borden Chemical Corporation,* 233 F. Supp. 53 (Penn., 1964). See also *Cova* v. *Harley Davidson Motor Co.,* 182 N.W. 2d 800 (Mich., 1970) (defective golf carts: losses recoverable under implied warranty theory); *Continental Copper and Steel Industries* v. *C.E. "Red" Cornelius, Inc.,* 104 So. 2d 40 (Fla., 1958) (defective cable: implied warranty). *Temple Sinai* v. *Richmond,* 308 A. 2d 508 (R.I., 1973) (defective bricks).

[9] *Inglis* v. *American Motors Corporation,* 209 N.E. 2d 583 (Ohio, 1965).

[10] *Thermal Supply of Texas Inc.* v. *Asel,* 468 S.W. 2d 927 (Tex. Civ. App., 1971).

[11] *Anthony* v. *Kelsey-Hayes Co.,* 102 Cal. Rptr. 113 (Cal. App., 1972) discussed further below, p. 342. See also *Hawkins Construction Co.* v. *Matthews Co.,* 209 N.W. 2d 643 (Neb., 1973); *Cooley* v. *Salopian Industries, Ltd.,* 383 F. Supp. 1114 (S.C., 1974); *McDonough* v. *Whalen,* 304 N.E. 22 199 (Mass., 1973).

[12] See, e.g., *Randy Knitwear Inc.* v. *American Cyanamid Co.,* 181 N.E. 2d 399 (N.Y., 1962); *Ford Motor Co.* v. *Lonon,* 398 S.W. 2d 240 (Tenn., 1966). The terms or *Restatement, Torts,* 2d s. 402B are set out above, p. 58.

[13] 148 N.Y.S. (2d) 284 (1955) (Sup. Ct. New York County), affd. 153 N.Y.S. (2d) 546 (1956).

the allegedly defective product itself?"[14] He held that it could not, and added that if the position were otherwise:[15]

"Manufacturers would be subject to indiscriminate lawsuits by persons having no contractual relations with them, persons who could thereby escape the limitations, if any, agreed upon in their contract of purchase. Damages for inferior quality, *per se*, should better be left to suits between vendors and purchasers since they depend on the terms of the bargain between them."

Different considerations were held to apply to the aircraft lost in the crash, although the physical damage was confined to the aircraft itself. The argument is a formidable (indeed an unanswerable) one. In so far as the loss was purely financial, there could be no conceivable justification for allowing the airline effectively to by-pass exemption clauses in its own contract with Lockheed by suing Curtiss-Wright in tort. Within English law the point retains its full validity in any non-consumer sale containing exemption clauses which are fair or reasonable as between the parties.[16]

The same considerations should apply under the more recent strict tort and implied warranty theories since the dispensing with a requirement of fault should not affect the type of loss compensated. However, there has been no consistency of approach. Two contrasting decisions may be cited by way of illustration. In the New Jersey case of *Santor* v. *A. and M. Karagheusian Inc.,*[17] the plaintiff had purchased some ninety-six square yards of carpeting manufactured by the defendant company and sold as Grade 1. It developed an unusual line which the retailer assured him would "walk out", but which in fact became worse. The retailer having gone out of business, the plaintiff sued the manufacturer alleging that the carpet was defective (which was conceded) and claiming that there had been a breach of an implied warranty of merchantability. The Supreme Court of New Jersey upheld the claim both on the basis of this theory and the strict tort theory and awarded damages equal to the difference between the price paid and the market value of the carpet at the time the plaintiff knew or ought to have known of its defective condition. In reaching this conclusion the court agreed that strict liability had hitherto been concerned primarily with compensating personal injuries[18] but denied that its application was limited to such cases. In the words of Justice Francis:[19]

---

[14] 148 N.Y.S. (2d) 284, 287.

[15] *Ibid.*, at p. 290.

[16] See above, ch. 8, pp. 150–158.

[17] 207 A. 2d 305 (N.J., 1965).

[18] *Henningsen* v. *Bloomfield Motors Inc.*, 161 A. 2d 69 (1960) above, p. 16, deciding in the Supreme Court of New Jersey itself was such a case.

[19] 207 A. 2d 305, 313 (1965).

"Existence of the defect means violation of the representation implicit in the presence of the article in the stream of trade that it is suitable for the general purposes for which it is sold and for which such goods are generally appropriate. As we have said, this representation is found in the law. If it is not a fact—if the article is defective and the defect is chargeable to the manufacturer, his must be the responsibility for the consequent damage or injury."

A more limited view of the proper scope of the strict tort theory was adopted by the Supreme Court of California in *Seely* v. *White Motor Co.*[20] Seely was purchasing a truck manufactured by the defendant company for use in his business as a haulier. It bounced violently or "galloped" and unsuccessful attempts were made over an eleven-month period to cure the problem. The truck finally overturned through a cause which was not shown to be related to the "galloping" and Seely sued to recover, *inter alia*, the money already paid under his conditional sale contract together with a further sum to compensate his loss of profits during the period in which he was unable to make normal use of the truck. He succeeded on the basis that the manufacturer was in breach of an express warranty[1] but would have failed under the strict tort theory. In the view of the majority of the court this theory applied only to physical injury and property damage and not to claims in respect of purely economic loss. Such claims fell within the province of warranty and were governed by its rules. Justice Traynor, the architect of the strict tort doctrine, justified the distinction by saying:[2]

"[The] manufacturer cannot be held liable for the level of performance of his products in the consumer's business unless he agrees that the product was designed to meet the consumer's demands. A consumer should not be charged at the will of the manufacturer with bearing the risk of physcial injury when he buys a product on the market. He can, however, be fairly charged with the risk that the product will not match his economic expectations unless the manufacturer agrees that it will."[3]

In a separate judgment Peters, J. disagreed with the majority view and held that the economic interests of the "ordinary consumer" were entitled to protection under the strict tort theory. He regarded Seely as an ordinary consumer rather than a commercial buyer in that he was the owner-driver of a single truck and not a fleet-owner who bought trucks

---

[20] 45 Cal. Rptr. 17 (1965).

[1] See further above, p. 62. Peters, J. dissented on this point holding that reliance on the warranty had not been established.

[2] 45 Cal. Rptr. 17, 23 (1965).

[3] On this basis *Santor* v. *A. and M. Karagheusian, Inc.*, above, note 17, was regarded as a case in which strict tort liability should not have been imposed, although the actual result was justifiable since the carpet had been warranted Grade 1: see 45 Cal. Rptr. 17, 23.

regularly in the course of his business.[4] In his view the objections of the majority were valid only when applied to an attempt to hold the manufacturer liable for the failure of his product to meet specific needs peculiar to the purchaser. They had no validity when applied to a case in which the gravamen of the complaint was that the product had failed to match up to the standard ordinarily to be expected of goods of that type. In short, he would hold the manufacturer strictly liable at the suit of an ordinary consumer in spite of the absence of physical damage, but only where the goods were of unmerchantable quality as opposed to being unfit for a particular purpose. In his opinion this was the type of case with which the court was dealing.[5]

This difference of opinion was also reflected in the subsequent Californian case of *Anthony* v. *Kelsey-Hayes Co.*[6] Here the owners of certain Chevrolet Trucks were suing the defendant manufacturers of the wheels which were mounted on the trucks and alleged to be defective. Chevrolet had repaired or replaced the wheels at their own expense. Hence the final claim was for compensation to cover the loss of a period of use and the general depreciation in the vehicle arising from its having been a serious safety risk. A majority of the Court of Appeal for the Second District treated the case as one in which property damage was not alleged, applied *Seely's* case and denied recovery under negligence, strict tort, and implied warranty theories. Stephens, A.J. dissented. He regarded *Seely's* case as being concerned with a product which was merchantable but unfit for a specific business need.[7] In his judgment a cause of action had been stated in both negligence and strict tort. Moreover he was of the opinion that "actual property damage" was in issue since tyres and springs required to be replaced and these were "property other than the defective product itself (the defective wheels)".[8]

---

[4] *Cf.* 45 Cal. Rptr. 17, 29–30 (1965). As the Law Commission notes in Working Paper No. 64, para. 91, Seely's purchase would not have qualified as a consumer transaction for the purpose of the Supply of Goods (Implied Terms) Act 1973 since he bought the vehicle for use in his business. On this point, see further above, p. 148.

[5] There is some difficulty on this point. The truck was resold subsequently to a third party (B) who drove it for some 82,000 miles without any particular problems. Traynor, C.J. agreed that it was possible that a cure had been found for the "galloping", but thought it more likely that B's use of the truck made demands on it which differed from those of the plaintiff: *cf.* 45 Cal. Rptr. 17, 22. Peters, J. dealt with this crucial point by saying that B's testimony went only to show that the truck *could* do the jobs for which it was built and that he had not apparently convinced the trial court: *ibid.*, at p. 28. The lack of clarity on this point was seized on by Stephens, J.A. dissenting in the *Kelsey–Hayes* case discussed in the text which follows.

[6] 102 Cal. Rptr. 113 (Cal. App., 1972).

[7] *Ibid.*, at pp. 119–120. See also above, note 5.

[8] *Ibid.*, at pp. 120–121. The general problems raised by the need to decide what constitutes "damage to property" are noted above, pp. 328–330.

Conclusions

In view of the dearth of English authority in point, any conclusions to be drawn from the above discussion can only be tentative. A manufacturer may clearly be held liable in tort where the claim is in respect of damage to property other than the defective product itself.[9] There may be considerable difficulty in deciding whether the damage was truly external to the product, but arguments on this point have still to be exploited successfully in an English case.[10] Secondly, English law would probably recognise a duty to warn of known dangers as in the *Rivtow Marine* case[11] with a consequent liability for the additional losses caused by breach of such a duty. Thirdly, a manufacturer might be held liable for impact damage suffered by the defective product[12] and perhaps also where the product damages itself through exploding or bursting into flames.[13] Fourthly, there is some sparse authority suggesting that a manufacturer might be held liable to compensate an owner or hirer who has incurred expenditure in neutralising a dangerously defective product.[14] It seems sensible to impose liability in such a case.

Fifthly, a manufacturer may be held liable to a person who has incurred loss through reliance on personal assurances or representations concerning the quality or suitability of the product.[15] This principle might, theoretically, be extended (whether the medium of the implied contractual promise or of an assumption of responsibility under *Hedley Byrne*[16]) to cases in which there is no direct personal communication. Liability to compensate economic losses might then arise where advertising or labelling claimed particular attributes for the goods or through the mere fact that they were present on the market. Depending on whether the contract or tort

---

[9] *Donoghue* v. *Stevenson*, [1932] A.C. 562, 599 *per* Lord Atkin.

[10] An unsuccessful attempt was made in *Dutton* v. *Bognor Regis Urban District Council*, [1972] 1 Q.B. 373; [1972] 1 All E.R. 462. See also *Anthony* v. *Kelsey-Hayes Co.*, 102 Cal. Rptr. 113 (Cal. App., 1972) above, p. 342.

[11] *Rivtow Marine, Ltd.* v. *Washington Iron Works* (1974), 40 D.L.R. (3d) 530.

[12] American cases accepting liability on such facts are noted above, p. 338, note 5.

[13] As in *Gherna* v. *Ford Motor Co.*, 55 Cal. Rptr. 94 (Cal. App., 1966).

[14] *Dutton* v. *Bognor Regis Urban District Council*, [1972] 1 Q.B. 373, 396; [1972] 1 All E.R. 462, 474 *per* Lord Denning, M.R.; *Rivtow Marine, Ltd.* v. *Washington Iron Works* (1974), 40 D.L.R. (3d) 530, 522, *per* Laskin, J. dissenting on this point. See, in general, above, p. 335.

[15] See, e.g., *Shanklin Pier, Ltd.* v. *Detel Products, Ltd.*, [1951] 2 K.B. 854; [1951] 2 All E.R. 471; *Wells (Merstham), Ltd.* v. *Buckland Sand and Silica, Ltd.*, [1965] 2 Q.B. 170; [1964] 1 All E.R. 41; *Sealand of the Pacific, Ltd.* v. *Ocean Cement, Ltd.* (1973), 33 D.L.R. (3d) 625 (B.C. Sup. Ct.); (1975) 51 D.L.R. (3d) 72 (B.C.C.A.); *J. Nunes Diamonds, Ltd.* v. *Dominion Electric Protection Co.* (1972), 26 D.L.R. (3d) 699 (Sup. Ct. of Canada). In the *Nunes Diamonds* case the claim failed on the facts.

[16] *Hedley Byrne & Co.* v. *Heller & Partners*, [1964] A.C. 465; [1963] 2 All E.R. 575, above, p. 337.

analogue is favoured the beneficiary would be anyone who had furnished consideration to support the promise or who had relied on the responsibility assumed. This position has been adopted in American case law where express warranties[17] have been made, but the conflict of opinion as to the proper scope of the strict tort theory is, as one would expect, paralleled in implied warranty cases.[18]

The present authors do not favour an extended non-contractual liability for economic losses but would favour the introduction of liability in respect of express misrepresentations of fact or "warranties". Liability might then be imposed on a manufacturer who, for example, had advertised his product as being "shrinkproof" or "waterproof" when it was not. In the absence of such representations a case could still be made for allowing purchasers in consumer sales[19] to sue the manufacturer directly even though the complaint was in respect of damage to or deterioration within the defective product itself. This would have the benefit of avoiding the circuity of action which one currently finds in English law. The extension of liability would, however, be open to the obvious objection that a manufacturer might thereby be deprived of the protection otherwise afforded by a fair or reasonable exemption clause in his own contract of sale.[20] It seems preferable that the position in such cases should be governed by the law of sale.

---

[17] See, e.g., *Randy Knitwear Inc.* v. *American Cyanamid Co.*, 181 N.E. 2d 399 (N.Y., 1962); *Inglis* v. *American Motors Corporation*, 209 N.E. 2d 583 (Ohio, 1965), and above, pp. 58–62.

[18] Thus recovery was permitted in *Continental Copper and Steel Industries Inc.* v. *E.C. "Red" Cornelius Inc.*, 104 So. 2d 40 (Fla., 1958) but denied in *Anthony* v. *Kelsey-Hayes Co.*, 102 Cal. Rptr. 113 (Cal. App., 1972), above, p. 342, on both the strict tort and implied warranty theories.

[19] For the definition of a consumer sale, see above, pp. 146–150.

[20] See above, pp. 150–158.

17 Conflict of Laws

There are two separate but connected issues in this chapter. One is the issue of jurisdiction which may not necessarily involve cases with a substantial foreign element. The other is that of choice of law, by which is understood the selection of rules by the court to deal with the various issues before it where such issues, because of a foreign element, cannot be resolved by the application of rules of domestic law. Recognition and enforcement of foreign judgments present no special problems in product liability cases and the reader is consequently referred to the standard texts on the conflict of laws.[1]

Jurisdiction

Jurisdiction presents no difficulty if the defendant is present in England so that process can be served on him in the normal way. Such presence may be of very short duration[2] but the court has an inherent discretion to stay proceedings if they are vexatious, oppressive or otherwise an abuse of process.[3] Apart from personal service, a defendant may submit

---

[1] Dicey and Morris, *The Conflict of Laws*, 9th edn., 1973; Cheshire, *Private International Law*, 9th edn., 1974; Morris, *The Conflict of Laws* 1971; Graveson, *Conflict of Laws*, 7th edn., 1974. I am indebted to my colleague, Michael Bridge, for his major contribution to this chapter. Responsibility for errors or omissions is mine alone.

[2] *Colt Industries* v. *Sarlie*, [1966] 1 All E.R. 673; [1966] 1 W.L.R. 440.

[3] *Logan* v. *Bank of Scotland (No. 2)*, [1906] 1 K.B. 141; *Egbert* v. *Short*, [1907] 2 Ch. 205; *Re Norton's Settlement, Norton* v. *Norton*, [1908] 1 Ch. 471; *Maharanee of Baroda* v. *Wildenstein*, [1972] 2 Q.B. 283; [1972] 2 All E.R. 689; *The Atlantic Star*, [1974] A.C. 436; [1973] 2 All E.R. 175; *McHenry* v. *Lewis* (1882), 22 Ch. D. 397; *St. Pierre* v. *South American Stores*, [1936] 1 K.B. 382, 398 *per* Scott, L.J.

to the jurisdiction of the English courts. This is commonplace in international contracts and provision for it is made in the Rules of the Supreme
Court.[4] Where the defendant is a company it obviously cannot be "present"
in England in the same way as an individual, but it will be held to be
present at common law if it carries on business in England.[5] Furthermore
any company incorporated outside Great Britain with a place of business
in Great Britain is obliged by the Companies Act 1948 to file with the
Registrar of Companies the name and address of someone authorised to
accept service of process on its behalf.[6]

In addition to the basic rule of jurisdiction governed by presence, the
High Court has a discretionary power to allow notice of the writ to be
served outside the jurisdiction if the case comes within any of the special
heads of jurisdiction set out in R.S.C. Order 11, rule 1. This discretion
is not exercised lightly.[7] Indeed the courts can be criticised for interpreting
the sub-rules of Order 11, rule 1 too restrictively, that is for blurring the
two separate legal and discretionary inquiries. This is particularly true
of rule 1 (*h*) which is the most important in product liability cases and
which states that service out may be allowed where the action "is founded
on a tort committed within the jurisdiction".

In a typical product liability case where the plaintiff will be suing in
negligence the courts have consistently refused to hold England to be the
locus delicti if the plaintiff has suffered damage in England but the other
elements of the tort were committed outside the jurisdiction.[8] The same
reluctance is to be seen where the action is founded on deceit.[9]

In *George Monro, Ltd.* v. *American Cyanamid and Chemical Corporation*,[10]
the plaintiffs had imported a quantity of the defendant manufacturer's
cynogas. It had been used by a local authority to "de-rat" a farm and
had caused loss to the farmer. The farmer sued the local authority in
negligence and the local authority recovered an indemnity from the
plaintiffs. The plaintiffs then sought leave to serve notice under Order 11
on the defendant manufacturer in New York, alleging, *inter alia*,
negligence. The application was supported by a grossly inadequate affidavit

---

[4] R.S.C. Order 10, rules 1–3; Order 11, rule 2.
[5] Cheshire, *op. cit.*, pp.81–2; *Dunlop Pneumatic Co.* v. *Actien Gesellschaft Cudell*, [1902] 1 K.B. 342.
[6] Section 407 (1) (*c*).
[7] *Cordova Land Co., Ltd.* v. *Black Diamond Steamship Corporation*, [1966] 1 W.L.R. 793, 801–2; *per* Winn, J.; *The Hagen*, [1908] P. 189; *Buttes Gas and Oil Co.* v. *Hammer*, [1971] 3 All E.R. 1025; R.S.C. Order 11, rule 4 (2).
[8] *George Monro, Ltd.* v. *American Cyanamid and Chemical Corporation*, [1944], K.B. 432.
[9] *Cordova Land Co., Ltd.* v. *Black Diamond Steamship Corporation*, [1966] 1 W.L.R. 793. But a different attitude is manifest in defamation cases: *Bata* v. *Bata*, [1948] W.N. 366; *Jenner* v. *Sun Oil Co.*, [1952] 2 D.L.R. 526.
[10] [1944] K.B. 432.

but the Court of Appeal nevertheless analysed this sub-rule of jurisdiction. Their lordships were unanimously of the opinion that the tort could not be said to have been committed in England simply because the damage was sustained here. Although damage was necessary to constitute the tort of negligence, the plaintiff could bring his action under this head of Order 11 only if he could establish a tortious act committed within the jurisdiction[11] or that the wrongful act from which the damage flowed occurred here.[12] In short, the plaintiff would have to show a breach of the duty of care taking place in England.

Cordova Land Co. v. *Black Diamond Steamship Corporation*[13] concerned, *inter alia*, a claim in deceit against a shipper for the allegedly fraudulent issue of clean bills of lading. Winn, J. was faced with three choices to determine the *locus delicti*: (i) the place where the allegedly fraudulent misrepresentation was made (Massachusetts); (ii) the place where the tort became complete by the plaintiff's reliance on the representation (probably England); or (iii) the place where the plaintiff suffered detriment because of his reliance (England). He chose the first because that was where "the substantial wrongdoing"[14] alleged to be a tort occurred. Accordingly he refused the plaintiff's application and indicated that he would in any event have exercised his discretion in the defendant's favour since the United States was the *forum conveniens*.[15]

In *Distillers Co. (Biochemicals), Ltd.* v. *Thompson*,[16] a child was seeking to bring an action against a British company for damages for negligence. The claim was in respect of pre-natal injuries caused by her mother's taking the drug Distaval which was manufactured and distributed by the defendants and the principal ingredient of which was thalidomide. In considering a head of special jurisdiction in the New South Wales Common Law Procedure Act 1899 similar to rule 1 (*h*), the Privy Council set out the following possibilities for determining the *locus delicti*. The first was that every ingredient of the cause of action had to be shown to have been committed within the jurisdiction. In the case of negligence, this would be duty, breach and damage. Such an approach has had the support of two judges in the Nova Scotia Court of Appeals[17] but has been criticised as "absurd" by the Saskatchewan Queen's Bench.[18] If a tort

---

[11] *Ibid.*, at p. 440 *per* Goddard, L.J.

[12] *Ibid.*, at p. 441 *per* Du Parcq, L.J.

[13] [1966] 1 W.L.R. 793.

[14] *Ibid.*, p. 800. But see *Original Blouse Co.* v. *Bruck Mills* (1964), 42 D.L.R. 2d 174 (B.C. Sup. Ct.).

[15] [1966 1 W.L.R. 793, 800–801.

[16] [1971] A.C. 458; [1971] 1 All E.R. 694.

[17] *Abbott-Smith* v. *Governors of the University of Toronto* (1964), 45 D.L.R. 2d 672, 687 *per* Ilsley, C.J., 695 *per* MacDonald, J.

[18] *Moran* v. *Pyle National (Canada). Ltd.* (1972), 25 D.L.R. (3d) 718, 723 *per* Disbury, J.

straddled the boundaries of two or more states, each of which adopted the *locus delicti* as a special head of jurisdiction and accepted this very restrictive interpretation, the plaintiff would be denied leave altogether. The Board considered this approach to be inconsistent with authority and "too restrictive for the needs of modern times".[19] The second possibility was that it was necessary and sufficient that the last act required to make the defendant liable should have occurred within the jurisdiction.[20] In the case of negligence, this would be the suffering of harm by the plaintiff as a result of the defendant's act or omission. Their Lordships rejected this possibility as being wrong in theory and we have seen that it was also rejected in both the *Monro* and *Cordova* cases. The final possibility was to require that the act of the defendant which gave the plaintiff his cause of complaint must have occurred within the jurisdiction.[1] In other words, the question to be asked was: "where in substance did this cause of action arise?" This was the approach adopted by the Board itself[2] and it is in line with earlier authorities.[3]

The authoritative approach may not always be apt to meet the needs of product liability cases. The typical plaintiff is a private individual and he may be trying to sue a foreign corporation. If he cannot obtain leave under Order 11, rule 1 (*h*) he will be faced with a very difficult claim perhaps thousands of miles from home. This problem was recognised implicitly by the Privy Council by the way in which it characterised the defendant's behaviour as negligent. The plaintiff had not alleged an act or omission arising from the *manufacture* of the drug Distaval but had complained rather that the drug had been distributed to pregnant women in New South Wales without any warning as to its dangerous properties. The defendants had failed in their duty towards the child by not giving this warning in New South Wales and that, said the Board, was where the substance of the cause of action arose.[4] Had the case involved a drug which was contaminated or wholly unsuitable for any purpose, it would have been artificial to regard the negligent conduct as consisting of anything other than the initial distribution of a dangerous product.[5] It is no answer to the demands of Order 11, rule 1 (*h*) to evade its requirements by an over-ingenious characterisation of the defendant's behaviour.

The problems facing a product liability claimant were recognised in a

---

[19] *Distillers Co. (Biochemicals), Ltd.* v. *Thompson*, [1971] A.C. 458, 467.
[20] This is the approach of the American *Restatement on the Conflict of Laws*, 1st section 377.
[1] *Distillers Co. (Biochemicals), Ltd.* v. *Thompson*, [1971] A.C. 458, 466.
[2] *Ibid.*, p. 468.
[3] E.G., *George Monro, Ltd.* v. *American Cyanamid and Chemical Corporation*, [1944] K.B. 432; *Cordova Land Co., Ltd.* v. *Black Diamond Steamship Corporation*, [1966] 1 W.L.R. 793.
[4] *Distillers Co. (Biochemicals), Ltd.* v. *Thompson*, [1971] A.C. 458, 469.
On this, see *Lewis Construction* v. *Tichauer Société Anonyme*, [1966] V.R. 341.

much more explicit and unconventional way by the Canadian Supreme Court in *Moran* v. *Pyle National (Canada), Ltd.*[6] A workman had died when he was changing a light-bulb at the potash mine where he worked. His dependants alleged that he had been electrocuted owing to the defective wiring in the base connection of the bulb. The accident occurred in Saskatchewan. The defendant company was resident in Ontario, sold all its products to distributors and had no salesmen or agents operating in Saskatchewan. Since the basis of the plaintiff's claim was that the defendant had failed to institute a proper system of safety checks at its Ontario factory, the death of the workman was the only part of the alleged tort which occurred in Saskatchewan. The Supreme Court allowed the plaintiffs' appeal against a refusal to allow service out of the jurisdiction and proposed the following test for determining the *locus delicti* where harm was suffered in one state as a result of the careless manufacture of a product in another:[7]

> "Where a foreign defendant carelessly manufactures a product in a foreign jurisdiction which enters into the normal channels of trade and he knows or ought to know both that as a result of his carelessness a consumer may well be injured and it is reasonably foreseeable that the product would be used or consumed where the plaintiff used or consumed it, then the forum in which the plaintiff suffered damage is entitled to exercise judicial jurisdiction over that foreign defendant."

In putting forward this test the court eschewed the need for arbitrary rules and showed considerable sympathy for an approach which required the plaintiff merely to show a real and substantial connection between the alleged tort and the country whose *locus delicti* rule he was invoking.[8]

It is submitted that this approach of the Canadian Supreme Court is logically the neatest and practically the most satisfactory that can be adopted. There is no need for a court to interpret its *locus delicti* head of special jurisdiction restrictively and at the same time exercise its discretion with great caution. The new approach, moreover, enables a court to adjust its approach to foreign defendants to fit changing social needs and tort patterns.

Another head of assumed jurisdiction that could be important in a product liability case is Order 11, rule 1 (*j*). If a party is properly served with a writ in the jurisdiction the plaintiff may apply for notice to be served on anyone outside the jurisdiction who is "a necessary or proper party" to the proceedings. So a foreign manufacturer could be joined as a co-

---

[6] (1973), 43 D.L.R. (3d) 239.

[7] *Ibid.*, pp. 250–251.

[8] *Ibid.*, p. 250. The court considered that this approach could be found in embryonic form in the *Monro* and *Cordova* decisions.

defendant to a negligence action brought against a distributor. The court
will not give such leave if the defendant within the jurisdiction is a man
of substance[9] or if the action has been brought against him solely for the
purpose of exploting rule 1 (*j*).[10]

It is also necessary to consider the special heads of jurisdiction in matters
of contract. A consumer is unlikely to sue a foreign manufacturer or
producer in contract. But it may happen that when a consumer sues a
retailer for breach of the implied terms of merchantability or fitness for
purpose[11] the retailer will join the wholesaler as third party who in turn
will join the importer as fourth party. The importer may then wish to pass
on liability to the manufacturer or producer. According to Order 11,
rule 1 (*f*) and (*g*), should he be unable to serve process in the normal way,
he may apply for leave to serve notice out of the jurisdiction in any
of the four following circumstances:

(*a*) Where the contract was made within the jurisdiction; or,

(*b*) where the contract was made by or through an agent trading or
residing within the jurisdiction on behalf of a principal trading or
residing out of the jurisdiction; or

(*c*) where the contract is by its terms or by implication governed by
English law; or

(*d*) where the action is brought on a breach of contract committed
within the jurisdiction even though a previous breach abroad rendered further performance impossible.

The last head is particularly interesting. In an international sale contract,
the importer will find it difficult to establish a breach of contract by the
seller (as opposed to the shipper) occurring within the jurisdiction. A
failure to deliver goods under a c.i.f. contract because of non-shipment
by the seller would come under this head.[12] But where the importer's
claim is for breach of express or implied terms relating to the quality of
the goods (whether under a c.i.f. or f.o.b. contract), such authority as
there is holds that the breach takes place at the port of shipment. In
Crozier, Stephens v. *Auerbach*,[13] the buyer complained that goods sold under
a c.i.f. contract failed to meet the contractual description and sought to
bring his claim under Order 11, rule 1 but was unsuccessful for this reason.[14]
Moreover the implied condition of merchantable quality does not demand
that the goods remain merchantable for any particular period after the
sale. The state of the goods is assessed at the time of the sale subject to

---

[9] *Chaney* v. *Murphy* (1948), 64 T.L.R. 489.
[10] *Witted* v. *Galbraith*, [1893] 1 Q.B. 577.
[11] Sale of Goods Act 1893 (as amended), s. 14 (2) and (3).
[12] *Cf. Johnson* v. *Taylor Brothers*, [1920] A.C. 144; Cheshire, *op. cit.*, pp. 90–91.
[13] [1908] 2 K.B. 161, C.A.
[14] See also *Cordova Land Co.* v. *Victor Brothers*, [1966] 1 W.L.R. 793.

hidden defects which may come to light later. Therefore the *time* of the breach is when the goods are sold and not when they break down.[15] By similar reasoning, we may conclude that the *place* of the breach is where the goods were shipped and the property transferred. If in a case of this kind the importer cannot serve process on his seller in the normal way he will probably have to take steps in a foreign forum.[16]

Choice of law

A plaintiff who wishes to sue a foreign manufacturer for his negligence in manufacturing a product abroad will probably not wish to plead and prove foreign law. The court will then apply English law on the assumption that it is the same as the foreign law. This goes some way towards explaining the dearth of product liability cases in the English conflict of laws. But it may sometimes be to the plaintiff's advantage to introduce evidence of the foreign law or the defendant manufacturer may plead a defence under that law unavailable in English law. This presents a choice of law problem.

The choice of law rule in tort laid down by Willes, J. in *Phillips* v. *Eyre*[1] was that as a general rule a plaintiff seeking to recover on a foreign tort would have to satisfy two conditions: first, that the wrong would have been actionable under English law (the *lex fori*) if committed in England; and secondly, that the act was not justifiable by the law of the place where it was done (the *lex loci delicti*). The second limb of Willes, J.'s rule has recently been modified by the House of Lords in *Chaplin* v. *Boys*.[2] It will no longer be sufficient for the plaintiff to show merely that the act is not justifiable under the *lex loci delicti*.[3] He must go further and

---

[15] See *Crowther* v. *Shannon Motors*, [1975] 1 All E.R. 139, 141, C.A.

[16] The EEC Judgments Convention should not be forgotten. The UK will probably become bound by this within the next few years. Under the Convention the major head of jurisdiction is that the defendant shall be sued in the courts of his "domicile" (art. 2). The Convention does not define "domicile" but leaves it to be resolved by the laws of the individual states. There are also a number of special heads of jurisdiction. Thus, the courts of the country where a contractual obligation has been or is to be fulfilled have jurisdiction in matters of contract (art. 5(1)). The courts of a country where a tort occurs (the Convention is deliberately vague on this point) have jurisdiction in tort (art. 5(3)).

[1] (1869), L.R. 6 Q.B. 1, 28–29.

[2] [1971] A.C. 356; [1969] 2 All E.R. 1085.

[3] In *Machado* v. *Fontes*, [1897] 2 Q.B. 231, the Court of Appeal in interlocutory proceedings held that the plaintiff had satisfied the second limb of Willes, J.'s rule by establishing that libel was a criminal offence in Brazil (the *locus delicti*). In *Chaplin* v. *Boys*, [1971] A.C. 356; [1969] 2 All E.R. 1085 Lord Hodson, p. 377 and Lord Wilberforce, p. 388, expressly declared that *Machado* v. *Fontes* should be overruled. Lord Guest, p. 381, did so implicitly by propounding a requirement of civil actionability under the *lex loci delicti*.

show that it grounds civil liability under that law.[4] Therefore the effect of this requirement of "double actionability" is that the plaintiff in a product liability action may well not benefit from a *lex loci delicti* which is more favourable than English law though he may be prejudiced by one which is less favourable.[5]

Although in *Chaplin* v. *Boys*,[2] their Lordships collectively were not clear on the matter, it seems that the doctrine of the proper law of tort as understood in the United States of America has not gained acceptance in this country.[6] According to this doctrine the appropriate law to apply to a tort or a tortious issue is the law which has the most real and substantial connection to the tort or issue. But one can infer a majority intention to apply the double actionability rule with flexibility in future to meet problems such as "forum shopping".[7] *Chaplin* v. *Boys*[2] also emphasised that the *lex fori* must govern all matters of procedure including the quantification (but not the availability of separate heads) of damages.[8] This reservation in favour of the *lex fori* may be extremely important in a product liability case. A plaintiff who might wish to sue a Californian aircraft-manufacturing corporation on a Fatal Accidents claim will not recover damages in this country on the generous California scale. He would be well advised to go to California and take advantage of the contingency fee system. The possibilities have recently been highlighted by the proceedings based on the allegedly defective design of a D.C. 10 aeroplane which crashed outside Paris in March 1974.

In applying the double actionability rule, an English court may be faced with a difficult problem of discovering the *locus delicti*. It is not safe to assume that the *locus delicti* for choice of law purposes is the same as for jurisdictional

---

[4] Lords Hodson, Wilberforce and Guest were agreed that the plaintiff need not show that the *lex loci delicti* characterised the cause of action in exactly the same way as the *lex fori*. Civil liability of one sort or another under the two laws would be sufficient.

[5] It is not clear whether an English court would apply the régime of double actionability in quite the same inflexible way as the Inner House of the Court of Session in *M'Elroy* v. *M'Allister*, 1949, S.C. 110. Lords Hodson and Wilberforce in *Chaplin* v. *Boys*, [1971] A.C. 356; [1969] 2 All E.R. 1085 considered the *lex loci delicti* to be the dominant partner in the double actionability rule. See also Lord Pearson's view, below, note 6.

[6] Lords Hodson and Wilberforce were prepared to accept a proper law doctrine to be applied by way of exception to the general rule in special circumstances as exemplified by *Chaplin* v. *Boys*, [1971] A.C. 356; [1969] 2 All E.R. 1085 itself. Their other Lordships were not so prepared, though Lord Pearson at p. 406 declared himself opposed to a rule demanding civil actionability under both laws and declared that, should such a rule be propounded, an exception would have to be created for cases such as *Chaplin* v. *Boys* itself to enable the plaintiff to recover adequate damages.

[7] See notes 5 and 6, above.

[8] Their Lordships agreed on this but a minority of two (Lords Guest and Donovan) considered damages for pain and suffering not to be a separate head but part of an ordinary claim for damages and hence regulated exclusively by the *lex fori*.

purposes. The English courts have shown themselves inclined to interpret Order 11, rule 1 (*h*) narrowly partly out of respect for the foreign sovereign. If a tort straddles both England and a foreign country the same desire may lead the court to rule that a significant connection of the tort with the foreign country is sufficient to establish that country as the *locus delicti* for the purpose of the double actionability rule. This differentiation has been accepted by Canadian courts[9] and there is recent English authority on the same lines. In the unreported case of *Bank Russo-Iran* v. *Gordon, Woodroffe*,[10] Browne, J., dealing with a complex problem of conspiracy and deceit crossing Iranian and British national frontiers, was prepared to treat Iran as the *locus delicti* for choice of law purposes and said so explicitly.[11]

The English choice of law rule in tort has been criticised as too forum-orientated. Even after *Chaplin* v. *Boys*[12] the forum's part in the proceedings will be very considerable.[13] For example, if an English plaintiff wanted to sue an American manufacturing company on a manufacturer's express warranty, he would fail because of the absence of such a theory of liability in the English law of tort.[14] In general there is much to be said for limiting the interest of the forum in the choice of law rule to the protection of English notions of public policy, but such a development is unlikely to come through the courts. A change of emphasis might, however, come through adherence to an EEC Convention on contractual and non-contractual obligations in the conflict of laws.

According to the current draft text of this EEC Convention the law governing tortious obligations shall be the *lex loci delicti*,[15] except where there is no significant connection between the tortious event and that country, and there is a closer connection with another country. In that event the latter country's law will apply as the proper law.[16] Furthermore the draft Convention reduces the pre-eminence of the *lex fori* even more in that it is the *lex loci delicti* (or the proper law as the case may be) which is to govern many procedural and remedial matters at present reserved to the *lex fori* under the English conflict of laws.[17] Since these

---

[9] *Abbott-Smith* v. *Toronto University Governors* (1964), 45 D.L.R. (2d) 672 (Nova Scotia Sup. Ct.) *per* MacDonald, J.: *Moran* v. *Pyle National (Canada), Ltd*. (1973), 43 D.L.R. (3d) 239 (Canadian Sup. Ct.)

[10] Browne, J., a 249-page judgment after a 62-day hearing.

[11] This appears neither in the *Times* report of 3 October 1972 nor in (1972), 116 Sol. Jo. 921.

[12] [1971] A.C. 356; [1969] 2 All E.R. 1085, H.L.

[13] See, e.g., *Bank Russo-Iran* v. *Gordon, Woodroffe* unreported, see note 10 above.

[14] For this theory, see above, pp. 58–62.

[15] Article 10 (1).

[16] Article 10 (2).

[17] Article 11.

include "the form of compensation and its extent",[18] this provision is likely to have a profound effect on product liability claims, more especially because the Convention is not confined to intra-EEC conflicts but will supersede the entire body of English conflicts rules in the areas covered by the Convention.[19] If our Californian aircraft manufacturer could be served with process in this or any other EEC country, damages would have to be awarded on the Californian scale. It is by no means easy to see how this could be achieved.

The Twelfth Session of the Hague Conference on Private International Law was convened in 1972 and produced a draft convention on the law applicable to product liability. The questions left to the law governing the tort are almost exactly those left to such law by the EEC Convention, and include "the form of compensation and its extent".[20] According to art. 4, the governing law shall be the *lex loci delicti* if that law is also either the law of the plaintiff's habitual residence or of the principal place of business of the defendant or of the place where the product was acquired by the plaintiff. By way of derogation from art. 4, art. 5 provides that the governing law shall not be the *lex loci delicti* but the law of the plaintiff's habitual residence if that law is also the law of the defendant's principal place of business or of the place where the plaintiff acquired the product. Therefore the most likely governing law in a product liability claim involving a consumer in this country would be English law as the law of the place where he habitually resides and acquired the product.[1]

Although most plaintiffs in product liability cases in England will probably attempt to recover in tort, it is quite possible that a consumer (where there is a direct sales operation by a foreign manufacturer or producer in this country) will wish to sue in contract. The law applicable to contracts in the conflict of laws is either the law chosen by the parties or, in the absence of such choice, the law which is most closely and substantially connected to the contract.[2] To prevent sellers from attempting

---

[18] Article 11, para. 4.

[19] Article 1 (1).

[20] Article 8, para. 4. See *Product Liability in Europe* (1975), pp. 11–14, 127–130.

[1] Where no law satisfies either art. 4 or 5, art. 6 provides that the plaintiff has the option of either the *lex loci delicti* or the law of the defendant's principal place of business depending on the way he grounds the claim. The defendant who could not reasonably have anticipated that his product would be distributed in another country is protected against the imposition of foreign law under arts. 4–6 by art. 7. Few manufacturers or producers are likely to be saved in this way.

[2] See Cheshire, *op. cit.*, ch. 8; *Vita Food Products Inc.* v. *Unus Shipping Co., Ltd.*, [1939] A.C. 277; [1939] 1 All E.R. 513; *The Assunzione*, [1954] P. 150; *Mount Albert B.C.* v. *Australasian Temperance and General Mutual Life Assurance Society*, [1938] A.C. 224; [1937] 4 All E.R. 206; *Bonython* v. *Commonwealth of Australia*, [1951] A.C. 201.

to exclude the terms implied by the Sale of Goods Act 1893, ss. 13–15, by the selection of a foreign proper law the Supply of Goods (Implied Terms) Act 1973, s. 5, introduced an anti-avoidance provision which limits their freedom to negotiate a foreign proper law. If, but for the choice of law clause, the contract would have been subject to the law of any part of the United Kingdom[3] and the contract is not one which is "international"[4] in character, then the provisions in the Sale of Goods Act dealing with the purported exclusion of implied terms shall apply regardless of the choice or incorporation in the contract of inconsistent foreign law. Where an importer is claiming against a foreign manufacturer or producer, his contract will be international in character and unaffected by the above provisions. The proper law of his contract will be assessed in accordance with normal principles.

To deal with the specific problem of mail order trading with consumers and direct solicitation of consumer orders by foreign suppliers, the latest draft of the EEC Convention makes special provision for the retention of "mandatory rules" of the law of the place of the consumer's habitual residence notwithstanding that the proper law of the contract is some other law.[5] The effect of this provision is similar to that achieved by s. 5 of the 1973 Act. Indeed it may go even further in that it would apply to contracts which might be classified as "international" and hence be excluded from the ambit of s. 5. If goods are shipped by a foreign manufacturer directly to a consumer in this country so that the goods cross national boundaries, the manufacturer is free to exclude his implied obligations under the Sale of Goods Act[6] but would be prevented from doing so by the new art. 4 bis in the draft EEC Convention. It is submitted that the new draft provision is preferable to s. 5 of the 1973 Act in this respect.

---

[3] Supply of Goods (Implied Terms) Act 1973, s. 5 (1).
[4] *Ibid.*, s. 6.
[5] Article 4, bis.
[6] Supply of Goods (Implied Terms) Act 1973, ss. 6–7.

18 The Reform of the Law

The purpose of this book has been to provide a statement of the law governing liability for defective products rather than of the way its authors believe the law should be developed. The book has, however, been written during a period in which proposals for reform have been in the air and it would be incomplete without some attempt to restate our own views. This will assume a continuation of the present system whereby compensation is through a process of inter-party litigation. The terms of reference of the Royal Commission sitting under the chairmanship of Lord Pearson admittedly cast doubt on the correctness of this assumption.[1] But the question whether we should abandon the present system for one similar to that operating in New Zealand whereby compensation is paid from a central fund run by a state agency is beyond the scope of the book.[2] Any such proposal is unlikely to be implemented in the case of product liability for many years though an earlier start might be made in compensating victims of road accidents.

Any reform of the law can hardly leave retail vendors of defective goods strictly liable for personal injury and property damage suffered by purchasers of such goods whilst continuing to absolve manufacturers unless negligence can be established. One possibility would be to remove the vendors' strict contractual liability for consequential losses whilst leaving intact the obligation to refund the purchase price of defective goods. But such liability existed even under the laissez-faire philosophy of the nineteenth century[3] and it could hardly be abolished today unless the change

---

[1] See above, p. 2.
[2] Accident Compensation Act 1972, as amended. See Harris, "Accident Compensation in New Zealand: a comprehensive insurance system" (1974), 37 M.L.R. 361.
[3] See, e.g., *Randall* v. *Newson* (1877), 2 Q.B.D. 102, C.A.

were accompanied by the imposition of strict liability on the manufacturer or producer.

The arguments for and against subjecting manufacturers or producers to strict liability have been rehearsed by the Law Commission in their working paper "Liability for Defective Products"[4] and it is not proposed to set them out *in extenso* here. The major argument in favour of such liability centres on the alleged ability of manufacturers to absorb the costs of compensation as an item in their overheads, pricing their goods accordingly. In the words of the explanatory memorandum accompanying the Commission of the European Communities proposed directive:[5]

> "The compensation paid forms part of the general production costs of the product. This increase in costs is reflected in the pricing. The damage is thus, from an economic point of view, spread over all the products which are free from defects."

Supporting arguments include manufacturers' moral responsibility to stand behind their products (even, presumably, where reasonable care has been exercised); the alleged difficulties of establishing fault; and the avoidance of suits involved in chain liability. Against such arguments are to be weighed, *inter alia*, the view that strict liability discourages the development of new products by manufacturers operating on the "frontiers of technology"; and the moral basis and content of the fault system of liability.

Whatever their intrinsic merits, it now seems likely that the former arguments will prevail. They have the advantage of being in step with the spirit of the age which generally favours compensating the victims of misfortunes. Moreover the adoption of a system of strict liability provides the basis for both the Strasbourg convention on Products Liability[6] and for the proposed EEC directive. Yet the reasoning which was accepted by American courts and commentators some ten to fifteen years ago does not have the same validity when applied to this country today. Where profit margins and price controls are tight the ability to distribute the loss is by no means apparent. Where medical treatment is provided by a national health service and welfare benefits are readily available, the justification for requiring manufacturers to shoulder additional burdens is not self evident. Matters are hardly advanced by bald assertions that differing bases of liability within the EEC "may distort competition" and that

---

[4] See Working Paper No. 64, paras. 34–38 especially.

[5] Proposal for a Council Directive relating to the approximation of the laws, regulations and administrative decisions of the member states concerning liability for defective products: Bulletin of the European Communities, supplement 11/76, p. 13.

[6] European Convention on Products Liability in Regard to Personal Injury and Death, DIR./Jur. (76) 5, above, p. 3.

legal systems based on a requirement of fault provide "completely in-adequate protection".[7] One is probably closer to the truth in suggesting that English law provides considerable protection even though the remedies are rarely used.[8] In any event strict liability is not a panacea which removes all barriers to successful claims. As American case law indicates there remains ample scope for argument over whether a product as designed and marketed is "defective" and over issues of causation.[9]

The types of damage or loss to be included within strict liability

If a system of strict tort liability for defective products were to be intro-duced, a key question would be the types of injury, damage or loss to which it should extend. The present authors would draw the line at death or personal injury and would not extend the system to property damage or economic loss. From the standpoint of the plaintiff or his dependants death or personal injury is that much more traumatic in its effect and that much more worthy of compensation. From that of the defendant, the sums involved in a claim for compensation for property damage are (exceptional cases such as drug disasters apart) potentially greater and so more expensive to cover by liability insurance. There would seem, how-ever, to be no valid reason for limiting an entitlement to sue to users or consumers in a narrow sense. Indeed a bystander who is injured by a defective product may be more deserving of protection since he will not have had the same opportunity to acquaint himself with the danger and so avoid the harm.[10]

In the USA, the formulation of strict liability in the Restatement of Torts, 2d, s. 402A, includes property damage. Similarly art. 6(*b*) of the proposed EEC directive covers:

> "damage to or destruction of any item of property other than the defective article itself where the item of property (i) is of a type ordinarily acquired for private use or consumption; and (ii) was not acquired or used by the claimant for the purpose of his trade, business or profession."

---

[7] See the explanatory memorandum accompanying the proposed EEC directive. Bulletin of the European Communities, Supplement 11/76, pp. 13 and 14 respectively.

[8] The willingness of the courts to infer negligence is well illustrated by cases such as *Grant* v. *Australian Knitting Mills, Ltd.*, [1936] A.C. 85, P.C., above, p. 256.

[9] See above, pp. 186–189 and 273–290 respectively.

[10] The *Restatement of Torts*, 2d, s. 402A, refers to "the user or consumer" and adopts a neutral position with respect to bystanders: see caveat (1) and comment O. American courts have made the extension in cases such as *Elmore* v. *American Motors Corporation*, 75 Cal. Rptr. 652 (1969) and *Passwaters* v. *General Motors Corporation*, 454 F. 2d 1270 (8th Cir., 1972).

This latter distinction between private and business assets is similar to the distinction between consumer and non-consumer sales in the Supply of Goods (Implied Terms) Act 1973[11] and it might be justified on a number of grounds. The sums involved in compensating damage to the domestic property and equipment of consumers are unlikely to be of the same order as in the case of business assets.[12] Moreover it is reasonable to expect the latter to be covered by appropriate loss insurance. Nonetheless it is submitted that in the absence of a contract between the parties the property interests of consumers are adequately protected by a system which requires proof of negligence.

Who should be held liable?

A further problem is to decide what categories of potential defendants should be subjected to any new system of strict liability. A number of solutions might be adopted. One would be to confine strict product liability to manufacturers of finished articles. Another, such as the proposed EEC directive, would limit liability to "producers" of defective products whilst defining this term in an extended sense. Thus producers of materials and components, those who market products under their own trademark, and importers into the EEC are all included as well as producers of finished articles.[13] The *Restatement of Torts*, 2d, s. 402A, goes further and extends liability to all who sell defective products whilst many American courts have imposed strict liability on other commercial suppliers.[14] The choice of the appropriate model is rendered especially difficult by the fact that the same general principle has to cater for situations which have little in common. A component producer may be manufacturing industrial fasteners to be used for a multiplicity of purposes or single purpose brandname products such as car tyres which are advertised in their own right and sold as replacement parts. A retail vendor of goods may be a small corner-shop or a giant supermarket chain.

If a system of strict product liability is to be adopted it is submitted that it should be extended to all commercial suppliers including component producers and those who retail and hire out products. Liability can be adjusted thereafter in accordance with normal common law and statutory principles. This might add marginally to the overall cost of the

---

[11] See above, pp. 146–150.
[12] Article 7 of the proposed directive places an overall limit on the compensation recoverable by individual claimants: see below, p. 360.
[13] Article 2.
[14] See, e.g., *Cintrone* v. *Hertz Truck Leasing and Rental Service*, 212 A. 2d 769 (N.J., 1965) (hirer-out), and cases cited above, p. 18, note 12.

product since all parties would then require to take out appropriate in-surance cover. But the interests of consumers are probably best served by having the maximum possible choice of defendants. Moreover, it has been said that retailers are "an integral part of the overall producing and marketing enterprise"[15] whilst their profit margins are frequently higher than those of the manufacturer whose goods they sell.

Should all products be included?

There is also the problem of whether all products should be subject to a regime of strict liability if this were to be adopted. The Law Com-mission has instanced a number of possible exceptions including im-movables, natural products and pharmaceuticals.[16] Certainly there is a strong case for exempting products which can be marketed only after they have satisfied the requirements of some official licensing or testing agency. Drugs are the obvious example. If such products nonetheless prove to be defective liability might be channelled to the testing agency rather than to the individual producer.[17] A difficulty about any such pro-vision is that it is apt to cover only those products whose risks are predictable in general terms. If the design, formula or ingredients or other products cause unpredictable and catastrophic results the manufacturer is left unprotected. With the problem of unlimited liability in mind, art. 7 of the proposed EEC directive provides that:

> "The total liability of the producer provided for in this directive for all personal injuries caused by identical articles having the same defect shall be limited to 25 million European units of account (E.U.A.). The liability of the producer provided for by this directive in respect of damage to property shall be limited
> —in the case of movable property to 15,000 E.U.A. and
> —in the case of immovable property to 50,000 E.U.A."[18]

It is envisaged that the overall limit for personal injuries would com-pensate several hundred average claims.[19] It would be understandable if a sense of grievance were felt by subsequent claimants suing in respect of

---

[15] *Vandermark* v. *Ford Motor Co.*, 37 Cal. Rptr. 896, 899 (1964) *per* Justice Traynor (Cal. Sup. Ct.).

[16] See "Liability for Defective Products", Law Com. No. 64, paras. 64–75.

[17] For an example of liability being imposed on a testing agency, see *Griffin* v. *United States*, 351 F. Supp. 10 (1972) (polio vaccine).

[18] The European Unit of account is defined by Commission decision No. 3289/75/ECSC of 18 December, 1975.

[19] See the explanatory memorandum accompanying the proposed directive. Bulletin of the European Communities, Supplement 11/76, p. 18.

injuries or illness which became apparent after the financial limit had been reached.

What defences should be available?

Any proposal for adopting a system of strict liability is also likely to meet with difficulty in deciding what defences, if any, should be available. A general defence exempting "development risks" would go a long way towards diluting the strictness of the liability imposed. But the product must nonetheless be shown to be defective and it is submitted that the appropriate standard to apply is the standard which prevailed when the product was marketed. If a reasonable manufacturer fully acquainted with the product's condition and capacity to cause harm would have continued to market the product at that time he should not be prejudiced by the fact that safety standards have increased in the meantime or because safer products have since become available.[20]

The availability of defences of *volenti non fit injuria* and contributory negligence is also controversial.[1] The present version of the proposed EEC directive does not make specific provision for the reduction of damages on the ground of contributory fault,[2] leaving the matter to be determined by the laws of individual states. On one view it might be argued that considerations of contributory fault should be excluded except in so far as the fault constitutes a truly subjective and voluntary assumption of the risk. But contributory negligence is interwoven inextricably with issues of causation and it must of course be shown that the product was defective and that this caused the damage. On balance it would seem preferable not to require an all or nothing solution, but to make provision rather for apportionment, as under the Law Reform (Contributory Negligence) Act 1945.

---

[20] See *Balido* v. *Improved Machinery Inc.*, 105 Cal. Rptr. 890 (1973) and above, p. 189.
[1] See above, p. 291 and pp. 293–296, respectively.
[2] Provision was, however, made in art. 8 of the second preliminary draft directive.

Appendix A
EEC Draft Directive

Proposal for a Council Directive relating to the approximation of the laws, regulations and administrative provisions of the Member States concerning liability for defective products

(Presented by the Commission to the Council on 9 September 1976)
[Bulletin of the European Communities, Supplement 11/76]

Article 1

The producer of an article shall be liable for damage caused by a defect in the article, whether or not he knew or could have known of the defect.

The producer shall be liable even if the article could not have been regarded as defective in the light of the scientific and technological development at the time when he put the article into circulation.

Article 2

"Producer" means the producer of the finished article, the producer of any material or component, and any person who, by putting his name, trademark, or other distinguishing feature on the article, represents himself as its producer.

Where the producer of the article cannot be identified, each supplier of the article shall be treated as its producer unless he informs the injured person, within a reasonable time, of the identity of the producer or of the person who supplied him with the article.

Any person who imports into the European Community an article for resale or similar purpose shall be treated as its producer.

Article 3

Where two or more persons are liable in respect of the same damage, they shall be liable jointly and severally.

Article 4

A product is defective when it does not provide for persons or property the safety which a person is entitled to expect.

Article 5

The producer shall not be liable if he proves that he did not put the article into circulation or that it was not defective when he put it into circulation.

Article 6

For the purpose of Article 1 "damage" means:
   (*a*) death or personal injuries;
   (*b*) damage to or destruction of any item of property other than the defective article itself where the item of property
      (i) is of a type ordinarily acquired for private use or consumption; and
      (ii) was not acquired or used by the claimant for the purpose of his trade, business or profession.

Article 7

The total liability of the producer provided for in this directive for all personal injuries caused by identical articles having the same defect shall be limited to 25 million European units of account (EUA).

The liability of the producer provided for by this directive in respect of damage to property shall be limited *per capita*
—in the case of moveable property to 15,000 EUA, and
—in the case of immoveable property to 50,000 EUA.

The European unit of account (EUA) is as defined by Commission Decision 3289/75/ECSC of 18 December 1975.

The equivalent in national currency shall be determined by applying the conversion rate prevailing on the day preceding the date on which the amount of compensation is finally fixed.

The Council shall, on a proposal from the Commission, examine every three years and, if necessary, revise the amounts specified in EUA in this Article, having regard to economic and monetary movement in the Community.

Article 8

A limitation period of three years shall apply to proceedings for the recovery of damages as provided for in this directive. The limitation period shall begin to run on the day the injured person became aware, or should reasonably have become aware of the damage, the defect and the identity of the producer.

The laws of Member States regulating suspension or interruption of the period shall not be affected by this directive.

Article 9

The liability of a producer shall be extinguished upon the expiry of ten years from the end of the calendar year in which the defective article was put into circulation by the producer, unless the injured person has in the meantime instituted proceedings against the producer.

Article 10

Liability as provided for in this directive may not be excluded or limited.

Article 11

Claims in respect of injury or damage caused by defective articles based on grounds other than that provided for in this directive shall not be affected.

Article 12

This directive does not apply to injury or damage arising from nuclear accidents

Article 13

Member States shall bring into force the provisions necessary to comply with this directive within eighteen months and shall forthwith inform the Commission thereof.

Article 14

Member States shall communicate to the Commission the text of the main provisions of internal law which they subsequently adopt in the field covered by this directive.

Article 15

This directive is addressed to the Member States.

Appendix B
European Convention on Products Liability in Regard to Personal Injury and Death

Preamble

The member States of the Council of Europe, signatories of this Convention,

Considering that the aim of the Council of Europe is to achieve a greater unity between its Members;

Considering the development of case law in the majority of member States extending liability of producers prompted by a desire to protect consumers taking into account the new production techniques and marketing and sales methods;

Desiring to ensure better protection of the public and at the same time, to take producers' legitimate interests into account;

Considering that a priority should be given to compensation for personal injury and death;

Aware of the importance of introducing special rules on the liability of producers at European level,

Have agreed as follows:[1]

Article 1

1. Each Contracting State shall make its national law conform with the provisions of this Convention not later than the date of the entry into force of the Convention in respect of that State.

2. Each contracting State shall communicate to the Secretary General

---

[1] The Convention was adopted by the Committee of Ministers of the Council of Europe, Strasbourg, at the session of 20–29 September 1976, and is open for signature on 27 January 1977.

of the Council of Europe, not later than the date of the entry into force of the Convention in respect of that State, any text adopted or a statement of the contents of the existing law which it relies on to implement the Convention.

Article 2

For the purpose of this Convention:
- (*a*) the term "product" indicates all movables, natural or industrial, whether raw or manufactured, even though incorporated into another movable or into an immovable;
- (*b*) the term "producer" indicates the manufacturers of finished products or of component parts and the producers of natural products;
- (*c*) a product has a "defect" when it does not provide the safety which a person is entitled to expect, having regard to all the circumstances including the presentation of the product;
- (*d*) a product has been "put into circulation" when the producer has delivered it to another person.

Article 3

1. The producer shall be liable to pay compensation for death or personal injuries caused by a defect in his product.
2. Any person who has imported a product for putting it into circulation in the course of a business and any person who has presented a product as his product by causing his name, trademark or other distinguishing feature to appear on the product, shall be deemed to be producers for the purpose of this Convention and shall be liable as such.
3. When the product does not indicate the identity of any of the persons liable under paragraphs 1 and 2 of this Article, each supplier shall be deemed to be a producer for the purpose of this Convention and liable as such, unless he discloses, within a reasonable time, at the request of the claimant, the identity of the producer or of the person who supplied him with the product. The same shall apply, in the case of an imported product, if this product does not indicate the identity of the importer referred to in paragraph 2, even if the name of the producer is indicated.
4. In the case of damage caused by a defect in a product incorporated into another product, the producer of the incorporated product and the producer incorporating that product shall be liable.
5. Where several persons are liable under this Convention for the same damage, each shall be liable in full (in solidum).

Article 4

1. If the injured person or the person entitled to claim compensation has by his own fault, contributed to the damage, the compensation may be reduced or disallowed having regard to all the circumstances.
2. The same shall apply if a person, for whom the injured person or the person entitled to claim compensation is responsible under national law, has contributed to the damage by his fault.

Article 5

1. A producer shall not be liable under this Convention if he proves:
    (*a*) that the product has not been put into circulation by him; or
    (*b*) that, having regard to the circumstances, it is probable that the defect which caused the damage did not exist at the time when the product was put into circulation by him or that this defect came into being afterwards; or
    (*c*) that the product was neither manufactured for sale, hire or any other form of distribution for the economic purposes of the producer nor manufactured or distributed in the course of his business.
2. The liability of a producer shall not be reduced when the damage is caused both by a defect in the product and by the act or omission of a third party.

Article 6

Proceedings for the recovery of the damages shall be subject to a limitation period of three years from the day the claimant became aware or should reasonably have been aware of the damage, the defect and the identity of the producer.

Article 7

The right to compensation under this Convention against a producer shall be extinguished if an action is not brought within 10 years from the date on which the producer put into circulation the individual product which caused the damage.

Article 8

The liability of the producer under this Convention cannot be excluded or limited by any exemption or exoneration clause.

Article 9

This Convention shall not apply to:
  (a) the liability of producers *inter se* and their rights of recourse against third parties;
  (b) nuclear damage.

Article 10

Contracting States shall not adopt rules derogating from this Convention, even if these rules are more favourable to the victim.

Article 11

States may replace the liability of the producer, in a principal or subsidiary way, wholly or in part, in a general way, or for certain risks only, by the liability of a guarantee fund or other form of collective guarantee, provided that the victim shall receive protection at least equivalent to the protection he would have had under the liability scheme provided for by this Convention.

Article 12

This Convention shall not affect any rights which a person suffering damage may have according to the ordinary rules of the law of contractual and extra-contractual liability including any rules concerning the duties of a seller who sells goods in the course of his business.

Article 13

1. This Convention shall be open to signature by the member States of the Council of Europe. It shall be subject to ratification or acceptance. Instruments of ratification or acceptance shall be deposited with the Secretary General of the Council of Europe.
2. This Convention shall enter into force on the first day of the month following the expiration of six months after the date of deposit of the third instrument of ratification or acceptance.
3. In respect of a signatory State ratifying or accepting subsequently, the Convention shall come into force on the first day of the month following the expiration of six months after the date of the deposit of its instrument of ratification or acceptance.

Article 14

1. After the entry into force of this Convention, the Committee of Ministers of the Council of Europe may invite non-member States to accede.
2. Such accession shall be effected by depositing with the Secretary General of the Council of Europe an instrument of accession which shall take effect on the first day of the month following the expiration of six months after the date of its deposit.

Article 15

1. Any Contracting State may, at the time of signature or when depositing its instrument of ratification, acceptance or accession, specify the territory to which this Convention shall apply.
2. Any Contracting State may, when depositing its instrument of ratification, acceptance or accession or at any later date, by declaration addressed to the Secretary General of the Council of Europe, extend this Convention to any other territory or territories specified in the declaration and for whose international relations it is responsible or on whose behalf it is authorised to give undertakings.
3. Any declaration made in pursuance of the preceding paragraph may, in respect of any territory mentioned in such declaration, be withdrawn according to the procedure laid down in Article 18 of this Convention.

Article 16

1. Any Contracting State may, at the time of signature or when depositing its instrument of ratification, acceptance or accession, or at any later date, by notification addressed to the Secretary General of the Council of Europe, declare that, in pursuance of an international agreement to which it is a Party, it will not consider imports from one or more specified States also Parties to that agreement as imports for the purpose of paragraphs 2 and 3 of Article 3; in this case the person importing the product into any of these States from another State shall be deemed to be an importer for all the States Parties to this agreement.
2. Such a declaration may be withdrawn at any time in accordance with the procedure laid down in Article 18.

Article 17

1. No reservation shall be made to the provisions of this Convention except those mentioned in the Annex to this Convention.

2. The Contracting State which has made one of the reservations mentioned in the Annex to this Convention may withdraw it by means of a declaration addressed to the Secretary General of the Council of Europe which shall become effective the first day of the month following the date of its receipt.

Article 18

1. Any Contracting State may, insofar as it is concerned, denounce this Convention by means of a notification addressed to the Secretary General of the Council of Europe.
2. Such denunciation shall take effect on the first day of the month following the expiration of six months after the date of receipt by the Secretary General of such notification.

Article 19

The Secretary General of the Council of Europe shall notify the member States of the Council and any State which has acceded to this Convention of:

(*a*) any signature;
(*b*) any deposit of an instrument of ratification, acceptance or accession;
(*c*) any date of entry into force of this Convention in accordance with Article 13 thereof;
(*d*) any reservations made in pursuance of the provisions of Article 17, paragraph 1;
(*e*) withdrawal of any reservations carried out in pursuance of the provisions of Article 17, paragraph 2;
(*f*) any communication received in pursuance of the provisions of Article 1, paragraph 2, Article 15, paragraphs 2 and 3 and Article 16, paragraphs 1 and 2;
(*g*) any notification received in pursuance of the provisions of Article 18 and the date on which denunciation takes effect.

In witness whereof, the undersigned being duly authorised thereto, have signed this Convention.

Done ... in English and French, both texts being equally authoritative, in a single copy, which shall remain deposited in the archives of the Council of Europe. The Secretary General shall transmit certified copies of each of the signatory and acceding States.

Index

373

Printed in Great Britain by Thomson Litho Ltd., East Kilbride, Scotland.